Brothers at Each Other's Throats

REGULARITY OF THE VIOLENT ETHNIC CONFLICTS IN THE POST-SOVIET SPACE

REVISED FIRST EDITION

Anatoly Isaenko

cognella®

SAN DIEGO

Bassim Hamadeh, CEO and Publisher
Jack Behrend, Associate Acquisitions Editor
Carrie Baarns, Manager, Revisions and Author Care
Kaela Martin, Project Editor
Rachel Kahn, Production Editor
Emely Villavicencio, Senior Graphic Designer
Alexa Lucido, Licensing Manager
Natalie Piccotti, Director of Marketing
Kassie Graves, Senior Vice President, Editorial
Jamie Giganti, Director of Academic Publishing

Cover image copyright © 2009 iStockphoto LP/busypix.
Cover image copyright © 2020 iStockphoto LP/TolgaMadan.

Printed in the United States of America.

3970 Sorrento Valley Blvd., Ste. 500, San Diego, CA 92121

TABLE OF CONTENTS

ACKNOWLEDGMENTS

In the effort of pulling together and presenting a model of the regularities of post-Soviet violent ethnic conflicts, I owe a great deal to many people whom I wish to personally thank.

I am grateful for the constructive comments on various sections of my previous and current works provided by my good friend and colleague Daniel Hoffman, emeritus professor of political science (PhD, MIT, 1977), who taught at Johnson C. Smith University for twenty-five years, including courses on comparative politics and on terrorism. Prior to his passing, Professor Hoffman encouraged me to pursue this goal and present my findings to the academic world. In his own words, he expressed how this model could be applicable to any and all ethnic conflicts from around the world, because the aspects that define it have universal characteristics in their own right.

For the rest of my life, I will be grateful for the involvement of Emeritus Professor Peter Petschauer, my constant partner and coauthor of many articles that helped me in formulating key parts of this model. He remained an enthusiastic and unrestrained helper throughout the development of this project and greatly helped in editing of the penultimate chapters of this volume.

Professor Wayne Morris, a specialist on the Ukrainian Holodomor, was also an invaluable advisor in working to understand and assess the importance of this tragedy as the key chosen trauma of the Ukrainian people. As a tenured fellow of the Center for Slavic, Eurasian, and East European Studies at the University of North Carolina at Chapel Hill, I want to thank the staff of the center for sharing invaluable materials pertaining to the Ukrainian crisis, inviting me to forums discussing these important issues, and providing the space necessary for this kind of research to thrive.

I extend my thanks to Emeritus Professor Daniel B. German, who published thoroughly analytical reviews of several aspects of my model as presented in preliminary publications on ethnic conflicts in the Caucasus. I am equally thankful for the input of Dr. Donald J. Raleigh, the Jay Richard Judson Distinguished Professor of History at UNC Chapel Hill, for his high assessment of my first presentation of this theoretical model at his university under the aegis of the Fulbright scholarship. I am grateful to Dr. John A. Berta, senior analyst, Ukraine desk, EUCOM, for our longtime partnership and co-participation in many conferences, including during my lectures, consultations, and presentations at the Advanced Analysis Course, United States Army JFK Special Warfare Center and School, and at Troy State University at Fort Bragg, North Carolina. He was an invaluable constructive critic and helper in understanding of the avalanche of current information relating to the important generalizations in this research.

I would also like to thank many of my other colleagues, including Professors Steve Bowers, Richard Giragosian, George Poteat, Dorothea Martin, York Norman, Garry Marotta, Andrew Nickols, and many others, from the bottom of my heart for providing invariably useful information, insights, and references for parts of this draft and presentations, as well as constructive comments on the proceedings of the model at large.

I especially wish to thank my industrious research and teaching assistant, Hedrick Leonard, a graduate student at Appalachian State University. He has done a tremendous job in helping me transcribe my handwritten manuscript into a digital format and prepare every one of these chapters for publication. Throughout this process, he has been an outstanding paragon of efficiency in polishing the textual and grammatical composition of this volume, as well as providing insight into some of the finer contextual details that I may have overlooked.

I would also like to thank my other teaching assistants, Joshua Waddell and Jeff Martin, also from Appalachian State, who shouldered a considerable workload during the arduous midterm transition to online instruction amid the COVID-19 pandemic. Thanks to their hard work, I was granted more of the valuable time needed to compose my handwritten manuscript. Additionally, I would like to thank my volunteer assistant, Robbie Pope, who took it upon himself to update me on several recent publications relevant to this subject, as well as assisting me in accessing them. I also extend similar thanks to my former student at Appalachian State (and now graduate student at the University of Uppsala in Sweden) McBarrett S. Good, who shared with me his own findings on the Russo-Ukrainian ethnic conflict, previously published in his honors thesis, which he had written under my supervision. My former graduate student Evan Wallace (he is currently working on his PhD dissertation) also provided me with important citations relating to his findings in the field of mystical political theology of Russia regarding the relationship between church and state in historical perspective, important to understand the religious building blocks of the current conflict in Ukraine. Having witnessed their superb academic capabilities firsthand, I wish all of these students and assistants the best of luck in furthering their own studies.

I will always be grateful to my longtime friend Barry Timberlake—a man possessing an incredible lifetime of experience—who served as a benevolent spiritual advisor and encouraged me toward this accomplishment through his words and prayers.

I am also grateful to Professor James Goff, the chair of the History Department at Appalachian State, for his all-encompassing support of this project.

The peer-reviewers, who in the process of preparation of the first national edition took upon themselves a great job of reading and providing invaluable notes and suggestions, which I have tried to thoroughly implement for the improvement of the text, certainly remain forever in my grateful thoughts and recollections, as well as the project coordinators and staff from Cognella Academic Publishing, who provided auspicious conditions for work on the manuscript and have patiently taken into account all my wishes as the author.

Finally, I wish to dedicate this book to the memory of my parents—Vladimir Spiridonovich and Yekaterina Davidovna Isaenko—as well as my mother-in-law—Valentina Stepanovna Sautina-Kalashnikova—veterans and survivors of World War II, whose remnants of the once-powerful Cossack families miraculously endured the tragic events of the 1930s and 1940s. Having survived many dramatic experiences in their own lives, they taught me to respect the different peoples among whom we lived, to learn their languages, and to value their unique ethnic cultures and traditions as much as our own.

A Necessary Note

Within this text, the reader may find several different spellings for the names of places and people that I have cited. This is because these names themselves are an important part of the nationality building block of ethnicity. During times of ethnic rebirth, each ethnic group would record these monikers in their own ethnic style and manner. But despite these changes, their older Russian and English translations would go unchanged in many sources, including my own respective citations. Out of respect, I cite them as they appeared in their original published source. However, if I cite them in the context of modern ethnic expressions, then I refer to them in their local ethnic variants. But even then, there sometimes exist certain variants and discrepancies in the spelling of place names—such as *Zakarpattia* and *Zakarpattya* or *Kiev* and *Kyiv*, and so on—and personal names—like *Andrii*, which may also be spelled as *Andryi*, and so on—that are essentially read/pronounced the exact same way. As a result, I aim to cite these terms as they are originally presented in the source or use the traditional transliteration of the sources in an ethnic context when it is most appropriate.

April 2020

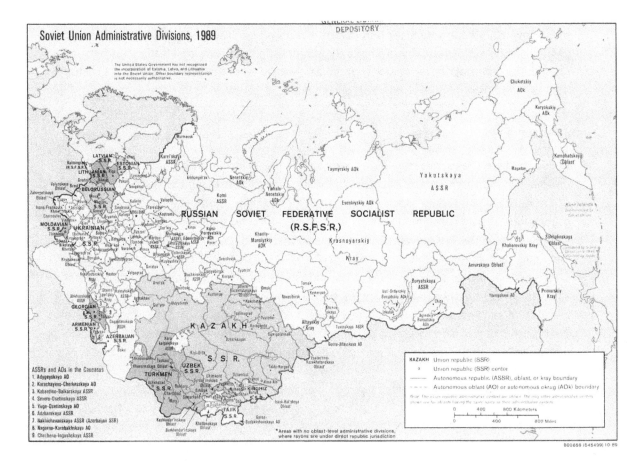

FIGURE 0.1   Map of the Soviet Union in 1989 on the eve of its collapse.

Geopolitical map of the Caucasus Region (2008)

FIGURE 0.2   Violent Ethnic Conflicts in the Caucasus

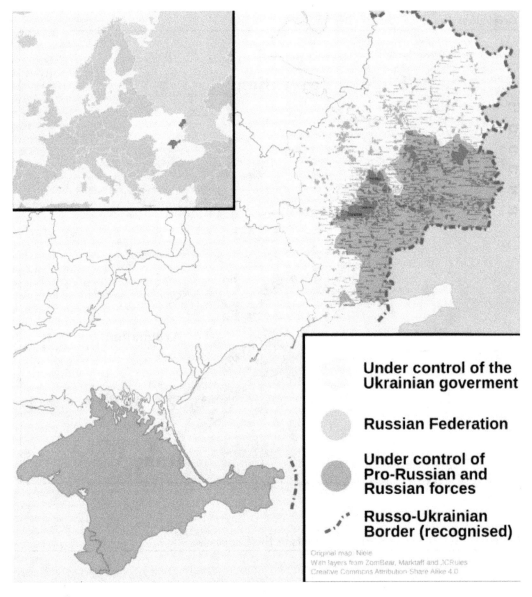

Under control of the Ukrainian goverment

Russian Federation

Under control of Pro-Russian and Russian forces

Russo-Ukrainian Border (recognised)

Original map: Niele
With layers from ZomBear, Marktaff and JCRules
Creative Commons Attribution-Share Alike 4.0

FIGURE 0.3   Ukraine: Who Controls What

Figure Credits

INTRODUCTION

S ince the end of the Second World War, more than ten million people have died due to ethnic strife. The end of the Cold War has been accompanied by the emergence of *ethnic conflicts* in Eurasia. New ethnic tragedies have subsequently erupted, with many thousands of casualties from former Yugoslavia added to this total. The collapse of the Soviet Union—a world superpower—considerably promoted and enhanced these types of conflicts. Since the late 1980s, ethnic conflict has emerged as one of the most serious obstacles to democratization in Eastern Europe and in newly independent states of the former Soviet Union. At first, said conflicts undermined and ruined attempts of Gorbachev's *Perestroika* (1985–1991) to "democratize" the Soviet system. Then they contributed to the demise of the Communist regime, virtually blowing it up and blossoming from its ruins. Under the motto of self-determination, "ethnic communists"[1] from "proud"[2] ethnic minorities plunged their compatriots into uncompromising stances for their "states'" independence, challenging the newly emerging *titular nations*.[3] In turn, former party bosses and Soviet bureaucrats who suddenly transformed from the devoted "Marxist internationalists" into embittered nationalists responded to *ethno-separatist* or *irredentist* challenges within the boundaries of their newly independent realms with even more harsh and brutal measures. They wanted to retain and increase their own power and privileges, which would allow them to tread the red carpets in foreign airports, even if for this they had to paint these carpets with the blood of their ethnic compatriots. At the same time, a lot of neighboring ethnic groups jumped at each other's throats for their "primordial" ethnic territories, without which they could not imagine their long-desired independence. Amid this mess loudly sounded a call from the first president of independent Russia, Boris Yeltsin, addressed to the elites of ethnic minorities: "Grab as much sovereignty as you may engulf!"[4] It was a vivid example of downplaying the risks and misjudging the destructive potential of emerging ethnic conflicts and of the nature of their ideology—*ethnocentric nationalism*.

In the meantime, ethnic conflicts, fed by the old traumas and hatreds that had remained suppressed before the collapse of the totalitarian regime, gradually became associated with ethnic cleansing, deportations, mutual destruction, and even genocidal explosions. Ethnic wars stretched like a giant bow along the fiery rim of the dying Soviet Empire and the disintegrating socialist world, from the Balkans, through the Caucasus, to the Near East and Central Asia and on to the Kashmir and Sinkiang. What is going on now in Ukraine is just another longstanding consequence of this yet-not-ended process, and its underestimated ethnic underpinning is vividly displayed and evolving along similar lines of regularities of the *theoretical model of ethnic conflicts* that I have been elaborating on while investigating the history and perspectives of ethnic conflicts in the Caucasus. Conclusions about the world perspectives until 2035 by the *National Council of Intelligence* state that "regional conflicts, both on the part of regional and local aggressors and on the part of nongovernmental structures threaten to become sharper. Terrorist threats will be strengthening."[5]

In his groundbreaking research, Professor Martin Miller of Duke University reveals the foundation of modern terrorism. Professor Miller argues that since the time of the French Revolution, "the tradition of state legitimacy was forever altered and terrorism became a part of violent contest over control of state power between officials in government and insurgencies in society. In the nineteenth and twentieth centuries everywhere in the world terrorism evolved into a way of seeing the world and a way of life for both insurgents and state security forces with the two sides drawn even closer in their behavior and tactics."[6] I intend to demonstrate the validity of this observation in numerous examples from the currently unleashing *hot stage* of Russo-Ukrainian ethnic conflict.

Many years of comparative analysis of the original materials, archival sources, and other primary sources from the areas of ethnic conflicts accompanied by ethnic terrorism; personal participation in the modern democratic movements; and the dramatic experience of survival in the ethnically torn regions of the former Soviet Union convinced me that the tendency toward interethnic tension throughout the world would increase in the twenty-first century. My comparative studies of ethnic conflicts show that the shift from relatively moderate manifestations of ethnicities gives way to more uncompromising ethnocentric behavioral patterns. For example, if co-ethnic ancestors had practiced genocide in the past against perceived (or real) ethnic enemies, their nowadays offspring not only justify it but elevate the perpetrators of monstrous crimes against humanity to the status of ethnic/national heroes. The entire architecture of the world's system of nation-states and their territorial integrity that has emerged in Europe since 1648 has met with this challenge, compared to that of the anti-colonial ventures post-WWII. Today, sixty-eight countries of the world are facing ethnocentric parochial secessionist or irredentist impulses in their most radical manifestations, and *ethnocentric nationalists* and *radical Islamists* represent a strong challenge to liberal and democratic alternatives.[7]

In the majority of ethnic conflicts, one of the sides represents local Islamic communities. This circumstance is gainfully exploited by professional jihadists. Such ethnic wars offer an extremely fertile recruiting ground. These professionals offer support to their brethren, skillfully manipulating the abused and humiliated freedom fighters and ordinary residents, turning them into embittered fanatics who seek "holy revenge" against their "oppressors." The perceived oppressors can conveniently be the Russians, other Christians (e.g. Americans, Europeans), the Chinese, and so on. Both radical Islamists and ethnocentric nationalists constitute insignificant minorities as compared to the entire population of ethnic groups/nations in conflict. But both groups are the most proactive and provocative, well-organized and purposeful, and passionate, and because of their ferocious energy, they exert a tremendous impression on the mind of a confused and sometimes disillusioned young generation.

Regressive dynamics of modern ethnic conflicts, to some extent, may be also conditioned by the uncertainty of their treatment by the international community. Since the beginning of the twentieth century, two fundamental paradigms and international norms have emerged: the concept of *national self-determination* and the doctrine of *nation-state sovereignty*.[8] Let us remind ourselves again that the current international system of national states began emerging in the West after the Peace of Westphalia in 1648. Whereas ethnocentric nationalists representing ethnic groups in the secessionist or irredentist territories refer to the first principle to justify their demand for secession and independence, nationalists in existing nation-states invoke the second doctrine to justify survival of their united states.[9] The tension between those who would like to maintain their territorial integrity and those who would like to assert their independence may be seen recently in the separation of a number of ethnic groups from their state entities. Ukraine, after obtaining its independence in 1991 as a result of the collapse of the Soviet Union, has been plagued both by ethno-separatist and irredentist challenges that were called into life by a variety of longstanding and immediate causal factors of internal and external character, which will be among the focal points of this research. To make things worse, international law does not fully answer the question of when, in what particular cases, and how one of the two principles takes precedence: the right to self-determination of an ethnic group or the right of a nation-state to its territorial integrity. However, as Raymond Taras and Rajat Ganguly have shown, in regard to the international framework, norms and actual state practice are generally averse to ethnic secession.[10]

All the same, some specialists, in view of a lack of clear legal precedent, continue to search for at least moral criteria that may justify secession. A leading contributor to the debate, political philosopher Allen Buchanan has managed to outline *five conditions* that *morally justify* those who seek separation:

> 1) The culture really is in peril; 2) less disruptive ways of preserving the culture do not exist; 3) the imperiled culture meets minimal standards of justice itself (that it does not represent a Khmer Rouge type of culture bent on genocide); 4) secession should not lead to the building of an illiberal state; and 5) neither the existing state nor any third party has a historic claim to the seceding territory.[11]

I will demonstrate that all sides in the Russo-Ukrainian ethnic conflict appeal to different moral criteria from the above-cited norms to justify their ethno-political agenda. Because the Ukrainian nation-state, with its present territorial boundaries, is a "relatively recent historical creation"[12] from the early 1990s, ethnic groups that have been living more or less compactly in their different regions are sharing very different ideas about certain ethnic issues.[13]

Overall, existing views underestimate the ethnic character of violent eruptions in the post-Soviet space. At present, economic motivations and individual ambitions are better analyzed than the psycho-historical or sociological factors. "Individual preferences in existing models typically include only material rewards and punishments."[14] However, an objective reality urges experts in different fields of study to reckon with the naked fact that *ethnicity* "has not disappeared as the result of modernization, globalization," or Sovietization.[15] Moreover, it has emerged even stronger in the beginning of the twenty-first century than early in the twentieth. Because of the relational nature expressed in the "us versus them" categories, and because of perceived inequality in access to economic resources, political and social power, ethnic identity, especially in transitional societies with vivid "ranked" ethnic relations, may reach dangerous potential of its radicalization fraught with sharp ethnic confrontation.[16] My studies of ethnic conflicts in the Caucasus, Central Asia, and in the former Yugoslavia confirmed that there is a direct connection between "the frustrations driving ethno-nationalist mobilization and violence" and socio-political and economic "horizontal inequality based on measures of ethnic groups' access to central executive power."[17]

Like Manning Nash aptly noticed, "most of the ethnically-oriented action lies in the nature of the case between the ends of the continuum. Mere symbolic recognition of ethnicity indicates a spectral and Cheshire cat-like existence of group difference, *while total absorption with ethnicity in political and social life* indicates an unstable state of crisis (the root of the crisis does not have to be, and frequently is not ethnic itself)."[18] In a situation of relative normalcy, when the political elite of a multiethnic nation-state can practically guarantee almost all ethnic rights, "the action of ethnicity can be as minimal as a national day of songs and costumes and then a disappearance of societal relevance of the ethnic group for another year or so (St. Andrew's Day and Von Steuben Day parades approach this action minimum for Scots and Germans in New York)."[19]

The Ukrainian reality, as well as that of the Caucasus and Central Asia, Moldova, and to some extent the reality in the Baltic States, has been very different. By the force of continuing all-sided societal crises, and especially by qualifications of existing ethnic elites, the latter gradually were able to propose to their ethnic compatriots *only ethnocentric projects* of building their independent states, with a vividly pronounced anti-Russian discourse or even Russo phobia. It was inevitably fraught with serious interethnic collisions, but without broad public support their projects were doomed to fail from the beginning. I will demonstrate further how an all-sided societal crisis has given rise to this opportunity.

In the early 2000s, while working on a book on ethnic conflicts in the Caucasus, I noticed that students and specialists demonstrate strikingly superficial knowledge of such vital issues as ethnic conflicts, along with remarkable ignorance of their history and psycho-historical underpinnings. In this regard especially vivid blank leaf in publications was, and still is, how the all-sided societal crisis of the super ethnic national/imperial construction of the Soviet Union affected separate ethnic groups and their ethnicities. At the same time, media coverage of ethnic conflicts in the 1990s and first decades of the 2000s were strongly biased and subjected to the dominating ideological thought, political stereotypes, and political order and sometimes had (and still have) true perjuries.[20] Most of the experts very convincingly (although in passing) had identified what I call *separate building blocks of ethnic conflicts*. However, they have not developed their findings into generalized, comprehensive, interactive, and dynamic models of evolving ethnic conflicts. Instead of such an attempt, they have focused primarily on their "ethno-territorial"/ "regional" dimension. At the same time, they have often separated "ethnic conflict" from "social," "linguistic," and "religious" conflicts. Thus they consider that all these conflicts are separate phenomena.[21] Such spontaneous and impulsive fragmentation of an organic socio-cultural phenomenon—a product of historical evolution and the interaction of concrete ethnic groups/peoples—proves that in the contemporary analytical literature, the dominating approach has been characterized by a general sense of unawareness and thus of underestimation of ethnic issues. It turns the subject of analysis into a cocktail of heterogeneous factors hectically colliding with each other and thus preventing diagnosing the societal disease correctly to outline the methods of its treatment. In my opinion, the root of the abovementioned imperfection lies in the fact that analysts had, and still have, difficulties in defining such concepts as *ethnié*, *ethnicity/ethnic group*, *nation*, *nation-state*, and so on.[22] Such uncertainty gives birth to many different labels as applicable to ethnicity: "primordial," "constructivist," "instrumental," "structuralist," "circumstantial," "situational," "interactionist," and so on.[23] Lowell Barrington in the above-cited article very objectively grouped theoretical approaches to "where ethnic identity comes from" around three sets: (1) *primordialism*, (2) *constructivism*, (3) *instrumentalism-situationalism*.[24]

Among the most famous creators of primordialism was Anthony Smith. He continued the logic of the arguments of his predecessors: anthropologist Clifford Geertz, influential sociologist Edward Shils, and Pierre L. Van den Berghe. Born in the Belgian Congo to Belgian parents and living through WWII in Nazi-occupied Belgium, Van den Berghe was an early witness to ethnic cleansing and racism. In agreement with the author of this "grouping," I consider Pierre Van den Berghe (who passed away in 2019) a leading authority among primordialists, who formulated "a socio-biological approach to ethnicity and ethnocentrism, while emphasizing its consistency with genetic programming in humans related to reproduction."[25] Primordialists were the first who expressed an idea that "ethniés," or ethnicities, "*share several common components*."[26]

The adherents of constructivism argue that ethnic identity or ethnic conflicts are not "natural" occurrences. Rather, they are "social constructions," just like some "markers of ethnicity": language or religion "are products of human agency."[27] In other words, constructionists propose that ethnic identity originates and then is passed on "from generation to generation through choice, effort and imagination."[28] Lowell Barrington further argues that according to instrumentalist and situationalist theoretical approaches, "ethnicity is seen as conditional and instrumental (either in the way it is led by individuals or in the way it is manipulated by elites)."[29] At the same time, such authors as John Comaroff and Crawford Young agree that primordialism and instrumentalism can be linked and are complementary. However, the majority of scholars argue in favor of more close links between instrumentalism and constructivism.[30] These are very important observations for my own model of ethnic conflicts. In my opinion, an unprecedented Soviet experiment aiming at creating a new *obshnost'*—a "super-ethnic" community known as the "Soviet people" and consisting of a new type of human beings known as "Soviet men," is one of the brightest examples of idealistic constructivism. This policy was in harmony with the greatest utopian Soviet dream, declaring that on the road to communism, all "nationalities"—that is, ethnic minorities—would unite around their "senior brothers," the so-called state-forming nations, first on the level of union republics. Later on, all of them, including those in the state-forming nations (such as Georgians, Armenians, Azeris, Ukrainians, etc.) would supposedly unite around Big Brother—the Russian people—because all of them share the same ideological paradigm: "Soviet internationalism." Then they would form an unprecedented new amalgamation: the *Soviet nation*. (During Brezhnev's period, some party propagandists argued that the process of the forming of the Soviet nation had been accomplished at the stage of "developed socialism" associated exactly with that period. Others promoted the thesis that the Soviet nation had already emerged by 1940.) In the process of such phased transformations, ethnic minorities (including titular ethnic groups in autonomous republics and autonomous regions and in the union republics) would subsequently abandon their languages and other ethnic components. Now we know that this Soviet utopia soundly failed.[31] However, it is not dead at all! From that point, the nowadays practice of nation-state building in the newly independent states by the ethnocentric political elites of the titular dominant ethnic nations regarding their peripheral ethnic minorities is nothing but the embodiment of old Soviet approaches under different ideological guise: their ethnocentric practices are in fact Soviet ideological approaches twisted inside out.

My analysis of the history of ethnic conflicts in the Caucasus led me to the understanding that all of them (Armenian-Azerbaijani, Ossetian-Ingushian, Russian-Chechen, Georgian–South Ossetian, and Georgian-Abkhazian ethnic conflicts) in their different stages had elements and typical characteristics of *all three* above mentioned theoretical approaches. I intend to demonstrate in this research that the Russo-Ukrainian ethnic conflict, which is currently passing through its *hot stage* in Donbas, also has almost all elements and characteristics of primordialist, constructivist, and situationalist-instrumentalist approaches.

The recent decade and a half have seen some really good reporting on different aspects of the Russo-Ukrainian conflict, and even general accounts belonging predominantly to political scientists.[32] Among the last ones especially important for my research are the above-cited books of Taras Kuzio; the monographs of Richard Sakwa, Serhy Yekelchyk, and Laada Bilaniuk; and that of Gwendolyn Sasse, dedicated to the Crimean question.[33] Earlier fundamental works on the history of Ukrainian nationalism are also very helpful for the context of this research, especially the books of Kenneth C. Farmer, Paul R. Magocsi, and Andrew Wilson and the publications of Dominique Arel, Bill Bowring, John S. Reshetar, Charles King, and many others.[34] For the convenience of presenting a new theoretical model, I will further discuss these and numerous other publications within the context of theoretical aspects of the new model. All the more, most of these literature sources explore separately this or that compound part of particular aspects. Beginning with exploration of ethnic conflicts in the Caucasus, and in the process of investigating Russo-Ukrainian conflict, I have been building my model on the verge of many disciplines: history, including psycho-historical studies; anthropology; ethnography; political science; philosophy;

sociology; geography; linguistics; economy; and others. Each publication greatly helped to fill the lacunas, and in the long run to complete the entire model.

Before I begin presenting concrete aspects of the theoretical model and applying them to the Russo-Ukrainian ethnic conflict, I want to cite several interviews of common people. In summer 2019, I recorded them while discussing the nature of this conflict with ethnic Russian and Ukrainian immigrants in Asheville, North Carolina, and Spartanburg, South Carolina. By the request of the interviewees, I will cite only given names, ethnic belonging, and in some cases occupations and places of origin. I conducted thirty-eight interviews with middle-aged people who had been still in Ukraine when the conflict erupted; twenty-three were Russians and fifteen were Ukrainians. For the sake of brevity, I will use the most typical and most clearly expressed and supply a numerical index to cross-reference them with principal/repeated ideas in other interviews.

Natalia, Ukrainian, L'viv, Western Ukraine, was clear about which outsiders and a person to blame:

> It is Putin who started all this mess. His lust for power over the new Russian Empire is to blame. Without Ukraine, this dream will never come true. We in Ukraine showed that people's power may have positive results, and Putin takes it as a threat. Ukrainian example may inspire Russians for resistance to his clique. That is why he wants to strangle Ukrainian freedom. But he is afraid to do it directly because of the Western reaction. That is why he currently and cunningly works with the Russians in our eastern areas, trying to set them against Ukrainians by exacerbating their fears of the so called Ukrainization. He has to be hanged by his balls. (9 out of 15) (Interview, June 3, 2019, Isaenko file II, list 10).

Nikolai, Russian, self-employed, a former resident of Gorlovka in Donbas (Donets'ka Oblast'), commended in Asheville, North Carolina:

> I agree with Putin: Ukrainians and Russians are one people. Ukrainian state and "mova" [the Ukrainian language] are artificial creations. They do it very simply: Vocabulary for the new Ukrainian language are being formed from the synonyms habitually used only in the western periphery, predominantly in Galichina [Ukr. *Halychyna*], and never used in southeastern or central regions. And now they enforce this new "mova" over the people who live there through coercion. My ancestors lived in Nikolaev and in Odessa, and on their graves; there are inscriptions on the Russian language. Ukrainization in these territories continues with certain breaks already for more than a hundred years. However, people there still speak Russian language. You have to understand that language is [the] most important foundation of cultural and personal identity. In February 2014, Rada [the Ukrainian Parliament] canceled the law about

the state linguistic policy, which had granted Russian language the status of regional in the 13 out of 27 Ukrainian regions. And after the two months of this crucial event, Donbas rebelled. I know that in LNR and DNR [non-recognized secessionist regions], more than 50 percent are native Ukrainians, but 90 percent of all people speak Russian at home. (19 out of 23) (Interview, June 3, 2019, Isaenko, file II, list 12).

Olga, Ukrainian, a university employee, former resident of Ternopil (Western Ukraine):

Russians and Ukrainians are completely different peoples. We speak completely different languages. German scientists in 2012 proved that many Ukrainians have unique genes, which allow them to digest milk and dairy products until old ages. Thus these peoples are biologically very different. Ukrainians are direct descendants of Kievan Rus', and Russians have roots in Finno-Ugorian world and Mongols' world, especially Russian political culture. All history of Ukrainians is the history of resistance to the aggression of Moscow and its annexation attempts. When they failed to subdue Ukrainian people, they purposefully tried to annihilate them, like in 1932–1933, during Holodomor—a targeted policy of genocide of the Ukrainian people by the Soviet Stalin's regime. In fact, if somebody says that Ukrainians and Russians are "brothers," then this is the story of Kane and Abel that had begun from time immemorial and continues to this day. (7 out of 15) (Interview, August 6, 2019, Isaenko, File II, list 18).

Olexandr, Ukrainian, vendor, former resident of Stryi (Western Ukraine):

Russians are different from us religiously. They have stolen from us our religious history. If we join European Union and reunite with the West, to which we belong historically, Russia will lose what they believe [is] its religious center, because as they say everything came from Kievan Rus'. By the same reason, they took the Crimea, where the most ancient religious shrines [are] locate[d]. (5 out of 15) (Interview, August 6, 2019, Isaenko, File II, list 19).

Yevgenii, Russian, former resident of Kharkiv, Eastern Ukraine:

Ukrainian oligarchs manipulate consciousness of both peoples to their own gains and benefits. Euromaidan is the biggest venture that had been designed here in America against Russia and realized by the local oligarchs. Whoever else helped [get] this war started, one thing is clear for now: neither Crimea nor Donbas by their own will would ever return to Ukraine. Overwhelmingly, their population hate Ukrainians, after Ukrainian army and "dobrobats" of

"Banderites" [paramilitary formations] killed their loved ones and after their pilots shot civilians in their cities. I talked to my friends who live there, and that [is] what they told me: "Blood is not water." Shared struggle for survival matters for them most. (18 out of 23) (Interview, July 30, 2019, Isaenko, File II, list 16).[35]

Andrii Sh., Ukrainian, former resident of Zaporijje (Central Ukraine):

This conflict has been always present, either openly or latently. And Ukrainian nationalism has always played a very positive role. It is only because of its nationalism that Ukraine managed to preserve its unique culture, language, and in the long run, was able (even under Communists) to carve out such a vast territory and build its own state, unlike many other peoples of the former Soviet Union. You ask why nationalism is not so broadly spread among Russians in Russia? I'll tell you what: because, unlike Ukrainians, most of the Russians are the descendants of slaves of Mongols and Tatars and then of Moscow lords. They continued to bend to the party line during the Soviet period too because of their slave-type nature. Ukrainians, when Moscow's grip on power is weakened, immediately rebelled. But Ukraine never had such a strong military force like their neighbors. That is why Ukrainians were often defeated and conquered. As a result, either Moscali [Muscovites] in Kyiv, or Lyahs [Poles] in western parts have always fixed their anti-Ukrainian puppet regimes, and ethnic Ukrainians have been always oppressed. Last example is Yanukovich's pro-Moscow rule. Ukrainian patriots responded to this corrupted regime with mass protests. Whoever is in power in Kyiv, if he or she really wants to defend and promote real Ukrainian values, he or she will always depend on the Ukrainian nationalism and on the support of this active part of Ukrainian people. Only they are ready no matter what to defend Ukrainian independence. And that [is] what has always taken place in history, especially against Moscow. (10 out of 15) (Interview, August 6, 2019, Isaenko, File II, list 20).

In the main part of this research, I'll return to these and other interviews. For now, a couple of the most obvious comments are important, which may also be backed by similar interviews that I recorded in the Caucasus during the *stirring up* and *hot* stages of ethnic conflicts there in 1988–1993.[36]

First, these interviews clearly show that the conflict between these peoples has undergone strong ethnicization and reached a very dangerous stage of regression. Many interviewees demonstrate total absorption with ethnicity while reproducing popular (sometimes absurd) political assessments that they have uncritically borrowed from ethnocentric media propaganda stereotypes. Second, none of these numerous interviewees have ever been acquainted with any of the theoretical approaches mentioned earlier. Now and then, in Georgia proper, South Ossetia, and Abkhazia; Karabakh and Chechnya; North Ossetia and

Ingushetia; and now with emigrants from Ukraine and Russia, I have listened to the opinions of ordinary people of all nationalities in the conflicts, of different ages and professions, and again I understand that all of them are victims of those who make up society's core and ultimately managed to dig the canyon of hatred that divides these ethnic groups. It is curious enough that, cumulatively, all these interviews virtually demonstrate combinations of *all three of the theoretical approaches* to ethnic conflicts that we have discussed above. Third, in these interviews, one may find *five repeatable components* that I call principal *building blocks of ethnic conflicts*—corresponding to the most important constituents of ethnicity, which I will discuss in chapter 1, corresponding to aspect one of the theoretical model. The building blocks remain the same, but their combinations may vary from conflict to conflict. Thus, comparative analysis of the interviews of ordinary people—witnesses, participants, and victims of ethnic conflicts—along with the experience of other explorers,[37] helped me to define and explain the first aspect of my theoretical model—the nature of ethnicity and principal characteristics of ethnic groups and nations. I will demonstrate that this and other subsequent aspects of a theoretical tool fit well into the evolution of the Russo-Ukrainian ethnic conflict. This instrument will also help to overcome the artificial fragmentation of this type of conflict into "cultural," "social," "political," "religious," "linguistic," and so on. Ultimately, it may pave the way toward defining a scope of holding and healing mechanisms for such a dangerous societal disease.

Notes

1   This term Ronald Suny very aptly applied to the Communist bureaucratic elite, whose leaders in the early 1990s burned their party cards and declared themselves sworn builders of capitalism and adepts of "liberal democracies" but in fact promoted ethnocentric nationalism. See Ronald Grigor Suny, *The Making of the Georgian Nation* (Bloomington: Indiana University Press, 1998), 290.

2   See Susan Goldenberg, *Pride of Small Nations: The Caucasus and Post-Soviet Disorder* (London: Zed Books, 1994).

3   In 1991, the collapsed USSR was replaced by fifteen independent nation-states. Their titles carry the name of the largest ethnic groups. The same is true for former Yugoslavia, which was also replaced by a number of titular nations.

4   Anatoly Isaenko, *Polygon of Satan: Ethnic Traumas and Conflicts in the Caucasus*, 3rd ed. (Dubuque, IA: Kendall Hunt Publishing House, 2014), chapters 1–3.

5   Cited in François Nordman, *Le Temps* (March 7, 2017).

6   Martin Miller, *The Foundation of Modern Terrorism: State, Society, and the Dynamics of Political Violence* (Cambridge, UK: Cambridge University Press, 2013).

7   Isaenko, *Polygon of Satan,* vii; see also Rohan Gunaratna, *Inside Al-Qaeda: Global Network of Terror* (New York: Columbia University Press, 2002); and Walter Laqueur (ed.), *Voices of Terror* (New York: Reed Press, 2004).

8   Anthony D. Smith, *The Ethnic Origin of Nations* (London: Blackwell, 1986); see also Anthony D. Smith, *National Identity* (London: Penguin, 1991); and Susanna Mancini, "Rethinking the Boundaries of Democratic Secession: Liberalism, Nationalism, and the Right of the Minorities to Self-Determination," *International Journal of Constitutional Law* 6, no. 3–4 (July—October 2008): 415–55.

9   Raymond Taras and Rajat Ganguly, *Understanding Ethnic Conflict: The International Dimension*, 3rd ed. (New York: Longman, Pearson Education, 2008), 43.

10 Taras and Ganguly, *Understanding Ethnic Conflict*, 50–52.

11 Allen Buchanan, *Secession: The Morality of Political Divorce from Fort Sumter to Lithuania and Quebec* (Boulder, CO: Westview Press, 1991); see also Allen Buchanan, "Theories of Secession," *Philosophy and Public Affairs* 26, no. 1 (1997): 31–61; and Taras and Ganguly, *Understanding Ethnic Conflict*, 50–52.

12 Vicki L. Hesli, William M. Reisinger, and Arthur H. Miller, "Political Party Development in Divided Societies: The Case of Ukraine," *Electoral Studies* 17, no. 2 (1998): 235–56.

13 See Lowell W. Barrington, "Examining Rival Theories of Demographic Influences on Political Support: The Power of Regional Ethnic, and Linguistic Divisions in Ukraine," *European Journal of Political Research* 41, no. 4 (2002):455–91; John A. Armstrong, *Ukrainian Nationalism and National Integration* (Englewood, CO: Ukrainian Academic Press, 1990); Dominique Arel and Andrew Watson, "The Ukrainian Parliamentary Election," *RFE/RL, Research Report 3000* (1994); Dominique Arel and Valerii Khmelenko, "The Russian Factor and Territorial Polarization in Ukraine," *Peoples, Nations, Identities: The Russian-Ukrainian Encounter, The Harriman Review* 9, no. 1–2 (Spring 1996):126-148

14 See Lars-Eric Cederman, Nils B. Weidman, Kristian Skrede Gleditsch, "Horizontal Inequalities and Ethno-nationalist Civil War: A Global Comparison," *American Political Science Review* 105, no. 3 (August 2011): 478–95.

15 Barrington, "Examining Rival Theories," 462.

16 Donald L. Horowitz, *Ethnic Groups in Conflict* (Berkeley: University of California Press, 1985); see also George I. Mirsky, *On the Ruins of Empire: Ethnicity and Nationalism in the Former Soviet Union* (Westport, CT: Greenwood Press, 1997).

17 Isaenko, *Polygon of Satan*, chapter 3; see also John G. Bullock, "Elite Influence on Public Opinion in an Informed Electorate," *American Political Science Review* 105, no. 3 (August, 2011): 496–515.

18 Manning Nash, *The Cauldron of Ethnicity in the Modern World* (Chicago: Chicago University Press, 1989), 16–17 (emphasis added); see also Manning Nash, "The Core Elements of Ethnicity," in *Ethnicity*, ed. John Hutchinson and Anthony Smith (Oxford: Oxford University Press, 1996).

19 Nash, *Cauldron of Ethnicity*, 15.

20 Isaenko, *Polygon of Satan*, vii.

21 See brief historiographic survey in Isaenko, *Polygon of Satan*, 6–15.

22 See Taras Kuzio, *Ukraine: State and Nation Building* (London: Routledge, 1998), chapter 1, 230f.

23 Barrington, "Examining Rival Theories," 462.

24 Barrington, "Examining Rival Theories," 463. Another discussion related to minor rival theories of ethnic conflict beyond this grouping may be found in Horowitz, *Ethnic Groups in Conflict*, chapter 1.

25 Barrington, "Examining Rival Theories," 463; see Pierre L. Van den Berghe, "Class, Race, and Ethnicity in Africa," *Ethnic and Racial Studies* 6, no. 2 (1983): 221–36; Anthony Smith, *The Ethnic Origins of Nations* (Oxford: Basil Blackwell, 1986); Edward Shils, "Primordial, Personal, Sacred, and Civil Ties," *British Journal of Sociology* 8, no. 2 (1957): 130–45; Clifford Geerts, *The Interpretation of Cultures* (New York: Basic Books, 1973).

26 Barrington, "Examining Rival Theories," 463(emphasis added).

27 See John L. Comaroff, "Ethnicity, Nationalism, and the Politics of Differences in an Age of Revolution," in *The Politics of Difference: Ethnic Premises in a World of Power*, ed. Edwin N. Wilmsen and Patrick McAlister (Chicago: University of Chicago Press, 1996), 162–63.

28 Barrington, "Examining Rival Theories," 463.

29 Barrington, "Examining Rival Theories," 463.

30 Crawford C. Young, "Evolving Modes of Consciousness and Ideology: Nationalism and Ethnicity," in *Political Development and New Realism in Sub-Saharan Africa*, ed. David E. Aptar and Carl G. Rosberg (Charlottesville: University Press of Virginia, 1994), 79; Comaroff, "Ethnicity, Nationalism, Politics," 165.

31 Compare Valerii A. Tishkov, *Ethnicity, Nationalism, and Conflict in and after the Soviet Union: The Mind Aflamed* (London: Thousand Oaks, 1997).

32 Along with the above-cited articles, most related to certain aspects of my model are the following: Robert H. Wade, "Reinterpreting the Ukrainian Conflict: The Drive for Ethnic Subordination and Existential Enemies," *Challenge* 58, no. 4 (2015): 361–71; Anna Fournier, "From Frozen Conflict to Mobile Boundary: Youth Perceptions of Territoriality in War-Time Ukraine," *East European Politics and Societies and Cultures* 32, no. 1 (February 2018): 23–55; Julia Strasheim, "Power Sharing, Commitment Problems, and Armed Conflict in Ukraine," *Civil Wars* 18, no. 1 (2016): 25–44; Ivan D. Loshkariov and Andrey A. Shushentsov, "Radicalization of Russians in Ukraine: From 'Accidental' Diaspora to Rebel Movement," *Southeast European and Black Sea Studies* 16, no. 1 (2016): 71–90; Huseyn Aliyev, "The Logic of Ethnic Responsibility and Pro Government Mobilization in East Ukraine Conflict," *Comparative Political Studies* 52, no. 8 (2019) 1200–1231; Oliver Boyd-Barrett, "Ukraine Mainstream Media and Conflict Propaganda," *Journalism Studies* 18, no. 8 (2017): 1016–34; Joseph Meyer, *Ethnic Conflict in the Former Soviet Union: Ethnic Demography and Its Influence on Conflict Behavior*, (unpublished manuscript, Murfreesboro, TN: Middle Tennessee State University, Spring 2015); Hans von Zon, "Ethnic Conflict and Conflict Resolution in Ukraine," *Perspectives on European Politics and Society* 2, no. 2 (2001): 221–40.

33 Richard Sakwa, *Frontline Ukraine: Crisis in the Borderlands* (London: IB Tauris, 2015); Serhy Yekelchyk, *The Conflict in Ukraine: What Everyone Needs to Know* (Oxford: Oxford University Press, 2015); Laada Bilaniuk, *Contested Tongues: Language Politics and*

Cultural Correction in Ukraine (Ithaca, NY: Cornell University Press, 2005); Gwendolyn Sasse, *The Crimea Question: Identity, Transition and Conflict* (Cambridge, MS: Harvard University, 2007). In addition, the following recent articles are valuable sources for the chapter on the Crimean and Donbas cases: Andrew Wilson, "The Donbas between Ukraine and Russia: The Use of History in Political Disputes," *Journal of Contemporary History* 20, no. 2 (April 1995): 269–71; Austin Charron, "Whose Is Crimea? Contested Sovereignty and Regional Identity," *Region* 5, no. 2 (2016); P. Terrence Hopmann, "Negotiating the Ukraine-Crimea Crisis," in *Tug of War*, ed. Osler Hampson and Mikhail Troitskiy (Montreal: McGill-Queens University Press, 2017); Andrei Zorin, "Eden in Taurus: The 'Crimean Myth,' in Russian Culture of the 1870s–90s," in *By Fables Alone: Literature and State Ideology in Late Eighteenth- and Early Nineteenth-Century Russia*, ed. Andrei Zorin (Brighton, UK: Academic Studies Press, 2014);Jane I. Dawson, "Ethnicity, Ideology and Geopolitics in Crimea," *Communist and Post-Communist Studies* 30, no. 4 (1998): 427–44; see also literature cited in endnote 2 of the conclusion to this book.

34 See Kenneth C. Farmer, *Ukrainian Nationalism in the Post-Stalin Era: Myths, Symbols, and Ideology in Soviet Nationalities Policy* (The Hague: Martinus Nijhoff Publishers, 1980); Paul R. Magocsi, *A History of Ukraine* (Toronto: University of Toronto Press, 1996); Andrew Wilson, *Ukrainian Nationalism in the 1990s: A Minority Faith* (Cambridge, UK: Cambridge University Press, 1997); Andrew Wilson, *The Ukrainians: Unexpected Nation* (New Haven, CT: Yale University Press, 2000); Dominique Arel, *Language and the Politics of Ethnicity: The Case of Ukraine* (PhD dissertation, Urbana-Champaign: University of Illinois, 1993); Dominique Arel, "Language Politics in Independent Ukraine: Towards One or Two State Languages?" *Nationality Papers* 23, no. 3 (September 1995): 597–622; Bill Bouring, "The Russian Language in Ukraine: Complicit in Genocide, or Victim of State-Building?" in *The Russian Language Outside the Nation*, ed. Lara Ryazanova-Clarke (Edinburgh: Edinburgh University Press, 2014); John S. Reshetar, "Ukrainian Nationalism and the Orthodox Church," *The American Slavic and East European Review* 10, no. 1 (February 1951); Aneta Pavlenko, "Linguistic Russification in the Russian Empire: Peasants into Russians," *Russian Linguists* 35, no. 3 (2011); Charles King and Neil J. Melvin, "Diaspora Politics: Ethnic Linkages, Foreign Policy, and Security in Eurasia," *International Security* 24, no. 3 (Winter 1999/2000): 108–38.

35 Compare these interviews with Anna Fournier, "From Frozen Conflict to Mobile Boundary," 36–40.

36 See Isaenko, *Polygon of Satan*, 143–49, 185–88.

37 See Anna Fournier, "From Frozen Conflict to Mobile Boundary," 26.

Figure Credits

CHAPTER ONE

The Meaning of Ethnicity

Principal Characteristics of Ethnic Groups and Nations

The contemporary reader who wanders into a bookstore or library to find books or journal articles about the nature of ethnicity, ethnic groups, and nations is likely to walk into a morass of contending views and competing prescriptions and cannot help but depart feeling more puzzled than enlightened. I agree with those who believe that contemporary thought regarding this vital issue needs to be put into historical perspective as a concise but respective sample of prevailing and diverging opinion that clarifies the issues, rather than adding to the confusion, all while presenting a balanced assessment that allows for the full spectrum of disagreement on the major issues to be considered.

Understanding the Terminology, Early Definitions of Ethnicity: First Recurrent Attributes

Common understanding of the term *ethnié*—an ethnic group/ethnicity—borrowed from French, descends down to Ancient Greek ἔθνος (*éthnos*)—*folk* in English, or народ (*narod*) in Russian. As such, ethnic groups are a "*narod*" (a group of people) who, according to Max Weber, "hold a common belief in their descent."[1] The tradition of defining ethnoses began in classical antiquity, after early authors like Anaximandr and Hecataeus of Miletus and Herodotus in c. 480 BC laid the foundation of both historiography and ethnography of the ancient world. While describing contemporary nations, the Greeks founded a concept of *their own ethnicity* under the name *Hellenes*. More importantly, in order to differentiate Greek (Hellenic) ethnic identity, Herodotus for the first time outlined its indispensable components/constituents: a) *shared descent* (ὅμαιμον—"of the same blood"); b) shared language (ὁμόγλωσσον—"speaking the same language"); c) shared sanctuaries and sacrifices (Θεῶν ἱδρύματά τε κοινά καί θυσίαι); and d) *shared customs* (ἤθεα ὁμότροπτα—"customs of the fashion").[2] Modern Western historiography, based on these findings of Ancient Greek thought, further developed its legacy by adding more recurrent attributes of *ethnié* to the fundamental constituents outlined above. Thus, Max Weber agreed with some other attributes further proposed by Anthony Smith: *shared history*, especially a common myth of descent; distinctive and *shared culture*; *specific territory*; *a sense of solidarity*; and a *collective name*.[3] Frederick Barth added that some sort of distinctive boundaries exist between ethnicities, too, arguing that "their 'We' is different to 'Others' beyond recognized borders."[4]

General Approaches to Ethnicity in the West

As is almost always the case in the *ethnic conflict* category, discussed in the introduction to this book, the study of *ethnicity* in the West until recently was dominated by two distinct debates: (1) between "primordialism" and "instrumentalism," and (2) between "constructivism" and "essentialism."[5] In short, "primordialists" insist that ethnicities are being perceived by members of the group collectively "as an externally given" social bond, while "instrumentalists" argue that ethnicity is being used as a resource for interest groups for achieving increases in wealth, power, or status.[6] "Constructivists" see ethnic identities as the product of historical forces, and even if these identities are presented as old, in fact they are very often fairly recent constructions. Yet "essentialists" view ethnic identities "as ontological categories defining social actors."[7] Debates over approaches to understanding ethnicity continue along further fragmentations of the abovementioned trends by different social scientists when trying to understand the nature of ethnicity as a factor in human life and society. Examples of the nuances within some of these various approaches, such as primordialism, essentialism, perennialism, constructivism, modernism, and instrumentalism, can be found in the cited literature.[8] In fact, World War II was a turning point for specialists of all the different disciplines in the West, due to Nazi racism discouraging essentialists' interpretations. Since that time, ethnic groups came to be defined more often as social rather than biological entities.[9]

Overall, for the present research, it is important to summarize the results of all the approaches to the study of *ethnié*/ethnicity/ethnic groups regarding the following principal attributes of coherence: *descent*, *kinship*, *a common place of origin*, *shared myths*, *language*, *religion*, *customs*, and *national character*. According to a consensus-like cumulative approach, ethnic groups are viewed as "mutable rather than stable, constructed in discursive practices rather than written in the genes."[10]

Initial Appearance of the Ukrainian Ethnos

Ethnicities/ethnic groups are also often considered "pre-national" forms of integration that represent "historical antecedents of the modern nations." Taras Kuzio argues that "all of these attributes of ethnoses existed in Ukraine to varying degrees by the seventeenth century and continued to exist until the nineteenth/early twentieth century. A people who described themselves as *rusyny* (Ruthenians), Ukrainians or Little Russians (then not yet a derogatory term), recalled history traced back to Kyiv Rus' and associated roughly with much of what is today Ukrainian territory, and exhibited a common culture and linguistic group (composed of a number of regional dialects)." Prior to 1917, anti-statism was their common characteristic, "as was their categorization into socio-economic and religious terms (peasant and Orthodox)." Interestingly enough, Ukrainians living in tsarist Russia shared this notion in terms of "Others": "few knew who they were, but 'most of them knew what they were not.'" And according to Kuzio, it was a typical "characteristic of pre modern nations" and could be seen in Ukraine since the seventeenth century.[11]

Approaches to Ethnicity in the Russian Empire: Imperial Categorization of Peoples

Since Russians and Ukrainians used to live together in the same state organizations during both the Imperial and Soviet periods (1711–1917; 1917–1991), it is also equally important to cast a brief look on the dominating ideas about ethnicity in these state entities. In one of my articles, coauthored with Peter Petschauer, I have demonstrated that during the later period of the Russian Empire, ethnic differences came to be conceptualized increasingly in forms of *language* and *religion*. The term *inorodtsy* ("aliens") was gradually used more to designate all (linguistically and sometimes religiously different) non-Russians. *Inorodtsy* generally were considered civilizationally more primitive than their native Russian-speaking contemporaries. Their paganism and Islam (such as in the Caucasus or in Central Asia, where it mixed with strong vestiges of paganism and traditional norms of common laws like the *Adats*) were not considered insurmountable obstacles to ultimate assimilation. Jews were considered to be an exception: their strict adherence to Judaism was alleged to be clearly opposed to Orthodox Christianity.[12] Yet even Jews were encouraged to assimilate, particularly the wealthy and other successful personages. The grandfather of Vladimir Lenin and the father of Leon Trotsky are two well-known examples of such assimilation. This displays a level of awareness in the Imperial Establishment upon the more important attributes of ethnicity and elaborated methods of their coercive amendment to pursue assimilatory politics.[13]

What was the reason for this drive? I have found that after 1897, the desire on the part of the imperial government to assimilate *inorodtsy* became even greater. Events in the first decade of the century drew further attention to the instability of the imperial regime and to the potential threat of the Empire's multiethnic character. Furthermore, the defeat of Russia in the Russo-Japanese war (1904–1905) reactivated racist fears on the part of Russians toward the Empire's huge Asian populations, as did stirrings of pan-Turkism, which were exemplified by the activities of Ismail Bey Gasprinskii. The widespread participation of the non-Russian population in the revolutionary activities of 1905–1906, particularly in Poland, the Baltics, Finland, and the Caucasus, put the ruling elite on alert and were seen as a perilous sign for the future of the state. Moreover, data from the census of 1897 (which were not published in full until 1907) gave clear demographic evidence of the near-minority status of ethnic Russians within the Empire. If one used native language (and sometimes religion) as surrogates for ethnicity, the census showed that Russians would not make up the majority of the Empire's population unless one added Belarusians and Ukrainians to their titular ethnic group/nation. In full knowledge of this reality, Belarusians and Ukrainians were officially defined as members of the Russian people (the *russkii narod*), and their languages were relegated to dialects. The authorities compounded this ethnic rearrangement by restricting the number of schools that could use native languages as the language of instruction and increasing the use of Russian as the dominant language for education in local schools. Today, things have curiously turned against Russians. Imitating their imperial and then Soviet predecessor governments, these newly independent states have begun to use language, history, and even religion to discriminate against Russians and other non-natives in their own states in less than a decade.

Soviet Definitions of Ethnic Group/Nation/Nation-State

During the Soviet period, theoretical approaches to ethnicity were dominated by Marxist "teachings" about the evolution of "social formations." According to the *Main Soviet Encyclopedia*, the principal conditions for the origin of an ethnic community were "the common territory and language." Then the latter served as its main indicators. A common religion, a propinquity of the components of an ethnic community in racial aspect, or the presence of considerable *Métis* (transitional) groups, also serve as the additional conditions for the composing of an ethnic group.[14] It should be said that from the 1920s to the 1930s, in the process of the so-called "Soviet State building," Stalin carved up the regions of the Soviet Union into separate units broadly along ethno-linguistic lines. This practice stemmed from equal parts administrative and practical/ideological considerations. Following the death of Vladimir Lenin in January 1924, Stalin's theory on "nationalities" acquired an official stamp. He developed his own definition of a *nation* (*natsiya* in Russian), which he argued was different from a *people* (*narod*). According to him, a nation is "a stable and historically developed community" based on a set of four general criteria: a *common language*, a *united territory*, a *shared economic life*, and a *shared psychological outlook* manifested in a *common culture*.[15] By comparing this definition of *natsiya* with that of *The Main Soviet Encyclopedia*, published in the 1970s, a still respected and unquestionable authority among Russian specialists, one can easily see that the latter almost textologically repeats Stalin's same outlook, several decades after his death. S.T. Kaltakhchyan, the author of the corresponding article in the encyclopedia, defined a nation as a "historically developed community composed through the formation of a common territory, shared economic ties, literary language, and some peculiarities of culture and character." Both the Marxist-Leninist and Stalinist views on what comprises a nation can trace their origins to the transitory period of overcoming "feudal parceling" and the strengthening of political centralization in Russian society on the basis of capitalistic (and "post-capitalistic," i.e., socialist) economic ties.[16]

As a matter of fact, all the territorial boundaries of the Soviet administrative formations that are currently recognized (autonomous republics, regions of the Russian Federation, and union republics, which have become fully independent states), with minor exceptions, are Stalin's legacy and were drawn arbitrarily by the man himself, within accord of his above-cited vision. An affected and far-fetched character of the Soviet definitions could be further demonstrated by the fact that despite the lack of any "feudal parceling" in China, nobody could deny the existence of a "Chinese nation" with origins rooted in remote antiquity and by how the clearly visible "post-capitalist reality" was disappearing in the eyes of the world after 1991. Nevertheless, S.T. Kaltakhchyan was absolutely correct when he argued that there exist no "pure" homogeneous nations, since all of them have been built from different tribes and "nationalities" (the terminology Soviet scholars used when referring to ethnic groups). The same source defines *narodnost'* (nationality or people) as a "historically developed *linguistic*, *territorial*, *economic*, and *cultural community* preceding the appearance of a nation." The beginning of a people is referred to the period of tribal consolidation characterized by "the gradual amalgamation of tribes and the replacement of previous blood relations by the territorial ties."[17] If we now compare these several definitions of *nation* and *nationality/people*, we may notice that the difference between them in the Soviet orthodoxy is relatively insignificant. If the first criterion for a nationality/people is "language," then the first for the nation is "literary language." In addition, the *Soviet Encyclopedia* attributes some "peculiarities of culture and character" to the concept of the nation. However, the same qualities are obviously inherent in the people too. In reality, Stalinist theory attributes the most significant difference between nation and people (ethnic group) to their "*materialistic nature*." Above all else, Soviet specialists valued "economic life" as a decisive criterion of such a difference. They argued that in contrast to the "feudal economic relations" of people, the inner economic ties of a nation are "capitalistic ties." The most critical consequence of this statement is that, according to Soviet orthodoxy, these ties (far more advanced than in the feudal formation) supposedly authorize the nation to exercise *self-determination* as a form of *political integrity*, and as such, seek its own statehood by incorporating the other peoples/ethnic groups into itself, even against their will, under more powerful economic forces. Ironically enough, this Soviet doctrine by antedate virtually justified the assimilatory politics of their imperial predecessors and "class enemies." As a matter of fact, Ukrainian dictionaries from the era of Soviet control strictly followed an identical discourse and defined *narod* (people/ethnic group) as a "*concrete historical form of society*" united through "*language, territory, economy*, and *race*."[18]

I agree with Taras Kuzio that the term *nation-state* is difficult to define in a post-Soviet space, especially in the case of Ukraine. It is better to use the term *state-nation*, as defined by Kuzio himself. Sometimes I also use the term *polity*. Bolsheviks expropriated the state as a result of a violent revolution in 1917. Then they initiated the process of building the Soviet nation within the framework of their own ideological dogmas by using all levers of state power at their disposal. After the collapse of this well-oiled "super-ethnic" machine, that independence fell into the hands of the titular ethnic groups appointed to such a high status by their Bolshevik predecessors. Now these "new" (and at the same time old, given that they belonged to a previously established political class) political elites have to begin building their new nations under a new ideological guise, using highly coercive state power once again. In its particular case, Ukraine would face a pressing dilemma, due to its large Russian population, with a significant level of self-awareness of the fact that in the recent past they themselves had been a state-forming ethnic nation. Thus, the dilemma is this: whether the ethnic component of the new Ukrainian political nation would be based upon Ukrainian or Ukrainian-Russian "cultural" criteria, with linguistic in first place. Through the entirety of his own book, Kuzio argues that "the Ukrainian political nation will be based upon Ukrainians as the titular, core ethnic group," as witnessed by the proclamation of the new Ukrainian constitution in June 1996.[19]

I will get back to the discussion of this crucial problem in the subsequent aspects of the theoretical tool and in the special sections dedicated to the linguistic building block of Russo-Ukrainian ethnic conflict. At this point, I want to express my conviction, based on the studies of ethnicity in historical perspective, that we need to exclude some of the more commonly attributed criteria from the definition of ethnic groups and nations. Particularly, the criterion of "economic ties" or "economic community" as a metric for evaluating an ethnic identity should be ignored, and for good reason. For example, an "economic community" never existed between the Spartans and Athenians of Ancient Greece or between the Assyrians and Babylonians of Ancient Mesopotamia. Nevertheless, the first pair constituted unalienable parts of the Greek people, while the latter pair both belonged to the Acadian/Akkadian people, with their ethnic backgrounds remaining solid despite the supposedly required economic connections as seen in more modern definitions.

Stalinist Categorization of Soviet Peoples

In contrast, very doubtful ideological dogmas were laid in the foundation of the Soviet state-building process. By the mid-1920s, Stalin had already established a hierarchy of ethnically defined autonomies headed by local socialist leaders with an almost knee-jerk acceptance of Stalin's policy. With little regard for the wishes and views of the peoples themselves, specific groups were selected to help realize Stalin's plan. If any territory, carved up along ethno-linguistic lines by the Soviets, lacked a sufficient amount of working-class people—a hegemon in the Soviet socialist quasi-state formation—the Soviet government arbitrarily added territories with considerable populations of the working class to the newly formed polities with the titular ethnic groups/nations or resettled people of certain working professions into such territories *en masse*. For example, it has been long accepted that during the period of collectivization, approximately 25,000 working class representatives were sent to head the collectivization efforts and to organize collective farms in the predominantly rural areas of the newly formed union and autonomous Soviet Socialist Republics. In the 1930s, more of these people were sent to the so-called national republics to bolster the workforce in the course of rapid industrialization. Sometimes entire regions were added to the newly formed "socialist" entities and would become historically industrially developed territories, as well as the home for the "proletariat" class, which were, for the most part, ethnically Russian.

This is how regions such as Donbas appeared within the newly established Ukrainian Soviet Socialist Republic (USSR). This same process would come to characterize almost all the emerging Soviet national administrative formations. By 1940, Stalin's Soviet state-building plan was accomplished and embodied by the specific administrative construction of the Soviet Union. Ironically enough, Stalin more or less continued the implementation of imperial categorization policies onto the Soviet peoples, albeit adding his own unique specificities. The people were divided into four categories:

> (1) The peoples of the first category consisted of the peoples that gave their *ethnic names* to the *Union Republics* (e.g., the Georgians in the Georgian Soviet Socialist Republic [GSSR], Latvians in the Latvian Soviet Socialist Republic [LSSR], Ukrainians in the Ukrainian Soviet Socialist Republic [USSR], etc.).
>
> (2) The peoples of the second category consisted of the peoples who gave their *ethnic name* to the autonomous republics (e.g., the North-Ossetian Autonomous Soviet Socialist Republic [ASSR] in the Russian Federation, or the Abkhazian Autonomous Soviet Socialist Republic in the GSSR, etc.).
>
> (3) The peoples of the third category consisted of the peoples that gave their *ethnic names* to the national autonomous districts (e.g., the Armenians in the Nagorno-Karabakh Autonomous District in the Azerbaijan SSR, or the South Ossetians in the South-Ossetian Autonomous District of the GSSR, etc.).
>
> (4) The peoples of the fourth category consisted of the peoples that gave their *ethnic names* to the autonomous (national) regions (*okrugs*) (e.g., the Buriats of the Aginsk Buriat Autonomous (National) region in the Chita District of the Russian Federation, etc.).[20]

The paradox of this construction in the long run, based on the ideological dogmas of Soviet interpretation of ethnicity, was in the fact that the officially declared goal of achieving "national equality" in reality led to the creation of hierarchically ranked concessions typically seen in the *imperial* and *mini-imperial* social organizations. In fact, the Armenians, the Azerbaijanis, the Georgians, the Ukrainians, and other titular ethnic nations often enjoyed more rights and privileges that the subordinate, non-titular ethnic nations/groups. These privileges were legalized in the Soviet variant of an affirmative action policy.

Stalinist Categorization and Radicalization of Nationality Constituent of Ethnicity

I will further demonstrate that ethnic names and territorial dimensions are very important parts of the *nationality* constituent of ethnicity, ethnic groups, and nations. For example, when Georgian ethnocentric nationalists came to power in their country in October 1990, they stripped the South Ossetians of their autonomous status as one of their first acts. They then replaced the more ethnic name of the region, given to it by the Soviets, with the Georgian name of this ethnic territory—Shida Kartly (Inner-Georgia).[21] Now we can see the implementation of a mass campaign of renaming Russian or Soviet place names with the titular ethnic nations in all the newly independent former Soviet Republics. States like Georgia and Ukraine, and even many of the former "autonomous republics" (now "sovereign republics") that constituted the Russian Federation share this trend almost unilaterally. Recently, Sergei Filatov, former head of President Boris Yeltsin's administration, while commenting on the visits of delegations from Donets'k, Luhans'k, and Crimea to the Supreme Council of Russia in autumn 1991, testified that the latter came to Moscow with the request not to leave them within the borders of Ukraine on the grounds that "these are primordial Russian lands that Bolsheviks had given to Kiev" out of ideological considerations. According to Filatov, the delegations humbly asked "not to leave them under Kiev's power" on the eve of the *Belovezhskoe Agreement.* He also related to them that "they [the delegates] have no equal rights with the Ukrainians." "We did not have time to deal with this request," continued Filatov, "at that moment we thought only how to preserve Russia itself."[22] A week before the *Belovezhskoe Agreement*, the document concerning the dissolution of the Soviet Union, was signed, there had been a referendum centered on the status of Ukrainian Independence on December 1, 1990. When it came time to vote, 90 percent of Ukrainian people voted in favor of the *Act o Nezalezhnosti Ukraini* ("Act about Ukrainian Independence").[23]

Such actions and other, similar facts will be more imperatively discussed within the relevant aspects of this and other chapters to indicate that the specific ethnically hierarchical Soviet construction was (and to some extent still is) a most *powerful historic prerequisite of modern ethnic conflicts in post-Soviet space.* In the long run, this division became a veritable landmine resting beneath the Soviet Union state. And during the time of the all-sided societal crisis from the late 1980s to the early 1990s, it finally went off, blowing the USSR to pieces along these well-established ethnic lines. The incorrect assessment of the nature of ethnicity, with an emphasis on "material culture" and "economic ties" serving as the most important attributes, worked alongside the belief in the gradual "atrophy" of other ethnic peculiarities in the creation of a "homogeneous socialist economy and society" in its further movement toward communism and cost all Soviet peoples dearly. It resulted in the loss of numerous human lives sacrificed on the altar of the blistery dream of revolutionary fanatics who secured the power of the government in 1917 and began the process that turned its self-confident sectarian virtue into a nationwide evil. To paraphrase Bertrand Russell's thought, in Russia, a new society has been created in much the same way that mythical Lycurgus supposedly created the Spartan polity; the ancient lawgiver was a benevolent myth; the modern Soviet lawgiver was (and under the new accoutrements of nationalism still is) a most terrifying reality.

Recurrent Constituents and Cultural Boundary Markers of Ethnicity as Demonstrated in the Caucasus Examples

My advanced studies of ethnicity came from the perspective of a professional historian and former native of the Caucasus. The Caucasus is easily one of the most topographically, climatically, and linguistically varied regions on Earth. With that in mind, it is a natural laboratory for ethnographic studies. All the same, the region attained a historical unity through its important position as a 600-mile-long mountain range between two seas and a crossroads of international trade. For these two major reasons alone, the Caucasus has been a battleground of peoples, cultures, and religions since ancient times. Cimmerians, Scythians, Sarmatians, Alans, Greeks, Romans, Byzantines, Persians, Arabs, Turks, Mongols, and Russians have all been involved in the Caucasus and have fought over it, leaving parts of themselves behind as a result. Those who retreated into the mountains built stone fortresses and established a mountain culture with horizontal social ties; those who cooperated with the conquerors remained in the fertile plains to the north and south and in time became ethnically mixed groups with a different feudal pattern and vertical social ties for sustaining themselves. The invasion, the lengthy occupation, and the rejection or accommodation of the various groups who then lived in the area became one anchor around which different ethnic identities were formed. I listened to the ballads of Shakespeare—like folk epics, in which various ethnic groups told their histories and began to understand that this was the method by which they tied their people together. In the same way, each group recalled and elaborated events that had taken place hundreds, or even thousands, of years earlier. In particular, the groups who retreated into the mountains recalled and constantly elaborated on the terrible defeats that they suffered at the hands of invaders—defeats so devastating that they could never be resolved. These memories, which one may call *chosen traumas*,[24] were readily substituted for an accurate and systematic written history and became a recurrent attribute and constituent of ethnic identity.

While visiting my friends of different ethnic groups, I became aware of yet another incredibly important attribute/constituent of their ethnicities. Many people's ethnic connection comes from the ruins of their clan's mountain cities, the eerie necropolis, and the abandoned clan's fields. Most modern residents have visited these ancient sites, where the bodies of their distant blood relatives still lie, and have looked out over the fields, where the traces of long-forgotten boundaries are still visible. Yet most know few facts about these remarkable vestiges beyond that they are the remnants of their brave kinsmen from the distant past. But on a more emotional level, the legacy of the ancient nests of these clans still resonates in the minds of the public. The ruins can even speak to outsiders, and I remember them giving my colleagues, Professors Peter Petschauer and Wayne Morris, a sense of the immense power they exert on every ethnic group in the region. The same impression came to Sebastian Smith, author of a wonderful book about the Caucasus titled *Allah's Mountains* and who I hosted in the mountains during the early 1990s.[25] The sacred nature of one of the most important attributes of ethnicity found its ultimate expression in the Caucasian proverb, "It is not a clan that owns land, but the land that owns the clan." Numerous Caucasian examples enabled me to understand why the traditional *Adats* (common laws of Caucasian peoples) and *Shariates* were primary targets of assimilatory attempts by super-ordinate powers and groups, be they historical incarnations of the Imperial or Soviet states. These codes represent a naturally emerged compendium of protective norms and values that, in fact, have legitimized specific stereotypes and behavioral patterns that fit alongside other ends for self-preservation of ethnic originality by securing sufficient ground for normal functioning of its *natural ethnic constituents* in all of their varieties.[26]

According to the Adats, *kinship* (common biological origins and/or ties) formed the main basis on which mountaineer societies were historically constructed and continue to function. The principal sacred duty of the living members of an extended family was and still is to produce offspring in order to preserve the clan's ability to both worship the dead and preserve its future. The terms for living members in Ossetia are *myggag* and *rvadalta*; in Chechnya and Ingushetia, *teip* or *teipa*; in Dagestan, *tukhum*; and in Kabarda, Adygea, *k'uae*. The biological force that keeps the clan alive, representing its living underpinning, is the sperm. Clan members believe it to be the link between past, present, and future generations. It is then by no means an accident that the Ossetian word *myggag* (family) originates from the root word *myg*, or sperm. Historically, the continuity of noble families and clans has been preserved and protected by mountaineer laws and expressed through the idea of "one blood" and "one bone." Members of each clan or tribe, and in the long run the entire folk/*adam*, constituted a blood community. According to one *Malsagov-Ingushian* family member, his clan numbers some 20,000 living members, and should he meet someone from this massive group in the distant lands, like Siberia or the United States, they will treat each other as brothers and help one another regardless of the circumstances. To impinge on the rights, dignity, or property of even the poorest member of any given family, even if the offense was no more than a rude comment or a man's awkward touch of a woman during a folk dance, could provoke a sharp reply from relatives and lead to a long and bloody vendetta against all members of the offender's own family.[27] My studies of the common laws in Central Asia (*Adats* in Central Asia and *Pashtu Vali* code in Afghanistan) reveal similar norms and important attributes of ethnicity in the local ethnic communities. Among them are also religious constituents of ethnicity and customs of a common cult.[28] However, the content of the formative evolution of ethnic groups in tandem with the historical and modern disputes in all these regions urges me to count *language* among the more important substances of ethnicity. It is very symptomatic that the silver-tongued Sheikh Kunta-Khadji Kishiev, founder of the popular *zikrism* mystical tradition and the brightest representative of the Sufi *naqshbandiya tariq* (order), during the first Caucasian War (1819–1859) taught his mountain dwelling followers,

> The ongoing Caucasian war does not please God. If they [the Russians] tell you that you should go to church, go, for it is merely a building. If they force you to carry a cross, carry it, for it is merely iron, in your hearts and souls, however, *you remain Muslims*. However, *if they touch your wife, force you to forget your native language, culture and customs, stand up and fight to the very last man!*[29]

One can see that in this sermon, the sheikh enumerated certain attributes/constituents of ethnicity, among them language, that are of a special value for the people's survival and continuity. In view of a longstanding governmental practice of suppressing native languages, one ought not be too surprised that right after the Russian Revolution of 1917, and again during Gorbachev's *perestroika* and *glasnost'* initiatives, the political struggle of various ethnic groups vying for independence began with efforts to enhance the status of their respective native languages as the most important indicators of ethnicity. They wanted "their" language to be the main means of communication in their areas and in their schools, ultimately trying to reduce the number of Russian-language schools. That is why eighteen of the twenty-three above-cited interviewed Russian emigrants and ten of the fifteen interviewed Ukrainians identified language as one of the most crucial building blocks of the current Russian-Ukrainian conflict.

All other secondary indicators of ethnicity could also be identified in close acquaintance with the common regulations of the *Adats*, particularly when concerning the tradition of hospitality. Traditional meals are occasions to celebrate, to receive a guest, to reaffirm the social and gender standing in the community, and to form or maintain alliances. For example, in the traditional cookery of the Caucasus, one can find a lot of special dishes that carry a vivid imprint of a concrete ethnicity and serve as classical secondary cultural markers of ethnic differentiation and subsidiary indices of separateness. Anyone in the Caucasus knows that *khinkali* (a sort of Caucasian dumpling) and *satsvii* (fried chicken in pecan gravy) are trademarks of Georgian cookery; that *wolibakhs* (round pies with special cheese stuffing, a Caucasian pizza) are a symbol of Ossetian hospitality; and that the Armenian *dolma*, Azerbaijani *liulya-kyabob*, and the Chechen *zhizhig-talnakh* all represent some measure of ethnic pride and belonging.[30]

Special arrangements of ritual tables and feasts and rituals of the traditional calendars are distinguished by peculiar specificities within different ethnic cultures. People who have lived in the Caucasus for a long time can merely glance at one of these ceremonies—even in fragmented forms imprinted in photographs or captured on film—and then tell you which particular ethnic community is holding it. For example, the *shashlyk* is the most famous traditional meal shared by all ethnic groups in the Caucasus and in almost all areas of the former Soviet Union. To an outsider, it looks like pieces of grilled meat on skewers. Yet an insider familiar with the local ethno-cultural diversity may be able to discern the origin of the particular *shashlyk* being served, be they Uzbek, Kazakh, Georgian, Ossetian, Armenian, Chechen, or other. Other details like the marinade, the meat itself, and even the flavor of smoke produced by the burning of different woods vary greatly within different ethnic cookeries. Using these "hints," a competent insider may correctly identify an ethnic variant of this dish, even to the point of recognizing it by the side dish or dressing paired with the main course.[31]

The same applies to *borscht/borsch/borsht/borshch*. This is a sour soup that is very popular throughout Eastern Europe, especially in the former Russian Empire and Soviet Union, and in many other countries, spreading by way of human migration. In English, the word *borscht* is most often associated with the Ukrainian variant, even if it is also commonly linked to either Jews or Mennonites, who were the first to bring it to the Americas from Europe.[32] Nevertheless, several ethnic groups claim *borscht*, in its various local guises, as their own *national dish*, consumed as part of ritual meals within Eastern Orthodox, Greek Catholic, Roman Catholic, and Jewish religious traditions. I met a lot of people from various ethnic communities who were ready and willing to physically fight another person if they dared to argue against their priority in inventing the most "genuine" and ethnically "correct" shashlyk or borscht. Recently, a similar event took place in the United States. Mr. Killian D. Hoffman, a thirty-seven-year-old New Yorker with Ukrainian roots, saw an advertisement in the window of a supermarket owned by a native Russian that said, "Borscht is a Russian dish." Hoffman was so infuriated by this claim that he filed a lawsuit against the owner of the supermarket, claiming that the latter had malignantly misled his customers and visitors with his signage. The courts sided with Hoffman and obliged the Russian owner to remove the advertisement from his store. Their decision was motivated by the highly respected *International ISBN Agency*, which stated that borscht "is a dish of Ukrainian origin."[33] It was at this point that I remembered the most delicious borscht I had ever eaten in my life was cooked by my grandmother Maria Isaenko, a hereditary Kuban Cossack woman (a lot of researchers consider that a part of the Kuban Cossacks stemmed from the Ukrainian Zaporijje Cossacks). She cooked it using pork and every time reminded me that this was genuine borscht, as Russians cooked it incorrectly by using "*korovyatina*" (beef).

Even this brief comparative survey demonstrates that ethnic groups are born, in part, of the space they occupy on the globe, the landscape that nourished them, the language that grants them access to the world, the songs that offer enjoyment in their adulthood, the God (or gods) who provides solace in their hardships, and the variety of rituals and common values that all members speak about frequently. They also become a distinct group by elaborating their own past and thereby separating themselves from others who live in the same area. By keeping past events and personages that focus them as a peculiar people alive, they are able to provide substance to the language they speak, the songs they sing, the prayers they offer, and the land that they populate.

Recommended Definitions of Ethnic Group (Including Ethnic Diaspora), Ethnic Nation

Raymond Taras and Rajat Ganguly have recently produced the most up-to-date definition of the term *ethnic group*. According to them, an ethnic group is

> a large or small group of people, in either traditional or advanced societies, who are united by a common inherited culture (including language, music, food, dress, and customs and practices), racial similarity, common religion, and belief in common history and ancestry and who exhibit a strong psychological sentiment of belonging to the group.

It is important for this research to note that ethnic groups can be of two types: *homeland societies* and *diaspora communities*. Homeland societies inhabit a particular territory that they claim to be their primordial ethnic land, and thus they claim "exclusive legal and moral rights of ownership over that land." More often than not, they develop historical and archaeological evidence, sometimes peppered with a mythological component, to prove their rights to any particular tract of land. Ethnic diaspora communities are members of a particular ethnic group who have found themselves in foreign countries as a result of population migrations or oppression in their home state. Ukrainian Diasporas are particularly strong in Canada, the United States, and, as of recently, other European countries. Taras and Ganguly, in reference to Ernest Barker, also indicate that ethnic groups may evolve into an *ethnic nation*. Such transformations may occur when "political and statist ideas develop within the group." It means that a significant number of people who form a community begin thinking of themselves as a nation and, consequentially, "behaving as if they were one."[34]

As we can see, the definition of ethnic group by Taras and Ganguly virtually embraces the same five aforementioned principal indications/attributes that I have found repeatedly displayed by most Caucasian ethnic groups in the course of their interaction between themselves and with the Russians.[35] Among them are (1) *language*; (2) *commonly shared dramatic history*, especially *mythologized memory of unresolved chosen traumas*;(3) adherence for or the right to particular *ethnic territories*, especially to those that have been taken by other ethnic groups; (4) *religion*; and (5) *biological origin* and *blood belonging*. All peoples have felt extremely uncomfortable and reacted sharply when any of these substantial attributes of their ethnicity were threatened.[36]

Five Principal Building Blocks, Three Principal and Three Secondary Cultural Boundary Markers of Ethnicity as a Living Organism

American anthropologist Manning Nash very aptly called these unalienable substances *"building blocks of ethnicity."*[37] Furthermore, he described them, in his own words, thus:

> (1) The *body* (a biological component expressed as blood, genes, bone, flesh, or other common "substance" shared among group members).

> (2) A *language* (some spoken and written forms of communications, meanings, essences, and stylistic elements unavailable in other languages).

> (3) A *shared history and origin* (this gives a sense of shared struggles, shared fate, common purpose, and the implication that personal and group fate are one and the same thing, with personal fate being itself dependent on group survival).

> (4) *Religion* (the set of beliefs and practices that purport to relate the group in a special way to the supernatural).

> (5) *Nationality* (this is the right to a territory, equality with the most powerful other nations, and all the symbolic and political accoutrements of a sovereign and independent people).[38]

> [I can add to this rubric also *ethnic name* as an important symbol of a sovereign people.]

Along with other cultural indicators mentioned in Taras and Ganguly's definition of ethnic groups, language can also play the role of an *ethnic boundary marker* that defines and marks off the groups from other, potentially similar groups.[39] Where there is a group, there exists some sort of boundary, and where there are boundaries, some mechanisms must act to maintain them. Nash defines these boundary mechanisms as "cultural markers of difference among groups." He had based his own conclusion on the study of African ethnic groups. For me, his observations and conclusions become convincing when I am aware of how my own perceptions about cultural boundary markers based on the study of ethnic communities in the Caucasus, including my native communities of Terek and Kuban Cossacks, which preserved the customs of their Ukrainian ancestors, found almost total coincidence with those described by Manning Nash. The most common and pervasive ethnic boundary markers are *kinship*, *commensality*, and a *common cult*.

The First Triad of Cultural Markers of Difference

According to Nash, *kinship* is a "presumed biological and descent unity of the groups implying a staff or substance continuity each group member has and outsiders do not."[40] In the Caucasus, within the communities of Terek and Kuban Cossacks, existed a traditional system of conflict prevention that helped to avert mutual hatred and extermination. Particularly, that system valued a standout custom relating to a cultural marker of *kinship*. By this, I am referring to the custom of creating an *artificial kinship*. This practice has not only marked off differences between ethnic groups but also performed the role of a cross-boundary mechanism of resistance to the feuds simultaneously. The practice of fraternization (*kunak*) was inherited by all ethnic groups in the Caucasus from their Scythian and Alan forerunners. The ritual aspect of the ceremony was first described by Herodotus and has not visibly changed since that time. The two participants each drop a small amount of blood and sacred personal items (like a cross in the Cossack communities, for example) in a cup—originally a horn—and drink from it. In this way they became *kinsmen* and accepted the obligations to each other's families in any and all situations. The sacred authority of the ritual was so powerful that a newly acquired relative was considered more reliable than a natural kinsman. Intermarriages and any resulting children brought up in the *kunak*'s families and estates were also welcome as part of their own. Such children learned the other clan's languages and traditions. The custom was called *atalychestvo* and the children *atalyks*. As adults, they could then become respected and skillful mediators for possible inter-clan conflicts. It is by this custom that mixed clans arose within ethnic vicinities, for example, *teips* of Arsenoi and Gunoi in Chechnya, which had historical relations to the Cossacks.[41]

Within Cossack communities were broadly spread such relationships as *kumovstvo*, which is inherited from their Ukrainian ancestors and still takes place in modern Ukraine. This is kinship specifically tied to blood, marriage, or the relationship of godparents. Today, such relationships characterize the system of mutual guarantees when relatives help each other in modern business, education, artistic endeavors, and in numerous other settings, as well as in state or political organizations, posing a genuine inhibition to hiring the most competent person. However, this habit leads to the overall spread of corruption, nepotism, and cronyism in the long run. One can find *kumoviya* and relatives well-established in the Ukrainian Parliament—Rada—as well as in the corresponding Russian political settings. Former Ukrainian President Petro Poroshenko and General Prosecutor Yury Lutsenko were both, in fact, *kums*. Such mutual guarantees may also lead to well-known criminals being protected by a powerful clan well-entrenched within the judicial system. An outsider unaware of such guarantees can draw assumptions and make statements detailing counterpoints of those in positions of power, questioning their appropriate background and training qualifications, all while ignoring the much more powerful clan connections that influence their decisions.[42]

Commensality is characterized as "the propriety of eating together indicating a kind of equality, peership, and the promise of further kinship links."[43] It greatly contributes to cohesiveness of ethnicity and works not only as a boundary mechanism but also as a constituent of ethnicity in its own right. It is so ingrained in ethnic culture that even today the most important agreement in the world of the ethnic decision-making elites is usually addressed and fixed during commensality-type table arraignments, dinners, or feasts.

A *common cult* is viewed as something "implicating a value system beyond time and empirical circumstances, sacred symbols and attachments coming from *illo tempore*."[44]

These three factors are grouped together into the *first triad* of "cultural markers of differences." Consisting of blood, substance, and deity, these three aspects symbolize the existence of the group and constitute it at the same time. It is therefore better to say that it helps the principal five building blocks of ethnicity to constitute it, because they serve as the basic (and for that matter—primordial) structure.

Second Triad of Cultural Markers of Difference

To use Nash's terms, the *second triad* of ethnic differentiation consists of "*index features*," which may include "1) *dress*, 2) *language*, and 3) culturally denoted *physical features*." The first rubric of this *secondary triad* of subsidiary indices of separateness, *dress*, is not simply limited to clothing. It also includes "house architecture and interior arraignments, ritual calendars, specific taboos in joint social participation, special medical practices, special economic policies, and a host of other secondary markers of differentiation."[45]

Language, or rather its ethnic vernacular variant, with a specific intonation, pronunciation, accent, and utterances used by the representatives of a primary group, may also be used as a marker of differentiation. When teaching at North-Ossetian State University in Vladikavkaz, Russia, I demonstrated this secondary index by asking students of a different ethnic origin within my multiethnic academic group to utter some phrases in Russian while I stood facing the wall with my back to the auditorium. They pronounced the conditional phrase in Russian, and by their accent, I was able to define from what ethnic community, and in some cases the form of the dialectical group, that student came from, all using my experience as a native of the Caucasus. With this experience, I could never confuse one specific "jargon" with another, be they townsman of Vladikavkaz, Grozny, Tbilisi, Baku, or central Russia, particularly Muscovites, and even Ukrainians, despite the fact that all of them were only speaking Russian.

Physical features may include skin color, hair form, height, density, eye shape, or whatever superficial details the culture stipulates as making the essential difference. It also includes less visible physical features, some of which are internal to the group, such as body mutilation (circumcision, scarification, or tattooing).[46]

Numeric Formula of a Viable Ethnic Group

All three of these secondary markers of differentiation and index features take their force of constituting and separating ethnic groups and persons within them only if they are originally linked to the core features of differences and if, through the *second triad*, they are also linked with the five basic building blocks of ethnicity. In this case, the entire ethnic construction as an organic and flexible living organism and a product of historical evolution may exist, function, and celebrate itself vis-à-vis other ethnic groups either independently or inside a pluralistic nation-state. If it does exist inside a larger nation-state that *declares its adherence to modern democratic political culture*, ideally the latter has to guarantee an ethnic group a "rightful place." This ensures that the sociopolitical and economic rules imposed by the titular ethnic nation and its policy of state building and modernization will allow ethnic minority groups equal access to the most important economic and sociopolitical and cultural resources and would not undermine even the least secondary constituent or element of differentiation inside the corresponding natural ethnic construction. Thus, the numeric index of a healthy and freely functioning ethnic group is effectively *5+3+3*. The more constituents of ethnicity and elements of differentiation that are being threatened as a result of realization of ethnocentric projects in the process of nation-state (or state-nation) building by more powerful titular ethnic nations, the higher the degree of absorption of ethnicity in political and social relationships between super-ordinate and subordinate groups occur, gradually leading to a regression into a more perilous phase of ethnic conflict. I will further discuss other details regarding principal factors and other circumstances leading to ethnic conflict in other aspects of the model.

Definition of a Nation

For now, I want to close out this aspect with a definition of *nation*, cited by Taras and Ganguly while rendering Barker's ideas:

> A *nation* is a body of people, inhabiting a *definite territory*, who normally *are drawn from different races*, but possess a common stock of thoughts and feelings acquired and trans-mitted during the course of a *common history*; who on the whole and in the main, though more in the past than the present, include in that common stock a *common religious* belief; who generally and as a rule use a *common language*, as the vehicle of their thoughts and feelings; and who, besides common thoughts and feelings, also cherish a *common will*, and accordingly form, or tend to form, a *separate state* for the expression and realization of that will.[47]

Notes

1   Max Weber, *Economy and Society: An Outline of Interpretative Sociology* (New York: Bedminster Press, 1968), 1:385–98, 2:221–26.
2   Herodotus argued that "The kinship of all Greeks is blood and speech, and the shrines of gods and the sacrifices that we have in common, and the likeness of our way of life." See Irene Polinskaya, "Shared Sanctuaries and the Gods of Others: On the Meaning of 'Common' in Herodotus 8.144," in *Valuing Others in Classical Antiquity* ed. Ralph M. Rosen and Ineke Sluiter (Leiden: Brill, 2010), 47–70; see also Athena S. Leoussi and Steven Grosby, *Nationalism and Ethno-Symbolism: History, Culture, and Ethnicity in the Formation of Nations* (Edinburgh: Edinburgh University Press, 2006), 115.
3   Max Weber, "The Origins of Ethnic Groups," in *Ethnicity*, ed. John Hutchinson and Anthony D. Smith (Oxford: Oxford University Press, 1996), 35; see also Anthony D. Smith, *The Ethnic Origins of Nations* (Oxford: Basil Blackwell, 1986), 21–31, 135–52. See also notes 5 and 6 in chapter 1 on Cynthya Enbe's criticism that "ethnicities do not necessarily hold single cultural characteristics" in Taras Kuzio, *Ukraine: State and Nation Building* (London: Routledge, 1998), 7, 237.
4   See "Introduction," in Frederick Barth, ed., *Ethnic Groups and Boundaries: The Social Organization of Social Difference* (Bergen-Oslo: Universitets Forlaget, 1990), 10–11.
5   See, Thomas Hylland Eriksen, "Ethnic Identity, National Identity and Intergroup Conflict: The Significance of Personal Experiences," in *Social Identity, Intergroup Conflict, and Conflict Reduction*, ed. Richard D. Ashmore, Lee Jussim, and David Wilder (Oxford: Oxford University Press, 2001).
6   Clifford Geertz, ed., *Old Societies and New States: The Quest for Modernity in Africa and Asia* (New York: Free Press, 1967); Cohen Abner, *Two-Dimensional Man: An Essay on Power and Symbolism*

in Complex Society (London: Routledge & Kegan Paul, 1974); Ernest Gelner, *Nationalism* (London: Weidenfeld &Nicolson, 1997).

7   Anthony D. Smith, *National Identity* (Harmondsworth, UK: Penguin, 1991).

8   Anthony D. Smith, *Nationalism and Modernism: A Critical Survey of Recent Theories of Nations and Nationalism* (London: Routledge, 1998), 159; Anthony D. Smith, *Myths and Memories of the Nation* (Oxford: Oxford University Press, 1999), 4–7, 13; Donald L. Noel, "A Theory of Origin of Ethnic Stratification," *Social Problems* 16, no. 2 (1968): 157–72; Gerald Sider, *Lumbee Indian Histories* (Cambridge, UK: Cambridge University Press, 1993).

9   See David Konstan, "Defining Ancient Greek Ethnicity," *Diaspora: A Journal of Transnational Studies* 6, no. 1 (1997): 97–110.

10 Konstan, "Defining Ancient Greek Ethnicity," 98.

11 See Taras Kuzio, *Ukraine: State and Nation Building*, 7. See also his references on: David Saunders, "What Makes a Nation a Nation?" *Ethnic Groups* 10 (1993): 119; Ihor Sevcenko, "The Rise of National Identity to 1700," in *Ukraine between East and West* (Edmonton: Canadian Institute of Ukrainian Studies, 1996), 187–96. See also Walter Schmidt, "The Nation in German History," in *The National Question in Europe in Historical Context*, ed. Mikulas Teich and Roy Porter (Cambridge, UK: Cambridge University Press, 1993), 151.

12 Alexander Gradovskii, *Nachala russkago gosudarstvennago prava* (St. Petersburg: Sytin, 1875), 1:394.

13 Peter Petschauer and Anatoly Isaenko, "Finding the Middle Ground: The Practical and Theoretical Center between Ethnic Ideal and Extreme Behaviors," *Mind and Human Interaction: Windows between History, Culture, Politics, and Psychoanalysis* 12, no. 1 (2001):52–74.

14 Vladimir I. Kozlov, "Etnicheskaya obshnost'," *Bolshaya Sovetskaya Encyclopedia* (1977),16:376.

15 Iosif V. Stalin, *Sochineniya* (Moscow: Gospolitizdat, 1946), 2: 273.

16 Stepan T. Kaltakhchyan, "Natsyia,"*Bolshaya Sovetskaya Encyclopedia* (Moscow: Gosizdat, 1977), 16: 375.

17 Stepan T. Kaltakhchyan, "Narodnost," *Bolshaya Sovetskaya Encyclopedia* (Moscow: Gosizdat, 1977), 16:280.

18 *Slovnik Ukrains'koi Movy* (Kyiv: Naukova Dumka, 1974), 5:232–33 (emphasis added).

19 Taras Kuzio, *Ukraine: State and Nation Building*, 8–11, 21–22.

20 See Valerii D. Dzidzoev, *Natsional'nye otnosheniya na Kavkaze* (Vladikavkaz, Russia: Ir Publishing House, 1995), 5.

21 In August 1990, the Georgian Parliament did not allow the Ossetian *Adamon Nykhas* popular movement to take part in Georgian elections. In response, the South-Ossetian Soviet declared the region the "South-Ossetian Soviet Democratic Republic" and appealed to Moscow to recognize it "as an independent subject of the Soviet Federation."After this, the Georgian government canceled all South-Ossetian autonomy. See Anatoly Isaenko, *Polygon of Satan: Ethnic Traumas and Conflicts in the Caucasus*, 3rd ed. (Dubuque, IA: Kendall Hunt, 2014), 165.

22 Several variants of this interview were published by many media sources. In this case, the author follows the one published by *Kommersant*.

23 See interview with Sergei Filatov, "Soratnik Yeltsina rasskazal o pros'be Donbasa i Kryma v 1991 godu ne ostavlyat' ikh v sostave Ukrainy," *Kommersant* (December 8, 2019), kommersant.ru/doc/4187488?utm_source=smi2_agr.

24 Vamik D. Volkan, "On Chosen Traumas," *Mind and Human Interaction* 3, no. 1 (1991): 13.

25 Sebastian Smith, *Allah's Mountains: The Battle for Chechnya* (London: I. B. Tauris, 2006), Preface.

26 Anatoly Isaenko and Peter Petschauer, "Traditional Civilization in the North Caucasus," in *Honoring Differences: Cultural Issues in the Treatment of Trauma and Loss*, ed. Kathleen Nader, Nancy Dubrow, B. Hudnall Stamm (Washington, DC: Taylor & Francis Group, 1999), 161–62.

27 Henry Field, *Contributions to the Anthropology of the Caucasus* (London: Cambridge University Press, 1953), chapter 1.

28 Anatoly Isaenko, "Family and Kinship in Central Asia," in Peter N. Sterns, ed., *Oxford Encyclopedia of the Modern World, 1750 to the Present* (Oxford: Oxford University Press, 2008), 3:263–64.

29 Emil Souleimanov, *An Endless War: The Russian-Chechen Conflict in Perspective* (Frankfurt, Germany: Peter Lang, 2007), 69 (emphasis added).

30 Isaenko, *Polygon of Satan*, 102–3.

31 Isaenko, *Polygon of Satan*, 102.

32 Nikolai Burlakov, *The World of Russian Borsch: Exploration of Memory, People, History, Cookbooks, and Recipes* (New York City, NY: Aelita Press, 2013); Lidiya Artyukh, *Ukrains'ka Narodna Kulinariya* (Kyiv: Naukova dumka, 1977).

33 "Bandera's Descendant in the USA Is Suing a Russian Store over Borscht," *Rusvesna*, December 1, 2019, https://rusvesna.su/news/1575194076?utm_source=smi.

34 Raimond Taras and Rajat Ganguly, *Understanding of Ethnic Conflict: The International Dimension*, 4th ed. (New York: Longman, Pearson Education, 2006), 1–3; see also Eric Hobsbaum, *Nations and Nationalism Since 1780: Programme, Myth, Reality* (Cambridge, UK: Cambridge University Press, 1990), 5.

35 Isaenko, *Polygon of Satan*, chapters 1–2.

36 Isaenko, *Polygon of Satan*, 98.

37 Manning Nash, *The Cauldron of Ethnicity in the Modern World* (Chicago: University of Chicago Press, 1989), 5.

38 Nash, *Cauldron of Ethnicity*, 5.

39 Taras and Ganguly, *Understanding of Ethnic Conflict*, 1–3.

40 Nash, *Cauldron of Ethnicity*, 10.

41 Isaenko and Petschauer, "Traditional Civilization," 171.

42 Isaenko and Petschauer, "Traditional Civilization," 162.

43 Nash, *Cauldron of Ethnicity*, 11.

44 Nash, *Cauldron of Ethnicity*, 11–12.

45 Nash, *Cauldron of Ethnicity*, 12; See also Manning Nash, "The Core Elements of Ethnicity," in *Ethnicity*, ed. John Hutchinson and Anthony D. Smith (Oxford: Oxford University Press, 1996).

46 Nash, *Cauldron of Ethnicity*, 13. See also Isaenko, *Polygon of Satan*, 98–103.

47 Ernest Barker, *National Character and the Factors in Its Formation* (London: Methuen & Co. LTD, 1927), 17, quoted in Norman D. Palmer and Howard C. Perkins, *International Relations: The World Community in Transition*, 3rd ed. (New Delhi: CBS Publishers, 1985), 19 (emphasis added, with the exception of "*separate state*"); see also Taras and Ganguly, *Understanding Ethnic Conflict*, 2.

CHAPTER TWO

The Place of Ethnic Groups in the Structure of the Modern World

Potential Transformation of Local Ethnic Conflicts into a Clash between More Powerful Units of the World Pyramid

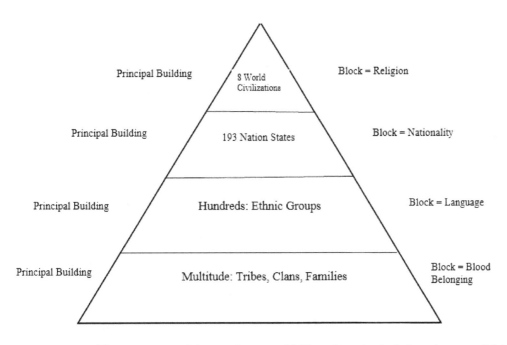

FIGURE 2.1   The structure of the modern world. The pieces included at the top of this "pyramid" are classified as *world civilization* units. A level beneath them are *nation-states*, which compose larger modern civilizations, and underneath them are *ethnic groups*, which similarly form the structure of *nation-states*. Finally, at the very bottom of the "pyramid" rest the pieces that historically constructed *ethnic groups*, which are *tribes*, *clans*, and *family groups*.

Definition of a World Civilization and the Most Important Building Blocks for Each Unit in the Structure of the World

According to Samuel P. Huntington, and as noted on the above diagram, eight *world civilizations* exist. These include the "Western, Confucian, Japanese, Islamic, Hindu, Slavic-Orthodox, Latin-American, and possibly African Civilization[s]."[1] A world civilization can be defined as

> an overlapping grouping of states brought together in varying degrees by history, culture, religion, language, location, and institutions.[2]

This definition indicates several things through its wording, the first of which is that civilizations "are differentiated from each other by history, language, culture, tradition, [territory], and, *most importantly, religion*."[3] Second, if to compare this definition to the above-cited definitions of ethnic groups and nation-states, each unit of this conditional pyramid consists of the same five principal building blocks that have been mentioned several times previously (except for a biological constituent, in the case of a civilization). Third, all of them are important constituents for each of these levels, but for the civilizations, the *religious building block* plays a vitally important defining and formative role. This importance is symbolically reflected in some of the names of these civilizations. Religious differences of this kind are products of centuries-long machinations, and they will be present well into the foreseeable future, but their fundamentally formative role is to define "relations between God and man, the individual and the group, the citizens and the state, parents and children, husband and wife, as well as different views of the relative importance of rights and responsibilities, liberty and authority, equality and hierarchy."[4]

Comparative research of interactions between *nation-states* in a historical perspective has allowed me to ascertain that, for them, the most important building block is *nationality*, especially in its territorial dimension. For the *tribes*, *clans*, and *families*, the importance of a *common biological origin* is foremost in defining themselves.[5] The content of formative evolution of both *ethnic groups* and modern ethnic disputes in the Caucasus and in other places within the former Soviet Union urges me to count *language* among the most important building blocks of ethnicity for ethnic groups.[6]

Where Do the Most Dangerous Ethnic Conflicts Originate?

A number of experts still share (even in a critical form) "this or that" aspect of the methodology proposed by Samuel Huntington. After the collapse of Communism, principal conflicts began to develop along the *civilization fault lines* while supplanting ideological conflicts and other forms of conflict (like between nation-states). These experts believe that "conflicts between groups in different civilizations will be more frequent, more sustained and more violent than conflicts between groups in the same civilization; violent conflicts between groups in different civilizations are the most likely and most dangerous source of escalation that could lead to global wars."[7] Reflecting on this methodology, R.C. Longworth stated that "there is a *cultural war* going on in the world, between globalism and tribal societies, between the tradition and information age, between ancient truths and the revolutionary ideas and technologies that are shattering societies shaped by those truths."[8]

While not arguing against the validity of this analysis and recognizing that this type of conflict exists throughout the world, I think that one does not need to disregard or underestimate the ethnic character of other violent eruptions on another level of the world "pyramid," including between ethnic groups *inside the same civilizations*. As a matter of fact, the father of the abovementioned methodology rather accurately assessed that "the end of ideologically defined states in Eastern Europe and the former Soviet Union permits *traditional ethnic identities and animosities to come to the fore*."[9] Yet he underestimated the depth of this "animosity," fed by the volumes of unresolved ethnic chosen traumas that remained suppressed under the totalitarian regime. Being preoccupied with the ideas of "civilizational clash" and "cultural conflict," he wrote: "While there has been serious fighting between Muslims and Christians elsewhere in the former Soviet Union and much tension and some fighting between Western and Orthodox Christians in the Baltic states, there has been *virtually no violence between Russians and Ukrainians*."[10] Now, we know that, after 2014, a bloody ethnic conflict between these ethnic nations has entered its *hot stage* in Donbas, in spite of the fact that they belong to the same Eastern Orthodox Christian civilization. As a result, this dangerous conflict is poisoning relations between the East and West, particularly between the United States and Russia, the strongest nuclear powers in the world.

My point is that in the modern world (which we hear about from the media every day), *the potential for conflict is accumulating on all levels and between all units of the world "pyramid."* It is very much akin to the name Huntington gave to conflicts on the upper floor of the world "pyramid," along the "fault lines" of civilizations: "The West versus the rest ... The very phrase 'world community' has become a euphemism to give legitimacy to the actions of the West."[11] However, in my opinion, the most dangerous conflicts are those taking place on the third floor of the "pyramid," *between ethnic groups, which are fraught with the potential to transform into a global war.* Bloody conflicts between ethnic groups may easily involve "kin"[12] nation-states who are supporting competing groups indirectly or even directly. Since the nation-states may be separated by different religious building blocks into separate world civilizations, especially sharp ethnic conflicts may flare up as a result. These would occur when certain ethnic groups with close connections to the most powerful nation-states (core states of civilization units, especially those at the head of military and political institutions and amalgamations of other "kin countries") trigger deterioration in the relationships between them and the other most powerful nation-states over their support of different ethnic groups. In a worst-case scenario, this *could provoke armed conflict*, with uncontrollable fatal escalation, leading to mutual destruction and the real "end of history" for humankind.

To demonstrate this possible transformation, we may refer to the latest cycle of ethnic conflicts between Georgia–South Ossetia and Georgia–Abkhazia, in which the West was indirectly involved and Russia, by 2008, was directly involved. One of the more recent and most well-prepared and well-funded Western projects of democratic state building in Georgia, regarding solving existing ethnic problems in the Georgian government, the primary recipient of generous Western help, has been carried out with an accord of notorious ethnocentric behavioral patterns. As my good colleague, well-studied expert Richard Giragosian, noted: "Rejection by the regional leadership of accommodation and compromise forms the basis for a new framework of post-Soviet politics that continues to favor the power of the pirate over the patriot. This distortion of democracy is rooted primarily in the *leadership's reliance on coercion (or the threat of coercion) as the dominant political institution*."[13] In the penultimate chapters of this book, I will specifically show that this is true in the case of the latest Russo-Ukrainian conflict, which has even more dangerous potential to transform into a fatal conflict between the East and West.

When Mikhail Saakashvili secured his position on the "Olympus of power" in Tbilisi, he began his state-sponsored activity by loudly voicing his determination to get "the mutinous outlying districts" under control. Using force, he quickly subdued Adjaria and declared that his next targets would be South Ossetia and Abkhazia.[14] In spite of the Abkhazian catastrophe of 1993, Saakashvili revitalized an old ethnocentric project, with all of its various stereotypes intact: (1) If war breaks out in South Ossetia, it would be a war between Georgia and Russia. He understood that North Ossetians who live in Russia would invariably interfere on the side of their co-ethnics, as well as the Russian Army's facing the threat of an all-Ossetian uprising if they refused to save kin Ossetians in the south. (2) He believed that Georgia needed to leave the control commission and cancel the Sochi Agreement, which had been concluded in the aftermath of the earlier *hot stage* of the conflict in South Ossetia, because Russia was declared Georgia's primary enemy. (3) Ossetians and Abkhazians are effectively the stooges of Russia and, therefore, the enemy. (4) The West is an ally of Georgia and, in the case of a war with Russia, will inevitably interfere *militarily* on the side of the Georgians. The last premise was (and still is) the most dangerous component of ethnocentrically twisted minds and mythology[15] and is once again developing in Ukraine and in Russia through machinations of nationalists and those in power in both states.

As a matter of fact, Ron Asmus, a US State Department official from the Clinton administration, alleged in his book *The Little War That Shook the World* that "President George W. Bush and his senior aides *considered*—and rejected—a military response to Russia's 2008 invasion of Georgia … Bush's national security aides outlined possible responses, including 'the bombardment and sealing of the Roki Tunnel' and other 'surgical strikes'" against the Russian Army coming to the rescue of the South Ossetians, who had been attacked by the Georgian Army on the order of Saakashvili.[16] One can only imagine what may have come to pass in Georgia if they had been allowed to join NATO. It is this very same situation that is ripening in Ukraine now. Let me repeat that the Ukrainian ethnic nation has a very strong and powerful amalgamation of Diasporas in the West, especially in the United States and Canada. Similarly, Russia also has a large population of their co-ethnics living in Ukraine. In the subsequent chapters, I will demonstrate that the modern political institutional design of post-Soviet Ukraine was (and increasingly is) unfavorable to the Russian Diaspora in the eastern and southern regions. After the tragic events of 2014, primarily in Euromaidan (better known in Ukraine as *Revolutsiya Hidnisti* ["Revolution of Dignity"]), and how these events went into the modern Ukrainian ethnic consciousness and mythology, the Russian Diaspora have undergone very heavy amounts of radicalization, especially when violence erupted in Donbas against their ethnic compatriots, who had been already in rebellion against the new government in Kyiv, instigated and reinforced by Russian nationalists from the territory of Russia. Volunteers, humanitarian aid, and even military personnel, just to name a few, are coming from Russia to support the co-ethnic rebels within Ukraine.[17]

Brief Outlook on Ukrainian Diaspora in the West

On the other side, the Ukrainian Diaspora has a long history in the West. The first wave of migrants was predominantly represented by young men from the Ukrainian territories, under the sway of the Austro-Hungarian Empire, who intended to earn some money and then return home. They congregated in the northeastern United States to work as coal miners and industrial laborers. However, many of these men chose not to return home, staying in America to be soon joined by their families. This is how such vibrant Ukrainian communities came to be in major American cities across the northeast, such as in Pittsburgh, Philadelphia, and Chicago.[18]

After the 1890s, this first wave was followed by a second wave of their peasant compatriots, once again from the territory of the Austro-Hungarian Empire. This time, however, they were coming with their entire families, all in a desire to secure arable lands in Brazil and Argentina, but eventually Canada became the most attractive place for them to immigrate to. Once there, they could also secure work in the construction of the massive Canadian Pacific Railroad. This enterprise required a large workforce to complete, and it is for this reason that the Canadian government welcomed the influx of Ukrainian peasants. According to Serhy Yekelchyk, "by the time of World War I, an estimated 500,000 Ukrainians" had already settled in the New World.[19] The third large wave of Ukrainian immigrants came at the end of World War II. This group consisted primarily of refugees of Stalin's regime and former Nazi slave laborers, predominantly coming from Galicia and other territories in Western Ukraine, which had been incorporated into the USSR on the eve of the war. These immigrants, totaling around 80,000 headed to the United States and 30,000 to Canada, were a "well-educated generation" of "displaced persons," who had suffered under both Stalin's and Hitler's totalitarian regimes. They became leaders in establishing more vibrant ethnic community organizations in North America with a very strong "anticommunist political profile." At the same time, small postwar Ukrainian communities would emerge in Great Britain and Australia.[20]

Based on recent census data, one may count approximately 1,209,000 people of full or partial Ukrainian descent in Canada and 961,000 in the United States. Most of the more recent arrivals, coming after the collapse of the Soviet Union in 1991, represent a generation of young professionals. During crucial events such as the Orange Revolution of 2004–2005 in Kyiv and the crises of 2013–2014, these young people were brought closer to the established Ukrainian community organizations and participated in public rallies and vigils in support of domestic ethnic forces in their conflict with Russians, especially in large cities like New York, Chicago, Philadelphia, Toronto, Edmonton, and Winnipeg.[21] It should then come as no surprise that Russia feels that her Diaspora in Ukraine, especially those in the south and east and Donbas in particular, are seriously threatened. In such cases, and as Charles King and Neil I. Melvin showed in their 2000 article, "Kin states may feel pressured to protect the interest of co-ethnics abroad."[22] I agree with both this and another of their conclusions, which saw that the conflict within a "host state" may enhance the "sense of attachment between homelands and diaspora" and that "ethnic ties *may be a catalyst for the spread of conflict across international borders.*"[23]

Of course, ethnic linkages and powerful diasporas will not be enough to urge a kin state to jeopardize their own political stability and "expend economic resources by plunging" into ethnic conflict, especially when it is within the *hot stage* of openly confrontational ethnic war. Along with other circumstances and factors, it may depend on how the entire ethnic community reacts to crisis situations of this kind. Thus, one may be interested in how particular ethnic groups used to react to such challenges in a more historical perspective. Hence, our next aspect of the theoretical model to be analyzed in the next chapter.

Notes

1   Samuel P. Huntington, "The Clash of Civilizations?" in *The Clash of Civilizations? The Debate*, ed. Samul P. Huntington (New York: Foreign Affairs, 1996), 3. Sometimes the "Western" civilization is

referred to as the "Judeo-Christian Western Civilization" and the "Slavic-Orthodox" as the "Eastern Christian Orthodox Civilization."

2   Samuel P. Huntington, "Response. If Not Civilizations, What? Paradigms of the Post–Cold War World," in *The Clash of Civilizations? The Debate*, ed. Samuel P. Huntington (New York: Foreign Affairs, 1996),63.

3   Huntington, "The Clash of Civilizations?"in *The Clash of Civilizations?*, 4 (emphasis added; bracketed term is my own addition).

4   Huntington, "The Clash of Civilizations?"in *The Clash of Civilizations?*, 4.

5   Anatoly Isaenko, *Polygon of Satan: Ethnic Traumas and Conflicts in the Caucasus*, 3rd ed. (Dubuque, IA: Kendall Hunt, 2014), 99.

6   Isaenko, *Polygon of Satan*, chapters 1–3.

7   Samuel P. Huntington, "The Clash of Civilizations?" *Foreign Affairs*, vol. 72, no. 3 (Summer 1993): 48.

8   R.C. Longworth, "America's Embrace Feels, to Some, Like a Fatal Squeeze," *The Charlotte Observer*, September 6, 1988, 1c and 4c.

9   Huntington, "The Clash of Civilizations?" *Foreign Affairs*, 29 (emphasis added).

10 Huntington, "The Clash of Civilizations?" *Foreign Affairs*, 38 (emphasis added).

11 Huntington, "The Clash of Civilizations?" *Foreign Affairs*, 39–40.

12 As the post–Cold War world evolves, civilization commonality, what H.D.S. Greenway has termed "kin-country syndrome," is replacing political ideology and traditional balance-of-power considerations as the principal basis for cooperation and coalitions. Cited in Huntington, "The Clash of Civilizations?" *Foreign Affairs*, 35.

13 Richard Giragosian, "Dead-End Politics in the South Caucasus," *Radio Free Europe/Radio Liberty, RFE/RLNewsline* 8, no. 78, part 1 (27 April, 2004): 2 (emphasis added).

14 Dmitrii Ivanov, "Natsional'naya gruzinskaya mifologia," *VIP Lenta RU*, (2004), http://vip.lenta.ru/news/2004/07/22/georgia.

15 Isaenko, *Polygon of Satan*, 175; see also chapters 4–5.

16 Cited in Ben Smith, "U.S. Pondered Military Use in Georgia," *Politico.com*, 4 February, 2010, http://www.politico.com/news/stories/0210/32487.html.

17 See Ivan D. Loshkariov and Andrey A. Sushentsov, "Radicalization of Russians in Ukraine: From 'Accidental Diaspora' to Rebel Movement," *Southeast European and Black Sea Studies* 16, no. 1 (2016): 71.

18 Serhy Yekelchyk, *The Conflict in Ukraine: What Everyone Needs to Know* (Oxford: Oxford University Press, 2015), 21.

19 Yekelchyk, *Conflict in Ukraine*, 22.

20 Yekelchyk, *Conflict in Ukraine*, 22.

21 Yekelchyk, *Conflict in Ukraine*, 23.

22 Charles King and Neil J. Melvin, "Diaspora Politics: Ethnic Linkages, Foreign Policy, and Security in Eurasia," *International Security* 24, no. 3 (Winter 1999/2000): 137.

23 King and Melvin, "Diaspora Politics," 137 (emphasis added).

CHAPTER THREE

Reaction of Ethnicity to Challenging Circumstances in a Historical Perspective

Ukrainian Interaction with Their Neighbors

I t has been previously stated that contemporary Ukraine is the product of many changes.[1] A complicated history of interaction of Ukrainian ethnos "in much of what is now independent Ukraine" with external powers ruling the country predetermined and varied forms and levels of its consolidation into an ethnic nation, depending on the different policies applied by outside powers onto Ukrainians. Taras Kuzio argues that hostile interethnic relations and military conflict, "important factors in the constructions of the nations," only played a noticeable role in Western Ukraine. In Eastern Ukraine, in his opinion, "the absence of such conflict did not lead to the clear *ethnic demarcation* found between, say, Poles and Ukrainians" in the West.[2]

Impact of Ukrainian Culture on the Rising Russian Ethnic Nation and State

As a matter of fact, at one time in the past, the Ukrainian ethnic community could boast a more advanced culture than its Russian neighbors. In the seventeenth century, when Ukraine and Russia signed the Treaty of 1654, also known as the *Treaty of Periaslav*—a hallmark event in the history of both peoples—westernization both prior to and after this treaty came to Russia via Ukraine. One of the major roles in this process was played by the famous *Kyievo-Mohylianska akademia*. It was the first and leading center of local high education and exerted a great deal of intellectual influence over the entire Orthodox Christian world throughout the seventeenth and eighteenth centuries. It had been established in the city of Kyiv in 1632 by the famous churchman Petro Mohyla through the merger of *Kyiv Epiphany Brotherhood School* (est. 1615–1616) and the *Kyivan Cave Monastery School* (est. 1631 by Mohyla himself). From the beginning, the founder conceived it as an academy, meaning that it had to be an institution of high learning "offering philosophy and theology courses and supervising a vast network of secondary schools." But Polish king Wladislaw IV Vasa, fearing this school would become a competitor to the Polish Jesuit academies, granted it the inferior status of a college and prohibited the teaching of philosophy and theology within it. It was only in 1694 that this college was finally granted the full privileges of an academy and was no longer restricted in such a way. In 1701, Tsar Peter I (also known as "Peter the Great") officially recognized it as an academy as well, further solidifying its place in the intellectual community.

Among the school's faculty were some of the most famous and accomplished scholars of the time, like Stefan Yavorsky, Ioan Maksymovich, Lasar Baranovich, Dymytrii Tuptalo, and especially Teofan ("Feofan" in Russian publications) Prokopovich. Among this group, the latter played a fundamental role in Peter I's educational reforms in Russia. For example, Moscow Academy was directly patterned after the Kyivan one, with most other Russian schools being established by bishops who themselves were alumni of *Kyievo-Mohylianska academia*. However, the golden age ended after the defeat of Hetman Ivan Mazepa, who had sided with King Charles XII of Sweden at the Battle of Poltava in 1709, by Peter I's army. From 1731 to 1742, in the aftermath of Peter I's death, the school witnessed a short period of revival. New courses in modern languages, history, mathematics, medicine, and geography were introduced and enriched its curriculum. At that time, the academy continued to educate the civil and ecclesiastical elite of the Hetman state and in the rapidly growing Russian Empire. In 1764, Russian Empress Catherine II (similarly known as "Catherine the Great") abolished the Hetmanate and secularized monasteries in 1786. These two changes crippled the academy by depriving it of its chief financial resources. In addition, the expansion of educational facilities in St. Petersburg and the opening of Moscow Imperial University in 1775 added momentum to this deterioration, and the Mohylianska academy became a "ward of the Russian imperial government and its importance declined rapidly."[3]

The particular history of the academy reflects a major process of drastic change in this period in both Ukrainian and Russian societies. In the mid-seventeenth century, the startup conditions for both Ukraine and Muscovy states were almost the same in many respects, with both countries having roughly the same population at around five million apiece. However, the successful westernization of Russia as a result of Peter the Great's reforms led to rapid expansion and achievements in all fields and respects under Catherine the Great, forming a foundation of steadfast growth for the Russian state. By the nineteenth century, the situation had drastically shifted in favor of Russia—"culturally, socio-economically, and demographically."[4]

Russian Expansion to the Southeast Territories of the Former Turkish Control and Interaction with the Ukrainian Cossacks

Here it is necessary to reiterate that, following the signing of the Treaty of Periaslav, "the Cossack lands that correspond approximately to present-day central Ukraine became a protectorate of the Russian tsars, who from then on referred to themselves as the rulers of Great and Little Russia (i.e., Russia proper and Ukraine)."[5] Since Cossacks frequently broke their conditional obligations to not interact with Poland and the Ottoman Empire without Moscow's approval, the tsars and then emperors were increasingly limiting the Hetmanate's sovereignty, which was ultimately ended with the complete abolishment of Cossack autonomy by Catherine II. In 1782, it was replaced by three provinces of the empire, and Cossack officers were incorporated into the Russian noble class. Preceding this event was the destruction of an old Zaporozhian Host fortress on the lower Dnieper River by the Russian Army.[6] At about the same time, the Russian Empire, as a result of the first partition of Poland, received Ukrainian land on the right bank of the Dnieper River and to the west of it, with an exception of Galicia (Halychyna in Ukrainian) and two other small adjacent historical regions, "which went to the Habsburgs instead."[7]

In the longstanding rivalry between the Ottoman and the Russian Empires for control over the Caucasus and for a vital presence in the Black Sea, Russia ultimately prevailed with their victory in the Russo-Turkish War of 1768–1774. In accordance with the *Kücük Kaynarca* (also spelled *Kuchuk Kainarji*) *Peace Treaty* (July 21, 1774), the Russian frontier was expanded to the southern Bug River, ceding to Russia the ports of Azov and Kherson (which would become the first base of Russia's Black Sea fleet), the fortress of Kerch and Yenikale on the eastern end of the Crimean Peninsula, a part of the province of Kuban (along the Kuban River in the North Caucasus, as well as the protectorates of Great and Little Kabarda and Ossetia), and the estuary formed by the Dnieper (*Dnipro*) and the Bug Rivers, which included the Kinburn fortress. The territory of the Crimean Khanate—a vassal of Ottoman Turkey—was to form an independent state that was only subject to the Ottoman sultan-caliph regarding religious matters.[8] Subsequent annexation of the entire Crimean Peninsula in 1789 and the abolishment of the Crimean Khanate allowed Russia to take full control over the vast steppe area to the north of it, scarcely populated by the remnants of the Nogai nomads and known as *Dikoe pole* ("Wild Prairie").

Catherine II's Program of Settling in the New Territories

Eventually, Catherine II opened a program to construct there flourishing agricultural settlements and urban settlements along the coast—ports in Kherson (1778), Nikolaev (1789) (Ukr. *Mykolaiv*), and Odessa (1794) (Ukr. *Odesa*). The empress's program presupposed the settling of people from a variety of ethnic stock in these locations. The first in consideration were those who could take the lead in developing productive agriculture in the region, those who could work in the shipyards at the ports, and a mix of artisans like those found in the urban centers of other cities. It is by way of these considerations that settlements populated by Greeks, Italians, German-speaking Mennonites, Moldavians, Jews, and other skilled foreigners came to be.

Eventually, Ukrainian peasant settlers moved to the region and were soon joined by Russians, who began settling in the newly emerging cities. As a result of the *Treaty of Yassy* (after the Russo-Turkish War of 1789–1792), Russia formally gained possession of the Sanjak of Özi (Ochakov, Ochakiv Oblast').[9] In 1792, it became a part of the Yekaterinoslav Viceroyalty. As a matter of fact, Zaporozhian Cossacks fought alongside Russian troops under Aleksandr Suvorov and Ivan Gudovich during this second conflict. On September 25, 1789, the combined forces took Khadjibey and Yeni Dünya for the Russian Empire. In 1795, Khadjibey was renamed Odessa, after the ancient Greek colony Odessos.[10] One of the Russian detachments that fought that day was even commanded by a Spaniard in Russian service by the name of José de Ribas (known in Russia as Osip Mikhailovich Deribas). Today, the main street of this glorious city—a capital of humor, of brilliant poets, writers, singers and actors, but also of the mafia—Deribasivska Street, carries his name. So this vast region, newly acquired by the Russian Empire from the very beginning of its modern history, was (and still is) distinguished by ethnic diversity, becoming nothing short of a melting pot of different peoples.

Resettling of the Cossacks to the North Caucasus and Establishment of the Kuban Cossack Host

In the late eighteenth century, a major part of the Zaporozhian Cossacks, at the behest of Catherine the Great, were resettled on the eastern shores of the Black Sea in the North Caucasus. There they eventually constituted an unalienable part of the Kuban Cossacks (who shared their name with a major local river) (Rus. *Kubanskiye kazaki*, Ukr. *kubans'ki kozaky*). Most of them are descendants of different major groups of Cossacks who were resettled to the western section of the North Caucasus in the late eighteenth century (the number of initial settlers was estimated to be from 230,000 to 650,000). The western part of this host populated the Taman' Peninsula and the adjoining region to the northeast and was originally known as *Chernomorskoye Voisko* ("Black Sea Cossack Host"). An original home of these Cossacks was in Ukraine. The eastern and southeastern part of the host carried the name *Kavkazskoye Lineinoye Voisko* ("Caucasus Line Cossack Host") and was previously administrated by the Khopyor and Kuban Regiments. The Don Cossacks composed a major part of these regiments, who had been resettled there in 1777 from the Don River area.[11] In 1860, both hosts were united into a distinct administrative and military unit under the name *The Kuban Cossack Host*. This union existed up until 1918, when during the Russian Civil War (1918–1920), the Kuban Cossacks proclaimed themselves the *Kuban People's Republic* and became a major force in the fight against the Bolsheviks. It is because of this revolt that the later Soviet authorities treated them so harshly, which saw them suffer heavy losses during *Holodomor* and subsequent crackdowns on their culture. This explains how and why Cossacks fought for both the Red/Soviet army and for the German Wehrmacht from 1941 to 1945 during the Great Patriotic War (the Russian name for that period of World War II).

Ordeals of Cossacks under the Soviet Regime and the Rebirth of Cossacks and Other Ethnic Communities in the Caucasus and in Modern Russia

At the end of the eighteenth century, some of the former Zaporozhian Cossacks and Cossacks from the Caucasus line reinforced the *Terek Cossack Host* in the towns (*stanitsas*) along the River Terek.[12] This Cossack Host was the first to be subjected to the genocidal policies carried out by the Soviet government in 1918–1921 with the utmost cruelty.[13] Recently, remnants of this targeted group were able to reconnect and amazingly declare their own cultural rebirth. At the fall of the Soviet Union, the author of this book took part in the constitutive *Congress of Terek Cossacks* on March 20, 1990, in their historical center—Vladikavkaz (the capital of North Ossentia–Alania), which put forth a legal basis for the rebirth of other Cossack hosts throughout modern Russia, with members of both the Don and Kuban Cossacks following suit soon after.[14]

However, the most important information relative to this research is the fact that, from the very beginning, both Ukrainian and Russian ethnic compound elements were among the Kuban and Terek Cossacks, who eventually grew into distinct sub-ethnic groups within the Russian state. Both communities have passed through their own terrible ordeals: revolution, civil war, "decossackization" and "dekulakization" campaigns—accompanied by the almost total annihilation of the most skilled and well-off farmers—the Holodomor Famine of 1932–1933 as a result of Soviet collectivization, the general destruction of their culture, and the targeted purge of entire family groups. Nevertheless, in March 1990, I and other members of the *Organizational Committee for the First Vladikavkaz Little Krug* (Circle, or Constitutional Congress) visited traditional *slanitsas* along the Terek River and witnessed the most incredible display of enthusiasm, hope, and the inexhaustible will to restore the traditional ways and frameworks of organizations. On the appointed day, several hundred delegates appeared, with some of them in their historic uniforms, dominated by the traditional blue of the Terek Cossack Host and insignias of traditional Cossack ranks, as well as awards passed down from ancestors, earned for taking part in numerous battles. Some of these most precious items had been kept hidden away by the remnants of Cossack families, kept hidden using underhanded methods throughout the entire seventy years of Soviet power. There is a Cossack proverb: "*Kazach' yemu rodu net perevódu*," which translates to "No end in sight to the Cossack might." Boris Pasternak, author of *Doctor Zhivago*, agrees with this phrase, saying that "even in indigence they were never servile."

It was an amazing time. Cossack rebirth set in motion similar renaissance events of many of the other ethnic communities in Russia. I have been invited to and visited informal constitutive forums in Ossetia, Ingushetia, Chechnya, Kabardino-Balkaria, Abkhazia, and Georgia ... and everywhere I went, I saw that all these peoples, who had passed through the same ordeals and had been met with the same challenges, had found a way to preserve *all five principal building blocks of their ethnicities*, albeit sometimes in a deformed way, as well as most cultural boundary markers of difference. In all such meetings, speakers articulated similar concerns about the necessity of building such conditions in their new polities that would help preserve and guarantee further development of their ethnic constituents and identities. All of them brilliantly, almost in a Shakespearean manner, rejuvenated countless chosen traumas that their people had suffered, including tsarist and Stalinist deportation and genocidal oppression at the hands of their more powerful ethnic neighbors. What was most striking about this was the manner in which these longstanding tragedies were presented, as it made them seem to have only just happened yesterday.[15]

Settling the Donbas Area

Until the revolution of 1917, Ukraine was predominantly an agrarian province and an economic backwater of the Russian Empire. Even as far back as 1926, only 20 percent of Ukraine's inhabitants lived in an urban environment. During the 1920s, most town residents were Russians, while the Ukrainians usually lived in the countryside.[16] The initial industrialization of the country began to spread slowly from the southeastern section of Ukraine in the second half of the nineteenth century. This process attracted many ethnic Russians to the region, especially in the Donbas area, which would be the most industrialized area of the state. In 1879, Welsh industrialist John Hughs, owner of the most productive coal mines, founded the city of Donetsk (originally named Yuzovka, after his last name in the Russian transliteration) (Ukr. *Donets'k*). However, the tsarist census taken in 1897 reveals that by the end of the century, the majority of the region's population identified themselves as *Malorussians* ("Little Russians"), which are the ethnic Ukrainians. It is important to note that they were not the ethnic Russians that would later adopt the Ukrainian ethnonym during the "Ukrainization" campaign efforts of the early Soviet period. I will address this discrepancy more thoroughly during a later section dedicated to the linguistic building block of Russian-Ukrainian ethnic conflict.[17] This and other facts mentioned above instigated the tsarist government to actively pursue the merging of Ukrainians, Russians, and even Belarusians through vigorous implementation of the policies of Russification, Little Russianism, and a "Russo-centric historiography that sought to blur any differences between the eastern Slavs."[18] By the mid-1860s, imperial officials had already banned the use of educational and religious books printed in Ukrainian. In 1876, the tsarist government took this a step further, prohibiting any publications written in the Ukrainian language.[19]

Andrew Wilson very specifically noted that "the various regions that make up modern Ukraine have moved in and out of Ukrainian history at different times, but *have never really interacted together as an ensemble* ... There are therefore serious difficulties in imagining Ukrainian history either as a temporal or a geographical continuity."[20] One result of this saw the eastern ethno-sociological and political boundaries between Ukrainians and Russians become blurred rather significantly. It slowed down the process of transformation of the scattered Ukrainian ethnos into an ethnic nation but did not stop it completely. However, it also did not lead to the total engulfment of the Ukrainians by the Russian nation. Rather, it resulted in the formation of local identities, laying the foundation for the emergence of the phenomenon of *regionalism*.

Ukrainian Ethnos in the West

Ukrainian historians actively promote the idea that, unlike in the "eastern Ukrainian territories" of the Russian Empire, Austrian Germans in the Ukrainian regions of the Habsburg Empire ostensibly adopted "liberal nationality policies," allowing the incorporation of a *rusyn* ethnos into a "Ukrainian Nation." In contrast, "in the areas controlled by the Hungarians, Magyarization and the maintenance of a *rusyn* ethnos was preferred policy." As a result, in northeastern Slovakia, which in the second half of the nineteenth century and early twentieth century was administered by Hungary, *Rusyny* preserved their ethnic identity and considered themselves "to be a part of the larger east Slavic *rus'kiy narod* rather than of a narrow Ukrainian nation."[21] However, when taking a closer look at the territorial patchwork of Ukrainian settlement in the west and its interaction with neighboring super-ordinate nations and powers, the picture becomes even more complicated, as its history is one of a space between the Habsburg, Russian, Ottoman, and Soviet Empires.

Three Major Regions of Settling of Ukrainians in the West and "Gathering" of Ukrainian Lands by the Soviet Leaders

In western Ukraine, at least three major regions of such interaction can be identified: (1) Halychyna, (2) Bukovina, and (3) Zacarpattya.

Halychyna

"Today's regions of L'viv, Ternopil', and Ivano-Frankivs'k" had belonged to the Polish-Lithuanian Commonwealth "from the fourteenth century onwards."[22] In 1772, during the partitions of Poland, the Habsburg Empire gained control of the region known as eastern Galicia (Ukr. *Halychyna*). Habsburg emperors and the following rulers of the Austro-Hungarian Empire continued to dominate this region until 1918. During the chaos at the end of World War I, there existed, albeit briefly, an independent West Ukrainian People's Republic (ZUNR). Then, once again, the region came under Polish control within the frames of the newly emerged and fully independent Poland. In September 1939, on the conditions of the "secretive protocols" of the Molotov-Ribbentrop Pact signed between Hitler's Germany and the USSR a month prior

(August 23), Western Ukraine (Galicia and Volhynia) was annexed by the Soviet Union and assigned to the Ukrainian Soviet Socialist Republic. Nevertheless, the Polish population was prevalent in the cities until the end of World War II.[23]

Bukovina

The region known as Bukovina had been in the possession of the Principality of Moldavia, which itself was a vassal of Ottoman Turkey. After 1774, Bukovina came under the control of the Habsburgs, who ruled until 1918. At this point, Northern Bukovina, alongside the administrative and cultural center of Chernivtsi, became a part of the independent state of Romania, which would last until 1940. This year saw the region annexed by the USSR and assigned to the Ukrainian SSR. During the course of the war, Romania regained control over the region, only to again lose it to the Soviets in 1944, who promptly incorporated it into the Soviet quasi-state of Ukraine.

Zacarpattya

The region of Transcarpathia (Zacarpattya) had been a part of the Hungarian Kingdom for around a millennium. In 1919, the victorious *Entente* assigned this region to the newly created state of Czechoslovakia "as punishment for Hungary's role in the Great War." However, the region was annexed by the USSR in 1945, where Stalin gave it to the Ukrainian SSR.[24]

In 1919, Vladimir Lenin had already assigned extensive territories to the east and south that had been known as *Malorossia* ("Little Russia") during imperial times "to what would become Ukrainian jurisdiction." But in agreement with Richard Sakwa, one can see that it was not Lenin but Stalin—the real designer of administrative composition of the USSR and the author of the previously mentioned system of categorization of the Soviet peoples—"who was the greatest Ukrainian state-builder, adding extensive territories to both the east and west" of what is the modern independent Ukraine.[25] The Crimean Peninsula, which "Russian historical mythology treats like the heartland of Russian nationhood" and glory, was presented to the Ukrainian SSR by Nikita Khrushchev in 1954. Thus, one can say that Lenin, Stalin, and Khrushchev were the real obstetricians and godfathers of the modern territorial building block of the independent Ukrainian nation.

Ethnic Policy of the Austro-Hungarian Empire

As to the policy of the Austrian Empire, it was typical for all empires. Many centuries ago, at the dawn of the Roman Empire, Julius Caesar founded the original policy of *Divide et Impera* ("Divide and Rule"), which set the standard for how future empires would manage their territories. However, the situation was quite tricky for the Habsburg Empire, as the super-ordinate ethnic nation of Austrian Germans constituted only a small minority of the total imperial population. That is why, unlike the Russian Empire, they could never hope, and therefore never tried, to assimilate other ethnic groups into their own to bolster strength. Instead, they skillfully exploited noteworthy tensions between the major ethnic groups. They also made attempts to ignite and fan out ethnic mistrust, and even hatred, in a classically constructivist way, targeting places where no tensions, even insignificant ones, had ever existed previously. Yekelchyk correctly noted that "this approach was particularly evident in the empire's Ukrainian lands."[26] In fact, "liberal measures" had been reserved for one particular group of Ukrainian ethnos, while at the same time other groups were treated quite harshly. This is especially true regarding the attitude of the imperial nation toward *Rusiny* (Ukr. *Rusyny*).

Rusiny/Rusyny

Rusiny is a people that specialists both in the USSR and modern Russia regard as an "ethnographic" compound sub-ethnic group of Ukrainians. In European historiography, they are known under different ethnonyms, including Ruthenians, Carpatho-Rusyns, Carpatho-Russians, and Ugro-Russians. The repeated prefix in all of these names—*Carpatho*—refers to Carpathian Ruthenia (Rusynia), a historical cross-border region encompassing parts of southwestern Ukraine, the northeastern regions of Slovakia, and the southeastern parts of Poland.[27] Sometimes Rusyny are referred to as Rusnaks or, in their own language, as *Rusnakÿ*. In the official Ukrainian context, the various subgroups of Carpatho-Rusyns are also collectively known as *Verkhovyntsi* ("Highlanders"). The national census only counts around 90,000 people within this group, yet the Rusyns themselves estimated that, from 2009–2015, 1.2–1.6 million people could trace their family origins directly from the group.

Recent genetic studies into the Rusyns' subgroups have yielded interesting results. It was found that the three major subgroups, the *Boykos*, the *Hutsuls*, and the *Lemkos*, have a greater genetic distance between themselves than other Central and Eastern European populations used in the comparison (including Belarusians, Croatians, Hungarians, Poles, Romanians, Russians, and Ukrainians). In particular, the *Boykos* show the greatest amount of genetic difference from all of these nations and failed to form a genetic cluster with any of their neighbors; the *Hutsuls* are closest to Ukrainians and Croatians; and the *Lemkos* to Czech and Romanian test groups.[28] The Zakarpattya and Chernivtsi Oblast (Bukovina) populations show insignificant difference from the typical Ukrainian population. Some percentage also relates these groups to Moldavians and Romanians, as well as Southern Slavs in the Western Balkans.[29]

As for their own self-identification, Rusyns often refer to themselves as Russians and trace their origin to the so-called "ancient Rusichy," or Eastern Slavs, who are the supposed origin ancestors of Russians, Ukrainians, and Belarusians. Some authors may see this as both an allusion to and the clear impact of both the Imperial and Soviet historiographical traditions. As a sample of some such sources, I can refer to the work of Aleksandr Dukhnovich, an Orthodox priest and writer famous for his work in the rebirth movements of the Carpathian Rus'. In his work *The True History of Carpatho-Rossov* (published in the middle of the nineteenth century), he promoted a thesis claiming that Carpathian Rusyns represented the nucleus of the ancient Rus's ethnos, from which originated the abovementioned trio of Eastern Slavic peoples. Based on comparative studies of ancient Greek and various Slavic chronicles of the medieval period, Dukhnovich defends an idea of the similarity between the languages of the Ancient Rus' and the contemporary language of the Rusyns.[30] The scholastic community rejected his ideas since he was not a professional historian and, therefore, unqualified. Yet they had to reckon with essentially the same opinion nearly half a century later, which would then go on to formulate an unquestionable authority among researchers through Moscow Imperial University professor Vasilii Osipovich Klyuchevsky and his five-volume *Course of Russian History*.[31]

Magocsi on the Origins of Rusyns

Among the diverse array of theories concerning the origins of Rusyns, Paul Magocsi authored the most balanced and well-founded one to date. His findings were among important supportive evidences that I placed as the basis of my own understanding of the nature of ethnicity (see chapter 1). Magocsi showed that the origin of the present-day Carpatho-Rusyns is neither simple nor related only to the Kievan Rus'. Their ancestors included the early tribes of Slavs who moved to the Danube Basin between the fifth and sixth centuries under pressure of the Huns and Avars from the east. Their ancestors would come to include the White Croats, who had occupied both slopes of the Carpathians and had built mountainous strongholds there, including Uzhgorod (Ukr. *Uzhhorod*), which was ruled by the mythical Laborec. The Rusyns of Galicia and Podolia and the Vlachyan shepherds of Transylvania also rank among the ancestors of modern Carpatho-Rusyns.[32] This is a strong confirmation of my thesis concerning the multi-tribal basis of modern ethnic groups and ethnic nations. As a matter of fact, the above-cited biological and genetic studies also produce strong evidence in favor of this conclusion, as well as of another one: that a biological component played a formative role for the tribes, clans, and families, while language played a bigger role in the establishment of ethnic groups.

Origin of the Ethno-Political Elite in Galicia (Halychyna)

Under the Habsburgs, the political elite in Galicia were Polish who had assimilated the Rus' nobility long before, and thus the single educated class of Ruthenians were those of the Ukrainian Catholic clergy. These clergymen recognized the authority of the pope but also shared Eastern Orthodox Christian rites which allowed them to marry and have children (with bishops and monks being the only exceptions). Gradually, the presence of such families would lead to the development of a "hereditary intelligentsia": teachers, lawyers, and other specialists. Thus, among Ukrainians in both the east and west, this group of Galician intelligentsia was historically the first to establish the tradition of enlightening the peasant population. The Magdeburg rights in Bohemia, Hungary, and Poland also helped this group of early scholars establish themselves in the blooming urban centers.[33] After the Polish Uprising during the revolution of 1848, Austrian authorities sought to create a counterweight to Polish separatism. For that purpose, they encouraged some prospectively loyal Ruthenian intellectuals to join their political life. The latter used this opportunity well, and by the second half of the nineteenth century, the first Ukrainian press had emerged, filling a vast network of reading rooms in the countryside. In the 1890s, the first political parties were established and in the typical constructivist way began promoting the ethnic designation of "Ukrainians" among the common people rather than Ruthenians/Rusyns.

Beginning of the Anti-Russian Discourse and Persecutions of the Local Pro-Russian Section of Rusyns

However, the attitude of the imperial authorities toward patriotic activists drastically changed. They became concerned that another sect of the Ruthenian/Rusyn activists was spreading ideas of a shared peoplehood with the Russians and the propinquity of the antiquated church vernacular of the Russian language among their folk. It is for this reason that Austrian authorities in eastern Galicia took all precautions to ensure that the language of instruction in the local schools was modern Ukrainian, which was just under construction. In contrast, after 1867 (in which the Habsburg Empire transitioned into the Austro-Hungarian Empire), Hungarian officials closed down all Ukrainian organizations in their region and began to enforce the assimilation of the local peasantry in the form of Magyarization.[34]

This shift in policies toward different sub-ethnic groups in the western regions is a bright illustration of how emerging geopolitics may interfere in the evolutionary process of ethnic groups and ethnic nations. With the creation of the Dual Union in 1879 between Germany and the Austro-Hungarian Empire and the conclusion of the secret military agreement between them against Russia and France, the ruling circles of the countries of Dual Union focused on the "Ukrainian Question." The newspapers of the countries of Dual Union unleashed intensive anti-Russian propaganda. In January 1888, the German journal *Gegenwart* published a programmatic article penned by the protégé of German Chancellor von Bismarck, a philosopher named Eduard von Hartmann, in which the author defended the thesis of the existential threat that Russia represented to the stability of European security. Ukrainian newspaper *Dilo* published a scope of Hartmann's ideas that "for the security of the rest of Europe, Russia should be divided without fail." Hartmann proposed that Russia should be divided thusly: "It is necessary to give Finland to Sweden, Bessarabia to Romania, Estonia, Courland, Lithuania, and Zhmud must create the Kingdom of Baltia under the German protectorate; and on the terrain between the Prut and Dnieper rivers should rise a separate kingdom of Kiev ... The Kievan Kingdom and Romania should be given guarantees from Austria, and in the case of war [with Russia] Austria would lead their troops."[35]

Famous Ukrainian writer Ivan Frankó, whom one could hardly rebuke in sympathy to the Russian Empire, very critically referred to Hartmann's plan in his own article "*Politychnii ohliad*," published in the L'viv journal *Pravda*. He wrote: "My God, what an honor for the lambs that a wolf shows interest in them ...Those in Europe who show interest in us are doing this while looking back to Russia, depending on how they build their relations to it. If one needs to threaten Russia—Bang!—one calls on stage Rusyns and Kyiv's kingdom ... So, jump my lambs! Master Wolf is pleased to show interest in your meat."[36] Some nationalistic parties in Germany planned to defeat Russia with the unwitting help of Ukraine, but after that, instead of giving independence to Ukraine in the aftermath, they planned to colonize Galicia and the Black Sea coast on their own. Another group of German politicians shared an idea about forming buffer states of "non-Russian peoples of the Russian Empire." The most famous intellectual of this group was Paul Rohrbach, who compared Russia to an orange and dreamt about dismembering it. (One might have an impression that the revolution of 2004 in Ukraine, which was called "the Orange Revolution," might reincarnate Rohrbach's metaphor, since it was in support of the anti-Russian candidate to the Ukrainian presidency.) Individual sections of Russia like Ukraine, the Baltic States, and the Caucasus should break away and become a series of hostile buffer states to help Europe lock the Russian bear in Asia and cut off their access to the seas, specifically warm-water ports.[37]

Split in the Western Ukrainian Ethno-Political Movement and Austrian Mass Terror Against "Moscowphile" Rusyns

Dmitro Doroshenko, a famous historian and political activist for the first Ukrainian patriotic organization *Soyuz Vizvolenn'a Ukraini (SVU)*, left a realistic description of the situation in Galicia on the eve of and in the initial stages of the Great War. According to him, "the misfortune of the Ukrainian people in Austro-Hungary was that it was deeply split into two parts along the lines of national ideas and in its political orientation: one bigger part wanted to live and develop as a separate Ukrainian nation, achieving full national and political rights within the framework of the Austro-Hungarian state; in conflict between Austria and Russia, this part hoped that with the help of Austria at least some parts of Great Ukraine, if not the whole, could be liberated from 'Moscow's yoke.'"

But a lesser part of the Galician-Ukrainian population did not consider themselves "Ukrainians," instead seeing themselves as "Russians." This minority saw their future salvation in the hands of Russia and, in the struggle between these two neighboring states, opted to side with Russia. These so-called "Moscowphiles" had their supporters not only among the intelligentsia but also among ordinary peasants. On the eve of war, some leaders within this movement had already escaped to Russia, anticipating, with the assistance of victorious Russian troops, to return to Galicia and "liberate" it from the "Austrian Yoke." However, a great majority of adherents of the "Moscowphile" trend never actively revealed themselves, keeping their sympathies in their souls and waiting for a clear indication on which side would emerge victorious, in a typical instrumentalist-circumstantial way.[38]

In reading this authentic and objective description of the situation at the beginning of World War I, I cannot shake the impression that I am reading a contemporary account of the current ethnic conflict in Ukraine. If one were to replace Austria and Germany with the United States, the European Union, and NATO on one side and modern Russia on another, then the split between *svidomye* ("conscious") Ukrainian patriots and "Moscowphile" Rusyns of Doroshenko's report during World War I can be extrapolated onto the intra-ethnic cleavage of the modern Ukraine between its western-central and Crimea-Donbas parts, and it makes for a stunning coincidence, to say the least. Symptomatically enough, the first president of an independent Ukraine, Leonid Kravchuk, now speaks about "three little Ukraines, with their different histories and mentality," while others speak about "regionalisms" of different levels and graduations.[39]

I will get to this in the next chapters, but for now I need to mention some facts that other analysts prefer to omit. After the first Austro-Hungarian defeat at the hands of Russia, there arose an open trend of repression within Galicia against "Moscowphile" Ukrainians, who were thereby accused of treason by imperial authorities. It was a campaign of mass terror against peasants, Orthodox priests, intellectuals, and so on. Thousands of Rusyns died in the executions and in Austrian jails. Dozens of thousands more were confined to concentration camps, like Telerhoff, Gnav, Terezin, and Gmündi. Some historians consider that the total number of victims of this terror reached about 70,000 civilians at the highest.[40] At the same time, approximately 28,000 Ukrainians, especially those who saw the war as "a means to liberate their brethren in Russia from an oppressive tsarist regime," volunteered in the Austro-Hungarian Army, yet only 2,000 were actually accepted. One may agree with Yekelchyk that, in the end, both groups would understand that the defeat of both imperial masters would be the most beneficial outcome for them all.[41] In the sections about the *commonly shared historical building block* of the Russo-Ukrainian ethnic conflict, I will show that the situation involving internal ethnic tensions would reproduce itself on a more tragic level during World War II.

Considerations Based on the Up-to-Date Analysis

The content of chapters 1, 2, and 3 enables me to make several important conclusions. An ethnic picture of Russia during both the Imperial and Soviet times shows many things. (1) The diversity of the groups that were being categorized was much greater than the simple categorization methods readily allowed. (2) There was a gradual awareness of the diversity of peoples and efforts to integrate the "least diverse" into the leading ethnic group. Similar attempts of integration were characterized by the beginning of building an ethnic Ukrainian nation in Galicia (Halychyna) under the Austrian/Austro-Hungarian Empire. Wartime challenges and ethnic conflicts with the neighboring super-ordinate nations served as a catalyst of this process. (3) There was a certain naïveté and unawareness surrounding the power of the principal constituents of ethnicity that, over a long period of time, allowed Imperial and Soviet administrators to assume that "lesser" ethnic groups (or sub-ethnic "compound parts") would continue to permit their own depreciation. The case of Rusyns in Galicia and in the adjoining regions shows that their religious and partially linguistic constituents/building blocks proved that sub-ethnic groups may preserve ethnic identity, even in the most challenging and unfavorable situations, generating enough energy to resist assimilation for an extended period of time. (4) Even though the approach was not overtly intended to lead to expulsion from jobs and definitely not to the trains and concentration camps of the Stalinist period (or Terezin and Telerhoff for the Rusyns during Austro-Hungarian domination), the ultimate outcome of this treatment of subordinate groups by the elite of powerful nations was instances of extreme ethnic abuse. Thus, what seemed to be rational categorizations (in terms of Enlightenment ideals or Stalinist practice based on reinterpreted dogmas of "Marxism-Leninism") in the long run became vehicles for ethnic hatred and abuse. The pogroms of the nineteenth and early twentieth centuries; deportations of Cossacks, Chechens, Ingushians, Kalmyks, Balkars, Karachais, Meskhetian Turks, (Baltic, Volga, and Crimean) Germans, Crimean Tatars, Greeks, and Bulgarians; "Russification," "Magyarization," and "Ukrainization"; and so on are in fact the culmination of the "enlightened" and Soviet categorization of peoples. (5) Where the conditions were allowed, groups of educated, patriotic intellectuals/activists of ethnic minorities emerged and began to generate ideas and plans of "national liberation" and building their own ethnic nations. Over time, ethno-political movements headed by these activists would appear, with some areas, like Galicia, became the hearths and citadels of local integral *ethnocentric nationalism*. (6) Ethnic (and sub-ethnic) groups led by such people in unfavorable circumstances adhered to a combination of methods, which may be characterized at specific periods of time as situational, constructivist, or instrumentalist tactics, in order to preserve their ethnic constituents and identities. Simultaneously, nationalists began to focus on obtaining complete independence from various super-ordinate powers in the future and then building their nation-states, where they might fully realize their ethnic and political rights as they understood them.

In *The Warrior's Honor*, Michael Ignatieff argues that the differences between ethnic groups that fight one another often appear insignificant to outsiders. He disagrees with others who maintain that in Yugoslavia or in the Caucasus, for example, the religious and other differences between groups are so great that they fight in order to determine which culture is superior and will succeed over the other. He describes an interview with a Serbian irregular who explains to him his hatred of Croats. The Serb makes several points, the most important of which is how he thinks that *everyone in the area is the same* (compare to my interviews with Russian emigrants, especially from Donbas, cited in the introduction). The differences between Croats and Serbs are not that great; that is indeed the point. But even small differences make for the development of interethnic strife. The cigarettes the Serb is smoking are Serbian-made, while those smoked by the Croats are Croatian. The Croats think that they are better than Serbs; they want to be gentlemen and think they are fancy Europeans. The Serbs believe that this is why they smoke a different brand of cigarette; they are different in the small things that matter. The Serb thinks he is different from everyone else, an attitude that gets to the heart of the conflict, namely that most non-Serb fighters saw themselves as Europeans and saw Serbs as mere farmers. By the very nature of the conflict, the Croat may have been at one time friends and classmates of the Serb soldier, but the differences between them became significant enough to turn them into enemies.[42] Thus emerged an enemy picture, or *Faindbild* in the poignant German phrase.

Finally, the point that small differences do indeed become enlarged and turn neighbors into bitter enemies can also be made about the low-level tension that characterized many former ethnic and sub-ethnic groups of Imperial Russia, Galicia under the Austro-Hungarian Empire during the nineteenth and early twentieth century, and of the former Soviet Union in the end of the twentieth and beginning of the twenty-first centuries. Neighboring ethnic peoples were similar in some areas, such as those in Russia and Ukraine, and very different in others, such as Russia and Uzbekistan, for example. Thus, some of these enemy images emerged because people knew each other well and lived side by side, while others emerged because people had hardly ever seen each other until modern work settings and transportation methods brought them closer.

My point is that whether the groups grew to dislike and hate one another by knowing the other well or not at all, the Russian Imperial and Soviet categorizations (or "balancing" policy of the Austrian Habsburgs) *predisposed* them toward attitudes and behaviors that produce disastrous expressions of ethnic prejudice and even the open ethnic conflicts that we see in the crossroads of the twentieth and twenty-first centuries.[43] Thus, one may consider these policies of super-ordinate powers toward ethnic groups in the past and the latter's reaction to these challenges as the *historical prerequisites of modern ethnic conflicts*. Now we need to examine the modern situation that fosters the reactivation of these prerequisites and prejudices in the new conditions and set in motion a new cycle of ethnic conflicts in a more regressive way.

Notes

1   Richard Sakwa, *Frontline Ukraine: Crisis in the Borderlands* (London: I.B. Tauris, 2015), 11.
2   Taras Kuzio, *Ukraine: State and Nation Building* (London: Routledge, 1998), 6 (emphasis added).
3   See Natalia Pylypiuk, "Kyivan Mohyla Academy," *Entsyclopedia Ukraini v itnteneti* (2005) ency-clopediaofukraine.com/display.asp?linkpath=pages%5ck%cy%5cKyivianMohylaAcademy.htm; V. Briukhovets'kyi et al., eds., *Kyevo-Mohylians'ka akademiia v imenakh XVII-XVIII st: Entsyclope-dichne vydannia* (Kyiv: Naukova dumka, 2001).
4   Kuzio, *Ukraine: State and Nation Building*, 7–8.
5   Serhy Yekelchyk, *The Conflict in Ukraine: What Everyone Needs to Know* (Oxford: Oxford University Press, 2015), 34.
6   Yekelchyk, *Conflict in Ukraine*, 37.
7   Yekelchyk, *Conflict in Ukraine*, 38.
8   Dale H. Hoiberg, ed., "Abdülhamid I," *Encyclopedia Britannica, vol. 1: A-ak Bayes*, 15th ed. (Chicago: Encyclopedia Britannica Inc., 2010), 22.
9   Spencer C. Tucker, *A Global Chronology of Conflict: From the Ancient World to the Modern Middle East* (Santa Barbara, CA: ABC Clio, 2011), 965; Yekelchyk, *Conflict in Ukraine*, 38.
10 Imperial Odessa Society of History and Antiquities, *Notes of the Imperial Odessa Society of History and Antiquites* (Odessa, Ukraine: Odessa City Typography, 2016), 183.
11 Modern Kuban Cossacks claim 1696 as the year of their formation, when the Don Cossacks from Khopyor took part in Peter the Great's Azov Campaigns. Jeffery Hays, "Cossacks," *Facts and Details*, retrieved 31 August 2018, factsanddetails.com.
12 Ivan L. Omel'chenko, *Terskoye kazachestvo* (Vladikavkaz, Russia: "Ir" Publishing House, 1991), 36–37.
13 About these repressions, see Anatoly Isaenko, *Polygon of Satan: Ethnic Traumas and Conflicts in the Caucasus*, 3rd ed. (Dubuque, IA: Kendall Hunt Publishing House, 2014), 234–39.

14 Anatoly Isaenko, "Rebirth of Terek Cossacks," *Terskii Kazak* 1 (April 1990): 1.

15 In my private archive, I keep a unique copy of the first printed issue of the newspaper *Kavkaz, No.1* (*The Caucasus, No.1)* (1 October 1990), an edition of *Assembly of Mountainous Peoples of the Caucasus* that had been formed in August 1989. This edition contains the layout to several ethnic programs, demands for the return of their native land to the descendants of deported ethnics, and a call to redress other "historical injustices" committed by the Russian and Soviet governments in the past, doing so in a special address to the president of the USSR, Mikhail S. Gorbachev. See "Table of Repressed Peoples" in Isaenko, *Polygon of Satan*, 84; see also Pavel Polian, *Against Their Will: The History and Geography of Forced Migrations in the USSR* (Budapest: Central European University Press, 2004).

16 Orest Subtelny, *Ukraine—A History* (Toronto: University of Toronto Press, 1994), 407; see also, Hans van Zon, "Ethnic Conflict and Conflict Resolutions in Ukraine," *Perspectives on European Politics and Society* 2, no. 2 (2001): 222.

17 Sakwa, *Frontline Ukraine*, 11.

18 Kuzio, *Ukraine: State and Nation Building*, 8.

19 Yekelchyk, *The Conflict in Ukraine*, 39.

20 Andrew Wilson, *Ukrainian Nationalism in the 1990s: A Minority Faith* (Cambridge, UK: Cambridge University Press, 1996), 25 (emphasis added).

21 Kuzio, *Ukraine: State and Nation Building*, 13.

22 Gwendolyn Sasse, "The 'New' Ukraine: A State of Regions," in *Ethnicity and Territory in the Former Soviet Union: Regions in Conflict*, ed. James Hughs and Gwendolyn Sasse (London: Frank Cass, 2002), 76.

23 Paul R. Magocsi, *A History of Ukraine* (Toronto: University of Toronto Press, 1996), 385.

24 Sakwa, *Frontline Ukraine*, 12.

25 Sakwa, *Frontline Ukraine*, 12.

26 Yekelchyk, *Conflict in Ukraine*, 39.

27 Paul Magocsi, "The Carpatho-Rusyns (Part 3)," *Carpatho-Rusyn American* 18, no. 4 (Winter 1995), 7; Paul Magocsi, *Our People: Carpatho-Rusyns and their Descendants in North America* (Toronto: Bolochazy-Carducci Publishers, 2005), 5.

28 Alexey Nikitin et al., "Mitochondrion DNA Sequence Variation in Boyko, Hutsul and Lemko Population of Carpathian Highlands," *Human Biology* 81, no. 1 (2009): 43–58.

29 O.M. Utevska et al., "Populations of Transcarpathia and Bukovina on the Genetic Landscape of Surrounding Regions," *Regulatory Mechanisms in Biosystems* 6, no. 2 (2015): 133–40.

30 Yarosalv Gorbunov, "Karpatskye Rusiny: Pochemu ikh schitayut istinnymi predkami russkogo naroda," *Kirilitsa*, October 12, 2019, https://cyrillista.ru/narody/125964-karpatskie-rusiny-pochemu-ikh-schitayut-i.html.

31 Vasilii Klyuchevskÿ, *Kurs russkoi istorii* (Moscow: Vysshaya shkola, 1957),1:56.

32 Magocsi, *Our People*, 5.

33 Jean W. Sedlar, *East Central Europe in the Middle Ages, 1000–1500* (Seattle: University of Washington Press, 1994), 3:328.

34 See Yekelchyk, *Conflict in Ukraine*, 40–41.

35 Eduard von Hartmann, *Das Judenthum in Gegenwart* und *Zukunft* (Whitefish, Montana: Kessinger Publishing LLC, 2010), 27.

36 Cited in I. Lysiak-Rudnits'kii, *Ukraintsi v Halychini pid avstriiskim panuvanniam*,vol. 1 (Kyiv: Naukova dumka, 1994).

37 Paul Rohrbach, *Der Krieg und die Deutsche Politik* (Dresden: Verlag "Das Groissere Deutschland," 1914), 32f.

38 Dmitri Doroshenko, *Voina i revolutsiya na Ukraine. Revolutsyia na Ukraine* (Moscow-Leningrad: Gozidat, 1930), 28; Doroshenko, *Moï spomini pro nedavnae minule (1914–1920), druge vidann'a* (Munich: N.P., 1969).

39 Leonid Kravchuk, *Interview to the Ukrainian TV Channel ZIK*, January 2, 2020: "We—the country of interests. Ukraine consists of three little Ukraines: The Southeast, West, and Center. They have different historical roots, a different mentality, and different historical memories." See also Lowell W. Barrington, "Examining Rival Theories of Demographic Influences on Political Support: The Power of Regional, Ethnic, and Linguistic Divisions in Ukraine," *European Journal of Political Research* 41 (2002): 455–49.

40 N.M. Pashaeva, *Ocherki istorii russkogo dvizheniya v Galichine v XIX—XX v.v.* (Moscow: GPIBR, 2001), 50.

41 Yekelchyk, *Conflict in Ukraine*, 41.

42 Michael Ignatieff, *The Warrior's Honor: Ethnic War and the Modern Conscience* (New York: Metropolitan Books/Henry Holt, 1998).

43 See Peter Petschauer and Anatoly Isaenko, "Finding the Middle Ground: The Practical and Theoretical Center between Ethnic Ideal and Extreme Behaviors," *Mind and Human Interaction* 12, no. 1 (2001): 64–65.

■ CHAPTER FOUR

The Impact of All-Sided Societal Crisis on the Peoples and Their Interactions

Definitions and Considerations on Collapse and Its Impact on Ethnic Interaction

Today, international relations specialists have come to a consensus-like conclusion that "a growing phenomenon of the post–Cold War is *state collapse*."[1] Ira William Zartman defines *state collapse* as "a situation where the structure, authority (legitimate power), law, and political order [within a state] have fallen apart and must be reconstructed in some form, old or new."[2] Some Sub-Saharan African states "suffered various degrees of collapse and have since grappled with the problems of reconstruction."[3] Among them are the states of Angola, the Democratic Republic of the Congo (formerly Zaire), Liberia, Sierra Leone, Somalia, and Sudan. The West Asian and Middle Eastern states of Afghanistan and Iraq (the latter following the US invasion in 2003) have been facing similar problems, namely "the onset of violent ethnic conflicts of various degrees of intensity."[4] This is not exclusive to the third world in any way, as the Central European state of Yugoslavia also collapsed as a result of bloody ethnic conflicts. In agreement with Taras and Ganguly, one can maintain that "the most dramatic example of this took place in December 1991 when the Soviet Union," a world superpower, "collapsed into fifteen new independent states."[5]

As was the case with the former Yugoslavia, bloody ethnic conflicts *had preceded* the collapse of the USSR and had become one of the reasons for it, with the collapse only fueling the intensity of ongoing ethnic wars. In 1989–spring 1991, ethnic conflicts in Georgia between South Ossetians and Georgians and between Abkhazians and Georgians had already entered the *hot stage*, accompanied by extreme forms of ethnic cleansing and terrorism, resulting in mutual destruction and heavy losses of human life. At the same time, the Armenian-Azerbaijani ethnic conflict over Nagorno-Karabakh had also entered the violent stage. These examples alone should be more than enough to show how these conflicts contributed to the hastening collapse of Soviet power. Other ethnic conflicts in Moldova (in Transnistria), the Russian Federation between Ossetians and Ingushians, and the Russian-Chechen conflict had passed through their own *hot stages* in 1992, 1994–1996, and 1999–2008, respectively,[6] while the Armenian-Azerbaijani violent ethnic conflict has passed through its next *hot stage* between September 27 and November 9–10, 2020.

Through this, one should understand that the collapse of centralized Soviet power strongly affected these conflicts and intensified their regressive dynamics. In other words, state collapse create an environment that is conducive to the transformation of relatively mild or middle-ground phases of ethnic conflicts to their more dangerous and uncompromising stages. The cruelties occurring all over the world during the last few decades, including those committed in former Soviet territory, remind us that humankind has the capacity to behave in very destructive ways. The boundaries of states and societies can contain destructive tendencies, but established laws and rituals of society usually help to defuse them. However, in an *all-sided societal crisis*, the boundaries are seriously weakened. In the case of the USSR, at the eclipse of Gorbachev's perestroika, the Soviet Federation, as formal as it was, met with an unprecedented crisis. In the long run, its collapse and ethnic conflicts were mere derivatives of the major crisis faced by all of its fundamental political, economic, social, cultural, and structural institutions, alongside its underpinnings and characteristics. I have thereby analyzed the risks of stressful changes in a multiethnic society, as the Soviet Union was, paying specific attention to how the crises in its society had prepared the way for a regressive psychological climate. Such a climate was, and still is, rife with a destructive political process that led to the total absorption of ethnicity of almost all manifestations of life and to an incredible level of ethnic hatred. It has been already said that the Soviet Union had unique cultural and structural characteristics and carries the notion that it is dangerous to generalize from one societal crisis to another. Yet in agreement with Marta Cullberg Weston, I consider that "when there are major crises in society, *some core patterns appear time and again.*"[7]

The Problems of Soviet Society on the Eve of Gorbachev's Perestroika

To understand the behavior of various ethnic groups during the crisis, one needs to assess the level of social regression in Soviet society at the time, because a new cycle of ethnic conflicts was (and is) merely an indication or symptom of unresolved problems in the whole area. Soviet society had slowly become more seriously ill from the middle of the 1960s onward.[8] The Brezhnev and Gorbachev eras witnessed an incredible jump in crime, poverty, violence, juvenile delinquency, divorce, theft from state enterprises of the so-called 'common property,' and so on. As sketchy and fragmentary as sociological data may have been at that time, some observers estimate that at least one-fifth of the Soviet population in the 1970s "lived at a minimal subsistence level, despite improvements in income, housing, food, and clothing since Stalin's day."[9] The general background that fed and maintained all the symptoms of the Soviet system's regression was defined by so-called *shady economics*. In the Caucasus and other places where previously mentioned traditions of "mutual guarantees" or "*kumovstvo*" were deeply engrained, it created an auspicious soil for the cancer-like manifestation of shady economics and corruption on a larger scale. Gradually, this led to the maximum reduction of the number of peoples engaged in "legal production" in some regions of the "national republics."[10] Clearly, an all-sided societal crisis in the Soviet Union had been built up over time. By the time it reached worldwide media coverage and became a local point of attention for researchers, it had already been brewing for years. The next stage of crisis came during the 1980s and coincided with Gorbachev's *perestroika/reconstruction* efforts. On the psychological level, "this gradual process wore people's normal defense mechanisms down and prepared the ground for a regressive process at individual and societal levels."[11]

The First Stage of Perestroika, a Different Assessment of the Term "Stagnation" of the Soviet Economic System

The economy, as per usual, was a central and critical factor. Research done by Michael Ross, Christopher Cramer, Paul Collier, and Anke Hoeffler provides strong arguments "holding that a necessary condition for societies to experience violent conflict is that groups have grievances and thus attempt to improve their situation through violence." Collier and Hoeffler also agree that societies more dependent on "primary commodity exports" and those "with low levels of per capita income have a higher risk of conflict."[12] Other scholars think that these conditions alone are not enough to trigger violence, but if such states with the appropriate economic conditions also have "weak formal state institutions," then violent conflict is almost unavoidable.[13]

When Mikhail Gorbachev declared his *perestroika/reconstruction* program in 1985, he motivated the necessity of drastic changes by stating that the Soviet Union had been through a long period of "stagnation." Now, this statement has become a stereotypical argument of some scholars who study this dramatic period, while other analysts doubted the legitimacy of the claim. For example, nobody ever once suspected *New York Times* correspondent Leslie H. Gelb of carrying pro-Soviet sympathies. Yet he reported that between 1960 and 1984 "real per capita income" in the USSR rose at an average annual rate of 3.47 percent, resulting in a tripling of the average standard of living.[14] In May 1990, the prime minister of the Soviet Union, and a close associate of Gorbachev, Nikolai Ryzhkov, stated that "the USSR's national income had increased 6.5 times in the past thirty-five years, equivalent to an average annual growth rate of 5.5 percent."[15] Today, the independent Russian Federation, Ukraine, and all other former USSR republics can only dream about such annual growth taking place in their national income. One would also be remiss to not know that in the United States, "over the same period, the increase was 2.8 times for an annual growth rate of 3.0 percent," which no expert or analyst has considered "stagnation."[16] This indicates that "stagnation" was more of an ideological term that characterized ideological confrontation both domestically and in the international arena during the Cold War period.

Negative Manifestations of Life in the Soviet Union in the Beginning of Perestroika

The aforementioned negative manifestations and tendencies that had appeared from the 1960s to the 1970s were ingrained, even broadened, in the 1980s, especially in the national republics: shady market economies, organized criminality forming into mafia networks, and increasing shortages in the consumer sector. The latter was especially vivid and caused inconveniences and irritating complications for many categories of Soviet people, primarily those who did not work in the spheres of trade and distribution of food, consumer goods, and commodities or did not belong to the privileged class of the *party*, the *Komsomol* (also known as the *All-Union Leninist Young Communist League*, a political youth organization), and Soviet *bureaucratic nomenclature*. As a former Soviet citizen, I remember the empty shelves in the state universal stores, especially in the grocery departments. During weekends, common residents of many cities and urban settlements around Moscow and other Union Republic capitals had to go and stand in long lines at these stores in order to buy deficit products and other necessities. This "event" would spark the colloquial term *sausage elektrichki* (literally "sausage commuter train") to describe the electrical trains bound for Moscow from places like Ryazan', Tula, or other cities around the capital. One could only buy deficit sausage (commonly known as *Kolbasa*) in Moscow, because, being a meat substitute, it would be completely sold out in many of the peripheral urban centers, where most of working class and budget institution workers lived. Another way to get deficit products and daily consumer goods (like soap, toilet paper, hosiery, quality clothes, shoes, building materials, household supplies, electronics, etc.), was to establish an informal connection with workers in the official system of trade and distribution enterprises. Alternatively, one could form a similar connection directly with "entrepreneurs" and their associates in the illegal sector of the previously mentioned "shady economy." From either of these options, one could basically get anything that he or she wanted, including modern items of foreign capitalist production, like American blue jeans, fancy Italian high boots, or women's pantyhose from Victoria's Secret. All of these goods would sell for either a high price or in exchange of "services," wherein buyers could pay the owners of deficit products by exploiting their own opportunities granted by their position in society.[17]

The Appearance of Illegal Soviet Businessmen and Ethnic Mafias

This situation led to the formation of a considerable class of illegal Soviet entrepreneurs known as *tsekhoviki* ("workshop men") engaged in illegal business practices. With time, many people with criminal intentions would enter this market and built criminal networks. At first, they would extort money from these shady local businessmen, and then later they could extend their reach beyond their home regions, usually developing their networks along ethnic lines. That is how Georgian, Armenian, Azerbaijani, Dagestani, Chechen, and other "ethnic mafias" began to appear. The Chechen criminal networks, in particular, "earned respect for their tenacity, solidarity, and unprecedented brutality relative early in Soviet ethnic criminal circles, particularly in Moscow and Leningrad (St. Petersburg)."[18] These would be the first glimpses of the delineations along ethnic lines in Soviet society and the first societal result of an impending economic crisis. As a matter of fact, it also found an expression in the more frequently pronounced grievances in the regions and national republics that Moscow supposedly drained of all resources, which is why the life of the common people in the periphery became so poor. Ultimately, such grievances transformed into accusations that Moscow was pursuing a policy of "internal colonialism," and by the end of the perestroika, many in the national republics circulated the slogan: "Enough to feed Moscow!"

Initial Goals of Perestroika and Modest Positive Results

This situation explains the initial goals of the first phase of perestroika from 1985 to 1988: while attempting to maintain socialist ideals and *central control* over primary societal goals, Soviet leaders aimed to *decentralize* economic activity and open the economy up to foreign trade. However, Gorbachev's policy simultaneously *legalized and encouraged private incentive*, initiatives, and created greater openness. As a result, a lot of shady enterprises became legal cooperatives. An important provision was the increase in the direct power of workers in economic policy and management. Gorbachev also wanted to accelerate economic progress, achieve world standards in technology through computerization, and eliminate housing shortages. He wrote: "We need real public involvement in administration. Such forms as the new management mechanisms, as election of managers, as setting up of work—collective councils at the work team, factory, shop, and enterprise level have been legitimately introduced."[19] Following this, steps were taken to reduce the suffocating details of centralized planning. As a result, the first phase of perestroika saw some economic growth, modest gains in living conditions, and a significant improvement in the international prestige of the Soviet Union. In 1986–1988, the annual growth rate of industrial production reached 4.0 percent, compared to 3.5 percent during the previous five years.[20] Additionally, housing construction went up by 17 percent.[21] A couple of years on, there would be a noticeable improvement in the traditionally bad Soviet agricultural sector. In particular, grain output constituted 39 percent above the level of the late 1970s, which was a good indication for the possible improvement in availability of much-desired meat and dairy products.[22]

Objective Setbacks and Decisional Mistakes

However, not all the negative tendencies were adequately addressed, with several mistakes and setbacks undermining this modest progress in short order. (1) The Cold War continued, and the limited success of nuclear arms reduction between the USSR and the United States did not end the arms race, which led to the siphoning of resources to maintain strategic military parity with the West. (2) After 1985, oil prices dropped, and the United States and its allies imposed a strict embargo that *blocked Soviet exports* to capitalist countries. This undermined their capacity to purchase grain and advanced technological products to further scientific-technological advances. (3) The Chernobyl disaster and a catastrophic earthquake in Armenia caused huge amounts of human, financial, and ecological losses. The nuclear tragedy also set back the overall Soviet electrification program. (4) Gorbachev's unconsidered anti-alcohol campaign based on reduced production and even the destruction of vineyard grape fields themselves ended in a costly failure, just like the American attempt at prohibition more than sixty years before. Paradoxically enough, this attempt to stem the tide of alcohol in the Soviet Union led to mass illegal production of moonshine and other dangerous surrogates of quality alcoholic beverages. It increased the illegal capital and untaxed profits of the ethnic mafias by an immense margin, ultimately leading to the spread of alcoholism among the Russian population. Naturally, it also reduced state income, due to the loss of the sales tax on alcohol, resulting in a considerable jump in the "state budget deficit." Due to this deficit, low-paid workers in the so-called "budget spheres," like education, scientific, and medical institutions, lost an opportunity and the hope of a raise in their salaries.[23] (5) Gorbachev's favorite entrepreneurial cooperatives also did not justify his high hopes. Even if their owners "combined with the wages of their workers, amounted to one-third of the total increase in consumer income in 1989," the paid taxes "amounting to only a quarter of one percent of the state budget."[24] Thus these new businessmen had already mastered the sophisticated methods of "withdrawing" their profits from revenue organizations, including the direct bribing of their inspectors.(6) By adopting existing technologies rather than developing its own, the Soviet Union failed to foster the user-friendly environment that could lead to further technological innovation and progress in their economy.

Deepening Crisis Became an All-Sided Societal Crisis during the Second Phase of Perestroika

During the second phase of perestroika (1988–1990), Soviet leadership further relaxed their control in order to save the faltering economic system but made the unintentional error of helping to create the conditions responsible for the country's dissolution. During this period, the existing economic crisis was augmented by and fostered in turn by fundamental *ideological*, *structural*, and *identity* crisis that would soon see rapid transition into an all-sided societal crisis.

Conservatives versus Radical Reformers; Beginning of Ideological Confrontation

The Communist leadership at this time was split into conservative hard-liners, headed by Politburo member Yegor Ligachev, and a group supporting the expansion of radical reforms, headed by Alexandr Yakovlev, former ambassador to the United States and member of the Politburo known to the Soviet people as a *Prorab perestroiki* ("Foreman of Perestroika"). Yakovlev, alongside Foreign Minister Edward Shevardnadze, leading intellectual Stanislav Menshikov, and editor-in-chief of the major theoretical edition of the CPSU *Problems of Economics* Gavriil Popov, began "rehabilitating" and justifying the social context of capitalism and foreign policy of Western countries within the framework of Gorbachev's *new thinking* ideological campaign. In the newest edition of *Problems of Economics*, Popov opened a campaign severely criticizing Marxism: namely, Marx's theory of surplus value, arguing that capitalists "earned their profits by mental labor."[25] Within another ideological campaign named *glasnost'* ("openness"), the USSR's media joined the fray and actively promoted Gorbachev's new thesis about the *stagnation* of the Soviet economy, which was a derivative of the highly centralized and planned economy while simultaneously propagating the advantages of a free market economy. Such a negative phenomenon as stagnation was declared innate to the socialist system. Jacob Keremetsky, another prominent Soviet economist, called on the vital necessity to convert "reconstruction" (i.e., perestroika) into a total destruction of public ownership and a planned economy.[26] Gorbachev would then drive the last nail in the coffin of the socialist economic system in mid-1990. According to the general secretary, the market in its contemporary interpretation "rejects the monopoly of one form of ownership and requires a diversity of such forms, vested with equal economic and political rights."[27] In February 1990, the Party Conference assumed the direction and adopted *The Communist Party Central Committee Platform*, which established the transformation of state property into one of the privately owned "modern forms" as their primary objective.[28] At the same time, the Conference purged "hard-liners" who opposed this new course of action from the party Central Committee.

At this point, it is important to remember that the cooperatives were only allowed to use their members as a workforce. However, and especially in the union and many of the autonomous republics, owners never observed this law and readily hired outside workers. By the end of 1990, five million such workers were employed at the cooperatives, yet they only produced 2.5 percent of the gross national product.[29]

Dismantling of the Planned System and Transition to Free Market Economy; Deepening Rivalry in the Political Leadership

In the meantime, the planned system entered into the process of dismantling: the 200,000 personnel of 1987 were reduced to 58,000 in 1989. In late 1990, Gorbachev became president of the USSR and, together with the radical reformers, instigated the transformation of state-owned enterprises to privately owned joint stock companies. Stock exchanges were established, where shares in these companies were traded, and new banks were opened. Russian Republic President Boris Yeltsin, a renegade of the Communist Party and rival of Gorbachev, used this opportunity to encourage secessionists in the governments of the union republics to interfere with deliveries across their boundaries. He headed radical reformers, like Grigory Yavlinsky, who planned "to shift seventy percent of industry and nineteen percent of construction and trade to private hands in 500 days; that would allow unbridled inflation; a sharp drop in real wages," and unemployment for millions of workers by closing inefficient factories.[30] Gorbachev tried to reach a compromise with this group, who enjoyed the support of secessionist forces in the various union republics and was strongly represented in the *Congress of Deputies*—a newly created representative organ. But in the long run and in many respects, the radical reformers would prevail. Gorbachev found himself balanced between this group, who enjoyed strong support from separatist forces in the national republics, and a group headed by Nikolai Ryzhkov, who proposed to extend the transitional process by six years at most to make the shift to capitalism less painful for the already considerably worn-out common people.[31]

In his book *Judgment in Moscow: Soviet Crimes and Complicity*, prominent Soviet dissident Vladimir Bukovsky tried to dismiss the Western assumption that the Soviet Politburo was becoming divided between "hard liners and liberals." He argued instead that its members "were generally united in its approach to both domestic and international problems."[32] However, some of the above-cited materials, in conjunction with the diary of Gorbachev's foreign policy adviser, Anatoly Chernyaev, indicate that fierce disagreements over the most vital components of perestroika had been a common occurrence between Edward Shevardnadze, Boris Yeltsin, and others on one side and Gorbachev and his supporters on the other. This is the main reason why Gorbachev ignominiously fired Boris Yeltsin from his job as Moscow Party chief and Politburo member in 1987. Yeltsin was soon joined by Shevardnadze, who, having resigned from both the Politburo and his position as foreign minister, like Yeltsin also defected from the Communist Party. Yet one can absolutely agree with Bukovsky's observation that "Gorbachev intended his reforms—which even the KGB considered necessary—only as expedient measures to maintain the leadership's grip on power."[33]

Denouncement of the Soviet Political System and Total Criticism of the Past Create Identity Crisis and Outbursts of Nationalism

In the meantime, rapid and immediate implementation of the three principal policies of perestroika continued to reinforce a dramatic pressure on the Soviet economic and political system. While "new thinking" fostered a significant rapprochement with the West, it simultaneously undermined and then ended Soviet control over the "socialist countries" of Eastern Europe. Glasnost gave the press and Soviet citizens alike unprecedented freedom to criticize both the past "crimes of the Soviet regime" and any issues they had with the Kremlin's more contemporary policies. These criticisms brought practically all Soviet historical narratives into question: revolution, collectivization, industrialization; all achievements and iconic heroes; crucial events on the eve of, during, and after Great Patriotic War; and so on were all put under a greater deal of scrutiny. From the pages of mainstream mass media and prime-time television programs, shocking stories about *gulag* (labor camps); the crimes of Lenin, Stalin, and other Soviet leaders; the oppressive Soviet psychiatry practiced by KGB against "twelve million people"; the deportation of entire ethnic groups; Stalin's ignominious deal with Hitler (the Molotov–Ribbentrop Pact of 1939) that was published by Alexandr Yakovlev; and many other stories crashed into the Soviet people like an avalanche. These stories, alongside countless others, were actively denounced and overturned official Soviet conceptions presented in their historical textbooks, which had been accepted by several generations of the Soviet people as unquestionable truth.

Other publications, in tandem with numerous radio and TV programs, also brought into question every aspect of the society's organizations and institutions. The constitution of the old system was now severely criticized, especially in the case of articles declaring the leading and directing role of the SPSU in Soviet society. The borders between both the individual units and the entire collective superstructure of the USSR were under similar scrutiny, especially in the national republics. Unsurprisingly, the Soviet people began to believe that the framework of their entire society was nearing total disintegration. This, of course, "created anxiety, and prepared the ground for the regressive acting out of inner impulses."[34]

Crisis of Soviet Identity Reinforced Ethnic Identities and Ethnic Tensions on the Background of the Secessionist Movements on the Republican Level

Professor Marta Cullberg Weston has left a remarkable description of the impact of Glasnost on Yugo-slavian society around this chaotic time. I want to cite it, since it perfectly matches similar authentic pictures of contemporary societies in the Caucasus and elsewhere in the Soviet Union that I observed myself in 1989–1990:

> With the end of the oppression also came a manic freedom-seeking *with ethnic underpin-nings*. When oppression is lifted, we often encounter a period of both *euphoria and anxiety,* and it is a common pattern to seek one's roots. Nationalistic identities had been suppressed during Communist rule, but like the opening of Pandora's box, nationalistic feelings awoke from a long Communist-induced narcosis. As most states have more than one nationality living within their borders, this can create serious problems. Minority groups often feel threatened by the outburst of nationalism in the majority group and their own nationalistic responses may align them with forces outside the state.[35]

This presented scenario is exactly the same as what occurred during the crucial period on the brink of perestroika in the Caucasus[36] and is the same process that has been taking place in Ukraine since 1991. In all union and in many autonomous republics, leaders soon understood that *playing the ethnic identity card* was an effective strategy when formulating viable solutions for the numerous economic and social problems that plagued their polities proved too difficult. This simmering unrest in the non-Rus-sian republics caught Gorbachev's leadership from behind, and tensions between the central Soviet government and ethno-political elites in their constituent union republics, especially in the Baltic and Caucasus polities, became increasingly strained. In 1989, the seats in the new Soviet Parliament—the Congress of the People's Deputies—were occupied by the representatives of informal public fronts (critics of Soviet institutions) and staunch partisans vying for the complete secession of their republics from the Soviet state. At the same time, Boris Yeltsin, a personal enemy of Gorbachev and self-declared liberal democrat, won a seat in this body as a representative of Moscow and adamantly reinforced republican critics of Gorbachev's policy and of the Communist regime. In spring 1990, he was elected chairman of the Russian Supreme Soviet, and in June of 1991, he became president of the Russian Republic, the largest and most powerful of the union republics.[37]

Everybody knew of Yeltsin's remarkable ability to gauge the mood of the populace. By building alliances with the nationalistic leaders of other republics and demanding autonomy for Russia, he seriously threatened Gorbachev's capacity to remain in control of the situation. The denouncement of the Soviet invasion of Afghanistan by the most prominent Soviet dissident and father of the hydrogen bomb, Andrei Sakharov, who openly called this invasion a crime of the Communist regime from the tribune of the Congress of the People's Deputies, was the last blow to the reputation of the Soviet state. Unsurprisingly, Yeltsin strongly backed Sakharov's accusations and denouncements, further empowering this already detrimental attack on the Soviet state.

Gorbachev's Unsuccessful Attempt to Deter Republics' Secessionism by Granting Equal Political Rights to the Autonomies

In view of the rising secessionist mood permeating the republics, most notably in the Baltics and Georgia, and facing the early stages of destabilization in the Caucasus because of the erupted ethnic conflict between Armenia and Azerbaijan over Nagorno-Karabakh, Gorbachev hastily promoted his new treaty-based "constitutional arrangement for power sharing between the federal center in Moscow and the constituent units of the federation." His efforts resulted in the Law on the Division of Powers between the USSR and the Subjects of the Federation, which was passed by the Congress of People's Deputies on April 26, 1990. It was a fundamental amendment to the previously established constitutional norms dictating that only union republics had the right to secede, which gave the autonomies no legal capacity in that regard. The new law "eradicated this distinction and treated both types of federal units as 'subjects of the federation.'"[38] James Hughes and Gwendolyn Sasse were completely right regarding the intentions of Gorbachev, who by "equalizing the status of union republics and autonomous republics, and making both equally subordinate to the federal government ... may have hoped to defer secessionism by the union republics and strengthen his leverage on them to negotiate a new Union Treaty."[39]

First Blood of Claimants of Independence Nearing the End of the Federal Center's Control and Reinforced Ethnocentric Groups That Begin to Take Power

This decision had been preceded by the tragic events in Tbilisi, the capital of the Georgian SSR. On April 9, 1989, following five days of anti-Soviet demonstrations by supporters of Georgian independence, the demonstrators and Russian troops clashed in the square adjacent to the government building in Tbilisi. By the time the dust settled, eighteen people had been killed and many more wounded.[40] The most common slogans of the rally were: "End discriminations against Georgians in Georgia," "Go home Russian invaders," and "Abolish the Abkhazian Republic."[41] This event played a mobilizing role for the most radical part of Georgian society, reconfirming recurrent Georgian suspicions over the aggressive intentions of their northern neighbors, the Russians.[42] I somewhat agree with the explanations of ethnic conflict that view ethnic groups as rational actors making carefully calculated choices to fight or to seek peace. However, they are only applicable to the initial stages of relatively mild and middle-ground interactions between both sides. I lived in the Caucasus among its peoples for a long time, and all of my experience convinces me that the side that adheres to outrage, commits violence, and sheds the blood of their opponents may forget the benefits of a peaceful resolution.

This crucial event *opened a completely different stage* in the interactions between the republics and the federal center, as well as between titular ethnic nations and ethnic minorities within the republics. From this tragic event onward, Georgian public opinion would drastically shift to the side of ethnocentric radicals seeking immediate independence from the Soviet Union, and many people (myself included) understood that Georgia would be independent. This event also triggered the radicalization of the public mood in all other republics and strengthened the position of the ethnocentric secessionist groups across the union. They had felt that they could quickly ascend to power through democratic procedures, specifically elections. And that is exactly what happened in Georgia and then later on in other republics. From that point onward, in the streets of Tbilisi and in many other places in the Soviet Union, I saw the dominating emotions that prevailed over any other manifestations of human nature: *fear*, *hatred*, *rage*, and *resentment*, all paired with the drive for immediate vengeance against real or imagined enemies.

With that in mind, I find myself agreeing with Roger Peterson, who defines emotion as "a mechanism that triggers action to satisfy a pressing concern."[43] Paradoxically enough, Gorbachev's maneuvers of implementing the abovementioned law and attempting to create a more powerful Soviet presidency were all aimed "at one union republic that was in the vanguard of the moves to decentralize the Soviet Union—Boris Yeltsin's Russian government—which contained the largest number of autonomous republics."[44] In reality, these ultimately strengthened the claims of secessionists across the entire Soviet Union, from the Baltic republics to Ukraine, Moldova, all the Caucasus, and Central Asia; from Crimea to Transnistria, Gagauzia, Nagorno-Karabakh, South Ossetia, Abkhazia, North Ossetia, Ingushetia, and Chechnya; and even in Tatarstan and Bashkortostan in Russia.

Interviews of Common People as Indication of Mistrust in the Soviet Political Authorities

As a result, Gorbachev, as the Soviet leader, began to personally and rapidly lose authority and respect in the eyes of the common people who suffered from the increasing hardships of daily life and ethnic wrongdoings. In 1989–1990, I recorded several interviews of commoner residents in South Ossetia, Georgia proper, and many other regions of the Caucasus already torn by ethnic strife. Here are some illustrations to this point:

Znaur G., Ossetian (aged seventy-four), said in Tskhinvali (South Ossetia) that,

> Some big shots in Georgia and here in Ossetia used the situation to their advantage. Gorbachev's power [after what happened in Tbilisi in April] is weakening, and our godfathers and party bosses understood that the time has come to strengthen their own power over us. They think only about their own fame and fortune. (Interview, June 29, 1989, Isaenko, file 1, list 20)

Others among them, Revaz Sh., a Georgian farmer (aged forty-nine), and five relatives of his wife, in Mukhrani (Georgia proper) observed that,

> This Ossetian old man [Znaur G.] is quite right. However, he must admit that in Moscow they have a lot of plunderers too. They will not let us go free. That is why they provoke quarrels between us [i.e., Ossetians–Georgians, and Abkhazians–Georgians]. They have already done so in the 1920s [during the civil war]. (Interview, June 30, 1989, Isaenko, file 1, list 25)

Vladimir P., a historian (aged forty-eight), made his comment in Dzawa (South Ossetia):

> I do not have any doubt that the Soviet Union is at its last breaths, and that very soon Georgia will be an independent state. They deserve it, but in this case we, the Ossetians, will be a divided nation. North Ossetia will stay with Russia ... Some of our intellectuals have already been talking about how to break away from Georgia as soon as possible and reunite with our northern brothers in Russia. They say that Gorbachev will support us. This is B.S.! Who will allow this? *Russians [Gorbachev] want to use us to exert pressure on Georgians, but in a decisive moment, they will turn their backs on us.*[45] Abkhazians tried to secede three times (in 1957, 1967, and 1978), and Russia did not accept this. *They know in Moscow that if they allowed this to happen, it could trigger a wave of some movements elsewhere.* Ukraine is an example of this. (Interview, July 3, 1989, Isaenko, file 1, list 41)

Similar mistrust was expressed by other thirty-nine interviewees in different regions of the Caucasus.[46] As a matter of fact, Gorbachev tried to avoid accepting responsibility for the bloody incident in Tbilisi, claiming that "he knew nothing about the plans to employ troops against civilians there, or that he at least disapproved of the assault." By citing Gorbachev's revelations to the leader of Germany's Social Democratic Party, Hans-Johen Vogel, Amy Knight shows that he lied about his noninvolvement. In fact, he actually justified the brutal suppression of demonstrators by telling Vogel that

> they speculate on democratic processes, inflame passions, and flaunt provocative slogans up to demanding the entry of NATO forces on the republic's territory. You have to put people in their place, actively counter these political adventurers, and protect perestroika—our revolution.[47]

The next year, amid growing public unrest in Azerbaijan, similar demands for independence would become prevalent there too. Gorbachev did not conceal the fact that he had ordered Soviet troops to crack down on these demonstrators. As a result, on January 19, 1990, 130 people were killed and thousands were arrested.[48] The same had happened in Vilnius, Lithuania, on January 13, 1990, which saw Soviet troops clash with protestors near the local television tower, killing thirteen civilians.[49] This was the final blow to both the authority of the Soviet government and Gorbachev's personal power. The imminent demise of the Soviet Union not only meant the loss of control of the federal center but also the advent of a resulting power vacuum in its wake. All of this happened amid an already-deepening crisis.

Deepening All-Sided Societal Crisis

Many people saw that the cumulative result of all Gorbachev's reforms in different spheres of life had provoked several unforeseen negative consequences: 1) Gorbachev dramatically diminished central state control over the allocation of consumer goods. But his government failed to replace it with an alternative supply-and-demand system. This led to dramatic shortages everywhere, which were by no means a result of "stock-jobbing, hoarding and speculation." Imports from former socialist countries and from capitalist countries alike fell 40–50 percent. 2) For the first time in Soviet peacetime history, production declined in 1990 and tumbled at a 10 percent rate in the first quarter of 1991. At the same time, the national income was also 10 percent below the 1990 average, resulting in a huge budget deficit. By March 1991, living costs were exceeding their original values from only a year before. Shortly after that, the government raised official prices on many items, sometimes by higher than 100 percent. Combined "with the increase only fractionally offset by raises in the low-end wages and pensions," even this modest raise seemed miserably miniscule.[50] 3) In a desperate attempt to finance this deficit, the authorities printed more rubles, causing a dramatic jump of inflation, "which in turn further aggravated shortages of consumer goods." According to Anatoly Chernyaev at the end of March 1991, Gorbachev relayed to him that "in 2–3 months ... we will not be able to feed the country."[51]

Psychological Impact of All-Sided Crisis: Radicalization with Ethnic Underpinnings

For the present aspect of my research, it is very important to understand what happens to people when society as they know it is dissolving in front of their eyes. How do people react when the economy of such a giant as the Soviet Union crumbles and they have difficulty surviving because their salaries no longer cover their basic needs? Psychological models provide an explanation that people in circumstances where they see their lives turned upside down naturally feel frustration and anger, with some even developing a depressive reaction. When people know that all their lives in the past—the lives and so many sacrifices of their ancestors—were inspired by false goals and values and spent in vain, a *crisis of identity* embraces *both individuals and entire groups*. When there is a breakdown of the habitual social order and a realization that the basic assumptions that people have built up over time are suddenly useless, it may seriously undermine people's coping capacity, both on an individual and on a group level. Thus, one may begin to address a collective crisis of self-efficacy.[52]

In the Soviet Union in 1991, the collective feelings of the confused masses readily spilled over into the political arena, "leading many people to attempt to deal with their own loss of control by trying to find someone whom they perceived as being able to handle the situation."[53] Paradoxically enough, people in such conditions will attempt to reestablish control "by transferring the control to someone else," which in this case were *ethnic secessionist elites* united into the new and powerful ethno-political amalgamations on both the republican and autonomous levels. The accumulated destructive energy and outrage of the common people became a looming threat not only for those in federally central positions but for the local elites as well. Because containing frustration is very difficult, people demand explanations from these new authorities, since the old ones have already completely lost their trust. Thus, in stressful situations people are inclined "to give up their individual norms, and rules and adopt the group rule" or delegate responsibility to their ethnic informal and sometime self-proclaimed authorities. Ethnic elites readily provided the explanation of who was to blame for the unbearable ordeals of their people by externalizing the cause of their problems, thus deflecting some tension outside the individual and their "ethnic or national group."[54]

Local leadership not only provided their respective populace with an explanation for the crisis (i.e., "the others"—ethnic neighbors and of course Moscow, who "have lined their pockets at our expense" through the draining and exploiting of local resources which can no longer be distributed effectively) but also "provided an outlet for feelings of frustration and anger." Vamic Volcan argued very specifically that an individual in a stressful situation tends to project aggression and anxiety onto someone else. As a result, one ethnic group may cope with frustration by utilizing ethnic minorities as "suitable targets of externalization."[55] If the political elite channel aggressive feelings that have been created by the crisis onto another ethnic group, and if it coalesces with their quest to strengthen their political power, then the road to ethnic conflict is inevitably opened. If the conflict has already erupted, then it may undergo regressive transformation into a more dangerous and volatile state.

"Parades of Sovereignties"

The rising might of these regional/republican ethno-political elites and their actually succeeding in acquiring popular support from their polities can be illustrated in 1988–1990 by the *Declaration of Sovereignty* of the union republics, which the Soviet press labeled "parades of sovereignties" (table 4.1):

TABLE 4.1

Union Republic	Adoption of the Declaration of Sovereignty
1) Armenian SSR	August 23, 1990
2) Azerbaijan SSR*	September 23, 1989
3) Belorussian SSR	July 27, 1990
4) Estonian SSR*	November 16, 1988
5) Georgian SSR*	November 18, 1989
6) Kazakh SSR	October 25, 1990
7) Kirghiz SSR	December 15, 1990
8) Latvian SSR*	July 28, 1989
9) Lithuanian SSR*	May 18, 1989
10) Moldavian SSR	June 23, 1990
11) Russian SFSR	June 12, 1990
12) Tajik SSR	August 24, 1990
13) Turkmen SSR	August 27, 1990
14) Ukrainian SSR	July 16, 1990
15) Uzbek SSR	June 20, 1990

Republics marked by asterisks are those in which ethno-political elites had already been well organized or had entered the stages of radicalization of ethnic interactions in the vanguard of a secessionist movement.[56]

Last Breaths of the Soviet Superpower

In March 1991, the last instance of the Soviet Union popular referendum showed that around 75 percent of the voters wished to preserve the USSR as a federation of equal and sovereign republics. However, even before this conclusion, the Lithuanian SSR (on March 11, 1990), the Latvian SSR (on May 4, 1990), and Georgia (on April 9, 1991, commemorating the deaths at the hands of federal troops in Tbilisi a year prior) had already declared their total and full independence from the USSR. At the same time of this multinational drive for independence, "Yeltsin defied the Kremlin by staging a large pro-democracy rally in Moscow in March 1991"[57] under the slogan "For your and our freedom!" After the June election, which saw Yeltsin become Russian president, the Kremlin's hard-liners, like KGB Chief Vladimir Kryuchkov, Defense Minister Dmitry Yazov, and Prime Minister Valentin Pavlov, were fearful that Yeltsin "would use his new position to transfer power from the Soviet center to Russia and other republics."[58] Under the pressure of this group, Gorbachev was forced to open negotiations with Yeltsin and other republican leaders (excluding those in Georgia, who held both anti-Russian and anti-Soviet agendas) to draw a new union treaty, which would grant the republics greater levels of autonomy, especially in the financial sphere. Had this treaty been signed, it would have simply reduced the federal center, and by extension Gorbachev, to a mere figurehead in terms of overall authority.

In August of 1991, Yeltsin and his supporters successfully repulsed and crushed the hard-liners' attempt to impose martial law. After that, each of the other republics declared their full independence, and in December of 1991, the three leaders of Russia, Ukraine, and Belarussia signed the abovementioned *Belovezha Accords* (also known as the *Belovezhskoye Agreement*), officially dissolving the Soviet Union.[59]

Conclusion

This analysis allows me to support those scholars who argue that a combination of ontological, decisional, and conjectural factors brought about the collapse of the Soviet Union.[60] This dramatic event pushed the ethnic activities that had been derivatives of the deepening all-sided societal crises with ever-increasing speed. It also brought many ethno-political elites to power and put before them a very complicated task: either to continue to play the ethnic identity card while building their new nation-states, where the titular ethnic groups would be politically dominant, or to build political nations where all ethnic groups would be guaranteed the rights to fully preserve and develop their principal ethnic constituents without hindrance and molestation. Hence, the next aspect of the theoretical model will be dedicated to the role of these political elites as the driving forces responsible for further supercharging ethnic tensions in their polities, as some of these elites adopted the first approach. These leaders headed down the road that led to the politicization of ethnic mobilization for conflict that came in the wake of the USSR's collapse. In fact, this factor alone supported the arguments of those who saw the shift from "inter-state conflicts within the international order to intra-state conflicts."[61]

As a matter of fact, during the processes of the abovementioned March 1991 referendum for renewing the union, 70 percent of the Ukrainian electorate (including the majority of Russians) voted for the union, and 80 percent of Ukrainians were wishing for an independent republic within such a renewed union.[62] However, in December of 1991, several months after the attempted coup, a staggering 90.3 percent voted for total independence, again including the majority of ethnic Russians and Russian-speaking representatives of other ethnic groups. All of them, nationalists and non-nationalists, were driven by "economic expectations." They believed in the promises of the Ukrainian ethno-political elite "that independence would free them of economic mismanagement from the part of Moscow"[63] and that their resources, when out of the hands of plundering federalists, would be enough to build a flourishing independent democratic state. These hopes, however, will be tested through a number of insurmountable difficulties, not the least of which being the effects of policies adopted by their dominant ethno-political forces in the long run.

Notes

1   Taras and Ganguly, *Understanding Ethnic Conflict*, 4th ed. (New York: Longman, Pearson, 2006), 18 (emphasis added). In an absorbing and generalizing historical survey, Taras and Ganguly in a well-funded and convincing way showed that the considerations of some international relations specialists "that the process of modernization would eventually lead to assimilation of minority ethnic groups within the dominant culture" had utterly failed. Equally wrong in this regard are those who believed in the capacity of capitalism in diffusing ethnic wrangling, Neo-Marxists who believed in the overwhelming impact of "class structure on society," and scholars (both western liberals and Soviet Marxists) who were "dismissive of ethnic sentiments in the contemporary world." Before the end of the Cold War, the focus of researchers was set on other issues: "East-West and North-South disputes, interstate conflicts, nuclear proliferation, disarmament, left-wing revolutionary movements, regional integration, and the global economy." All these led to the underestimation of ethnic issues. See Taras and Ganguly, *Understanding Ethnic Conflict*, 4th ed. (New York: Longman, Pearson, 2006), 18; 25–26.

2   Ira William Zartman, "Introduction: Posing the Problem of State Collapse," in *Collapsed States: The Disintegration and Restoration of Legitimate Authority*, ed. William Zartman (Boulder, CO: Lynne Rienner, 1995), 1.

3   Taras and Ganguly, *Understanding Ethnic Conflict*, 18.

4   Taras and Ganguly, *Understanding Ethnic Conflict*, 18.

5   Taras and Ganguly, *Understanding Ethnic Conflict*, 18.

6   Anatoly Isaenko, *Polygon of Satan: Ethnic Traumas and Conflicts in the Caucasus*, 3rd ed.(Dubuque, IA: Kendall Hunt Publishing House, 2014),chapters 4, 5, 7, 8; Steven D. Roper, "Regionalism in Moldova: The Case of Transnistria and Gagauzia," in *Ethnicity and Territory in the Former Soviet Union: Regions in Conflict* (London: Frank Cass, 2002), 108–9.

7   Marta Cullberg Weston, "When Words Lose Their Meaning: From Societal Crisis to Ethnic Cleansing," *Mind and Human Interaction* 8, no. 1 (Winter/Spring, 1997): 21 (emphasis added).

8   In a concentrated and comprehensive form, all the breakdowns of socialist societies and economies have been analyzed in John M. Thompson, *A Vision Unfulfilled: Russia and the Soviet Union in the Twentieth Century* (Lexington, MS: DC Health and Co., 1996), 446–65.

9   Thompson, *Vision Unfulfilled*, 446.

10 Isaenko, *Polygon of Satan*, 3rd ed., 121; in Georgia, for example, this reduction was down to 17 percent.

11 Weston, "When Words Lose Their Meaning," 21.

12 Michael Ross, "Oil, Drugs and Diamonds," in *The Political Economy of Armed Conflict: Beyond Greed and Grievances*, ed. Karen Ballentine and Jack Sherman (Boulder, CO: Lynne Reinner, 2003), 47–72; Christopher Cramer, "Homo Economicus Goes to War: Methodological Individualism, Rational Choice, and the Political Economy of War," *World Development* 30, no. 11 (2002): 143–64; Paul Collier and Anke Hoeffler, "Greed and Grievance in Armed Conflict," *Oxford Economic Papers* 56, no. 4 (2004): 563–95.

13 James D. Fearon, "Primary Commodity Exports and Armed Conflict," *Journal of Conflict Resolution* 49, no. 4 (2005): 483–507; Julia Strasheim, "Power-Sharing Commitment Problems and Armed Conflict in Ukraine," *Civil Wars* 18, no. 2 (2016): 27.

14 Leslie H. Gabe, *The New York Times*, October 28, 1984, cited in: "The Economic and Political Crisis in the USSR," *Marxism-Leninism Today, US Classics*, 1 August, 1991, https://mltoday.com/the-economic-and-political-crisis-in-the-ussr.

15 Nikolai Ryzhkov, Interview to *Pravda*, May 25, 1990.

16 ML Today, "The Economic and Political Crisis in the USSR," *Marxism-Leninism Today, US Classics*, 1 August, 1991, https://mltoday.com/the-economic-and-political-crisis-in-the-ussr.

17 See Hedrick Smith, *The New Russians* (New York: Random House, 2012); see also Hedrick Smith, *The Russians* (New York: Random House, 1976).This is the best and most authentic description of Russian face-to-face interaction and the texture of life as Russians lived it.

18 Emil Souleimanov, *An Endless War: The Russian-Chechen Conflict in Perspective* (Frankfurt, Germany: Peter Lang, 2007), 79–80.

19 Mikhail Gorbachev, *Perestroika* (New York: Harper & Row, 1987), 42–44.

20 *Narodnoye Khozyaistvo SSSR* (Moscow: Gosizdat, 1989), 8–9.

21 *Narodnoye Khozyaistvo*, 7.

22 *Narodnoye Khozyaistvo*, 458.

23 *Narodnoye Khozyaistvo*, 76–77.

24 *Narodnoye Khozyaistvo*, 77.

25 Gavriil Popov, "Glavnye vyzovy perestroiki," *Problemy economiki*, no. 1 (1990), cited in ML Today, "The Economic and Political Crisis in the USSR"; see also Raymond L. Garthoff, *The Great Transition: American Soviet Relations and the End of Cold War* (Washington, DC: Brookings Institution, 1994), 432.

26 "Editorial Article," *Pravda*, July3, 1990.

27 *Pravda*, July 3, 1990.

28 *Pravda*, February 13, 1990.

29 *Narodnoye Khozyaistvo*, 268–69.

30 *Pravda*, December 14, 1990.

31 *Pravda*, December 14, 1989.

32 Cited in a very thorough review, Amy Knight, "The Secret Files of the Soviet Union," *The New York Review*, January 16, 2020, 28.

33 Knight, "The Secret Files of the Soviet Union," 28.

34 Weston, "When Words Lose Their Meaning," 21.

35 Weston, "When Words Lose Their Meaning," 21–22 (emphasis added).

36 Isaenko, *Polygon of Satan*, chapter 3.

37 Amy Knight, "The Mysterious End of the Soviet Union," *The New York Review*, April 5, 2012, 74.

38 James Hughes and Gwendolyn Sasse, "Comparing Regional and Ethnic Conflicts in Post-Soviet Transition States," in *Ethnicity and Territory in the Former Soviet Union: Regions in Conflict*, ed. James Hughes and Gwendolyn Sasse (London: Frank Cass, 2002), 19.

39 Hughes and Sasse, "Comparing Regional and Ethnic Conflicts," 19.

40 Amy Knight indicates that there may have actually been twenty-one fatalities. See "The Secret Files of the Soviet Union," 28.

41 Zvaid Gamsakhurdia, "We Have Chatted Too Long with the Separatists: A Conversation with the Chairman of the Georgian Supreme Court," *Moscow News*, December 2, 1990, 11.

42 Ghia Nodia, "The Conflict in Abkhazia: National Projects and Political Circumstances," in *Georgians and Abkhazians: The Search for a Peace Settlement*, ed. Bruno Coppieters, Ghia Nodia, and Yuri Anchabadze. Published online in *Caucasian Regional Studies* 3, no. 2/3 (1998): http://poei.vub.ac.be/publi/Georgians/chp0201.html.

43 Roger D. Petersen, *Understanding Ethnic Violence: Fear, Hatred and Resentment in Twentieth-Century Eastern Europe* (Cambridge, UK: Cambridge University Press, 2002), 1.

44 Hughes and Sasse, "Comparing Regional and Ethnic Conflicts," 19.

45 Around the same time, Anatoly Chekhoev, a deputy of the Soviet Parliament, told me that Gorbachev assured the Ossetian delegates that he "would never leave the Ossetians alone against the Georgian nationalists." My research did not allow me to verify this information, but the *Soyuz* ("Union") hard-line faction in the Soviet Parliament did, in fact, promise this to the Ossetians in the Vladikavkaz rallies, at which I was present.

46 First published in Isaenko, *Polygon of Satan*, 143–44, 146.

47 Cited in Knight, "The Secret Files of the Soviet Union," 28. The author witnessed the outrage of Georgians in Tbilisi in 1990, "when it was announced that Gorbachev was awarded the Nobel Peace Prize."

48 Isaenko, *Polygon of Satan*, 332. Twenty-one soldiers also died in this incident. See also Thomas De Waal, *Black Garden: Armenia and Azerbaijan Through Peace and War* (New York: New York University Press, 2003), 93.

49 Knight, "The Secret Files of the Soviet Union," 28.

50 "Editorial Article," *Izvestia*, April 20, 1991; *Nardodnoye Khozyaistvo*, 8–9.

51 Cited in Knight, "The Mysterious End of the Soviet Union," 74. Anatoly Chernyaev's diaries can be found in English on the National Security Archive website at www.gwu.edu/nsarchiv.

52 The author behind the concept of "self-efficacy," Albert Bandura, showed the impact of a crisis on the capacities of both the individual and a group. See Albert Bandura, *Self-Efficacy in Changing Societies* (Cambridge, UK: Cambridge University Press, 1995).

53 Weston, "When Words Lose Their Meaning," 22–23.

54 Weston, "When Words Lose Their Meaning," 23.

55 Vamic Volcan, *The Need to Have Enemies and Allies* (Northvale, NJ: Jason Aronson Inc., 1988), 35f.

56 Mikhail Stoliarov, *Federalism and the Dictatorship of Power in Russia* (Washington, DC: Taylor & Francis, 2014), 56.

57 Knight, "The Mysterious End of the Soviet Union," 74.

58 Knight, "The Mysterious End of the Soviet Union," 74.

59 Amy Knight cited interesting documentary evidence that does not depict Gorbachev a victim of the attempted coup. Rather, it argues that he was actually one of the conspirators. See Amy Knight, "The KGB, Perestroika, and the Collapse of the Soviet Union," *Journal of Cold War Studies* 5, no. 1 (Winter 2003): 67–93.

60 Richard Sakwa, *Soviet Politics in Perspective* (London: Routledge, 1998), 285–86. "Foreman of Perestroika" Yakovlev insisted on ontological reasons in this travail: "As soon as we began to make really radical reforms, in foreign policy say, we immediately came up against the resistance of the system. It began to resist ... And from that moment on people began to say that *the system is irreformable* and the party is irreformable. Although there did remain some illusions, some hopes, but it could all be done without major conflict" (emphasis added). Cited in Thayer Wattcins, *The Economic Collapse of the Soviet Union* (Silicon Valley, CA: San Jose State University, 2019), sjsu.edu/faculty/Watkins/sovietcollapse.htm.

61 David Carment and James Patrick, "Ethnic Conflict at the International Level: An Appraisal of Theories and Evidence," in *Wars in the Midst of Peace: The International Politics of International Conflict*, ed. David Carment and James Patrick (Pittsburgh: University of Pittsburgh Press, 2000); David Carment and James Patrick, "Explaining Third-Party Intervention in Ethnic Conflict: Theory and Evidence," *Nations and Nationalism* 6, no. 2 (2000): 173–202.

62 See Ilya Prizel, "Nation Building and Foreign Policy," in *Ukraine—The Search for a National Identity*, ed. Sharon Wolchik and V. Zviglyanich (Lanham, Maryland: Rowman & Littlefield Publishers, 1999), 14.

63 Hans van Zon, "Ethnic Conflict and Conflict Resolutions in Ukraine," *Perspectives on European Politics and Society* 2, no. 2 (2001): 224.

CHAPTER FIVE

Driving Forces of Ethnic Conflict

The Role of Ethno-Political Elites and Charismatic Leaders

In one of his many verses, the famous Russian revolutionary poet Vladimir Mayakovsky warned Soviet workers to beware the "canaries who may guzzle socialism." In 1991, this prediction came true in a resounding fashion. I demonstrated in the previous chapter that an unusual alliance between Yeltsin's self-proclaimed liberals-democrats and nationalists in the Caucasus, Baltic republics, and Ukraine successfully put an end to the Soviet empire and socialism. The immediate result was a phenomenon that Taras and Ganguly cleverly dubbed "matryoshka nationalism," in which, like the brightly painted Russian nesting dolls that contain smaller dolls within them, anti-Soviet Russian nationalism "spawned lower-order nationalisms and with them, ethnic conflicts."[1] The same people who set the centrifugal tendencies of titular and subordinate groups in motion used dying Soviet federalism as an instrument to reinforce ethnic identities and advance ethnic mobilization amid a deepening all-sided societal crisis, effectively "sweeping them into office might."[2] However, by the time they had achieved their goal, consolidating both economic and political power, their polities encountered the cascading social and economic problems that had been aggravated by the collapse of the Soviet Union. Suddenly, they realized that they were in no position to formulate and pursue the comprehensive policy required to meet these powerful challenges. They had no clear strategies or coherent programs on how to promote social and economic reform. In these unfavorable circumstances, they instead decided to read reality in coalescence with their claims to preserve the political power that had suddenly fallen into their hands. It was for this purpose alone that they drew on each ethnic groups' own uncertainties and fears. Thus, with ethno-political elites and their charismatic leaders "using such a situation for their own political purposes and playing different groups against each other—a fact suggestive of their own individual regression—the road was destined to warfare."[3]

In this chapter, I want to identify and scrutinize certain groups of people who, before and especially after the collapse of the Soviet Union, became driving forces behind the ethnic conflicts that arose from the ruins of the super-state and are ultimately responsible for their regressive development and disastrous results.

Ethnic Mafias

Within the previous chapter, I indicated that *ethnic mafias* were the first social groups with anti-Soviet sentiments and had already begun building their own underground networks along ethnic lines. Their activity, aimed at putting lucrative business ventures under their control, had led to the creation of a "shady" economy, which had provoked clashes between different ethnic groups early on. These groups of new people had quickly established corrupt connections to co-ethnic members of the earlier mentioned *ruling party*, *Komsomol,* and *state nomenklatura* by bribing and buying off its cadres and functionalities, as well as those in the disparate law enforcement structures of the national republics and in the new Russia. Many of these people were connected by blood, usually belonging to the same extended families. This is especially true in societies where clans and tribes, even for those shattered during the Soviet period, remained the basic structures of ethnic communities. By the end of the 1980s, so-called "rent economics" had already been formed among ethnic nomenclature elites. These powerful and highly privileged people—together with ethnic criminalities and a cohort of shady businessmen who had become wealthy off of the accumulation of illegal capital—represented an early *amalgamation* that would be the first real driving force of ethnic mobilization.

The ethnic criminal syndicates have increased in both power and scope in the intermittent years, flourishing within the conditions of spontaneously emerging free market economies. It is important to understand that these new ethnic criminalities were, and still are, rather different from the so-called *Thieves World*—organized groups of career criminals headed by the "crowned Thieves-at-Law." These new ethnic criminalities quickly picked up on the most ruthless methods from their professional predecessors, succeeding them in the long run regarding both unrestricted aggressiveness and brutality. Therefore, one should be fully aware that we are dealing with two completely different breeds of organized crime, even if both of them—the Thieves World and ethnic criminalities—have been ubiquitously labeled as "the Russian Mafia" or "the Russian Mob" in the West.[4] In fact, many leading cases of criminal activity in Western countries were not perpetrated by native Russians but by representatives of other, more well-organized ethnic criminal groups from the former Soviet Union.

The amalgamations that I refer to as *ethnic mafias* were, and still are, representatives of a vicious new form of emerging frontier capitalism. My studies of ethnic mafias in the Caucasus during the late 1980s and early 1990s allowed me to identify *four principal subgroups* among their ranks: 1) members of the Soviet underground business world; 2) Soviet and ex-Soviet officials; 3) newly legal post-Soviet entrepreneurs; and 4) a new type of ethnic criminal who did not originate from within the classical Thieves World and were not restricted by its rules and traditions, ultimately distinguished by their unprecedentedly ruthless ways of achieving their interests, known in the post-Soviet lexicon as *bespredel'shiki* ("without limits" or "bullies"). This amalgamation became one of the first major forces behind crime, corruption, and ethnic conflicts in the post-Soviet landscape. In the case of Russia, these mafia groups became an absolute nightmare for Yeltsin's government, so much so that in February 1993, Clair Sterling quoted Yeltsin as saying:

> Organized crime is destroying the economy, interfering with politics, undermining public morale, threatening individual citizens, and the entire Russian nation ... Our country is already considered a great Mafia power.[5]

On January 26, 1994, Russia's leading media resource, *Izvestia* (*The News*), reported that the Russian mafia (including ethnic mafias from the Caucasus republics) controlled "70 to 80 percent of all private businesses and banking."[6]

One can therefore agree with Marshall Goldman that "the East Europeans and the Chinese were able to avoid many of Russia's problems with the mafia because they *moved gradually* or because *they already had many market-type institutions in place*. But Russia [and other post-Soviet polities], like a deep-sea fish, is exploding because it has not had time to build up the institutions it needs to cope with market process."[7]

In 1994, official Russian estimates regarding the number of penetrated state institutions, including the army, indicated that organized criminal groups controlled some 40,000 state and private organizations. These included hundreds of state enterprises, joint-stock companies, cooperatives, banks, and markets. Specialists argue that, at the time, over 2,500 organized criminal groups were operating within Russia alone, "many with international connections and structures that became increasingly sophisticated." Unsurprisingly, the most ruthless of these groups fit under the umbrella of the so-called "ethnic mafias."[8]

Ukraine's first president, Leonid M. Kravchuk, once expressed "dismay at the levels of organized crime" and how "corruption and bribes were penetrating into structures of [Ukraine's] ministries and departments."[9] In the second half of the 1990s, the situation worsened as, alongside other organized crime issues, growing criminality in Crimea and waves of attempted assassinations and bombings would become an ever-present headache for subsequent Ukrainian administrations.[10]

I witnessed first hand how an ethnic mafia acted in Vladikavkaz, North Ossetia-Alania (Russian Federation), at that time. I had a good friend who lived there who belonged to an extended Azerbaijani family of six brothers whom I had known since childhood. In the early 1990s, they had been one of the first in the entire republic to set up a vegetable trading cooperative. Then one of the brothers opened a universal store on the main avenue, the most prestigious place in the city. Well-organized and well-equipped, it was a place where visitors could try wonderful Azerbaijani tea and tasty pastries in the lobby while their companies could peruse the various items that the owner brought in from Turkey and the Arab Emirates. Soon, however, local mobsters, who had been hired by a competitor belonging to the titular (Ossetian) ethnic nation, began demanding weekly "protection" money in gradually increasing payments. When my friend ultimately refused to pay the next increase, his son was kidnapped and other relatives were likewise threatened. After several failed attempts by the police to find the abducted son on their own, and only with the assistance of the same mafia who had committed the crime in the first place, they eventually managed to secure the son's release. However, the conditions of this release forced my friend to move his business into the suburbs of the city. After his departure, another store belonging to an entrepreneur with "the proper ethnic credentials" opened in the same location. When I asked this man, who was actually a former student of mine, why he would do such a thing, he told me in confidence that very soon all lucrative businesses in the republic would be solely run by his own co-ethnics. "Let Azerbaijanis go and open their businesses in Azerbaijan, Ingushians in Ingushetia, Russians in Russia, etc. ... and Ossetia must belong to the Ossetians." By that time, I had already heard a similar slogan from Zviad Konstantinovich Gamsakhurdia (March 31, 1939—December 31, 1993), the first president of a newly independent Georgia, who openly and proudly declared: "Georgia for Georgians!" I suspect that neither of these men could have guessed that they were echoing Hitler's own Nazi motto: "*Nur für Deutsche!*" ("Only for Germans!").

At this point, I had recorded many stories in different places within the Caucasus that shared this sentiment. They reflected on the idea that one's own titular ethnic group's members/relatives should hold greater legal access to the more valued space in a society than other ethnicities. They affirmed these ethnic preferences in the distribution of awards and recognitions; the allotment of funding; and the promotion of relatives, kinsmen, and fellow nationals to key positions within a society, in both semi-legal and illegal lucrative mafia-style businesses. They encouraged the reinstating of mutual guarantees while resisting or avoiding proper legal procedures of an ethnically dominated state order for the sake of protecting their kinsmen or ethnic co-nationals from legal prosecution. Families and clans revealed a tendency to partially transform into post-Soviet mafia-type economic units of frontier capitalism, monopolizing entire branches of lucrative consumer production, like legal or semi-legal vodka production in Ossetia, or industrial production, such as oil refineries, oil fields, and long stretches of pipeline, in Chechnya. They then directed a portion of their "uncontrolled" income to provide kickbacks for the local corrupted bureaucracy, to finance informal ethnocentric movements and paramilitary organizations, and to manipulate local elections and appointments for governmental positions within local political structures.

Cases of the Direct Involvement of Ethnic Mafias and Other Forces in Interethnic Clashes

The earliest case of Mafia involvement in ethnic conflict was the *Fergana Massacre*. In spring 1989, the Uzbek SSR exploded with several mass pogroms organized by the local Uzbeks against the Meskhetian Turks. In the ensuing chaos, 103 people were killed, more than 1,000 were wounded, and 750 households were burned to the ground.[11] According to the 1989 census, around 207,500 Turks lived in the USSR.[12] More than 90 percent of these former Soviet Turks originally inhabited the five administrative districts of Southern Georgia near the Turkish border. These districts constitute a significant part of the historically Georgian region of Meskheti, which is why these particular Turks bear the "Meskhetian" moniker. In 1944, they, along with other Muslim groups living in Meskheti at the time (including Kurds and Karakalpaks), were deported at the behest of Stalin to the rural areas of Uzbekistan, Kazakhstan, and Kyrgyzstan under the status of "special settlers." Twelve years later, Khrushchev would release them from the bonds of administrative surveillance, though they were not allowed to return to their original homelands. While some of these people had migrated to Azerbaijan and the North Caucasus in the 1950s and 1960s, the majority were left to live in Central Asia and Kazakhstan. By 1989, the biggest regional group of these Meskhetian Turks—numbering around 106,700—lived in Uzbekistan, with 13,600 living in the Fergana Oblast' in particular.[13]

In 1990, I recorded the story of two refugees from the Fergana Valley, a father and daughter pair of Meskhetian Turks who settled in the Mozdok District of North-Ossetia-Alania following the massacre. The principal details of their stories share several coincidental parallels to accounts of professional analysts.[14] The duo told me that all the Meskhetian Turks used to live compactly in special blocks of their designated settlements known as *makhallyas*. The former represented the self-organization of communities or neighborhoods that were typically populated by large and closely related families, usually headed by elected councils of elders or *aksakals* (lit. "gray-bearded" in Turkish). Relationships between relatives were traditionally characterized by a high degree of mutual guarantees. Uzbeks made a habit of avoiding these blocks out of fear of being confronted by very well-organized groups of young Turks who called the block home. The daughter, a young lady named Fatima, admitted that her younger co-ethnics used to behave rather "cheeky" by going out to public dance parties in groups of twenty to thirty individuals. Once they had arrived at these public places, these young Turks would usually perform their traditional folk dances and bully or abuse any local Uzbeks that were present. According to Fatima, it was in this way that these young people demonstrated their "*jigitism*" (from the Turkish word *jigit*, meaning "bold, audacious warrior").

More importantly, some of the well-organized minority family groups put the trades of local markets of urban settlements, including Fergana, under their control. These families were more successful and well-off when compared to those of the Uzbeks. I have already mentioned that scholars specializing in ethnic conflicts argue that access to vital material recourses, especially amid an economic crisis, is the most common reason for ethnic mobilization and the gradual transformation of mundane quarrels into full-on interethnic clashes.

However, my interviewees were very critical of these "economic" discrepancies, arguing that the majority of both Turks and Uzbeks lived in the same worsening conditions and that the level of control that Meskhetian Turks had over certain spheres of trade and distribution of vital products was inordinately exaggerated. Instead, they proposed their own version of what had transpired, which I believe deserves serious attention. Fatima's father, who himself was a historian and a teacher at the local high school, told me about the situation in Fergana Valley and the republic at large, which he characterized as "pre-conflict," describing it as a "dense atmosphere of social depression caused by the deep crisis of the official and traditional institutions, which were deaf to the needs of the common people." He asserted that the people "had lost confidence in the future and lived in constant fear, always thinking that something terrible may happen at any moment." In such an overheated atmosphere, each and every instance of violence could pull the trigger on an uncontrollable escalation in conflict.

And this is exactly what happened. The pogroms began on the evening of May 31, 1989, in the Kuvasai urban settlement. Near the local pub, a mass street fight broke out between two groups of young, and thoroughly drunk, Turks and Uzbeks. After the dust settled, twenty-five civilians and two police officers were injured, with one of the Uzbek lads later dying in the hospital from his injuries. Overall, the Turks would prevail, but the Uzbeks mobilized forces in response and attempted to force their way into the Turks' *makhallyas*. The attackers would be beaten once again, with the caveat of the "victors" promising to rape them and their wives the next time they tried.

After this, the entire Fergana Oblast' erupted, and like a mass conflagration, the wholesale slaughter of Meskhetian Turks rolled from one town to another. Mobilization leaflets circulated among some Uzbek populations bearing calls "to expel the newcomers from Uzbekistan." Rumors began to spread that these calls were created by several informal organizations like the *Union of Uzbeks* and *Birlyk ("Unity")*. Unknown activists began compiling lists of volunteers and ordered them to wait for the proper signal to begin, instructing them to prepare weapons, explosives, and Molotov cocktails in the meantime.

May 23–25, 1989, was what one may call an "active phase" of attacks against the Meskhetian Turks, taking place in Kuvasai, Fergana, Margelan, Kokand, Tashlak, and other nearby towns and cities. June 3–12 that same year saw the most horrific of these ethnic cleansings, when well-organized crowds of young Uzbeks from the surrounding rural areas came into the cities by the truckload. Armed with knives, clubs, and firearms, they broke into the Turkish *makhallyas* and began killing random inhabitants, only to then set their homes and cars alight. On June 7, the city of Kokand became the center of these pogroms, as huge trucks, buses, and tractors brought in thousands more to join the mobs already roaming the streets. They even stormed the police station and released those who had been arrested for various crimes committed during the earlier pogroms. This bloody mess continued until June 9, when 16,282 Meskhetian Turks were evacuated into Russia proper with the assistance of the Soviet Army.

The pogroms triggered a mass exodus of not only Meskhetian Turks but also Russians, Tatars, and representatives of various other ethnic groups from Uzbekistan, all motivated by the imminent dangers brought about by the rise in nationalism.[15] Ridiculously, the official explanation of this massacre put forth by the local authorities, namely Secretary of the Central Committee of the Communist Party of Uzbekistan Rafik Nishanov and Council of Ministers Chair Gayrat Kadyrov, indicated that the interethnic clashes began in a local market, when a Meskhetian Turk cursed at an Uzbek woman who wanted a higher price for her traded strawberries.[16] Stranger still, modern textbooks that detail the history of Uzbekistan (written around 2005) assert that this tragedy was supposedly a gainful experience for "the long hand of Moscow," which had provoked the slaughter to preserve Soviet Union control over Uzbekistan.[17]

It has been a little over thirty years since the tragedy in Fergana. By the time I had sufficiently prepared to compare this atrocity with analogies of other early interethnic conflicts to reveal the repetition of patterns, the news reported that other interethnic incidents had broken out in South Kazakhstan.

The authors behind the telegram channels in the various forms of social media stated that "an interethnic conflict between Kazakh and Dungan youths" had occurred. According to local police reports, on February 7, 2020, a road patrol stopped a car near the town of Sortobe for speeding. Supposedly, the driver had previously committed several administrative misdemeanors and, while arguing with the police, called for relatives to come to his aid. When they arrived, they severely beat the police officers and damaged their vehicle. Following this incident, conflict would spill over into the adjacent town of Masanchi, where, as a result of the fighting, an eighty-two-year-old elderly man was hospitalized. Some of the people who witnessed the fighting managed to make a video of the incident and subsequently uploaded it onto several social media platforms. After this, around 300 young people came from neighboring villages, and unsurprisingly, the conflict flared up vigorously: eight people died and forty more were wounded by firearms, including two police officers. The conflict continued in the villages of Auhatty and Bulan-Batyr until local police and internal ministry reinforcements secured the perimeter of the entire region and regained control of the situation.

For context, the city of Masanchi is known by locals as an informal capital for the Dungan ethnic minority in Kazakhstan, supporting a population of approximately 13,000. In terms of ethnic distribution, roughly 90 percent belong to the Dungan diaspora, 5 percent are Russians, and the remaining 5 percent are the titular Kazakhs. The primarily Muslim Dungans had resettled in Masanchi and Sortobe in the nineteenth century from China due to the persecutions of the Qing Dynasty.

Kazakhstani President Kassym-Jomrat Tokayev officially blamed this incident on unknown provocateurs who took a simple "domestic accident" and transformed it into "an interethnic conflict." However, Khusei Daurov, head of the *Association of Kazakhstan Dungans*, argued that the conflict was interethnic from its inception. According to Daurov, young Kazakhs, under the cover of night, entered Masanchi and arranged a horrific pogrom: they set fire to dozens of Dungan homes, beat and shot at any Dungans they could find, and destroyed the town's House of Culture, nearby shops, and the town center at large. The main roads were blocked and patrolled by bands of armed Kazakhs, which prevented the Dungans from leaving their homes. Supposedly, the Dungans attempted to save themselves by fleeing to Kyrgyzstan;

however, the Kazakh police argue that this was false information spread through social media by those same "malignant provocateurs" and in a more traditional manner by intellectuals, all in an effort to explain the events as being caused by the "unresolved socio-economic problems in the Dzhambul region of Kazakhstan."[18]

Alexandr Grozin, one of the leading specialists of the Department of Central Asia and Kazakhstan at the Institute of the Union of Independent States, weighed in on this incident:

> Even if the triggering moment was a domestic accident, it rather quickly transformed into an interethnic pogrom ... Look at the lists of casualties: all of them are Dungans, and all the houses, shops, and cars are also Dungans' ... Such things happen periodically: Kazakhs attack Armenians, Uighurs, Meskhetian Turks, Uzbeks, Uighurs again, etc. ... They do not beat the Russians only because they live dispersed throughout the urban centers—the urbanistic environment, so far, keeps them in relative safety ... The problem lieson the sur-face: Kazakhs have become the absolute majority in the state. They are being reminded of this all the time and everywhere they go they hear that they played an important role in world history, and that all other ethnic groups are spongers and parasites; that all the land belongs to the Kazakhs and the others moved onto it. That is why all who have "doubts" must be put in their places ... Kazakh society is ill with nationalism.

Essentially, the problem is that after the collapse of the Soviet ideology and political culture, in both the post-Soviet space and within the independent states themselves, local political elites are building ethnocratic regimes.[19]

Considerations Regarding Recurrent Behavioral Patterns of Interethnic Clashes

Both of these cases, separated by a period of thirty-one years, share many parallels between not only themselves but among a litany of interethnic clashes in the former Soviet Union, the post-Soviet landscape, and beyond. This is true in the cases of ethnic conflicts that stem from a long history, have a long course of existence through the latest and future cycles of violence, contain vivid ideological components, and in which the opposing sides have quantitatively comparable forces. Not only do these factors apply to conflicts like the Armenian and Azerbaijani schism over Nagorno-Karabakh or the current Russo-Ukrainian conflict, but they also apply in those ethnic conflicts between super-ordinate titular groups and ethnic minorities, who are usually well-organized and supported by outside ethnic diasporas. These factors also apply to situations of "ethnic violence" that are usually much smaller in scale, such as mass riots and pogroms, which usually stand alone and are not a component of a more intense and prolonged conflict.[20]

I compared both of the previous cases to those of the Armenian pogroms that took place in Sumgait on February 27–28, 1988, and similar events in the Prigorodnyi District of North-Ossetia-Alania and Vladikavkaz from October 31 to November 3, 1992. Both of these incidents were enacted as well-structured and vividly ideological/formally recognized ethnic conflicts, which bears a striking resemblance to two separate cases of ethnic violence and rioting in Grozny (capital of the Chechen-Ingushian ASSR) in August 1958. These two separate incidents share a common motive, as both were brought about due to Chechen and Ingushian resettlement following their exile to Central Asia. Similar still was the short period of heightened "ethnic violence" seen in the Ossetian riots provoked by the October 1981 murder of Ossetian taxi driver K. I. Gagloev by Ingushians. In 1958, the Russian participants of the Grozny riot demanded that the repatriation of Chechens and Ingushians exiled in Central Asia to the Chechen-Ingushian ASSR cease in order to "defend the Russian population." Ossetians made nearly identical demands in 1981, with a call to end the continuous resettlement of Ingushians into the Prigorodnyi District of North-Ossetia and to "defend the Ossetian population."[21]

While analyzing the Fergana pogroms, one can attract similar outside events for the sake of comparison, such as the mass violence against ethnic Germans suspected of spying for the Nazis during the early German onslaught of Europe from 1940 to 1941.[22] Further similarities can be found in South Asian inter-communal clashes, particularly the Hindu pogroms against Sikhs between October and November 1984, following the assassination of Indian Prime Minister Indira Gandhi.[23] Some analysts also cite several cases of riots and racial violence in both the United States and Great Britain from the 1960s to 1990s as viable incidents for comparison.[24]

When you ignore the obvious differences among all of these cases, one may identify certain behavioral patterns that appear within them time and again. Among these are:

- the escalation of disturbances that began as small quarrels, skirmishes, or protest actions;
- the rapid structuralizing of crowds along *ethnic lines* and the appearance of leaders /ethnic activists/ organizers;
- the rapid spread of rumors and their successful competition with official information in explaining the nature of the events;
- the rapid escalation and multiplication of targets of violence, increasing involvement by activists, who transition into acts of violence;
- the ambivalent positions taken by those in power: they may sometimes be the objects of aggression and demands, but some of them turn into *active supporters of co-ethnic pogrom-makers* or share some of the key demands, especially those instances regarding the deportation of the targeted ethnic group from their own "area," which is essentially ethnic cleansing;
- a lack of clear strategies by official social structures to handle the riots and pogroms, usually resulting in them lagging behind during the bloodier phases;
- the appearance and circulation of statements about various *"plots"* by the unknown forces and provocateurs in the official structures, resulting in seemingly random arrests of participants and bystanders alike;
- a number of indispensable demands issued by the pogrom-makers for the release of detained co-nationals or to give up their targets who are protected by the power structures, sometimes resulting in the storming of police stations, other places of confinement, and even government complexes.[25]

Additionally, there are several identifiable patterns and immediate consequences that repeat over and over again in interethnic clashes and violence throughout the post-Soviet space specifically:

- the increasing exodus of members of the targeted ethnic minority groups and non-titular groups who, in a regressive atmosphere of interethnic clashes, fear that they may soon be the next target of hostility by the dominating ethnic nations; particularly, such uncertainty and fears were (and still are) spreading among the many fragmented Russian family groups who could not compete with the very well-organized extended clans of titular groups and thus tended to leave the national republics as a precaution;

- the abovementioned exoduses are enticed by the splash of *radical ethnocentric nationalism* in the midst of titular ethnic nations heavily buttressed by conspiracy theories about "the long hand of Moscow"—the source of all malice—maintained and spread by the ethno-political elites and the mass media outlets under their control;
- cases of interethnic violence spurning further regressive development of existing ethnic conflicts and triggering their transition into the more dangerous *"hot stages"*;
- *the ethnic mafias of the titular ethnic nations becoming the principal beneficiaries of the resulting mass migration of the targeted ethnic groups, filling in the resulting gaps within the most lucrative spheres*; and
- cases of interethnic violence leading to the deterioration of the norms of traditional *Adats* (mutual guarantees) into more mafia-style relations; the contamination of social/political institutions by *pervasive corruption, nepotism,* and *protectionism*; the lack of social mobility; increasing emigration of a Slavic/Russian-speaking population; and the *demodernization of emerging mono-ethnic societies*.

This section's analysis of the role of ethnic mafias is quite revealing in the context of the previously mentioned ethnic violence between Kazakhs and Dungans in the Dzhambul District of Kazakhstan. On the eve of these quite recent pogroms, the competition over control of "shady economics" between these ethnic groups reached its most dangerous level. According to Marat Shibutov, a member of the Almaty (formerly Alma-Ata) City Public Council, the border between the Dzhambul District and China supports a flourishing illegal contraband trade centered around smuggled Chinese goods that are monopolized by Dungan families, who in turn command the lion's share of trade within the flea markets of Almaty. These families live in highly enclosed enclaves, well within the tradition of "hard solutions to economic disputes" between ethnic owners of the most ingrained and lucrative illegal and semi-legal businesses in the area, and with "very low respect toward corrupt representatives of the law-enforcement agencies and local courts." Shibutov's opinion is quite valid as, during the pogroms, over fifteen Dungan shops, later found to be trading smuggled Chinese commodities, were specifically targeted and burned to the ground.[26]

Back in 1989, the Meskhetian Turks, their businesses, and their workplaces were being broadly replaced by those of the titular ethnic Uzbeks during the post-pogrom period throughout the Fergana Valley. This same process of replacement also befell Armenians from 1988 to 1989 after the previously mentioned pogroms in Sumgait and Baku resulted in numerous vacancies. Prior to the pogroms in Sumgait, the crowd became incensed and multiplied after hearing stories of Azerbaijani refugees from Kafan (Armenia),describing how the Armenians had expelled them from their homes and businesses.[27] The most recent events in the Dzhambul District and other similar cases illustrate that this process, which began in the late 1980s–early 1990s, is still very much underway throughout the post-Soviet space of the twenty-first century.[28]

Pick of Activity of Ethnic Mafias, Case of Chechnya

Overall, the peak of this activity was in the mid-1990s. According to the Russian Interior Ministry's Main Administration for Criminal Investigations, around 31,500 murders or attempted murders connected to the illegal distribution of properties and businesses occurred in 1995 (~32,300 cases in 1994), compared to approximately 15,600 recorded cases in 1990. This explosion of crime in the post-Soviet space "disgruntled many Russians with democracy, leaving many yearning for the security of communist rule."[29] In the words of General Alexandr Gurov, a leading specialist on Russian organized criminality and author of the book *Red Mafia*, "mobsters have killed 600 entrepreneurs and bombed or raided 700 company offices in the span of one year."[30]

The Ministry of Internal Affairs maintains that by the end of the 1990s, roughly 4,300 organized criminal groups were operating in Russia "with a total of 40,000 members (with 600 groups formed on an ethnic basis)," which account for the majority of serious crimes, including ethnically targeted criminal actions. Organized groups had about 150 large associations, with 170 individual groups having international ties and 275 possessing interregional ties. The average size of such a gang is fifteen people, while their associations usually number between 100 and 150 members. All ethnic associations belong to the same extended clans, tribes, or home regions. Famous Russian entrepreneur and president of both the Party of Economic Freedom and the Raw Materials and Commodities Exchange Konstantin Borovoi even once stated that "all major and small commercial structures pay tribute to the criminal world."[31]

I have already published many different works that provide evidence of direct mafia involvement in the Russian-Chechen ethnic conflict (1991–2009) and about the close ties that these organizations had to officials on both sides. Initially, Dzhokhar Dudayev, president of the separatist Chechen Republic of Ichkeria, and the semi-criminal elements within his entourage successfully ascended to power, in no short part due to the support of the criminal elements within the Moscow-based Russian *nomenklatura*. After 1991, a heavy degree of lawlessness spread throughout the republic, and "leaders of the Russian criminal underworld transferred business holdings to Chechnya and continued their business outside the republic or became involved in criminal business there."[32] The famous oligarch Boris Berezovskii, once deputy chairman of the Russian Security Council, collaborated with Chechen warlords who had made a lucrative business out of kidnapping people and holding them for ransom by acting as the middleman for transactions between the criminals and the victims. In the well-spoken words of ethno-historian Valery Tishkov, the Chechen breakaway story shows how "Moscow lost sight of the important distinction between seeking to impose legality and undermining it."[33]

A plethora of information also exists proving that Yeltsin's administration intentionally helped elements of these ethnic mafias come to power as a counterbalance against pro-Communist conservative forces in the wake of the USSR's dissolution. Aside from the well-known fact that the entire Soviet arsenal in Chechnya was given to Dudayev and his political party, I can provide additional and less obvious pieces of evidence. For instance, I refer to the testimony of Nickolai M., who at the beginning of the 1990s was in charge of the minute books and other documents relating to the monthly meetings of the Terek Cossack administration. According to him, they had detailed evidence regarding the amounts/routes of supply shipments and the locations of weapons and munitions stores purchased with stolen oil money and gold from the coffers of the Chechen and Ingushian mafias. He claimed to have shared this evidence with Russian law enforcement agencies (including the FSB, the successor to the KGB), who then made no attempts to intercept the arms from being smuggled into Chechnya. Their inaction was motivated by a share of the resulting profits in the form of payoffs and bribes provided by the ethnic mafias and their counterparts—radical international Islamist organizations like Al-Qaeda.[34] Russian officials and oligarchs assisted local mafia groups in transforming the Grozny Airport in Chechnya into "a transit site of smugglers, with thousands of flights carrying various types of contraband to the Middle East and other countries" and bringing weapons and Islamists back to the republics of the North Caucasus.[35] In this way, Victor Yassmann was correct in saying that "the desire to have greater Russian control over the businesses that developed from Chechnya's special status probably played at least as big a role as the publicly stated reasons in leading Yeltsin to invade [Chechnya] in December 1994."[36]

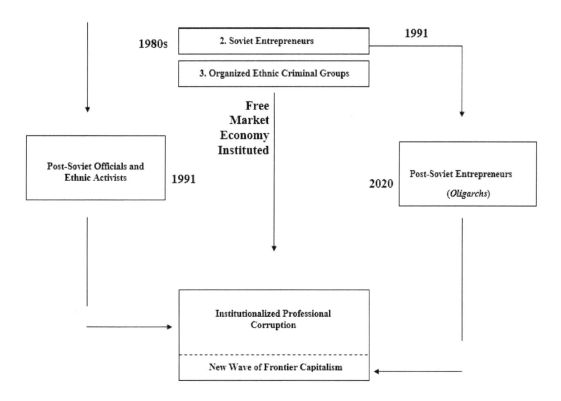

FIGURE 5.1   This diagram depicts the actual amalgamation of ethnic mafias and their internal links among the various subgroups that form their structural components in both the Soviet and post-Soviet periods.

The Role of Post-Soviet Ethno-Political Elites in the Supercharging of Ethnic Tensions

The process that transformed the elites of the Soviet regime into those of the independent states was rather heterogeneous. For example, in Armenia, Georgia, the Baltic republics, and Azerbaijan (partially), the transition was rather quick. The anti-Soviet elites within these various regions had already been very well-organized prior to the collapse of the Soviet Union. For the most part, they had already accomplished the latent transformation from the typical schema of Soviet Communist elites into so-called "national communists," establishing connections for the development of alternative economics and the absorption of anti-Soviet activists. Ronald Suny outlined certain conditions that allowed national communists in Georgia specifically to strengthen them (similar conditions could also be found in Armenia and the Baltic States long before their own independence):

> First, the reduction in political penalties with the relaxation of the Stalinist terror had made it easier for the people to express *long-latent national feelings* ...
>
> Second, the national elite in Georgia [as well as Armenia and the Baltics] used the opportunity offered by the Khrushchev years to consolidate local power and *with the backing of the local ethnic majority* legitimized its rule and gained support vis-à-vis Moscow ... *Ethnicity in turn became an important criterion for success*, as the Georgian leadership patronized members of its own nationality to the exclusion of others ... That nationalism was expressed in culture, in cadre favoritism, and in the economic "exploitation" of the Soviet system.
>
> Third, nationalist expression is a genuine indicator of the historic fear of small nations that they will be swallowed up by larger nations in the process of modernization ...
>
> Finally, the erosion of Marxist ideology within the Soviet Union cleared the way for its replacement by patriotic nationalism.[37]

In Armenia, Georgia, and Azerbaijan, the titular ethnic nations were the overwhelming majority, and this circumstance helped in the realization of the full potential of the abovementioned conditions. An influx of a Russian-speaking population into the Baltic republics and Ukraine after 1945 during the Soviet modernization process served as an additional factor in the long-term consolidation of national communists due to fears of gradual Soviet/Russian assimilation (see the third condition in previous citation).

In the Central Asian republics, however, this process has not moved as briskly, as the consolidation of post-Soviet ethno-political elites has been stretched over a number of years. This is especially true in Kazakhstan, where ethnic Russians have made up a significant percent of the population since its creation, and further complicated following the Virgin Land campaign of the 1950s–1960s. It is worth remembering that thousands of Russians migrated to Kazakhstan during the Imperial period and that by the Soviet period, over 40 percent of the population of the Kazakh SSR were ethnically Russian. The exodus of a large portion of this population after the fall of the USSR eased tensions between the remaining Russians and titular Kazakh ethnicity, as the latter no longer feared Russian preeminence in politics. The previously cited cases of violence against other minorities, alongside historical and religious factors, are well-discussed in the research of Anara Tabyshalieva, who confirms that this process is slowly nearing completion but is still very much underway.[38]

On the other hand, the Caucasus republics and Moldova saw a rather quick consolidation of power by post-Soviet nationalist elites ("counter elites"), which in turn became a catalyst for the regressive development of ethnic conflicts there. As ethnic minorities were treated harshly by the new powers, they simply had no other alternatives but to rebel and desperately attempt to defend the principle building blocks of their ethnicities, which were under threat of complete destruction.[39]

In Ukraine, its own multiethnic character and the previously mentioned historical complications in its evolution into an ethnic nation and, later on, into a Soviet quasi-nation-state predisposed the transition of elites from Soviet to independent as a long and arduous process. It was more or less inevitable that the new post-Soviet elite would be primarily composed of the two primary elements: first that of the "*ancien régime*" (to use Kuzio's term)—economic, political and cultural, and second- a slowly growing political oppositional "anti-elite."[40] Kuzio himself cites Dmytro Vydrin and Dmytro Tabachnyk, who believed that the formation of Ukraine's new elite would be undertaken in four stages:

- 1990–1991: *nomenklatura* (a "formal elite");
- 1992: politicians who explained what had happened (a "pre-elite");
- 1993–1994: politicians who performed the role of guides (a "corporate elite");
- ?: integral politicians (an "elite").[41]

The socioeconomic background for such a long-running and complicated transformation was deftly illuminated by Serhy Yekelchyk in the following travail:

> From its Soviet predecessor Ukraine inherited an economy dominated by heavy industry, much of it simply incapable of being reformed. Large, inefficient factories produced military hardware for the Soviet army and in turn depended on dirt-cheap fuel from elsewhere in the Soviet Union. Huge, obsolete mines were kept running, in part to keep alive the Stalinist myth of model Soviet proletarians, the Donbas miners. In the 1990s *the economic ties among the former Soviet republics loosened*, leaving much of the Ukrainian-made machinery idle. The reorientation towards the production of consumer goods proved slow and painful.[42]

Thus, a very different task fell upon the shoulders of the "formal elite," sometimes also called "pre-elite" and "corporate elite," which represented the "*ancien régime*" and the slowly appearing elements of "integral politicians"—champions of change based on radical nationalism. Roman Szporluk formulated it as "an undertaking to transform the peripheries of several nations ... into a sovereign entity able to communicate directly with the larger world."[43] As will be shown in the next chapters of this book, an old and new compound parts of ethno-political elite in Ukraine managed to only partially cope with this monumental task and, regarding the establishment of ethnic peace, have so far performed rather poorly.

The Three Groups of the Post-Soviet Ethno-Political Elites

First Group

The policy of the Communist leadership of the USSR had always pursued a proportional participation of Ukrainians in the national elite. In 1989, 76.4 percent of the political elite and 68.9 percent of the managerial elite in Ukraine were ethnic Ukrainians.[44] From the early 1990s to early 2000s, this subgroup included many party, state, and Komsomol functionaries referred to as *apparatchiks*, "atavistic heavy industrialists—known as *Red directors*—and downwardly mobile military officers," all collectively known as *nomenklatura*. Until the dawn of the new millennium, this subgroup of post-Soviet ethno-political elite in Ukraine typically constituted the overwhelming majority of the former Soviet states. By the end of the 1990s, only Estonia, Latvia, and Armenia had leaders who did not originate from the former Communist *nomenklatura*, and among them, only Armenia was headed by the now-typical anti-elite—a former Soviet dissident.[45]

Within the Soviet Union existed three principal "clans" of Communist Party *nomenklatura-apparatchiks* that could enter the Politburo and become general secretary, with all of them located within the Russian Federation (Moscow, Leningrad [now St. Petersburg], Kuban, the Urals) and in Ukraine. Moscow, Leningrad, and Kiev (Kyiv) constituted the three principal centers from which these privileged party clans were concentrated. All local party secretaries were members of or connected to one of these clans. After the death of Konstantin Chernenko, the post of general secretary of the Communist Party was set to be handed to the party boss of Leningrad, Grigory Romanov. However, Romanov lost this chance when he disgraced himself by holding extravagant Lucullus-esque feasts in the Hermitage—the former Winter Palace of the Romanov Dynasty of tsars. Following this, longtime Ukrainian Party boss and veritable "dinosaur" Volodymyr Shcherbytsky cast a challenge to fill the position. However, the three clans quarreled over the post, and the gerontocratic Politburo members elected Gorbachev to the post instead. For all intents and purposes, his ascension and subsequent political actions were an accident, as he was originally seen as a compromise that appeared out of nowhere, had little political weight on his own, and was thought to be easily manipulated. If it were not for this, then Shcherbitsky would have been given the chance, like Khrushchev and Brezhnev before him, to represent the Ukrainian Clan at the Olympus of power in the Kremlin. Had he done so, the fate of the Soviet Union would have been far different then it came to be.

At that time, and alongside its sheer political strength, Ukraine provided 40 percent of the grain supplies across the union. This is why the Kievan Clan had more opportunities to exert influence on the central power structure. When Gorbachev suddenly gained power and shifted the course of the union to fundamental party reform and a Western-style reorientation, alongside the appearance of the far more radical Yeltsin (also out of nowhere), a plan appeared within the sophisticated minds of the experienced Kievan *apparatchiks*: they would help overthrow Gorbachev and help Yeltsin come to power, and in turn they would have Ukraine at their disposal as an independent state. Specifically, they hoped to reduce or eliminate Moscow's share of (as they saw it) the immense resources within Ukraine. As we all know, this plan worked out quite well, as Yeltsin also wanted to secure more power rather than to preserve the crumbling Soviet Union. It is through this that Yeltsin and his own supporters, with the assistance of the Ukrainian Clan of *apparatchiks* (alongside the tangential support of Belarusian Party Boss Stanislav Shushkevich), initiated the dissolution of the USSR in order to gain control over vast amounts of territory. That is what my perspicacious interlocutor Andrii Sh.—a former resident of Zaporijje whose interview I cited in the introduction—meant when he said that Ukrainian national communists were so smart "to carve out such a vast territory and build its own state, unlike many other peoples of the former Soviet Union." Yet in the long run, these people began to understand that the only alternative to the disgraced aspects of socialism and Sovietism—"as an integral ideology for the Ukrainian state building could only be *Ukrainian nationalism*" (interview, August 6, 2019, Isaenko, File II, list 20).

However, it would take a long time for such a transformation to take hold, especially in terms of lacking elites capable of driving it forward. Based on the data concerning the origin of the approximately 1,300 names listed in Ukraine's *Who Is Who?* book from 1995, Kuzio calculated that only a miniscule percent of the Ukrainian intelligentsia—1.89 percent—and among writers 2.29 percent, belonged to an aristocratic lineage or could trace their family line to the Cossack *Starshina* ("elite").[46] This entails that the genuine Ukrainian elites "had been either assimilated or annihilated by Polish, Tsarist Russian, and Soviet rule. Ukraine therefore had to devote greater energy and scarce resources than Russia *to create a new ruling elite*."[47]

Therefore, the early days of the post-Soviet period saw a greater part of the abovementioned subgroup of post-Soviet ethno-political elites realize that "only *nationalism* could provide an alternative set of myths and symbols to succeed the now discredited Soviet and Marxist-Leninist legacy and hold together an atomized society. The absence of proletarian internationalism as a guiding ideology could only be filled by national values, cultural and linguistic demands, long repressed and neglected."[48] Hence, the principal characteristic of the ruling ethno-elites following the collapse of the USSR, in terms of their ideological transformation, might be described as the gradual transformation of "proletarian internationalists" into moderate nationalists, which for some would roll over into the modern embittered ethnocentric nationalists. Such can be seen in the communities historically devoted to the teachings of Islam, moving from Marx to Muhammad and even to Islamists; a similar transition exists in historically Christian-dominated territories, turning "dedicated" militant atheists into "exemplary" Christians. In the 1990s, I witnessed this process in the Caucasus, when former party bosses, many guilty of severely persecuting religious organizations and destroying their associated shrines, began receiving mass baptisms, standing with candles in the solemn liturgies of Easter Sunday, or bowing in the front-most rows for Friday prayers in the numerous reemerging mosques and along the Caucasus range. In Christian communities, many people began to refer to such elite converts as *podsvechniki* (Rus. "candlesticks" or "candleholders").

While these leadership groups have transformed, the governments have remained unstable. And as economic sureties began to disappear, the old nomenclature of elites transitioned into that of new feudal-type leaders. The entire Caucasus region (as well as Central Asia, etc.) had regressed into a society more commonly imagined in an earlier, more medieval time. Given the lack of democratic leadership, the regions of the Caucasus declined into various forms of what leading historian Mark Bliev described as the "dispositions and habits of tribal aristocracy."[49] Another well-informed and perceptive analyst in the region, and also the longtime head of the Republic of Dagestan, Ramazan G. Abdulatipov, wrote:

> The ethnic elites, as well as many intellectuals, proved themselves unable to elaborate and realize adequate socio-political, economic, ethno-cultural, and moral mechanisms of self-preservation ... because they closed themselves off in their own highly narrow political interests.[50]

In my book on ethnic conflicts in the Caucasus, I shared particular territories claimed by both Armenia and Azerbaijan on the grounds of their "historical legacy." Among them are the western part of the Echmiadzin District, the southern part of the Erevan (now Yerevan) District, the Surmalinsky District, the Sharur-Daralagez District, the Zangezur District, the mountainous part of the Kazakh District, the Nakhichevan District, and the more mountainous sections of the Shusha and Jevanshir districts that constitute parts of Nagorno-Karabakh.[51] In his recent monograph, Farid Shafiyev demonstrated how the Russian imperial resettlement policy and the subsequent creation of the pockets of "loyal" Christian populations (composed particularly of Armenians) seriously altered the demographic profile of these former colonial territories. Additionally, it explained how the uneven distribution of privileges between different ethnic communities in favor of Christians put "Muslim inhabitants in a disadvantageous situation" in these contested territories and urban centers like Baku and Tbilisi. Exposure to this situation acted as a catalyst for the regressive development of interethnic relations, which, during the revolutionary crisis of 1905–1906, resulted in a "bloodbath of interethnic clashes between Armenians and Azerbaijanis."[52] At that time, parties of radical nationalists, namely the Armenian *Dashnak Tsutiun* and the Azerbaijani *Musavat*, acted as the driving forces of these violent episodes. Almost amazingly, history repeated itself to an insane degree, with conflict stretching throughout the 1990s and 2000s.

Second Group

Shortly after 1991, a portion of a previous *nomenklatura* regrouped and absorbed new activists into their folds. From this amalgamation would emerge the beginnings of *the second group of the post-Soviet ethno-political elites*. For the first decade of the 2000s, the overall correlation between the old compound elements of the "*ancien régime*" and the new regime within these emerging subgroups varied greatly between various independent states. Regardless, many members of the old *nomenklatura* would use this synthesis to, rather smoothly, transition into post-Soviet officials, entrepreneurs, and even oligarchs (similar to the abovementioned transformation schemes of ethnic mafia groups). For example, specialists calculated that in Russia, 75 percent of the new political elite and 61 percent of the new economic elite originated from the former *nomenklatura*. Among the new Russians, former Komsomol functionaries, members of the economic *nomenklatura*—"Red Directors" and other former Soviet managers—would constitute around 38 percent in each group.[53] At the same time, in Ukraine "only 40 percent of its elites originated in the *nomenklatura*."[54] The central Russian government hosted up to 74.3 percent of the "*ancien régime*" and, at their highest, 83.3 percent of previous government and regional elites.[55] In the North Caucasus (except for Chechnya) and autonomous republics of Central Russia, members of the latter stratum of this second subgroup of post-Soviet elites still retained Soviet ways. If one were to use the abovementioned Vydrin-Tabachnyk classification, this second amalgamation represented a kind of transitional subgroup that moved between "formal" elites and "integral politicians." At the same time in Ukraine, this transformation process was still underway, having only reached the middling stages. In Russia, the previously powerful democratic elite suffered repeated defeats, allowing the second group to flourish under Putin's authoritarian rule.

Essentially, a majority of the second subgroup of ethno-political elites in all the independent polities of the former Soviet Union (with some minor exceptions) were, and still are, too poorly equipped to understand and implement real principles of democracy or democratic leadership and administration. They had no sense or skills pertaining to the art of compromise, accommodation, peaceful resolution of differences, the rule of law as an inclusive and systematic set of legal procedures, or basic human rights consisting of unilateral respect regardless of ethnic belonging. While they quickly learned democratic rhetoric, it was inadequately understood and, instead, skillfully used to attract the support of constituents during electoral cycles, garner outside support, or discredit rivals in the eyes of the local and international communities. Additionally, few of the newly emerging leaders from this subgroup have shown the ability to grasp economic realities. It was only in the recent past that republics like Adygea, Karachai-Circassia, Kabardino-Balkaria, North Ossetia–Alania, Dagestan, Bashkortostan, Tatarstan, and so on were headed by former party leaders and the *nomenklatura*.

Third Group

"New activists," or as some specialists previously addressed them, "*national democrats*" or "*anti-elites*," constitute *the third group* of post-Soviet elites. Regretfully, some of the previously mentioned characteristics can be attributed to this group as well. After 1991, the organizations composing this subgroup became either "parties of power" or very influential ethno-political movements that, to a large extent, defined and (where they still hold some leadership positions) define the sociopolitical agenda in their respective polities. Sometimes, powerful individuals from the younger generations (those within their thirties and forties) joined this subgroup as leaders of existing ethnic networks. These individuals started their careers in the post-Soviet era and, through personal resolve and skillful exploitation of their regions' economic and social chaos, made their way up the sociopolitical ladder. In the 1990s, Gadji Makhachev, former chairman of Dag Neft' in Dagestan, and Khozh-Akhmet Nukhaev, the former chairman of the Caucasus Common Market and previous deputy prime minister of Chechnya, were the most frequently cited examples of this upward momentum. Many of these men had criminal convictions on record, often for violent crimes, and sometimes even emerged from their respective ethnic mafia groups.[56] Currently in Ukraine, President Vladimir (Ukr. Volodymyr) Zelensky and his cohort of activists from the new *Sluga Naroda* ("Servants of the People") Party perfectly personify this subgroup of newer integral ethno-political elites in the post-Soviet independent states.

In the early 1990s, Paul Henze explored the situation and presented a key characteristic shared by these new ethnic activists who had finally managed to join this category and attain political power during the state formation process:

> One is struck in all these Caucasian societies [and one can add in other parts of the former Soviet Union] by the large number of specialists in linguistics, literature, folklore, archeology, and history who are now active in politics. After decades of suppressing their ethnic pride and national feelings, they have now moved into the forefront of political movements *asserting ethnic rebirth and national self-determination*. Many of them, alas, are ill-equipped to understand the principles of democracy or even of simple leadership and administration in any form.[57]

Additionally, Henze would state that "attitudes of responsibility, forms of local initiative, and forms of discipline and control inherent in most free-market societies (and even in many ... authoritarian systems) are largely absent" in regard to membership of this particular group.[58]

The careers of Zelensky and his closest associates originally stemmed from more show businesses in the entertainment industry. Early on, many Ukrainians became tired of the seemingly permanent all-sided societal crisis spurred on by the devastating interethnic conflict in Donbas, a confrontation with Russia, and the incompetence and pervasive corruption of many previous administrations. This pushed many people (more than 73 percent of the voting population) to vote this newer political force, brandishing promises of peace and prosperity in the near future, into power. After several months, however, the president, whose party also controls the parliament (*Rada*), was forced to reshuffle his own government due to ongoing incompetence. In a speech to the parliament on March 3, 2020, Zelensky admitted that his appointed head of the government, thirty-four-year-old Alexii Goncharuk (who has since been dismissed by the *Rada*), "managed to achieve certain success, including uprooting the corruption in its midst. But this is too little. Not to steal is not enough. New faces—it is not enough. We need new brains and new hearts. Economics have started up but have stumbled and risks smashing its face against the ground once again." He then presented severe criticism of the government itself, stating that it is their fault that industry continues to shrink, Ukrainians continue to suffer from high tariffs and communal payments, minuscule pensions have continued to be indexed, medical reform "bursts against the wall; miners have not seen their salaries, and law-enforcement structures do not fulfill their obligations properly."[59]

While reading this revelation, one may begin feeling a strong sense of *déjà vu*. In the 1990s–2000s, a number of analysts, on more than one occasion, stated that the economic situation in Ukraine had been dismal. This downturn was most clearly evident in the working class, particularly miners. In Eastern Ukraine, Russian-speaking workers and managers in the decaying state enterprises "had natural interests in strong economic ties with the Russian firms." The economic interests of the Russian-speaking population, influenced by both close cultural/kinship ties to Russia and the ever-present conditions of a crisis, were easily swayed by ethno-political demands to promoting Russian as a second state language and possessing "little interest in state building at the expense of economic well-being."[60]

In fact, this serves as a bright illustration of how these same continuing economic hardships and the failure of incompetent/inconsistent reforms to improve the situation led to the development of highly negative views of the political system and the gradual worsening of interethnic relations between the titular ethnic nation and, predominantly in the case of Russians, other ethnic groups. This is especially true when the ethno-political elite, rather than concentrating efforts in elaborating a comprehensive sociopolitical, cultural, and economic transitional policy that accounts for regional ethnic peculiarities, continue to vehemently pursue the project of building a unitarian state based on their own specific *ethnic criteria*. Lowell Barrington demonstrated that "support of the government and support for the regime scales indicate strong discontent in Ukraine in the latter years of the 1990s."[61] Throughout the 2000s and 2010s, administrations were changing rapidly, especially with the explosive revolutions of 2004 and 2014. However, economic hardships have persisted and even worsened, with the prospect of viable reforms having not improved due to the continuing onslaught against the cultural rights of ethnic minorities (including a large Russian-speaking population) raging in the background. This has ultimately resulted in a recursive political crisis becoming a part of the all-sided societal crisis while the Ukrainian economy has been sliding deeper into the morass, which has been recently confirmed by President Zelenksy, in the previously cited address to the Ukrainian parliament.

Overall, the most authentic characteristic of the modern Ukrainian/post-Soviet elite (as an amalgamation of the three primary groups) is presented by Yekelchyk:

> What emerged in Ukraine in the 2000s was *crony capitalism at its worst*. The new rich usually owed their instant wealth to their government connections, if not their political appointments, but some of them also came from gangster backgrounds. Organized crime merged with big business and the political class to create an impenetrable ruling elite concerned only with its own enrichment. Its ostentatious display of wealth brought to Kyiv and other big cities brand-name boutiques and luxury cars, but social tensions were simmering in residential neighborhoods. The gap between the rich and the poor grew rapidly, exacerbating popular resentment against rampant corruption and political manipulation.[62]

One may also extrapolate this remarkable and honest characteristic onto both the majority of ethno-political elites and the leadership of many other post-Soviet states. From 1991 onward, violent solutions became the norm for Russia and other post-Soviet countries. No matter the official rhetoric, the Russian and non-Russian publics alike understood that their political elites and leaders would take the most ruthless measures to attain their personal goals. This was, and still is, a devastating blow to the emerging civil societies and to interethnic relations in the post-Soviet space. This resulted in the fragmentation of the Russian populations, who, lacking their own organizations, responded with ever-growing political apathy and exodus. It also saw the oligarchs, tycoons, godfathers, bureaucrats, and regional ethnic elites take advantage of the situation, specifically the unrestricted and unprecedented expropriation of the so-called common property that had been opened for them. This culminated in a final development as the oligarchic regimes rose in strength and *ethnocentric nationalism* swelled within the polities.

Slowly, many people began to realize that a return to real economic progress and true modernization would be arduous and time-consuming. The long-term stress evoked by economic and political uncertainty threatened to revive unresolved conflicts that had lingered just below the surface. Few realized that these longstanding Imperial and Soviet legacies were much stronger than they could have ever imagined or that within Russia, and many other former Soviet republics, a new, unprecedented variety of authoritarian rule was beginning to emerge. Volodymyr Polokhalo, an observing analyst, went so far as to call it "*post-communist or pseudo-democratic neo-totalitarianism*" and argued that

> this form of government can be characterized as a political system in which overall control over individuals and society is exercised by a combination of familiar and new techniques. Control is not exercised through ideology, as in the past, but through other means. These means may include elections, for example, but these are merely used as a way to exert total control over citizens and tend to undermine this process itself, the social fabric, and consensus in general.

Polokhalo further argued that in post-Soviet societies a "multidimensional dependency had begun to assume both obvious and latent economic (social, cultural, legal, traditional, religious, etc.) and extra-economic forms. Such forms determine the numerous power relationships associated with coercion, violence, and the constant threat of the use of either."[63]

So by the force of the stated objective circumstances, an obvious lack of the experience and capacity required to elaborate concrete plans on building viable modern economics and civic democratic nations, and the poor qualifications of existing ethno-political elites (which was previously detailed through President Zelensky), these leaders were able to propose the construction of mono-centric states to their ethnic compatriots, just like their historical predecessors had previously done following the collapse of the Russian Empire in 1917. Similarly, this process was, and continues to be, fraught with serious ethnic collisions.

Violent Ethnic Conflicts in the Post-Soviet Space

Since the collapse of the Soviet Union, there have been a total of *seven violent ethnic conflicts* within its former borders, and *eight significant potential conflicts that have not regressed into the violent stages*. Instead, some of them have produced sporadic episodes of interethnic clashes, like those in Uzbekistan and Kazakhstan that were previously discussed.[64] In this part of the chapter, I will deal with, in the most general terms, the radical ethno-political organizations whose policies led to a regressive development of ethnic conflicts in their corresponding polities, plunging them into the aforementioned same violent stages. This group of conflicts includes the following:

1) Armenian-Azerbaijani ethnic conflict in and around Nagorno-Karabakh
2) "Russo"-Moldavian conflict in Transdnistria/Transnistria (Romanian)
3) Georgian–South Ossetian ethnic conflict
4) Georgian-Abkhazian ethnic conflict
5) North Ossetian–Ingushian ethnic conflict
6) Russian-Chechen ethnic conflict
7) "Russo"-Ukrainian ethnic conflict

For numbers two and seven on this list, I apply the term "Russo" to one side of the conflict in order to differentiate it from "Russian," as seen in number six. This is because these sides of both former cases include not only ethnic Russians but also significant numbers of Russian-speaking ethnic Moldavians and Ukrainians, respectively. Similarly, the "Russo"-Ukrainian ethnic conflict sees an equally significant number of ethnically Russian combatants fighting on behalf of the Ukrainian side. In Donbas, for example, there are Russians fighting not only in the Ukrainian Army proper but also in several of the radical nationalistic paramilitary formations. In the next chapter, we will deal with what one might call a *phenomenon of ethnic defections*.

Ethnic Paradigms of the Conflicts

As previously said, it was an all-sided societal crisis, aggravated by the collapse of the Soviet Union and socialist system that accumulated the destructive energy and outrage of the common people. This incited danger not only for ethnic neighbors but also for the positions of local ethnic elites, who responded almost immediately in five distinct ways:

Some leaders and organizations (1) shifted the blame of economic and political collapse onto the rule of Moscow, as in the case of Chechnya. Ethnocentric Chechen elites skillfully propelled the anti-Russian drive by reopening several specifically chosen events, including unresolved historical traumas, unfinished territorial claims, competition over resources, and fears of cultural vulnerability.[65]

The Ingushian and Abkhazian ethnic elites (2) offered resolution through the restoration of "historical justice" through "territorial rehabilitation." This comprised the return of the Prigorodnyi District of North Ossetia and part of its capital, Vladikavkaz, to the Ingushians, whence they had been deported by Stalin in 1944, and the Abkhazians regaining their status as a union republic, which had been reduced by Stalin to the status of an ASSR in the 1930s, and gradually becoming independent, similar to Georgia.

In Armenia, Azerbaijan, and Georgia, ethnic organizations and leaders (3) developed a rhetoric that created an enemy or "other" mentality with another ethnic group; in North and South Ossetia, the elites used these same feelings of national insecurity and fear to perpetuate an atmosphere akin to a "besieged fortress" surrounded on all sides by ethnic enemies.[66]

Moldavian ideologues and ethno-national movement leaders formed a mono-ethnic government and, in 1990, (4) declared a return to the Transnistria doctrine (1941–1944) of former Romanian dictator

Ion Antonescu. This provoked the rise of a secessionist movement among the resident ethnic Russians and Russian-speaking Moldavians, who did not want to become Romanians. This movement based itself around the right bank of the Dniester River, with its center being the city of Tiraspol', and triggered a bloody ethnic conflict throughout Moldova.[67]

Finally, the ruling ethno-political elite in Ukraine set a long-term plan by (5) adopting a modernized variant of "Ukrainization" based on the renewal of the Ukrainian nation-building project, started, as we remember, by a part of the Galician intelligentsia at the turn of the 20th century. However, one should recall that the 2004 Orange Revolution had initiated a rather peaceful transition into democracy, because it provided credible guarantees for the already-weakening party, which at that point was Viktor Yanukovych's political constituency backed by the majority of ethnic Russians in Eastern Ukraine. In contrast, during the 2014 *Revolutsia Hidnisti*, the leadership behind the *Euromaidan* movement assumed a vividly confrontational policy against ethnic Russians by repelling a law securing Russian as a second state language and demonstratively incorporating radical ethnocentric nationalists from the *Svoboda* organization into the cabinet of ministers. These actions radicalized an ethno-separatist drive in the southeastern oblasts and "without credible guarantees to prevent their future marginalization, it became rational for (some of) them to mobilize for secessionist violence in April 2014." Additionally, the transitional government, composed of Ukrainian nationalists in Kyiv, failed to consolidate its grip on power throughout the Donbas territory. Prior to these events, ethnicity played a rather muted role in social relations and policy. Soon, however, the ethnic policies of the interim government triggered a rapid absorption of ethnicity in these separate spheres, and Russia (as an outside exacerbating factor), could use them for its own gain by showing direct support for its co-ethnics. As Julia Strasheim and other analysts argue, the latter did this by "opening new strategies to portray military intervention as humanitarian aid."[68] This is in the same vein as its interference in the Crimean Peninsula, where Russia ostensibly shifted as a response to the promotion of radical Ukrainian nationalists from the *Svoboda* into the workings of the interim government.[69]

However, in my opinion, it was not the beginning of the conflict but rather the end of its preliminary stage. In the subsequent chapter and aspect of the theoretical model, I will demonstrate that the process of gradual ethnicization of a conflict had been building up since the early 1990s. Its evolution reflects the corresponding transformative process of the political elites in both Russia and Ukraine, as well as the formation of *a completely different* ethno-psychological paradigm of their nation-state-building process. It should therefore come as no surprise that the building of party systems along ethnic lines had begun before their conflict in 2014. I agree with those who argue that ethnic heterogeneity does not increase the risk of a sharp uptick in violence per se, but "ethnic *dominance and exclusion*" certainly increases the risk of opening the door for ethnic confrontation.[70]

The Georgian Example: Organizations, Leaders, and Intellectuals Responsible for the Regressive Development of Ethnic Conflicts

The nation of Georgia provides an excellent example of what may happen when the "new activists" and their organizations ascend to power. In my book on ethnic conflicts in the Caucasus, I collected several pieces of evidence regarding the ethno-political organizations on both sides of the Georgian–South Ossetian and Georgian-Abkhazian conflicts. Pertaining to their principal programmatic ideas and methods of realization, I decided to classify them as "moderate," "radical," and "extremist," respectively.

Groups I considered to be "moderate" included *The People's Front*, *The Society of Ilya Chavchavadze*, *The Society of Saint Ilya the Pious*, and *The Society of Rustaveli*. Notable among the ranks of "radicals" was *The Roundtable Block for Independent Georgia*, which successfully rose in power in 1988–1989 under the leadership of former Soviet dissident, scholar, and writer Zviad Gamsakhurdia. By riding this wave of general enthusiasm, Gamsakhurdia would eventually become the first democratically elected president of Georgia on April 14, 1993. "Extremist" organizations and armed paramilitary formations were primarily represented by Jaba Ioseliani's *Mkhedrioni (Riders)*, *White Legion*, and *The Forest Brothers*. In particular, South Ossetians were headed by *The People's Front of South Ossetia* (a.k.a. *The South Ossetian Popular Front)—Adamon Nykhas* (lit. "People's Assembly") and included both radical and moderate national activists.

In Abkhazia, Georgian nationalists (the prewar Georgian population was originally the majority) created their own *Progressive-Democratic Union of Abkhazeti* (1992). They directly confronted Abkhazian nationalist-separatists from the organization *Aidgylara* (*Unity*), who were led by writer Alexei Gogua and Professor Vladislav Ardzinba. The Abkhazians were heavily supported by North Caucasian ethnic groups united under the banner of the *Confederation of Mountain Peoples* and the *International Circassian Association*, which represented a foreign Diaspora of Circassian people, who are ethnic relatives of the Abkhazians. The *Confederation* also included Chechens and other non-Circassian groups who supported Abkhazian efforts for their own purposes, such as Chechens wishing to be trained by former Russian military specialists in order to use those skills in their own fight against Russia. Surprisingly, some Ossetians even joined the *Confederation*, fighting for the Abkhazian cause due to their own previous confrontations with Georgia. Finally, the *Confederation* also hosted representatives of Russian Cossacks, who joined in response to the vivid anti-Russian and pro-West rhetoric of Georgian nationalists.

In June–July 1989, I conducted and recorded a large collection of interviews in all the ethnic communities within the Caucasus, which gave me a chance to observe how the hard will of ethnic confrontations began to quickly unravel along issues of nationality, predominantly among younger nationalists.[71] But even during this crucial period of rapid ethnic delineation, a less aggressive lifestyle was still available to middle-aged South Ossetians, Abkhazians, Georgians, and everybody else, because they had grown up in the relatively quiet Soviet period of the 1950s–1980s. To their credit, some moderate leaders within the Georgian National Democratic Party intended to soothe the rising tensions between ethnic Georgians, Ossetians, and Abkhazians that had been generated by radical ethnic organizations. In the pages of *Zarya Vostoka* (lit. "The Dawn of the East"), the primary Georgian media resource, liberal activists and moderate intellectuals published a joint *Appeal of the "Georgian Society Named for Ilya Chavchavadze" and The Peoples Front of South Ossetia, Adamon Nykhas to the Georgian and Ossetian People*:

> Interethnic relations in our republic have just entered a dangerous phase of tension. Radical forces are interested in further supercharging tension between our people. They spread false and provocative rumors about the creation of armed paramilitary formations and attacks on populated areas [unfortunately, these facts *did* take place]. *Judging from the present level of anxiety and perturbation among common residents, we may conclude that our society stands on the verge of psychosis.* It can be averted only by our joint, reasonable actions. Therefore, we call our people not to yield to the provocations: we beg our people *not to estrange based on fear of each other and to not think about what is dividing us but*

to concentrate on what is uniting us. We are very proud of our wise ancestors, who knew how to find ways into each other's hearts. And we will not allow bad people to infringe upon this, our common achievement. We are aware that only enemies of both of our people are interested in worsening the relations between us.[72]

Unfortunately, ethnocentric nationalists from Gamsakhurdia's *Roundtable Block*, whom even the highly objective Georgian analyst Ghia Nodia called "fascists" (see note 72), drowned out the calls of moderates and began to dominate Georgian society. Almost simultaneously, in the Prigorodnyi (Suburban) District of North Ossetia, the tension was growing between Ingushians and Ossetians. That is why most of the radical Ossetian representatives in both the North and South revitalized and spread an ethnocentric phobia of living in a "besieged fortress" surrounded by enemies who "are about to attack." For many, a suitable container, "safe keeper," or safe place had become the dream of a united Ossetia—this is the dream on which to project the split-off (good) part of the self or society—as Georgians and Ingushians were perceived as "plotting traitors."[73] Ethnocentric representatives of Ossetian intellectuals began to argue in favor of restoring the famous old name of Alans in order to give it over to the dreamt reunion or at least to the existing "inseparable" part of it; to them, the name "Ossetia" has negative connotations "because of its Georgian origin."[74] Until now, they believe that whatever has been fixed by this name might one day be the reality. After all, both Alania and Ossetia (prior to its division in the 1920s) had existed as united and powerful states in their own right. It is for this same reason that they call the South Ossetian capital "Tskhinval," rather than the Georgian name "Tskhinvali." A similar mindset is why separatist Abkhazians call their capital Suhkum instead of the current Georgian designation of "Sukhumi." In Ukraine, all of the previously Russian names of major cities were replaced with those of a local, in this case Ukrainian, style. This same process also took place in almost all of the former Soviet republics. The significance of this in relation to the latest developments in the Russo-Ukrainian ethnic conflict will be demonstrated later in this research, with the added implications regarding the repetition of similar regularities of ethnocentric mobilization in the Caucasus as described in the third edition of my book *Polygon of Satan*.

Both in the Caucasus and currently in Ukraine, amid the continuing all-sided societal crisis, nationalists exploit ethnocentric myths, thus exacerbating their chosen traumas from history and reinforcing the troubled consciousness of their already anxious people with the idea of "historic enmities." In particular, Georgia has cultivated the concept of the Georgians themselves as a "host people," with the other ethnic groups within their territory being "guest peoples." However, I insist that, in such conflicts, the supercharging of ethnic tensions lies on both sides of ethnocentric nationalists and their charismatic leaders. Nodia is probably correct when he speculates that "one can only guess at how the independent Georgian state would have treated the Abkhazian and Ossetian minorities if their leaders had not opposed Georgian independence and sought protection in Moscow from the beginning."[75]

Moscow's ambiguous and vacillating policy only added fuel to the fire. Lavished with promises of support for the Ossetians and Abkhazians, the Kremlin never took practical steps toward this end; such proposals, like the creation of commissions on ethnic groups and minorities, were never adopted before the collapse of the USSR.[76] Nevertheless, the Ossetian and Abkhazian ethnic leadership continued to cherish the illusion that Moscow, in the most decisive moment, would interfere on their behalf. I vividly recall how in 1988–1989, Anatoly Chekhoev, deputy of the Soviet parliament and one of the leaders of *Adamon Nykhas*, plied between Moscow, Vladikavkaz, and Tskhinvali/Tskhinval in a disturbing atmosphere. Thousands of Ossetian refugees who had been forced out of Georgia began to participate in mass rallies and to support *Adamon Nykhas*. Slowly, they began influencing the crowd with their stories describing their treatment at the hands of the Georgians and belief in the empty promises that the Soviet parliament "would never leave the Ossetians and Abkhazians alone against the Georgian nationalists." Even if such aid never came about, the role of Russia in aggravating these conflicts was rather provocative and should be characterized as an *outside enticing* or *exacerbating factor*. In fact, they played this very same role in all of the above-cited ethnic conflicts, especially the one between Russia and Ukraine. I will demonstrate this more appropriately in the corresponding parts of the research findings.

Gamsakhurdia and his *Round Table Block* animated the xenophobic "theory" of philologist Pavle Ingorokva. In the 1950s–1960s, this theory served as the primary ideological foundation of the assimilation policies belonging to the Georgian national communists. As a result, and with the help of mass media under Gamsakhurdia's control, this idea was crystallized in a number of stereotypes within the Georgian national consciousness:

> The first and most important of these was the belief that the Georgian nation had a "historic past" that predetermined that it would flourish as an independent, united nation in the future. The clearest manifestation of this stereotype was the idea of the "historical right of Georgians to Georgian lands" and the related concept of "guests" who should know their place, as opposed to "hosts."[77]

Nodia wrote about how Gamsakhurdia believed that "ethnic sentiment was a level suitable for helping him to achieve popularity" and did not hesitate to pronounce vehement threats against minorities who "would not behave in a proper manner." Nodia also noted that Gamsakhurdia's rhetoric strikingly recalled postulations similar to Stalin's own classical clichés from the 1930s. He used these to label ethnic minorities and his political opponents as "enemies of the nation" (Stalin: "enemies of the people") or "agents of the Kremlin" (Stalin: "agents of imperialism"). Interestingly enough, Ukrainian nationalists and mass media also adopted a similar rhetoric regarding rebels in Donbas, ultimately accusing them of being champions of the Kremlin's policy within Ukrainian territory. Both examples are very symptomatic and serve as a bright confirmation of my thesis regarding the strong legacy of Sovietism in the minds of modern sculptors of independent nation-states, and that their version of nationalism, as a principal ideology of state-building, is merely the same intolerant Stalinist "Sovietism" turned inside out.

This approach was one of the few ways to mobilize ethnic feelings to such an extent that it allowed ethnocentric nationalists to lead people in whatever directions they desired. Barry R. Posen showed, for example, that newly independent ethnic groups often turn to "history" in order to assess the danger of potential opponents, asking, "How did the other group behave the last time it was unconstrained?" and "Is there a record of offensive military activity by the other?"[78] Georgian ethnocentric nationalists, in an attempt to provide pivotal answers to the questions of their compatriots, eventually mobilized well-known members of the Georgian intelligentsia, including notable professors like Bakradze, Chkvanava, Kharadze, Loumouri, and Sturua. Their tracts regularly appeared in the more popular editions of Gamsakhurdia's *Roundtable Block: Literaturi Sakartvelo* (Tbilisi) and *Zarya Vostoka*.

On September 30, 1988, Professor Kvanchilashvili published a piece in *Literaturi Sakartvelo* entitled "What Would Happen Afterward?"[79] In this article, the professor severely criticized both the theoretical and practical aspects behind Communist internationalism, reasoning that it had damaged the Georgian nation by forcing it to accept large groups of "national minorities." Additionally, he condemned "a broad settling of Ossetians in Shida Kartli [South Ossetia], and in Georgia proper" as absolutely inadmissible, arguing that the practice preceded the "degeneration of the Georgian nation." To rectify this, he insisted on "the necessity of artificially limiting childbearing among ethnic minorities in Georgia." Other prominent historians accused the Ossetians of helping the Bolsheviks successfully, and violently, end the previous independent Georgian state in March 1921, thus confirming and fully permitting the absolute worst of individual assessments and fears that surrounded this "fifth column of Russian Imperialists."[80] I remember how, at the culmination of this campaign, Gamsakhurdia called on his loyal subjects "to sweep all rubbish out of Mother Georgia." As previously stated, his slogan "Georgia for Georgians" was an eerie echo of the ethnic exclusionary verbiage spouted by the Third Reich. As a result of such an intensive and extensive deployment of ethnic domination rhetoric and other propaganda, common people came to fully adopt the hostile ethnocentric ideas of their political and intellectual authorities and were ready to engage in more directly destructive behavior. This is fully confirmed thanks to a litany of interviews of the common residents of Georgia, Ossetia, and Abkhazia. Here are a few of the very symptomatic samples:

Izolda M., Georgian (age forty-six) housewife, said in Sukhumi (Abkhazia):

> We gave the Ossetians and Abkhazians everything. We fed them well and gave them culture and religion. They started to multiply like chickens. Now they have grown so proud that they want to fly away with our property. You know that in the autumn, a good host counts his chickens and separates the good from bad, and he puts the bad ones under his knife. Those who are grateful and love the Georgian nation should forget Russian and learn the Georgian language. To prove their loyalty, they must stop their connections to Russia at once and help us build our state. Then they will be citizens like us, and they don't need any "autonomies." To those who would not do so, *we'll show the way to the places whence they came from a couple of hundred years ago.*(20 out of 23) (Interview, July 30, 1989, Isaenko, file 1 list 60)

This next example prominently expresses the most highly distributed ideas and emotions of that time:

Boris Sh., Abkhazian (age twenty), said in Sukhumi (Abkhazia):

> The Georgian chief fired my father from the locomotive depot because he listened to our writer, Alexei Gogua, at the meeting of the People's Forum *"Aidgylara"* [on December 13, 1988]. The Georgian bosses are firing all the Abkhazian patriots. I am a student. They segregate us at the university and are building their own separate university. Their mobsters have beaten my friend only because he wanted to take a picture of their meeting. But it's okay. Let them now abuse us as much as possible. It will help us awaken our people and mobilize them for one last battle. Even the girls will fight. We will not be alone. Our brothers from the North Caucasus will help us. *They will pay dearly for all the humiliations that our people*

suffered for decades at their bloody hands. We will restore our Abkhazian Republic and get rid of them once and for all. (17 out of 18) (Interview, July 30,1989, Isaenko, file 1, list 57)

Organizations, Leaders, and Intellectuals Responsible for the Regressive Development of Other Violent Ethnic Conflicts in the Post-Soviet Space

In the early years of the 1990s, within the rest of the Caucasus and Moldova, the atmosphere surrounding interethnic relations had also reached the boiling point, which one may fittingly characterize as *ethnocentric hysteria*. In *Polygon of Satan*, I collected a large amount of evidence regarding ethnocentric nationalist organizations and their methods, both of which helped to set the stage for ethnic confrontation and hatred. This would then, gradually, slide into the kind of uncontrollable bloodbaths, purges, and pogroms that have become a staple of this model. The readers may find all the necessary details regarding the evolution of each violent ethnic conflict within their dedicated chapters.[81]

On the Armenian side of the Armenian-Azerbaijani ethnic conflict, the most provocative organizations include: a reborn *Dashnak-Tsutiun* (*Dashnaks*), *Karabakh Committee*, *Krunk* (*The Crane*), the *Armenian Pan-National Movement* (APNM), the *Armenian National Army* (ANA), and the violent guerilla formations of *Fedayins*. On the Azerbaijani side of things was a modern reincarnation of the *Musavat Party*, and other organizations such as *Varlyg* (*Reality*) and the *Azerbaijani Popular Front*. Additionally, the Mujahedeen distinguished themselves as the primary player within the realm of the more violent organizations.

In terms of ideological foundations, Zorii Balayan and noted academic Zia Buniatov, for the Armenians and Azerbaijani respectively, were famous for producing the previously mentioned mythologies and paradigms for both peoples. As for leadership, Genrikh Pogosian, Levon Ter-Petrosian, and Serj Sargsian were the leaders of the abovementioned Armenian organizations, while Neimat Panakhov, Etibar Mamedov, and Abul'faz Elchibey did the same for their Azerbaijani counterparts.

In the North Ossetian–Ingushian ethnic conflict, the Ossetian part of the titular role was played by the previously mentioned *Adamon Nykhas*, which had the leading intellectuals of the republic at its head. There was also the *National Guard of Ossetia-Alania*, an armed formation headed by the charismatic Bibo Dzutsev and sided with their Ossetian compatriots the *Vladikavkaz Circle of Terek Cossacks* (later on, the *Otdel*). The first president of The Republic of North Ossetia–Alania, professor of philology Akhsarbeck Khadzhimurzaevich Galazov, provided a strong level of leadership in this tumultuous time.

On the Ingushian side, the collective role of leadership was fulfilled by the *Congress of the Ingushian People*, the *National Guard of Ingushetia*, an armed paramilitary organization, and *Niiskho* (*Justice*), an ethno-political organization with the charismatic Magomet Kostoev as its leader.

In Moldova, ethnic organizations greatly contributed to the conflict and included the *Democratic Movement in Support of Perestroika*, the *Musical-Literature Club*, and the very radical *People's Front of Moldova*, which concentrated the political power that they possessed and took up the direction of building nationalist ethnic criteria. Romanian-Moldavian nationalist forces confronted the self-proclaimed Pridnestrovian Moldavian Republic, otherwise known as Transdnistria (September 1990), headed by Igor N. Smirnov and a separatist movement of the Gagauz ethnic group based around their capital, Komrat.[82]

In the Russian-Chechen ethnic conflict, the radical Chechen ethnocentric paradigm had been built through the efforts of the *National Congress of Chechen People* (OKChN), the *Executive Committee of*

Congress, Vainakh Democrats, the *National Guard* (1991), and *Bakó* (*Right*), as well as the later *People's Army* (1993), headed by the, again, charismatic Dzhokhar Dudayev, a former general-major of the Soviet Army Air Force. Violent extremist organizations included the *"Warriors of Righteous Caliphs" Battalion* (1994), *"Abd al-Kader" Battalion* (1994), *"Party of Islamic Liberation" Brigade* (1994), *"Islamic Jamaat" Brigade* (1994), *Riyadh as-Saaliheen* (*The Meadows of Righteousness*) (2002, 2009), the *Caucasian Front* (2002), and *Imarat Kavkaz* of Dokku Umarov (2008). All of these organizations were jointly responsible for the gradual transformation of a typical radical ethnic movement into part of a regional and global jihad not only against Russia but to ensure the construction of a worldwide Islamist power—the Caliphate. These formations were coordinated and led by Aslan Maskhadov, former colonel in the Soviet Army; an Arabic representative of Al-Qaeda al-Sulbakh Amir Khattab; and the commander Shamil Basaev.

On the Russian side, Boris Yeltsin was soon replaced by Vladimir Putin, who has remained in power since then.

The people listened to charismatic leaders and believed in their "magical" solutions. Nationalistic intellectuals preyed on the genuine antipathies and fears of ordinary citizens, exacerbating their chosen traumas and encouraging and redirecting ethnic hatred with the aid of absurd "historic" myths and conceptions. Ethno-political elites not only provided a respectful populace with an explanation for the crisis ("the others" having lined their pockets at our expense) but also created an image of the ethnic enemies as suitable targets for the externalization of accumulated feelings of frustration caused by the all-sided societal crisis.

Beginning of the Process of Ethnicization of Politics, an Impact of Post-Soviet Ethno-Political Elites' Policies on Building Blocks of Ethnicity at the Initial Stages of Ethnic Confrontation

At this point, I want to share some of the more important results of the analysis of the various interviews that I have taken from common people living in the above-listed affected areas, immigrants from Ukraine, and also from the Moldavian and Baltic students and visitors whom I met at the Appalachian State University between 2001 and 2019. In order to explain these conclusions, I have correlated my findings with numerous publications spread across the totality of local mass media, research publications from these same areas, and interviews published in other sources by some of my colleagues.

All of these stories and materials remarkably show the situation within the *five principal building blocks of ethnicity*, which are paired by the state politics and economic measures that affect them. These policies reflect both the mild and middle-ground forms of ethnic discrimination.

(I) *Regarding the biological building block of ethnicity*, I ascertained the most frequently met forms: (1) increasing use of ethnic styles to assert one's ethnic background. (2) Use of specific ethnic clothing as a way of affirming one's ethnic affiliation. (3) Viewing the dominant groups' male and female bodies as the expression of aesthetic fulfillment. (4) The search for an "ethnically pure" style of housing, etiquette practices of public ceremonies, calendars, receptions, and so on. (5) Policy of intentional change in demographic composition of the territories of ethnic minorities in favor of the representatives of titular ethnic nations by their mass resettling in such territories. All of this, obviously, is strongly based to favor one's titular nation, which I refer to as a manifestation of ethnic narcissism.

(II) *Regarding language as the most important formative building block of ethnicity*, I mark off the following forms of ethnic discrimination: (1) The denial of access to government positions due to language. (2) Promotion of the dominant ethnic group's language in a state or a subdivision of that state's infrastructure and, usually, in education. (3) Denial of access to prominent social positions because of language. (4) The adoption of constitutional norms more or less forbidding those who do not speak the dominant language to hold elected or appointed offices. (5) Educational facilities sometimes do not provide opportunities for minorities to learn the titular national language, in order to ensure the other conditions.

(III) *Regarding the religious building block*, I have noticed the following: (1) The tendency of some ethnic groups to prefer a particular form of religious expression. (2) Some efforts by some religious groups to assert the preeminence of their particular religious affiliation. (3) Some hostility of some religious groups in titular nations against the other, non-dominating religious groups and even separate denominations of their own religion.

(IV) *Regarding the building block of commonly shared history*, the following forms encouraged by ethnocentric nationalists are the most provocative: (1) The creation of, in the earlier stages, an established image of a historical "ethnic enemy." (2) The creation of an official nationalistic history/mythology that looks to defend a glorious past, ethnic territories, ethnic exclusiveness, and superiority. (3) Creation of a version of a society's history that does not include the experience of all ethnic groups. (4) The supporting and promotion of the cultural inheritance of the dominant ethnic group. (5) The spread of so-called "domestic nationalism" being directly aimed at "ordinary persons" of their respective titular nations. (6) The invention and prolific spread of humiliating jokes and anecdotes against the non-dominant ethnic groups.

(V) At the same time, *state organizations of the dominant/titular ethnic nations increasingly practice such forms of collusion*: (1) Preference is given to a person with the proper ethnic credentials—representatives of the leading ethnic group will be more desirable for positions in government, business, law enforcement and judicial agencies, various elected offices, and so on. (2) The replacement of local and regional territorial officials by ethnically "reliable" leaders of the titular ethnic group. (3) The limited practice of individual and small-group humiliation, harassment, assault, battery, robbery, and kidnapping. (4) The seating of certain ethnically afflicted students in specific areas within educational institutions. (5) The implementation of state laws that require schools to be separate but equal.

(VI) The more *economic measures* include the following: (1) The spread of corruption (alongside the imitation of state agencies "fighting" against it) through nepotism, protectionism, and the hoarding of positions and honors by a dominant group. (2) Preference in the distribution of grants, awards, promotions, recognitions, the allotment of funding, and so on. (3) Preferential treatment for hiring ethnic majorities who have proved their loyalty to the ethnic group at large. (4) The rejuvenation of clan and kinship ("*kumovstvo*") ties and partnerships. (5) Firing of all non-majority ethnics from their positions in order to be replaced.[83]

When a societal crisis begins to penetrate deeper into a society, these practices of dominating/titular ethnic groups are ushered into law and then enforced by them with all the power at their disposal. Ethnic minorities, whose principal and secondary building blocks/constituents of ethnicity (especially language) are hurt and threatened with destruction, may be led to rebel due to the rise in tensions. Overall, such practices are not typical for more modern states with properly developed civil societies. If the ethno-political elites are the ones enforcing such ethnic restrictions in the initial stages of ethnic conflicts, one may refer to them as the driving forces of ethnic conflict in its regressive dynamics. In this case, their driving ideology may be defined as *ethnocentric nationalism*, as opposed to the far *civic nationalism*, which itself is a healthy and helpful aspect of constructing a viable modern democratic society.

Notes

1   Raymond C. Taras and Rajat Ganguly, *Understanding Ethnic Conflict*, 4th ed. (New York: Longman, Pearson Education, Inc., 2006), 116.

2   See Gregory Gleason, *Federalism and Nationalism: The Struggle for Republican Rights in the USSR* (Boulder, CO: Westview Press, 1990), 135; Jack Snyder, "Nationalism and the Crisis of the Post-Soviet State," in *Ethnic Conflict and International Security*, ed. Michael E. Brown (Princeton, NJ: Princeton University Press, 1993), 95–96.

3   Marta Cullberg Weston, "When Words Lose Their Meaning: From Societal Crisis to Ethnic Cleansing," *Mind and Human Interaction* 8, no. 1 (Winter/Spring 1997):25.

4   For example, see Arkady Vaksberg, *The Soviet Mafia* (New York: St. Martin Press, 1993); Stephen Handleman, "The Russian Mafia," *Foreign Affairs* 73 (March–April 1994): 83–96.

5   Clair Sterling, *Thieves World* (New York: Simon and Schuster, 1994), 34.

6   Front Page "Editorial Article," *Izvestia*, January 26, 1994; see also Marshall I. Goldman, "Why Is the Mafia So Dominant in Russia?" *Challenge* (January/February 1996), 125; also Marshall I. Goldman, "Is This Any Way to Create a Market Economy?" *Current History* 94, no. 594 (October 1995), 305–10.

7   Marshall I. Goldman, "Organized Crime's Role in the Russian Economy," excerpted from "Why Is the Mafia So Dominant in Russia?" *Challenge* (January/February 1996), reprinted by permission, emphasis added.

8   Joseph Serio, "Organized Crime in the Soviet Union and Beyond," *Low Intensity Conflict and Law Enforcement* 1, no. 2 (Fall 1992), 127–51; Mark Galeotti, "Organized Crime in Moscow and Russian National Security," *Low Intensity Conflict and Law Enforcement* 1, no. 3 (Winter 1992), 237–52.

9   Leonid M. Kravchuk, *Imenem zakonu*, January 15, 1993, translated in FBIS Vienna message 2513402, January 1993.

10 See "Minimalization of the Russian Armed Forces," *Foreign Military Studies Office Publications,* http://call.army.mil/call/fmso/fmsopubs/issues/mafia.html.

11 Mikhail A. Zhyrokhov, *Semena raspada: Voiny i konflikty na territorii byvshego SSSR* (St. Petersburg: BHV—Petersburg, 2012), 57f; see also Alexandr G. Osipov, "Ferganskie sobytiya: Konstruirovanie etnicheskogo konflikta," *Ferganskaya dolina: Etnichnost', etnicheskie protsessy, etnicheskie konflikty* (Moscow: Nauka, 2004), 164–233.

12 *Natsional'nyi sostav Naselenya SSSR.. Po dannym Vsesoyuznoi perepisi naseleniya 1989g.* (Moscow: "Finansy i statistika," 1991), 22.

13 *Natsional'nyi sostav Naselenya SSSR*, 92–100.

14 In addition to the above-cited publication, see also Maks Lurijie and Petr Studenikin, *Zapah gari i gorya (Fergana, trevozhnyi iyun'1989g.)* (Moscow: "Kniga," 1990); V. Mukomel, "Vooruzhyonnye mezhnatsional'nye i regional'nye konflikty: Lyudskie poteri, ekonomichskii usherb i sotsial'nye posledstviya," *Identichnost' i konfliky v postsovetskikh gosudarstvah* (Moscow: Moskovskii Tsentr Karnegi, 1997), 298–324; Shahobitdin Ziyamov, "O mezhetnicheskom konflikte 1989 goda v Uzbekistane," *Tsentral'naya Azia i Kavkaz* 6 (2000); Anatoly Golovkov, "Ranenie," *Ogonyok* 29 (July 1989): 28–31.

15 K. Myalo, P. Goncharov, "Zarevo Fergany," *Novoye vremya* 37 (September 8, 1989): 31.

16 Alexandr G. Osipov, "Ferganskie sobytiya: Konstruirovanie ethnicheskogo konflikta," *Igrunov*, 2004, igpi.ru/info/people/osipov/1172304934.html.

17 See also Alexandr G. Osipov, "'Ferganskie sobytiya' dvadtsat' let spustya. Istorya bez uroka?" *Fergana. Informatsionnoe agenstvo*, February 9, 2020, fergananews.com/articles/6197.

18 See Ksenia Loginova, "'Selom bit': s chem svyazan konflikt na juge Kazakhstana," *Izvestia* (*The News*), February 8, 2020, https://iz.ru/973832/ksenia-loinova/selom-bit'-s-chem-svyazan-konflikt-na-juge-kazakhstana?utm_source=smi2.

19 An interview with Alexandr Grozin, "Pravda, kotoruyu skryvaiyut ot nas v Kazakhstane: massovaya draka byla ne bytovoi," *Tsargrad,* February 9, 2020, tsargrad.tv/articles/pravda-kotoryu-skryvajut-ot-nas-v-kazakhstane-massovaja-draka-byla-ne-bytovoj_238120.

20 Osipov, "Ferganskie sobytiya," 207.

21 See the description of the course of these ethnic pogroms and riots in Isaenko, *Polygon of Satan: Ethnic Traumas and Conflicts in the Caucasus*, 3rd ed.(Dubuque, IA: Kendall Hunt Publishing House, 2014), 243–44;250–65; 320–23.

22 See Liudvig de Yong, *Nemetskaya pyataya colonna vo Vtoroi mirovoi voine* (Moscow: Gosizdat, 1958).

23 V. Das, "Official Narratives, Rumor, and Social Production of Hate," *Social Identities* 4, no. 1 (1998): 109–30; V. Das, ed., *Mirrors of Violence: Communities, Riots, and Survivors in South Asia* (Delhi: N.P., 1990).

24 See note 199 in Osipov, "Ferganskie sobytiya," 222.

25 Some of these behavioral patterns have parallels in the recursive analogs outlined by Osipov in the above-cited article, "Ferganskie sobytiya," 207–9.

26 See "Chinese Muslims Appeared in the Center of the Riot in Kazakhstan," *Vzglyad*, February 8, 2020, https://vz.ru/world/2020/2/8/139494.html?utm_source=smi2.

27 Isaenko, *Polygon of Satan*, 320; Thomas de Waal, *Black Garden: Armenia and Azerbaijan Through Peace and War* (New York: New York University Press, 2003), 32.

28 For more about similar ethnic violence in other areas of Central Asia, see Anara Tabyshalieva, *The Challenge of Regional Cooperation in Central Asia: Preventing Ethnic Conflict in the Fergana Valley* (Washington DC: United States Institute of Peace, 1999), 19–30.

29 Penny Morvant, "Crime, Fire Figures Released," *OMRI Daily Digest* 12, part 1, January 17, 1996; "Excess in a Time of the Redistribution of Property," *Izvestia*, October 18, 1995; Glen R. Page, *What is the Russian Mafia?* (graduate thesis, North Carolina State University, 1996), 10.

30 Cited in Page, "What Is the Russian Mafia?," 11.

31 Page, "What Is the Russian Mafia?," 12–13.

32 Page, "What Is the Russian Mafia?,"14.

33 Valery Tishkov, *Chechnya: Life in a War-Torn Society* (Berkeley: University of California Press, 2004), 74.

34 Isaenko, *Polygon of Satan*, 366.

35 Page, "What Is the Russian Mafia?,"15.

36 Victor Yassmann, "The Russian Mafia and the Chechen War," *Prism, Part 2*, June 24, 1995.

37 Ronald Grigor Suny, *The Making of the Georgian Nation* (Bloomington: Indiana University Press; Stanford, CA: Hoover Institution Press, 1988), 205 (emphasis added).

38 Tabyshalieva, *Challenge of Regional Cooperation in Central Asia*, 5–10; Julduz Smagulova, "Kazakhstan: Language, Identity, and Conflict," *Innovation* 19, no. 3–4 (2006): 306; Neil J. Melvin, "Patterns of Center-Regional Relations in Central Asia: The Cases of Kazakhstan, the Kyrgyz Republic and Uzbekistan," in *Ethnicity and Territory in the Former Soviet Union: Regions in Conflict*, ed. James Hughes and Gwendolyn Sasse (London: Frank Cass, 2002), 165–94.

39 Isaenko, *Polygon of Satan*, chapters 4–7.

40 Taras Kuzio, *Ukraine: State and Nation Building* (London: Routledge, 1998), 23.

41 Dmytro Vydrin and Dmytro Tabachnyk, *Ukraiina Na Porozi XXI Stolittia. Politychnyi Aspekt* (Kyiv: Lybid', 1995), 170; Kuzio, *Ukraine: State and Nation Building*, 23.

42 Serhy Yekelchyk, *The Conflict in Ukraine: What Everyone Needs to Know* (Oxford: Oxford University Press, 2015), 77, emphasis added.

43 Roman Szporluk, "Ukraine: From an Imperial Periphery to a Sovereign State," *Daedalus* 126, no. 3 (1997): 86; see also Roman Szporluk, "The Politics of State Building: Centre-Periphery Relations in Post-Soviet Ukraine," *Europe-Asia Studies* 46, no. 1 (1994): 47–68.

44 Mark Altshuler, *Some Soviet and Post-Soviet National and Linguistic Problems in the Slavic Republics (States): Russia, Ukraine, Belarus* (Bergen: Slavic Research Center, 1998), 4.

45 See "Ex-Communist Bosses Still in Majority in Ex-USSR," *Reuters*, December 2, 1996; Kuzio, *Ukraine: State and Nation Building*, 27–28.

46 Serhiy Bilokin', "Dolia Ukraiins'koi National'noiAristokratii," *Heneza* 4 (1996): 144–45.

47 Kuzio, *Ukraine: State and Nation Building*, 26, emphasis added.

48 Kuzio, *Ukraine: State and Nation Building*, 29.

49 Mark Bliev,*Ossetia, Kavkaz: Istoria i sovremennost'* (Vladikavkaz, Russia: North-Ossetian University Press, 1999), 249.

50 Ramazan G. Abdulatipov, "Kavkazskaya tsivilizatsiya: Samobytnost' i tselosnost'," *Nauchnaiya mysl' Kavkaza* (Rostov-on-Don, Russia: North Caucasian Scientific Center, 1995), 57–58.

51 Isaenko, *Polygon of Satan*, 284.

52 Farid Shafiyev, *Resettling the Borderlands: State Relocations and Ethnic Conflicts in the South Caucasus* (Montreal: McGill-Queen's University Press, 2018), 223.

53 Kuzio*, Ukraine: State and Nation Building,* 28-9. .

54 Natalia Boyko, "Uriad: shtrykhy do sotsialnogo portretu," *Den'*, February 15, 1997, cited in Kuzio, *Ukraine: State and Nation Building*, 28.

55 Kuzio, *Ukraine: State and Nation Building*, 28.

56 Robert Bruce Ware and Enver Kisriev, *Dagestan: Russian Hegemony and Islamic Resistance in the Northern Caucasus* (Armonk, NY: ME Sharpe, 2010), 73–74.

57 Paul Henze, *Conflict in the Caucasus* (Chapel Hill, NC: UNC Library, Rand Library Collection, 1995), 12, emphasis added.

58 Paul Henze, *Conflict in the Caucasus*, 9–11.

59 Cited in Anna Juranets, "'Not Stealing Is Not Enough': Zalensky Changed the Government," *Gazeta.ru*, March 4, 2020, https://www.gazeta.ru/politics/2020/03/04_a_12988813.shtml?utm_source=smi22utm_medium=exchange&es=smi2.

60 Stephen Crowley, "Between Class and Nation: Worker Politics in the New Ukraine," *Communist and Post-Communist Studies* 28, no.1 (1995): 68–69.

61 See Lowell Barrington, "Examining Rival Theories of Demographic Influences on Political Support: The Power of Regional, Ethnic, and Linguistic Divisions in Ukraine," *European Journal of Political Research* 41 (2002): 458; see also Dominique Arel, "Ukraine: The Middle Way," *Current History* (October 1998): 342–46.

62 Yekelchyk, *Conflict in Ukraine*, 78, emphasis added.

63 Volodymyr Polokhalo, *The Political Analysis of Post-Communism* (College Station: Texas A&M University Press, 1997), 7.

64 Compare these numbers to the *List of Post-Soviet Conflicts* in James Hughes and Gwendolyn Sasse, eds., *Ethnicity and Territory in the Former Soviet Union* (London: Frank Cass, 2002), XIII. In 2002, when this collection of articles was published, Russo-Ukrainian ethnic conflict had yet to enter its *hot stage* in Donbas, which is why the authors included it on their list of nonviolent conflicts and instead indicated that this potential conflict would center around Crimea.

65 See Jane Ormond, "The North Caucasus: Confederation in Conflict," in *New State, New Politics: Building the Post-Soviet Nations*, ed. Ian Bremmer and Ray Taras (Cambridge, UK: Cambridge University Press, 1997).

66 Isaenko, *Polygon of Satan*, 128.

67 Pavel M. Shornikov, *Polya padeniya. Istoriographiya moldavskoi ethnopolitiki* (Kishineu: n.p., 2009); Nikolai V. Babilunga and Boris G. Bomeshko, *Pridnestrovskii konflikt: istoricheskiye, demographiches-kiye, politicheskiye aspekty* (Tiraspol': RIO PGU, 1998): Mikhail A Zhirokhov, *Semena raspada: voiny i konflikty na territorii byvshego SSSR* (St. Petersburg: "BHV—Petersburg," 2012), 76–77.

68 Julia Strasheim, "Power-Sharing, Commitment Problems, and Armed Conflict in Ukraine,"*Civil Wars* 18,no. 1(2016): 38–39.

69 See, for example, Lawrence Freedman, "Ukraine and the Art of Limited War," *Survival* 56, no. 6 (2014):7–38; Elizabeth Cullen Dunn and Michall S. Bobick, "The Empire Strikes Back: War without War and Occupation without Occupation in the Russian Sphere of Influence," *American Ethnologist* 41, no. 3 (2014): 405–13; Michael Rywkin, "Ukraine: Between Russia and the West," *American Foreign Policy Interest* 36, no. 2 (2014): 119–26; and especially Jeffery Mankoff, "Russia's Land Grab: How Putin Won Crimea and Lost Ukraine," *Foreign Affairs* 93 (2014): 60.

70 See James D. Fearon and David Laitin, "Ethnicity, Insurgency, and Armed Conflict," *American Political Science Review* 79, no. 1 (2003): 75–90; Jose G. Montalvo and Marta Reynal-Querol, "Ethnic Polarization, Potential Conflict, and Armed Conflicts," *The American Economic Review* 95, no. 3 (2005): 796–816; Andreas Wimmer, Lars Eric Cederman, and Brian Min, "Ethnic Politics and Armed Conflict: A Configurational Analysis of a New Global Data Set," *American Sociological Review* 74, no. 2 (2009): 316–37.

71 Isaenko, *Polygon of Satan*, see the interviews in chapter 4, 143–49; see also chapter 5, 186–88.

72 "Appeal of the "Georgian Society Named for Ilya Chavchavadze" and The Peoples Front of South Ossetia, Adamon Nykhas to the Georgian and Ossetian People," *Zarya Vostoka*, Tbilisi, July 23, 1989, 2, emphasis added. Ghia Nodia, one of the most informed and objective Georgian analysts, estimated a high level of effort from the "moderate opposition of ethnocentric nationalists, who had united into a block called *Democratic Georgia*, who was more sensitive ... to ethnic populism, regarding [it] as an *indication of a threatening fascism*." Ghia Nodia, "Political Turmoil in Georgia

and the Ethnic Policies of Zviad Gamsakhurdia," in *Contested Borders in the Caucasus*, ed. Bruno Coppieters (Brussels: VUB University Press, 1996), 78, emphasis added.

73   John Mearcheimer, "Back to the Future: Instability in Europe after the Cold War," *International Security* 15, no. 1 (Summer 1990). Reprinted in Sean M. Lynn-Jones and Steven E. Miller, eds., *The Cold War and After* (Cambridge, MA: MIT Press, 1991), 157. For the details of this period, see *Yuzhnaya Osetia: krov'i pepel* (*South Ossetia: Blood and Ashes*) (Vladikavkaz, Russia: Assotsiatsia tvorcheskoi i nauchnoi intelligetsii, Ir, 1991), 40–55.

74   About the importance of an "ethnic name" in the process of ethnocentric mobilization among the Ossetians, see Victor Shnirelman's very absorbing article, "The Politics of a Name: Between Consolidation and Separation in the Northern Caucasus," *Acta Slavica Iaponica* (2005) Tomus 23:37–73; see also Bruno Coppieters, *Federalism and Conflict in the Caucasus* (London: Royal Institute of International Affairs, 2001) 54–55.

75   See Nodia, "Political Turmoil in Georgia," 83.

76   Isaenko, *Polygon of Satan*, 163.

77   See Olga Vasileva, *Gruziya kak model' post-kommunisticheskoi transformatsii* (Moscow: s.p., 1993), 43.

78   Barry R. Posen, "The Security Dilemma and Ethnic Conflict," in *Ethnic Conflict and International Security*, ed. M.E. Brown (Princeton, NJ: Princeton University Press, 1993), 107.

79   Anzor Kvanchilashvili, "Chto budet potom?"*Literaturi Sakartvelo*, September 30, 1988.

80   Nikolai V. Siukaev, *Dve tragedii Yuzhnoi Osetii* (Vladikavkaz, Russia: North Ossetian State University Press, 1994), 7.

81   For full detail, see chapters 4–8 in Isaenko, *Polygon of Satan*.

82   Zhirokhov, *Semena raspada*, 78–83.

83   Isaenko, *Polygon of Satan*, see the interviews and documentary materials cited in chapters 4–7; Refer also to the table "Mild and Middle Ground Levels of Ethnic Discrimination," 407–408, and in the introduction of the present research.

■ CHAPTER SIX

Ideology of Ethnic Conflicts

Ethnocentric Nationalism and Behavioral Patterns

Using the above-cited examples that set the stage for violent ethnic conflicts, I want to demonstrate how they all stem from (1) a combined presence of long-term *mass hostility*, defined by the impact of an all-sided societal crisis, within ethnic groups; (2) *enhanced*, *reinvigorated*, and *redirected ethnic hostility by ethno-political elites* leading these ethnic groups; and (3) a rejuvenated *security dilemma* that, in an uncertain situation, increases collective ethnic fears for the future. While I intend to present examples from the Russo-Ukrainian conflict in subsequent parts of this research, it is important to note that all of these conflicts have and continue to display these three factors throughout their miserable tenure. Woven together in such a way that "helped to exacerbate the other two," each individual factor inevitably led "to an increasing spiral of ethnic violence."[1] Parallel to Stuart Kaufman's considerations regarding the Russo-Moldavian conflict, I had a chance to personally observe how in all of these conflicts, to use his words, "belligerent leaders stoke mass hostility; hostile masses support belligerent leaders; and both together threaten other groups, creating a security dilemma which in turn encourages even more mass hostility and leadership belligerence."[2] Later on, I will show how the different phases of escalating violence within ethnic conflicts can be either mass-led, elite-led, a joint effort driven by a common psychosis, or even blame on one another for failure, as masses reject their leadership when a "national cause" is a failure. In my own book, I figuratively described Kaufman's previously mentioned "spiral" of violence as a *handwheel of Satan*, indicating that the policies of the post-Soviet ethno-political elites ultimately set this cycle of violence in motion. While aiming at the establishment of ethnic dominance and exclusion, these choices also affected the *principal building blocks of ethnicity within targeted groups*.[3]

Two Types of Modern Nationalism

According to Jack Snyder, a political scientist at Columbia University, ethnic nationality is based on the consciousness of shared identity within a group, rooted in a shared culture and a belief in common ancestry. By contrast, civic nationality is inclusive within a specified territory. Membership in a national group is generally open to everyone who is born within or is a permanent resident of the outlined national territory, *irrespective of language, culture, or ancestry.* In the late 1980s–1990s, ethnic elites in all former Soviet republics, but especially in the Caucasus, Baltic, and Central Asian states, advanced (and continue to advance) the use of *ethnic criteria* for group membership. In fact, only former Russian President Boris Yeltsin and Ukrainian President Leonid Kravchuk "generally argued for *civic criteria.*"[4] However, when Professor Snyder published these assessments in 1993, he could not have known that subsequent Ukrainian administrations would slowly begin drifting away from the more liberal, civic criteria. Instead, these administrations began to build their nation-state on the grounds of total dominance of the titular ethnic nation in those spheres vital to the survival of all ethnic groups within the country, beginning first and foremost with language—as it is *the most important building block of ethnicity.* As we now know, the choice between the *civic-type nationalism* and the *ethnic-type nationalism* as the possible ideological paradigms of state-building gradually shifted toward the latter. Some specialists, such as Kathryn Manzo, argue against a binary classification of nationalism on the grounds that such a dichotomy does not fully match the reality of this phenomenon.[5] However, most specialists in this field consider it appropriate to make a distinction between *civic* and *ethnic* types of nationalism. Some authors from this cohort refer to civic nationalism as *liberal, benign, positive,* and so on, while its opposite is sometimes defined as *authoritarian, integral, malignant,* and so on.[6]

Dusan Kecmanovic, an Australia-based psychiatrist and author of several groundbreaking mass psychology research studies, labeled the latter strain of nationalism as "*ethnic,*" or as some experts in 1987 called it, *ethnonationalism.*[7] In my recent publications, I introduced the term *ethnocentric nationalism,* which I feel more precisely describes the nature of the dominating form of ideology driving violent ethnic conflicts.[8] It indicates the *highest degree of absorption by ethnicity* through politics, especially (such as in the interviews and examples in previous chapters) when this malignant type of ideology embraces the ethno-political elites and the masses alike while simultaneously manifesting in all the spheres corresponding to the five principal building blocks of ethnicity. *The more constituents/building blocks and cultural markers of ethnicity of targeted groups are affected by the practical implementation of this ideology, the more sharp and violent the resulting ethnic conflict will be.*

Defining Ethnocentric Nationalism

Based on the exploration of this type of nationalism in its practical realization (as manifested in repeated behavioral patterns displayed by ethnic groups/nations during violent conflicts in the Caucasus, Moldova, and now Ukraine), I propose the following definition for this phenomenon:

> Ethnocentric nationalism expresses itself in a collective conviction that one's own ethnic group/nation is an exclusive people and has a special mission, which is the way that each individual has to subjugate themselves to the collective will and show absolute loyalty to their ethnic group/nation; all members of this group are united by an unquestionable conviction that their language, religion, national version of history, heroes, symbols, names, and all other characteristics of a distinct people and a sovereign nation, which includes the supreme right to "primordial ethnic territories," must reign above all as an integral manifestation of the collective will of the chosen people.

In social psychological terms, originating from the precedence of absolute loyalty to the ethnic/national group, Kecmanovic defines three other distinctive features of ethnocentric nationalism (or as he puts it, "ethnonationalism"). They are generally symptomatic in the way that they do not contradict the above characteristics, as they are usually complimentary in disclosing some immanent details in the above definition. According to these terms, "ethnonationalists" believe the following:

> (1) That co-nationals are in one or many regards superior to members of other ethnonational groups; (2) the ethnonationalists' disregard for the rights and interests of, and hostility toward, people of other ethnonational backgrounds [sic]; (3) that individual destiny is, by and large, determined by and dependent on the destiny of one's own ethnonational group.[9]

All of the above convictions are noticeably present in the latest interviews of some Ukrainian emigrants, previously cited in the introduction. As a matter of fact, the idea of absolute loyalty can be properly identified in the records of history since time immemorial. It is present in the common law, such as the Adats, and in the rites of Bedouins of pre-Islamic Arabia regarding loyalty to the tribe, which later entered Sharia'h as absolute devotion to Umma. But in truth, the object of this loyalty may have changed throughout different periods of history: it may have been for their tribe, polis/city, ethnic or religious community, empire/nation-state, revolutionary or criminal group, political party, leaders, and so on. One could even continue this list of objects of loyalty further into the stratum of any particular society. Yet an overall obvious conclusion in all of these examples may be its representation of a universal human potential that has been realized, both inwardly and outwardly, under certain social, political, economic, and other circumstances/conditions. However, I agree with Kecmanovic that "in modern times, historically one and the same pattern becomes evident on the social and political stage" and that this same pattern has now emerged under the guise of ethnocentric nationalism. It is an ideology that, following the collapse of the Soviet Union and the socialist system amid a continuing all-sided societal crisis, represents one of the strongest *stimuli* that dormant characteristics of human nature "actualize at maximum."[10] It also represents a full-fledged form of *behavioral patterns totally defined by this integral ideology*. In 1987, experts within the *Committee on International Relations* had already come to the conclusion that "the biopsychosocial forces that underline group-belonging are crystallized in our times as ethno-nationalism."[11]

Objective Conditions for Different Types of Nationalism

Before discussing the behavioral patterns of ethnocentric nationalism that span the concrete historical circumstances and ethnic conflicts driven by the post-Soviet transition of polities into nation-states, it is important to outline certain auspicious conditions that must exist in a society to facilitate the rise of these types of nationalism. With this connection, I need to remind the reader that the starting conditions of the national state-building process were *relatively* the same across all post-Soviet societies and could be accurately defined as an all-sided societal crisis.

The comparative analysis of life in different groups of nation-states belonging to different world civilizations shows that the *civic* type of nationalism is dominant (1) when the society is relatively prosperous, stable, and developed; (2) when it has a sizable and robust middle class—the social backbone of democracy; and (3) when it has a long and ingrained tradition of being a civil society. In contrast, ethnocentric nationalism generally rises to prominence (1) when the society in question is suffering from an all-sided economic and political crisis, leaving it polarized and fragmented; (2) when it possesses a minuscule and feeble middle class; and (3) when it has long held authoritarian/totalitarian traditions.[12]

If one takes into account both Polohalo's above-cited definitions pertaining to the post-Soviet space (excluding Russia after 2000) and those of Yekelchyk pertaining to Ukraine in particular, then a conclusion favoring the three societal conditions responsible for the rise and reproduction of ethnocentric nationalism would be more than obvious. Understandably, this becomes even more noticeable in regard to the strife in Ukraine.

The Role of Putin's Reforms in Creating Alternative Conditions for the Development of Civic Nationalism in Russia

Regarding the middle class, Russian President Vladimir Putin recently assured his public that "70 percent of Russian citizens belong to the middle class." Supposedly, this would fall in line with the requirements as defined by *the World Bank*, who defines this category as people whose income is at least 1.5 times more than the minimal monthly wages established in the country (which is currently ₽17,000 Rubles or $210 USD).[13] However, it seems that President Putin delivered the desirable state of affairs rather than the actual one, considering he inaccurately rendered the *World Bank's* method of quantifying the middle class. Some journalists with experience delving into the specificities of their subject matter noticed that the World Bank ranks a person as a member of the middle class if their personal income is 1.5 times larger than the cumulative minimal income of the entire household, not the "minimal wage level." Combine this with the simple reality of how, rather than the average income, the price of consumer goods and services have been steadily increasing in Russia over the last few years, one can safely assume that the Russian middle class must be considerably less than 70 percent of the population. In fact, according to experts at the World Bank, as well as the *Global Wealth Report 2015*, published by the *Credit Suisse* bank in Switzerland, the "classical middle class" in Russia constituted 9.5 percent of the total population in 2009 (compared to 12.6 percent prior to the 2008 economic crisis) and a staggering 4.1 percent by 2015—i.e., approximately five million people. At the same time, they counted less than 1 percent of the Ukrainian population as belonging to the middle class (for the sake of comparison: in the United States—38 percent, in China—11 percent, in Africa and India—3 percent). According to *Credit Suisse*, an individual must make the equivalent of $18,000 USD annually to qualify as part of the middle class.[14] Given this, one can conclude that the Ukrainian middle class embodies an "embryonic" status. While the middle-class situation in Russia is better, it still lags far behind the more developed capitalist and democratic societies.

To Mr. Putin's credit, however, one could feasibly argue that, over the last fifteen years, he has reduced the arbitrary role of those oligarchs who dominated the 1990s and redistributed the power behind the most vital resources in favor of a group of loyal corporations and tycoons. Under this new management, loyal oligarchs have preserved (and even increased) their economic privileges, though in exchange of sacrificing their political influence while leaving the vital spheres to the competence of the president. Putin also successfully crushed and constrained ethnic separatists in the North Caucasus, forced radical Islamists into hiding or out of the country entirely, and relatively stabilized the economy.

As James Hughes demonstrated, the so-called "partial asymmetric federalism" born out of Putin's reforms during the early 2000s "has had an important stabilizing effect on the management of federal relations with the key ethnic republics" within the Russian Federation. This in turn has created *several important objective conditions* that, in the long run, promote the development of *civic* nationalism. Among them, Hughes emphasizes significant institutional arrangements: (1) "By decentralizing power over a wide range of policy domains, the [system] of treaties have been important institutional counterweights to the powerful residues of a centralizing unitarist state tradition in Russia, which has historically practiced ethnic control, assimilation, and oppression against its national [ethnic] minorities." (2) The treaties between Moscow and titular ethnic elites in the republics "have engineered a new institutional structure for the accommodation of Russia's multi-ethnic society." It is, in fact, "a critical element in the construction of the federal process in politics itself." In response to the arduous nature of the bargaining process, Putin has demonstrated not only patience and tact but enough charisma to understand and persuade ethnic contemporaries that "institutionalizing elite bargaining" ultimately leads to *democratic consolidation*. If some disparities in federal revenue distribution that favor the ethnic republics, like Tatarstan, Bashkortostan, or Chechnya, come about, they are compensated by the huge concentration of wealth in Moscow held by the ethnic Russian elites, who are now mostly loyal to the president. (3) Hughes also specifically denotes "a lack of transparency" in the "bilateral power-sharing treaty process." Yet he argues that secrecy itself gives flexibility to both sides of the negotiation and provides the ethnic leadership of those key ethnic republics an illusion, albeit sometimes a real feeling, of hope that, depending on the case of the negotiations, they can "extract the most concessions." (4) Russia's successful management of separatist/regionalist challenges *sets a model* for an "asymmetrical type of solution" in the above-mentioned violent ethnic conflicts in the Caucasus, Moldova, Ukraine, and places beyond (like Bosnia). (5) Asymmetric federalism allowed local ethnic and regional elites to play an ever-increasing role in the so-called "marbled diplomacy of international relations."[15]

In my opinion, the system of institutional arrangements of partial asymmetric federalism that have been built and successfully implemented by Putin helped to create a rather firm foundation that avoids the prospect of violent ethnic conflicts within Russia in the near future. Particularly, the nature of this *consociational* type of arrangement demonstrates to ethnic elites/groups that they would retain the right to block any possible moves of the center that they deem injurious to their vital interests, as well as guaranteeing the right to withdraw or secede from the joint arrangement. In the grand scheme, such guarantees are crucial "to get ethnic groups to credibly commit to peace."[16]

It is with this bargaining process that Putin was able to persuade his counterparts in Tatarstan and Bashkortostan (as well as other potential secessionists throughout Russia during the 1990s) that the cost for choosing war over peace might have "increased substantially for them to make credible commitments toward peace."[17] In addition, the bloody stages of the Russian-Chechen ethnic conflict, with their terrible destruction of human life and material resources, were still a gaping wound in front of their eyes.

As a matter of fact, Russia-Tatarstan and Russia-Bashkortostan finally found a solution to their nonviolent conflict, which began in March 1990. Through long negotiations within the framework of the new institutional arrangements, the parties were successful in establishing "*Treaty Autonomies*" without the need for any mediators. Ukraine-Crimea contradictions (beginning in 1990) and Moldova-Gagauzian ethnic tensions (beginning in August 1990) found similar resolutions through the establishment of *constitutional autonomy* with the international mediation of the *Organization for Security and Cooperation in Europe (OSCE)* and *High Commissioner for National Minorities (HCNM)*, respectively. (As one may have guessed, the Crimean arrangement would last until 2014.) In the section dedicated to the *nationality building block* of the Russo-Ukrainian ethnic conflict, I will discuss in more detail why this compromise could not last. A similar constitutional autonomy regime was established in Ajaria by Georgian President Mikhail Saakashvili in 2004 and has lasted as a policy in Georgia to this day. Potential conflicts between titular ethnic nations and ethnic Slavic minorities also began to bubble up in Estonia and Latvia. Yet with the help of the OSCE, HCNM, and the European Union, they avoided regression into the more violent stages by, again, adopting elements of a *consociational ethnic democracy.*[18]

In Ukraine, regionalism, with distinctively ethnic underpinnings, serves as a recurrent challenge whenever the titular ethnic nation (and its elite) has the opportunity to begin the nation-state (or state-nation, to use Kuzio's term) building process. It occurred following the collapse of the Russian Empire in 1917, during the short-lived *Hetmanate* under General Pavlo Skoropads'kyi, with his proclamation of a *Ukrains'ka derzhava* ("Ukrainian State"), and during Ukraine's federation with the anti-Bolshevik Russian government of Anton Ivanovich Denikin. In January 1919, the so-called *directorate* under Volodymyr Vynnychenko and Hetman Symon Petliura declared *sobornost'* ("unity") between the *Ukrains'ka Narodna Respublica* (UNR; lit. *Ukrainian People's Republic*), and the *Western Ukrainian Peoples Republic* (ZUNR). This union was to formally ratify by the *Ukrainian Constituent Assembly*, at which point until then the ZUNR continued to exist as the "Western Oblast" of the Ukrainian People's Republic (ZOUNR). Thus, even from the first attempt to build an independent Ukrainian state, an immanent *confederal element* had already appeared—stemming from the very multiethnic nature of these territories.[19] As illustrated by Alexander Motyl, and later by Gwendolyn Sasse, this early Ukrainian *derzhava* ("state") soon fell apart due to Petliura's political games: he tried to "secure Poland's political and military help against Russia in return for granting Poland Eastern Galicia and the Western half of Volhynia."[20] The collapse of the Russian and Hapsburg Empires, alongside the ambivalent policies of the UNR's leaders, caused the Ukrainian territories, as demonstrated previously, to become parts of Poland, Slovakia, and Romania until 1945, when they were then incorporated into the Ukrainian SSR at the behest of Stalin. Sasse also specifically showed how "the debates over Crimea's status—independence vs. autonomy within Ukraine vs. integration with Russia—in the aftermath of the revolution [of 1917] and under the German protectorate during World War I *offer some striking parallels* with the post-Soviet struggles over Crimea."[21] We have previously discussed the Rusyns' question: how, despite being Magyarized after 1867 and persecuted under Austro-Hungarian rule, they were able to preserve the basic building blocks of their ethnicity and revived their claims for autonomy in the region, though some gradually joined the Czechoslovak Federation in 1919. One should keep in mind that the Soviet Bolsheviks (by exploiting regional ethnic identities against the nationalist *Central Rada* in Kiev) had created a short-lived *Donets'k-Kryvi Rih Republic* in 1918, which also has many parallels to the struggles over the Donbas region after 2014.

My point is that all of these cases, alongside other unmentioned ones, are historical precursors/prequisites of modern problems, indicating that whoever revives the state-building process in Ukraine will eventually face the political significance of the country's regional diversity with ethnic underpinnings and peculiarities. And it is this, despite all manner of turmoil, tragedy, and idealistically constructivist experiences that remains *the biggest challenge when attempting Unitarianism.*

Ethno-Political Challenges in the Regions of Post-Soviet Ukraine (Hungarian Case)

After Ukraine gained its independence, the earliest ethno-political regional challenge came by way of ethnic Hungarians. At this time, they were "living in multi-ethnic communities in Romania, Slovakia, and Transcarpathian Ukraine." Their ethno-political elite were remarkably successful in creating *ethnic parties/organizations* in order to institutionalize their own ethnic interests, concerns, and identity.[22] Thus, in Ukraine, they were the first ethnic minority, like the Chechens in Russia, who displayed (according to Nash's definition) a "total absorption by ethnicity" of their politics.[23] As I previously demonstrated in chapters 1 through 4 and 5 of this research, "ethnic parties/organizations" emerge from the inherent cleavages of societies and regularly manifest themselves. However, this is not the result of malignant plots and the "manipulation" of ethnic groups by their elites, as some authors and specialists argue.[24] Rather, it is, as we have previously seen, a certain issue of *resonance* between elites and populations at some point during an all-sided societal crisis, especially when titular ethno-political elites begin vigorously promoting their own ethnocentric policies. In agreement with Sherrill Stroschein, and in conformation with previously cited examples, a majority of individuals within ethnic minorities are usually "concerned about the language used in their children's schools, the version of history their children will learn, the statues in public places in their cities, and who controls their local governments. Ethnic parties may facilitate political mobilization along these lines, but they are not solely responsible for the importance of these issues to ethnic populations."[25] Stroschein cited Jon Elster, Claus Offe, and Ulrich Preuss, who also noticed that, regarding these crucial ethnic issues (which I refer to as the principal building blocks of ethnicity), if the dominating ethno-political force of the titular ethnic nations put ethnic groups in the position of "either-or" instead of "more or less," categorical conflicts "undomesticated by rules" can "lead to civil wars."[26] Yet, as the above-cited Russian experience shows, this kind of projection *is not inevitable.* Even if ethnic parties/organizations "domesticate" ethnic issues—stemming from the concerns surrounding sensitive constituents of a particular ethnicity that require the respect and protection of an institutional form—they may be able to find a solution *through bargaining.* And much like the asymmetric federalist system built in Russia; these bargains address ethnic issues through consociational institutional arrangements. Thus, the problem rests against the political wills of both sides: at first place of the titular ethnic nation and then of the ethno-political parties/organizations/movements of ethnic minorities concerned with the preservation of their ethnic identities. In the Ukrainian case, we see such political will on the part of some ethnic minorities.

For example, Hungarians constitute approximately 12.5 percent of the population within the Ukrainian Transcarpathian Oblast. The Berehovo *raion* ("district") and its center—Berehovo-city (also known as Beregovo)—is the home to the Hungarian majority in Western Ukraine (Berehovo—about 72,000 or 63.1 percent of the population; Berehovo-city—16,310 or 55.8 percent of people, according to data from 1994).[27] On December 1, 1991, when the Ukrainian population of multiple ethnic groups voted for Ukrainian independence, 78 percent of voters in the Zakarpattya Oblast also supported a call for *self-governing powers* for their region "within the structure of independent Ukraine."[28] At the same time, the Hungarian-dominated district held a referendum, in which 81.4 percent of voters approved the creation of a *Hungarian National District (Magyar autonóm körzet).*[29] So, if the Hungarians constituted only 63.1 percent of the district's populace, then who made up the remaining 18.3 percent? Based on data collected and thoroughly analyzed by Stroschein, I formulated several important generalizations regarding this outcome:

(1) Despite absolute minority status and the small number of Hungarians in Ukraine, they appeared as the first regional ethnic group in the independent Ukrainian state that showed the highest level of ethnic mobilization relative to other ethnic groups in Zakarpattya Oblast. In particular, I explained this through the tragic experiences following both World Wars, wherein Hungarians were repeatedly punished by the Allies and lost a large swath of their territories; these are profound *chosen traumas*—which are critical factors of ethnic mobilization amid all-sided societal crisis.

(2) Ethnic organizations of minority groups, especially those with traumatic experiences in the past, tend to prioritize the interests of their own particular groups over those of the society as a whole. As Stroschein showed, the "Hungarian parties in Romania and Slovakia have been using their recent inclusion in the coalition governments of each country *to improve the legal status of the Hungarian language in schools, universities, and other official circles.*"[30] But in Ukraine, similar demands from the respective Hungarian ethnic organizations were staunchly ignored. Even the *Hungarian Cultural Organization* (*KMKSz/TUKZ*) was denied registration as a political party because it had little to no support from outside regions. Thus, titular ethnic nations have a partial tendency to ignore the vital interests of ethnic minorities when they have proved their local significance but, in the grand scheme, comprise only a small part of the national population. Generally, these are the first signs of rising ethnocentric nationalism. As a matter of fact, the earliest modern ethno-political party in Ukraine—*The People's Movement of Ukraine* (*RUKH*)—as a combination of both highly radical and moderate adherents of a Ukrainian ethnonational idea, was pre-occupied with suppressing the Russians. They viewed these people as loyal to Russia, which presented a danger to the success of Ukrainian statehood, and they paid little attention to Hungarians.[31]

(3) The case of Hungarians in Zakarpattya, as well as my own exploration of the minorities in the Caucasus, demonstrates that their ethno-political elites adopt rather sophisticated policies when facing a more powerful ethno-political force of dominating ethno-political aggregates, resulting in relatively *unfavorable circumstances*. First, they often experience ethnic voting and develop a party/organization system *based on ethnicity*. Such shared identities allow their political leaders to gain mass amounts of support from within their particular ethnic group.[32] Rather creatively, ethno-political elites of minority groups use instrumentalist and situational methods to pursue their tactical ethnic interests. Second, Hungarians, particularly those living in the Berehovo District, understand that the RUKH, as the most organized party within their region, did not consider them as the primary political foes of the Ukrainian cause. This is why they voted for presidential candidate Vyacheslav Chornovil, a former political prisoner who, on October 14, 1991, was elected as the hetman of Ukrainian Cossacks at their great council. (In the presidential elections, he received the second-largest number of votes—7,420,727, or roughly 23.27 percent).[33] When voting at the state level, Hungarians were made to choose between the two major political forces as if they were choosing between two great evils: in the end, they would rather vote for the RUKH than for the socialists. After all, the RUKH shared a clear Western orientation of international discourse within the Ukrainian politicum. However, when given the option on the local level, they would infallibly vote for their own ethno-political organization, the KMKSz.[34]

(4) Overall, ethnic minorities in the post-Soviet space, vis-à-vis titular ethnic nations, hoped that the latter party would guarantee the free functioning of their primary constituents of their ethnicity/identity (especially language) and all attributes of nationality, ranging from autonomy rights (such as political autonomy of their areas/regions) to the most ideal federalist system in the multiethnic states (like they were accustomed to having, at least formally, in ethnic quasi-state formations in the USSR), all to ensure

the procreation of elements of consociational democratic representation in all national power structures under the imagined (and promised) ideal conditions of modern democracy.

(5) The levels of their ethno-political demands and activities are dependent on one side on what project—civic or ethnocentric/unitarianist—would choose the ethno-political elites of titular ethnic nations in their state-building discourse, and on the other side on the level of support of their ethnic diasporas in adjacent or far-off nation-states, as well as on support of the international organizations and amalgamations of military-political alliances of powerful kin actors, and each ends up representing contesting civilizations.

(6) As the Hungarian case in the Berehovo District suggests, the most important building blocks of their ethnic mobilization were language, nationality, and a commonly shared history, which, as they felt, may be vulnerable for attack during the process of Ukrainian ethnonational construction.

(7) In the long run, the Ukrainian ethno-political elite ignored most Hungarian concerns. Yet ethnic mobilization and radicalization later emerged in Crimea and Donbas along the same principal constituents of ethnicity, and also with a lower level of intensity among other, smaller ethnic communities over the perimeter of the boundaries of the Ukrainian state.

Recent Manifestations of the Aforementioned Behavioral Regularities of Ethnocentric Nationalism

In the last few years, the challenges facing the Hungarian ethnic minority received another continuation that proves the validity of the abovementioned behavioral regularities. On September 5, 2017, the Supreme Rada—the Ukrainian parliament—adopted a new edition of the *Law about Education* (*Zakon pro osvitu*), which was signed by then Ukrainian President Petro Poroshenko on September 25, 2017.[35] This document did not specifically outlaw instruction in other languages, as students could still learn their native languages as a separate subject. However, this did little to assuage the fears of ethnic minorities like the Hungarians, Poles, Romanians, Bulgarians (all of whom have sizable ethnic communities in Ukraine), and, of course, the Russians—the largest ethnic minority group. Russia immediately jumped on this with vociferous criticism, with the Foreign Ministry issuing a statement that month decrying that the law hoped to "forcefully establish a mono-ethnic language regime in a multinational state."[36] As a matter of fact, this bill's language requirements overturn a 2012 law passed by Moscow-friendly President Victor Yanukovych, who was overthrown by Revolutsiya Hidnisti and Euromaidan in 2014 and subsequently fled to Russia. In its wording, this law allowed for minorities to teach their languages in regions where *they represented more than 10 percent of the population.*

As one may have expected, Poroshenko and Ukrainian ethnocentric nationalists summarily ignored the Russian diplomatic démarche and protests of the state Duma—the Russian parliament—alongside the resentment of the Russian and Russian-speaking populations in the eastern and southern regions of the country (all the more, the rebel breakaway areas of Donbas—Donets'k and Luhans'k). Yet the resulting storm of criticism blowing in from the Eastern European capitals took Poroshenko and his *European Solidarity* party aback.

To cite Olga Shumylo-Tapiola, those supporting the overturn of the 2012 law had previously tried to explain to other European nations the necessity of its revocation. If this law was allowed to properly function, then it "would mean the adoption of *regional languages* in about 13 of Ukraine's 27 regions ..."

which "may ultimately bring about the demise of the Ukrainian language and strengthen the split between western and eastern Ukraine."[37] The adepts of the 2017 law counted on receiving support from Washington, DC, which had largely praised the package of educational reforms of the Poroshenko administration, including the language clause. However, arguments from Ukrainian ethno-political leadership in favor of the newer law have been mostly drowned out by the general uproar surrounding the language requirements. Looking past the political battle, everyone understood that this law was primarily aimed at the Russian language. This was evident given that ethnic Russians account for 17 percent of Ukraine's 41.87 million people, while other minorities, such as Hungarians and Romanians, make up less than 1 percent.[38] However, this reality did not quell the criticism of ethno-political organizations within these smaller minority groups, which was strongly buttressed by the negative reaction of their respective European *metropoli/ kin states*. As stated by these language requirements, only two or more subjects could be taught in any of the languages of the EU by grade five. While this may rule out the use of Russian in schools, it would also seriously damage Hungarian, Polish, Bulgarian, and Romanian as cultural languages when the requirements took full effect in 2020.

Of the approximately 15,000 schools in Ukraine, 581 use Russian as the primary language of instruction, with seventy-five using Romanian, seventy-one using Hungarian, and five using Polish, respectively. Together, all 732 schools host some 400,000 students.[39] I personally do not remember any other single issue during the Russo-Ukrainian ethnic conflict where, regardless of their level of hostility toward one another, officials from Russia, Poland, Romania, and Hungary "have all heaped vitriol on it."[40]

In response to this law, Romanian President Klaus Iohannis canceled his official state visit to Kiev. On September 21, 2017, he issued a statement to the press in New York that he "would not travel to Ukraine next month in protest over a bill that obliges schools to teach the Ukrainian language only." He also added that the bill drastically limits "the access of minorities to education in their native language." Hungary, Moldova, and (unsurprisingly) Russia called for this legislation to be revised. Hungarian Prime Minister Viktor Orban said that "withdrawing existing minority rights are not usual in European culture" and that "it drives Ukraine further from European Union membership." In a more personal equivocation, Hungarian Minister of Foreign Affairs Péter Szijjártó remarked that, by passing this law, Ukraine had effectively "stabbed Hungary in the back."[41]

This story continued for more than two years. On December 4, 2019, Szijjártó, in response to numerous complaints from Hungarian compatriots from the Zakarpattya Oblast, threatened that Budapest would block Ukrainian efforts to join NATO until Kiev restored the Hungarian minority's right to teach their children in their native tongue without hindrances or restrictions. Szijjártó sounded this ultimatum following a statement he had made a few months earlier on October 3, according to which Ukraine did not take any steps to revise the norms of the legislation that outrightly violate the rights of all ethnic minorities in the country.[42] In support of the concerns of Eastern European leaders, the *Venice Commission* of the *European Council* (*The European Commission for Democracy Through Law*) issued a statement on December 6, 2019, calling for Ukrainian officials to revise the requirements of this law and immediately elaborate a new line of legislation regarding the rights of linguistic minorities.[43] Overall, this criticism, combined with the continuing protest of Eastern European leaders defending the most crucial building block of ethnic identity of their corresponding ethnic diasporas, were also pertinent to the totality of Ukrainian linguistic legislature. Namely, this concerns another law *About the Provisions of Functioning of Ukrainian as the State Language*, which had been signed by President Poroshenko on May 5, 2019, just five days before the end of his term (and was slated to be put into effect on July 16, 2020). In fact, all this criticism objectively undermined the longstanding linguistic policy of Ukrainian ethnocentric nationalists (referred to as "patriots" by their supporters). Following their rise to power in the aftermath of the Euromaidan movement in 2014, these nationalists began working toward the demise of the *Law About the Foundation of State Policy of 2012*, which had been specifically created to expand the rights of regional languages in Ukraine and was severely criticized by the "patriotic" opposition of Yanukovych's regime as a part of "Russification."[44]

I plan to return to these peripeties pertaining to the *linguistic building block of Russo-Ukrainian ethnic conflict* in the subsequent chapters. However, at this point it would be far more interesting to describe more of the behavioral reactions to the European criticisms on the part of ethnocentric nationalists within the Ukrainian ethno-political elite. In their case, they were especially infuriated by the very well-organized Hungarian protests in the Berehovo District and their renewed claims for territorial autonomy, as well as a corresponding address of the Hungarian National Assembly to the Russian State Duma to coordinate their efforts.

Oleg Soskin, politologist and advisor for former Ukrainian President Leonid Kuchma, supposedly told the *National News Agency* (*NSN*):

> [The] process is underway, [the] National Guard is deploying, and helicopters are in the air around Berehovo, this address is an interference of Hungary into the internal affairs of Ukraine. I think that soon there will be sending an "Alfa" Spetznaz of the (SBU- Security Service of Ukraineand maybe a tank division … If the interference [of Hungary] continues, then Ukraine will deploy middle-range missiles "Ol'ha," etc. … In this particular case, Hungary has supported [our] Russian enemy, hence now it will be an escalation of Hungarian-Ukrainian relations. Ukraine is 42 million strong and Hungary is only 8 million. America and NATO will support Ukraine. Naturally, [the] Hungarian army will not stand against [the] Ukrainian army. It is ridiculous … Kiev will undertake sanitation measures, which had not been undertaken in Crimea, Donets'k, and Luhans'k, to cleanse separatists when they are still in minority.[45]

At the same time, Vyacheslav Kovtun, another Ukrainian politologist, echoed these claims on a Moscow-based Russian talk show.[46]

In addition to the regularities outlined above, this story also serves as a visual confirmation of my own thesis regarding the dangers of the *potential transformation of local ethnic conflicts when principal building blocks of ethnic identity are jeopardized* into a regressive confrontation between kin states to the sides in conflicts. This is especially apparent when one or multiple kin states are supporting their ethnic minority diasporas and have real political weight and military tools at their disposal.

Fortunately, from the beginning of this recent crisis among the Ukrainian ethno-political elite, including regional representatives, there were those who did not share the militant zeal of ethnocentric nationalists. Hennadiy Moskal', governor of Zakarpattya Oblast, was one of the first and most vocal critics of the linguistic legislation and has been arguing that this policy vividly contravenes the *European Charter for Regional or Minority Languages* since 2017. (Later I will further demonstrate how this legislature contradicts several articles of the Ukrainian constitution as well). Moskal's spokesman, Yaroslav Halas, told *RFE/RL Ukrainian Service*: "We understood that *this law is primarily directed against the Russian language*, because it dominates the capital, the eastern regions. But in Transcarpathia, it hits the national minorities."[47] Still, some other politicians were allowed to, rather poorly, conceal their mocking ethnocentric positions. For instance, former Justice Minister Serhiy Holovaty told Tony Wesolowsky—senior correspondent for *RFE/RL*—the following: "If private individuals in Ukraine, or Governor Moskal', want, they can establish a private Hungarian school and fund it."[48]

Popular Ideas of Ethnocentric Nationalists and the Introduction of Modern Categorization of Peoples of Different Ethnic Backgrounds in the Ukrainian Linguistic-Educational Sphere

One could understand why, in the 2019 presidential elections, the majority of Russian-speaking populations of eastern, southern, and even central Ukraine would vote against Poroshenko in favor of Volodymyr Zelensky, who personifies the new wave of young politicians. Additionally, this surge of support comes from a campaign built on slogans that accumulated the broad public protest against the system, with the primary factors being disappointment with Poroshenko's ethnocentric linguistic policy and his failure to resolve the bloody conflict raging in Donbas. Zelensky lavishly peppered his speech with promises to promote both the restoration of peace and the revision of linguistic legislation following a popular referendum. He also vowed to suppress all piercing corruption within the state and bring the oligarch Poroshenko to justice. Naturally, these promises made him invariably popular and, out of those who made their way to voting stations, more than 73 percent lent their voices to him: he won in all Ukrainian regions except for Lviv Oblast, where Poroshenko still held a majority (elections did not take place in Crimea or the breakaway areas of Donets'k and Luhans'k).

The disappointments of the latter's supporters were brightly expressed by one Andrii Drozda. I allow myself to summarize his insights because they actively illustrate the typical conceptual ideas of the Ukrainian nationalists/patriots and their ethnocentric project of state-building, as well as their resentment of any hypothetical alternative discourse. Elements of both were also skillfully sounded out by Zelensky and his team of pragmatic young activists from *Sluga Naroda* (*People's Servant*), thereby exploiting popular sentiments of the electorate during the campaign. According to Drozda:

> Lvivians were shocked by the results of the elections, we are scared and lost. One can understand the reasons of the fright. Since the end of the 1980s, it was predominantly Lvivians who have been actively pushing the country forward: first towards independence, and then to Europe. They were starving on the granite and sleeping in the tents in Maidan, went against bullets courageously. In the end, the country recognized their weightful contribution ... and elected "a clown" as President. It is a knife at the back, a control bullet in the head. ...
>
> The worst thing is that our compatriots voted for him. The catastrophe is that the Ukrainians rose in opposition to our candidate ... It had happened before, but we have been patiently doing our bid. Chornovil had not become our President. [Viktor] Yushchenko had not done well, but after the second Maidan in 2014 it seemed that at last everything had been going our way. We have been moving toward Europe, our culture and language have

been strengthening; we have beaten the Moskal's! We have overcome! Corruption—it is OK for now—we'll settle this once we are in the European Union … But now these illusions are evaporating. After the elections, it has appeared that 14.5 million Ukrainians are thinking differently than the majority of Lvivians… Even in Lviv about a third of its electorate supported Zelensky. And in Ternopil and Ivano-Frankivs'k Oblasts he won. Does it mean that Halychyna [Galicia] is no more!? … An irony is that Lvivians believed that conservatism, faith in blameless traditions and patriotic morals are omnipotent … Yet Lviv's historian Yaroslav Hrytsak has been telling us for ten years that "moral values must be spread over the bread."[49]

However, the recent course of events has vividly displayed that the disappointment of Halychyna national patriots was rather premature. Though lacking any serious political experience, Zelensky, for those citizens of the ethnically and socially torn country polarized and fragmented amid tamping corruption and a continuing economic crisis, has become a candidate for being "the last hope."

The masses tired of the hardships and losses for which they had blamed the oligarch Poroshenko and his administration quickly put forth their unwarranted emotional expectations for wide-scale normalization. From settling the dialogue with Donbas to the revision of otherwise destructive initiatives within the socioeconomic, humanitarian, and linguistic spheres, they invested their trust in this sparkling showman and his command of young activists. Together with his one-party-led parliamentarian majority, this new president received, for the first time in the modern history of Ukraine, a full *carte blanche* in order to "correct" the most odious elements in the heritage of his predecessors. Instead, he soon became indistinctive from Poroshenko, both in terms of rhetoric and practical implementations of policy.

On March 26, 2020, Zelensky's representatives departed from the *Three-Side's Contact Group* in charge of facilitating negotiations over Donbas (later he elevated their status by incorporating high-profile officials from executive branch and deputies of parliament). Even minimal measures, such as a second long-awaited exchange of detained individuals, had been toppled (later it happened, with big difficulties, on a minimal level). Under pressure of ethnocentric nationalists, Zelensky fired Serhy Sivokho, who was both a moderate advisor to the secretary of the National Security Council and head of the peacekeeping efforts in Donbas. Nationalists were incensed by his calls "to correct mistakes, forgive, and ask forgiveness" from the civilians of the uncontrolled areas. Following this, on March 31, 2020, Zelensky'sparty sided with the *Block of Petro Poroshenko*, and radical deputies of the parliament from *Golos* (*Voice*) adopted a highly controversial and unpopular law concerning the creation of a free land market in Ukraine. Farmers in Ukraine are afraid that the rich black belt of soil shares within this land—the last richness of Ukraine left after years of deindustrialization and demodernization—would end up easily expropriated by rich oligarchs and foreign companies alike. In fact, this law has been adopted under unprecedented pressure exerted by the *International Monetary Fund* (*IMF*). This organization has gone so far as to threaten a complete halt in any and all monetary traffic into Ukraine, which the country's ill economy desperately needs, if this law is not adopted. In response, Zelensky gave into this blackmail, which vividly indicates his volatile position of dependency on one part of the international conjuncture, as well as radical nationalist groups. But Zelensky is also afraid of the popular outrage that may spring up as a result of this law's adoption. It is for this reason that before the last reading, an article allowing for the trade of large shares of this precious land to foreigners mysteriously disappeared from the final variant of the bill. Unsurprisingly, the *IMF* was livid with this outcome, with the repercussions essentially resulting in political deadlock.

The other milestone of the ethnocentric nationalists can be found through their minority within parliament and other representative structures. Despite their small size, this group has the support of the most proactive, well-organized, armed, vocal, purposeful, and passionate ethnic mob organizations that control the streets. They enjoy lavish support from the oligarchs, including the seemingly omnipotent Minister of the Interior Arsen Avakov, and can easily intimidate, or even physically remove, any critics or opponents while going virtually unpunished. Once again, this results in another form of deadlock.

The most significant victory of those in favor of an ethnocentric project of state-building was a "new variant" of Poroshenko's education law, which was signed by President Zelensky with nary a murmur on March 13, 2020, and had significant social consequences. This law, whose full name was *Zakon pro povnu zahal'ny serednyu osvitu* (lit. The Law about Full General [and] Middle Education) had been previously adopted by the *Rada* (parliament) two months earlier on January 16. According to the Presidential Office, "it introduces practical instruments that would help to put in action an educational reform that had been founded in 2017."[50]

This "new variant" of Poroshenko's law provides "three adaptation cycles of teaching: in 1st–2nd forms, 5th–6th forms, and in 10th form." It also introduces "three models" of study of the Ukrainian language at schools.

The "*first model*" is for the "indigenous"/"native" peoples of Ukraine who do not live in their linguistic environment and/or have no state structure to protect and develop their languages. The authors of this model aimed this stipulation, first and foremost, at the Crimean Tatars. According to the plan, they may instruct their children in their own language from the first to the eleventh (a total of twelve) forms, along with a substantial study of the Ukrainian language.

The "*second model*" is reserved for those schools where the instructed language of ethnic minorities *is one of the official languages of the European Union* (Russian is not among them). Depending on the particular linguistic group and their surrounding environment, they may use their mother tongue, along with the study of the state language (Ukrainian) in elementary school. Following the fifth form, 20 percent of the annual volume of study hours in all disciplines must be instructed in Ukrainian, with a gradual increase to 40 percent by the end of the middle grades (at the start of the ninth form). This increases in high school, where no less than 60 percent of every subject's curriculum must be taught in Ukrainian.

The "*third model*" will apply to the remaining ethnic communities—ethnic minorities whose language *belongs to the same linguistic family as Ukrainian* and/or who predominantly live compactly within their own linguistic environment. Based on previously presented information, it should come as no surprise that this categorization is reserved almost exclusively for ethnic Russians. Regardless, this group is allowed to use their native language along with Ukrainian only during the elementary grades. But from the fifth form onward, an astonishing 80 percent of school disciplines should be taught in the state language of the titular ethnic nation.[51] When paired with the aforementioned state language law, which came into effect on July 16, 2020, this linguistic policy will have several significant consequences:

(1) First and most importantly, it has officially introduced an original *categorization* of the peoples of different backgrounds in the linguistic-educational sphere. The order of most to least privileged groups in this regard is as follows: Ukrainians, then Crimean Tatars, followed by ethnic minorities with strong

support from their kin states/metropoli in Europe, with the Russians at the bottom as the most denigrated ethnic group. The irony of this situation is that this kind of policy is typical for a totalitarian or imperial absolute monarchical state. In particular, it harkens back to the Russian Empire, with the categorization of its various peoples along linguistic lines, and Stalin's delineation of territorial polities that were, to a large extent, arbitrarily drawn by the *"Father of all the Soviet Peoples"* along these same linguistic principals. Such categorization is atypical for the European democracies whose "family" Ukraine officially craves to join. However, it does share many similarities with the policies of other ethnocentrically nationalistic ideologies and their respective state-building projects.

(2) The primitive categorization of people into "we–them" groupings is also a characteristic feature of so-called *bytovoi natsionalism* (an informal nationalism of everyday life among common people) that was highly pervasive within the post-Soviet space and encompasses more intense feelings of mistrust toward some outsiders. Amid the instability of everyday life in this transitional period, outsiders are usually considered *ne svoi—chuzhie—*"aliens," which stunningly resembles *inorodtsy*, a term dug up from the long-forgotten oblivion of the Imperial era holding a pejorative connotation of outside ethnics who lack culture and are generally uncivilized. For example, in the Caucasus, Russians, who came to the region during the Soviet period, have been considered as such for the longest time. It was only until very recently, however, that they were perceived as noticeably different from the so-called "root Russians," who had lived in the region for generations and practice the same customs/way of life as their neighbors. For the most part, these "root Russians" have been loyal to the region, became familiar with its various traditions and practiced them in their households, learned to speak the native languages, and willingly serve the society in a multitude of capacities. As applicable to Ukraine, in particular, noted scholar Dr. Huseyn Aliyev recently published an interesting bit of research dedicated to this phenomenon, which he has dubbed "ethnic defection." Based on "micro level interview data from Ukraine," he clearly demonstrated that a lot of "Ukrainian Russian-speakers mobilized for the government" during the recent ethnic conflict, "driven by the strong sense of ethnic responsibility, engendered in the perception that" pro-Russian separatists "misrepresented ethnic values of Ukraine's Russian-speakers." The rebels in Donbas "are suspected by their co-ethnics of violating or disregarding socio-cultural, ideological, or religious values of their ethnic group." Until now, these Russian "ethnic defectors" loyally served as officers and soldiers not only in Ukraine's official military forces but also in the ranks of voluntary nationalistic paramilitary formations—*dobrobaty*, or Battalions of Volunteers—like *Azov, Donbas,* or *Dnipro.*[52] In the early 1990s, I saw how many of my Cossack co-ethnics served and died in the Ossetian or Abkhazian paramilitary groups, not as mercenaries or soldiers-for-hire, but out of respect and devotion for the "causes" of those ethnic groups, their friends and neighbors, whom they had lived among for ages. Of course, this is not to say that some such people, especially those in the state military, are not ruled by a variety of personal or situational considerations (career perspectives in the military, for example). But, as my personal investigations have shown, the most common consideration was formulated by my interview of Valerii, a former resident of Mariupol' City in Donbas (who arrived in America in June 2018). Valerii told me that he and his Russian-speaking comrades had fought against the rebels because many of them were "bad and violent people," with him also believing that, unlike Russia, "Ukraine is a democratic state that had many important guarantees to preserve Russian-speaking culture and language that are being taught to their children" (interview on June 26, 2019, Isaenko, File II, list 23).

As such, this new linguistic policy and the act of ethnic categorization may estrange such people from pro-government support and will certainly deepen the ethnic split between Ukrainians and "root Russians."

(3) It will further undermine the Russian-speaking population's trust in the Ukrainian political system, President Zelensky, and his promises by negatively affecting his personal rating.

(4) It further estranges the population of rebel areas in Donbas and shuns perspectives of a peaceful resolution of the conflict there. Additionally, a majority of the Crimean population will be hard-pressed to rejoin Ukraine as part of the lowest sociolinguistic cast.

(5) It reinforces the legalization of an informal ethnocentric subdivision of people onto the so-called "*svidomye*" ("conscientious" patriot), "real" native Ukrainians actively supporting the efforts of national organizations, who necessitate building Ukraine as a unitarian state for the total domination of the titular ethnic nation in all spheres and over all other people—not reliable, or even pro-Russian, elements.[53]

(6) It may end up stimulating mass appeals to the European Court on Human Rights from those who see the new linguistic-educational legislation as a transgression against basic human rights, which are protected by the European Charter for Regional or Minority Languages and Articles 10, 11, 24, and 53 of the Ukrainian Constitution, which are "guaranteed and cannot be amended." Article 10 specifically assures the "free development, use, and protection of Russian and other languages of the national minorities of Ukraine. The state is conductive the learning of languages of international communication," of which Russian is among them as an official language of the United Nations.[54]

(7) It may promote an increase in outmigration from the Ukrainian state, resulting in the repatriation of ethnic minorities to their kin states out of fear of escalating hostilities.

(8) An ethnocentric linguistic-educational policy (which is totally absorbed by ethnicity) sends a plain signal that those who still cherish the illusion of possibly developing regional rights in the linguistic-cultural sphere inevitably abandon this goal under the threat of persecutions, according to the newly established legal norms. Therefore, they are symbolizing *the end of a federalist state-building project* (which has been intact as an alternative to the unitarist plan since the early 1990s) and consociational power—which translates as the sharing of guarantees with the ethnic Russian minority. (Currently Rada stipulates an adoption of the new law of Zelensky about the *koreynne narody* (indigenous peoples) which are referred to only Ukrainians, Crimean Tatars, Karaims, and Krymchaks. No doubt this law will deepen the split in the relationship between them and Russians and other ethnic minorities who were excluded from this category).

Those responsible for elaborating these laws had hoped to persuade the European organizations that they would bring more homogeneity and integrity to the Ukrainian state. In reality, however, they achieved the opposite result. It ultimately strengthened the position of separatist forces, as well as those in Donbas insisting on the irredentist plan to "reunite" with Russia, because they now were able to more effectively manipulate the consciousness of their compatriots. In turn, these same compatriots (as shown through my interviews taken from the area) fear "total Ukrainization" in the sphere pertaining to the most critical building block of their ethnic identity—their language. Comparative studies of ethnic conflicts indicate that *highly energetic and uncompromising enforcement* of such a policy, especially in those regions where a particular ethnic group (a national ethnic minority) constitutes a decisive majority of the population, is doomed to fail. As we have seen, ethnocentric politicians have to reckon with this reality in the Hungarian-dominated Berehovo District, where they assigned this minority to the second category, with fewer ethnocentric linguistic requirements; in the case of the Russians, they would prefer exerting as much pressure as they can. This means that they scorn the regularities of ethnic mobilization, even in the case of Crimea and Sevastopol, where Russians constitute the ethnic majority and the prevailing precedent. As a result, Russian propaganda can be easily planted and exponentially grown in the "freshly manured soil" put in place by Ukrainian nationalists.

The Case of Crimea in 2014 through the Prism of Ethnocentric Behavior

In the sections dedicated to the *nationality building block* in relation to the current Russo-Ukrainian violent ethnic conflict, I plan on putting all aspects of this complicated case under greater scrutiny. In the context of this part, however, it is important to demonstrate how particular attributes of ethnic identity promoted radicalization within the principal sides of the Crimean conflict that are responsible for the "rapid absorption of ethnicity" into political and social life prior to the annexation of this strategically vital territory.

As of 2014, the combined population of the *Republic of Crimea* and *Sevastopol* totaled around 2,248,400 people (with 1,889,485 and 395,000 people, respectively).[55] These numbers are down from the 2001 *Ukrainian Census* data, which put the population closer to 2,376,000 (Autonomous Republic of Crimea: 2,033,700, and Sevastopol: 342,451).[56] Within the combined 2014 population, 67.9 percent (1,432,078) were Russian, 15.7 percent (344,515) were Ukrainian, and 10.6 percent (232,340) were native Crimean Tatars. In comparison to the 2001 Ukrainian census data, the size of the Russian and Crimean Tatar populations remained relatively stable, while the Ukrainian population had dropped dramatically from a previous total of 24 percent (576,600).[57] Further corresponding with this data, the 2014 Russian census indicated that *84 percent* of Crimea's inhabitants identified Russian as their native language, with 11.4 percent citing Crimean Tatar (also known as "Crimean"), 3.7 percent citing Tatar proper, and 3.3 percent citing Ukrainian.[58] One has to agree with Yekelchyk that this "discrepancy between self-identified ethnicity and mother tongue is indicative of the cultural assimilation of Ukrainians during the late Soviet period." The resulting "hybrid identity" in places like Crimea and Donbas (as well as in the southeastern regions of Ukraine) was due to both longstanding cultural assimilation (during the imperial and late Soviet period by Russians and during the early Soviet period via Ukrainization) and "an allegiance to the Soviet version of modernity and, following its disappearance, to the strong paternalistic regime in Russia."[59] The fact that both Russian and Ukrainian peoples belong to the same linguistic family only further cemented this impact over time. Thus, a lot of people in both ethnic nations, especially those who lived in regional proximity to one another over a long span of time, may choose to identify themselves either as Ukrainian or Russian depending on the changing political circumstances auspicious to the preservation of social privileges and the retention of access to vital societal resources and executive power.

When Russian political domination was restored following the 2014 Crimean *Anschluss*, many Ukrainians left for Ukraine. This was not necessarily done in response to "persecution" by Russian authorities (as some propagandists stated when interpreting the above-cited statistics), but rather because they simply chose to identify themselves as "Russians" in the Russian census taken that same year. Similarly, the Russians, who (via the same kind of pragmatism) had previously identified themselves as "Ukrainians" in 2001, did so in the midst of Ukrainian domination (which was at its highest from 1991 to 2014).

When the tide shifted, they simply "became Russians" again. I had many acquaintances, especially those from families with mixed origins due to intermarriages, from Crimea and Donbas who told me about such "ethnic defection" or "hybrid identity" with a good sense of humor. In the words of Valerii, the previously mentioned Mariupol' resident: "What can we do if the politicians are so crazy that they have begun again playing the ethnic identity card and the success in your life now depends on your ethnic credentials? If the Ukrainian side prevails, we'll greet it: 'Glory to Ukraine!' 'Glory to the Heroes!' If it would be the Russian side on top, then we'll cry out: 'Glory to Russia!' 'Glory to Putin!'" (interview, June 26, 2019, Isaenko, File II, list, 43).

Based on her own recorded interviews of common people in these same regions, Anna Fournier points toward a variety of perspectives on both language and "territoriality" (the latter as a part of a nationality building block of ethnicity). In a 2017 publication, she came to the conclusion that "language and identity in Ukraine may or may not intersect" and "that *territory* and identity may also intersect or diverge in interesting ways." Some of her informants, who supported Ukrainian independence, spoke "of the congruence of territory and national/cultural substance." Other informants combined "a concern with preserving Ukrainian territorial sovereignty with a *supranational* identification." Still, there are others for whom "the preservation of territorial sovereignty is compatible with a belief that the boundaries of the *'real Ukraine' exclude the Donbase.*"[60]

Interestingly enough, in December 2019, Alexander J. Motyl, a famous American historian with Ukrainian origin, strongly supported this very idea. He argues that "reintegration would be too costly; beyond an expensive reconstruction, it would entail reintegration of a deeply pro-Russian region at a time when Ukraine is finally moving West." He further states that this region constantly supported the most retrograde and pro-Russian forces in Ukraine; without Donbas, Ukraine has become more transparent and liberated itself from the tenets of corruption and criminality.[61] This last statement is rather disputable, if one remembers the aforementioned negative characteristics of the current situation as presented by President Zelensky.

In the final chapter of this book, I will demonstrate that, by 2014, linguistic and other ethnic concerns, especially *geopolitical cleavages/security dilemmas* (with economic concerns playing a subsidiary role), had been supercharged by the ethnocentric factions on both sides of the Russo-Ukrainian violent ethnic conflict. Ethno-political entrepreneurs managed to reshape their own interests while simultaneously exploiting the ethnic identities of their respective communities, bringing them into an alignment that allowed ethnic tensions in Crimea to reach its boiling point. All of this took place amid what Ukrainian historians call the Revolutsiya Hidnisti in Kyiv, which their Russian colleagues and opponents refer to as an "illegal *coup d'état.*"[62]

In the beginning of 2014, the majority of the international Commonwealth refused to recognize the incorporation of the Crimean Peninsula into Russia within the administrative boundaries of two recognized Ukrainian regions: the Autonomous Republic of Crimea (ARC) and the city of Sevastopol.[63] Both the Russian Federation and Crimean authorities claimed that the "reunification" of these regions with "Mother Russia" was "legal." According to the official Russian position, this annexation was the result of a broad "public dissatisfaction" with "the illegal actions" of the adherents of Euromaidan, who had staged a "forceful change of power in Ukraine" that February. It was also spurred on by the subsequent refusal of the authorities of both the autonomy and Sevastopol to recognize the legitimacy of the new Ukrainian provisional government, which they labeled as a "junta."[64]

On March 27, 2014, the 80th Plenary Meeting of the 68th Session of the UN General Assembly adopted Resolution A/RES/68/262 regarding the territorial integrity of Ukraine. In it, the UNGA reconfirmed the sovereignty of Ukraine over both the ARC and Sevastopol and refused to recognize any changes in the status of these territories, including those based on the results of the March 16 "all-Crimean Referendum" as it "has no legitimate bases" (though 96.77 percent of voters of ARC and 95.6 percent of Sevastopol residents supported "reunification with Russia").[65] According to the official position of the Ukrainian authorities, including present ones, the annexation was an act of "armed aggression of Russia against Ukraine."[66] As professor of law at George Mason University Ilya Somin states: "There was a referendum … and those who participated overwhelmingly voted for unification with Russia. However, that referendum was fraudulent, and conducted under Russian military occupation, combined with intimidation of opponents."[67]

International legal institutions and Western specialists (with minor exceptions) share a common consensus and consider the joining of these territories to Russia as illegitimate and a violation of international law, specifically as annexation or *Anschluss*. Thus, the major bulk of outside observers supports the Ukrainian side of this ethnic conflict in terms of both *de jure* and *de facto* law. This approach reflects, in part, the ambivalent treatment of such cases by the standards of international law, the imperfections of which I have discussed in the introduction of this volume. In the absence of a clear legal framework that allows for the *self-determination* of an ethnic group (the majority of ethnic Russians in Crimea) or the right of a nation-state (Ukraine) *to its territorial integrity*, which was previously agreed upon and guaranteed through bilateral Ukrainian-Russian agreements, the powerful actors within the international arena are usually ruled by geopolitical interests as they understand them.[68]

In the case of Crimea, the driving forces of ethnocentric mobilization on the Russian side were (1) Sergei Aksyonov's "*Russian Unity*" political party, (2) the "*Russian Block*" party, (3) Cossack paramilitary formations, (4) so-called armed "groups of self-defense, including Cossack and Serb volunteers," and, of course, (5) Russian authorities in Moscow.[69] The Ukrainian and pro-Ukrainian side consisted of (1) Mustafa Dzhemilev and Refat Chubarov's "*Mejlis of the Crimean Tatar People*," (2) the "*All-Crimean Ukrainian Rada*" popular movement, (3) an organization known simply as "*Ukrainian House*," (4) the "*Euromaidan Krym*" movement, (5) a subsect of fanatical fans—also known as "ultras"—of the "Tavira" football team, and (6) ethnocentric authorities in Kyiv.[70] Both sets of organizations were themselves responsible for the ethnocentric interpretation of contemporary current events and political decisions made by both the Russian and Ukrainian leadership, and are thus responsible for the regressive development of the entire conflict.

In the report of the Crimean *OSCE Mission*, who were present within the region from March to April of 2014 and investigating the human rights situation during the conflict, one may make an important observation. The OSCE report states that a controversial decision made by the Supreme Rada of Ukraine concerning the cancellation of the acting "[2012] law concerning language" and the preparation of a "lustration law" directed at Russian activists supercharged existing ethnic tensions on the peninsula. Even if these measures "were not the decisive factors that caused turmoil in Crimea," they nevertheless promoted the mobilization of a considerable part of the "*ethnic Russians*" against the newly formed provisional government in Kyiv.[71] Regarding language (as an important ethnic building block of ethnicity), political measures proposed by ethnocentric nationalists in the Ukrainian legislature included the following: (1) denying access of Russian-speaking representatives to governmental positions; (2) making Ukrainian the sole language in both state functionality and education; and (3) prohibiting the election/appointment of officials who could not speak Ukrainian.[72] These intentions awakened and rejuvenated the fear of

Ukrainian political revanchism within the hearts of the Russian majority in Crimea. These reasonable fears, which are rather typical of ethnocentric behavioral patterns, were then fed by both enormously exaggerated, almost gossip-like, alarmist reports in mass media and the radical and/or ethnocentric statements of politicians on either side of the conflict.[73] However, this should come as no surprise, as it has already been explained how real wars fought along ethnic lines, like the previously discussed clashes and pogroms, are usually preceded by a fictitious war of lies and half-truths in the media.[74]

The above-cited OSCE report further stated that, within the atmosphere of ethno-nationalist hysteria, the Crimean Tatars and ethnic Ukrainians, especially those who actively supported the territorial integrity of Ukraine, also found themselves in a very vulnerable position.[75] Many ethnic Ukrainians were fearful of targeted ethnic persecutions because they believed (not without reason) that the Russian majority, feeling the impact of ethnocentric propaganda, held the entirety of the Ukrainian community as "choleric and violent" in the adherence to Ukrainian territorial integrity. The presence of several unaffiliated armed groups, the appearance of Russian and Crimean Tatar paramilitary "self-defense" formations, and the red-hot situation over Ukrainian military bases (peppered by rumors that the Ukrainian authorities wished to invite American/NATO forces to the peninsula) only added fuel to the rising ethnic tensions.[76]

The *Mejlis of Crimean Tatar People* joined the fray in February 2014, where it proceeded to loudly support European integration and Ukrainian activists in Euromaidan—which itself was in direct opposition to the pro-Russian ARC supreme council, where ideas of Russian reunification were dominant. Sociologists V. I. Mukomel and S.R. Hikin outlined the principal interests of the Crimean Tatar ethnic elite thusly: (1) in the case of reunification with Russia, they would lose many things, considering their occupation of prominent positions in the politico-economical spheres of the peninsula; (2) the vast majority of them shared similar optimism in and expected benefits from European integration via Turkey and Ukraine; (3) they had the *Mejlis* acting as a quasi-state organ; (4) they had a vested interest in the lavish monetary grants from both the West and Turkey; and (5) their ideological loyalty to the Ukrainian authorities was vivid, in large part due to their hostile attitude toward Russia, whom they considered responsible for their biggest chosen historical trauma—Stalin's deportation of their people in 1944. The reason why the new Russian Federation inherited this ire is because it declared itself the legitimate "heir" of the former USSR.[77] The Mejlis would regularly dispatch groups of activists to Kyiv in order to reinforce Ukrainian nationalists and their standing against the *spetznaz* "Berkut" police force of President Viktor Yanukovych, who was later forced to flee. In the grand scheme of things, the Ukrainian government and press actively exploited Tatars within the country as the "anti-Russian" factor by exacerbating their underlying acute historical trauma of victimization suffered at the hands of the Soviet/"Russian" government.

Before staging the referendum and deploying the troops in unmarked green fatigues (which spawned the colloquialism—"polite green little fellows"), Russia unleashed a massive informational campaign directed toward the Russian majority in Crimea (as well as the rest of Russia). To this end, the Russian authorities aimed to convince their audience that these radical Ukrainian nationalists—dubbed "Ukrainian Nazis"—were poised to inevitably attack them. In particular, the Russian press was actively circulating a statement made by Ihor Mosiychuk, a leader within the ultra-radical Ukrainian ethnocentric nationalist organization *Right Sector*, threatening to send an ironically named "train of friendship" to suppress Crimean separatist activity. In fact, this was the last bit of evidence required to fully legitimize the worst Russian ethnic phobias regarding their Ukrainian neighbors.[78] Another stereotype installed into the Russian collective mind centered on the threat of NATO's engulfment of the peninsula with the aid of the "junta" in Kiev. President Putin, his political elite, political analysts, and press commentators from presidential pull began propagating the thesis that the West had cultivated and "tamed" ethnocentric nationalists in the Ukrainian Maidan to secure Crimea for NATO (invoking the name of prominent Euromaidan activist Oleksandr Turchynov), culminating in Russia being declared an "aggravated party" and a victim of NATO's expansionism. The Russians were reminded that their country had been treacherously invaded by Western armies through many overland campaigns: by the Nazis in 1941; by the Central Powers in 1915; by an alliance of "Western" powers in 1853 (in Crimea specifically); by Napoleon-led European invasion; by the Swedish in 1709, assisted by Ukrainians of Hetman Mazepa; and even by the Poles in 1610. In the repulsion of the "most recent" act of Western aggression (with Putin pointing out that detachments from several conquered Western countries had been integrated into Hitler's army), Soviet Union had paid a nigh unfathomable price—27,000,000 lives, predominantly those of civilians, were annihilated as a result of collateral damage and crimes against humanity, in fact racial war on annihilation- the genocide. Now, with the armed forces of NATO positioning themselves along the Russian border to the Baltic States, Romania, and Bulgaria, it only serves to further call upon a memory of the catastrophic consequences of Operation Barbarossa. In short, this acute chosen trauma of the Russian people was exacerbated, sparking epic Shakespearean recollections of past crises during the present crisis.

And so, fueled by these stereotypical ethnic phobias, Putin began justifying Russia's actions in the peninsula as a form of "self-defense" driven by the need "to deter the West." This is what he meant on March 18, 2014, when he invited Russia's elite to the Kremlin's gilded hall to solemnly announce the "reunification" with Crimea. He told those who had gathered: "Like a mirror, the situation in Ukraine reflects what has been happening in the world over the past several decades [following the collapse of the USSR]. Our Western partners, led by the United States of America, prefer not to be guided by international law, but by the rule of the gun." He also reiterated that *the West had crossed the red line in Ukraine*, leaving Russia no choice but to deploy its troops to Crimea.[79]

Thus, one may say that even if *ethnic phobias* were not the overall decisive factor in the Crimean Anschluss, they obviously promoted the ethnocentric mobilization of the Russian population within and outside Crimea and eased *a strategic goal of the Russian government to secure control and sovereignty over this vital area* by a considerable margin, setting the stage for a potential military confrontation with the West.[80] Certainly this campaign, enhanced by the active exploitation and radicalization of another important building block of ethnicity—*a commonly shared history*, especially one of acute chosen traumas—mythologized collective memories of victimization by the old and the presence of "ethnic enemies" reemerging on all sides. For the Russian side of this conflict, these behaviors essentially predetermined the result of the referendum before it even hit the floor, if one may take into the bargain that a considerable part of the Russian-speaking population belongs to the retired and acting Russian military and their families, who fully share Putin's historical narrative.

In the aftermath, Putin continued this campaign with ever-increasing efforts. During a televised Q&A session on April 14, 2014, he reintroduced the old imperial concept of *New Russia* (*Novorossiya*) into modern Russian political discourse. In particular, he said:

> It is not Russia who is guilty in this conflict, but Ukraine with its nationalistic moods and also indirectly the West that encouraged the present state of affairs ... Concerning the feeling

regarding Crimea, we have no right to fall into euphoria. Other territories (Khar'kov, Lugansk, Donetsk, Kherson, Nikolaev, and Odessa [here the Russian spellings of these place names are cited]) the Soviet government transferred [to Ukraine] in the 1920s … God knows why. They were originally known as Novorossiya with the capital in Novorossiysk. Ethnic composition there was approximately 50/50. This situation differs greatly from that of Crimea [where the Russian population constitutes an overwhelming majority].[81]

It should come as no surprise that the taking of this position incensed the regressive development of the conflict in Donbas. In fact, both the Crimean case and the subsequent separatist revolt in Donbas would open a new bloody stage of the overall Russo-Ukrainian violent ethnic conflict, this time harboring the potential to spiral out into a full-scale confrontation between the East and West, with unpredictable consequences. From that point on, in comparison to the other violent ethnic conflicts in the post-Soviet space, this one in particular became the most dangerous form of ethnic collision. This danger came both in terms of the potential carnage that violence would bring as well as the inherent difficulty in finding a possible solution or plan of reconciliation. As written in the Adats of the Caucasus, "blood spilled by the native brothers against each other has no ransom." The ethnic cleavage between Ukrainians and Russians began with the *linguistic building block*, then, as we have seen, the building blocks concerning *nationality* and a *shared history* were radicalized, which called for the beginning of a bloody stage of conflict. Gradually, the *biological building block* was brought to bear with the appearance and circulation of thoroughly absurd "ethno-genetic populist" theories regarding the varied biological origins of these peoples. Ultimately, the very provocative *religious building block* added its own momentum in 2018, leading to the split in the Orthodox Church. All of this only served to fan the flames of the current ethnic conflict, to the point where it became almost irreconcilable for the foreseeable future. However, as other violent ethnic conflicts in the post-Soviet space in which *all five principal building blocks of ethnicity* were radicalized can demonstrate, the intermediation efforts of the international community could put an end to the unrestricted violence of the "hot stages." In fact, the long-term impact of this kind of intervention may actually lead the conflict into a "frozen" (or, in my own terminology, "smoldering") phase. But this is only a stopgap measure, as the complete reestablishment of "normal" interaction between the two sides holds an indefinite period of time between the cooling of heads and proper reconciliation.

Concerning the "commonly shared history" building block, an amazing stage was opened when the presidents themselves began interfering with and interpreting events of the past to garner justification of their present political discourse. Both sides recite historians with academic degrees and (mostly) with the correct ethnic credentials to construct "nationally oriented" histories that must help to "restore the historical justice" that was mutilated by Communist totalitarianism. The idea was to impress the necessity to rewrite (or defend) "history," to "undo" previous injuries and/or change borders. History was being weaponized by both individuals and leaders alike, while at the same time these people had become prisoners of their supposed "history." Such "historical narratives" aim to refurbish old grudges and spare no efforts to reassert one's victimization under recent policies forged through ethnic rivalries. I personally found that this "victim position" in all nationalistically interpreted "histories" brought about by these post-Soviet conflicts is usually linked to ideas of entitlement. Such "histories" thereby served as effective platforms "to legitimate excesses against those whom one believes have wronged one's own group in the past."[82]

On May 31, 2006, in order to deal with the construction of a nationally oriented history, Ukraine formed a special organization for the restoration and preservation of national memory of the Ukrainian people—*Ukraïns'kii Institut Natsional'noï Pam'yati* (*Ukrainian Institute of National Remembrance*). As previously seen in Russia, President Putin himself laid down ruling directions for the "correct" interpretation of the past. In the sections dedicated to the *commonly shared history building block* of the Russo-Ukrainian violent ethnic conflict, I will return to this problem with greater detail. But in more general terms, some specialists have already noticed that both sides have managed to form completely opposite and mutually exclusive "historical narratives" using the same sources and events but interpreted from drastically different ethnic orientations.[83] According to numerous examples from nearly every violent ethnic conflict, one can decisively prove that those seized by ethnocentric nationalism *do not want to have their history rendered accurately.* "Histories" of chosen traumas are not written to shed more light on a historical event from every then-present perspective but rather to defend a specific point and legitimize certain feelings and emotions toward it, which are capable of mobilizing and uniting the "victimized" people behind charismatic leadership for the "last battle" against their new, yet historically old, enemies. Joseph Brodsky eloquently exposed these kinds of rationalizations, noting: "Evocations of history are bare nonsense. When one pulls the trigger in order to rectify history mistake one lies. One always pulls the trigger out of self-interest and quotes history to avoid responsibility or pangs of conscience"[84] In an objective sense, such "histories," when taught on a daily basis at schools and universities or spread by mass media, indisputably strengthen those same ethnocentric ideologies and behavioral patterns of common people that have been legitimized by this malignant form of nationalism.

Ethnocentric Nationalism as a Consequence of a "Polarized and Fragmented Society": The Role of Oligarchs

Oligarchs are usually defined as businessmen who hold a considerable level of influence on both politics and the economy. Since the advent of independence in 1991, Ukraine's internal political life has, to a large extent, been directed by the contradictions and rivalries between different oligarchic groups. The process of transitioning political power from one group to another can assume many forms, ranging from standardized democratic elections to "people's revolutions," the latter of which sees the active involvement of highly organized ethnocentric organizations. Alongside these rivalries, international contradictions also play a major role. It was by no means an accident that the *Revolutsiya Hidnisti* took place after autumn 2013, when pro-Moscow President Viktor Yanukovych (who is himself an oligarch) postponed the signing of an *Association Agreement* with the European Union in exchange for a lavishly promised subsidy of fifteen billion rubles from Russia. However, this was not the primary cause of the revolution. Rather, this event can be more appropriately described as a pretext—a triggering moment—for the revolution as a whole. Protests on *Maidan* (lit. "Square," the colloquial name for Kyiv's central square) began in October 2014, as a peaceful demonstration organized by middle-class representatives. The primary drive behind the popular unrest was due to a deep and longstanding dissatisfaction with the corrupt oligarchic regime of Yanukovych's Donbas clan. In fact, he and his closest associates were striving to recreate an older model of an oligarchic state originally created by former Ukrainian President Leonid Kuchma, with themselves at the head.

These collected events, now better known as "Euromaidan" (a combination of the setting and the participants' desire for the *Association Treaty* between the EU and Ukraine) brought many different people and perspectives together in a profound way. Serhy Yekelchyk points out that "few protesters knew the details of the proposed Association Agreement, but 'Europe' served as a popular short-hand slogan implying democracy, rule of law, and economic opportunity—all the things ordinary citizens found lacking in Yanukovych's Ukraine."[85] Indeed, European integration inspired a large number of people, especially those from the newly spawned post-Soviet middle class. They sincerely believed that this agreement would make the Ukrainian state effective enough to prevent oligarchs from looting the economy, which they had effectively been doing since the dawn of Ukrainian independence through massive kickbacks (bribery), intentional inflation of costs, and outright embezzlement for the instant enrichment of their respective clans.[86] No matter which group of oligarchs rose to prominence under whatever political regime they helped come to power, these clans, without fail, strove to maintain conditions for the reproduction of wild frontier capitalism, or as other specialists call it, "crony capitalism." In order to maintain the auspicious conditions for this kind of capitalism, in which they saw themselves as proverbial ducks on the pond, it became necessary to play ethnic identities against one another. As such, they did not hesitate to invest huge sums of money to support the corresponding ethnocentric groups and political movements. Additionally, the faith held by most of the protestors that European integration could put an end to the vicious cyclical rise of oligarchic regimes was so strong that they did not care to read the original text of the Agreement itself. If they had, then they would have quickly noticed the rather controversial articles contained within regarding the minuscule "quotas" on Ukrainian products that would be allowed in European markets, which would, in fact, be monumentally detrimental to the long-term health of the country's economy.

Ukrainian historians also tend to underplay the fact that the Maidan also hosted another category of groups and individuals who combined the ideas of social protest and European integration with their own personal agenda, including stunningly ethnocentric (if not completely jingoistic) doctrine. Despite the fact that ethnocentric activists from *Right Sector or Svoboda* (*Freedom*) were the minority in Maidan, they were, as Yekelchyk admitted, "the best organized and the most visible" force on display. Their slogans revived nationalist greetings from the 1940s, namely "*Slava Ukraini*!" ("Glory to Ukraine!") and its response, "*Heroiam slava*!" ("Glory to the Heroes!"). These cries were joined by the return of the red-and-black banner of the *Organization of Ukrainian Nationalists* (*OUN*), while images of its leader, Stepan Bandera, "became widespread."[87] More importantly, however, is that the ferocious energy of these well-organized activists, who continuously received reinforcements from ideological supporters located predominantly in the western provinces, gained momentum week after week. This continued until it finally fanned out into the highest degree of bloody clashes with law enforcement on February 19, 2014. Led by these activists, Euromaidan protestors (much like the Bolsheviks in St. Petersburg almost a century prior) seized control of strategic locations around Kyiv, which led to the collapse of Yanukovych's oligarchy-laden political regime. The new authorities were first headed by Speaker of the Rada Oleksandr Turchynov and, from June 2014, by elected President Petro Oleksievych Poroshenko, another oligarch. Both men fully supported the ideas of Euromaidan's radical vanguard and used them to formulate the institutional design of the new regime, making it unfavorable to the Russian population in the eastern and southern regions.

During the above protests, the Russian Diasporas in these areas began to evaluate the rapidly changing political situation, ultimately finding it an unpleasant fit to its own ethnic identity. After a few months of exploring the extent of their own identities and sociopolitical interests, and under the impact of violent actions attributed to the newly assembled authority in Kyiv, the most active among them began building their own alternative authorities, setting themselves on a course for radicalism. Soon, it became evident that this course of action was only possible in regions in which the new government, who was acting at the behest of mobile ethnocentric nationalist groups, did not hold a monopoly on the use of violence. As Ivan Loshkariov and Andrey Sushentsov showed in a 2016 publication, "the involvement of Russia and international volunteers complexifies the situation in Donbass and the identity formation process in unrecognized republics also known as *DNR* and *LNR*"—the *Donetsk People's Republic* and the *Lugansk People's Republic*, which appeared as a result of all these calamities (here these authors spell the place names according to the Russian linguistic standard).[88]

I'll get back to the important details regarding the radicalization process of the Russian Diasporas at this stage of the conflict in the next chapters. At this point in the analysis, and as a part of a macro-background of its regressive development, one should heed the fact that during its many years of independence, Ukraine (unlike Russia) failed to consolidate its political elite into a single entity that could encompass the entire country. The current political system is such that the winner of its elections gains almost absolute power within the country, alongside those tycoons that stood behind the winner. This pattern returns time and again, due in large part to the lack of inherent checks and balances within the system.[89] As a consequence, the victorious group and its leader usually replace top authorities in the capital and regional heads with those who are loyal to them. This is how the leader forms his new elite over a period of time, usually representing groups of discrete regional interests (recently dubbed "Donetskie," "Dnepropetrovskie," etc.), and why Russians tended to support political parties and presidential candidates from eastern Ukraine (the *Communist Party*, Yanukovych's *Party of Regions*, etc.).

When the victor and his "discrete" people begin forcing out local authorities in order to spread their control over vital businesses, resources, and managerial positions, they effectively raise the stakes so high that the following elections, as Andrew Wilson indicated, turn into a dangerous crisis.[90] Richard Sakwa also noted that nearly all nationwide elections were accompanied by and resulted "in divisions between the east and west."[91]In contrast with the Russian political system, all of these peculiarities and repeating patterns make the Ukrainian oligarchs and outside powers put more priority on the acquisition of personal profit rather than national interests. As such, they funnel their financial resources to promote their "placemen" into key political positions. They then continue to abuse the central executive authorities' inability to consolidate power in order to exploit all manner of societal divisions, especially regional ones, with vividly marked ethnic and sub-ethnic connotations. These oligarchs do not care about these ethnic concerns in any moral regard and cynically support whichever side can produce the largest amount of personal profit through new business opportunities and provide more comfortable conditions for their companies following their political ascension. For example, Petro Poroshenko, Ihor Kolomoyskyi, and Serhy Taruta supported several 2004 pro-democratic protests in favor of Viktor Yushchenko, whom they believed would grant them and their businesses beneficial concessions.

The Three Major Ideological Streams in Modern Ukraine

Both before and after Euromaidan, there existed three major ideological streams in the Ukrainian politicum, the first of which is the Ethnocentric Nationalists. This stream is the most well-organized and best represented in the world of mainstream media resources/outlets. This is owed to the fact that some of these groups previously "belonged" to a particular set of oligarchs, thereby earning their financial and political support. As one may have guessed, their programs usually aim to create a Ukrainian nation-state for people who ascribe to the Ukrainian identity, which are based on the core elements and ethnic attributes historically formed in western Ukraine. Gradually (especially after 2014), this stream would become the nucleus of mainstream ideology, uniting both Ukrainians and even a number of Russian-speaking representatives who are loyal to the national cause (with the hope of including elements of *civic nationalism* into the state-building project) under a common *political identity*.[92] Overall, this leading group sees their country as a part of the EU and NATO and "in the avant-garde of the West's confrontation with Russia."[93] (President Zelensky and his cohort gradually have adopted many of these principal goals and ideas of ethnocentric/integral nationalists). They tolerate the notion that the conflict in Donbas should be settled through the use of force, with the most radical of them ready to take extreme measures to force the disloyal population out of the country. This process, which also includes the exclusion of the "alien" Luhans'k and Donets'k from Ukraine, is aimed at consolidating a homogeneous ethnic community in the remainder of the Ukrainian state.

The second stream is working to unite ethnic Russians and Russian-speaking Ukrainians (alongside representatives of other ethnic communities) who *reject most of the goals and values of Euromaidan*. Originally, such people had been loyal to the Ukrainian project. However, following 2014, many of these people began to rally against many of the movement's accomplishments regarding language and other ethnic attributes, as they increasingly lose the perception or desire to be associated with Ukraine.

The third group of the politicum is what I define as the supporters of *civic nationalism*, who insist on "inclusive statehood as a precondition for the territorial integrity" and sovereignty of Ukraine. They reject radicalism of all kinds, instead promoting an idea of "national interest," which they understand as a preservation of the Soviet legacy (in terms of territory and economy), east–west geo-economic ties, Ukraine's neutral status, and the diversity of the population with a strong localist/regionalist component.[94] In addition, this stream also seeks "balanced policies on culture and language" and the reassurance "that the Galician way of life not be imposed on the populations of Donetsk and Crimea."[95] Oftentimes, ethnocentric nationalists refer to members of this group as "Russians" and subject them to various forms of badgering and slurs, even if most of them are ethnic Ukrainians from different regions.

The Corresponding Support of Oligarchic Groups

The value of the combined assets of the 100 richest Ukrainians is equivalent to 23 percent of the entire country's GDP, totaling $34.8 billion. Of that, $30.6 billion (roughly 79.7 percent) is split among the top fifty. To this end, the *Kyiv Post* once wrote, "At least one thing in Ukraine shows enviable stability from year to year—the list of the wealthiest [Ukrainian oligarchs]."[96] Although the six richest have remained in their positions since 2018, their fortunes have seen a significant decrease in the last five years, due in part to the continuing conflict in Donbas and the shift away from collusion with the previous presidential administrations.

Rinat Akhmetov remains the richest oligarch in Ukraine (with an estimated worth of US $9.63 billion), who primarily made his capital through the iron, steel, and thermoelectric industries. His holdings include the industrial giant *Systems Capital Management*, stakes in the mining and steel firm *Metinvest Group*, and energy firm *DTEK*. He owns important media holdings and the *Shahtar Donets'k* football team. He had also "smoothed over an early reputation for mixing with tough street operators."[97]Subsequently, Akhmetov consolidated his wealth due to his longtime ties with Ukraine's top officials and was an outspoken supporter of the ousted President Yanukovych, for whom he "bankrolled" his *Party of the Regions* as an MP for it. Soon after, he'd drastically change sides and began supporting Poroshenko's government, which was "calling for national unity."[98] If one takes his influence on the Russian-speaking East into account, it may be fair to assume that his support is desired by Zelensky's administration as well.

The son-in-law of former President Leonid Kuchma, Viktor Pinchuk, is worth around $2.31 billion. He is a cofounder of the steel producer *Interpipe*, the *Bank Credit Dnipro*, and a pair of philanthropic organizations (*Pinchuk Art Center* and the *ANTIAIDS Foundation*) in Kyiv, which are both headed by his wife, Olena Pinchuk (the daughter of Leonid Kuchma). More importantly, he owns several major media resources, including the *ICTV* and *STB* television channels. Pinchuk also funds *Blair's Faith Foundation* and, according to Nick Kochan, "treads a fine line between east and west."[99] Thus, he might (if he so chooses) be helpful in promoting elements of civic nationalism within the abovementioned spectrum of Ukraine's ideological streams.

Another oligarch, who allegedly holds a pro-Russian position, is Vadim Novinsky. He owns *Smart Holding Group*, which invests in mining, oil and gas, banking, agriculture, retail, shipbuilding, and real estate, which is worth an estimated $1.76 billion (which is actually down 22 percent from last year).[100]

Last year, Ihor Kolomoyskyi and his partners in the *Privat Group*—Henadiy Boholyubov (reinforced by Oleksiy Martynov)—switched places on the wealth list in third and fourth, with fortunes of $1.48 billion and $1.37 billion, respectively. Kolomoyskyi owns the famous 1+1 Channel and, until recently, was a longtime associate of Volodymyr Zelensky. He was a fierce opponent of the Yanukovych regime, serving as an informal head of the Dnipropetrovs'k clan (who own *F.C. Dnipro*), and was once allied with the "Gas Princess," Julia Tymoshenko—former Prime Minister and Yanukovych's political prisoner. In short, he is a typical political opportunist and adventurist, even if he is, according to *The Guardian*, the most professionally qualified.[101]

Kolomoyskyi was a crucial figure in aiding Ukrainian *Dobrobats*—pro-government volunteer paramilitary formations following the far-right ideological stream—in preventing the advance of pro-Russian forces in 2014 by investing millions of dollars to equip them. He was also on good terms with the president, at one point taking up President Poroshenko's offer to serve as governor of his home province of Dnipropetrovs'k. However, this would not last in the long run, as Kolomoyskyi's financial interests eventually led the two into becoming rivals and, eventually, enemies. He would later gain the informal status of the most powerful figure "outside government, given his role as the patron of the President Volodymyr Zelensky."[102] As previously mentioned, the latter garnered a massive level of popularity among the Ukrainian populace, who were worn down by the rampant corruption of Poroshenko's regime, in large part thanks to the exposure granted on Kolomoyskyi's Channel 1+1. However, the long-term effects of close proximity to the controversial tycoon eventually put Zelensky in a highly impractical position. Specifically, it played a part in his troubles with the IMF, who were holding up their monetary transactions to Ukraine. Not only was this due to the lagging passage of the previously mentioned free land market law, but also because of the required promotion of the so-called "anti-Kolomoyskyi law," which had yet to be adopted as well (the litigation around this law is still underway). The IMF voiced their avid concerns that Zelensky "is not doing enough to recover funds that Mr. Kolomoyskyi is accused of stealing from his Ukrainian Bank, *Privatbank*, which cost the government in Kiev $5.6 billion to bail out in 2016."[103]

Needless to say, Mr. Kolomoyskyi denied all accusations of embezzlement. He is also openly frustrated that both Western diplomats and the IMF itself have been urging Zelensky to prevent him from regaining control over *Privatbank*, which had been seized from him and his co-owners by Poroshenko in 2016. In an act of vengeance, he drastically altered his political rhetoric from unquestionably supporting the ethnocentric/anti-Russian nationalists and the West to vying for peace talks in Donbas. He allegedly said that it is high time for Ukraine "to give up on the West and turn back towards Russia." He continues, saying that "they're stronger anyway. We have to improve our relations ... People want peace, a good life; they don't want to be at war. And you [America] are forcing us to be at war, and not even giving us the money for it."[104] This serves as a transparent hint that this alleged "stolen money" of his was real and that he spent it on the Ukrainian paramilitary militia fighting pro-Russian separatists in Donbas.

It was at this point that American diplomats began to worry, as no matter what Kolomoyskyi's motivation might be, he still has an extensive level of influence on the Zelensky administration. As a matter of fact, during past impeachment hearings in Washington DC, American officials "have described Mr. Kolomoyskyi's influence as one of the biggest problems facing Mr. Zelensky's administration."[105] Kolomoisky controls the news media and finances a lot of deputies from Zelensky's *Sluga Naroda* party in the parliament, and thus exerts certain influence, which he may use at odds with American and European efforts to further strengthen Ukraine's pro-Western geopolitical orientation. Thus, the United States has vacillated for a long time on how to handle Mr. Kolomoisky. Ultimately, America struck back. On March 5, 2021, the United States placed sanctions on the tycoon and members of his family. Some of Mr. Kolomoisky's assets (his American real estate is worth several hundred million dollars) have already been seized in separate actions by the US Justice Department. According to Secretary of State Antony J. Blinken, Mr. Kolomoisky posed a risk for "ongoing efforts to undermine Ukraine's democratic process and institutions." It is a plain signal that the new American administration of Joe Biden has assumed an aggressive new approach in dealing with corruption in Ukraine.

For the "statists"—or civic nationalists in my terminology—an unexpected wave of support came their way when pro-Russian oligarch Viktor Medvedchuk—"*kum*" of President Vladimir Putin (meaning that Putin is the godfather of Medvedchuk's daughter, Daryna)—returned to Ukrainian politics in the summer of 2018 as a member of Vadim Rabinovich's *For Life* party. Doing so was only part of an ambitious plan to unify every politician on the pro-Russian spectrum regardless of individual specificities. The RosUkrEnergo group of "gas workers," representing the *Opposition Block* (15 members of the parliament) and headed by Yuri Boyko and Serhy Lyovochkin—who themselves are business partners of known oligarch Dmyro Firtash—joined this alliance on the eve of the 2019 presidential elections. The resulting *Opposition Block–For Life* political party has since garnered a presence in the Rada, with backing from 13 percent of voters as of the last parliamentary elections, and promotes the idea that negotiations on the status of peace in Donbas should be conducted in the Kyiv-Moscow-Donets'k-Luhans'k quadrangle, which is utterly inadmissible for ethnocentric nationalists.[106] Additionally, MP Taras Kozak, creator of the *Noviny* (*News*) holdings company—which includes several media outlets, such as *112 Ukraine*, *News One*, and the *ZIK Channel*—and Medvedchuk's political comrade, also took part in this new alliance. As of now, the ideas of this political force, strongly buttressed by the informational backup of these popular media outlets, have won on its side a considerable part of the population in the southeastern regions, and at one point, the ratingof the new *Opposition Block* has even exceeded that of presidential party *Sluga Naroda* in these areas.

Former President Petro Poroshenko is the only billionaire in Ukraine who did not lose any wealth within a couple of last years, in spite of the fact that he soundly lost the presidential election to Zelensky. Regardless, the *Petro Poroshenko Block–European Solidarity* party remains a major player in the parliament and is still a political vehicle for the ethnocentric nationalist ideological stream within Ukrainian society. Poroshenko, who is often called the "Chocolate King," on account of his ownership of the Roshen Confectionary Corporation (a name derived from his own [Poroshenko]),which is worth $1.25 billion. Additionally, and like any self-respecting oligarch, he also owns his very own media broadcaster—Channel 5.

Last, but certainly not least, is Mykola Zlochevsky, who Natalia Datskevich cites as owner of the oil and gas company *Burisma Holdings*, which is entangled "in the recent Trump–Ukraine whistleblower scandal" and thus hosted an enhanced polarization of the American political establishment.[107]

Overall, this brief survey demonstrates that the Ukrainian oligarchs constitute relatively a small group of people in opposition to standard democratic trends, as they use their economic opportunities and disproportionally strong political influence to pursue their own narrow and highly egotistical interests. To promote the latter, they subjugate and privatize mass media outlets and, through them, never hesitate to play into matters concerning ethnic identity so long as it fits their immediate interests. Thus, they actively contribute to the further polarization of Ukrainian society along these same regional/ethnic lines.

A sworn enemy of Poroshenko and "omnipotent" Interior Minister Arsen Avakov, former president of Georgia (who is currently wanted on criminal charges in the same country) and former governor of the Odesa Province, Mikhail Saakashvili (who was recently appointed as chair of the Council on Reforms by Zelensky) allegedly said that "it is necessary to reform [the] Ukrainian political system," as Ukrainian oligarchs "are overgrown with private armies" and are preparing an infrastructure to divide the country "into five different Ukraines."[108]

In view of rapidly losing popular support domestically because of his failure to achieve any progress in Donbas (which he blamed on Russia, rather traditionally repeating Poroshenko's mantras), and because of his abovementioned ethnocentric linguistic policy, alienating the Russian-speaking population, Zelensky quickly caught the new wind from Washington, DC. He understood that he could get strong international support for making a clean break with Mr. Kolomoisky, and especially cracking down on the other oligarchs, who can be accused of collusion with Moscow's interests, since it would be perfectly reflecting Mr. Biden's long-term strategy "to clean up Ukraine's internal politics as the best protection against Russian influence." In a lightening move (though in a plain violation of constitutional norms), he closed all oppositional media outlets belonging to Taras Kozak (*112 Ukraine*, *News One*, *ZIK Channel*) and imposed sanctions on their owner. In doing so, he has got a sound appraisal from Washington, DC, for this action of closing down the "Russian propagandistic speaking trumpets," with a silent approval from the EU too. In a further blow, by the approval of Zelensky, the *Security Service of Ukraine* (SBU) placed economic sanctions on the leader of *Opposition Block*, Viktor Medvedchuk, and his wife, Oksana Marchenko. However, it did not bring the desired internal consolidation of ethno-political elite around the president, but rather alerted other oligarchs like Poroshenko that he might be next. More importantly it did not elevate a deep ideological split in the society, since it had been instigated by much more fundamental causes pertaining to the major track of present research.

Overall Ideological Polarization in Modern Ukraine in the Context of Russo-Ukrainian Ethnic Conflict

The struggle between the lasting legacy of Soviet/Communist totalitarianism and the push toward ethnocentric (anti-Soviet and then anti-Russian) integral nationalism is an all-encompassing reality in modern Ukraine.

As stated above, the presentation of chosen traumas amid the current societal crisis and the steadily rising number of negative ethnic interactions hold a much greater potential for spurring on ethnic mobilization. In almost all of the sixty-eight ethnic conflicts taking place across the world at this very moment, we can observe how entire groups of peoples are uniting around mythologized collective memories of one (sometimes several, depending on the length of the conflict) key traumatic events. During the conflict, this helps people to find some manner of expression through campaigns against the "victors"—those who had caused losses so painful that they entrenched themselves into the very essence of the ethnic group. Hundreds of years may have passed since any given event's occurrence—such as when the Turks defeated the Serbs at Kosovo in 1389 or during the conquest of Constantinople in 1453—yet the need for atonement persists throughout the centuries. Serbs and Greeks, who were unable to mourn those abovementioned momentous events, have woven them into a clearly visible and tangible thread of their ethnic identity by hoping and working toward some manner of revenge. Historians within these slighted ethnic groups write volume upon volume of work centered on such traumas in order to keep them relevant in the collective ethnic memory as images of inhumane monstrosities—alien ethnic neighbors who had malignantly, cunningly, and purposefully caused these defeats in the first place. Similarly, playwrights and other artistic members of the group create Shakespeare-esque masterpieces to dramatize (both literally and metaphorically) these very same tragedies and, by extension, the "evil" set upon them. Both contributions then serve as the reason behind the unification of the group, as they must all help to achieve any form of atonement, revenge, and/or compensation against their ethnic enemy that they feasibly can.

The Jews will never forget nor forgive the horrors of the Holocaust. Armenians will do much the same for the 1915 Genocide. Arabs will forever remember the loss of Jerusalem (Al-Kuds in Arabic) in 1967. The Irish—the Drogheda Massacre, Penal Laws, and the Potato Famine; the Azerbaijanis/Azeris—the loss of Nagorno-Karabakh to Armenia in the previous ethnic war of 1991–1994; the Georgians—the loss of South Ossetia (Shida Kartli in Georgian) and Abkhazia (Abkhazeti); the Crimean Tatars, Karachays, Kalmyks, Balkars, Chechens, Ingushians, and numerous others—their deportation by Stalin during World War II; the Cossacks—the Decossackization Genocide; and so on and so forth. It is by no means a difficult task to find such key chosen traumas in the collective memories of all peoples living on our planet. But those groups embroiled in ethnic conflict are especially interested in rejuvenating, exacerbating, and redirecting these key ethnic traumas in order to rally the masses behind their charismatic leaders. All of this is done in order to repulse the modern "aggression" and "plotting" of new, yet distinctly familiar, ethnic rivals/enemies once and for all, thereby "cleansing the infection" and allowing them to build their mono-ethnic home. Usually, the interpretations of these rejuvenated traumas are shared by the entire people during times of ethnic conflict against real or perceived perpetrators of their particular traumatic events.

Since gaining its independence, "nationally oriented" Ukrainian historians have put forth a great deal of effort to give/recreate/rejuvenate an underlying chosen trauma—the premeditated and genocidal *Holodomor* Famine of the early 1930s—within the collective memory of the people. As a matter of fact, one of the earliest accounts of this tragedy to appear in recent historiographies belongs to my longtime colleague and friend Professor Wayne M. Morris.[109] His book, *Stalin's Famine and Roosevelt's Reconstruction of Russia*, is well written and based on the primary sources available from the records of the United States Congress. In 1992, I witnessed Wayne's presentation on the famine in the USSR to the students and faculty of North Ossetian State University (NOSU) in Vladikavkaz, Russia. It is worth pointing out that, before this point, many Soviet/Russian/Ukrainian students and researchers alike had been effectively excommunicated by attempting to study this tragic event (as well as any other part of the "dark side" of controversial Soviet history). A model of clarity, Wayne's presentation, backed by the precise citations of the original source material, depicted horrendous scenes of mass starvation, hecatombs of dead bodies that blocked the rivers of the North Caucasus (particularly the Kuban region), the desolated landscapes normally home to the nomadic inhabitants of Northern Kazakhstan, the depopulated Volga regions, the death of entire Ukrainian villages, the cynical reaction of Stalin and his party bosses, and the unprecedented cruelty of Red Army units firing upon a people desperate to escape their famine-ridden homes. All of this was taken in by the packed auditorium, which itself was dead silent. Students had never heard about such things from their professors, so to them it was a major shock. A veritable bomb of reality ...

In June 2019, while recording the previously referenced interviews, I contacted a former Ossetian student of mine, a woman named Olga who now resides in Asheville, North Carolina. Twenty-seven years ago, she had also attended Wayne's presentation, and it had left a lasting impression. Olga recounted that she and her schoolmates, whom she was still in touch with, remember his lecture as one of the brightest and most memorable aspects of their time in the History Department of *NOSU*. In Olga's words, it divided both the students and faculty alike into antagonistic groups. The young people were in favor of the necessity to study the history of the *Holodomor* from all perspectives, including the one as demonstrated by Professor Morris. On the other hand, the faculty, who represented the older Soviet school of thought, utterly resented the presentation, its perspective, and the desire to explore this incident. One among them—who was a decorated veteran of the Great Patriotic War (WWII), highly respected in the Republic of North Ossetia–Alania, and a Hero of the Soviet Union (the highest distinction one could receive in the USSR)—told those who opposed the faculty's viewpoint that if such "truths" had been taught so broadly in the Soviet Union then "we would have never won the war."

Instead of this, Soviet students were taught that rich peasants—"*kulaks*"—resisted collectivization by concealing grain and slaughtering both domestic and draught animals rather than surrendering them to the collective farms, as well as initiating open rebellions against the newly established Soviets. Supposedly, this was the "primary reason" for the famine that spread over some parts of the USSR in the early 1930s. Students never learned about the abovementioned horror or the bone-chilling figures of the dead in these areas. Ukraine and the Kuban region of the North Caucasus, as well as the Don and Volga areas, were among the traditional grain-producing domain and, according to Soviet historians, were home to the largest concentration of *kulaks* and displayed a severe resistance to collectivization efforts. This particular depiction of the area was so highly spread thanks in part to the impact of *Podnyataya tselina* (*Raised Virgin Land* or *Virgin Soil Upturned*), a novel written by Nobel Prize winner Mikhail Sholokhov, which was a required reading in all Soviet high schools. Simply put, this book depicted the exact same story of the Don Cossack *stanitsas* ("villages") in accordance with the aforementioned "official" history.

Questions surrounding Stalin's intentions during this tragedy have been discussed among foreign historians since the enactment of Khrushchev's 1956 "de-Stalinization" campaign at the 20th Communist Party Congress. Some authors argue that Stalin was equally oppressive to all people who stood in the way of the general party line and rapid modernization, regardless of their ethnic/regional identity. Collectivization and the high quotas mandated by the Kremlin to the grain-producing regions (in complete disregard for the environmental or human conditions) were put into place to achieve one overarching goal: feed the cities initiating the gigantic construction effort aimed at industrialization. After a plentiful harvest in 1930, the following years saw the normally rich soils of Ukraine and the North Caucasus fail to produce enough crops for the farmers to meet their quotas (which Stalin and his party bosses did not want to reduce accordingly). This resulted in "death by starvation for many of the farmers of the southwestern Soviet states."[110] In his essay on the topic, Hiroaki Kuromiya found "no evidence to substantiate the claim that Stalin, and by proxy the Kremlin, intentionally starved millions of Ukrainians to death."[111]

Today, Ukrainian historians estimate the number of losses from the Holodomor in the republic "at between 3 and 3.5 million famine deaths." According to Stanislav Kulchytsky, in tandem with demographers and taking into account the number of unborn children, the figure must be at least 4.8 million in Ukraine alone.[112] This constitutes a little over 68 percent of the approximately seven million people that died across the entirety of the USSR.[113] Ukrainian historians began building their current concept of the Holodomor by pushing off the following line from Khrushchev's 1956 *Secret Speech* to the Party Congress: "The Ukrainians avoided meeting this fate [mass deportation, as seen with other nationalities] only because there were too many of them and there was no place which to deport them [*sic*]."[114]

The idea that Stalin genuinely wanted and deliberately planned to eliminate the entire Ukrainian ethnic nation cannot be fully substantiated through the existing documents, much like another of Khrushchev's claims from that same speech, in which he insisted that "the Father of the Soviet People" had planned his military operations with the globes normally reserved for geography classes, wherein this remark was heavily criticized by the "Marshal of Victory," General Georgy Zhukov.[115] The point of this is the realization that *there is no direct evidence to either substantiate or refute this claim.* To this end, I agree with McBarrett S. Good, a well-dressed student of mine from Appalachian State University, who wrote in his thesis: "Despite historical facts, the truth will be manipulated to fit the ideas of the one who tells it. In this case, the nationalist groups that are attempting to rally the Ukrainians against the Russians will do what is necessary to prove that they were intentionally targeted to create a sense of victimhood amongst the populace."[116] Thus, in contrast to the above-cited arguments of other historians, Ivan Drach states that the famine was "just one stage in the planned eradication of the Ukrainian nation."[117] In fact, Khrushchev had given a great deal of validation to this claim.

Bohdan Klid and Alexander Motyl compiled a previously cited collection of documents, including numerous survivor recollections of the Holodomor (a Ukrainian term meaning "extermination through starvation") and a large body of other sources and literature. Both this and all other efforts made by Ukrainian historians have helped to establish a firm foundation for "seeing that the man-made famine was a part of a broader attack against the Ukrainian nation." In the 2000s, this development allowed Ukrainian authorities to enact an international campaign to recognize the Holodomor as genocide of the Ukrainian people. Soon after, Canada and the United States both passed legislative acts to the effect and recognized it as such. As one might have expected, Russian authorities were strongly opposed to recognizing the Holodomor, as well as other terror tactics employed against the Ukrainian political and cultural elite, as a premeditated act of genocide, and according to Yekelchyk, they (the Russian authorities) estimated this as a move by the Ukrainian authorities to intentionally "distance modern Ukraine from its Soviet past—and from historical ties with Russia."[118] Therefore, within these circumstances, they consider these movements a "constructivist activist" approach to ethnocentric mobilization.

However, and unlike other ethnic groups in the post-Soviet space who found themselves embroiled in conflict and united by the mythologized chosen traumas, Ukrainians have been more polarized than united in regard to the Holodomor. In my opinion, this occurred because Ukraine, since the first dawning of independence arrived in the country, has been constantly and periodically failing to form a fully fledged national political spectrum in which the political forces of diverse trends, ethnic backgrounds, and orientations might be formally recognized. So, under any political administration, the above-cited principle of "more or less" eventually regressed into the more divisive "either-or." In the context of chosen traumas as important vehicles for ethnic mobilization, one may go so far as to say that Soviet Communist totalitarianism traumatized one part of the Ukrainian socium, while the system implemented by the Nazis wounded another part for generations to come.

One part of the country ideologically resents everything that, to even the slightest extent, resembles "radical [or in my terminology—ethnocentric] Galician Nationalism," while another part resents everything of the Russian Imperial/Soviet (i.e., "leftist") legacy. Both sides do not tolerate the presence of "statists" or even politically neutral people, who are finding themselves stuck between these two political poles as if they were milestones. However, I am not necessarily implicating those crazed marginal groups stationed at the extreme flanks of either side who carry the key notions of a "master Aryan race" or a "dictatorship of the proletariat," respectively. Rather, I am talking about the solitary and relatively large contingent of the populace for which organizations like trade unions and ideas of solidarity, equal rights (including ethnic minorities and individual rights), the rights of sexual minorities, feminism, ecology, and so on, are alien notions being enforced by either outsiders—mainly from the West—or through the legacy of Soviet dictatorship. Further still, there is another relatively sizable part of the population for which the importance of the state language, an autonomous Ukrainian church, the traditions of integral patriotism, or anything else related to the titular ethnic nation are identified with the columns of torchbearers crying out "*Ukraina po nad use*!" ("Ukraine is above all!"), in which this people hear "Zig Heil!"

This polarization and connected perception of a threat on an individual or group level is closely related to the responses garnered from the actions of any given regime that hurts one's family or group more than others or in support of whichever regime's ideology proved more convincing for this or that family/group. Only in recent times has such a dichotomy found a form of expression in the popular perceptions of the Ukrainian socium, which is to say that it has been reduced into a battle of *pro-Ukrainian* versus *pro-Russian*.[119]

That is how the corresponding representatives of those same antagonistic groups label all views on the five building blocks of ethnicity; their leaders, oligarchs, political parties ("leftists" or "rightist"), churches, their professional art masters and producers of creative works, and even down to such minuscule aspects as their dress and food—everything must relate to the two distinct triads denoting the cultural markers of difference. *This means that we are, in fact, dealing with a typical ethnic conflict at full sway in which both active sides profess a kind of ethnocentric nationalism that, in Ukraine specifically, has a long-established historical tradition.*

The Tradition of Ethnocentric Nationalism in Ukraine: A Brief Survey of "Pro-Ukrainian" Integral Nationalism

In a combined effort, Paul Magocsi, Kenneth Farmer, and Andrew Wilson compiled one of the most comprehensive and unbiased accounts regarding the history of Ukrainian nationalism during the three distinct periods of the country's existence: the Imperial, the Soviet, and the post-Soviet (1990s) periods, respectively.[120] Within the context of this chapter, in which I elaborate on a particular aspect of a theoretical tool, I need to provide a brief outlook on this type of ideology that Andrii Bilec'kii, the founder and leader of the "nationalist front," the *Social-National Assembly* (*SNA*), defines as a "self-dependent, great powerful, *ethnocentric*, authoritarian idea."[121] In his own words, this nationalism "is based on the three pillars: racialism, sociality [social instinct], and great powerfulness," which, according to him, serves as the modern continuation of the same nationalist traditions laid out by Ukrainian leaders in 1930s.[122]

Ideologues

One may trace the gnoseological roots of Ukrainian nationalism to the ideas of the historian Nikolai Kostomarov and the poet Taras Shevchenko—members of the first organization dedicated to the political character in the empire, *Kirillo-Mefodievskoye Bratstvo*. Kostomoarov penned a thesis that detailed the "two Russian peoples," wherein "Southern Russians" constitute a separate ethnic nationality. In the 1890s, Halychyna [Galicia] played host to Boris Grinchenko, Ivan Franko, and Mykhailo Pavlyk, who founded the *Russo-Ukrainian Radical Party*. At the dawning of the twentieth century, the previously demonstrated split in the Ukrainian national movement spawned many different trends, with the struggle among them resulting in the idealization and politicization of the very notion of "nationalism." Representatives of the *narodovsty*—the general term for precursors of modern ethnocentric nationalists—received a great deal of support from the Austrian-Hungarian Imperial government based on their own resentment toward the Russian Empire and their hatred of "Russophile" movements within their sphere. The *Revolutionary Ukrainian Party* would debut in 1900, only to have the *Ukrainian People's Party* split off from it two years later under the leadership of founder Mykola Mikhnovs'ky (1873–1924). Like many other *narodovsty*, Mikhnovs'ky descended from the line of an old Cossack family of Greco-Catholics. A lawyer, journalist, and social activist, he became a cofounder of the first political party in East Ukraine—the *Revolutionary Ukrainian Party* (*RUP*) and later became the leader of the aforementioned *Ukrainian People's Party*, a prominent member of the *Brotherhood for Self-Determination*.[123] He was also one of the many organizers behind the Ukrainian national armed forces—a prototype of which was his *Polubotok Military Club*, who later joined the renowned *Sichovykh striltsiv* (*the Sich Riflemen*) under the command of Yevhen Konovalets. On May 3, 1924, Mikhnovs'ky was found hanged on the property of his longtime political ally, Volodymyr Shemet. Officially, his death was ruled as a suicide, but there were rumors that the Soviet secret service (*GPU*) was involved. This could very well be true, especially given Mikhnovs'ky's political ideas and activity prior to his death. As a member of the Ukrainian national independence movement, he actively took part in organizing terror attacks against Russian monuments. Within the pages of his "Ten Commandments" of the Ukrainian People's Party—a highly programmatic document in its own right—he named Jews, Poles, and Russians as the primary enemies of the Ukrainian people "for as long as they ruled and exploited us." In addition, he also condemned intermarriage between Ukrainians and individuals of these three groups, as well as those with other foreigners.[124]

It is very symptomatic that contemporary Ukrainian ethnocentric nationalists consider Mikhnovs'ky worthy of being added to the government cohort of Ukrainian national heroes, who themselves have been honored through the opening of monuments and memorials. In his article devoted to Mykola Mikhnovs'ky, Victor Rog lists him among the "prophets" of the Ukrainian people, like Taras Shevchenko and Lesya Ukraïnka, who "had passed ahead of his time" in order "to reunite the followers from the coming generations." He wrote, "The ideas of Mikhnovs'ky and his followers eventually gave birth to the legendary ranks of both the Sichovykh striltsiv and the Cossacks of the Army of the Ukrainian People's Republic," and "warriors of the Ukrainian armed organizations—*Organization of Ukrainian Nationalists (OUN)—Ukrainian Insurgent Army (UPA)*."[125] It is interesting to note that, during this early period, Ukrainian integral (ethnocentric) nationalism also absorbed many socialist and even Marxist ideas into their port-folio. This was particularly apparent in 1900, when Mikhnovs'ky became one of the founding members of the *Revolutionary Ukrainian Party* stationed in Kharkiv (East Ukraine).

One of the most important figures during the Ukrainian national revival, whose ideas would have a great impact on the structure of Ukrainian integral (ethnocentric) nationalism during the early twentieth century, was the country's greatest modern historian, leader of the pre-revolution Ukrainian national movement, and head of the Central Rada (1917–1918), Mykhailo Serhiyovych Hrushevsky (1866–1934). As a historian, Hrushevsky authored the first detailed synthesis of Ukrainian history—the ten-volume *History of Ukraine-Rus'*: the most comprehensive account of the ancient, medieval, and early modern history of the Ukrainian people. These writings are relevant to this chapter because they provided Ukrainian nationalists with a version of their anthropological heritage that was separate from the Imperial Russian narrative. According to Hrushevsky, the Ukrainian lineage could be traced to long before the time of the Kyivan Rus'.[126] His narrative asserts that the *sole* successors to the Kyivan Rus' were the ancestors of the modern-day West Ukrainian—the Halychyna and the Volhynia—and that the Vladimir-Suzdal' princi-pality had been populated by a completely different set of people, which biologically separates ethnic Ukrainians from ethnic Russians.[127]

This theory is seen in a more active application among the present-day ethnocentric nationalist dis-course. As an extension of this theory, one may find its modern embodiment within the theory of direct origin of Ukrainians from the Trypillian culture (c. 4800 to 3000 BCE), which is included in the national curriculum for children by the Ukrainian Ministry of Education.[128] Thus, it was Hrushevsky who origi-nally laid the historical foundations of what would become the biological building block of the modern Russo-Ukrainian ethnic conflict.[129] I will return to discuss the details of these theories in a section dedi-cated to this ethnic building block of conflict.

As it has been already stated, many of the organizations that existed in western Ukraine during the early twentieth century had a strong socialist component in their ideology. However, between the two World Wars, when Poland was dominant in Halychyna, the autonomous rights granted to the Ukrainians by the Austrians were canceled. In the midst of this formed the idea that the democratic and socialist worldviews were actively hindering the movement "to get [a] Ukrainian state." In the 1930s, the combination of Stalin's mass repressions and the Holodomor completely undermined anything resembling Communist ideas. Following this, a strong anti-Communist and anti-Soviet discourse would be an indispensable part of Ukrainian integral (ethnocentric) nationalism. An example of this transformation comes by way of another pillar of Ukrainian ethnocentric nationalism—a man named Dmytro Dontsov (1883–1973). He was a member of the Revolutionary Ukrainian Party and later the *Ukrainian Social Democratic Workers' Party (USDRP)*. After 1908, he began drifting away from socialism when he fled from St. Petersburg to Kiev and then Galicia (Halychyna) to avoid persecution and when he studied law in Vienna from 1909 to 1911. In 1913, at the *Second Student Congress* in Lviv, he had already severely criticized the Russophile intelligentsia for its "Little Russian" orientation, as well as those views held by Ukrainian socialists and even Vladimir Lenin. The following year, he broke off all ties to the USDRP and joined the *Union for the Liberation of Ukraine*. During the period of revolutionary turmoil, Dontsov traveled between Kiev and Bern, Switzerland, and by the early 1920s "had rejected all of his earlier socialist and Marxist ideas and has become a leading ideologue of Ukrainian anti-democratic integral nationalism."[130]

While serving as an associate professor at Lviv University between 1922 and 1939, Dontsov edited *Literaturno-naukovyi vistnyk* (1922–1932), *Zahrava* (1923–1924), and the journal *Vistnyk* (1933–1939), while also publishing numerous books and articles. Among them was programmatic work—*Natsionalism (The Nationalism)* (1926). Based on the principles of social Darwinism, he stated that the nation must be headed by "the special strata of the best people," who are ultimately responsible for the implementation of a "creative violence" against the major bulk of the populace. He asserted that hostility between nations is a natural occurrence and that the outcome of such a fight must undoubtedly allow the "strongest" nations victory over the "weak" peoples.

He openly condemned any and all examples of Russophilia, Polonophilia, and Austrophilia found within the various segments of contemporary Ukrainian society. Dontsov also stated that a national culture is something sacred and must be protected by all possible means from all possible transgressions.[131] All of these ideas had been firmly adopted by the OUN, with his writings themselves inspiring the actions and policies of its younger members throughout Galicia (Halychyna) and Volhynia. These papers are currently preserved in the National Archives of Canada, as he died in Montreal, Quebec, in 1973.

One of the men who most critically defined the goals of the OUN (based on the ideas of Mikhnovs'ky and Dontsov) was Yaroslav Stetsko (1912–1986). He was the leader of Stepan Bandera's OUN from 1968 until his death eighteen years later. Stetsko and Bandera (1909–1959) were both descendants of the most prominent Greco-Catholic families in Galicia (Halychyna).

Organization and Leadership of the OUN

The OUN (*Organizatsiia ukrainskykh natsionalistiv*) arose from the merger of the *Ukrainian Military Organization (UVO)*, the *League of Ukrainian Nationalists*, and a collection of several nationalist student associations. Conferences held in Berlin (November 3–7, 1927) and Prague (April 8–9, 1928) paved the way for the founding of the First Congress, which was held in Vienna on January 27 to February 3, 1929. The first leader of this newly founded organization was Yevhen Konovalets (1891–1938), a former colonel in the army of the aforementioned Ukrainian National Republic (UNR). Notably, he also spent some time in North America, helping the Ukrainian Diaspora organize into the nationalist *Organization for the Rebirth of Ukraine* in the United States and the *Ukrainian National Federation* in Canada.[132]

Under the direction of Stetsko, who himself edited the main publications of the Ukrainian nationalists; the OUN followed the principal ideas of Dontsov by stressing the importance of a strong political elite that would ensure national solidarity by relying on its own forces. The older leadership supported the stark principles of militaristic authoritarianism and accepted the use of "creative" violence or, in Dontsov's words, "*direct action*" as a political tool against both domestic and foreign enemies of the national cause. Meanwhile, the younger members were more inclined to proliferate and share a more romantic view of nationalism. In both Galicia (Halychyna) *and* Volhynia, the OUN performed hundreds of acts of sabotage against Polish landowners and businessmen. They also carried out around sixty assassinations, with their targets including Polish officials Tedeusz Holowko and Interior Minister Bronislaw Pieracki (who was responsible for the persecution of nationalists in Lviv, Volhynia, and Polisia from 1930 to 1932), as well as Soviet consular official Alexei Mailov, who was killed in 1933 as an act of retaliation for the Holodomor. In 1934, the lead OUN activists, including Bandera (head of the *Western Ukrainian Territorial Executive* of the OUN), were arrested by Polish police and imprisoned until the start of the Second World War. In 1938, while holding out in Rotterdam, Holland, Yevhen Konovalets was assassinated by Stalin's agent, Pavel Sudoplatov. After his murder, the organization split into two separate factions: the *Revolutionary OUN* or *OUN(r)/OUN-R*, better known as the *OUN(b)/OUN-B*—*Organization of Ukrainian Nationalists* (*Bandera Movement*)—or "*Banderites*," after their leader, Stepan Bandera; and the *OUN(m)/OUN-M*—headed by Andriy Melnyk (1890–1964)—otherwise known as "*Melnikites*." The primary discrepancy between the two saw the latter faction take a "softer" approach regarding the use of "creative" violence or "direct actions" in achieving their goals.[133]

In the early stages of WWII, both factions of the OUN collaborated with the Third Reich for tactical reasons in order to help establish an independent Ukrainian state. Around 1942–1943, during Nazi occupation, the *Ukrainian Insurgent Army* (*UPA*) was formed. Officially, its primary goal was to engage in guerilla warfare campaigns against the German Army, detachments of the Polish Underground State (specifically the *Ludova Army* and *Kraiova Army*), the Red Army, and all manner of Soviet partisans. As it mentioned before, up until that point, the capital of Galicia had been under the direct dominion of Poland. However, it was later captured by the Red Army during the Soviet invasion of 1939. The city would again change hands when the Wehrmacht invaded Soviet-controlled Lviv on June 30, 1941. Before they left the city, however, the Soviets entered the local prisons and shot many of the inmates, a majority of which were Ukrainian nationalists.

Regarding the OUN's tactics, it is worth remembering that these plans had been properly elaborated in April 1941, on the eve of Hitler's invasion of the Soviet Union, at the Second Congress of the OUN(b) in Krakow, wherein Yaroslav Stetsko was elected deputy of Stepan Bandera. The Congress would then denote and formally adopt the expected program of actions that the OUN(b) would follow through the course of the war. They stated that "OUN (b) is fighting for the independent Ukrainian state and for [the] liberation of the enslaved by Moscow peoples of Eastern Europe and Asia." A month later, Stetsko published his directives, which would constitute the foundations of the "state" policy. Within the rhetoric, he assigned the fledgling Ukrainian state to use "war with the USSR for deploying struggle for the Ukrainian state." He also recommended the propagandizing of the OUN(b), who "under the leadership of Bandera struggle not only for [a] self-dependent Ukrainian state but also for the total disintegration and destruction of the Muscovy Empire, for the creation of independent national states on its ruins." It is important to note that the Third Reich was looked upon as an instrument, whose military forces would create the favorable conditions to facilitate the rise of an independent Ukrainian state. In other words, the OUN(b)'s tactic was based on a theoretical alliance with Hitler's Germany, as opposed to their subjection by it.

On June 23, 1941, a day after the commencement of Operation Barbarossa, a force of 5,000 OUN activists followed the Wehrmacht's path into Galicia (Halychyna) in order to construct the Ukrainian authorities, law enforcement, miscellaneous social agencies, and press to enable their propagandistic goals while the area was an occupied German territory.

On June 30, 1991, the city of Lviv saw the organization of "people's assemblies," in which anywhere from fifty to 200 (depending on the source) representatives of Lviv's society participated. There, Stetsko declared *The Act of Restoration of the Ukrainian State*, also known as *The Act of Proclamation of Ukrainian Statehood*. As a result, Stetsko would become the prime minister, and Kost' Levitsky became head of the Council of Seniors.[134]

Initially, a segment of the Ukrainian populace greeted the Germans as liberators. Stalin's repressions and the application of a scorched-earth policy—as seen through the murder of political prisoners during the Red Army's hasty retreat, the removal of local industrial plants, and the destruction wrought on the crops and food reserves, and the flooding of mines—created an atmosphere in which the OUN's propaganda held firm to the Ukrainian population of Halychyna. Because of this, Germany—as the sworn enemy of both Poland and the USSR—was seen as a natural ally in their quest for independence. That same day, while Stetsko prepared to officially declare the implementation of Ukrainian statehood, the OUN simultaneously began plastering the city with leaflets calling for ethnic cleansing and formed a militia that initiated the persecution of the local Jews. Their "work" began that day (June 30) and died down on July 2, only to flair back up again from July 25 to July 29. At this time, Lviv was populated by multicultural communities: out of the city's 312,211 residents, 157,490 (a little over 50 percent) were ethnic Poles, 99,565 (or around 32 percent) were Jews, and 49,747 (roughly 16 percent) were Ukrainians.[135]

According to the *Encyclopedia of Camps and Ghettos, 1933–1945*, the first pogrom resulted in approximately 2,000 to 5,000 Jewish deaths, followed by another 1,000 deaths during the so-called "Petliura Days" at the end of July. Another figure comes by way of historian Peter Longerich, who argues that the first pogrom cost 4,000 lives, followed by another 2,500 to 3,000 arrests and executions by the Nazi mobile death squads of the *Einsatzgruppen*, with the "Petliura Days" resulting in more than 2,000 additional deaths.[136]

Determining the degree of involvement that these Ukrainian nationalist organizations had in the Holocaust in Eastern Europe has given rise to a prominent controversy among a plethora of historians and authors hailing from several different ethno-political orientations.

One group of specialists, who count many Russian historians and publicists among their numbers, label all Ukrainian nationalist organizations as "Nazi collaborators and vehement anti-Semites by nature." They usually cite Yaroslav Stetsko's "autobiography," allegedly written in August 1941, as the most damning evidence in this regard. In particular, they call attention to his statement that Marxism was "a product of Jewish thought" and that it was put into practice by the Muscovite-Asiatic people with Jewish assistance; despite the fact that he considered Moscow the primary enemy of the Ukrainian people, he still staunchly endorsed the idea "of the indubitably harmful role of Jews in the enslavement of Ukraine by Moscow." Supposedly, he also stated that he "absolutely endorsed the extermination of the Jews," as well as the "rationality of the German methods of extermination of Jews, instead of assimilating them."[137]

On the other side of this controversy, Ukrainian historians in Diaspora, as well as a majority of their colleagues in the West, consider the depth of collaboration between the Ukrainian nationalists and Hitler's occupational forces to be over-exaggerated. In particular, OUN veteran and historian Taras

Hunczak argued that the veracity of the aforementioned document, and especially Stetsko's authorship, is highly questionable.[138] The process of "whitewashing" the OUN's role in the Holocaust had already begun in 1943, when, following the Wehrmacht's defeat at Stalingrad, it became clear that Germany would inevitably lose the war. This would begin the process of nationalist rehabilitation that continues well into the modern day. From this, Per Anders Rudling, Jeffrey Kopstein, Jason Wittenberg, and a host of other specialists have demonstrated that, throughout the entire postwar period, the OUN drastically changed its paradigm by describing its legacy as a "heroic Ukrainian resistance against the Nazis and the Communists."[139] This was augmented by a great number of memoirs penned by various veterans of the OUN, the *Ukrainian Insurgent Army* (*UPA*), and the *SS Division Galicia*. Since 2008, the *Secret Service of Ukraine* (*SBU*) has also joined this effort, releasing a collection of documents titled *For the Beginning: Book of Facts* (*Do pochatku: kniha factiv*), in an attempt to show that the OUN's involvement in the horrors of the Holocaust was to a lesser degree than originally thought, ultimately hoping to dis-associate the OUN from a legacy of anti-Jewish violence.

This scholarly battle is yet another confirmation that the historical building block is one of the most provocative and mobilizing factors of an ethnic conflict, which is especially true for the recent Rus-so-Ukrainian ethnic conflict. Both sides utilize reinterpreted and/or mythologized histories to discredit one another and to attract outside support.[140] Every time I see this take place, I cannot help but remem-ber a line from George Orwell's book *1984*: "Who controls the past controls the future. Who controls the present controls the past." This very much rings true, as the falsification of history is a typical and recurrent behavioral pattern exhibited through ethnocentric nationalism, especially when it is a driving ideology of ethnic conflict.

That being said, there exist more balanced accounts of the OUN's involvement in the Holocaust, due in part to the work of historians like John-Paul Himka, Wendy Lower, Grzegorz Rossolinski-Liebe, Gabriel Finder, Alexander Prusin, Vladimir Melamed, Karel C. Berkhoff, Marco Carynnyk, and many others.[141] The last pair of authors, in particular, established the authenticity of Stetsko's autobiography and that of the above-cited passage. In particular, Himka stated: "The fundamental point of contention between the adherents of the national myth [ethnocentric nationalists] and me is whether or not the Organization of Ukrainian Nationalists and its armed force, the Ukrainian Insurgent Army ... participated in the Holo-caust. They deny this entirely. My research indicates, however, as does the research of scholars around the world, that *the participation was significant*."[142] In line with this, their studies on the pogroms in Lviv indicated that the Germans created conditions favorable for the outbreak of violence, essentially encour-aging them in the first place. As such, Ukrainian nationalists and their militias were arresting Jews and subsequently present at their executions, in which the Nazis shot them *en masse* during and after the first pogrom. At the same time, the urban crowd, mainly comprising Poles and Ukrainians, "took advantage of the particular conjuncture of high politics to act out an uninhibited script of robbery, sexual assault, beating, and murder. Germans filmed all of these actions and this irrefutable documentary proof of this tragedy." The OUN cooperated with these anti-Jewish actions in order to curry favor with the Germans, in hopes of gaining official recognition for the proclaimed Ukrainian state. Therefore, its anti-Semitism "was not an independent factor in the decision to stage a pogrom."[143]

However, the illusion of German support for their cause was quickly shattered. Within days of the pogrom, many of the organizers behind the proclamation of the Ukrainian state (including Bandera, Stetsko, and Melnyk) were separately arrested. On July 5, 1941, Bandera was placed under "honorary arrest" in Krakow, only to be later transferred to Berlin, where he was joined by his deputy, Yaroslav Stetsko. Once there, the two received various proposals of cooperation from the Gestapo and their various subdivisions in regard to providing them information on various officials under Melnyk. After the inevitable assassination of various high-ranking members of the OUN(m), the pair was held at Spandau Prison in Berlin until January 1942, at which time they were transferred to the Zellenbau barrack of *Sachsenhausen Concentration Camp*, which hosted 180 isolated cells for high-profile political prisoners.[144]

With the nationalists out of the way, the Nazis placed Galicia (Halychyna) under the general governorship of Poland and returned Bukovina to Romania. Additionally, Romania was given the region between the Dniester and Southern Bug Rivers as the province of *Transnistria*, with Odessa being made the local capital. What remained was reorganized as *Reichskommissarriat Ukraine* under Erick Koch—the governor of East Prussia. The Nazis would then proceed to implement their racial policies within these "new" territories, resulting in the death of an estimated 1.5 million Ukrainian Jews, with an additional 800,000 being displaced to the east.[145]

On July 11, 1943, various Ukrainian nationalist formations attacked 150 Polish settlements in the Volhynia area, Eastern Galicia, segments of Polesia, and the Lublin region. This action would later be known in Polish as *"rzeź wołyńska,"* (lit. *Volhynian Slaughter*). The announced goal of this action was the "total extermination of hostile elements"—which is a roundabout way of saying the entirety of the local Polish population. As a result, between February 1943 and February 1944, units of the UPA brutally killed up to 100,000 Polish civilians, with Polish retaliatory efforts at the end of 1943 leading to numerous deaths among the Ukrainian population. This mutual brutality between the two sides would continue until order was restored in 1945. Recently, the Upper House of the Polish Seim passed legislation to officially qualify the Volhynian Slaughter as an act of Genocide.[146]

The *Babi Yar ravine* (Ukr. *Babyn Yar*) in Kyiv became known worldwide as the execution grounds for countless civilian lives. According to different sources, from 1941 to 1943, there were anywhere from 100,000 to 150,000 civilians shot. The victims came from a wide spread of society, consisting of Jews (with 33,771 being killed September 29–30, 1941, alone), Roma People, Kyivan Karaims, Soviet POWs, and Ukrainian nationalists. History has preserved the names of those responsible for these monstrous crimes: General-Major Kurt Eberhardt, Chief of the SS *Einsatzgruppen* Paul Blobel, Chief of the SD Police Otto Rush, and the Ukrainian Chief of the Kyiv Police Andriy Orlik (real name allegedly Dmitrii Miron), who was later shot by the Gestapo in 1942.[147]

Ukraine's human and material losses during the course of the war were astronomical: some five to seven million people perished, 2.2 million were forced to resettle throughout Germany and occupied Europe as an exploitable labor source by the Nazis (the latter of whom abolished schooling beyond the fourth grade of and denied medical treatment to Ukrainians). More than 700 cities and towns, as well as 28,000 villages had been destroyed, leaving ten million people homeless.

The Sovietization of western Ukraine only added momentum to this suffering, with the postwar dislocations and the drought/famine of 1946–1947 claiming nearly one million lives. Additionally, the purges of Ukrainian "bourgeois nationalists" and others with "questionable" loyalties—numbering in the hundreds of thousands—were sent to GULAG camps in Siberia. In such conditions, the UPA, under the leadership of Roman Shukhevych (until he was killed in 1950), continued to inflict painful losses on Soviet troops and activists alike, all while receiving support from the local rural population of Western Ukraine, who had become embittered due to the aggressiveness of forced collectivization. The former persecutions were also joined by a host of them aimed at Ukrainian Greek Catholic Church hierarchies, such as Metropolitan Yosif Slipy, as well as the entire hierarchy in the region of Galicia.[148]

Ukrainian Nationalists in the Soviet Ukraine after Stalin's Period

Within the framework of the abovementioned campaign of "further rapprochement of socialist nations," the postwar decrees of the Communist party never technically referred to the process as Ukrainization, nor had they "formally decreed assimilation into Russian culture." But in reality, they clearly promoted the latter. As such, the Ukrainian language only held ground in the western, central, and scattered rural areas of the country, while to the east (especially in the cities) and in the 1970s–1980s, Russian was steadfastly expanding as the official language of the party and all facets of the state apparatus. Unsurprisingly, this resulted in the appearance of Ukrainian dissident movements to defend their native tongue. In 1966, Ivan Dziuba, a Ukrainian literary critic, wrote a pseudo-dissident manifesto titled *Internationalism or Russification?* Interestingly enough, he criticized the Russification of the Ukrainian language and culture, trying to appeal to a Marxist-Leninist viewpoint. He believed that the ideas and practices of Leninist proletarian internationalism had been corrupted by the myth of Russian primacy as an "elder brother" around whom all people must be united at the cost of their linguistic cultures. Thus, in order to restore the state to its pristine purity of Leninist Soviet federalism, Dziuba insisted that the state should provide the conditions to develop the national potential of the Ukrainian people. In other words, Dziuba, alongside other "reformists," wanted to return to the practices of Ukrainization as set forth by Mykola Skrypnyk—a Ukrainian Communist leader who, in the early years of Soviet Ukraine (especially from 1927 to 1930), led the policy and practice of facilitating and using the Ukrainian language on a much wider scale. This not only entails the development of the language as a tool but also elevating the influences of Ukrainian ethnic culture into the various spheres of public life: education, publishing, government, and religion, as well as the promotion of ethnic Ukrainians into key positions within the party and Soviet nomenclature. All of these measures were both intact and actively enforced until 1930, when Stalin abruptly reversed this policy.[149]

Kenneth Farmer referred to activists like Dziuba as "Ukrainian nationalist dissenters." This considers how they essentially exhausted any and all *legal methods* to achieve their goals, such as petitioning "for the realization of rights that are constitutionally guaranteed, but known to be punishable." However, it also accounts for their creation of alternate channels of communication known as *samvydav* (Rus. *samizdat*) in order to spread their views through self-made pamphlets, manifestos, and manuscripts.[150] These efforts were severely repressed by the Soviet regime, who took to sending those they captured in the act to prison. But during the 1970s, Petro Shelest, who was in charge of Ukraine at the time, protected some of these "reformists" from the threat of open persecution. These instances indicated that Ukrainian nationalism has a respectably long history and set of traditions, which prevented Russian Communist leadership from solving the *nationalities problem*. However, this form of nationalism was not a complete incarnation of the integral (ethnocentric) nationalism touted by the OUN. In agreement with Farmer, who roughly explained the philosophy of dissidents like Dziuba and Valentine Moroz, one may conclude that this was "a highly demotic form of ethnic nationalism, which does not set the nation up as superior to all others, nor necessarily destined by history to fulfill some mystic mission, but rather as an entity necessary to the spiritual health of its people, and deserving an equal place among the other nations of the world."[151] Therefore, we can observe a graduation of sorts between typical civic and ethnocentric (integral) forms of nationalism.

Traditions of Integral Nationalism Matured Abroad

The traditions of ethnocentric nationalism throughout the postwar Soviet and post-Soviet periods had been preserved and maintained by members of the OUN outside of Ukraine. Afterward, the internal conditions following the collapse of the Soviet Union allowed for this mindset to return to its birthplace in Ukraine. After 1991, this nationalism, as previously shown, slowly but steadily went back into the Ukrainian state, only to be embraced by the severe, and seemingly permeant, all-sided societal crisis. This results in most of their modern history being a depiction of their painful search for their own identity. In the West, this nationalism had been forged and matured by the conditions of a different kind of war—the Cold War—which pitted East against West and, by the 1990s, had emerged ready to enact a spectacular revanche.

Between 1940 and 1958, some groups of the OUN–UPA continued their activities within the Donbas region. Their primary goal was to resist the Soviet Union's "Russification" policy by any means necessary. As a result, many of them were heavily repressed by the Soviet NKVD/KGB.[152] After WWII, leaders from both factions of the OUN collaborated with American and British intelligence agencies, directly participating in the Cold War on the side of the West. By 1956, however, a third faction, *OUN(3)/OUN(z)/OUN-Z* (or, as a number of leaders called it, "*dviika*")—headed by Zinoviy Matla and Lev Rebert—splintered off into their own movement. Allegedly, this new division of the OUN would gradually begin phasing out the more radical methodology of their parent organization, though the specifics are notably shady.[153]

In February 1945, a conference in Vienna, Austria, saw older leaders of the OUN(b), including Bandera, Stetsko, and other *providniki*, formally establish their connections with the special services of the United States and Great Britain. Additionally, they also adopted an official foreign policy for the postwar period. However, their most pressing decision was the creation of a broad *Anti-Bolshevik Front* (*ABN*), a structure built around the Ukrainian cultural nucleus that could unite all other ethnic groups with anti-Soviet sentiments under a single banner. Within a more widespread perspective, this organization might have very well been the coordinating center of all anti-Communist organizations around the world. On April 16, 1946, a Congress in Munich, Bavaria, announced the formation of the *Anti-Bolshevik Block of Nations* (*ABN*). The structure of this organization supported military functionality and an international legal committee alongside an intelligence service and the so-called "Black Committee"—a terrorist cell in charge of liquidating traitors among their ranks. Yaroslav Stetsko became the head of this international organization at its inception, which at the time included Romanian national-tsaranists, Serbian monarchists (*Chetniks*), Lithuanian and Slovak emigration groups, and various others with like-minded desires. Throughout the 1970s, anti-Communist Vietnamese and Cuban organizations would also join the ABN in search of mutual support.[154] Yaroslav Stetsko headed the ABN until his death in 1986, when he was succeeded by his widow, Slava Stetsko. In 1996, following the dissolution of the USSR and the elimination of their primary threat, the group officially disbanded.

As for the OUN(b), their story is far less clear-cut. Following Bandera's assassination on October 15, 1959, perpetrated by KGB defector Bohdan Stashynsky on the order of Nikita Khrushchev, the OUN(b) was subsequently headed by Stepan Lenkavsky (until 1968), Yaroslav Stetsko (until 1986), Vasil Oleskiv (until 1991), Slava Stetsko (until 2001), and Andriy Haidamakha (until 2009), after whom came the current leader, Stefan Romaniv.[155] On the other side, the OUN(m) has been headed by Bohdan Chervak since 2012. Regarding the treatment of non-Ukrainians, the First OUN Congress in 1929 vehemently stated that "only the complete removal of all occupiers from Ukrainian lands will allow for the general development of the Ukrainian nation within its own state." Additionally, their previously cited "Ten Commandments" required them to "aspire to expand the strength, riches, and size of the Ukrainian State even by the means of enslaving foreigners."[156] However, this was modified in the 1950s and simply read: "Thou shalt struggle for the glory, greatness, power, and space of the Ukrainian state."[157] Per Anders Rudling defines the overarching ideology of the OUN as sharing the "attributes of anti-liberalism, anti-conservatism, and anti-communism, an armed party, totalitarianism, anti-Semitism, *Führerprinzip*, and an adoption of fascist greetings."[158] As stated above, the most radical principles of this ideology have undergone major reconstruction after 1943, which was reflected by the Third OUN Congress (in August 1943) proclaiming that all minorities inhabiting Ukraine would receive equal rights in the eyes of the law.[159] Another major shift was expressed in the OUN's clandestine journal, *Idea i Chyn*, which specifically called for an active resistance to the manifestation of anti-Semitism.[160]

However, as seen with Andrii Bilec'kii's SNA, the newer ethnocentric Ukrainian nationalist organizations have adopted many of those same radical ideas left behind by their OUN predecessors.

New Organizations of Ethnocentric Nationalists in Modern Ukraine

Since around 1989–1991, Ukraine has seen a rapid rebirth of nationalistic movements. The following organizations are especially active in spreading an ethnocentrically nationalistic ideology within a vivid anti-Russian discourse: *The Ukrainian National Assembly–Ukrainian People's Self-Defence (УНА-УНСО, UNA-UNSO)* is a Ukrainian political organization seen as far-right in Ukraine and abroad. Although the Ukrainian National Assembly was the organization's political wing, on May 22, 2014, it merged with *Right Sector*; the UNA-UNSO continues to operate independently. Other ethnocentric organizations include: "*White Hammer*" (2013–2014); Dmytro Korchynsky's *Brotherhood* (2004); *PSO "Karpathian Sich"*; the "*People's Front of Poltavshina*" (2011); the *OUN*; the *Patriots of the Ukraine*—an ultra-radical paramilitary organization (Kharkiv, 2006); *Right Sector, Svoboda* (Freedom)—a formal political party; *S14 (Sich)*; Andrii Bilec'kii's *Ukrainian Nationalistic Movement SNA* (2008); *VO "Trizub"* (named after Stepan Bandera [1991]); and the "*Dnipro*," "*Azov*," "*Aidar*," and "*Vostok*," and other battalions (who are active participants at the front in Donbas). These groups, at some point or another, played a part in many unpunished rampages against their oppositional groups, including the intimidation and murder of activists, journalists, or any others who disagree with their ethnocentric discourse.[161] One may demonstrate the activity more effectively through the following examples, which also illustrates how more official state establishments tend to buttress some of the views and/or methods of the ethnocentric nationalists.

In 2017, the local authorities erected a monument at Babi Yar honoring the death of Olena Teliha during the 1942 pogroms (though it is unclear whether she was shot by the Germans or committed suicide to avoid such a fate). However, Teliha, who was a well-known poet, conversely played the part as an outspoken propagandist for the OUN and its radical ideals during its early days. Presiding over the ceremony was Mayor of Kiev Vitali Klichko, then Ukrainian Minister of Culture Yevhen Nishuk, and Chief Head of the Ukrainian Institute of National Memory Volodymyr Viatrovych. This event was primarily organized by the present head of the OUN(m), Deputy Chairman of the State Committee of TV and

Radio Broadcast Bohdan Chervak. During his opening remarks at the ceremony, Chervak said: "Babi Yar—is the Ukrainian land. Here perished Ukrainian heroes. Ukrainian authorities and Ukrainian people should honor not only [the] memory of the Jewish victims of genocide, but most of all they have to honor the memory of the Ukrainians." In the words of Avigdor Eskin, no one in Europe at that time had ever attempted, so openly and on the state level, to glorify the perpetrators of crimes against humanity "and elevate them above their victims."[162]

That very same year, an Israeli newspaper reported the tragic death of Mendel Daich—a famous activist for the Hasid movement and father of eleven children—in the Ukrainian city of Zhitomir. A few weeks later, the Holocaust monument in Ternopil (Western Ukraine) was desecrated by graffiti of swastikas. Recently in Lviv (on the day set aside to honor victims of the Holocaust), nationalists paraded around while wearing the uniforms of the Ukrainian *Nahtigal* Battalion,which had during WWII participated in punitive and persecutory police operations against civilians. Alongside this, there was a rise in anti-Semitic incidents in many places around the country, with Odesa being a frequent hotspot of activity. Eduard Dolinsky, director of the *Jewish Committee of Ukraine*, wrote an article for *The New York Times* arguing that this level of hatred only became possible due to the *state laws* adopted by President Yuschenko between 2006 and 2010, which glorified OUN-UPA founders Stepan Bandera and Roman Shukhevych. By Dolinsky's words, "these laws forbid any criticism of these formations." At some point in the recent past, sixty-two deputies of the Knesset—the Israeli parliament—sent a letter to the European Parliament in which they expressed a deep amount of concern regarding the seemingly uncontrolled growth of anti-Semitism and Russophobia in Ukraine. They received only silence in response.[163]

In keeping with "tradition," the major factors of the OUN continue to insert themselves into a multitude of political fronts. For instance, the Melnyk faction of the OUN threw its support behind the *Ukrainian Republican Party* when it was being headed by Levko Lukyanenko throughout the 1990s and 2000s. The OUN(b), on the other hand, reorganized itself into the *Congress of Ukrainian Nationalists* (*CUN*), which would be officially registered as a political party in 1993.[164] Conversely, some leaders of the Diaspora attempted to imbue the party with a more modern façade; however, this only served to attract the attention of ethnocentric nationalists in Ukraine.[165] With this newfound political influence, the OUN forced President Yanukovych to finish building the "Hero of Ukraine" statues dedicated to Bandera and Shukhevych, which he previously planned to cancel. Moreover, they enforced the practice of recognizing those who fought for Ukrainian independence as "Heroes of Ukraine," notably awarding the title to Symon Petliura and Yevhen Konovalets, the first head of the OUN.[166] During the 2019 presidential elections, Ruslan Kashulynsky was the chosen candidate of the CUN, Right Sector, and S14, receiving 1.6 percent of the votes.[167]

Andrii Bilec'kii continues to propagandize his claim to the importance of Ukrainian racial purity.[168] Bilec'kii was one of the original leaders of the Azov Battalion, which became the tip of the spear in the Ukrainian military struggle against pro-Russian separatist forces in Donbas. In January 2019, this battalion was attached to the 30th Mechanized Brigade of the Ukrainian Armed Forces in order to carry out active combat missions in the region.[169] In reviving the racial theories of his forerunners, Bilec'kii writes: "Ukrainian social-nationalism considers the Ukrainian nation to be a society based on a common bloodline and race ... Race is paramount for the genesis of a nation."[170] In an interview with *Telegraph* reporter Tom Parfitt, a twenty-three-year-old Azov commando was quoted as saying, "Personally, I'm a Nazi," and, " I do not hate any other nationalities, but I believe each nation should have its own country"(in comparison to my previously cited interviews from Georgia and elsewhere).[171]

My previously mentioned student McBarrett Good also shared with me another highly indicative example of the open manifestation of ethnocentric nationalism among the active political scene in Ukraine. In a video taken at a Ukrainian primary school, Iryna Farion, a member of the Ukrainian Parliament, "is seen asking five-year-olds their names. Those whose names are Russian, she gives the Ukrainian translation and for the one child whose name is Ukrainian, she gives her congratulations." In response, McBarrett said: "Imagine a kindergarten teacher here in America asking Mexican-American children their names and then correcting them to their English equivalent: telling young Marco that he will be called Mark and Angelica that her name is Alicia. The implications of taking the ethnic divide into the classrooms of such young children are frightening."[172]

With that in mind, why is this type of "minority faith," to use the subtitle of Andrew Wilson's 1997 book, so powerful and proactive in modern Ukraine?

In my opinion, aside from the other objective circumstances that I have discussed earlier in this study, this comes about in response to the major political forces in Ukraine lacking a well-articulated ideology. The previously cited examples, which one may multiply on their own accord, and the gradual emergence of the Svoboda Party (which shares many of the abovementioned ideas regarding the principal building blocks of ethnicity) and its presence in the Rada since 2001 is a flagship of the core extreme-right ideology, successfully integrating it into the political mainstream. The economic crisis, unemployment, and corruption have enabled ethnocentric organizations to add a socioeconomic dimension to their ultranationalist agenda. They have also been more apt to communicate with the grassroots movements rather than their elite political counterparts. That is why Svoboda, for example, could gain regional power among the political bodies of western Ukraine. In agreement with Mridula Ghosh, one may then consolidate that instead "of distancing themselves from the rhetoric of Svoboda [and similar ethnocentric organizations], the mainstream political parties [including the currently ruling *Sluga Naroda* party] have entered into situation-dependent and other tactical alliances with it [them]" regarding reforms in the spheres with direct ties to the major building blocks of ethnicity in order to win the nationalist support/vote necessary to maintain their higher ratings. "The lack of consensus among the major political actors on how to combat right-wing extremist ideas has legitimized Svoboda [and similar ethnocentric organizations] in the public perception."[173]

Pro-Russian Ethnocentric Organizations in Ukraine and Their Principal Ideas

In 2009, the organization known as the *Cossack Union "Oblast' of Don Host"* (KSOVD) was, according to local information and sources, registered "by the residents of Donbas" as a territorial community. In 2014, KSOVD hetman Yuri Safonenko said that his organization had been "re-registered" into the self-proclaimed *Donetsk People's Republic* (DNR). According to him, the KSOVD's militants took an "active part in the military actions against [the] Kievan junta together with volunteers from different countries: Russians, Serbs, Brazilians, Belarusians, Moldavians, and even Americans." He estimated that the number of militants in his organization was at about 3,500 armed individuals, with a "major part of them from Donetsk and Luhansk Oblasts and from Ukraine proper." It is estimated that around 130 of the KSOVD's militant branch died in combat in the span of a year from 2015 to 2016.[174]

On December 5, 2019, the General Prosecution's Office of Ukraine announced their submission of documentary materials regarding the extrajudicial executions of nine Ukrainian servicemen during the battles of Ilovais'k and Debaltsevo, taking place in Donbas in 2014 and 2015, respectively, to the International Criminal Court in The Hague, Netherlands. According to the Ukrainian sources, these executions had been carried out by the militant forces of the KSOVD. The Prosecution's Office submitted video, photographic, and testimonial evidence depicting that the executions of these Ukrainian soldiers took place while they were in captivity.[175] The hetman of the KSOVD denied these accusations and stated that they do not recognize the legitimacy of the Ukrainian judicial system "because they belong to the state in which the leaders came to power as a result of armed coup d'état and used [the] army against civilian people that rejected this coup."[176] In his publication "War Crimes Committed during the Armed Conflict in Ukraine," Rustam Atadjanov concluded that the armed formations of "pro-Russian separatists" committed the following crimes during the conflict: "crimes committed against persons," "crimes against property," and "employing prohibited methods of warfare."[177]

On the KSOVD's website, one reads that the original goals of this organization included "the rebirth of the traditions on the primordial Cossack lands," the "defense of [ethnic] rights of Cossacks," and ensuring the "social-economic development of their region." However, "the most important goal of KSOVD is the creation of [Putin's above cited] *Novorossiya* as a strong, sovereign, socially oriented state aiming at [the] realization of natural, societal, and highest demands of its citizens." Their political programs pursue the self-determination of the territories of Ukraine, the independence of Novorossiya, and the "liberation of Donbas." The KSOVD also demands the prohibition of private banking institutions within the self-proclaimed republic of Donbas, nationalization, and a ban on the exploitation of the schistose gas fields. The latter demand is supposedly directed against the alleged intentions of the Ukrainian government to rent these fields, and thus give away their resources, to American companies. These ideas are in harmony with the principal ideological postulates propagating by other militant groups which I mention in the chart of Russo-Ukrainian ethnic conflict in chapter 9 operating on the territories of non-recognized pro-Russian enclaves of Donbas, and especially those nationalistic organizations that are active in Russia. Their ideas are thoroughly analyzed by one of the foremost authorities on the nature of Russian nationalism Marlene Laruelle, with an emphasis on the ideologies of Russia's ultra-nationalist and far-right groups. Three pertinent and overlapping paradigms constitute a scope of their doctrines: (1) great-powerness incarnated in the socially varied visions of Novorossiya/ "Large Russia"/ "Eurasian Russian World;" (2) anti-Westernism as an embodiment of anti-Western geopolitics; and (3) anti-liberalism in the form of a political Orthodoxy that found its accomplishment in confirmation of "Russia's status as the herald of conservative Christian values" in their contrast to Western liberal "decadent" values.[178] In the penultimate chapter I'll return to the detailed discussion of the gnoceological roots of the Russian political nationalism in the form of its Eurasian paradigm.

In Lieu of a Conclusion: Recurrent Behavioral Patterns of Ethnocentric Nationalism

In my book *Polygon of Satan*, I was able to denote the following patterns based on the observations of recurrent collective and individual behavior during different phases of violent ethnic conflicts in the Caucasus: (1) a group mentality as manifested by a sense of belonging; (2) self-assertive/integrative tendencies in collective behavior; (3) "mass behavior"; (4) "conformity"; (5) mutually displayed ethnic prejudices; (6) "brotherhood within/war-likeness without"; (7) uncritical obedience to charismatic leaders; (8) "authoritarianism"; (9) unrestricted aggressiveness; and (10) regression to a "paranoid-schizoid behavioral pattern" on a group level.[179] The above-cited examples of interethnic clashes within other parts of what was once the Soviet Union, as well as the historical perspectives of theoretical and practical manifestations of ethnocentric nationalism in the state of Ukraine, give me a firm foundation to confirm that these behavioral patterns are, in fact, both regular and regulatory norms of behavior, elements of which can be found within all violent ethnic conflicts.[180] Additionally, nine of these ten forms of ethnocentric behavior correspond to similar behavioral patterns of "*ethnic*" nationalism as laid out in the original research classification of author Dusan Kecmanovic.[181]

Group Mentality—Group Belonging

If one agrees with the thesis that a human being is "a social animal," then he can be, as Carlton Hayes argues, "particularly social with a particular group of men." In this sense, an ethnic group/nation—acting as an extended "super-family"—is a perfect association to fall in line with. After all, this is a social group that most of the people have been raised by, have continued to be closely familiar with, and share the same principal building blocks of ethnicity (as well as most of the same cultural boundary markers of difference) with one another. Thus, it is a natural occurrence to be drawn into this particular group and to show "marked loyalty to it."[182] As Harold Isaacs demonstrated: "at present, the 'nation or 'nationality' appears as the ultimate, the most inclusive, even the 'terminal' form of the basic group identity itself."[183]

At this point, it is once again worth citing Andrii Bilec'kii in order to demonstrate how this ethnocentric behavioral pattern finds its way into the Ukrainian socium. The leader of the Azov Battalion argues: "The major part of the Russian minority are patriots of such places of Ukraine like Slobozhanshina, Donechina [Donets'k], Zaporizhia, and even Kyiv [Kiev]—'mother of all Russian cities.' Overall, they are patriots of Little Russia and, in [a] more general sense, of 'Great Russia.' Hungarians, who live in Mukachevo and in [the] Berehovo District, are patriots of Zakarpattya, but without Ukrainians and with the name of South Hungary ... All of them are enemies of Ukraine and Ukrainians, lustful for pieces of our territory ... Ukraine needs only one single, Ukrainian integral, national state patriotism that [all the Ukrainians must be attached to] that discerns a single whole, territorial, powerful, national, and cultural integrity. All other 'patriotisms' are mere fakes—lies."[184] That is how Bilec'kii promotes this behavioral pattern among his followers and co-thinkers.

"Self-Assertive/Integrative Tendencies"

In his research, Arthur Koestler brought up several viable examples of how "the greatest human achievements and sacrifices, but also most monstrous crimes against humanity, come from one and the same source."[185] In agreement with the first part of this thesis, one can point to examples of how people who were not completely possessed by ethnocentric nationalism ultimately risked their lives to protect the people of the persecuted ethnic group amid the more violent stages of ethnic conflict. During the *hot stages* of the Ossetian-Ingushian conflict (October 31–November 3, 1992), I witnessed this action firsthand, as I saw my Ossetian neighbors usher Ingushians into the relative safety of their homes. This occurred despite the fact that they generally agreed with the highly proliferated opinion that, within the Republic of North Ossetia–Alania, Ingushian nationalists were guilty of sparking the regressive development of the conflict. It is also a well-known fact that, on January 1, 2019, the state of Israel honored 2,619 Ukrainians as *Righteous Among the Nations*. These people were recognized because they risked their lives to aid the Jews during the Holocaust, with some of them being killed as a result.[186] This is by no means a scattered phenomenon, as I have collected and cited numerous other examples of this behavior from every violent ethnic conflict to take place in the Caucasus.[187]

At the same time, I also cited a plethora of examples detailing the opposite behavior: people who have become unwaveringly possessed by the zeal of ethnocentric nationalism.[188] Unfortunately, they were the more numerous than those abovementioned acts of compassion and serve to confirm the second half of Koestler's thesis. Just as Koestler formulated, ethnocentric nationalism veritably destroys a human's capacity to make critical assessments of their ethnic group's behavior at moments where the integral tendency transcends individuals and merges them with "some supra-individual datum." If individual members of any given ethnic group in conflict find themselves absorbed by a self-assertive and integrative behavior, then, in the words of Ervin Staub, "human beings have the capacity to experience killing other people as nothing extraordinary"—especially when it is presented as beneficial to a "higher cause"—because there is supposedly no other way to save their own ethnic group from "malignant ethnic aliens."[189]

As previously stated, ethnocentric identities had been actively suppressed during the era of Communist rule. But now, like the opening of Pandora's box, these ethnocentric feelings awoke from a long, Communist-induced hibernation to ravage the world. Surrounded by the conditions of a seemingly permanent all-sided societal crisis, these ideas are able to spread and influence more people within ethnic groups, given that "people tend to give up their individual ideas, norms, and rules, and adopt the group rule" in stressful situations. As I already cited from Dr. Marta Weston's arguments, there is only one tentative way to "enhance our self-esteem" in such situations: to "value the groups to which we belong and to devalue other groups."[190] In chapter 3, I demonstrated that even groups who share minimal differences can develop an in-group bias that "is related to people's need for a social identity."[191] Therefore, these conditions increase the prevalence of group mentality and inter-operative tendencies as behavioral aspects of ethnocentric nationalism.

"Mass Behavior"

Of course, both forms of nationalism (civic and ethnic) are manifestations of a group phenomenon/mass phenomenon. As seen with previous examples of ethnic clashes, and within the writings of ethnocentric nationalist ideologues (both old and new), there exist a great number of distinguishing common characteristics and manifestations fixed in this way. As noted by Kecmanovic, these consist of: "anti-individualism, a call for uniformity, a low tolerance threshold for any different attitude or view, the degradation of the rational, a reluctance to consider alternative views, highly polarized mental energy," and "a readiness to act out."[192] One may also share the considerations of John Breuilly that "even if nationalist movements do not have active support, they claimed to speak for the whole nation. In this sense, nationalist politics is always mass politics."[193]

"Conformity"

The next behavioral pattern of ethnocentric nationalism is defined by both Kecmanovic and various other specialists as an aspect of "conformity." As can be gleaned from the above-cited interviews, as well as those cited in the research of Huseyn Aliyev (see note 52), there are several sources of motivation that pushes an individual to conform to the group. As we grow up as a member of certain ethnic groups, we as people naturally tend to adopt the underlying ideas and biases regarding our own and neighboring ethnic groups. However, we will also invariably pick up on the commensality customs, etiquette, situational behavioral mannerisms; the traditional observation of local calendars, rituals, dress, cuisine, accent; and even the phraseology of the certain ethnic group or sub-ethnic group that we belong to. Once we enter a period of crisis, we begin to become more aware of the time it would take to return to a more rational ethno-political interaction, and these qualities suddenly acquire a vital importance. This stems from the base understanding that without the support of our families and ethnic groups, who act as an extended family, we cannot survive. We also understand that, in return for the favor, we have to pay our ethnic communities back with loyalty, thereby showing the utmost conformity to all constituents and cultural markers/symbols of the group as a whole. Thus, we demonstrate that conforming to these attributes within a group, thereby achieving the basic and urgent needs of being liked, being in the right, being rewarded amid a time of trouble by a primitive political life, being positive, showing solidarity, being at ease with our compatriots for the sake of survival, and, eventually, being able to move on from this difficult period. When ethnic conflict deepens the regressive tendencies of any given group, the level of conformity to the group and its ethnocentric nucleus deepen as well. The more a group is imperiled by an ethnic rival group, especially if the latter is notably powerful, the greater the pressure put on members to conform. Then, based on a close acquaintanceship with these ethnic groups in conflict, one can easily recognize all of those circumstances in the times when ethnocentric tensions run high. Once set in motion, this behavioral pattern and other associated sentiments cyclically boost ethnocentric nationalism while simultaneously being "produced by it, created by its instigators and proponents."[194]

Mutually Displayed Ethnic Prejudices

Ethnocentric nationalism is also a set of ethnocentric prejudices concerning one's co-ethnics and members of other ethno-national groups, especially those who are embroiled in conflict. This pattern helps broad masses of common people adopt ethnocentric nationalism as a driving ideology of ethnic conflict. It is here that the ethnocentric nationalism of the ethno-political elite merges with the so-called informal nationalism of "grassroots" movements—the common people. That is why ethnocentric leaders, oligarchs, and intellectuals make a great deal of effort to encourage and spread the popular stereotypes of ethnic prejudices through the various means of communication they control, including popular media outlets and even the word of researchers pretending to act with some manner of scientific authority. Ethnocentric intellectuals also value popular prejudices because they are an easily accessible vehicle to imbue their ideological paradigms (mostly concerning the exclusiveness of race, nation, *vozhd'* [Führer or leader], etc.) into the popular consciousness.

Using a reference from Stuart Sutherland, Kecmanovic indicated the following reasons as to why people hold ethnocentric stereotypes as a cognitive dimension of prejudice:

> Because they are convenient ... because we tend to notice anything that supports our own opinions; because we notice the actions of members of a minority group much more readily than those of a larger group; because people are likely to exaggerate the difference between one set of objects (or beings) and another set when labels are attached to them; because stereotypes can be self-fulfilling; because if someone has a salient feature, he or she is,

due to the halo effect, seen as having other features which are believed to be associated with the former.[195]

By utilizing several distinct examples, I will demonstrate this behavioral norm in a more practical way. During the buildup prior to the 1991 Ossetian-Ingushian ethnic conflict, I asked my students of both Ingushian and Ossetian origin to anonymously describe what they believed to be the most important qualitative characteristics of their respective peoples. Remarkably, the responses from both groups unanimously noted the same positive qualities that are normally considered natural for their groups: *honesty, generosity, hospitality, trustworthiness, faithfulness, valor and bravery, sobriety, pride, self-esteem, integrity*, and so on. They were equally unanimous regarding the negative qualities of their co-ethnics, namely citing their "long-standing *soft-heartedness* and *patience*." However, when characterizing the opposite group, they did not spare them the most humiliating qualitative descriptors, like *unreliability, thieving, archness, cruelty, hardheartedness, rapaciousness, perfidy*, and so on. Interestingly enough, *soft-heartedness* and *hardheartedness*, despite being obvious antonyms, were estimated as negative qualities all the same. However, the former was marked as applicable to their own group as a sort of self-rebuke that shows the apparent necessity of ridding them of this "weakness." Essentially, the respondents hardened themselves in view of a cruel adversary who imminently lacks this "weak," chimera-like remorse or pangs of consciousness, thereby displaying them as an accomplished, unfeeling, and Hollywood-movie/Tolkien-esque aggressor. In fact, this reflected the vivid ethnic division into the categories of "good/bad," and "we" are human/"they" are not, indicating a perilous level of regression in the development of ethnic conflict.[196]

Regarding these prejudiced perceptions, I found a stunning amount of similarities shared among all of the violent ethnic conflicts that I had observed, as well as displayed in the interviews of common people from these conflicting groups at the same time. As one may expect, almost everyone idealized their own ethnic group and outright demonized others. Ethnocentric leaders further encouraged these ghastly images, alongside the strict model of mirror-reflected prejudiced thinking that propagates them. Mass media was inundated with stories that did little more than spread these ethnocentrically prejudiced stereotypes. For example, during the disintegration of Yugoslavia in the early 1990s, Dr. Weston reported that Serbian leader Slobodan Milošević portrayed Croatians as "*Ustasha*," a reference to Ante Pavelić's fascist "Ustaša/Ustaše" regime, which led to Croatia's collaboration with Germany during WWII (notably, their use of a concentration camp system to kill or confine hundreds of thousands of Serbs, as well as Vlachs, Jews, Bosnians, and Croats). In this case, Milošević's stereotyped and prejudicial label imbued the minds of loyal Serbs with the idea that all modern Croats were still "Ustasha" and that they were once again looking for an opportunity to enact genocide against the Serbs.

According to Weston, "the irony was that Milošević, while warning the Serbs in Croatia about the hostile intentions of the Croats, was himself actively preparing for a genocidal campaign against Croats and Bosnian Muslims."[197] This example illustrates a classic case of projection that can be found within the context of any and all ethnic conflicts.

At the same time, ethnocentric leaders in Croatia and Bosnia—Franjo Tudjman and Alija Izetbegović (author of the radical *Islamic Declaration*), respectively—similarly portrayed all Serbs as "Chetnics," which were Serbian nationalist monarchists who also saw action during WWII. With his control over mass media, Tudjman spread this prejudiced stereotype among these two populations. This would more or less allow the Croatian army to kill tens of thousands of civilians during genocides in the proto-state of Serbian Krajina. Serbs, who had been convinced that they were betrayed by Bosnians at the Battle of Kosovo in 1389, then massacred the entire Muslim male population of the Bosnian town of Srebrenica. One may continue to cite examples of how ethnic prejudice lowered the threshold of compassion toward the targets of an ethnic cleansing in this and many other ethnic conflicts. But the point is that prejudiced stereotypes, fostered by crisis and skillfully projected onto the other side, are an effective means to instigate aggressive feelings within an ethnic community.

Ever since violence first erupted in Donbas in 2014, I have watched political talk shows on both Russian and Ukrainian television channels. Russian political analysts often portray the Ukrainian side of the issue as "Nazis" or "Banderites" who aim to "genocide" the Russian-speaking population in Donbas. Their Ukrainian colleagues return the compliment one hundredfold, denouncing the "Russian imperialism," which carries a campaign of direct aggression against the heroically resistant Ukraine. Through both this desire and the exploitation of Ukraine's weaknesses, the Russians "had stolen Crimea" and now strove for "the disintegration of the entire Ukrainian state." While recording the previously cited interviews with Russian and Ukrainian immigrants, I noticed that almost all of them shared these prejudices regarding each other's intentions and propagated the reflected stereotypical characteristics of one another. If you were not perceived as "in favor" of the group in question, then you were seen as an enemy.

During more informal speech (though it sometimes breaches into public statements and discussions), the two sides allow themselves to utilize abusive sobriquets (such as the Russian *hohly* and *ukropy* for Ukrainians or the Ukrainian *katsapy*, *kolorady*, and *moskali* for Russians), slurs, and humiliating and/or mocking jokes and anecdotes regarding one another.

Social networks and even some editions of more formal publications are loaded with prejudiced stereotypes. Here are some examples: According to many Russians, Russian culture during most of the Soviet period (as well as in the modern day) is regarded as "urban," "advanced," and "progressive," while Ukrainian culture is characterized as that of "peasants," being "reactionary," and "retrograde." The pronunciation of the fricative sound *g* as *h*—as it is in Ukrainian (i.e., "Lugansk" in Russian versus "Luhans'k" in Ukrainian)—in Russian speech is considered to be a sign of belonging to the "uncultured plebeians" or "primitive bureaucrats." Thus, many Russians declare that it is inappropriate to associate Ukraine with anything and everything pertaining to the spheres of science, education, entertainment, and general mode/lifestyle. In turn, prolific Ukrainian bloggers ascertain that everything connected with Russian culture from the Imperial and Soviet periods is of an alien and hostile nature to genuine Ukrainian culture, such as literature, music, art, and so on. Therefore, this outside cultural influence, including the works of Pushkin, Tolstoy, Bulgakov, and numerous others, must be forbidden.

In comparing the folklore trends of Russians, Ukrainians, and Belarusians, one of these bloggers promotes the following prejudiced stereotype: a hero of the Russian tales tends to willingly enter battle and suffer some manner of temporal injury from the superior forces of evil. But by mobilizing every available resource during a period of unbelievable privation, the hero ultimately defeats his powerful enemy and celebrates in triumph. Supposedly, Russians like to construct artificial difficulties for themselves in order to overcome them. In contrast, a Ukrainian hero utilizes the ruse of war and natural sophisticated finesse that, in the long run, brings about the desired result. A Belarusian hero, in stark opposition to the previous two examples, essentially invites "the devil" into his own home, giving him shelter, warmth, and food. As a result, the tensions of the enemies are relaxed, thereby "destroying" said enemy by making him a friend. Interestingly enough, the Russian lexicon possesses no positive connotation for the more "cerebral" notions, such as "cunning," "sophisticated finesse," or even "ruse." According to these stereotypes, Russians lack cunning and are constantly warring—for them, it is crucial to prove that they are strong and important, as being humiliated and not getting what they want are equally unbearable to them; Ukrainians move to outwit and overreach their foes tactically; and Belarusians are good at "warming up" friendlier relationships.[198]

In the long run, all of the previously mentioned behavioral patterns of ethnocentric nationalism, including mutually displayed ethnic prejudices, serve the purpose of ethnic delineation and dehumanization of ethnic aliens. Tom Campbell and Chris Heginbotham argued that "the division between 'us' and 'them,' together with the assumption and assertion of 'our' superiority, seems endemic to human society."[199] During the more relatively mild conditions of a crisis, as well as during the conditions of normalcy, this might very well be a natural occurrence. However, in the conditions presented by an all-sided societal crisis, this division between "us" and "them" rapidly regresses from the love of one's own ethnic group to sharp, opened hostility toward another group(s). This exceptionally dangerous pattern of ethnocentric behavior was defined by Kecmanovic as such:

"Brotherhood Within/War-Likeness Without"

This behavioral pattern serves as a dividing line between the relatively mild/middling phases of ethnic conflict and the more outstanding violent stages, where dehumanization, as practiced by ethnocentric nationalists, becomes the tantamount form of ethnic interaction, laying the auspicious groundwork for extreme forms of ethnic cleansing, including some elements of full-on genocide. In such conditions, "crimes against humanity" committed by these ethnocentric nationalists against their ethnic enemies are not regarded as something extraordinary, as the enemy population is "not necessarily defined as humanity."[200] During the more violent stages of ethnic conflicts in the Caucasus, I saw how individual and group dynamics were invariably linked, with the aggression of the leaders augmented by the aggression of the masses, thereby opening the door for the abovementioned vicious interactions. The propaganda apparatuses of rival ethnic groups send waves of hysteria crash into their respective populace by depicting their own ethnic nation as a singular living organism under attack by an "infection." At the end of the 1980s, I observed how Armenians and Azerbaijanis used these methods to project an extreme level of aggression toward one another. This was so vitriolic that they began to actively perceive one another as truly dangerous, necessitating a breach of all shared ties and ultimately initiating the removal of one another from their own territories. They then began arguing about the necessity of cleansing their respective nations from any and all earlier ethnic mixtures. This in turn led to the previously addressed Armenian pogrom in Sumgait, which then spiraled into the bloodiest hot stage of ethnic conflict in the post-Soviet landscape. The Ukrainian case also shows that these efforts usually begin as a surge to cleanse the language and culture of "alien" influence, but it may itself regress into the complete removal of the "foreign element" from their respective territories. This is no better seen than during the Caucasian and Yugoslavian conflicts, which demonstrated some of the heaviest implications of this behavioral pattern of ethnocentric nationalism and garnered these same horrendous results.

Uncritical Obedience to Charismatic Leaders

When ethnic identity has already become integrated into the "core identity" of a group; when the next wave of a societal crisis has already undermined a group's "coping strategy"; when the resources are scarce and both envy and distrust between ethnic neighbors are growing in prevalence; when ethnocentric propaganda has already dehumanized ethnic groups into beings bent on lining their pockets at the expense of a "host" group, thereby defining them as "suitable targets" of righteous wrath; when fear, resentment, and hatred have endorsed a "brotherhood within/war-likeness without" mentality; when the most passionate part of an ethnic group are armed and ready "to defend" its principal ethnic constituents from the "contamination" of both internal and external "infections"—it needs only a charismatic leader to set off the violence. This kind of leader is willing to take full responsibility, presents himself as being able to handle the situation, and, if necessary, could lead an ethnic crusade to establish a border between one's group and the groups of their neighbors/enemies, who have been totally demonized by the projective process. This is especially true if such a leader's command stems from a place of *legitimate authority*.

Much to the chagrin of those who believe that people under such circumstances tend to behave more humanely, Max Rosenbaum reminds us all that "the history of our century [the twentieth century] is one of heinous acts committed by men *obeying authority*."[201] As the leaders of post-Soviet countries rose to power during the first truly free elections, they found that, aside from their new stations, the circumstances of their ascension "further gave them a special position often beyond approach."[202] A combination of these two factors effectively grants them a *carte blanche* to act in accordance with their own inner aggressive tendencies.

"Authoritarianism"

This pattern of ethnocentric behavior is closely linked with the previous concept of obedience. In the above-described circumstances, which fall along the above-stated prevailing feelings and emotions in group behavior, a lot of people feel threatened by the unstable reality of a prolonged transitional period at an individual level. Unlike others, they cannot adjust themselves to the challenges of the rapidly changing conjecture and, as a result, feel insecure, marginalized, incompetent, and "unable to find a point of support in themselves." To that end, I agree with the argument that such people may find a means of overcoming these internal issues within a more authoritarian pattern of leadership.[203]In the previously mentioned social conditions of Russia, Ukraine, and many of the other transitional post-Soviet societies, such people constitute a "silent majority"—otherwise known as "statists" or "lost people." They willingly and positively react to the *social promotion* of the authoritarian agendum of an ethno-political party/movement or charismatic leader, like, for example, Vladimir Putin in Russia. As I have previously pointed out, Putin reestablished a relatively stable sense of order, constrained the influence of independent oligarchs, and forced others to share pieces of their immense riches with the more desperate parties struggling to find a place in the turbulent ocean of frontier capitalism.

This is very symptomatic of how Andrii Bilec'kii describes a possible advent of a new leader and his cohorts in Ukraine. In his article, "How to Recognize the Leader?," he writes:

> From many citizens whom you can meet, one may hear that they regret that, already for the fourth time, they have elected the wrong candidate. But an absolute majority of our caste firmly knows that only an integral, strong, and willful one may lead them out of [their]

miserable existence ... Mediocratists could elect only a mediocratistout of them. That is why today the guarantee for all nations and classes appears to be a declassed element of nobody knowing what nationality he is [a rude hint to President Zelensky].

But a real leader cannot be elected or appointed; he can come forward himself. A superior force of the world (God, Nature, Providence, and History—whatever you may call it) simply sends the chosen one into our world with a special mission ... The leader has beforehand formed a militant armed column for the foray of invasion into the coming [reality] and one may know him only by following him on his march to the future ... The leader can be seen only where gathers the best of the best—into the column of conquerors of tomorrow's light ... Soon, the leader of the devoted patriots will change history.[204]

It is not difficult to notice how Bilec'kii (as well as the leaders of similar ethnocentric organizations mentioned previously) revitalized and practiced some of the basic principles of the OUN-UPA when leading their own movements. Namely, they push an agenda of anti-liberalism, Russophobia, authoritarianism (with a vivid tendency to develop into totalitarianism), *Führerprinzip*, an armed party column, and the adoption of fascist symbols and greetings. During the 2009 and 2010 municipal elections, *Svoboda* (*Freedom*), which was originally founded as the *Social-National Party of Ukraine*, received a third of the seats in Halychyna and officially adopted the Neo-Nazi "*Wolfsangel*" symbol. Though they later tried to discard the symbol, the anti-Semitic and anti-Russian rhetoric that it represented remained intact. The red and black banners of the OUN have become the official banners and colors of *Right Sector*, while nationalist greetings have been adopted by the Ukrainian military. Further still, the Azov Battalion has continued to use the *Wolfsangel* as their official emblem.

Unrestricted Aggressiveness

By its very nature, ethnocentric nationalism is a highly aggressive ideology. The previously cited examples clearly indicate that militancy is an inherent aspect of it and is both intricately and mutually conditioned. Kecmanovic outlined three distinct ways to connect ethnocentric nationalism with latent aggression or active aggressiveness as a behavioral pattern. (1) It *raises* human aggressive potential. (2) Ethnocentric nationalism "triggers" the implementation of aggressive potential, converting it into unrestrained aggression. (3) It provides an ideological platform—justification—"for aggressive acts against people of other ethno-national backgrounds, legalizes and legitimizes such acts, absolving perpetrators of any responsibility whatsoever for their misdeeds."[205]

In that same vein, Robert Cullen reported on an interesting letter sent by Albert Einstein to Sigmund Freud in 1932. By then, Einstein may have already envisioned the destructive power that physics was about to place in humanity's hands. He was also troubled that totalitarians who had made racial and ethnic hatred the basis of their official policy were ascending into positions of power. As such, Einstein asked Freud if psychoanalysis could devise a kind of vaccination to prevent the horror he foresaw: "Is it possible to so guide the psychological development of man that it becomes resistant to the psychoses of hatred and destruction?" he wondered. Freud's reply should give pause—he said that men make war because it feels good. Killing one's enemies, and thus satisfying the dead calling out for revenge, gratifies a fundamental aggressive instinct. That instinct would never go away, and Freud saw no sense in wishing that it would or could. He wrote: "Why don't we accept it as we do so many other painful calamities of life? It seems to be a natural occurrence, biologically well-founded and … scarcely avoidable."[206]

My point is that even if such an aggressive instinct is imminent to human nature, there is another instinct, that of self-preservation, which serves as counterbalance during times of normalcy, thereby giving a person the ability to control aggressive drives. Early on, I demonstrated how this opposing part of human nature had found a practical embodiment in the norms of the Adats, who were (and still are) creating special mechanisms to reconcile or even outright prevent the enactment of vendettas. Soviet leadership rejected common laws like retrograde heritage of the past and replaced them with new ideological paradigms containing proletarian internationalism as a substitution for the preventative and cross-boundary mechanisms of the Adats' way of thinking. When this ideology collapsed with the USSR itself, and during its subsequent replacement by nationalism, the remnants of these homespun ways of thinking amazingly emerged from their Soviet-induced narcosis. However, the only parts to survive this time were those aspects that called for "blood revenge" in its most hideous of forms. When previously covering aspects of the overarching theoretical model, I tried to demonstrate how, in most post-Soviet societies, the complexities of both the objective and subjective socioeconomic and political conditions are what sired ethnocentric nationalism, which, aside from other destructive tendencies, has the remarkable potential and ability to exacerbate the dark side of human nature while suppressing all other holding instincts and control mechanisms. Thus, it enables the enactment of fully gratifying and unrestricted aggression, which during the course of the hot stages of an ethnic conflict can potentially regress into the following:

"Paranoid-Schizoid Behavioral Pattern"
Virtually all of the interviews of common people that I recorded at a time when ethnocentric nationalism engulfed nearly every conflicting ethnic community in the Caucasus revealed obsessions and desires for vengeance against their "malignant" ethnic neighbors. These were expressed through phrases like "They were and are our enemies," "We'll never forget or forgive," "Nothing has changed in these 70 years," "We will not allow genocide again," "We need to be prepared to fight," "They will pay dearly for all humiliations," "We will teach them a lesson," "The bad ones will be put under the knife," and "We'll show them the way back to their places." These statements sound less like an utterance of a "modern" person and more akin to the incantations of some barbarian ancestors who, on the graves of their murdered kinsmen, vowed to gratify their consuming thirst for sacred retribution. The entirety of this society stood on the brink of complete psychosis. Each community had armed cohorts of people ready and willing to perform unbelievable atrocities against each other through acts of ethnic cleansing. And, unfortunately, they followed through.

The model that best describes how many ordinary Caucasian ethnics behaved in these disparate stressful situations originates from the field of child development, called the *paranoid-schizoid model*, which was originally conceived by Melanie Klein.[207] In this instance, however, the behavior exhibited is not a child's regression but an ethnic group's "regression to a paranoid-schizoid phase."[208] The model was first applied to ethnic strife in particular by Dr. Marta Weston, who used it to describe the ethno-nationalist behavior of Serbs and Croats during the Bosnian War.[209] And in the Caucasus, it is once again applicable.

Klein devised the paranoid-schizoid model as a way to explain the behavior of children when processing internal, irreconcilable conflict. She argued "that small children, when dealing with incompatible and conflicting aspects of themselves, resorted to a paranoid-schizoid position." This process includes a set of certain phases: (1) the splitting off of incompatible parts of the self into good/bad to protect the good part from destruction; (2) the building of a "container" as the "safe keeper" of this "good" part of themselves; and (3) the transformation of the "split off" part into an enemy of the "self," which perceives the "other" as a threat. The "self" then feels "persecutory anxiety," which is an exaggerated feeling of dread based on projection. In this phase, the dominant emotions are envy, greed, and fury, which are very easily evoked by frustration. During the course of normal development, especially after maturation, a child is better able to handle this frustration and display a more complex perception of both themselves and others, including the ability to feel empathy, guilt, and a desire for selfless reparation. However, in *stressful situations*, children/groups can regress into their earlier childhood stage of a "paranoid-schizoid pattern," which can have dangerous consequences.[210]

When comparing the evolutionary course of the violent ethnic conflicts in the Caucasus with that of the current Russo-Ukrainian violent ethnic conflict, I noticed that all of them have passed through certain similar stages/phases. Each stage contains certain prevailing behavioral patterns of ethnocentric nationalism that endorsed and legitimized particular forms of ethnic cleansing. If the conflict has passed through all the stages within a certain accomplished cycle, then it will have stunningly similar analogues to those in the past that also did so. After considering this, I then began comparing violent ethnic conflicts in the post-Soviet space with other famous analogous events in Ireland, Rwanda, the Arab-Israeli conflict, conflicts during the collapse of Yugoslavia, and so on. As a result, I found that all of them also possess these cyclical patterns, with each having passed through roughly the same stages as one another. All of them are obviously different in terms of the specific socio-cultural causal factors, but they all share the same building blocks that correspond with the five principal building blocks/constituents of ethnicity. From conflict to conflict, they are all the same, albeit in many different combinations and with the significance of the primary and secondary mobilizing factors being placed in different ranking concessions.

Hence, the task of the next aspect of this theoretical model: to describe the cyclical patterns found within those violent ethnic conflicts in the post-Soviet space, define their typology, and build individual charts, or "passports," with their unique combinations of building blocks.

Notes

1   Raymond C. Taras and Rajat Ganguly, *Understanding of Ethnic Conflict*, 4th ed. (New York: Longman, Pearson Education, Inc., 2006), 22–23.

2   Stuart J. Kaufman, "Spiraling to Ethnic War: Elites, Masses, and Moscow in Moldova's Civil War," *International Security* 21, no. 2 (Fall 1996): 109, cited in Taras and Ganguly, *Understanding of Ethnic Conflict*, 23.

3   Anatoly Isaenko, *Polygon of Satan: Ethnic Traumas and Conflicts in the Caucasus*, 3rd ed.(Dubuque, IA: Kendall Hunt Publishing House, 2014), Table 3-3, 130.

4   Jack Snyder, "Nationalism and the Crisis of the Post-Soviet States," *Survival* 35, no. 1 (Spring 1993): 7.

5   See Kathryn A. Manzo, *Creating Boundaries: The Politics of Race and Nation* (Boulder, CO: Lynne Rienner Publishers, 1996).

6   See, for example, Majid Tehranian, "Ethnic Discourse and the New World Disorder," in *Communication and Culture in World and Peace*, ed. Colleen Roach (London: Sage, 1993); Ghia Nodia, "Nationalism

and Democracy," in *Nationalism, Ethnic Conflict, and Democracy*, ed. Larry Diamond and Marc F. Plattner (Baltimore: John Hopkins University Press, 1994); Charles A. Kupchan, ed., *Nationalism and Nationalities in the New Europe* (Ithaca, NY: Cornell University Press, 1995).

7   Dusan Kecmanovic, *The Mass Psychology of Ethnonationalism* (New York: Plenum Press, 1996); Dusan Kecmanovic, "Nationalism and Psychiatry," *Journal of Medicine and War* 10, no. 2 (1994): 127–32; Dusan Kecmanovic, "Ethno-Nationalism: Between the Normal and Pathological," *Australasian Psychiatry* 3, no. 3 (1995), 180–85; see also Walker F. Connor, *Ethnonationalism: The Quest for Understanding* (Princeton, NJ: Princeton University Press, 1994).

8   I first introduced this term in an article with Peter Petschauer, "A Failure That Transformed Russia," *International Social Science Review* 75, no. 182 (2000):3–16; See also Anatoly Isaenko, *Polygon of Satan: The Ethnocentric Nationalism in the Caucasus,* First (2010), Second (2012), and Third Editions (2014), in the latter, table 3-2, 129–30.

9   Kecmanovic, "Ethno-Nationalism: Between the Normal and Pathological," 181.

10 Kecmanovic, "Ethno-Nationalism: Between the Normal and Pathological," 180–85.

11 See Group for the Advancement of Psychiatry, *Us and Them: The Psychology of Ethnonationalism* (New York: Brunner/Mazel, 1987), 3.

12 Numerous examples can be found in Taras and Ganguly, *Understanding of Ethnic Conflict*, 3–35; see also Fredrik Barth, ed., *Ethnic Groups and Boundaries* (Boston: Little, Brown, 1969), 5, 9, 11, 15–17, 19–20; Abdula A. Said and Luiz R. Simmons, *Ethnicity in an International Context* (New Brunswick, NJ: S.N., 1979), 16–47; Daniel Chirot, ed., *The Crisis of Leninism and the Decline of the Left: The Revolution of 1989* (Seattle: University of Washington Press, 1991); Charles Tilly, *Democracy* (Cambridge, UK: Cambridge University Press, 2007); Tilly and L. Walker, eds., "Special Issue on Ethnic Conflict in the Soviet Union," *Theory and Sociology* 20, no. 5 (1991): 569–724.

13 "Putin nazval dolyu srednego klassa v Rossii," *RT*, March 18, 2020, russian.rt.com/Russia/news/729528-putin-srednii-klass.

14 "Global Wealth Report 2015," *Credit Suisse*, January 12, 2015, 32–35; World Bank ,"Report on Economics in Russia," June 2009, 1–18; the Russian translation of this report was prepared by a team of experts at the World Bank headed by the head Russian economic specialist and coordinator of sector in world countries, Zhelko Bogetich.

15 James Hughes, "Managing Secession Potential in the Russian Federation," in *Ethnicity and Territory in the Former Soviet Union: Regions in Conflict*, ed. James Hughes and Gwendolyn Sasse (London: Frank Cass, 2002), 62–63.

16 Taras and Ganguly, *Understanding of Ethnic Conflict*, 19.

17 Taras and Ganguly, *Understanding of Ethnic Conflict*; see also the list of resolved "nonviolent" ethnic conflicts in the post-Soviet space as documented in Hughes and Sasse, eds., *Ethnicity and Territory in the Former Soviet Union*, xiii. The Russia/Tatarstan and Russia/Bashkortostan conflicts entered the initial stages of conflict in March 1990 and were resolved with the establishment of "treaty Autonomies" within the framework of asymmetric federalism and consociational arrangements under Putin, without any mediation.

18 For details concerning the role of international organizations in finding compromises between competing ethnic parties in post-Soviet countries, see Walter A. Kemp, *The OSCE in a New Context: European Security Towards the Twenty-First Century* (London: Royal Institute of International

Affairs, 1996). An assistance group of the OSCE was also present in Chechnya during both violent phases of the respective conflict. In particular, following the first hot stage in 1996, an OSCE group was present at the Khasav-yurt truce talks.

19   See Alexander Motyl, *The Town to the Right: The Ideological Origins and Development of Ukrainian Nationalism, 1919–1929* (Boulder, CO: East European Monographs, 1980), 17; A.H. Slyusarenko and M.V. Tomenko, eds., *Istoriya ukrains'koi konstitutsii* (Kyiv: Znaniya, 1993), 123–24; Gwendolyn Sasse, "The 'New' Ukraine," in *Ethnicity and Territory in the Former Soviet Union*, ed. James Hughes and Gwendolyn Sasse, 78.

20   Motyl, *The Town to the Right*, 18–19; Sasse, "The 'New' Ukraine," 78–79.

21   See Gwendolyn Sasse, *Bringing the Regions Back In: The Crimean Issue in Post-Soviet Ukraine, Doctoral Thesis* (London: University of London, 1999), 216–26; Sasse, "The 'New' Ukraine," 79; see also Igor Torbakov, "Russian-Ukrainian Relations 1917–1918: A Conflict over Crimea and the Black Sea Fleet," *Nationalities Papers* 24, no. 4 (1996): 679–88.

22   See Sherrill Stroschein, "Measuring Ethnic Party Success in Romania, Slovakia, and Ukraine," *Problems of Post-Communism* 48, no. 4 (July/August 2001): 59.

23   In the early 1990s, the same ethno-political regionalist movement was formed by the Chechens, and they had built their own "ethnic parties," challenging the territorial integrity of the Russian Federation. See Isaenko and Petschauer, "A Failure that Transformed Russia," 5–6.

24   For example, see Jack Snyder, *From Voting to Violence: Democratization and Nationalist Conflicts* (New York: Norton, 2000), 20f.

25   Stroschein, "Measuring Ethnic Party Success," 60; Donald Horowitz even proposed some manner of institutional structure that may constrain the formation of ethnic parties as obviously damaging to the democratic process in multiethnic states. Donald L. Horowitz, *Ethnic Groups in Conflict* (Berkeley: University of California Press, 1985), chapter 15, 348. Additionally, a reminder of the pessimism regarding the ability of multiethnic states to "support stable democracy" is recommended, see Juan J. Linz and Alfred Stepan, *The Breakdown of Democratic Regimes: Crisis, Breakdown, and Re-equilibration* (Baltimore: John Hopkins University Press, 1978).

26   Jon Elster, Claus Offe, and Ulrich K. Preuss, *Institutional Design in Post-Communist Societies: Rebuilding the Ship at Sea* (New York: Cambridge University Press, 1998), 147–48; cited in Stroschein, "Measuring Ethnic Party Success," 61, note 13, 69.

27   Stroschein, "Measuring Ethnic Party Success," 67.

28   "Editorial Article," *Novini Zakarpatia*, November 30, 1991.

29   See Alfred Reisch, "Transcarpathia's Hungarian Minority and the Autonomy Issue," *Radio Free Europe/ Radio Liberty Research Report*, February 7, 1992; Stroschein, "Measuring Ethnic Party Success," 68.

30   Stroschein, "Measuring Ethnic Party Success," 61.

31   Stroschein, "Measuring Ethnic Party Success," 62.

32   Isaenko, *Polygon of Satan*, chapters 4–7.

33   Vasil' Derevins'kyi, *Viacheslav Chornovil: Narys portreta politika* (Ternopil, Ukr.: n.p., 2011).

34   Stroschein, "Measuring Ethnic Party Success," 62.

35   "Ukrainian President Signs Controversial Language Bill into Law," *Radio Free Europe/Radio Liberty*, September 26, 2017, rferl.org/a/ukrainian-poroshenko-signs-controversial-language-bill-into-law/28757195.html.

36   "Ukrainian President," *Radio Free Europe*.

37   "Ukrainian President," *Radio Free Europe*. See also Olga Shumilo-Tapiola, "The Ukrainian Language: LosingIts Voice," *Carnegie Europe*, August 31, 2012.

38   *Derzhavna sluzhba statistiki Ukraïni, Naselennya Ukraini*, Chislenost' naselennya (za otsinkoyu na 1 lyutogo 2020 roku ta serednya chisel'nist' u sichni 2020 roku—41,879,904). This is the total population minus those living in Crimea and Sevastopol, database.ukrcensus.gov.ua/PXWEB2007/ukr/news/op_popul.asp.

39   "Editorial Material," *RIA Novosti Ukrainy*, September 14, 2017, RIAN.com.uza.

40   Tony Wesolowsky, "Ukrainian Language Bill Facing Barrage of Criticism from Minorities, Foreign Capitals," *Radio Free Europe/Radio Liberty*, September 24, 2017, rferl.org/a/ukraine-language-legislation-minority-languages-russia-hungary-romania/28753925.html.

41   "Kyiv 'Disappointed' as Romanian President Cancels Ukraine Visit over Language Bill," *Radio Free Europe/Radio Liberty*, September 27, 2017, rferl.org/a/ukraine-romania-president-cancels-visit-over-language-law/28751116.html.

42   "Vengriia nazvala usloviia dopuska Ukrainy v NATO," *Izvestia*, December 4, 2019, https://iz.ru/950770/2019-12-04/vengriia-nazvala-usloviia-dopuska-ukrainy-v-nato?utm_source=smi2.

43   Editorial: "Venetcianskaya komissiia prizvala Kiev podgotovit' zakon o iazykovykh menshinstvakh," *Izvestia*, December 6, 2019, https://iz.ru/951636/2019-19-06/venetcianskaia-komissiia-prizvala-kiev-podgotovit-zakon-o-iazykovykh-menshinstvakh?utm_source=smi2.

44   Roman Huba, "Why Ukraine's New Language Law Will Have Long-Term Consequences," *Open Democracy: Politica*, May 28, 2019, https://inosmi.ru/politic/20190528/245163604.html?utm_source=smi2.

45   "Kiev gotovitsya k zachistke 'vengerskikh separatistov' v Zakarpattye," *Natsional'naya sluzhba novostei*, December 3, 2019, https://nsn.tm/policy/na-ukraine-nachalas-voemaya-eskalatsiya-protiv-vengrii?utm_source=smi2.

46   *Vremya pokazhet Talk Show*, December 4, 2019, Channel 1, RT.

47   Cited in Wesolowsky, "Ukrainian Language Bill" (emphasis added).

48   Cited in Wesolowsky, "Ukrainian Language Bill."

49   Andrii Drozda, "Strakh i nenavist'u Lvovi," *Zahid*, April 24, 2019.

50   "V Ukraïni nabuv chinnosti zakon pro serednyu' osvitu," *UNIAN Information Agency*, March 18, 2020, unian.ua/politics/10920005-v-ukraiini-nabuv-chinnosti-zakon-pro-serednyu-osvitu.html?_ga=2.157642874.1912961417.1586630503-990977929.1586207445.

51   "V Ukraïni nabuv chinnosti zakon pro serednyu' osvitu," *UNIAN Information Agency*.

52   See Huseyn Aliyev, "The Logic of Ethnic Responsibility and Pro-government Mobilization in East Ukraine Conflict," *Comparative Political Studies* 52, no. 8 (2019): 1200–1231; see the especially meaningful interviews of Russian speakers on pages 1219, 1220, 1221, 1223.

53   Regarding informal nationalism, see Abel Polese, Oleksandra Seliverstova, Emilia Pawlusz, and Jeremy Morris, eds., *Informal Nationalism after Communism: The Everyday Construction of Post-Socialist Identities* (London: I.B. Tauris, 2018).

54   *Ukrainska Konstitutsiya (Constitution of Ukraine)*, 1996 (rev. 2014), Article 10, constituteproject.org/constitution/ukraine_2014.

55   "Region of Ukraine/Autonomous Republic of Crimea," *2001 Ukrainian Census*, retrieved December 16, 2006, 2001.ukrcensus.gov.ua/eng/regions/reg_crym.

56   *Dzerkalo Tzhnia*, September 20, 2013.

57   *Itogy perepisi naseleniya v Krymskom Federal'nom Okruge*. Table 4.1, *Natsional'nyi sostav naseleniya* (2014).

58   *Dzerkalo Tzhnia*, September 20, 2013.

59   Serhy Yekelchyk, *The Conflict in Ukraine: What Everyone Needs to Know* (Oxford: Oxford University Press, 2015), 116.

60   Anna Fournier, "From Frozen Conflict to Mobile Boundary: Youth Perceptions of Territoriality in War-Time Ukraine," *East European Politics and Societies and Culture* 32, no. 1 (February 2018): 47, emphasis added.

61   See Alexander J. Motyl, "It's Time for Ukraine to Let the Donbass Go," *Foreign Policy*, December 6, 2019.

62   In her early publications, Jane Dawson contrarily considered that during the 1990s, "political entrepreneurs" formed from competing ethnic elites failed "to correctly identify and skillfully manipulate existing ethnic, ideological, and geopolitical cleavages" and at that point had "played a central role in deterring violent conflict in the region." See Jane I. Dawson, "Ethnicity, Ideology, and Geopolitics in Crimea," *Communist and Post-Communist Studies* 30, no. 4 (1998): 427, 443. In a 2002 publication, Gwendolyn Sasse similarly believed that "de facto the federal principle is already inscribed in Ukraine's Crimean Autonomy, and the regional diversity which permeates its policy-making, political bargaining, electoral politics and has left its mark on the transition process in general." See Sasse, "The 'New' Ukraine," 96.

63   "Disputed Territories," *The Territories of the Russian Federation 2015*, 16th ed. (London: Routledge, Taylor & Francis Group, 2015), 307, 346.

64   "An Address of the President of Russian Federation on 18 March 2015," Kremlin.ru/events/presidents/news/20603; *Crimea: Russia's Little Pawn,* worldview.stratfor.com/article/crimea-russias-little-pawn

65   UN General Assembly, *Resolution adopted by the General Assembly on 27 March 2014*, undocs.org/en/A/RES/68/262.

66   Vedomosti Verhovnoi Rady, *Procedures of Supreme Rada*, no. 12 (2015), 77.

67   Ilya Somin, "The Dubious Crimean Referendum on Annexation by Russia, "*The Washington Post*, March 17, 2014, https://www.washingtonpost.com/news/volokh-conspiracy/wp/2014/03/17/the-dubious-crimean-referendum-on-annexation-by-russia. All aspects of this case from the perspectives of both Ukraine and international law were investigated in Sergey Sayapin and Evhen Tsybulenko, eds., *The Use of Force against Ukraine and International Law* (The Hague, Netherlands: Asser Press Springer, 2018); James Hughes and Gwendolyn Sasse, "Power Ideas and Conflict: Ideology and Leverage in Crimea and Checnya," *East European Politics* 32, no. 3 (2016): 314–34; Francois Gruber-Magitot, *The Crimean Referendum: A Democratic Secession or an Imperial Annexation? Dissertation* (School of Politics and ZR, Spring 2017); see also an interesting publication on this matter by Qumars Aria, *Was the Russian Annexation of Crimea in 2014 Contrary to International Law* (London: London Metropolitan University, May 24, 2017); in defense of the right of the Russian population of eastern and southern Ukraine to secede grounding on moral consideration, see John Ja Burke and Svetlana Panina, *Eastern and Southern Ukraine's Right to Secede and Join the Russian Federation: A Text Based Argument* (Le Buisson, France: Publications on the International Law, 2014), Burke_Panina_WPS_Ukraine_Secession_21102014; Sansiro Hosaka, "The Kremlin's

"Active Measures" Failed in 2013: That's When Russia Remembered Its Last Resort—Crimea," *Democratizatsiya: The Journal of Post-Soviet Democratization*, 26/3 (Summer 2018): 321–64.

68 Paul Kubicek, "Structure, Agency, and Secessionism in the Soviet Union and Post-Soviet States," in *Secession as an International Phenomenon: From America's Civil War to Contemporary Separatist Movements*, ed. Don H. Doyle (Athens, GA: University of Georgia Press, 2010), 210.

69 In this and in the next endnotes were cited editorial articles of the following editions: *Focus.ud*, February 27, 2014; *New Sebastopolis*, February 3, 2014; *Segodnya.ua (Today.ua)*, February 20, 2014.

70 *Ukrinform*, February3, 2014; *The Moscow Times*, February 25, 2014; *Euronews*, February 25, 2014.

71 "The Situation with the Human Rights and the Rights of Ethnic Minorities in Ukraine," *OSCE Office for Democratic Institutions and Human Rights* (hereafter *OSCE/DIHR*), 2014, 115–16.

72 *OSCE/DIHR*, 116.

73 *OSCE/DIHR*, 115–16.

74 Isaenko, *Polygon of Satan,* 300ff.

75 *OSCE/DIHR*, 115–16.

76 *OSCE/DIHR*, 115–16.

77 Vladimir I. Mukomel' and Sergey R. Hikin, "Crimean Tatars after 'Crimean Spring': Transformation of Identities," *Monitor of Public Opinion: Economic and Social Changes* 33, no. 3 (2016): 51–68; see also Sergei Markedonov, "God Krima" ("A Year of Crimea"), *Politicom.ru*, December 29, 2014.

78 See *OSCE/DIHR*, 116.

79 Arkady Ostrovsky, "Inside the Bear," *The Economist*, October 22, 2016, 11.

80 It is worth noting that Barry Posen was the first to draw a direct correlation between ethnic conflict and the security dilemma in former Yugoslavia and in the post-Soviet space when the Cold War ended due to "the emergence of nationalist, ethnic, and regional conflict in Eurasia." Additionally, the Crimean Case of 2014 fully confirmed his vision. For details, see Barry Posen, "The Security Dilemma and Ethnic Conflict," *Survival* 35, no. 1 (Spring 1993): 27–47.

81 "Question-and-Answer Session," *RT, Channel 1*, April 14, 2014; "Putin: Khar'kov, Donetsk, Lugansk, Kherson, Nikolaev, Odessa ne vhodili v sostav Ukrainy," *Segodnya*, April 17, 2014, http://www.segodnya.ua/politics/pnews/putin-harkov-lugansk-doneck-herson-nikolaev-odessa-ne-vhodili-v-sostav-ukrainy-513722.html. According to the 2001 Ukrainian Census, specifically in Donbas, ethnic Ukrainians made up 56.9 percent of the Donets'k Oblast, with Russians making up 38.2 percent. In the Luhans'k Oblast: 58 percent and 39.1 percent, respectively. Despite this, 74.9 percent of Donets'k and 68.8 percent of Luhans'k residents claimed Russian as their mother tongue. See Yekelchyk, *The Conflict in Ukraine*, 116.

82 Isaenko, *Polygon of Satan*, chapter 4–7; see also examples of such "histories" in the former Yugoslavia, as cited in Marta Cullberg Weston, "When Words Lose Their Meaning: From Societal Crisis to Ethnic Cleansing," *Mind and Human Interaction* 8, no. 1 (Winter/Spring 1997): 26.

83 For an example, see Anna Wylegala and Malgorzata Glowacka-Grajper, eds., *History, Memory, and Identity in Contemporary Ukraine* (Bloomington: Indiana State University Press, 2020).

84 Joseph Brodsky, "Blood, Lies, and the Trigger of History," *TheNew York Times*, August 6, 1993, c8.

85 Yekelchyk, *The Conflict in Ukraine*, 102.

86 Yekelchyk, *The Conflict in Ukraine*, 103.

87 Yekelchyk, *The Conflict in Ukraine*, 105–6.

88 Ivan D. Loshkariov and Andrey A. Sushentsov, "Radicalization of Russians in Ukraine: From 'Accidental' Diaspora to Rebel Movement," *Southeast European and Black Sea Studies* 16, no. 1 (2016): 71.

89 Loshkariov and Sushentsov, "Radicalization of Russians in Ukraine," 73.

90 Andrew Wilson, *Ukrainian Crisis*: *What It Means for the West* (New Haven, CT: Yale University Press, 2014), 39f.

91 Richard Sakwa, *Frontline Ukraine*: *Crisis in the Borderlands* (London: I. B. Tauris, 2015), 58–59.

92 Wilson, *Ukrainian Crisis*, 149.

93 Loshkariov and Sushentsov, "Radicalization of Russians in Ukraine," 74.

94 Mykola Riabchuk, "'Two Ukraines' Reconsidered: The End of Ukrainian Ambivalence?" *Studies in Ethnicity and Nationalism* 15, no. 1 (2015): 83–99.

95 UNIAN.2014b.,"Intelligentsiya lvova vyskazalas' protiv travli russkoyazychnih ukraintsev," June 29, 2015, http://unian.net/politics/889778-intelligentsiya-lvova-vyskazalas-protiv-travli-russkoyazichn-nyih-ukraintsev.html, cited in Loshkariov and Sushentsov, "Radicalization of Russians in Ukraine," 75. These authors refer to representatives of this ideological stream as "statists."

96 Natalia Datskevich, "New Ranking, Same Oligarchs: Meet Ukraine's Richest People," *Novoe Vremya*, October 3, 2019, retrieved by *Kyiv Post*, *Ukraine's Global Voice*, April 23, 2020, kyivpost.com/business/new-ranking-same-oligarchs-meet-ukraines-richest-people.html?cn-reloaded=1.

97 See Nick Kochan, "Ukraine's Oligarchs: Who Are They—and What Side Are They On?" *The Guardian*, March 9, 2014, theguardian.com/world/shortcuts/mar/09/ukraines-oligarchs-who-are-they-and-what-side-are-they-on.html.

98 Kochan, "Ukraine's Oligarchs."

99 Kochan, "Ukraine's Oligarchs."

100 Datskevich, "New Ranking, Same Oligarchs."

101 Kochan,"Ukraine's Oligarchs."

102 See Anton Troianovski, "A Ukrainian Billionaire Fought Russia. Now He's Ready to Embrace It," *The New York Times*, November 13, 2019, nytimes.com/2019/11/13/world/Europe/ukraine-ihor-kolomoyskyi-russia.html.

103 Troianovski, "Ukrainian Billionaire."

104 Troianovski, "Ukrainian Billionaire."

105 Troianovski, "Ukrainian Billionaire"; several facts in the subsequent abstracts about the recent US sanctions against Ihor Kolomoisky are cited in Andrew E. Kramer, "U.S. Sanctions Key Ukrainian Oligarch," *The New York Times*, March 5, 2021.

106 Viktor Medvedchuk's pro-Moscow *Opposition Block–For Life* party won 13 percent of the vote, allowing the otherwise unsanctioned Medvedchuk to return to Ukraine's parliament after more than a decade. See "Parties' Funding: How Pro-Russian Oligarch Viktor Medvedchuk Is Regaining Power in Ukraine," *Hromadske International*, July 19, 2019, en.hromadske.ua/posts/how-pro-russian-oligarch-viktor-medvedchuk-is-regaining-power-in-ukraine.html.

107 Datskevich, "New Ranking, Same Oligarchs."

108 "Saakashvili predrekaet raspad Ukrainy," *Argumenty i Facty*, February 2, 2020, aif.ru/politics/world/Saakashvili_predrekaet_raspad_ukrainy.html.

109 Wayne M. Morris, *Stalin's Famine and Roosevelt's Reconstruction of Russia* (Lanham, MD: University Press of America, 1994), 47–59; This book was followed by Stanislav Kulchytsky's Ukrainian

publication, "Terror holodom iak instrument kolektyvizatsii," in *Holodomor 1932–1933 rr. v Ukraini*: *Prychyny i naslidky*, ed. Stanislav Kulchytsky (Kyiv: Instytut istorii Ukrainy NANU, 1995), 34f. See also Yekelchyk, *The Conflict in Ukraine*, 47–49. The most thorough collection of related documents, including memoirs of the survivors and other sources and assorted literature, may be found in *The Holodomor Reader*, compiled and edited by Bohdan Klid and Alexander J. Motyl (Edmonton, Canada: Canadian Institute of Ukrainian Studies Press, 2012); see also, Stanislav Kulchytsky, "The Ukrainian Holodomor Against the Background of the Communist Onslaught, 1929–1938," translated from Ukrainian by Ali Kinsella and Marta D. Olynyk, Holodomor.ca/wp-content/uploads/2017/09/kulchytsky-holodomor-and-communist-onslaught.pdf.

110 Peter Kenez, *A History of the Soviet Union from the Beginning to the End*, 2nd ed. (Cambridge, UK: Cambridge University Press, 2006), 98–99. My student McBarrett S. Good collected numerous references from other accounts in his Honors Thesis, *How to Alienate a Culture*: *Soviet and Imperial Russia's Role in the Current Russo-Ukrainian Conflict* (Appalachian State University, 2019), 20–22.

111 Hiroaki Kuromiya, "The Soviet Famine of 1932–1933 Reconsidered," *Europe-Asia Studies* 60, no. 4 (June 2008): 665; cited in Good, *How to Alienate a Culture*, 21.

112 Stanislav Kulchytsky, "Terror holodom iak instrument kolektyvizatsii," 34.

113 Yekelchyk, *The Conflict in Ukraine*, 48, (see the second citation in the endnote 109).

114 See Zhores and Roy Medvedev, *N.S. Khrushchev: The "Secret" Speech* (Nottingham, UK: Spokesman Books/Bertrand Russell Peace Foundation, 1976), 58. Quoted in Andre Wilson, *The Ukrainians*: *Unexpected Nation* (New Haven, CT: Yale University Press, 2000), 132–33.

115 Georgy Konstantinovich Zhukov, *Memuary* (Moscow: Gosizdat, 1968), 72.

116 Good, *How to Alienate a Culture*, 22.

117 Ivan Drach, "Chy pokaiet'sia Rosiia? Vystup na mizhnarodnii naukovii konferentsij 'Holod 1932–1933 rr. v Ukraiini,'" in *Polityka* (Kyiv, Ukraine, 1997), 354–58, 354, and 357. Quoted in Andrew Wilson, *The Ukrainians*: *Unexpected Nation* (New Haven, CT: Yale University Press, 2002), 144–45.

118 Yekelchyk, *The Conflict in Ukraine*, 49.

119 See Nazarii Zanos, "Ukraïna mizh travm natsizmorn ta komunizmom," *Zaxid.net*, March 14, 2020.

120 See Paul Robert Magocsi, *The Roots of Ukrainian Nationalism*: *Galicia As Ukraine's Piedmont* (Toronto: University of Toronto Press, 2002); Kenneth C. Farmer, *Ukrainian Nationalism in the Post-Stalin Era: Myths, Symbols and Ideology in Soviet Nationalities Policy* (The Hague, Netherlands: Martinus Nijhoff Publishers, 1980); Andrew Wilson, *Ukrainian Nationalism in the 1990s: A Minority Faith* (Cambridge, UK: Cambridge University Press, 1997); also Andrew Wilson, *The Ukrainians*: *Unexpected Nation* (New Haven, CT: Yale University Press, 2000).

121 Andrii Bilec'kii and Golovnii Providnik SNA, "Chomu sotsial'nii natsionalizm?" *Zbirki ideologichnykh robit i programovykh dokumentiv "Ukrains'kii sotsial'nii natsionalizm"* (Kyiv: Sotsial-Natsional'na Assamblea Sila-Dobrobut-Poriadok, 2012), 24, www.sna.in.ua, emphasis added.

122 Bilec'kii and Providnik, "Chomu sotsial'nii natsionalizm?," 24.

123 "Ridna vira-Mykola Mikhnovs'ky," svit.in.ua, retrieved June 18, 2017.

124 S. Shemet, "Mykola Mihnovs'ky," *Khliborobs'ka Ukraïna*, no. 5 (1925).

125 Victor Rog, "Mykola Mikhnovs'ky, 1873-03.05.1924r.Vaga velikogo zapovity," *Rus'ke Pravoslavne Kolo*, http://www.svit.in.ua; see also *100 vidatnikh ukraïntsev* (Kyiv: Vydavnitstvo Arii, 2006), 325.

126 Paul Magocsi, *A History of Ukraine* (Toronto: University of Toronto Press,1996), 21.

127 See Ilya Prizel, "The Influence of Ethnicity on Foreign Policy: The Case of Ukraine," in *National Identity and Ethnicity in Russia and the New States of Eurasia* Vol. 2, ed. Roman Szporluk (Armonk, NY: M.E. Sharpe, 1994), 115.

128 See Roman Lyah and Nadiya Temirova, *Istoria Ukraïni, Pidruchnik dlya 7-go classu* (Kyiv: "Geneza," 2005), 6.

129 For an explanation of the complexities surrounding the topic of Russo-Ukrainian lineage, see "Part Two: The Kievan Period" in *A History of Ukraine*, ed. Paul Magocsi, (Seattle: University of Washington, 1996), and "Ukraine: Historical Roots of Diversity" in *Ukrainian Nationalism in the 1990s: A Minority Faith*, ed. Andrew Wilson (Cambridge, UK: Cambridge University Press, 1997).

130 Volodymyr Yaniv, "Dontsov, Dmytro," *Entsyklopediya Ukraïni v interneti* (2002), encyclopediaofukraine.com/display.asp?Linkpath=pages%5CD%5CO%5CDDontsovDmyro.htm. The most comprehensive and detailed biography of Dontsov was compiled by Mykhailo Sosnovs'kyi, *Dmytro Dontsov: Politychnyi portret* (New York: Canadian Institute of Ukrainian Studies, 1974).

131 Dzmitra Dantsou, *Natsyianalizm* (in Belorussian), trans. Yura Agievich, ed. Miraslav Peremibida, web.archive.org/web/20080801082612/http://lukveritatis.at.tut.by/ddnacblr.pdf, chastka drugaya, razdel VI, 185–191.

132 Volodymyr Yaniv, "Konovalets, Yevhen," *Encyclopedia of Ukraine* Vol. 2 (1989).

133 Myroslav Yurkevich, "Organization of Ukrainian Nationalists," *Encyclopedia of Ukraine* Vol. 3 (Toronto: Canadian Institute of Ukrainian Studies, 1993).

134 V. Lysyi, "Do istorii 30 chervnia," *Vil' na Ukraïna* 11 (1956); Magocsi, *The Roots of Ukrainian Nationalism*, 33.

135 See John-Paul Himka, "The Lviv Pogrom of 1941: The Germans, Ukrainian Nationalists, and the Carnival Crowd," *Canadian Slavonic Papers* 53, no.2–4 (Special section: Twenty years on: Slavic Studies Since the Collapse of the Soviet Union, 2011): 210.

136 Christine Kulke, "Lwów," in *Encyclopedia of Camps and Ghettos, 1933–1945,* Vol. 2, ed. Geoffrey P. Megargee (Bloomington: Indiana University Press, 2012), 802; Peter Longerich, *Holocaust: The Nazi Persecution and Murder of the Jews* (Oxford: Oxford University Press, 2010), 194. The "Petliura Days" carried on until the end of July 1941, commemorating the assassination of Symon Petliura on May 25, 1926, at the hands of Sholom Schwartzbard—an anarchist of Jewish descent who sought revenge for the Jewish pogroms perpetrated under Petliura's government in 1918.

137 See citation in Alexi Kalinovskii, "Antibolshevistskii block: Fashistskie korni sovremennoi Ukrainy," *Regnum Informatsionnoe agenstvo*, August 18, 2018, 5, https://regnum.ru/news.polit/2466793.html; "Lvivski pogrom 1941-go: Nimtsi, ukraïns'ki natsionalisti i karnaval'na yurba," *Istorichna pravda*, December 20, 2012, iskpravda.com.ua/research/2012/12/20/93550/; see also John A. Armstrong, *Ukrainian Nationalism*, 2nd ed. (Littleton, CO: Ukrainian Academic Press, 1980), 77–84; Karel C. Berkhoff and Marco Carynnyk, "The Organization of Ukrainian Nationalists and Its Attitude Towards Germans and Jews: Iavoslav Stets'ko's 1941 Zhyttiepys," *Harvard Ukrainian Studies* 23, no. 3/4 (December, 1999): 171.

138 Taras Hunczak, *My Memoirs: Life's Journey through WWII and Various historical Events of the 21st Century* (Falls Village, CT: Hamilton Books, 2015), Part 1.

139   See Per Anders Rudling, *The OUN, the UPA, and the Holocaust: A Study in the Manufacturing of Historical Myths: The Carl Beck Papers in Russian and East European Studies*, no. 2107 (2011): 14–15; Jeffrey S. Kopstein and Jason Wittenberg, *Intimate Violence: Anti-Jewish Pogroms on the Eve of the Holocaust* (Ithaca, NY: Cornell University Press, 2018), 92. For the Ukrainian perspective, see D. Vedeneev and G. Bistrukhin, *Dokumental'na spadshina pidcozdiliv spetsial'nogo priznachennia OUN ta UPA, 1940–1950—ti roki* (Kyiv: Geneza, 2006).

140   Per Anders Rudling argues that the SBU relied on the "memoirs" of one Stella Krenzbach—a Ukrainian Jew fighting in the ranks of the UPA. Rudling concludes that these "memoirs," as well as the figure of Krenzbach herself, "were likely post-war falsifications by the nationalist Ukrainian Diaspora." See Rudling, *The OUN, the UPA, and the Holocaust*, x.

141   Himka, "The Lviv Pogrom of 1941," 209–43; Wendy Lower, "Pogrom, Mob Violence, and Genocide in Western Ukraine, Summer 1941: Varied Histories, Explanations, and Comparisons," *Journal of Genocide Research* 13, no. 3 (2011): 217–46; Grzegorz Rossolinski-Liebe, "Debating, Obfuscating, and Disciplining the Holocaust: Post-Soviet Historical Discoveries on the OUN-UPA and Other Nationalist Movements," *East European Jewish Affairs* 42, no.3 (2012): 199–241; Gabriel N. Finder and Alexander V. Prusin, "Collaboration in Eastern Galicia: The Ukrainian Police and the Holocaust," *East European Jewish Affairs* 34, no.2 (2004): 95–118; Per Anders Rudling, "Historical Representation of the Ukrainian Accounts of the Activities of the OUN-UPA," *East European Jewish Affairs* 36, no.2 (2006): 163–89; Vladimir Melamed, "Organized and Unsolicited Collaboration in the Holocaust," *East European Jewish Affairs* 37, no.2 (2007): 217–48.

142   Himka, *Challenging the Myths of Twentieth-Century Ukrainian History*, emphasis added. The text of this work is based on an address delivered at the second annual Celebration of Research and Creative Work Faculty of Arts, University of Alberta, Canada, March 28, 2011, 3.

143   Himka, "The Lviv Pogrom of 1941," abstract.

144   O.I. Stasiuk, "Bandera, Stepan Andriiovich," *Entsiklopedia istorii Ukraïni*, t.1 (Kyiv: "Naukova dumka," 203), 688.

145   "Murder By Bullets: The Einsatzgruppen and Their Fellow Mobile Killers," *Encyclopedia Britannica*, Britannica.com/event/Holocaust/murders-by-bullets-the-Einsatzgruppen-and-their-fellow-mobile-killers. Out of a pre-war population of around three million, Yekelchyk estimates that "900,000 to a million" Ukrainian Jews were killed. See Yekelchyk, *The Conflict in Ukraine*, 52.

146   See Grzegorz Motyka, *Wolyn' 43 Ludobójcza Czystka-fakty, analogie, politica, historoyczna* (Cracow, Poland: Wydamnictwo Literackie, 2016), 85, 124; Yekelchyk estimates that there were approximately 50,000 Polish victims. See Yekelchyk, *The Conflict in Ukraine*, 55.

147   Ilya Levitas, "Mify i pravda o Bab'em Yare," *Jewish Observer*, no. 15/57 (August 2003); see also A. Anatoli (Kuznetsov), *Babi Yar: A Document in the Form of a Novel. New, Complete, Uncensored Version* (any edition); Ilya Levitas, ed., *Entsyclopedia Holokosta*, Yevreiskaya entsyklopediya Ukrainy (Kyiv: Geneza, 2000).

148   Orest Subtelny, *Ukraïna. Istoria* (Kyiv: Lybid, 1993); *Letopis Ukraïns'koi povstans'koi armii*, t. 21 (Toronto, Canada: n.p., 1991); Yekelchyk, *The Conflict in Ukraine*, 51–52.

149   Farmer, *Ukrainian Nationalism in the Post-Stalin Era*, 208.

150   Farmer, *Ukrainian Nationalism in the Post-Stalin Era*, 212.

151   Farmer, *Ukrainian Nationalism in the Post-Stalin Era*, 209.

152 S. Dobrovols'kii, *OUNovs'ke pidpilya Donechini* (Pavlograd, Ukraine: s.n., 2009).

153 Magocsi, *The Roots of Ukrainian Nationalism*, 100f; the last member of the Donetsk Region chapter of the OUN was arrested in 1958. At that point in time, OUN membership totaled around 300,000 individuals. *SBU Declassified Documents on OUN's Activity in Southern and Eastern Ukraine in 1939–1950s*, http://www.ukrainews.com/eng/article/109073.html.

154 V. Markus, "Anti-Bolshevik Block of Nations," *Encyclopedia of Ukraine*, encyclopediaofukraine.com/pages/A/N/antiBolshevikBlockofNations.htm.

155 "The Poison Pistol," *Time Magazine*, December 1, 1961.

156 See Timothy Snyder, *The Reconstruction of Nations*: *Poland, Ukraine, Lithuania, Belarus, 1569–1999* (New Haven, CT: Yale University Press, 2003), 143.

157 Ivan Gamza, "The Elusive Proteus: A Study in Ideological Morphology of the Organizations of Ukrainian Nationalists," *Communist and Post-Communist Studies* 48, no. 2–3 (2015): 9.

158 Rudling, *The OUN, the UPA, and the Holocaust*, 3 (6 of 76 in pdf).

159 Taras Hunczak, "Ukrainian-Jewish Relations," cited in "Organization of Ukrainian Nationalists." See note 133.

160 Hunczak, "Ukrainian-Jewish Relations," 51.

161 Loshkariov and Sushentsov, "Radicalization of Russians in Ukraine," 73–74.

162 Avigdor Eskin, "In Babii Yar the State Outraged on the Victims of Nazism," *RIA Novosti*, February 2, 2017, 1–3.

163 Eskin, "In Babii Yar the State Outraged," 1-3..

164 *Kongress Ukraïns'kikh Natsionalistiv*, da-ta.com.ua/mon_mainnews/815.htm.

165 Wilson, *Ukrainian Nationalism in the 1990s*, 100f.

166 "OUN Rejects Tymoshenko's Calls to Form United Opposition," *Kyiv Post*, March 9, 2010, kyivpost.com/article/content/ukraine-politics/oun-regects-tymoshenkos-calls-to-form-united-oppos-61306.html.

167 Mattia Nelles, "Zelenskiy Wins First Round but That's Not the Surprise," *Atlantic Council*, April 4, 2019.

168 "Ukraine's Future Nazi Leader," *Oriental Review*, January 4, 2018, https://orientalreview.org/2018/01/04/ukraines-future-nazi-leader.

169 Illia Ponomarenko ,"After More Than Three Years in Bases, Azov Regiment Returns to Front," *Kyiv Post: Ukraine's Global Voice*,February 1, 2019, https://www.kyivpost.com/ukraine-politics/after-more-than-three-years-in-bases-azov-regiment-returns-to-front.html?cn-relaoded=1.

170 Cited in Good, *How to Alienate a Culture*, 24.

171 Tom Parfitt, "Ukrainian Crisis: The Neo-Nazi Brigade Fighting Pro-Russian Separatists," *The Telegraph*,August 11, 2014, cited in Good, *How to Alienate a Culture*, 24.

172 Good, *How to Alienate a Culture*, 26.

173 See Mridula Ghosh, *The Extreme Right in Ukraine* (Berlin: Frederich Ebert Stiftung Department for Central and Eastern Europe, 2012), 3–12, library.fes.de/pdf-files/id-moe/09407.pdf.

174 See Artem Afonskii and Georgii Tadtaev, "Pro-Russian Cossacks Responded to the Accusations of Ukraine about Executions in Donbass," *Politica, RBC*, December 6, 2019, https://www.rbc.ru/politics/06/12/19/5deau7ef9a79472db59726ef?utm_source=smiz8.utm_medium=smi28.utm_campaign=smi2.

175 Rustam Atadjanov, "War Crimes Committed During the Armed Conflict in Ukraine: What Should the ICC Focus On?," in *The Use of Force Against Ukraine and International Law*, ed. Sergey Sayapin and Evhen Tsibulenko, 388–408.

176 Afonskii and Tadtaev, "Pro-Russian Cossacks."

177 Atadjanov, "War Crimes," 398–404.

178 Afonskii and Tadtaev, "Pro-Russian Cossacks"; see Marlene Laruelle, *Russian Nationalism: Imaginaries, Doctrines, and Political Battlefields* (London, UK and New York, NY: Routledge, Taylor & Francis Group, 2019), 195–208; see also Yulia Mikhailova, "Electronic Media and Popular Discourse on Russian Nationalism," *Nationalities Papers*, vol. 39, no. 4 (2011), 523–46.

179 See Isaenko, *Polygon of Satan*, and Table 3-2, 129–30. Some of the original titles of these behavioral patterns (in the apostrophic commas) indicate that they had been themselves borrowed from another specialist.

180 Marta Cullberg Weston found all these forms as they manifested in the former Yugoslavia specifically, while Taras and Ganguly deduced them in a more general sense from their appearances in all other ethnic conflicts around the world. See Weston, "When Words Lose Their Meaning," 20–32; Taras and Ganguly, *Understanding of Ethnic Conflict*, especially 19–20.

181 See Kecmanovic, "Ethno-nationalism: Between the Normal and Pathological," 180–85.

182 Carlton Joseph Huntley Hayes, *The Historical Evolution of Modern Nationalism* (New York: Russell and Russell, 1968), 1.

183 See Harold Robert Isaacs, *Idols of the Tribe: Group Identity and Political Change* (Cambridge, MA: Harvard University Press, 1989), 171f.

184 Bilec'kii, "Patriotism proti natsionalizmu," *Zbirki ideologichnykh robit*, 14.

185 See Arthur Koestler, *The Ghost in the Machine* (London: Hutchinson & Co., 1967).

186 *Yad Vashem. The World Holocaust Remembrance Center*, righteous.yadvashem.org/index.html.

187 For example, see Isaenko, *Polygon of Satan*, chapter 7.

188 Isaenko, *Polygon of Satan*, chapters 4–8.

189 Ervin Staub, *The Roots of Evil: The Original Genocide and Other Group Violence* (Cambridge, UK: Cambridge University Press, 1990), 13.

190 Weston, "When Words Lose Their Meaning," 23.

191 Weston, "When Words Lose Their Meaning," 23.

192 See Kecmanovic, "The Ethnonationalism-Like Behavioral Pattern," *Mind and Human Interaction* 8, no. 1 (Winter/Spring 1997): 4.

193 John Breuilly, *Nationalism and the State*, 2nd ed. (Chicago: Chicago University Press, 1994), 300 and following pages.

194 Kecmanovic, "The Ethnonationalism-Like Behavioral Pattern," 5.

195 Kecmanovic, "The Ethnonationalism-Like Behavioral Pattern," 4; see also Stuart Sutherland, *Irrationality* (London: Constable, 1992).

196 Isaenko, *Polygon of Satan*, 246.

197 Weston, "When Words Lose Their Meaning," 25.

198 "5 Traits of Primordial Russian Culture That Distinguish Russians from Ukrainians," *Yandex.Zen*, October 24, 2019, https://zen.yandex.ru/media/russian_friends/5-chut-iskonno-russkei-kultary-katorye-otlichaiut-otoukrainecev-5dad131678125e00ad553114; Meir Brook, "Osobennosti trioh

narodov-russkogo, ukrainskogo, beloruskogo i ikh yevreiskie prelomlenia," *Yandex.Zen,*April 19, 2020.

199 Tom Campbell and Chris Heginbotham, *Mental Illness: Prejudice, Discrimination, and the Law* (Dartmouth, UK: Dartmouth Publishing Company, 1991); cited in Kecmanovic, "The Ethnonationalism-Like Behavioral Pattern," 3.

200 Liah Greenfield and Daniel Chirot, "Nationalism and Aggression," *Theory and Society* 23, no. 1 (February 1994): 79–130.

201 Max Rosenbaum, "Compliance," in *Compliant Behavior: Beyond Obedience to Authority*, ed. Max Rosenbaum (New York: Human Science Press, 1983), 33, emphasis added.

202 Weston draws a comparison to the development of these same conditions in the former Yugoslavia. Weston, "When Words Lose Their Meaning," 28.

203 Kecmanovic, "The Ethnonationalism-Like Behavioral Pattern," 6.

204 Bilec'kii, "Yak piznati vozhdia?," *Zbirki ideologichnykh robit*, 10–11.

205 Kecmanovic, "The Ethnonationalism-Like Behavioral Pattern," 6.

206 Robert Cullen, "Cleansing Ethnic Hatred," *Atlantic*, no. 2 (1994), 30–36.

207 Melanie Klein, *Envy and Gratitude and Other Works (1946–1963)* (New York: Delta Books, 1975).

208 Klein, *Envy and Gratitude*, 30f.

209 Weston, "When Words Lose Their Meaning," 24f.

210 Weston, "When Words Lose Their Meaning," 24.

CHAPTER SEVEN

Cyclical Pattern and Typology of Violent Ethnic Conflicts in the Post-Soviet Space

In comparing the exact chronology of seven distinct ethnic conflicts in the post-Soviet space, I noticed that the previous ones each passed through three distinct stages and that the current Russo-Ukrainian conflict is itself passing through its second phase. In addition, both sides of the conflict, as well as members of the wider international community, have (at this current time) made failing efforts in order to allow this conflict to enter into its less violent and relatively peaceful stage.

In *Polygon of Satan*, I introduced a set of specified designators for each stage of the final cycle of violence in post-Soviet ethnic conflicts that has analogues in the rest of the sixty-one ethnic conflicts taking place around the world. Surprisingly, this even applies to very old conflicts (such as the Arab-Israeli and Irish conflicts) that have already passed through multiple historical cycles on their own. Furthermore, within each of these cycles exists a set of three distinct stages with their own associated lengths, sometimes including breaks and interruptions that define the bloody stages of these confrontations.

Some violent ethnic conflicts end with the "total victory" of one side and the crushing defeat of the other. For example, the Serbo-Croatian conflict concluded in 1995 when Serbian Krajina was leveled and around 200,000 Serbs were violently purged from their ethnic territory. However, this is far from being a cut-and-dried affair. Currently, other conflicts rest in the beginning, in the midst of, or close to the end of these stages, thereby embodying the specific qualities of each.

I define the first distinctive stage of each violent ethnic conflict cycle as the *stirring-up stage*; the second is the *hot stage*; and third, assuming that certain conditions are met, the conflict may enter the *smoldering stage*. If certain holding conditions are in place that continue to reproduce the same constraining effect, then the *smoldering stage* may gradually cool and see the conflict enter its *frozen period*. Alternately, if either side or other international actors are interested and willing to continue promoting certain "holding mechanisms" and build a more viable democratic/liberal political culture, one side of the conflict may find a peaceful resolution. At the end of this project, I will discuss such possible holding and healing mechanisms that may prove effective in the current Russo-Ukrainian conflict.

The Stirring-Up Stage

The beginning of the stirring-up stage in many post-Soviet conflicts temporarily coincided with Gorbachev's "Perestroika" policy (1986–1991), which resulted in the collapse of the old system and an all-sided societal crisis that triggered the long, arduous, and controversial transitional period. Recurrent and highly complex, periodic waves of this complicated crisis (including a crisis of morals) still shake the unstable and fragile economies and societies of the wild frontier, oligarchic crony capitalism, and the sociopolitical systems of many post-Soviet states. More importantly, they reproduce the same auspicious conditions for the rise and subsequent spread of ethnocentric nationalism within most multiethnic societies. These three conditions are identical to the ones I highlighted in the previous chapter and still hold a great deal of influence in these countries today.

As an analysis of the current course of the latest cycle of violent ethnic conflicts in the post-Soviet landscape may suggest, the stirring-up stage usually begins with a *triggering event*, which delivers a veritable jolt to any given ethnic nation that resonates within the collective mind of the population and specifically exalts emotions like fear, hatred, and resentment. Roger Peterson defines them as "a mechanism that triggers actions to satisfy a pressing concern." He further argues that "it helps the individual and groups to meet situational challenges" by (1) raising "the saliency of one desire/concern over others" and (2) by heightening "both cognitive and physical capabilities necessary to respond to the situational challenge."[1]

Such events set in motion the ethnicization of sociopolitical life within these countries, thereby enabling the later development of strife. At this point, ethnocentric nationalism takes root and gradually embraces a considerable part (in not the majority) of familiar co-ethnics, their ethno-political elite—former "national communists"—and new kinds of activists that produce the embitterment that predisposes its audience into becoming ethnocentric nationalists. These groups then begin crystallizing the *ethnic paradigms* (see the corresponding paragraph in chapter 5) used to mobilize the masses in times of action. In a more practical sense, these strategies share similarities with those of former Yugoslavian ethno-political elites who, in the words of V.P. Cagnon, were "a response ... to shifts in the structure of domestic challengers who seek to mobilize the population against the status quo and can better position themselves to deal with future challenges."[2] Thus, a contingent of these ethno-political elites—who tend to be avid ethnocentric nationalists—use a triggering event to redirect the preferences of the masses and the behaviors of the remaining elite, simultaneously "proving" that only they can feasibly provide the outside support of international forces and co-ethnic diasporas for the sake of the "national cause." For instance, Russian nationalists cursed the Yeltsin administration, which supposedly "betrayed Serbia" and allowed "[the] Serbs' enemies to tear them to pieces" with the aid of "Western predators." Similarly, Putin has, on multiple occasions, reiterated that he "would not allow" Ukrainian forces in Donbas to recreate the "scenario" surrounding the previously discussed "slaughter in [Srebrenica]."[3]

At this stage, and while interpreting a triggering event, ethnocentric nationalists raise and consolidate the *fear* that increases the desire of their respective populace for security, the *hatred* that allows for the articulation of historical grievances and injustices, and the kind of *resentment* that prepares individuals and groups to address status and self-esteem shortcomings. Essentially, a triggering event serves to assist ethnocentric nationalists in building an image of their concrete "ethnic enemy/enemies"—who are "guilty" of manufacturing the misfortunes, hardships, and privations that plague their co-ethnics—within the common ethnic consensus.

If this provocative part of the ethno-political elite already holds power, then they will begin to mobilize all facilities they have at their disposal in order to propagate ethnically biased ideas, organize broad ethnocentric movements, and equip armed formations to "defend" their co-ethnics from internal and external "enemies."They begin incorporating ethnocentric paramilitary formations into the official state armed forces and promoting those loyal officers who share these dominating ethno-political paradigms into key positions in the chain of command. They will do the same for law enforcement agencies, the secret police, and the judicial system, ultimately reformatting the civic structures of their society to better suit their ideological goals.

If ethnocentric forces are not yet in power by this stage, then they will focus their efforts on acquiring these positions of authority. One such way sees them build their ethno-political organizations to a more formidable level and utilize democratic processes to penetrate the more crucial political structures of the state. Another method sees these elites craft highly attractive social demagogy, containing vivid ethnic/ethnocentric underpinnings and redirecting the social indignation of the masses. This then allows them to stage popular revolutions or coups in order to ascend to power. Alternatively, both courses of action can be undertaken simultaneously, with those in the government provoking ethnocentrically based social unrest in order to supplant current leadership.

At the same time, they encourage and instigate the previously detailed behavioral patterns of ethnocentric nationalism that have been spontaneously generated by the objective reality of a devastating all-sided societal crisis. With this, the stirring-up stage sees the emergence of the aforementioned effects of "a combined presence of mass hostility within ethnic groups, ethnic outbidding and out flank-ing by [ethno]political elites within the groups, and a security dilemma that increases collective fears for the future." In the long run, these factors would lead to an "increasing spiral of ethnic violence," as demonstrated by Stuart Kaufman's examination of the "ethnic civil war" in Moldova.[4] This *ethnocentric consolidation* helps these nationalists unite more people under their banner and encourage them to join their organizations, parties, and armed groups. In these machinations, ethnocentric nationalists pay special attention in presenting themselves to the youth and, in some cases, children, as they are the most fragile and vulnerable section of the population amid a crisis and, as a result, the most susceptive to the effects of radical behavior.

Various interviews I have taken from common people living amid this stage of ethnic conflict, coupled with the analysis of media reports, the legislative practices of the titular nation's ethno-political elites, and their vividly underpinned socioeconomic policies, show the deteriorating conditions of the principal and secondary constituents of ethnicity for targeted ethnic minorities. I previously mentioned these recurrent practices—which rest in the spheres of linguistic culture, history, common biological origin, nationality, and religion—as well as the sociopolitical measures undertaken at this stage during the conclusion of chapter 5. In a publication written in conjunction with Peter Petschauer, we demonstrated that at this stage of a conflict, any undertakings pertaining to the principal building blocks and cultural boundary markers of ethnicity correspond to *mild and middle-ground forms of ethnic cleansing*. These actions, which oppose the ethnic building blocks of targeted groups, are initiated by the ethno-political elites through sociopolitical machinations. Simultaneously, considerable groups of their co-ethnics commit mild and middle-ground actions against the people and property of these same dehumanized/targeted ethnicities.[5]

Samples of Mild and Middle-Ground Forms of Ethnic Cleansing during the Stirring-Up Stage

In a period between late 1988 and early 1989, the first large group of South Ossetian refugees arrived in North Ossetia after fleeing from inner Georgia. All hotels, health resorts, rest homes, and many other tourist centers, which at one point had provided the republic with significant income, were subsequently provided to these traumatized and poverty-stricken refugees; even the residence halls of North Ossetian State University (in the capital of Vladikavkaz) were reassigned for this purpose. Uniformly, these same refugees would report many uncomfortable or traumatic encounters with Georgians in the country during their temporary tenure. The following is a sample of the accounts and tales that I collected between 1988 and 1989.

A former student at Tbilisi University told me that one day, as he was walking across the campus, he found himself being accosted by a group of young Georgians in a jeep. They used the wheels to splash him with water and mud while shouting, "Go back to your pigsty and trade with your stinking corn moonshine!" ("*Araka*" is a maize liqueur that Ossetians drink at all traditional celebrations.) Similarly, a father of two complained of how he was unable to help his daughter, who had graduated from high school with honors, enroll in the Department of Economics at this same university because the professors in charge of admissions claimed bribes for admission from Ossetians needed to be twice as much as those of Georgian students. A former attorney from Tbilisi reported that he and three other Ossetian lawyers lost their jobs for what they considered far-fetched accusations. Following their release, their Georgian bosses filled the now-vacant positions with relatives who possessed the "proper" ethnic credentials. A former highway patrol officer said that there were many Ossetians working within the department prior to 1988. However, that year saw all of them fired under the pretense of an agency-wide "staff reduction." An older woman from Marneuli told me that she had not seen her own pension for nearly seven months, while her Georgian neighbors regularly received their stipends. Another woman recounted how, when attempting to sell her property in Kakheti (Georgia), she received mockingly low prices from every prospective buyer. Additionally, she heard other Georgians offensively remark, "Don't buy from Ossetians. Wait a bit. Soon all their belongings will be ours without payment."[6]

If history shows anything, it is that some kind of backlash has never lagged behind a perceived slight. In 1950, my parents befriended a Georgian named Rezo and his family in Vladikavkaz. They were wonderful people, who for many years ran a very successful café in one of Vladikavkaz's most prestigious establishments. This would change in 1988, when the Ossetian municipal authorities abruptly curtailed their rent and sank the business. Afterward, and with great difficulty and several huge bribes, Rezo managed to find a job at a gas station. This would not last long, however, as his Ossetian boss soon accused him of stealing gas and summarily fired him. Simultaneously, his two sons, who had both graduated cum laude from university, repeatedly failed to find jobs in Ossetia.

In the meantime, mobsters threatened their other family members, demanding that they pay some nonexistent debt. Finally, and as a result of all these pressures, Rezo was forced to sell his magnificent property for a modest sum to a buyer with the "proper" ethnic background, and his family traded their native home of Vladikavkaz for Georgia. Rezo's son Misha told me how his university professor, himself a Western Ossetian, once began a test with an unusual remark. Whether or not he was joking was unknown, though he seemed serious in saying: "To Digorians [Western Ossetians], I give As; to Ironians [Eastern Ossetians], I give Bs; to Kurdarians [South Ossetians], Cs; and to the rest, according to their knowledge, what is left" (recorded by author, July 1, 1989, Isaenko, file 1, list 38).

Through the interethnic clashes in Uzbekistan and Kazakhstan, I have already demonstrated what I call the process of "*homogenization and/or exchange of population,*" which started under the direct pressure of ethnocentric nationalism. The former examples show that a part of this process is embodied by the forcible outmigration of non-titular ethnic groups (like Meskhetian Turks, Dungans, etc., and, as a byproduct, the "volunteer outmigration" of Russians). In other cases (like those cited above), this process comes by way of a *mutual compulsory exchange of ethnic populations* as a result of implementation during the stirring-up stage of mild and middle-ground ethnic cleansing on both sides of the conflict. By the end of this stage, the process catapults total ethnic delineation and further escalates existing ethnic tensions: the brotherhood within/warlikeness without behavioral pattern becomes the prevailing form of ethnic interaction. Careful monitoring of the situation then leads into the increasing frequency and intensity of physical, verbal, and moral abuses/attacks at the hands of ethnocentric mobs. Concerningly, these tensions have the capacity to spontaneously explode into sporadic ethnic pogroms, with devastating results. The blood of innocent civilians haphazardly spilled by these driven mobs predetermines further deterioration of the courses of ethnic conflicts, leading them into the most dangerous and violent stages accompanied by *extreme forms of ethnic cleansing with elements of genocide.*

Hot Stages

Similar to the preceding stage, the hot stages of violent ethnic conflicts also tend to begin with *triggering events.* In fact, it is because of the hot stage as a concept that ethnic conflicts have accrued their standard connotation as overly violent, as incredible acts of violence occur on a regular basis at this stage, as opposed to their sporadic appearances in the stirring-up stage.

In an overheated atmosphere of ethnocentric hysteria, which by the end of the stirring-up stage has engulfed whole ethnic groups into conflict, it only takes one lit match of discontent to ignite the social gasoline and trigger the avalanche-esque and mirror-reflected dynamics of ethnocentric behavioral patterns. This entails a gradual slide from brotherhood within/warlikeness without to the development of unrestricted aggressiveness characteristic of the third phase of Kline's model, with subsequent regression into a paranoid-schizoid pattern at the group level and all accompanied by *extreme forms of ethnic cleansing.* I will cite the specific triggering events pertaining to each of the seven main violent ethnic conflicts of this study within their respective charts in the next chapter. But regardless of these specifics, they have all had the same effects in electrifying the conflicting ethnic societies in ways akin to "The Shot Heard round the World" in Lexington, Massachusetts, and the "Boston Tea Party" of the eighteenth-century American Revolution. These events in hand, the elites of those titular ethnic nations call their respective masses of co-ethnics to arms and mobilize any and all efforts (mostly the deployment of armies) to utterly destroy "ethnic enemies" and to "get rid of them once and for all, no matter what." During the hot stages, both sides of the conflict use these highly radicalized mantras to bolster their legitimacy and harden the resolve of their followers.

Extreme Forms of Ethnic Cleansing during the Hot Stages of Violent Ethnic Conflict

Stories set during the hot stages of the different post-Soviet ethnic conflicts allow me to identify the following forms of strife corresponding to the principal building blocks of ethnicity, state organizations, and socioeconomic practices.

(I) Regarding the *common biological origin building block* are these: (1) the assertion that the biological nature of one's ethnic enemies is generally inferior and reproduces inferior abilities in kind; (2) the general reemergence of absurd racist theories.

(II) The use/abuse of *language* includes the following: (1) linguistic chauvinism; (2) the neglect, hindrances, prohibitions, or oppression of non-dominant languages, sometimes on a legal basis; (3) the reduction in the number of schools operating in non-dominant languages; (4) the introduction of methods of categorization of peoples based on linguistic culture in the educational sphere.

(III) Regarding *religious expression*, ethnocentric nationalists practice the following: (1) the prohibition of minorities from their places of worship, the destruction of their temples and churches, or the expropriation of parishes by contesting confession; (2) the restriction of minority religions to operate their own organizations and councils; (3) disapproval and prohibition of marriages between dominant and minority groups; (4) the radicalization—almost pre-pogrom-like—of dominant religious teachings, such as sermons and publications of inciting character; (5) the assertion of supposedly malignant/evil characteristics of minority religions by the dominant religious group; (6) the restriction of minority religions to create/maintain their own charitable institutions, communities, and so on; (7) if either side of the conflict belongs to the same religion, one of them will attempt to form autonomous structures with different administrative structures loyal only to them.

(IV) The act of *sharing histories* has produced (and continues to produce) the following extreme forms: (1) the rehabilitation, mass glorification, and state glorification of the dominant ethnic groups' historical personages—who are the perpetrators of crimes against ethnic enemies—and the simultaneous degradation of the historical heroes of ethnic minorities; (2) the falsification of the history of the dominant ethnic group by their respective ethnocentric intellectuals; (3) the falsification of the history of minority groups, including the projection of negative components onto supposed enemies.

(V) The *nationality building block* manifests itself in the following: (1) the mass relocation of minorities, accompanied by ethnically charged statements, policies, and activities; (2) claims of how "primordial ethnic territories" should be returned or retained by force: (3) calls for territorial readjustments or the realignment of borders by both public or state officials; (4) the removal of autonomy status of minority groups by the dominant ethnic nations and the subsequent prohibition of symbols and accoutrements of their independency and the ethnic names of particular territories; (5) the assertion of the dominant group's rights through the change of place names that carry traces of "alien" presence; (6) the implementation of restrictions on available living spaces for minorities; (7) the desecration or total destruction of the burial sites, memorial places, cultural monuments, museums, and so on belonging to or servicing ethnic enemies.

(VI) Oftentimes, *state organizations intensively practice* the following: (1) the open persecution of minority leaders, public persons, and activists; (2) organized and state-sponsored defamation of a particular ethnic group and its leadership; (3) the organization of campaigns to boycott certain ethnic minorities, including the imposition of blockades of their territories by cutting off supplies, energy, water or other vital resources, as well as access to social programs and earned benefits (pension payments, stipends, etc.); (4) the use of intimidation tactics and terrorist attacks on minority leaders and activists; (5) the organization and enactment of campaigns of mass murder/extermination against "alien" populations by armed paramilitary formations, random attacks on random civilians, crimes against persons and their properties and extrajudicial executions (this can include military functions, including the regular targeting of civilian settlements by artillery barrages, the use of prohibited weapons, the intentional destruction of civilian infrastructure [including power plants, hospitals, schools/kindergartens, etc.], and the creation of minefields and atypical booby-traps); (6) the appearance of organized or encouraged actions aimed at the destruction of ethnic minorities by creating inhospitable or unbearable living conditions; (7) the suppression and elimination of groups of unwanted people, dislocations, and ethnically targeted banditry; (8) the creation of state-sponsored conditions of everyday life that encourage ethnic groups to return to live in their former ethnic homeland; (9) the denial of minority access to key political, economic, and social resources via ethnically controlled state organizations, as well as closing down oppositional media outlets; (10) the active enslavement and exploitation of "aliens" within the households of the dominant group; (11) separate yet interconnected cases of massacres and pogroms against the minority/ethnic enemy by the dominant majority.

(VII) The *economic practices* of ethnocentric nationalists of titular nations include the following: (1) the imposition of restrictive measures on representatives of the "unwanted groups"; (2) official and nonofficial measures that exclude minorities from working in specified professions; (3) unequal and unfair taxation of ethnic minorities; (4) the protection of fellow ethnics from the official laws and regulations of their society, especially when contesting with a member of an ethnic minority; (5) the confiscation of property from non-dominant ethnics and its subsequent redistribution to fellow dominant ethnics.

It is important to note that such extreme forms of ethnic cleansing during the hot stages of ethnic conflicts were (and in some cases, still are) carried out by state military detachments, paramilitary volunteers, and mobs of armed people, all inspired and led by ethnocentric nationalists. The dominating behavioral patterns, at this point being *blind obedience to charismatic leaders*, *authoritarianism*, *unrestricted aggressiveness*, and ultimately *regression to a paranoid-schizoid behavioral pattern*, allow them to commit the most monstrous of crimes, which are easily identified as key elements of genocide.[7]

Additionally, this selection is based primarily on the analysis of the hot stages in all seven violent ethnic conflicts in the post-Soviet space specifically. That being said, it is by no means far-fetched to infer that, in these particular conflicts, the combination of these forms of extreme character are themselves varied, though some extreme forms are omnipresent among them. This is especially true regarding the "organized mass murder and extermination of [an] 'alien' population by armed forces and paramilitary formations," "random and indiscriminate attacks on civilian settlements," "crimes against persons and their properties," and "extrajudicial executions" (see section VI. 5 above).

Within these many intermittent periods of strife, including 1989 to 1994, 1996 to 2009, August 2008, and from 2014 to the current day (in Ukraine), the recurring cycle of hot stages of the latest ethnic conflicts (particularly between Azerbaijanis and Armenians, Ossetians and Ingushians, Georgians and South Ossetians, Georgians and Abkhazians, and Russians and Chechens) has resulted in almost two million people being forcibly displaced, tens of thousands murdered, and hundreds of thousands wounded, alongside a litany of psychological traumas and the demodernization of their societies.[8] Regarding the hot stage burning in Ukraine since 2014, specifically, more than 13,000 have been killed, 30,000 wounded (predominantly civilians, just as in the abovementioned conflicts), and nearly five million people have been displaced from the affected territories. This last ethnic conflict vividly displays all of the currently mentioned regularities and features of the central theoretical model of this work, including the very high possibility of a gradual escalation/transformation into a calamitous global clash between the West and Russia well past the end of the Cold War.

The estimated number of casualties in the "Moldovo-Transnistrian" conflict (or in my terminology, the "Russo-Moldovan" conflict) currently rests near 1,400 total deaths. Moldova's losses come to about 286 dead and 284 wounded, while Transnistria's ("Pridnestrovie") account for 826 casualties, 310 of which were civilians.[9]

Volunteers/Mercenaries: Their Motivations

Both I and my colleague Steve Bowers recognize the high volume of volunteer combatants from different countries and ethnic diasporas who have actively participated on either side of the various ethnic conflicts in the post-Soviet space, with the most prominent figures stemming from the Georgian-Abkhazian conflict. The participation of ethnic/national Russians in this instance was considerable, making up as much as a third of the overall troops who fought for the Abkhazians. They included highly skilled military personnel consisting mostly of ex-Soviet soldiers possessing the training and skills granted by a professional military background, which was sorely lacking among other volunteers. This even included specialists like pilots, demolitionists, trainers, and other valuable military professionals. Their skill was helped along by the fact that all the weapons and equipment were Soviet-made, giving them a familiarity with their implements. Also, and despite a large number of "adventurers" in their ranks, some Cossacks were ideologically biased via "anti-Imperialistic" or "anti-Georgian" sentiments, which the Abkhazians made good use of.

North Caucasian volunteers, which included Kabardians, Circassians, and Adygeans, had myriad potential reasons for joining the military action in Abkhazia, with the strongest being nationalism, given the general proximity between their cultures and that of the Abkhazians; though in the case of the Chechens, it might have been based more on religion (the struggle for Islam) and/or political motives (the independence of the North Caucasus as a whole). However, I think that the Chechen motivations, regardless of their origin, had been enhanced by a desire to use the conflict to cultivate much-needed military experience in anticipation of an armed conflict at home. Some Ossetians from South (and even North) Ossetia also took part in the war against Georgia. On the other side of things, the Georgian side saw an influx of Ukrainian volunteers from the *UNA-UNSO* ethnocentric nationalist organizations.[10] Later on, some of these same Ukrainians fought for the Chechens in the Russian-Chechen conflict. In both accounts, the staunchly anti-Russian (i.e., "anti-imperialist") sentiments of these particular volunteers were strikingly obvious and primarily corresponding with the ancient proverb: "the enemy of my enemy is my friend."

Mujahedeen Mercenaries in the Russian-Chechen Conflict

By 1994, Dzhokhar Dudayev, president of the secessionist Republic of Ichkeria, had failed to obtain any direct support from either the West or the governments of Muslim countries. He wished to build an army of guerilla partisans capable of traditional "hit-and-run" tactics, which are officially regarded as actions of a "low-level guerilla war" in the West. For that express purpose, he wanted to attract the support of both experienced and novice mujahedeen fighters from across the Islamic world. To do so, he had Chechen Mufti Akhmad-Haji Kadyrov proclaim their resistance against Russia a *jihad*.

Simultaneously, the Pakistani ISI (Inter-Services Intelligence) began sponsoring a "Taliban" offensive, which jeopardized the flow of heroin shipments from Afghanistan that served to finance the Chechen revolt. Some Islamabad authorities intervened to ensure the continued movement of drugs and, by using Gulbuddin Hekmatyar's *Hezb-e-Islami* political party as a front, encouraged the already strengthening ties with Chechen leadership. Between April and June of 1994, the Chechen delegation, headed by Dudayev's first lieutenant, Shamil Basayev, visited the ISI's sponsored terrorist training infrastructure in both Pakistan and Afghanistan. According to Yossef Bodansky, Pakistani General Hamid Gul and his aid, Colonel Imam, would assist the Chechens in arranging local connections and contracts for their drug and weapon smuggling operations. The first hundred Chechen terrorists were trained in camps located near Khōst, Pakistan, which is where Osama bin Laden himself received his "elementary" terrorist education.[11] Additionally, the Chechen jihad gained several powerful patrons within Pakistan, including retired Major-General Naseerullah Babar (minister of internal security), Aftab Shahban Mirani (minister of defense), and General Javed Ashraf Qazi of the ISI. In particular, these benefactors arranged for the establishment of a comprehensive training and arming program for the Chechens in Pakistan and Afghanistan.[12] In the autumn of 1994, in an attempt to expedite the flow of expertise to Chechnya, the ISI organized mixed detachments of recently trained Chechen fighters and Pakistani mujahedeen veterans. Together with a heavily armed battalion of the ISI's Afghan mujahedeen, they were quickly dispatched to Chechnya in late 1995. Bin Laden dispatched his bosom friend and treasure of Al-Qaeda, Samer bin Saleh as-Suwailem, better known as Emir al-Khattab, to the Caucasus alongside them. To ensure the safe passage of money, as well as hundreds of Afghan Arabs, Talibs, and other mercenaries from across the world into the area, Khattab bribed local officials across Azerbaijan, Georgia, and Dagestan. Later on, this force would build terrorist camp infrastructures within Chechnya itself, turning it into a veritable staging ground to spread jihad throughout the Caucasus and beyond. As a result, most acts of terrorism committed within Russia from the late 1990s into the 2000s were carried out by the "graduates" of these training camps.[13]

Both the foreign mujahedeen and their local adherents actively participated in the *hot stages* of the Armenian-Azerbaijani conflict (for the Azerbaijanis) and in Abkhazia (on the side of the Abkhazians), notably committing many horrendous crimes against civilian populations. According to my own calculations, these mujahedeen fighters constituted approximately 10 percent of Dudayev's ragtag army in Chechnya. Additional information comes by way of Igor Girkin, one of the primary organizers of the Donbas rebellion and a former colonel of the Russian FSB-GRU with experience fighting in Chechnya (and who recently took "moral responsibility" for the Malaysia Airlines Flight 17 disaster in 2014). According to Girkin, approximately 10 percent of the DNR-LNR (Russian acronyms for the self-proclaimed Donetsk Peoples Republic and Luhansk Peoples Republic) rebels are former Russian military specialists who joined the fighting under the guise of being foreign volunteers. He also provided highly pejorative characteristics of the former leadership of the self-proclaimed republics in Donbas, as well as to many rebels who fought as a part of their paramilitary formations.[14]

Samples of the Crude Forms of Ethnic Cleansing Carried Out in Chechnya and Abkhazia during the Hot Stages

There exists a category of lesser-known and -published instances of ethnic cleansing deployed by the ethnocentric nationalists (as well as by volunteers/mercenaries) during the hot stages of these and other violent ethnic conflicts. I want to cite them in full in order to provide a real measure of the horror and consistently recurrent traumas that they have inflicted throughout their miserable existences. There is not a shred of doubt that these acts, and others like them, generated further acts of vengeance in kind. But it should be noted that, throughout their progression, they were peppered with and reinforced by tales and histories detailing distinct traumas. During the Chechen *hot stages* (1994–1996 and 1999–2009), ethnocentric nationalists and Islamists, in their attempts to demoralize the "alien population" and force it out of the area, usually set their sights on the brightest and most well-known representatives/leaders of the so-called Russian-speaking communities: professionals, doctors, academics, priests, and so on. Specifically, I point to the example of Nina Vasil'evna Potokova, history professor and chair of the Modern and Most Recent History Department at Grozny University. She is also well-known among the students and faculty of Texas State University in Houston, where she spent ten months as a visiting professor. She had been also invited to serve as a chair of the State Examination Commission at North Ossetian State University, which is where I first met her. In the spring of 1996, several masked individuals broke into her apartment in downtown Grozny, killed both her son and her mother, and left her seriously wounded. She somehow managed to survive her injuries, only to later end up homeless in Vladikavkaz for a time. Another acquaintance of mine, a renowned representative of the Jewish community and chancellor (rector) of Checheno-Ingushian State University in Grozny, Professor Kankalik, was kidnapped and beheaded.

As one of the few samples that break the defining silence around the gruesome fate of the Terek Cossacks, I point to the testimony of American journalist Mike Edwards, published in *National Geographic*. He visited the area in the 1990s and left this account of his experiences:

> Despite the tensions, Cossacks and other Russians have long lived among the Chechens. Now the Cossacks stream into Terskaya [a Cossack *stanitsa* in the territory of North Ossetia–Alania] with stories of being harassed by the bandit gangs. Tatiana, who had lived there alone, told me: "They came with rifles in the middle of the night. I cried and begged them not to kill me—I had some carpets that looked nice and a nice table. They took them. They even took my old broken cups." Terrified, she set out walking to North Ossetian territory. Tatiana is seventy-two.[15]

Currently, only Chechens live in the abandoned houses of the Cossacks, the legacy of their former occupants indicated by the traditionally ornamented window frames.[16] Terek Cossacks managed to survive the Bolsheviks' genocide in 1918–1921 and the subsequent deportations of collectivization and "dekulakization" efforts of the 1930s. Yet, as a sub-ethnic group, they failed to survive during the latest round of ethnic cleansings and subsequent cover-up at the hands of local Islamists' disciples and ethnocentric nationalists. This marked the end of the centuries-long Cossack history, which had been nestled in the banks of their native Terek River. And almost no one paid enough attention to notice. As did no one notice the dreadful fate of the other small ethnic communities, like the Jews and Armenians, within the independent Chechen Republic of Ichkeria.

Another extreme form of ethnic cleansing broadly practiced by ethnocentric nationalists and Islamists in Chechnya, as well as beyond its borders, was mass enslavement. Thousands of Russian slaves were exploited in the mountainous households of local citizens. During the mid-1990s, there existed in Grozny—the capital of the breakaway Republic of Ichkeria—an openly operated and functioning slave market. Effectively flying under the radar of most people, cases of kidnappings and assassination only became prevalent in global media when foreign nationals found themselves victims of Islamists ploys (for example, the kidnappings and assassinations that befell Red Cross personnel in 1996 or the beheadings of New Zealander and British specialists). Regarding slavery, one of my Chechen contacts suggested an explanation that sounded contextually symptomatic to my theoretical exploration of ethnic conflicts. He relegates this treatment of Russians as a form of retaliatory humiliation for all past and present offenses suffered by any given Chechen individual and his compatriots at the hands of the Russian military during the Imperial period, Stalin's deportations, and the current conflict.[17]

When discerning the exact nature of the atrocities committed by the Russian military during the hot stage of the Russian-Chechen conflict, one may cite the following examples. Besides the broadly publicized and reported excesses committed by Colonel Budanov and Captain Ulman against civilians in Chechnya, there were other similar atrocities known only to human rights centers and aid groups. Maura Reynolds of *The Los Angeles Times* published a slew of documentary materials that dealt with the astounding revelations of Russian troops openly admitting their part in committing atrocities against civilians and soldiers alike during the intermittent *hot stages* of the conflict. To cite a few of the most notable ones:

> "I remember a Chechen female sniper. We just tore her apart with two armored personnel [carriers], having tied her ankles with steel cables. There was a lot of blood, but the boys needed it."
>
> "The main thing is having them die slowly. You don't want them to die too fast, because a fast death is an easy death."
>
> "The summary executions don't just take place against suspected fighters. One 33-year-old army officer recounted how he drowned a family of five—four women and a middle-aged man—in their own well."
>
> "You should not believe people who say Chechens are not being exterminated. In this Chechen war, it's done by everyone who can do it ... There are situations when it's not possible. But when an opportunity presents itself, few people miss it."
>
> "I would kill all the men I met during a mopping-up operation. I didn't feel sorry for them one bit."
>
> "It's much easier to kill them all. It takes less time for them to die than grow."
>
> "So there will be one Chechen less on the planet, so what? Who will cry for him?"[18]

Reynolds herself further testifies that "servicemen say atrocities aren't directly ordered from above: instead, they result from a Russian military culture that glorifies ardor in battle, portrays the enemy as inhuman and has no effective system of accountability."[19] However, one may say the same military culture permeates traditional Chechen warfare as well. Russian television reports have repeatedly broadcasted footage depicting the alleged atrocities committed by the Chechens, including mutilations and beheadings. This behavior walks the very same line as the seemingly "routine" implementation of horrendous torture performed in the numerous Russian "filtration camps" and the disgraceful practice of trading the bodies of victims or kidnapped hostages back to their relatives on both sides. This, in and of itself, promotes a vicious cycle of mutually unrestricted violence, which accounts for the gradual regressive degeneration of the conflict. These varieties of extreme ethnic cleansing were some of the more notable characteristics of the punitive military operations known to Russian commanders as *zachistki* ("mopping-up" operations predominantly performed by the military forces of the Interior Ministry in retaliation for the diversions and raids carried out by rebel brigands).This back-and-forth behavior between the sides of the conflict, which I refer to as the "balance of terror," is typical of the hot stages of all violent ethnic conflicts in the former USSR.

Abkhazia

The following interviews from residents of Abkhazia vividly and similarly address these same issues from another perspective:

Known simply as A., this Abkhazian woman, a resident of Sukhumi, recounted:

> On August 29, 1992, together with [another] twelve servicemen of the regiment of the Abkhazian Interior Ministry, [a] Georgian guardsman captured my son. They put all of the captives on their knees. They asked only one question: "In what republic do you live?" If somebody answered that they lived in the Republic of Abkhazia, they beat him. When a resident of Ashara village, B. Kvarchia, answered the same, they shot him. Then they asked one lad about his name, when he said "Kvizinia," one guardsman laughed and said to his company, "Shoot him; he'll be the fourteenth Kvizinia." Then they grabbed my son and started to beat his head against the wall. When he answered that he lived in Abkhazia, the brother of the commander-in-chief of the Georgian troops in Abkhazia, Karkarashvili, started to cut my son's back and shoulder with a razor.[20]

S., another Abkhazian woman and resident of Gulripsh, reported:

> Georgian guardsmen raped a twenty-five-year-old woman and her five-year-old daughter. When the child was taken to the hospital, the Georgian doctors refused to treat her, saying that they did not have enough [medication] for their own guardsmen. I saw how [some] people buried three five-year-old girls: [an Armenian, Russian, and Ukrainian] who had been raped by a group of Georgian guardsmen. Nine of them [the guardsmen] also raped a three-year-old daughter of Irina G. After that, her child died, and two months later she [Irina] died.[21]

K., a Russian woman and resident of Sukhumi, had this to say:

> Twelve Georgian guardsmen came to my friend's home. She was a Russian who worked at the drugstore. They killed her husband immediately. Then they raped her and her daughter, [who was] a student in the eleventh grade of the local high school. They continued to torture

them until dawn. Another group of guardsmen tortured a woman to death at the seashore beside the lighthouse. They made a fire and [burnt her breasts with a red-hot metal rod]. Then, they shot her, put her body in [a] boat, and sent it sailing. In our city of Sukhumi, a lot of old retirees died from hunger and their relatives were not allowed to bury them in the cemetery. That is why people buried their loved ones in backyards (For this citation see the previous endnote 21).

Stanislav Lacoba noticed another of the Abkhazians' noticeable losses that threatened their cultural index features, writing:

The purposeful destruction of the historical and cultural centers and monuments of the Abkhazian people resulted in the burning down of the archives, institutes, libraries, and theaters. The museums and art galleries have been plundered. The university and institutions carrying manuscripts, historic documentation, folklore and linguistic records perished in the flames. Every possible human thing is being done to deprive the Abkhazian people of their history.[22]

It is said that the hot stages of the Abkhazian conflict ended on September 30, 1993. On that day, Abkhazian paramilitary formations, reinforced by mercenaries form the Confederation of the Peoples of the Caucasus, gained a decisive victory over the Georgian guardsmen. And thus, per the previously mentioned "balance of terror," it was now the turn of ordinary Georgian residents of Abkhazian towns and villages to suffer inhumane treatment at the hands of vengeful mountaineers. Thousands of Georgians were brutally killed by these uncapitulating ethnocentric murderers. Witnesses reported incidents where Georgian residents of Abkhazian villages unlucky enough to not have escaped in time were forced to eat dirt. The Abkhazian paramilitaries then killed them, their deaths accompanied by shouts of, "You wanted our land, eat it!" They then slit their throats, shot them point blank, or simply beat them to death, before moving on to the next.[23]

This was similar to an incident nearly a year prior. On October 1, 1992, the Abkhazians launched a full-scale offensive on Gagra, a town in Northwestern Abkhazia resting on the edge of the Black Sea. The attack was well-coordinated and primarily carried out by Chechens (under the direct command of Shamil Basayev) and North Caucasian militants. The assault resulted in the removal or cleansing of most of the Georgians living in that area. The lengths of these ethnic hostilities are fully expressed in subsequent reports. In one such record, a Georgian woman testified:

My husband, Sergo, was dragged out and tied to a tree. An Abkhaz woman named Zoya Tzvizba brought a tray with lots of salt on it. She took a knife and started to inflict wounds on my husband. After that, she threw salt into my husband's exposed wounds. They tortured him like that for ten minutes. After [that], they forced a young Georgian boy (who they killed afterwards) to dig a hole with [a] tractor. They placed my husband in this hole and buried him alive. The only thing I remember him saying before he was covered with gravel and sand was "Dali, take care of the kids!"[24]

Mikhail Demianov, "a Russian military observer who was accused by the Georgian side of being the advisor to the separatist leader Ardzinba," told Human Rights Watch:

> When [the Abkhaz] entered Gagra, I saw Shamil Basayev's battalion. I have never seen such a horror. They were raping and killing everyone who was captured and dragged them from their homes. The Abkhaz commander Arshba raped a 14-year-old girl and later ordered her [execution]. All day, I could only hear the screams and cries of the people who were brutally tortured. The next day, I witnessed the mass execution of people in the stadium. They installed machine guns and mortars on the top and placed people right on the field. It took a couple of hours to kill everybody.[25]

As indicated by these testimonials, the *hot stages* of the Georgian-Abkhazian conflict in particular resulted in thousands of victims from both ethnic communities, around 200,000 refugees, and thousands upon thousands of properties being plundered or outright destroyed. In spite of the Abkhazian military victory, the conflict saw no moral or long-term "winners" (as compared to Allen Buchanan's moral criteria in justifying rightful secession). There is not a shred of doubt in my mind that both peoples, regardless of the overarching circumstances and mutual violence, can and will add this tragedy to their long list of chosen traumas, thereby poisoning interethnic relations between the two communities for the fore-seeable future. As such, this discontent led into another *hot stage* in August 2008, which continued to permeate this relationship until recently, when they entered one of the two final stages of ethnic conflict.

The Smoldering and Frozen Stages

Using examples from all violent ethnic conflicts, there is a noticeable pattern showing that, under cer-tain conditions, the hot stage of any given conflict may transition into a far less intense, yet still vividly hostile, *smoldering stage*. This new stage is usually ushered in with the decisive prevalence of one side over the other (such as a military victory), which results in the cessation of regular military action and the total withdrawal of extreme forms of ethnic cleansing. After this point, there tends to be a concerted and intensive diplomatic effort to rally outside support for the "winner." In nearly every post-Soviet violent ethnic conflict (barring the Ukrainian case, which is still currently in its *hot stage*), the prevailing side begins this process either on its own or with assistance from outside parties—like volunteers/mercenaries or a powerful nation-state, who move to either aid the victor or for the sake of containing the violence and protecting their own vital national/strategic goals and interests. As a result, intervening parties may force both sides into open negotiations. Groups of interested nation-states (sometimes with the aid of international organizations) elaborate on the specifics of the constraining mechanism needed to maintain the status quo and prevent the reemergence of open confrontations. Metaphorically speaking, this stage very much resembles the suppression of a blaze by "firefighters," resulting in an area filled with nothing more than red and smoking charcoal. It is by this logic that I refer to this time as the *smoldering stage*.

Conversely, there is the gradual reemergence of the "losing" party, who, after capitulating to the inten-sity of the hot stage and having suffered massive losses in human lives and/or territory, will invariably move to avenge/retake what it had previously lost. This is especially true when the slighted party has powerful kin states/ethnic diasporas on its side or when international political and military amalgamations are interested in the continued presence of this conflict for the sake of recruiting allies. Regardless, if members of the international community (or any other powerful global actors) hold these same concerns and do not recognize the "winner's organization"—especially if they do so in the form of diplomatic maneuvers in accordance with international law while rebuilding the military potential of the "defeated" side—then the smoldering stage may very well reignite into a second hot stage. Furthermore, prolonged assistance convinces this newly revitalized and encouraged party that their "allies" would not abandon them in their attempt to retake what they believe is rightfully theirs

There also exists a variant of this situation, which comes about when a hot stage concludes with the victory of a more witting and potentially weaker party. In such a case, the "defeated" stronger party would invariably regroup and attack the "winner" once more, taking advantage of its remaining strength and their target's potential lack of balancing outside support. This is exactly what occurred in the case of the Russian-Chechen conflict, with the seemingly defeated Russians quickly regrouping and reopening the front.

However, if the still fragile "peace" negotiations following the end of any ethnic conflict reach any sort of compromise (even if both parties are still "rivals" in the international arena) and there is continuous effort to maintain the holding and healing mechanisms preventing them from backsliding into open conflict, then the smoldering stage will more or less "chill out." As a result, the conflict will then enter the aptly named *frozen stage*. If the quality of the agreements/control mechanisms and the level of coordination in their implementation continue to aid in the building of viable democratic political cultures—prompted by and based on socioeconomic, socio-cultural, and sociopolitical characteristics—remain relatively high, then the conflict can, eventually, reach a formal resolution.

Despite this, I am fully aware that in the current world situation, based on the chaotic attempts of powerful international forces to create a new order, such an outcome would be preferable, though bordering on nothing more than an idealistic dream. In this modern day and age, the core states of world civilizations and their military alliances seem to ignore the application of a holding and healing strategy. Rather, these forces tend to incite and exacerbate the roles of the parties involved in these types of conflicts to consolidate their own interests. I will discuss their resulting impact on conflicts in the last chapter. For now, it is important to demonstrate the individual courses of particular ethnic conflicts in the post-Soviet landscape by building timelines (see the timelines of violent ethnic conflicts in chapter 8) for each in order to define more specific qualities.

Types of Violent Ethnic Conflicts in the Post-Soviet Space

First of all, it is imperative to remember that an ethnic conflict is roughly defined as *a prolonged altercation between two or more contending ethnic groups that are expressly fighting for the preservation of their groups' identity and position within society.*[26] Second, and in complete agreement with Yurij Matsievsky, I believe that before defining where on the scale this or that post-Soviet violent conflict actually lies, one must consider the following conditions within which the conflict initially developed:

1. Whether it is a conflict between ethnic groups [that] belong to one political system.
2. Whether it is a conflict between at least one ethnic community and one independent state.
3. Whether it is a conflict between independent political actors (sovereign states).

4. Whether it is a conflict [that] occurs as a result of the collapse of the political system in the broad territory where those groups in conflict are primarily located.[27]

Regarding condition four, all of the previously mentioned ethnic conflicts, violent and nonviolent alike, chronologically stem from the final breaths of the Soviet Union, taken during the eclipse of Gorbachev's perestroika. However, many experts and specialists, whom I have respectfully cited in the previous chapters, have had the tendency to make a certain mistake, especially when, for example, they date the Russo-Ukrainian ethnic conflict to having started in 2014—marking its beginning with the Russian Anschluss of Crimea and the pro-Russian rebellion in Donbas. These specialists (as well as the wide-scale media coverage of the event) make such an error because they associate ethnic conflict with a kind of openly vivid violence. An aspect of my postulations regarding the *cyclical patterns* of ethnic conflicts within my theoretical model better demonstrates that, by the time the Russo-Ukrainian ethnic conflict entered its *hot stage* in 2014, the necessary tensions had already been building up over an extended period. In the individual chart of this particular conflict, I will show how a triggering event during the *stirring-up stage* relating to the linguistic building block (and later on, the nationality building block) had already occurred in 1990.

Thus, regarding Matsievsky's fourth condition, all ethnic conflicts "in the broad territory where those groups in conflict" were "primarily located"—i.e., within the territory of the former Soviet superpower—occurred as a result of the previously analyzed conditions, which led to the collapse of its overarching political system and, in turn, these conflicts contributing to the eventual collapse of the USSR.

After 1991, these same ethnic conflicts would continue their regressive development within conditions one, two, and three of Matsievsky's scheme. First and foremost, all of them were either passing through the stirring-up stages or were just entering the hot stages within the same transitional political system, only to later emerge in the era of the independent post-Soviet states, as cited previously in the works and definitions of Volodymyr Polokhalo and Serhy Yekelchyk. Second, the political systems of these newly independent states resembled (and to some extent, still do) mini Imperial structures, seeing how they inherited the hierarchical ranking concessions of ethnic groups living within them from their Imperial and especially Soviet predecessors. By this, I refer to Stalin's abovementioned categorization of the Soviet peoples and the establishment of a hierarchy of different Soviet administrative formations centered on the titular ethnic groups/nations. This legacy was handed down to the newly independent states, not only in the vein of preserving Stalin's (and Khrushchev's) established boundaries between these formations but also in terms of the intrastate attitudes ingrained on a psychological level between super-ordinate/ titular ethnic nations and subordinate ethnic groups/minorities within the framework of the new polities. All titular groups, regardless of category, were (and are) accustomed to thinking of themselves and about their respective republics/autonomies/districts in terms of ethnic "proto-political formations."

To hold the status of a titular, or root, people ("*korennye narody*"—a term which existed in the political lexicon of the Soviet Union that was, again, put into habitual circulation by Stalin, and under different ideology of ethnocentric nationalism amazingly reemerging in modern Ukraine in its legislature) is considered to be a "historical foundation" of being a privileged nation, on the grounds that they constitute the ethnic majority. Alternatively, if they are not in the majority yet hold the status of being a "titular" or "root" people, such groups try to create the majority through mild and middle-ground acts of ethnic cleansing against any and all "aliens" through various forms of assimilation (such as linguistics). This course of action inevitably leads to an ethnic conflict. The status of the majority, especially amid the emergence of democratic procedure within a country, has been considered the most important mechanism in defending collective ethnic rights.[28] Therefore, ethnocentric leadership within the schema of hierarchical titular groups with the full backing of an obedient and respective people (both super-ordinate and subordinate within the framework of newly formed, independent, and multiethnic states) tend to elevate their own status or, alternatively, degrade the status of an ethnic rival to such an extent that the resulting concentration of power guarantees the titular group an exceptional level of priority within the contesting territories. By this logic, I choose to refer to this process as *the privatization of state power by the corporation of ethnocentric nationalists.*

Thus, it is hardly a surprise to learn that the most frequent type of both violent and nonviolent ethnic conflict in the post-Soviet states is that *between super-ordinate and subordinate ethnic groups within one and the same multiethnic nation-state* (or in terms of Soviet categorization, between ethnic nations of the first category—i.e., "titular nations" of the former union republics—and those "ethnic nations" of the second and third categories—i.e., those populations living within the former autonomous republics or districts). Such is the case with the latest ethnic conflicts to pass through all the cyclical stages, including those between (1) Georgians and South Ossetians; (2) Georgians and Abkhazians; (3) Moldavians and the Russian-speaking population of Transnistria (*Transdnistria*); (4) North-Ossetians and Ingushians in the Prigorodnyi District of North-Ossetian-Alania; and (5) Russians and Chechens.

In the meantime, specifically during the eclipse of Gorbachev's perestroika, a different type of conflict had been ripening in the South Caucasus between Soviet ethnic nations of the aforementioned first category and, following the collapse of the USSR, "independent political actors"—primarily the sovereign states of Armenia and Azerbaijan in and around Nagorno-Karabakh—corresponding with Matsievsky's third condition.

In August 2008, during the *second hot stages* of the Georgian–South Ossetian and Georgian-Abkhazian ethnic conflicts, Russia interfered on the side of the Ossetians and Abkhazians, both in terms of direct military aid and by providing munitions/supplies. Prior to Russian involvement, these conflicts represented the first type of ethnic conflict. However, these hostilities would eventually carry both parties into the Georgian-Russian ethnic conflict, allowing it to simultaneously represent the second type of conflict, which is between different independent and sovereign states. Equally, the conflict between the Ukrainian titular ethnic nation and the Russian-speaking minority following the Russian annexation of Crimea in 2014 (an act of direct interference on behalf of the Russian majority living there) and their indirect support of the rebels in Donbas has undergone a similar transformation. Again, it has slowly escalated from an ethnic civil war, described by the first type of conflict, into a clash between sovereign states in a sort of "hybrid war" (with the only exception being a lack of direct military confrontation between the *regular* armed forces of Russia and Ukraine).

The above-cited first type of ethnic conflict may also be defined as "intra-system" conflicts. This is because all of them saw ethnic minority groups strive to win political autonomy/independence or affirm the recognition of previous declarations that were ignored by the political body of the super-ordinate titular ethnic nations. Such conflicts are often referred to as an *ethno-secessionist* or *ethno-separatist* type of conflict, with the classic example being the violent ethnic conflicts between Russia and Chechnya.[29]

While I agree with this definition, I also recognize that, regarding other conflicts within this first type, their individual courses represent more complicated characteristics that exceed such a relatively simple definition, as it rather statistically fixes them in place during one particular moment of their overall regressive evolution (or rather, devolution). The violent ethnic conflicts in Georgia and Ukraine are, once again, useful indicators of this, as they both exhibit the transition of an intra-system conflict into an inter-system conflict. This mainly occurred when primarily internal struggles boiled over into neighboring Russia, who then directly (in the case of Georgia) or indirectly (in the case of Ukraine) interfered in order to "prevent further civilian slaughters, [the mass exodus of refugees,] and chain reaction effects" on its own territory.[30]

As a response to this, I have formatted this particular aspect of my theoretical approach to be flexible enough to overcome the limits of a static assessment and to examine these conflicts, and their evolution, more succinctly. If one were to apply this tool in such a way, then they would find that, during the stirring-up stages, ethnic minorities prevalently exhibit elements typically associated with secessionist claims, mild demands to confirm their autonomous rights previously enjoyed under the Soviet regime, or even attempts to obtain or petition for these same qualities within a desired consociational democratic federalist system. At one point, such projects were the most attractive options, given that these people had already seen their fellow co-ethnics (mainly Abkhazians and Ossetians) enjoy these very same privileges while living in Russia. But by the end of the stirring-up stage of their respective conflicts, these groups had been met with little more than overwhelmingly negative reactions from the dominant titular ethnic nations, which (at that point) culminated in middling acts of ethnic cleansing that threatened their most important ethnic constituents. This led to a dramatic transformation of their expectations, which in turn shifted their previously subdued *ethno-secessionist/ethno-separatist* tendencies into *irredentist* paradigms of the conflict as a whole.

Scholars define *irredentism* as a "territorial claim based on a national, ethnic, or historical basis. The term irredentism is derived from the Italian word *irredento* ("unredeemed"). It originally referred to an Italian political movement during the late 1800s and early 1900s that sought to detach predominantly Italian-speaking areas from Switzerland and the Austro-Hungarian Empire and incorporate these territories into the new-Italian state, thus "redeeming" these territories.[31] So an irredentist paradigm of an ethnic conflict presupposes the existence of a third party in which an ethno-political movement, primarily composed of an ethnic minority, may recognize a *revisionist* power of an ethnic, cultural, or political persuasion. As a result, these same movements may seek to occupy a part of the territory of an oppressive "status quo" state, stemming from geopolitical and/or strategic-security considerations, which look upon such territory as "lost" or "unredeemed" based on "history or even legend."[32]

Myron Weiner summarized the conditions defining the "*status quo*" *state* as an auspicious set of characteristics that indicate the onset of an "*irredentist–anti-irredentist*" struggle with a neighboring (or, to use his term, a "*revisionist*") state. According to Weiner, there are *three conditions* that set this kind of ethnic struggle in motion. Coincidentally, they fit perfectly within the gradual evolution of the aforementioned ethnic conflicts in both the Caucasus and Ukraine:

(1) When (and if) "the neighboring irredentist power presses its claims and express [concern] for the plight of its ethnic kin, usually a minority in the status-quo state, it could raise expectations among that ethnic minority that it will either be incorporated into the revisionist state or at least will be able to form an independent state of its own with support from the revisionist state." The previously mentioned project of *Novorossiya*, which has been declared by both the Russian ethno-political elite and President

Putin himself (especially following the Crimean Anschluss), raised these exact expectations among the Russian-speaking population in the southeastern regions of Ukraine, especially in Donbas. In that same vein, the irredentist actions of Ingushians in Ingushetia brought about the development of such expectations by the Ingushian minority living in the Prigorodnyi District within the "status-quo" state of North Ossetia–Alania. Equal expectations became cherished and championed by the Armenian population of Nagorno-Karabakh of the Azerbaijani "status-quo" state after this same kind of irredentist demonstration entered the country via the adjunct Armenia. By that time, South Ossetians and Abkhazians living in Georgia had already been acquiring Russian Federation passports, emboldened by the hope of "reuniting" with their native Ossetian kinsmen in a "greater Alania," while the Abkhazians hoped that, at the very least, Russia would assist them in forming an independent state.

As a matter of fact, my own explorations of the effect of irredentist conflicts in the post-Soviet space and in the former Yugoslavia (as well seen in the experiences of other scholars studying similar conflicts in other parts of the world) show that, under the claim of "redeeming" these "lost" territories, these irredentist movements usually conceal the desire to create greater nation-states. The quest for a "Greater Serbia," "Greater Croatia," "Greater Albania," "Greater Armenia," and so on are the most frequently cited examples of this, but this also includes the "Greater Romania" project (*România Mare*), which was partially responsible for Romania's decision to join the Axis Powers during World War II. Nowadays, the latter concept has reemerged regarding the incorporation of Moldova into the modern Romanian nation-state, mostly at the hand of Romanian ethnocentric nationalists residing in both countries.

(2) According to Weiner, the next condition required to facilitate the rise of irredentist conflict arises when the "demands for revising boundaries persist on the part of [an] irredentist state," in which the "status quo" state is likely to view minority ethnic groups as a grave risk to their territorial integrity. Therefore, the "status quo" state may try to accelerate those programs established to "nationalize" the "schoolchildren belonging to the minority ethnic group," as well as any other coercive measures and repressive policy, in order to extort "expressions of loyalty from the group members to the national government" through intimidation. For a more practical example, one only needs to look to Ukraine, as all of these "measures" have been utilized at one point or another (as discussed in the previous chapter).

(3) "Finally, as a result of [the] status-quo state's crackdown, significant numbers within the minority ethnic group may come to regard the status-quo state as the oppressor and an obstacle in the path to its merger with the revisionist state or to its full independence."[33]

As previously demonstrated by the mild and middle-ground forms of ethnic oppression during the stirring-up stage, and especially with the extreme forms of ethnic cleansing at the opening of the hot stages, the crackdown of the "status-quo" states tends to be so heavy that every ethnic minority fighting in these conflicts gradually adopts their own irredentist plans.

A good example can be seen in how Zviad Gamsakhurdia, the ethnocentric leader of Georgia, explained the "necessity" of suppressing the South Ossetians, who by that point had elevated the status of their autonomy inside Georgia from "Autonomous District" to full-on "Republic." In an interview with *Moscow News* in December 1990, he stated, "Yes, I organized the Tskhinvali [the capital of South Ossetia] campaign. We wanted to persuade the Ossetians to give in. They took flight, which is quite logical because they are criminals … The Ossetians are uncultured, wild people—clever people can handle them easily."[34] During his unsuccessful talks with Major General Kim Tsagalov, Ossetian representative and hero of the

Soviet-Afghan War, Gamsakhurdia, boastfully moved to intimidate this decorated warrior, threatening, "I shall bring a 200,000-strong army. Not a single Ossete will remain in the land of Samachablo [the Georgian term for South Ossetia]."[35]

The heavily referenced linguistic-educational policy, as well as other undertakings in the spheres directly relating to the principal building blocks of ethnicity of the ethnic minorities within the Ukrainian nation-state (especially Russians) placed them in a similar position, with three potential alternatives: (1) *to give in and eventually be assimilated*, (2) *to strive to improve their status inside of the existing "status-quo" state*, or (3) *to create a completely independent state and later merge with Russia*.[36] In both Crimea and Donbas, the majority of residents made their preference abundantly clear and strove to merge with the neighboring "revisionist" state of Russia. South Ossetians similarly declared their desire for an irredentist reunification with their kinsmen in Russia to facilitate a "Greater Ossetia–Alania," while the Armenians of Nagorno-Karabakh wished to merge with their compatriots into a "Greater Armenia." Abkhazians strove to build their own independent state under the aegis of the Russian Federation by completely merging with it, especially when a Georgian attack reignited the *hot stage* of their shared conflict; along those same lines, the Ingushians also rely on Moscow's aid in returning their refugees to the Prigorodnyi District of North Ossetia–Alania. As a result of the *stirring-up stages* and, more crucially, the *hot stages* of the above-cited violent ethnic conflicts, these *irredentist paradigms* became more ideologically prevalent.

Notes

1   Roger D. Peterson, *Understanding Ethnic Violence: Fear, Hatred, and Resentment in Twentieth-Century Eastern Europe* (Cambridge, UK: Cambridge University Press, 2002), 17–18.

2   See V.P. Cagnon, Jr., "Ethnic Nationalism and International Conflict: The Case of Serbia," *International Security* 19, no. 3 (Winter 1994/1995): 131.

3   See Taras Kuzio, "Putin's Imperial Ambitions Mean Ukraine Must Learn to Live with Frozen Conflict," *Atlantic Council*, December 19, 2019, atlanticcouncil.org/blogs/ukrainealert/putins-imperial-ambitions-mean-ukraine-must-learn-to-live-with-frozen-conflict/; Gennadii Sysoev, "Scenarii dlia Donbassa," *Kommersant*, December 16, 2019, kommersant.ru/doc/4196316#id1135790.

4   Raymond Taras and Rajat Ganguly, *Understanding of Ethnic Conflict*, 4th ed. (New York: Longman, Pearson Education, Inc., 2006), 19, 22.

5   Peter Petschauer and Anatoly Isaenko, "Finding the Middle Ground: The Practical and Theoretical Center Between Ethnic Ideal and Extreme Behaviors," *Mind and Human Interaction* 12, no. 1 (2001):55–59.

6   Anatoly Isaenko, *Polygon of Satan: Ethnic Traumas and Conflicts in the Caucasus*, 3rd ed. (Dubuque, IA: Kendall Hunt Publishing House, 2014), 144; for examples from the Georgian perspective, see Vamik Volkan, *Killing in the Name of Identity: A Study ofBloody Conflicts* (Charlottesville, VA: Pitchstone Publishing, 2006), 21–85.

7   Isaenko, *Polygon of Satan*, Table 3-3, 130.

8   Women Aid International, *Conflict in the Caucasus* (2004), www.womenaid.org/press/info/aid/conflict.html.

9   This data is cited in the daily internet journal *Locals* (June 19, 2017), "Kolichestvo zhertv pridnestrovskogo konflikta," locals.md/2015/tsitra-dnya-kolichestvo-zhertv-pridnestrovskogo-konflikta/. However, some experts believe that these figures may be larger than presented.

10   This passage has been modified from the corresponding section of an article manuscript discussing mercenaries in the Caucasus that Professor Bowers and I are preparing for publication.

11   Yossef Bodansky, "Chechnya: The Mujahedin Factor," November 6, 1998,http://www.amina.com/chechens/article/muj-fact.html. Shamil Basayev was born in 1965 in Vedeno (Checheno-Ingushian ASSR). A former fireman and computer salesman, he earned recognition as a military commander when he led a battalion of Chechen volunteers in support of the Abkhaz side of the Abkhazian-Georgian war (1992–1993), at which point, ironically, he and his men received support and possibly training from the Russian Army as part of its anti-Georgia strategy. After the Russian invasion of Chechnya in 1994, Basayev quickly emerged as the bravest and most brilliant of the Chechen field commanders. In 1995, he led a raid on the Russian town of Budyonnovsk, Stavropol Krai, that killed dozens of Russian civilians and took hundreds more hostages. Though the raid helped to persuade the Russians to call for a ceasefire, Basayev has since been considered an arch-terrorist by Moscow authorities. In January 1997, he ran for president of Chechnya-Ichkeria but was soundly defeated by Aslan Maskhadov. Basayev would later organize numerous terrorist attacks across the North Caucasus and beyond, with the biggest being the attack on Beslan High School #1 on September 1, 2004. Two years later, he would be killed by Russian forces.

12   Isaenko, *Polygon of Satan*, 375–76.

13   Isaenko, *Polygon of Satan*, 387–88. Khattab was a Bedouin from northern Saudi Arabia. His combatant, American mujahedeen Aukai Collins, who took the name Abu Mujahid (and who fought in Chechnya against the Russians from 1995 to 1999), argues that Khattab joined the professional jihadists in Afghanistan at the age of sixteen or seventeen, where he had been fighting the Soviets under the command of bin Laden. As a result of this, Khattab would end up fully adopting the ideas of the latter. Using his family's money, Khattab established his own organization and fought in Tajikistan, only for bin Laden to later redirect him to Chechnya. Like many other Al-Qaeda–aligned Arabs, he married a local girl in the Karamakhy Wahhabist jamaat (from Nadir Khachilaev's clan). After this point, Khattab fraternized with Shamil Basayev, whose father also adopted Khattab as his own son. In May or June 2002, he was supposedly killed by a Russian artillery shell.

14   Igor Strelkov (Girkin), "Rano ili pozdno eta voina pereydet v goryachuyu stadiyu," *Moskovskii komsomolets*, August 15, 2019, mk.ru/politics/2019/08/15/igor-strelkov-rano-ili-pozdno-eta-voina-pereydet-v-goryachuyu-stadiyu.html. Strelkov/Girkin served as the minister of defense for the self-proclaimed Donetsk People's Republic in 2014.

15   Mike Edwards, "A Comeback for the Cossacks," *National Geographic*, November 1998, 57.

16   Maria Bondarenko, "Poslednie Kazaki Terskogo Kazach'ego voiska," *Nezavisimaya gazeta*, April 14, 2003, 2.

17   Isaenko, *Polygon of Satan*, 377–78.

18   See Maura Reynolds, "War Has No Rules for Russian Forces Battling Chechen Rebels," *The Los Angeles Times*,September 17, 2004, 1.

19   Reynolds, "War Has No Rules,"2–3.

20   Vitalii Sharia, ed., *Abkhazskaya tragedia* (Sochi, Russia: Department of Mass Media of Krasnodar Oblast, 1993), 90.

21   Sharia, *Abkhazskaya tragedia*, 95.

22   Stanislav Lacoba, "Abkhazia Is Abkhazia," *Central Asian Survey* 14, no. 1 (1995): 101.

23 Isaenko, *Polygon of Satan,* 215-16.

24 *Human Rights Watch* [1993]. See also US Department of State, *Country Reports on the Human Rights Practices for 1993* (February 1994), chapter II, 96.

25 US Department of State, *Country Reports*, chapter II, 96.

26 See Ashutosh Varshney, *Ethnic Conflict and Civic Life: Hindus and Muslims in India* (New Haven, CT: Yale University Press, 2002); Stuart Kaufman, *Modern Hatreds: The Symbolic Politics of Ethnic War* (Ithaca, NY: Cornell University Press, 2001), 17.

27 See Yurij Matsievsky, "Ethnic Conflicts: Typology, Causes and Forms of Manifestations," *Naukovi zapiski* 18(2000): 63.

28 See Isaenko, *Polygon of Satan*, 152.

29 Taras and Ganguly, *Understanding Ethnic Conflict*, 130–39.

30 Matsievsky, "Ethnic Conflicts," 64.

31 See Thomas Ambrosio, "Irredentism: Territorial Claim," *Encyclopedia Britannica*, Britannica.com/topic/irredentism.

32 Markus Korrnprobst, *Irredentism in European Politics: Argumentation, Compromise and Norms* (Cambridge, UK: Cambridge University Press, 2008), 8.

33 Myron Weiner, "The Macedonian Syndrome: An Historical Model of International Relations and Political Development," *World Politics* 24, no. 4 (July 1971): 673–74; Taras and Ganguly, *Understanding Ethnic Conflict*, 16.

34 Zviad Gamsakhurdia, "We Have Chattered Too Long with the Separatists: A Conversation with the Chairman of the Georgian Supreme Soviet," *Moscow News*, December 2, 1990, 12.

35 Isaenko, *Polygon of Satan*, 165.

36 Regarding similar alternatives, see Weiner, "The Macedonian Syndrome," 674.

CHAPTER EIGHT

Timeline of Violent Ethnic Conflicts in the Post-Soviet Space

FIGURE 8.1   Flag of Azerbaijan

FIGURE 8.2   Flag and Coat of Arms of Republic of Armenia

FIGURE 8.3   Flag of Nagorno-Karabakh Artsakh

(I) Armenian-Azerbaijani Violent Ethnic Conflict: 1984-Present

(1) The Previous Cycle as a Historical Prerequisite: 1885–1921

1885–1890: Stirring-Up Stage

- 1885: Rising radicalization among the Armenian population.
- 1885–1890: Initial emergence of underground paramilitary groups and armed nationalist revolutionary societies (*Armenakans of Van, Hunchaks*) (1887); *Armenian Revolutionary Federation—Dashnak-Tsutiun (Dashnaks)* (1890).

- 1885: *Triggering Event*—Armenian intelligentsia and *Armenian Apostolic Church* formulated the concept of "lost ethnic territories" of a "Great Armenia" that had been taken over by "Turkish enemies," including the lands previously abolished by the Russians of the Azerbaijani Khanates. Then came the emergence of the *commonly shared history* and *nationality* building blocks of ethnic conflict, which were aggravated by their *chosen traumas*.
- 1885–1890: Azerbaijanis began to discover their "Turkish [biological] brothers," forging links with Turkey and militarizing in order to secede from Russia. Then followed emergence of the *biological* building block of the conflict.

1890–1895: Hot Stage of the Armenian–Turkish Conflict

Ethnocentric Armenian nationalist groups unleash a campaign in defiance of both the Ottoman government and local Kurdish overlords, performing a series of terrorist attacks against Turkish authorities.

In retaliation, Sultan Abdul Hamid "armed the Kurds, and encouraged them to attack the Armenian villages. In 1891, he formed the Kurdish [*Hamidiye*] regiments, which terrorized the Armenian civilian population."[1]

- 1891–1895: A series of localized and bloody Armenian uprisings and terrorist attacks, followed by retaliatory massacres of Armenian populations organized by the Ottoman imperial authority.
- 1895: The Armenian Sasun Rising was followed by a series of massacres throughout Turkish Armenia lasting from October to December 1895. Dashnak terrorists seized the Ottoman Bank in Istanbul, threatening to blow it up unless European powers intervened to ensure the fulfillment of Armenian political demands. When the armed men retreated, another massacre of Armenians broke out in the capital.
- 1894–1895: The utilization of extreme forms of ethnic cleansing, including the grimmest massacre of Armenian civilians, taking place at Urfa on December 29, 1895. Around 3,000 Armenians were burned alive while taking refuge in the local cathedral. It saw the emergence of the first acute underlying chosen trauma in the Armenian collective consciousness.
- 1894–1895: The overall casualties of the first *hot stage* of the Armenian-Turkish conflict estimated up to 300,000.[2]

1895–1905: Smoldering Stage

Mild and middle-ground forms of ethnic cleansing prevailed, resulting in waves of out-migration of the Armenian population to different countries. Armenian Diasporas grew at the cost of the refugees.

This stage also saw the emergence of outside exacerbating factors: (1) At this point, the Russian empire continued to enforce a rather intense resettlement policy, based around creating pockets of "loyal" Christians (Armenian refugees from Turkey in particular), which they had begun after the incorporation of the Khanates of Sheki, Karabagh (or Karabakh), and Kuba, in 1813 and especially their victory in the Russo-Turkish War of 1877–1878.[3] Since that time, the logic behind the further building of radical nationalist philosophies and their radical realization would develop in the background of the "*Big Game*"—which encompassed the competing interests/rivalries of *Turkey*, *Russia*, and the other major *European powers*.

(2) In particular, the hopes and nationalist inspirations of the more radical sect of Armenians became aggravated by the position of Great Britain, whose prime minister, Benjamin Disraeli, thought that any

pressured reforms in the wake of the Russian victory over Turkey would only serve to advance Russian power. In terms of maintaining British interests, this was, of course, entirely unacceptable. Thus, Disraeli and Lord Salisbury utilized political maneuverings to force the Russians into evacuating Erzurum—an important strategic center with a notable Armenian population (though the Russians retained both Kars and Ardagan). However, any and all Armenian hopes to promote some modicum of self-administration in those territories under Turkish control evaporated when, in 1882, half a dozen of the British consuls within the empire were ordered to return home. As former Prime Minister David Lloyd George admitted in 1938, "Armenia was sacrificed on the triumphal altar we had erected. The Russians were forced to withdraw: the wretched Armenians were once more placed under the heel of their old masters," namely, the Turks and the Kurds.[4] For the Turkish Armenians, this "betrayal" was even more painful due to the realization that the policy promoting Christian elites in the Caucasus was still being implemented by their "next-door neighbors" in the Russian-controlled "Armenian province." The resulting stream of Armenian settlers into the territories of the abolished khanates would drastically shift the demographic situation within the region. By 1895, the Armenians constituted around 58 percent of the entire population of Nagorno-Karabakh.[5]

In his most recent book, Farid Shafiyev showed how this period oversaw serious changes to the demographic profiles of many territories, including the western part of the Echmiadzin District, the southern part of the Yerevan (sometimes spelled "Erevan") District, the Surmalinsky District, the Sharur-Daralagez District, the Zangezur (the mountainous part of the Kazakh)District, the Nakhichevan District, and the mountainous parts of the Shusha and Jevanshir Districts (constituting parts of Nagorno-Karabakh). He further illustrated how the ruling imperial power unevenly distributed privileges between different ethnic communities with a bias toward Christians (Armenians). This in turn put the remaining "Muslim [particularly the Azerbaijani] inhabitants in a disadvantageous situation," especially those living in Baku and other urban centers.[6]

All of this—the combination of nationality, commonly shared history (aggravated by chosen traumas), and biological building blocks (the latter in its more *demographic* dimension)—served as a catalyst in charging the ethnic tensions between Armenians and Azerbaijanis during this period.

Concerning the general impact of the commonly shared history building block of ethnicity (and of ethnic conflict) during the *smoldering stage*, both ethnic groups began to actively develop the perception of a "historical homeland" among Armenian settlers and their Azerbaijani neighbors. During this period, Prince Grigory Golitsyn, the new Russian governor-general in Transcaucasia, closed all Armenian schools and considerably reduced the number of Armenians working in the civil service. Incensed by this, Dashnak-Tsutiun organized myriad protests, shootings, and bombings in and around Baku.[7]

- 1905: First Russian Revolution/First *hot stage* of the Armenian-Azerbaijani ethnic conflict. The imperial governor of Baku encouraged the local Azerbaijani nationalists into a four-day-long slaughter of Armenians. Mob violence from both sides continued through September, resulting in fires throughout the famous Baku oilfields. Gradually, the more organized Armenians, led by the armed Dashnaks, gained the upper hand during these vicious clashes against the far less centralized Azerbaijanis. Hundreds died, thousands more were wounded, and the entire incident left a profound legacy of hatred between these ethnic communities.

- 1907–1917: *Frozen period* of the Russian-controlled South Caucasus. The defeat of the first Russian revolution resulted in the mass persecution of revolutionaries and the strengthening of the tsarist regime in the South Caucasus. In 1911, the Dashnak party was put on trial, though the case would collapse before charges were filed. This is because in 1912, on the eve of World War I, Russian policy shifted back to a pro-Armenian (i.e., Christian) stance, as the primarily Muslim Turks (who were co-religious to the Azerbaijanis) had once again become the open enemy of Russia.[8]

- 1911–1913: The foundation of the *Musavat Party (Equality Party)* in Baku by Mammed Amin Rasul-zade, his cousin Mammed-Ali, Abbasgulu Kazimzade, and Taghi Nagioglu. While focused on restoring the independence of all subjugated Muslim nations, *Musavat* also supported several pan-Islamic and pan-Turkish ideas that complimented those of the *Young Turk* revolution in the Ottoman Empire.[9]

- 1915: Establishment of the Armenians' underlying acute *chosen trauma—The Genocide* in Turkey. Following the Young Turk revolution of 1908, Turkish ethnocentric nationalism began to take shape, as reflected in the doctrine of *pan-Turkism/pan-Turanianism*, according to which:

> First, Ottoman Turks had to consolidate their grip over the empire and *Turkicize its minorities*. In the second, "pan-Turkic," phase, the closest relatives of the Ottoman Turks—the Azerbaijanis of Russia and Persia (the south-eastern group of Turkic peoples)—were to be taken into the *Turkic state*. The third step would be the uniting of all the Turanian peoples of Asia around the *Turkish core*.[10]

Supposedly, and unsurprisingly, the Armenians stood in the way of realizing this plan. In discussing a nonbiased and fully impartial assessment of the subsequent tragedy of 1915, I fully support the opinion of Richard Hovannisian, who is the chair of the Department of Modern Armenian History at UCLA:

> Some renowned American and European scholars do not object that Young Turks had some aggressive plans regarding the Armenians but by no means did not want total annihilation of the Armenian people. However, there are some historians who with great confidence ascertain the opposite opinion. Yes, the Genocide of Armenians took place, but in order to understand whether it has been planned before or [during] the deportation of the Armenians from [their lands], it is necessary *to get and study all the historical documents*.[11]

Armenian historians claim that, during the course of this event, "the Armenian nation lost a million and a half persons by gun or bayonet, by deliberate starvation, and by privation and disease."[12] (On the other hand, Turkish historians argue that the actual figures were considerably less than those professed by their Armenian contemporaries.) In their historical ideology, the Armenians depict this *chosen trauma* as the destruction of Anatolian (Western) Armenia, which "ended centuries of Armenian life in Turkey and turned Russian Armenia into a land of refugees."[13]

- 1917–1921: *Second hot stage* of the Armenian-Azerbaijani ethnic conflict. This conflict was a part of (i.e., took place in the midst of) the Russian Civil War of 1918–1920 which saw the Bolshevik "Reds" face off against a conglomerate of opponents collectively dubbed the "Whites." The total collapse of the Russian Empire in 1917 was the *triggering event*. The Armenians "fought the Azerbaijanis and the Georgians; the latter were also at war with the Abkhazians and the Ossetians; the Chechens took on the Cossacks, while the Ingushians fought the Ossetians"; all the while, the Armenians and the Turks were once again at each other's throats.[14] A few years later, when "Russia" returned to this area under the ideological guise of the Soviet regime, these ethnic scrapes abruptly concluded. Interestingly enough, one can see a very similar series of events taking place during the decline of the Soviet empire during the late 1980s, where both the Russians and the people of the Caucasus went down the same road, leading to the *next cycle of ethnic violent conflicts* (including additional *hot stages*) within the framework of the same ethnic configuration. This consistency gave me a firm historical foundation to develop this aspect of my theoretical model regarding the repeatable/recurrently cyclical pattern of ethnic conflicts in the pre-Soviet and post-Soviet space.

It also shows how this territorial dispute transitioned into the most important building block (*nationality*) between the Armenians and Azerbaijanis, as well as the preceding conflict between the Armenians and Turks, at this *hot stage* of its earliest cycle.

- May 22–24, 1918: Armenia managed to avoid total destruction and occupation by Turkish forces; Armenian commanders Tomas Nazarbekov, Drastamat Kanayan (better known simply as "Dro"), and Movses Silikov led their detachments in repulsing the Turks at the Battle of Sardarabad.
- May 28, 1918: An Independent *Armenian Republic* was proclaimed under the leadership of the Dashnaks. At the same time, the Musavat Party declared the creation of a *Democratic Republic*. The initial name for this new "state" was the *Azerbaijan—ADR*.
- 1918: The partition between the three youngest nation-states in the South Caucasus—Georgia, Armenia, and Azerbaijan—begins in earnest.

The development of outside exacerbating factors for each country, from Germany in Georgia, Turkey in Azerbaijan, and the Triple Entente (Russia, France, and the United Kingdom) in Armenia, added momentum to each country. Briefly it resulted in a near-total German/Turkish hegemony throughout Transcaucasia.

- June 4, 1918: The signing of the *Treaty of Batumi/Peace of Batumi* officially ended the Georgian-Armenian–Turkish War. One of the conditions saw the Kars Province (which had been invaded by Russia in 1915), as well as a considerable part of the former imperial *Erivan Governorate* (including the Surmala, Sharur, and Nakhichevan Districts), go to Turkey.
- September 1918: Turkish-Azerbaijani forces occupied the predominantly Russian city of Baku (specifically for the Caspian Sea oil production centers), thus fulfilling the second phase of the Young Turks' plan—using the Musavat Party to build a self-sustaining pan-Turkic state. (Their rule would be followed by that of British troops and then the Baku Committee of Bolsheviks.)

  - April–November 1918: Period of Ottoman domination.
  - December 1918–September 1919: Period of British domination.
  - April 1920 and onward: Period of Soviet domination.

Following the Battle of Sardarabad, Armenia would lose the abovementioned territories in eastern Armenia. However, it was able to combine what remained into *a nucleus of a nation-state*.

Woodrow Wilson would submit his *Fourteen Points to the Paris Peace Conference*. This doctrine, combined with promises of British assistance, revitalized the Armenian and Dashnak expectations for territorial acquisitions.

- Summer 1919 (and since March 1920): Armenia clashed with Azerbaijan over the disputable areas in the areas of Nakhichevan and *Karabakh*. This resulted in brief Armenian control over Surmala, Sharur, and the Zangezur.
- 1920: Rise of the Soviets in the North Caucasus. Many key military victories, coupled with the simultaneous success of Kemalists in Turkey, gradually *excluded Western powers from interfering in the South Caucasus*.
- April 1920: The Sovietization of Azerbaijan and the establishment of a Soviet-Turkish diplomatic partnership left the Armenian Republic surrounded by enemies. The end of the *second hot stage* of the Armenian-Azerbaijani conflict resulted in the occupation of disputed territories (namely the Shusha, Nakhichevan [Nakhjevan], and Zangezur Districts) by the Red Army and Azerbaijani forces.
- 1920: Under the aegis of Western powers, *The Treaty of Sèvres* discussed the division of the former Ottoman Empire, which included large swaths of territory in Anatolia going to Armenia. However, ethnic purges within these territories—performed by the Young Turks in 1915—and the 1920 political advancements of the Kemalists made the realization of these plans impossible. Yet in October 1920, the Dashnaks attempted to realize these provisions of the Sèvres Treaty by force. This would result in a *third hot stage* of the supposedly dormant *Armenian-Turkish War*, which completely wore down the Dashnaks' army. Blows from the Kermalist forces in the south, the 11th Soviet Red army from Baku in the north, and a pro-Soviet revolution within the nation-state itself, led to the ultimate demise of the independent Armenian Republic. Following this, the Soviet Bolsheviks, in order to exert even more pressure on the weary Dashnaks, proclaimed the creation of a *Soviet Republic* in the Yerevan District between November 29 and December 2, 1920. At this point, the Dashnaks would hand themselves over to the Soviets, all the while falling back on the classic mantra: "Better Red than Dead."[15]
- 1921: Creation of the *Moscow* and *Kars Soviet-Turkish Treaties*. The new Armenian Soviet Republic was declared to rest within the so-called "zone of Soviet control," while the "zone of Turkish control" (which included the Kars and Ardagan Districts) was incorporated into the state of Turkey. The Nakhichevan Province (including the former Sharur and Nakhichevan Districts) was melded into the autonomous status of their new protectorate, the *Azerbaijan Soviet Republic*. They were soon after joined by the city of Baku, which would become the republic's new capital.

Losing Nagorno-Karabakh in 1921 was the most painful loss for the Armenians, as it was the last territory containing a large Armenian majority. Bolshevik leadership based their strategy of "obtaining allies of [the] Socialist October 1917 revolution among the peoples of the East" by exporting "revolution in the Islamic world," reckoning with the fact that the "geopolitical weight of Armenia was incompatible with the weight of Muslim solidarity with [Soviet Russia]."[16] In addition, Soviet Russia was critically dependent on oil supplies from Baku, which became even more obvious during their war with Poland in 1920. This, when combined with the prevailing political-ideological considerations of the time, shows that purely economic and pragmatic reasons *sealed the fate of Karabakh Armenians*. Gradually, the *Nagorno-Karabakh Autonomous Oblast (NKAO)* was left within the "third category" of Stalin's Soviet formations as an enclave within the Azerbaijan Soviet Socialist Republic—which was a "first category" member republic of the USSR. And so these tensions would become a veritable landmine buried beneath the feet of the Armenian-Azerbaijani relationship, where it would threateningly rest for a long time. Since then, the loss of Karabakh became *the second underlying acute chosen trauma for Armenians*, as "the perceived injustice of the international treaties" of 1920–1921 "ensured border divisions within the region, reinforced the Armenian determination to hold on to Karabakh, which was viewed as *the only part of historic Armenia* outside the republic's borders still populated by an Armenian majority. Thus, Karabakh represented both a *raison d'être* of the Armenian national [ethnocentric] project and a *centerpiece* of the Azeri [Azerbaijani] one."[17]

During the collapse of the USSR, this landmine finally went off. The Kremlin's inability to satisfy the demands of these contesting ethnic nations set in motion *another cycle of violent ethnic conflict* between the Armenians and Azerbaijani both in and around Nagorno-Karabakh.

In summation, 1921 would see the end of the first cycle of ethnic conflict. However, the irredentist and anti-irredentist struggle was not concluded but merely postponed. The principal building blocks of this particular conflict were: (1) *Nationality* (in terms of territorial hypostasis); (2) A *commonly shared history* aggravated by the *acute chosen traumas* of the Armenians (namely the Genocide of 1915 and the territorial losses during the *second* and *third hot stages* of their conflicts with Turkey and Azerbaijan); (3) *religion* (particularly the pan-Turkic state project).

(2) The New (Modern) Cycle: 1984 to the Present

1984–April 30, 1991: Stirring-Up Stage

- 1984: *Triggering Event*—the publication of *Ochag (The Hearth)*, a highly provocative book penned by well-known Soviet-Armenian journalist and author Zori Balayan.

This book quickly became a best-seller among Armenians throughout the USSR; it is by no means an exaggeration to say that, at some point, nearly every Armenian family had it as a table-reading book. "While describing his travels around Armenian lands, he [Balayan] provocatively included as Armenian landmarks such territories as Nakhichevan and the Araxes River (which he called *Arake*), which marks the southern border of Azerbaijan."[18] Based on his interpretations of medieval Armenian inscriptions that cover many older monuments, Balayan argued that the territory of Azerbaijan had been known as "Aghvank" earlier in its history. However, this would change when the Turkish masses invaded and destroyed the cultural legacy of the native Armenians during the fourteenth century. From that point onward, Armenian *historical mythology* regarded the Armenian Genocide of 1915 as the culmination of *Turkish* intermittent violence against Armenia (as, according to Balayan, the name "Azerbaijan" was not applied to any territory at the inception of the violence). Additionally, he pushed that the Soviet-built boundaries of the Armenian SSR, which did not include its historical lands of Nagorno-Karabakh, Nakhichevan, Surmala, Kars, and Ardagan, were the end of a similarly drawn-out process of (Soviet-Turkish) "division of the Armenian historical territories."[19]

Balayan then took the pseudonym Gaik Karabakhtsi, thereby emphasizing the special importance of this territory to Armenians and its return under the historical name of *Artsakh*. He wrote that "out of all rights and before any other human rights, I prefer the right for the heyday of [a] nation. And only he who carries it into life could be called a citizen and a patriot. All the rest is treachery and immorality."[20] Stunningly, this revelation resembles those of Andrii Bilec'kii, which were extensively covered in the previous chapter. In both cases, this kind of rhetoric vividly demonstrates the resurgence of ethnocentric nationalism, with individual human dignity and rights being fully sacrificed at the triumphant altar of radical integral nationalism, which, in the latter half of the 1980s, was quickly embraced by Balayan's co-ethnics. The long-dormant dreams of the Dashnaks were revitalized within the collective psyche of ethnocentric Armenian patriots: "that is to realize an idea of a 'united Armenia,' even if without Armenians by tearing away from Turkey all [of] Eastern Anatolia well off [into the] Mediterranean Sea ... in [what] would be great military clashes."[21] And the first step to realizing this plan necessitated that, first and foremost, Karabakh must be taken back.

- 1984–1986: Reemergence of acute chosen traumas of the *commonly shared history building block of the ethnic conflict*. Revitalization of the *nationality building block* centered around the area of Nagorno-Karabakh, Nakhichevan, and the other aforementioned disputed regions, especially regarding their "*ethnic names*." This period also saw the beginning of the "group mentality," "self-assertive/integrative tendencies," and "conformity" behavioral patterns of ethnocentric nationalism in Armenia.

Needless to say, this book, in the words of Thomas de Waal, "caused a storm of protest in Azerbaijan as no doubt he [Balayan] intended."[22] This publication, alongside other similar Armenian works, was called upon to prove the Armenians' right of primogeniture within the territories of what once constituted the historical "Greater Armenia."[23]

- 1984–1988: An event that I refer to as the "*war of pamphlets*" saw the appearance of numerous pseudo-historical publications in both countries that garnered the involvement of leading scholars, writers, poets, publicists, and amateurs. Within my files, I have collected samples of 128 of these publications, with eighty-one published during the *stirring-up stage* in Armenia and forty-seven from Azerbaijan.

All of these interpretations, regardless of which side produced them, aimed to remove the difficulties in building a *popular conception* of their respective autochthones living within the contesting territories. Both Armenian and Azerbaijani authors used their work to make exclusive legal claims and moral rights concerning the ownership of the land by, more often than not, developing "historical" and "archaeological evidence" (peppered by a mythological component) to prove themselves as the primogenitures of their homelands. Thus, I wish to once again emphasize that, in examining all of these violent conflicts, one does not deal with "history," per se (to the point that my book does not strictly define itself by the "history" alone). Rather, I focus on the "*historical*" *mythological component* of the *commonly shared history building block* of ethnic conflict as a part of the kind of ethnocentric ideology that drives the concept of ethnic hatred.

Countering the veritable landslide of work ushered in by Balayan, the Azerbaijani historical-mythological conception ultimately came into its own through the framework of the so-called *Albanian Theory*, written by the leading specialist at the Azerbaijani Academy of Sciences, Ziya Buniatov, and his disciple Farita Mamedova. Their most lasting impact saw Azerbaijani schoolchildren learning, from grade school onward, how the Azerbaijani ethnic nation emerged during the Turkish assimilation of the Albanian autochthones and other Caucasian/Irano-speaking (Aryan) ethnic elements, as well as their own cultural heritage and settlements. As a result, the Armenians did not have any viable attitudes or claims in deciding the allotment of the contested lands, which included Karabakh.[24]

- 1986–1988: Reemergence of the *religious building block*. Representatives of the Armenian intelligentsia, who were summarily reinforced by their liberal Russian colleagues—such as Dmitry Likhachov—repeatedly expressed their cultural complaints, the most painful of which were the grievances concerning dozens of medieval Armenian churches and religious monuments—khachkars (stone crosses)—in Karabakh that "were falling down from lack of upkeep." Additionally, many other churches were closed for worship due to similar issues, though Azerbaijani authorities outright denied these facts.[25] In the pages of *Literary Newspaper*, Russian intellectual Igor Belyaev allowed himself to directly insult the religious feelings of the Azerbaijani people. As such, the main point of his article, which written in one of the foremost liberal publications in the USSR, carried the allegations that Muslims "are insidious and treacherous people."[26]
- 1986–1988: Emergence of the *linguistic building block*. Armenian ethnocentric nationalists broadened their list of cultural accusations against their ethnic rivals. They complained of the lack in Armenian-language television within Nagorno-Karabakh and that "the history of Armenia was not allowed to be taught [in the Armenian language] in the Armenian-language schools."[27]

In Karabakh, these emotions would become even more inflamed, especially when the local Armenians "contrasted their situation to that in [the next door] Armenia where national culture was undergoing its officially sanctioned revival."[28]

The authorities of both republics encouraged intellectuals to prove that Karabakh was culturally—as in, *linguistically* and *religiously*—a distinctive subset of Armenia or Azerbaijan, respectively.[29] With that, both republics then saw an unprecedented resurgence of nationalistically mythologized history, national literature, poetry, and journals glorifying their nations and cultural origins while simultaneously demonizing their neighbors.

- 1986–1988: Reemergence of a *biological building block*. Azerbaijani ethno-political elites revitalized a concept detailing that during the Turkish domination (of 1918), which came following the disintegration of Imperial Transcaucasia, the Azerbaijani ethnic nation had already manifested itself within a stable Turkish/Muslim nucleus religiously, linguistically, and biologically. In that sense, they were effectively coterminus to the ethno-cultural and ethno-political markers of the larger nation-state itself. *Azeri-Turk* became synonymous with the traditional ethnic name— *Azerbaijani*—and gradually became the moniker of the titular-super-ordinate nation as a union nation-state. In accordance with Buniatov's Albanian (Aryan) theory, this biological "type" was then used to populate the lands to the west of and in and around Nagorno-Karabakh (which was a regional focal point) since time immemorial.[30]

Prior to his Albanian theory, Buniatov had been publishing anti-Armenian materials since the 1960s, only to effectively double his activity when he became head of the Academy of Sciences in Baku. In his own writings, de Waal provides a scandalous example of Buniatov's anti-Armenian campaign. In 1990, on the eve of the new *first hot stage* of this conflict, 30,000 copies of a racist opus named *The Caucasus*, first published in 1904 and written by the controversial Russian polemicist Vasil Velichko, were reissued under Buniatov's supervision. In it, this radical monarchist and racist (according to de Waal) "had argued that the Armenians' short skulls, like those of the Jews, make them a politically unreliable race and praised the obedience of Azerbaijanis to the Tsarist regime."[31]

- 1986–1988: The meteoric rise of popular campaigns. Mass behavior, mutually displayed ethnic prejudices, uncritical obedience to charismatic leaders, and authoritarianism began to prevail within the inner workings of both ethnic communities. In this case, the *triggering event* came by way of a petition written by Igor Muradian, a thirty-year-old Armenian activist with Karabakh origins. Following his first attempt in 1983, this second attempt, given the auspicious atmosphere of perestroika, moved to persuade the highest Soviet authorities to transfer the NKAO to Armenia. The petition was signed by nine highly regarded members and scientists of the Armenian Communist Party, including Gorbachev's leading economic reform advisor, Abel Aganbegyan. This petition immediately became a rallying point, as a great collection of Karabakh and Armenian activists rapidly mobilized, with the support of Karabakh Communist leader Karen Demirchyan. Simultaneously, Karabakh-based irredentist circles and the national communist leadership of Armenia added their own influence by contributing to the demise of the longtime Azerbaijani communist leader, Geidar Aliyev. Through this, Muradian would establish close connections with the underground Dashnak cells in Yerevan—the capital of Armenia—who then mobilized the Diaspora populations in turn.
- August 1987: A ten-volume petition for the Armenian annexation of the NKAO was submitted to the Kremlin, bearing over 75,000 signatures.
- October 1987: Muradian and would-be Armenian leader Levon Ter-Petrosyan formed the ethnocentric organization known as *The Karabakh Committee* in Yerevan and organized mass demonstrations and meetings began in both Yerevan and Stepanakert—the capital of the NKAO. A subdivision of The Karabakh Committee called *Krunk* (lit. "Crane")—a symbol of longing for one's homeland—was soon formed and headed the demonstrations in the NKAO.
- November 19, 1987: Aganbegyan traveled to Paris, where he began mobilizing the resources of the local Armenian Diaspora in support of the "Karabakh national cause." Radio Free Europe/Radio Liberty and the Voice of America translated and openly broadcast his calls for support. The Armenian Diaspora, with its many political organizations/parties—such as *the Revolutionary Dashnaks*, *the Union of Armenian Revolutionaries*, *Peasant's Freedom*, *Eastern Armenians of the USA*, *Cilicia*, *Zhirair*, *Armenian Defense*, and the *Young Armenian Dashnaks*—then entered the fray. Soon enough, an illegal flood of money and weapons were making their way into the NKAO.
- 1987: Excluding the areas around Karabakh, approximately 350,000 Armenians lived in Azerbaijan. At the same time, around 200,000 Azerbaijani lived in Armenia. Meetings and activist-led attacks on civilians became more and more frequent as disputes erupted throughout both republics. Of particular note was a spat between Azerbaijanis and Armenians in the northern Azerbaijani village of Chardakhlu (Çardaqlu) in October 1987. This unrest, which stemmed from a disagreement regarding the appointment of a new Azerbaijani collective farm director, ended with the beatings of several Armenians at the hands of the local Azerbaijani militia—which essentially served as the police. This incident triggered mass protests throughout Armenia.
- October 18, 1987–February 1988: Violent clashes broke out in the southern adjunct areas of the Armenian SSR—the Meghri and Kafan Districts—which encompassed many Azerbaijani villages. The brotherhood within/warlikeness without behavioral pattern became prevailingly recurrent in

the mass fights and attacks perpetrated by the Armenian mobs on the Azerbaijani villages. Azerbaijani refugees, carrying their stories of humiliation, destruction of their property, and beatings, began arriving in Baku and the neighboring industrial city of Sumgait, where many Armenians occupied a myriad of jobs in the industrial, trade, and service sectors. Therefore, the influx of 10,000 desperate and unemployed Azerbaijani refugees from the Gugark District of Armenia supercharged the already dense atmosphere of ethnic hatred among the distressed masses of the city and the surrounding villages.[32]

- February 20–25, 1988: Mass rallies and demonstrations in Yerevan grow by exorbitant amounts. What was originally a crowd of 30,000 people numbered 300,000 the very next day, and then perhaps even a million the day after that. At its peak, more than a quarter of the entire population of Armenia, comprising men, women, and children, were gathering and demanding the return of Karabakh.

- February 20, 1988: At almost the same time as these meetings, Armenian deputies of the Stepanakert Regional Soviet (NKAO) adopted a resolution regarding the transference of Karabakh from Azerbaijan to Armenia. Armenian authorities began to replace Azerbaijani flags and the signboards of administrative buildings/enterprises with the banners and symbols of the Armenian SSR, while also building parallel power structures.

The events in Yerevan and Karabakh effectively stood the needle on its head, ultimate requiring only the slightest touch to set these strained and frayed nerves loose. And a few days afterward, the trigger was pulled in Sumgait.

- February 27–29, 1988: The ethnic pogroms in Sumgait would begin as a small demonstration against the events in Karabakh. The crowd of Azerbaijanis would continuously grow in size, especially with the addition of the homeless and unemployed refugees from Armenia, whose stories of the horrors they suffered at the hands of the Armenians gradually electrified the protestors. Second Secretary of the Sumgait Communist Party Committee Bagirova added fuel to the fire by reporting that Armenians would have to leave Azerbaijan as a result of growing tensions. The few violent incidents that sprang up resulted in the connivance of the local law enforcement organizations, which were overwhelmingly composed of Azerbaijanis. Yet the event that would truly set off the situation was a public statement made by the military prosecutor of the Soviet Union (and broadcast on both TV and radio) stating that, five days previously, two young Azerbaijani men had been killed by Armenians in Karabakh.

The day after this announcement, the brotherhood within/warlikeness without behavioral pattern of the crowd accommodated a higher level of unrestricted aggressiveness and, in accordance with the Kleinian model, regressed into paranoid-schizoid behavior. By this, the crowd went on an unrestricted rampage, which resulted in the random killings of any and all Armenians they could get their hands on within the city. Later on, a documentary film of the incident was created and shown in Sweden in 1989. It provided just a measure of the horror and depth of the near chosen trauma, which, in and of itself, generated further revenge and unleashed a vicious cycle of ethnic violence at this stage of the conflict. One of the heroes of the film, a witness named Gabrielian, captured and shocked the European audience by speaking about the brutal murder of his friend, Misha, and his wife, both of which he allegedly witnessed. After Misha and his wife were beheaded, thirty Azerbaijanis rushed their young daughter. With her defenseless, they raped her in turns and then cut her flesh into small pieces; after making a fire, they then prepared *shashlyk* (a Caucasian dish of skewered and grilled meat) out of her flesh and ate it.

In the long run, this film was also presented throughout Europe and even made its way to America, which, as we have previously discussed, hosted sizable Armenian populations and communities. Therefore, it should come as no surprise that, following the end of these "demonstrations," there was a significant amount of sympathy and support for the Armenian cause and an overwhelming desire "to oust the savage cannibals not only from [Nagorno-Karabakh], but also from the entire South Caucasus."[33] Ultimately, on February 29, a well-armed detachment of marines from the Caspian flotilla arrived in the city, and their commander, General Krayev, established a curfew to curtail the violence. Soon enough, the pogroms ceased. The official death toll reached thirty-two men and was accompanied by more than 400 arrests. While many of the witness testimonies described incidents of slaughter, robbery, rape, and savage assaults, some even went so far as to describe the self-sacrifice of some Azerbaijanis who incurred the wrath of the crowd for attempting to shelter and save their Armenian neighbors.[34]

- 1988–1991: Ethnocentric consolidation, as well as further ethnic delineation, became prevalent among both republics (and, after 1991, as independent states). As a result, both entities participated in a forcible exchange of ethnic populations. A chain of violent cases of ethnic cleansing based on the "interplay of three distinct strata of [the] population": (1) the "city mob," which consisted of low-level, almost plebian social elements thrown out of rural places that tend to be religiously conservative; (2) the considerably Russified bureaucratic national communists and new anti-Soviet/anti-Russian ethnocentric activists; (3) the pan-Turkic and anti-Soviet/anti-Russian ethnocentric intelligentsia.[35] (Specific organizations and their leadership—who were/still are the driving forces behind many of these ethnic conflicts—are listed in chapter 5).
- January 13–15, 1990: This period highlighted the exacerbating role of Gorbachev's government in this conflict. Primarily, this is seen in their relatively late reaction to Armenian pogroms in January (in which ninety Armenians died and thousands more were beaten and injured—as a result from the indictment of the *Azerbaijani People's Front*). Only on January 15 did the overarching authorities of the USSR impose a state of emergency, though it was not applied to the tenuous city of Baku. Instead, Soviet troops marched into the city and clashed with demonstrators. When the dust settled, 130 civilians and twenty-nine soldiers lay dead.
- Summer 1990: An ethnocentric Armenian pan-national movement won the election and threatened to secede from the Soviet Union. In contrast, August 1991 saw the Azerbaijani People's Front side with Gorbachev's administration.
- August 1991: End of the *stirring-up stage*. It was at this point that mild and middle-ground forms of ethnic cleansing prevailed and set the stage for the emergence of more extreme forms of cleansing, which came about during the pogroms in Sumgait and Baku, as well as during the sporadic interethnic incidents leading up to the end of this stage.

During the *stirring-up stage,* and based on the previously presented list of mild and middle-ground forms of ethnic cleansing (see chapter 5 under the subheading "Beginning of the Process of Ethnicization in Politics," in which certain numbers refer to particular building blocks of ethnic conflict, state and economic policy; and numerals in each rubric refer to certain mild and middle-ground forms of ethnic cleansing performed by ethnocentric nationalists during stirring-up stages and fixed in the abovementioned list in chapter 5). In this particular conflict at this stage I recorded: regarding the biological building block that both ethnic nations practiced—I(4); regarding language—II (2, 5); regarding the religious building block—III(2, 1); regarding the commonly shared history building block—IV(1, 2, 3, *4, 5); the efforts of the state organizations of both titular ethnic nations, as they increasingly practiced such* forms of collusion—V(1, 2, 3); and economic measures—VI(1, 2, 3, 4, 5).

During the pogroms themselves, as well as in the grand scheme of the conflict by the end of this stage, there appeared elements of extreme forms of ethnic cleansing. Based on the list of extreme forms of ethnic cleansing (published earlier in the previous chapter 6), one may identify the following forms, which are generally accompanied by the *unrestricted aggressiveness* of the perpetrators, spurred on by the informal and even official state organizations. Regarding the *common biological building block,* both groups practiced: I (1, 2); *language:* II (2, 3); religion—III (1, 2, 5); *commonly shared history—*IV (2, 3); *Nationality:* V (1, 2, 3, 5, 7); *state organizations practiced—*VI (1, 2, 3, 4); *economic measures* include—VII (5).[36]

April 30, 1991–May 12, 1994: The First Hot Stage

At the end of the *stirring-up stage,* many Azerbaijani villages in Nagorno-Karabakh, including the principal settlement of Susha, had been plundered by the local Armenian militia and the units of the so-called *fedayins*—armed ethnocentric guerillas that penetrated the countryside in the guise of protestors from Armenia.

- April 30, 1991: *Triggering Event*—a pair of attacks on the Armenian villages of Getashen (*Chaikent* in Azerbaijani) and Martunashen (now known as *Qarabulaq*) took place within the boundaries of the *state-organized deportation operation* under the name "Operation Ring" (which would continue until the August 1991 coup in Moscow). These attacks were perpetrated by the Azerbaijani *OMON (Detachments of Militia for Special Operations)* and Soviet Army units.
- April 1991–August 1991: The abovementioned forces would establish a blockade of the NKAO and deported around 10,000 people (out of an approximate population of 130,000) from twenty-six villages, all while killing anywhere from 140 to 170 Armenian civilians (thirty-seven of which were killed during the attacks on Getashen and Martunashen). In the end, Soviet Army units were demoralized by the incident due to their involvement in the interethnic clashes and the execution of civilians, alongside other unbelievable atrocities. More crucially, however, it triggered the openly armed phase of the Karabakh conflict, which itself contributed to the demise of the Soviet Union in general.
- August 31, 1991: The Azerbaijani Supreme Soviet passed a declaration by which it reestablished the independent Republic of Azerbaijan.
- September 2, 1991: A joint session of the NKAO Soviet and the Soviet of the Armenian-populated Shaumyan/Goranboy District (which had not been previously a part of the NKAO and was captured by *fedayins*) adopted its own declaration that elevated its autonomous status to that of a *sovereign Nagorno-Karabakh Republic (NKR)* with a prospectively irredentist project of "reunifying" with Armenia proper.
- September 28, 1991: Armenia declared its independence from the USSR.
- September 1991: The first steps toward the *internationalization of the conflict*. In the town of Zheleznovodsk (a part of Stavropol Krai in the Russian North Caucasus), Boris Yeltsin attended a

meeting with Ayaz Mutallibov—the president of Azerbaijan—and Levon Ter-Petrosyan—the president of Armenia—in the presence of Kazakhstani President Nursultan Nazarbayev, where they signed the so-called "Zheleznovodsk Declaration," a sort of cease-fire and/or peace agreement. With this action, Russia demonstrated that it had reinserted itself into the affairs of the South Caucasus, wearing the halo of a peacemaker. However, this was only the first in a long series of similarly worded "agreements" under different schools of thought, in which neither side's desires ever were (or will never be) fulfilled.

- November 20, 1991: Interpersonal actions would wreck this agreement when Armenian fedayins downed an Azerbaijani helicopter in the Martuni region of Karabakh. All twenty-two passengers, including President Mutallibov's press secretary, head of the Shusha District Vagif Dzhafarov, and an assortment of Russian and Kazakhstani officials, died in the crash.
- November–December 1991: The army of the NKR would grow into a force of 7,000 troops who were well-armed, equipped, and trained due to the monetary support of Armenia and Armenian ethnic Diasporas.
- February 26, 1992: *The Day of the Khojaly Tragedy*—for Azerbaijanis, this town in Karabakh, home to many modern apartment complexes, which housed around 6,300 Azerbaijani people (whose original homes had been previously plundered and/or destroyed in Stepanakert), symbolizes *a new unresolved acute chosen trauma* akin to Srebrenica for Bosnian Muslims, Beslan High School #1 for Ossetians, or Sumgait for Armenians.

The strategic location of Khojaly, which was a mere five miles from the NKR capital of Stepanakert, effectively sealed its fate. It was not a matter of if something would happen, but merely when. By that point, Armenians had already gained control over all the other towns and villages around Karabakh's capital, and the only remaining settlement connecting it to Azerbaijan proper was Khojaly. On the night of February 25, 1992, an Armenian detachment surrounded the town from three sides, with a single corridor being left open for the inhabitants and the local Azerbaijani OMON forces, commanded by Alif Hajiyev, to escape toward the Azerbaijani town of *Ağdam (Aghdam)*. However, the refugees were ambushed on the road. What followed was an appalling display of carnage of defenseless people as, after the deaths of a few militiamen, *613 were killed* (including *63 children, 106 women, 70 senior men, and two whole families* [who were completely annihilated]), *with an additional 487 wounded* (including *76 children*), *1,275 taken prisoner*, and *750 missing*.[37]

In contrast to the slow goings of earlier stages, 1993 saw the relatively rapid advance of the Armenian forces in and around Nagorno-Karabakh:

- June 27: Armenian forces in Karabakh recaptured the previously lost city of Martakert. They would then strike deep into Azerbaijani territory and, on July 23, capture the town of *Ağdam*.
- August 23: *Füzuli* (Armenian: *Varanda*) fell to Armenian units.
- August 25: Armenians would capture the city of Jabrayil.
- August 31: The forces would quickly advance and take *Qubadlı* (Armenian: *Vorotan*).
- September: The Armenians began their offensive, moving toward the Iranian border at Horadiz. For their efforts, they gained control of over 160 km of the Azerbaijani-Iranian border.

- October 24: After the capture of Horadiz, the Armenian units cut off the Zangilan region, which they would completely overtake five days later (see Fig. 8.4).[38]

During the *first hot stage of the modern cycle,* several extreme forms of ethnic cleansing became prevalent among the combatants, including: III (5); IV (1); V (6, 7); VI (3, 4, [and especially] 5, 6, 7, 8).

- 1992–94: Further *internationalization of the conflict*—Russia and her international partners decided to physically step in to prevent the further destabilization of the region and any areas beyond the South Caucasus.
- March 1992: The *Minsk Group* was formed in the titular Belarusian capital under the authority of the OSCE in order to better organize various peacemaking conferences between the two sides.
- May 8–9, 1994: The parliamentary delegations of the CIS countries would convene in Bishkek, the capital of Kyrgyzstan. Once there, they would draw up a document known as the *Bishkek Protocol*, which called on both sides of the conflict to initiate a cease-fire at midnight on May 8. Six representatives, including Russia's Vladimir Kazimirov and various Armenian representatives, signed the protocol. As the first tenuous step toward peace, this was a crucial moment in the history of the region. That same day, Azerbaijani Defense Minister Mamedrafi Mamedov endorsed the protocol with his own signature, signing it in Baku on May 9; the next day, Serzh Sargsian, the Armenian defense minister (who would later become president of Armenia), signed the document from his office in Yerevan. At midnight on May 11–12, 1994, the cease-fire officially took effect. Suffice to say, this one event put an end to the bloody *first hot stage of the modern cycle* of the Armenian-Azerbaijani ethnic conflict.[39]

But despite the advent of peace, *the casualty figures* of this conflict still looked miserably bleak. Between 1991 and 1994, through the course of both military action and various forms of ethnic cleansing, it is estimated that 22,000–25,000 people perished between the two countries. Additionally, the devastation wrought in the wake of the violence left more than 1 million refugees and displaced persons behind to try and rebuild their lives. Several armed Armenian forces had secured control over Karabakh, as well as occupying considerable territory within the adjoining internal Azerbaijani regions. Until recently, Azerbaijan has continued to insist that Karabakh is an indispensable part of its territory and identity/ statehood. In turn, Armenia firmly states that the Armenian majority living within Nagorno-Karabakh possess all rights regarding self-determination and independence.[40]

May 11–12, 1994–September 27, 2020: Smoldering Stage

From time to time, this stage was interrupted and examined by peaceful consultations organized through the *Minsk Group*, which comprises those countries that host significant Armenian and Azerbaijani Diasporas: the United States, Russia, and France. This group's principles for crafting possible resolutions include the following:

- the return of occupied territories around Nagorno-Karabakh;
- providing Nagorno-Karabakh an intermediate status with a warranty regarding its sovereignty and self-government;
- preserving the Lachin corridor [see figure 8.4] linking Nagorno-Karabakh to Armenia;

- the possibility of firmly defining the final status of Nagorno-Karabakh by the popular will and reinforcing it with a legally binding power;
- granting the right of return to all internally and internationally displaced persons/refugees; and
- providing guarantees of international security, including the execution of a full-scale peacekeeping operation.[41]

So far, none of these points have been fulfilled in any capacity by either side or the *Minsk Group*. Instead, the sides of the conflict have increasingly dedicated the lion's share of the budget to their military spending and fortification programs. For instance, Russia is essentially playing both sides, trading weapons to either side while simultaneously maintaining their military base in Armenia. In is own part Turkey did the same for Azerbaijan. From time to time, both sides also provoke armed "accidents" along the line that separated their armed forces at the moment of the cease-fire in 1994.

The last summit between Azerbaijani President Ilham Aliyev (son of the previous leader, Heydar Aliyev) and former Armenian President Serzh Sargsyan took place on October 16, 2017, and was organized by the *Minsk Group* in Geneva, Switzerland. Both presidents agreed to take appropriate actions in order to reinforce the negotiations process and decrease tensions on the *Line of Contact*. However, the situation has seen no significant change since that point and was still characterized by mutual hostilities. As of now, the most recent clash took place on June 1 (and then in July- August), 2020, on the border with the Nakhichevan region, where Armenian armed forces targeted and destroyed Azerbaijani military vehicles.[42] Clearly, increasing mutual provocations, skirmishes along the contact line, and provocative statements of leadership of both countries (Ilham Aliev, Nikola Pashinian, and Karabakh/Artsakh's leader, Araik Arutunian, as well as that of Turkey) in July–August 2020 indicated that the *smoldering stage* of the conflict was still well underway and at any moment could regress to another *hot stage*, with potentially dangerous involvement in it of a number of regional nation-states and even global powers.

On September 27, 2020, when this edition was signed for publication, a new *hot stage* rather predictably erupted at full strength, as has been a logical outcome of the previously cited provocative actions of the two sides and enticing exacerbating policy of Turkey. This *second hot stage of the modern cycle* of violent ethnic conflict ended with the catastrophic military defeat of Armenian forces (thousands were dead and wounded on both sides) and the loss of the key Karabakh city of Shusha, which opened a direct way for the advancing Azerbaijani army to capture the capital city of Stepanakert (Azerbaijani *Khankendi*). At this point, Putin interfered, and under his pressure, the two sides and Russia signed a *Trilateral Agreement* on the night of November 9, 2020, about stopping the military action from November 10, 2020. Under the conditions of the treaty, Azerbaijan received back almost all regions that since 1994 had been under Armenian military control, restoring its territorial integrity. Russia deployed a 1,960-strong, fully equipped military peacekeeping contingent to Karabakh (including a special PK Brigade that had been taking part in the operation against Georgian forces in the 2008 war in South Ossetia), thus reinforcing its military presence in the South Caucasus, effectively breaking the arc of instability along the perimeter of the former Soviet border, saving the remnants of the Karabakh territories for the Armenian population. Turkey, by helping Azerbaijan, has blistering perspectives in the area and via Azerbaijan forges a link to the Turkic (Turan) space in Central Asia. And only Armenia is in shock and disarray amid the acute internal political crisis caused by the humiliating defeat, with unclear perspectives of physically surviving in the hostile environment under Russian tutelage. As a result of resolute Russian actions, one of these oldest and most complicated violent ethnic conflicts in the post-Soviet space has a perspective of, after the current *smoldering stage*, entering its *Frozen Phase*, at least for the next five-year period of the Russian presence, as granted exclusively to Russia's peacekeeping forces by the aforementioned *Agreement* (with subsequent automatic prolongation with the consent of the contractual sides). The political status of what is left from Nagorno-Karabakh under Armenian control is currently unclear, with the Azerbaijani resolute unwillingness to discuss any variants of a political status of this territory after Azerbaijan's undisputable victory. As to the casualties of the *Second hot stage*, military authorities of Armenia have reported so far about 3,439 fatal losses of their servicemen, and the Azerbaijani side about 2,855.

- **Type of Conflict:** Irredentist, interstate violent ethnic conflict
- **Principal Building Blocks of the Armenian-Azerbaijani violent ethnic conflict in terms of overall importance:**
  - **Primary Building Blocks**
    - 1.1.1. Nationality (most important and mobilizing)
    - 1.1.2. Commonly shared history aggravated by historically *unresolved acute chosen traumas* (as per their *ethno-historical mythology*)

  - **Subsidiary Building Blocks**
    - 1.1.3. Religious
    - 1.1.4. Linguistic
    - 1.1.5. Biological

FIGURE 8.4   Map of Nagorno-Karabakh

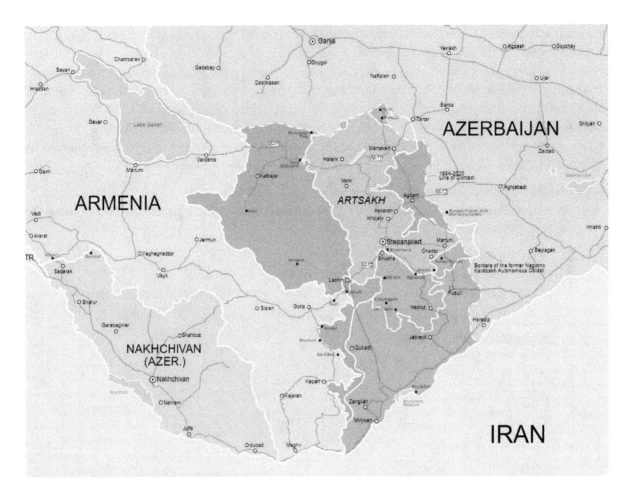

FIGURE 8.5   Map of What Is Left of Nagorno-Karabakh under Armenian Control after the Second *hot stage* of the modern cycle and Crushing Defeat of the Armenian Side; Adapted from 2020 Nagorno-Karabakh War.

(II) "Russo"-Moldovan Violent Ethnic Conflict in Transnistria/ Transdniestria: May 20, 1989–Present

(1) Current Cycle: May 20, 1989–Present

May 20, 1989–November 2, 1990: Stirring-Up Stage

- May 20, 1989: *Triggering event*—Ethnocentric Moldovan (pro-Romanian) nationalists from the *Democratic Movement in Support of Perestroika* united with the similarly thinking members of the *Musical-Literary Club,* forming the *People's Front of Moldova (PFM).* In the national elections held shortly thereafter, the leaders of this organization found themselves holding positions in the Supreme Soviet of the Moldovan SSR.

FIGURE 8.6   Flag of Transnistria-Transdniestra

FIGURE 8.7   Flag and Coat of Arms of Republic of Moldova

- 1989–1990: The process of ethnicization of politics and delineation along ethnic lines began in force. The conflicting sides of this conflict emerged. The *First Congress of PFM* adopted a program and formed a mono-ethnic leadership structure within the republic. This movement exhibited ethnocentrically nationalistic sentiments and expressed their intent to leave the Soviet Union in favor of uniting with Romania, thus creating the foundation for their brand-new *irredentist project*. It is worth remembering that, prior to the Soviet Occupation of Bessarabia and Northern Bukovina, Stalin's creation of the ("first category") union *Moldavian SSR* in 1940, as well as the partitioning of territory to the west of the Dniester (Moldovan/Romanian *Nistru*) River as a part of Romania (1918–1940). Later on, the ethnocentric, mono-ethnic government of Moldova would declare the Molotov–Ribbentrop Pact between the USSR and Germany "null and void," despite Moldova's retention of additional territory resulting from the terms of the agreement.
- April 1990: *The XIIIth Session of the Supreme Council of the MSSR* (which was characterized by a campaign of intimidation and physical abuse against the representatives of other political and ethnic groups unleashed by ethnocentric nationalists) adopted a law functionally establishing "Romanian" as the official state language, with the Cyrillic alphabet being replaced by a Latin one. Simultaneously, the Session adopted a new name for the titular ethnic nation—*Romanians*.[43] Thus, and in addition to the *commonly shared history* and *linguistic building blocks,* there emerged a *nationality building block*. That same Session also adopted a new Romanian flag with the traditional blue-yellow-red color scheme in the "Pales" pattern, as well as a Romanian emblem featuring the head of an ox, which was popularized in Romanian Moldova during the Revolution of 1848.

At the same time, opposition to these new ethnocentric trends and other potential acts of "Romanization" was on the rise in the region of Transnistria—also known as *Pridnestrovie* (Russian). Unlike the rest of the MSSR, ethnic Moldovans only constituted 39.9 percent of the population there, with most of them speaking Russian. Additionally, they were handily outnumbered by the combined populations of Russians and Ukrainians (who also primarily spoke Russian), which rested at 53.8 percent as reported by the 1989 Transnistrian census. But they were not a lone exception, as there was a reasonably sized opposition to these policies forming in Moldova proper.[44]

- June 2, 1990: *The First Congress of the People's Deputies of Pridnestrovie*, consisting of 673 delegates, declared their independence from Moldova and triggered a massive anti-irredentist (separatist) struggle within the country. The congress elected a new *Coordinational Soviet of Socio-Economic Development of the Region,* with the new government headed by Igor Smirnov. In response, Mircea Snegur, leader of the MSSR and a typical representative of the nomenclature of the late Soviet Communist Party, and other "national communists" quickly transitioned into full-on ethnocentric nationalists.
- June 5, 1990: Under the supervision of Chairman Snegur, the *Supreme Council* (*SC*) of the MSSR renamed the country the *Republic of Moldova (RM)*, effectively subsuming the August 2, 1940, formation of the MSSR.
- August 19, 1990: Local Soviets proclaimed the formation of the *Gagauz Republic* (from its capital of Comrat). By this point, armed groups of ethnocentric Moldovans, headed by Mircea Druk and loaded into the backs of trucks and tractors (just as during the previously described interethnic riot between Uzbeks and Meskhetian Turks), began their march against Gagauzia, threatening a massacre like the one seen in Fergana. Fortunately, General Aleksandr Lebed' of the Russian (Soviet) 14th Army, which was stationed in Transnistria, deployed his Spetznaz units to handle the situation, thereby preventing any ethnic collision.[45]
- September 23, 1990: Shortly thereafter, the *Pridnestovskaya Moldavskaya Respublika* (in Russian) or *TDMSSR*—better known as the *Pridnestrovian Moldavian Republic (PMR)*—was officially declared and comprised the Grigoriopol, Cocieru-Dubossarskii (left bank), Rîbniṭa, and Slobozia Districts, which encompasses the cities of Bender (Rus. *Bendery*), Dubăsari (Rus. *Dubossary*), and Rîbniṭa (Rus. *Rybnitsa*), with Tiraspol serving as the capital.

November 2, 1990–July 21, 1992:The Hot Stage

By this point, the pro-Russian forces included the *Transnistrian Republican Guard, local militias, Cossack Units* (of the Don and Kuban Cossacks), and *elements of the Russian 14th Army*, with the addition of *Ukrainian volunteers from the UNA-UNSO.* As for the pro-Moldovan force, they consisted of Moldovan troops, police forces, and Romanian volunteers.

- November 2, 1990: *Triggering event*—the first clash between these opposing forces erupted in Dubăsari/Dubossary, leaving three dead and sixteen wounded. An attempt to hold formal negotiations—under the protection of Leonid Kravchuk—fell through when Igor Smirnov, Chairman of the Supreme Soviet of the PMR Grigory Marakutza, and several deputies were kidnapped from their hotel in Ukraine (they were later released).[46]
- August 21, 1991: The RM officially declared full independence from the USSR.
- September 1991: The second onslaught against Dubăsari by Moldovan police forces failed.
- December 26, 1991: The *Cossack Circle* (a Congress) declared its intention to create a *Black Sea Cossack Host* and elected Hetman Aleksandr Rudskikh to oversee it.
- January–April 10, 1992: The regular armed forces of both the RM and PMR were formed. Fighting further intensified after March 1.
- March 2–July 21, 1992: Intense fighting accompanied by *extreme forms of ethnic cleansing.*

- June 19, 1992: A battle in Bender city results in 500 deaths. By that time, the Moldovan armed forces had numbered 25,000–35,000 professional soldiers, with arms, munitions, and military instruction provided by the Romanians. Opposing them were 9,000 PMR militia men, who were trained and armed by the Russian 14th Army (under the command of General Lebed').
- June 19–20, 1992: According to the Human Rights Center's *Memorial* report, Moldovan troops riding in armored vehicles began deliberately firing at houses, courtyards, and cars in Bender with heavy machine guns. As a result, many civilians taking refuge in these buildings or attempting to escape the city were shot.[47]
- June 21–22, 1992: Both sides engaged in severe close-quarters street fighting punctuated by random fire from tanks, artillery, and grenade launchers. Many PMR soldiers captured by the RM were later tortured, in some cases being beaten by clubs and the butt stocks of rifles. However, the similar treatment of Moldovan POWs was reported by PMR forces.[48]
- July 21, 1992: End of the *hot stage*. PMR forces gained the upper hand in military confrontations after the battle.

July 21, 1992–Present: Smoldering Stage

- July 21, 1992: *Internationalization of the conflict.* A cease-fire and subsequent peace talks between Boris Yeltsin and Mircea Snegur concluded with the signing of the *Agreement about the Principles of a Peaceful Resolution of Military Conflict in Pridnestrovie.* A *Security Zone* was created and would be patrolled by peacekeeping forces from both sides of the conflict (five Russian battalions, three Moldovan battalions, and two PMR battalions) under a joint military command structure—the *Joint Control Commission (JCC)*. Since then, the conditions of the cease-fire have been upheld by both sides, which technically classifies this conflict as having entered the *Frozen Stage.* However, the conflict at large has not been fully resolved, seeing as the PMR still maintains an otherwise unrecognized independence and cherishes irredentist hopes to reunite with Russia well after the conclusion of the *hot stage.* At the same time, Moldova insists on the reincorporation of the PMR into its national territory. And while Russia disbanded the 14th Army stationed within the PMR as a sign of solidarity, it still maintains a garrison of 1,300 men within their borders that constitutes a part of the JCC.
- The new president of Moldova, Maia Sandu (since December 24, 2020), a leader of the *Party of Action and Solidarity*, has assumed a rather radical approach to the problem of Transnistria/Pridnestrovie. The Constitutional Court of Moldova added fuel to the fragile situation of balance in the republic. On January 21, 2021, the majority of its members, who are Romanian citizens, canceled a special status of the Russian language as a language of intercourse between ethnic groups in Moldova. It immediately revitalized a *linguistic building block* of ethnic conflict. Furthermore, backed by the amalgamation of ethnocentric pro-Romanian parties standing for a unification with Romania (*National-Liberal Party, Romanian People's Party, Liberal Party, Union of Salvation of Bessarabia, Democracy at Home Party*—headed by the unionist movement—*Unirea* [Union]), President Sandu outlined as one of her new strategic preferences a withdrawal of the Russian peacekeeping contingent from the Security Zone in Pridnestrovie. If forcibly realized, such a radical plan may easily destabilize the situation in the entire area, and in the worst case scenario

may result in a direct clash with the forces of the Russian Federation. Besides, in Pridnestrovie exists a huge storage of military ammunition and explosives as a legacy of the former Soviet Union, once predestined for a number of the fully filled-up Soviet Armies. Nobody knows how to utilize it, and there are no comprehensive plans whatsoever for how to deal with this problem. One can only imagine what might happen if a full-fledged *hot stage* were to reignite in the area, which literally lives on a powder keg. If it goes off, the entire Republic of Moldova will be in great danger.

The primary behavioral patterns of ethnocentric nationalism during the *smoldering stage* of this conflict in particular include *mass behavior, conformity, authoritarianism, self-assertive and integrative tendencies*, and *brotherhood within/warlikeness without*.

The *smoldering stage* also saw the development of mild *and* middle-ground forms of ethnic cleansing: regarding *language*—II (1, 2); regarding the *commonly shared history building block*—IV (1, 2, 3); *state organizations practiced*—V (1, 2, 3); and *economic measures*—VI (1, 4, 5).

Interestingly, the previously mentioned behavioral patterns would eventually coalesce, with the primary behavioral pattern during the *hot stage* being *unrestricted aggressiveness*.

In that same fashion, the *extreme forms of ethnic cleansing* undertaken during the *hot stage* would also simplify and consist of two primary aspects: regarding the *nationality building block*—V (2, 5) and *state organizations practiced*—VI (1, 4, 5).

- **Type of Conflict:** Irredentist violent ethnic conflict
- **Casualties:** Moldova had 286 killed and 284 wounded (other estimates count 279–324 dead and 1,180 wounded). Transnistria lost a total of 826 lives, 310 of which were civilians (though some estimates indicate 364–913 deaths and 624 wounded).[49]
- **Principal Building Blocks of the Russo-Moldovan Violent Ethnic Conflict Ranked by Importance:**
  - Nationality
  - Linguistic

FIGURE 8.8   Map of Transnistria

(III) Georgian–South Ossetian Violent Ethnic Conflict: June 1988–Present

(1) Historical Prerequisites of the Modern Conflict: 1918–1921; 1930s–1950s

- 1918–1921: Period of independence of the Georgian state, which was recognized by Western powers. The Menshevik government faced off against the Bolsheviks over control of the country.

FIGURE 8.9   Flag and Coat of Arms of Republic of Georgia

FIGURE 8.10   Flag and Coat of Arms of South Ossetia

During the course of the conflict, the Georgians came to believe that several South Ossetian partisan groups had betrayed them and sided with the Bolsheviks.

- 1920: A South Ossetian proclamation of Soviet power assumed the form of Ossetian ethno-political self-determination well outside the Georgian state. By announcing the formation of a new Soviet republic, the Ossetians expressed their desire to remain a part of Russia, as opposed to the pro-Western orientation of their Georgian neighbors.

- June 1920: The Georgian army of Valiko Dzhugeli launched large-scale punitive actions against South Ossetian civilians, ultimately killing 5,000. Additionally, more than 50,000 were forced to flee across the Caucasus mountain range into North Ossetia, during which time another 15,000 died due to hunger, cold, or the poor conditions of precarious mountain roads. For the Ossetians, who at that time numbered nearly 200,000 strong, these deaths/relocations have become their unresolved and acute chosen trauma.[50] Unsurprisingly, this effectively created the *commonly shared history building block* of the Georgian–South Ossetian ethnic conflict. For the Georgians, their chosen trauma was the destruction of their independence by the 11th Red Army in 1921 and the subsequent creation of the "artificial" autonomy of South Ossetia by the Russian Bolshevik government in 1922–1923. Therefore, this slight predicated the emergence of the nationality building block of the conflict at large.

- 1930s–1950s: Georgian national communist authorities would begin closing Ossetian-language schools in the South Ossetian Autonomous Soviet Socialist District. From this, the *linguistic building block* of this conflict would emerge by assuming the form of yet another chosen trauma. (For more context, refer to the previously cited interviews of common people during that time.)

- 1950s: Georgian anthropologists developed a theory that the Dwali (Georgian)/Tualta (Ossetian)— the cultural and genetic ancestors of both groups—supposedly belonged to the same *Kavkasion* anthropological type of ancient population.[51] Furthermore, it suggested that, during the early medieval period, the nomadic Alans people exposed this group to the Iranian language, which influenced their own. Therefore, Ossetians (at least those in the Southern half of the region) could not be a separate nation form the Georgians, as they came from the same stock. The Ossetians, of course, opposed this idea, insisting that they stemmed both anthropologically and linguistically from the Scythians, Sarmatians, and Alans–North Iranian/Aryans, who had arrived in the area before the Georgians. As a result, the *biological building block* of the conflict emerged in earnest.

(2) Current Cycle: June 1988–Present

June 1988–November 10, 1989: First Stirring-Up Stage

Triggering event—the gradual formation of an independence movement in Georgia. The first demonstrations of this movement were organized by Nodar Natadze and Merab Kostava of the *Roundtable Block for Independent Georgia*. A short time after this, ethnocentric organizations would begin emerging in both Georgia and Ossetia (see list of organizations and leadership in chapter 5).

- 1988–1989: All of the previously mentioned building blocks reemerged in all public discourse regarding the ethnic relations of both nations and in their most radical reinterpretations (see above-cited interviews).[52]

Georgian ethnocentric nationalists adopt the concept of "Host-Georgians versus guests/ethnic minorities" into their public discourse.

Prevalent behavioral patterns of the ethnocentric nationalists at this time include *group mentality/group belonging*; *self-assertive and integrative tendencies in the collective behavior*; *mass behavior*; *conformity*; *mutually displayed ethnic prejudices*; *brotherhood within/warlikeness without*; *uncritical obedience to charismatic leaders*; and *authoritarianism*.

Mild and middle-ground forms of ethnic cleansing in Georgia, Ossetia, and Abkhazia (as cited in chapter 5) include the following: regarding the *biological building block*—I (2, 4); regarding *language*—II (1, 2); regarding the *commonly shared history building block*—IV (1, 2, 3, 4, 5*); state organizations practiced*—V (1, 3, 4, 5); and *economic measures*—VI (1, 2, 3, 4, 5).[53]

- 1989: Ethnocentric representatives of the Ossetian intelligentsia began arguing to restore the old name of "Alans" in order to assign it to either the idealized union of Ossetia-Alania or, at the very least, to the currently existing and "inseparable" parts of it. From this, an *irredentist* project emerged.
- 1988–1989: The *ambivalent policies of the Gorbachev administration* became an outside exacerbating force of this conflict. At this point, the Soviet government positioned itself as a natural ally of the irredentist (or in Abkhazia's case, secessionist) autonomies in order to better exert political pressure on ethnocentric authorities in Georgia to not secede from the USSR. But despite this pressure, the Soviet government failed to implement any practical measures to prevent or mitigate mild and middle-ground forms of ethnic cleansing in this stage. Yet it readily provided Zviad Gamsakhurdia the necessary pretext to accuse the Ossetians and Abkhazians of being "champions of the Kremlin's policy on the territory of Georgia."[54]
- April 9, 1989: Anti-Soviet demonstrations (which had begun in Tbilisi only five days before) were brutally suppressed by Russian troops: eighteen people were killed, many others were wounded, and a new chosen trauma was added to the Georgian self-perception. By the *fall of 1989,* the individual characterizing factors of the long-standing building blocks, the chosen traumas, the media, the destructive out-behavior of both the masses and ethnocentric nationals and of the

charismatic political leadership on every side of the conflict, all had become so tightly interwoven that it had irreversibly put their people on the road to disaster. The fragmented and demoralized forces of both the democratic (liberal) and conservative (pro-Soviet) camps proved unable to resist the overwhelming onset of the ethnocentric nationalists and their venomous rhetoric. Local Communist leadership, fearful of the passionate ethnocentric nationalists, sided with and supported these movements and associated ethno political organizations. (See chapter 5 for more in-depth examples of the driving forces behind these ethnic conflicts.)

November 10, 1989–June 24, 1992: First Hot Stage

- November 10, 1989: *Triggering event*—the South Ossetian Supreme Soviet passed a motion that upgraded its political status, declaring South Ossetia an autonomous republic within the Georgian SSR. As a result, this unilaterally transformed the entire region's status from that of the fourth category (an autonomous district) into the second category (an autonomous republic) of Stalin's aforementioned ranking concession of the Soviet people. The Georgian parliament immediately revoked the South Ossetian parliamentary decision. This rejection set off avalanche-like and mirror-reflected dynamics, with the behavioral patterns of both sides sliding from *brotherhood within/ warlikeness without* to *unrestricted aggressiveness*, as characterized by phase three of Klein's model. This transition also defined a subsequent regression into a *paranoid-schizoid behavioral pattern*, generally accompanied by *extreme forms of ethnic cleansing*.

- November 23, 1989: About 30,000 Georgian nationalists, including the illegally armed paramilitary formations of the *Legion of Georgian Hawks* (*Mkhedrioni*), advanced on the South Ossetian capital of Tskhinvali (Georgian)/Tskhinval (Ossetian), aiming to take the entire region. Several hundred Ossetian picketers stopped them and held their advance. At the end of this twenty-four-hour confrontation, many of the Georgians were forced to retreat. However, several of the armed formations stayed behind, organizing a prolonged blockade and occasionally engaging in clashes with the local Ossetian population. As a result of these skirmishes, six people would die and around 500 more would be wounded.

- November 23, 1989–January 1990: Armed clashes between these forces would continue in the area surrounding Tskhinvali.

- August 1990: The South Ossetian Soviet declares the reorganization of the region into the *South Ossetian Soviet Democratic Republic (YuOSDR)*, applying for Moscow to recognize it as an "independent subject of [the] Soviet federation."[55]

- October 1990: The Georgian Supreme Soviet abolishes the legal grounds for South Ossetian autonomy.

- December 1990–July 1992: The Georgians would continue to hold their positions around Tskhinvali and the republic at large. The blockade would eventually be joined by both artillery barrages and sniper fire from the surrounding heights, killing many civilians and devastating the urban infrastructure. With no other options, the people of Tskhinvali began burying their loved ones in the yard of City High School #5.

- January 5–6, 1991: Under the cover of night, a detachment of the newly organized Georgian National Guard, flanked by Georgian police forces, invaded Tskhinvali. However, Ossetian paramilitary formations would respond and subsequently push them out of the city. Afterward, Georgian forces would begin to continuously harass Ossetian civilians and their villages, primarily operating out of neighboring Georgian villages.

- March 17, 1991: 99 percent of the YuOSDR voted in favor of keeping the USSR together, as per Gorbachev's all-Soviet referendum. The Georgians would respond to this by cutting off Tskhinvali's electricity and water systems. Additionally, 20,000 people fled to Georgia and North Ossetia following a famine in conjunction with the Georgian stranglehold on the burgeoning republic. Fifty-three Ossetian civilians died, 230 were injured, fifty Ossetian villages were pillaged and burned to the ground, and the whole economic and social structure of South Ossetia had been effectively destroyed.[56]

There was also a *forcible exchange of ethnic populations* with the advent of mass persecutions of Ossetians living in other parts of the country: only 65,000 Ossetians lived in the autonomy, while another 160,000 lived in villages within Georgia proper. The Georgian government seized local food supplies and cut off utilities and transportation methods to all of these villages. Any and all lands leased to Ossetian peasants, some of which were leased less than a year beforehand, were stripped away.[57] As a result, around 60,000 Ossetians were forced from their homes in Georgia and South Ossetia into North Ossetia, while 10,000–20,000 Georgians moved from South Ossetia to inner Georgia. Following this mass migration, ethnic place names assigned by the Ossetian autonomy were forbidden and soon replaced by Georgian ethnonyms.[58]

- May 26, 1991: Zviad Gamsakhurdia is elected the first president of Georgia.
- December 1991: Gamsakhurdia's apparent inability to quell the Ossetian resistance efforts and capture Tskhinvali led to a mutiny within the Georgian Army and his removal from power. These rebels then promoted Eduard Shevardnadze, the chair of the Georgian Soviet and former Soviet minister of foreign affairs—wherein he had a well-kept relationship with the West—as the second president.
- May 20, 1992: The true summit of horror. A bus filled with thirty-nine children and several older Ossetian refugees traveling to North Ossetia along the *Zar Road* bypass was intercepted by armed Georgians, who mercilessly shot every passenger. Suffice it to say, this coldhearted murder shook the country of Ossetia to its very core.[59] Soon after, South Ossetian leader Torez Kulumbegov was kidnapped and arrested.
- May 29, 1992: The Republic of South Ossetia officially declares its independence.
- June 1992: The *internationalization of the conflict*. Seeing the high potential for the outbreak of mass rioting in North Ossetia—located in Russia—following the *Zar shootings*, President Yeltsin decided to intervene in the conflict. Meanwhile, the West preferred to keep their distance from internationalization of the conflict in this understandably delicate situation.
- June 24, 1992: End of the *first hot stage*. A quadrilateral meeting was held at Dagomys in the Russian city of Sochi to work out a settlement to the conflict. In the end, a comprehensive plan for peace was signed by Yeltsin, Shevardnadze, and several representatives from both North and South Ossetia. A joint peacekeeping force made up of four battalions totaling 2,000 men—with an additional 1,000 in reserve—from Russia, Georgia, and both Ossetias was deployed in the vicinity of Tskhinvali. A Mixed Control Commission was put in charge of administrative and decision-making efforts involving the zone of ethnic conflict.

Extreme forms of ethnic cleansing during the *hot stage*: Regarding the *common biological building block—*I (2); regarding use/abuse of *language—*II (1, 2); regarding the *commonly shared history building block—*IV (2, 3); regarding the *nationality building block—*V (1, 2, 4, 5, 6); *state organizations practiced—*VI (1, 2, 3, 5, 6, 7, 8, 9); and *economic measures—*VII (2, 5).

Casualties of the hot stage and outside orientations of either side of the conflict: More than 1,000 Ossetian civilians were killed in this conflict, with an additional 18,000 wounded and 120 still missing. Anywhere from 40,000 to 100,000 people (including those who had been expelled from the inner regions of Georgia) became refugees. Between 10,000 and 20,000 Georgians similarly fled from South Ossetia to Georgian territories. More than 80 percent of the most important installations within the city were completely destroyed. The situation was by no means limited to the city, as ninety-three villages from around the region were raided and burned to the ground. Because of this, the industrial infrastructure of South Ossetia effectively ceased to exist.[60]

In that same vein, Ossetian historians publicly cite the following facts: In 1770, the population of South Ossetia numbered at approximately 35,000. In 1993, after the conclusion of the *hot stage*, it was found that the prewar population of 65,000 had been reduced back to this same eighteenth-century figure. This means that for more than two centuries, the Ossetian population within South Ossetia, supposedly under the aegis of Georgia, saw no increase in their population. For the sake of comparison, North Ossetia, which primarily existed within the Russian Empire/Soviet Union/Russian Federation, saw its Ossetian population grow to 300,000 people from the comparatively measly 50,000 they had when they first united with Russia in 1784.[61]

By the end of this *hot stage* the *irredentist* projects taking place in both parts of Ossetia, as well as in its final *outside orientation on Russia*, firmly held their ground. Simultaneously, the Georgian orientation toward the West and the desire to join NATO as a way to dissuade Russian interference was heavily propagated under Shevardnadze's leadership. Therefore, joining NATO would supposedly helpGeorgia to reassert control over the entire territory of South Ossetia (*Shida Kartli*—Samachablo-Georgian name).

- June 24, 1992–August 8, 2008: *Second smoldering stage*. By this stage, the conflict had transitioned from an *intrastate* to an *interstate* status; ultimately, it would assume a new "form" as the Georgian-Russian conflict over both South Ossetia and Abkhazia, especially after Mikhail Saakashvili's rise to power in Georgia following the 2003 Rose Revolution. As previously stated, Saakashvili did everything in his power to territorially reincorporate South Ossetia (and if at all possible, Abkhazia) back into Georgia through force. These ostentatious efforts were bolstered by the thought that, in the case of possible Russian interference, the West was willing and able to directly confront Russia on their behalf. In 2004, I warned several of my colleagues here in America of the high probability of this issue developing into something much worse. However, many of them skeptically rejected the idea, stating that "he [Saakashvili] is not insane." To this, I told them that they severely underestimated the influence of *ethnic hatred* and the *thought processes of ethnocentric nationalists*, both of which demonstrate the abovementioned deterioration of the *self-preservation instinct* and the capacity for rational decision-making brought about by these scenarios, which, under certain conditions of outside support/encouragement, may gradually degrade into unrestricted aggressiveness and even into paranoid-schizoid repression on the individual and/or group level.

Between the middle of 2004 and August 2008, I counted 124 separate armed "accidents" that took place in the *South Ossetian Security Zone* between Georgian police and armed bands of South Ossetians. This even included the use of artillery stationed in Georgian villages and settlements on the perimeter of Tskhinvali, such as Tamarasheni, Kehvi, and others like them. However, the Ossetian side was not entirely innocent themselves, as they were similarly involved in provoking several skirmishes and shootings in the area. From time to time, groups of people from either side were captured and humiliatingly forced to their knees until they were released thanks to the intervening peacekeeping force. Both Georgian and Ossetian mass media outlets were undisciplined in their handling of social hysteria, essentially fueling the situation by providing mutually exaggerated and one-sided accounts that did little but stoke the fears of either side. These civilian populations, who were already disoriented with fear and paranoia, were effectively bombarded with messages claiming how their ethnic enemies "could attack us again at any moment."

In the meantime, ethnocentric nationalists in South Ossetia continued to reproduce the situation in which history, myth, and group identity were (and always will be) intertwined with the still relatively recent losses of the *Zar Road executions.* A statue of the *Crying Father* was soon erected in the yard-turned-makeshift-burial-ground of Tskhinvali's City High School #5. It is absolutely critical to understand that in the traditional male-dominated mountain society of the Caucasus, which carries strict norms regarding "masculine" behavior, the *sight of a crying man* will invariably *stir up* feelings of entitlement and, according to the Adats, the "sacred right" for merciless revenge—distinctly lacking any concept of forgiveness or empathy for those victims on the other side. That is why this stage, which saw the Russians effectively turn South Ossetia into a protectorate—by distributing supplies and granting Russian passports to the majority of the population—saw these vengeful mountaineers carefully work toward a decisive round of confrontation, while the Georgians, who were receiving material aid from the West, similarly worked toward revenge.

This "process" would continue until 2008, wherein the self-proclaimed Republic of South Ossetia had more or less become a de facto Russian protectorate inside of the otherwise-recognized boundaries of the Georgian state.[62]

The *religious building block* of this conflict would also emerge at this time. Though both Ossetians and Georgians were (and still are) primarily Orthodox Christians, South Ossetian parishes were administratively directed by the Orthodox Patriarchate of Georgia. However, after the brutality of the *first hot stage* and the actions of Georgian Patriarch Elias II—who did not openly condemn the shooting on Zar Road—Ossetians sought to separate themselves from the Georgian Orthodox Church. Ultimately, the Russian Orthodox Church Abroad and the older-style Greek Orthodox Church, then headed by Metropolitan Kiprianus, took the Ossetians under their wings. Kiprianus went so far as to establish a *separate Alanic Diocese of the Republic of South Ossetia.*

Throughout the *smoldering stage*, Charles King, a professor at Georgetown University, demonstrated that "during the eleven years of Shevardnadze's tenure … Georgia became one of the world's largest per capita recipients of American democracy assistance and economic development aid, totaling nearly a billion dollars."[63]

- January 2004–2006: Saakashvili closed the huge market in the South Ossetian/Georgian village of Ergnety, where both groups were engaged in heavy trade (sometimes with contraband or other illegal commodities), thereby cutting of the last "economic bridge" of spontaneous rapprochement.

By 2007, Saakashvili would hold absolute presidential power, and he used it to subdue all manner of public protests within his country. He also began hoping that a "small victorious war would restore his reputation." This unfortunate idea was inspired by the 2005 visit of American President George Bush, who praised Georgia as "an island of freedom" and lavishly promised to provide any help that they could. However, the rather inexperienced diplomatic nature of the Georgians caused them to misinterpret the messages they had received from Washington, DC, and the US president. Altogether, these factors "furthered Saakashvili to make up his [ethnocentric] mind to begin an operation against Tskhinvali in the beginning of August [2008]."[64]

August 8, 2008–August 13, 2008: Second Hot Stage

Overall, the war—known simply as the *"Five Days' War"* due to its brevity—would throw these people back into their medieval past of collecting their "well-deserved" and bloody revenge according to the traditions of the Adats. All parties involved in this *second hot stage* blatantly ignored the norms and conditions of international law, which resulted in irreparable consequences.

In the aftermath of this brief yet devastating conflict, an international team of experts, under the tutelage of the impeccable Swiss diplomat Heidi Tagliavini, established a loose timeline of the events as they transpired:

- August 7–8, 2008: Under the cover of night, Georgian armed forces fired a barrage of "Grad" artillery shells into Tskhinvali and subsequently attacked the Russian peacekeeping forces stationed in the area. This would mark the beginning of this newly revitalized violent conflict.[65] Russia would soon join the fray, quickly moving a pre-prepared force of the 58th Army through the Rocky Tunnel and into South Ossetia. Simultaneously, Abkhazian military units (with Russian support), engaged Georgian forces in the Kodori Valley in Abkhazia. Russian Naval dominance was soon established, as the Black Sea fleet would quickly dispatch the relatively weak Georgian vessels.
- August 12, 2008: Five days later, the war was essentially over. After being repelled from Tskhinvali and attacked from both the south and west (Abkhazia), the Georgian Army was in full retreat, which left the capital of Tbilisi wide open. No serious impediments, including any worthwhile military resistance, stood before the advancing Russian tank columns on their way to the Georgian capital. It was only thanks to an intermediate mission led by French President Nicolas Sarkozy that the entire country of Georgia did not end up fully occupied by the otherwise victorious Russians and their allies. (For information about the United States' position during this crisis, see above).
- August 26, 2008: Russian President Dmitry Medvedev signed an order officially recognizing the independence of both South Ossetia and Abkhazia.

Casualties resulting from the *second hot stage*: Under the cover of the advancing Russian Army, vengeful Ossetians enacted extreme (and total) measures of ethnic cleansing against the Georgian population in its wake. A massive amount of Georgian property and fortune was looted, with their villages subsequently burned to the ground.

The Russian human rights centers *"Memorial"* and *"Demos,"* in conjunction with *Human Rights Watch*, determined that 162 Ossetians (predominantly civilians) died during this stage of the conflict, while 273 were wounded. At the same time, the Georgians lost 224 civilians (sixty of whom were killed during the pogroms in Georgian villages) and around 150 soldiers (Russian military losses were about the same).[66]

August 26, 2008–Present: Second Smoldering/Frozen Stage

Since the "end" of the official demarcation of violence, this conflict has gradually entered the *frozen stage*. Georgia, alongside most of the international community, declared both South Ossetia and Abkhazia as occupied and annexed territories of the Russian Federation. Fittingly, Russia has since organized and fortified military installations within these territories.

Between 2008 and 2018, several incidents have occurred along the de facto border between Georgia and the Republic of South Ossetia. These disputes have centered around the border itself, with the specific issues including the deployment of frontier guards, the building of monitoring stations, and sometimes even the demarcation of the border itself.

While the EU, NATO, OSCE, and US have subsequently voiced their concerns and displeasure with Russia's decision to fully recognize South Ossetian and Abkhazian independence, other countries have themselves decided to recognize the independence of these territories in the intermittent years:

- September 5, 2008: Nicaragua.
- September 10, 2009: Venezuela.
- December 15–16, 2009: The Republic of Nauru (an island country in Micronesia that recognized South Ossetia on December 15 and Abkhazia on December 16).
- May 23, 2011: The Republic of Vanuatu
- May 29, 2018: Syria

South Ossetia and Abkhazia themselves have recognized the independence of one another, as well as that of Transnistria, the Republic of Artsakh (Karabakh), and the Sahrawi Arab Democratic Republic. Conversely, most of the nation-state members of the UN (and many other international organizations) do not have any intention to recognize the independence of either territory.

- **Current Status of the Conflict:** Frozen
- **Type of Conflict:** Initially *separatist/intrastate*. After the *first hot stage*, it transitioned into an *irredentist/interstate* violent ethnic conflict.
- **Principal Building Blocks of the Georgian–South Ossetian violent ethnic conflict (prior to its transformation into the Russian-Georgian War) in ranking of importance:**
  - **Primary Mobilizing Building Blocks**
    - 1.1.6. Nationality
    - 1.1.7. Commonly shared history aggravated by acute chosen traumas
    - 1.1.8. Linguistic
  - **Subsidiary Building Blocks**
    - 1.1.9. Biological
    - 1.1.10. Religious expression

(IV) Georgian-Abkhazian Violent Ethnic Conflict: December 13, 1988–Present

(1) Historical Prerequisites of the Modern Conflict: 1918–1978

1918–1931: Emergence of the Nationality Building Block and Connected Chosen Trauma

FIGURE 8.11   Flag and Coat of Arms of Republic of Georgia

FIGURE 8.12   Flag and Coat of Arms of Abkhazia

- Autumn–Winter 1918: Fighting breaks out between Georgia, Anton Denikin's White Guard, and later on, the Bolsheviks as a result of territorial disputes over the Sochi and Sukhum (Russian: *Abkhaz*; Georgian: *Sukhumi*) Districts. In the end, a new border between Abkhazia and Georgia was established in accordance with the Soviet-Georgian Treaty of 1920, whereas the old boundary between the Sochi and Sukhumi Districts ran southward along the Bzyb' River.[67]
- March 31, 1921: An *independent* Soviet Socialist Republic under the direct control of Moscow and with no links to the Georgian SSR is created in Abkhazia. Later on, and due to political pressure from both Stalin and prominent Georgian Bolshevik Grigory (Sergo) Ordzhonikidze, Abkhazia was compelled to enter a contractual relationship with the Georgian SSR. But despite becoming a Contractual Soviet Socialist Republic, Abkhazia was able to retain a status *equal to that of a fully endorsed union republic.*
- February 19, 1931: Once again under pressure from Stalin, Abkhazia's status within the union was downgraded, and it was formally incorporated into the Georgian SSR as an autonomous republic. This reduction in status, and the loss of power that came with it, served as the first chosen trauma for the Abkhazians during the subsequent ethnic conflict.

1937–1950s: Emergence of the Biological Building Block

Demographic dimensions. At the behest of Stalin, Lavrentiy Beria (who himself was of Mingrelian-Georgian descent) organized the mass resettlement of Georgian peasants to the subtropical areas of Abkhazia to bolster the workforce within the highly lucrative citrus and tea plantations (which would continue well into the 1980s). The long-term result of this movement saw a massive drop in the local Abkhazian population in percentage to the total population of the republic. In fact, by 1989, Abkhazians would make up only 17.8 percent of the total population, whereas the Georgians held an overwhelming majority. The following table (table 8.1) more accurately demonstrates what the Abkhazian intelligentsia called a "demographic catastrophe."

TABLE 8.1 The Dynamics of Ethnic Composition of Abkhazia (1897–1989)[68]

Years	1897		1926		1939		1959		1970		1979		1989	
Thousands and %	106.2	100%	212	100%	311.9	100%	404.7	100%	487	100%	486.1	100%	525.1	100%
Abkhazians	58.7	55.30%	55.9	26.4%	56.2	18%	61.2	15%	77.3	17.1%	83.1	17.10%	93.3	17.80%
Georgians	1.2	1.70%												
Megrelians/ Georgians*	23.8	22.40%	67.5	31.8%	92	29.50%	158.2	39.10%	199.6	41%	213.3	43%	239.9	45.70%
Russians	6	5.70%	20.5	9.60%	60.2	19.20%	86.7	21.40%	92.9	19.4%	79.7	16.40%	74.9	14.30%
Armenians	6.5	6.10%	30	14.2%	49.7	15.90%	64.4	15.90%	74.8	15.2%	73.3	15.10%	76.5	14.60%
Greeks	5.4	5.10%	27.1	12.8%	34.6	11.10%	9	2.20%	13.1	2.40%	13.3	2.80%	14.7	2.30%
Others	3.9	3.70%	11	5.20%	19.2	6.20%	24.1	6%	29.1	5.90%	23.5	4.80%	25.8	4.90%

*After 1926, the Georgian Communist leadership stopped counting Mingrelians/Megrelians as a separate ethnic group and began counting them as Georgians.

This loss of control over their homeland would become another underlying trauma for the Abkhazians (for a more interpersonal perspective of this trauma, see the interviews in my book *Polygon of Satan, Third Edition*, 186–88).

- 1940: Alongside the internal relocation of Abkhazians from their fertile homelands, there was also an outspoken campaign to replace Abkhazian place names with their Georgian equivalents.
- 1930s–1950s: At this time, the official Georgian anthropological theory of "double originality" stated that the original medieval Georgian population living in the territory of *Abkhazeti* (the Georgian name for Abkhazia; known as *Apsny* in Abkhazian) was gradually assimilated by the Abkhazians' ancestors, who had come in from the North. Abkhazians, on the other hand, claimed that they originated from the aboriginal Meotian tribes, which had no connections (and therefore nothing in common) with the Georgians.[69]
- March 13, 1945: Emergence of the *Linguistic Building Block*. All Abkhazian language schools had been closed by this date.
- June 1978: Two new journals written in and centered on the Abkhazian language enter publication. Additionally, the first broadcasts of Abkhazian TV hit the airwaves for the first time. These palliative measures were implemented as a result of the periodic protests of the severely persecuted Abkhazian intelligentsia and in order to mitigate the damages that these protests produced.

December 13, 1988–August 14, 1992: Stirring-Up Stage

- December 13, 1988: *Triggering event*—the creation of the *Abkhazian People's Forum–Aidgylara* (*Unity*), headed by Alexi Gogua, a popular Abkhazian writer.

At the same time, a highly propagandist campaign among the Georgians effectively dehumanized Abkhazians, convincing many that they were, in fact, nothing more than "ungrateful barbarians."[70]

- March 18, 1989: *Aidgylara* assembled 30,000 followers at the historical field Lykhnashara in the village of Lykhny, where in 1866, the first anti-Imperial uprising of the Abkhazian people began. The resolution generated by this assembly (known as the *Lykhny Appeal*) called on Soviet authorities to restore "union republic" status to Abkhazia—the reemergence of the *nationality building block*. The request ultimately did gain some traction, as thousands of Armenians, Russians, Greeks, and even Georgians willingly signed the petition.
- March 25–April 1, 1989: A number of Georgian-centric mass meetings took place in Abkhazia, sporting anti-Soviet, anti-Communist, and anti-Abkhazian slogans. This generated tension within the Georgian population, so much so that on April 9, 1989, they clashed with Soviet troops in the streets of Tbilisi, demanding that the Soviets "abolish [the] Abkhazian republic."
- July 16, 1989: Clashes between the Abkhazians and Georgians take place over "segregation in [the] educational sphere" (specifically due to the establishment of a branch of Tbilisi State University in Sukhumi). By the time the smoke cleared, twelve people were dead and nearly 200 were wounded. Disorder of all kinds subsequently spread across Abkhazia and throughout Western Georgia.
- August 25–28, 1990: On the 25th, the *Declaration on the Sovereignty of Abkhazia* was adopted by the deputies of the *Abkhazian Supreme Soviet* in an act excluding their Georgian peers. In response, the Georgian parliament passed an election law that outright banned the *Aidgylara* movement from participating in politics.
- December 24, 1990: The *Abkhazian Supreme Soviet* elected Vladislav Ardzinba, an Abkhazian professor of philology, as its new head. Ardzinba (whom I personally knew very well as well as his wife Svetlana Dzhergenia who had been my co-student mate), was staunchly adherent to the idea of an Abkhazia with full independence from Georgia. Following this, *a full-on separatist project emerged.*
- Spring 1991: New elections for the Abkhazian Supreme Soviet were held, all of which were based on ethnic quotas.
- January 6, 1992: Ardzinba won the position of chairman of the Supreme Soviet. However, his deputy, Tamaz Nadereishvili, was an embittered Georgian ethnocentric nationalist.
- April 1992: The Georgian population of Abkhazia, led by the newly formed pro-Shevardnadze *Progressive-Democratic Union of Abkhazia*, began forming armed paramilitary units, including *Mkhedrioni*, Jaba Ioseliani's "*Riders*," and other groups. On the Abkhazian side, Ardzinba announced the mobilization of Abkhazian reservists into the *Abkhazian Regiment of Interior Ministry*. In response, the *Confederation of Mountainous Peoples of the Caucasus* promised to rescue their "Abkhazian brothers" if they ended up in over their heads. (For information about the specific groups of mercenaries and other ethnic detachments of the *Confederation* that sided with the

Abkhazians, see the previous section of chapter 6.) Volunteers from the disparate Abkhazian Diasporas in Near East and Arab countries began to arrive in force to support their co-ethnics.

- July 23, 1992: Abkhazian members of the parliament (Supreme Soviet) abrogated the Georgian Soviet constitution of 1978 and restored the 1925 Abkhazian SSR contractual constitution written prior to its incorporation: in fact, this move essentially served as a *declaration of independence*.

Behavioral patterns of ethnocentric nationalism and mild and middle-ground forms of ethnic cleansing during the *stirring-up stage*: please see the previous chart (III), with the additional inclusion of the biological building block—V (5).

August 14, 1992–September 30, 1993: First Hot Stage

- August 14, 1992: *Triggering event*—an armed group of "Zviadists"—rabid supporters of the overthrown Georgian president Zviad Gamsakhurdia—entered the predominantly Georgian-populated Gali District of Abkhazia, hijacked a train carrying a group of high-ranking Georgian officials, and disrupted railway traffic. This gave Tengiz Kitovani—the commander of the Georgian Gossoviet armed forces—the pretext to invade Abkhazia. With the support of several tank columns, he entered Sukhumi and engaged the Abkhazian National Guard.
- August 25, 1992: The relatively new Georgian commander, Ghia Karkarashvili, threatened to exterminate all 97,000 Abkhazians, which was in fact their total population, if they continued to resist.
- August 31–September 27, 1992: *Internationalization of the conflict*: Using his influence, Russian President Boris Yeltsin held preliminary negotiations between the two sides. However, these efforts failed to garner any worthwhile results, and fighting continued.
- October 2, 1992: Abkhazian forces, with support from Confederate troops commanded by Shamil Basayev, successfully recaptured Gagra city.
- October 6, 1992: Abkhazian forces recaptured Gantiadi (Abkhazian: *Tsandryphsh*).
- October 7–8, 1992: The *World Congress of Abkhazo-Abazin People* took place in Lykhny and was attended by delegations from the diasporas in Turkey, the Middle East, Western Europe, and the former Soviet Union in support of the Abkhazian cause.
- December 4–14, 1992: A session of the Supreme Council of the Republic of Abkhazia (RA) restored all previously removed Abkhazian names to settlements within Abkhazia's borders.
- January 18, 1993: Georgian guardsmen shot down a helicopter bringing humanitarian aid to the besieged city of Tkvarcheli (Abkhazian: *Tkuarchal*).
- March 23, 1993: The Abkhazian Supreme Council ratified the *Treaty of Friendship* with the self-proclaimed Transnistrian-Moldovan Republic and the Gagauz Republic.
- June 9, 1993: Abkhazian and Confederate forces surrounded Sukhumi.
- June 13–July 27, 1993: The consultations regarding a peace settlement between the Abkhazians and Georgians were renewed under Russian political oversight.
- September 27, 1993: After a prolonged siege, the Abkhazian forces successfully captured the capital (Sukhumi).
- September 30, 1993: End of the *first hot stage*. Due to the crushing weight of numerous critical military defeats, the Georgian troops essentially collapsed, and the Abkhazians claimed victory.

The ambivalent role of Russia during this conflict (aside from their attempts to negotiate peace): On one hand, Russia officially supported Georgia's territorial claims over Abkhazia. But on the other, Russia supplied weapons and munitions to both the Russian and Confederate forces during the fighting.

Extreme forms of ethnic cleansing during the *first hot stage* (accompanied by a behavioral pattern of unrestricted aggressiveness): Regarding the *common biological building block*—I (2, 5); regarding the use/abuse of *language*—II (1, 2, 5); regarding the *commonly shared history building block*—IV (1, 2, 3); regarding the *nationality building block*—V (1, 2, 3, 4, 5, 6, 7); *state organizations practiced*—VI (1, 2, 3, 5, 6, 7, 8) (see above-cited interviews); and *economic measures*—VII (5).

Casualties resulting from the *first hot stage*: More than 10,000 people were killed through both the fighting and punitive expeditions, while anywhere from 140,000 to 160,000 civilians (predominantly Georgians) were forced to flee their homes; the material damages in this conflict amounted to more than 500 billion rubles.[71]

April 1994–August 8, 2008: First Smoldering Stage

- April 1994: *The Collective Peacekeeping Forces*(specifically the Russian military contingent of these forces) were stationed in Abkhazia.
- 2006: Saakashvili's forces moved into and occupied the Kodori River Valley, ultimately crushing the Emzar Kvitsiani's band of Svanetian rebels (who were supported by the Abkhazians).
- 2006: Georgia attempted to organize an Abkhazian blockade through the *Commonwealth of Independent States (CIS)*. At the same time, several different peace settlement projects began falling apart due to the demands of either side.
- 2007-2008: Russia used its influence in the CIS to break the fledgling Abkhazian blockade, then later granted many residents legal Russian citizenship.
- 2008: Georgia made moves toward total integration with NATO and the EU, hoping that, in the long run, Russia would eventually weaken. When that time came, Georgia would then be able to reclaim its territorial integrity under the forcible cover of the West.[72]
- 2008: Skirmishes on the contact line within the Gali District continued to occur.
- August 8, 2008–August 13, 2008*: Second hot stage*—the transformation of an *intrastate conflict* into an *interstate conflict* (see previous chart [III]).
- August 26, 2008–present: *Second smoldering/frozen stage*—(see previous chart [III]).

The principal and mutually exclusive demands of both sides remained relatively unchanged following the conclusion of the *second hot stage*.

The underlying interests of the parties were far from achieving any actual semblance of compromise. While talking to Abkhazians, I compiled the following list of primary interests that dominated their rhetoric: (1) independence for Abkhazia; (2) the punishment of war criminals and Georgia's signing of official documents regarding the nonuse of force in bilateral relations with Abkhazia; (3) the preservation of their ethnic group; (4) opening the border with Russia; (5) economic and political prosperity; (6) the demilitarization of the Caucasus region; and (7) equal membership in the global community.

Conversely, the Georgians almost unanimously promoted the following list of priorities during *their* interviews: (1) the unconditional return of Georgian refugees to Abkhazeti (Abkhazia); (2) the reinforcement of territorial integrity; (3) the possibility of Abkhazian broadcast autonomy inside of Georgia; (4) the replacement of the Russian peacekeeping contingent by an international force and the extension of their zone of responsibility that includes the whole of Abkhazia; and (5) the enactment of constitutional reform within Georgia, ultimately resulting in it becoming a confederation.

- **Current Status of the Conflict:** A *frozen stalemate* with a strong military presence in Abkhazia, paired with a weak economy that is totally dependent on Russia and recurrent social unrest propagated on the basis of clan loyalty, leading to a struggle for political control and power.
- **Type of Conflict:** *Separatist intrastate*, then transitioned into an *interstate* (and potentially *irredentist*) conflict with the advent of the *second hot stage*.
- **Principal Building Blocks of the Georgian-Abkhazian violent ethnic conflict ranked by overall importance:**

  o Nationality
  o Biological (especially in its demographic dimension)
  o Commonly shared history aggravated by unresolved acute chosen traumas
  o Linguistic

(V) | North Ossetian–Ingushian Violent Ethnic Conflict: January 1988–Present

(1) Historical Prerequisites of the Modern Conflict: 1918–1988

Emergence of Nationality Building Block and Connected Chosen Traumas

- 1918–1921: *The Russian Civil War*—Fighting broke out between the Ossetians, who sided with the Terek Cossacks, and the Ingushians, who sided with the Bolsheviks, with the Cossacks' land on the line. As this progressed, the Bolsheviks exploited existing land disputes between these people to initiate a classic imperial political maneuver: *Divide et impera* ("Divide and conquer").

FIGURE 8.13   Flag and Coat of Arms of North Ossetia–Alania

FIGURE 8.14   Flag and Coat of Arms of Ingushetia

- January 27, 1919: After being signed into law by Yakov Sverdlov, the Directive of the Central Committee of the Russian Communist Party authorized any and all actions aimed at unleashing "merciless terror against all the Cossacks who directly or indirectly participated in the anti-Soviet activity."

Measures included disarmament; the confiscation of bread supplies to Cossack settlements [stanitsas near the Sundzha River, in an area commonly referred to as the *Sundzha Line*]; shooting; [delivering] weapons to the non-Cossacks [primarily the Ingushians and Chechens]; occupation of Cossack stanitsas; measures for a mass resettling of the poor non-Cossacks [Ingushians and Chechens] onto Cossack Lands.[73]

- April–May 1919: The first mass deportation of Terek Cossacks from their four stanistas (located within part of what would later become the Prigorodnyi District of North Ossetia–Alania and the subject of a territorial dispute between Ossetians and Ingushians). Ingushians were then resettled onto these newly "ethnically cleansed" locales (though Ingushian historians claim that, prior to the Cossacks' construction of the first three towns, the land had originally belonged to their ancestors).[74]
- October 1920: The beginning of the second wave of deportation targeting Terek Cossacks. Under the orders of Ordzhonikidze, the Supreme Commissar of the North Caucasus, a total of 9,000 Cossack families living near the *Sundzha Line* (around 45,000 individuals) were deported to the Donbas region and the Arkhangel'sk Gubernia (Archangel Governate).
- April 17, 1921: Mass execution (i.e., outright murder) of deported Cossacks traveling on the road, followed by the mass execution of the remaining population within the stanitsas (totaling 35,000). These attacks were carried out by the Special Task Units (*ChON*) of the Red Army, as well as by armed groups of Ingushians and Chechens.
- April 25, 1922: The Central Executive Committee of the Mountain Republic renamed all former Terek Cossack stanitsas in the Sundhza Line, giving them Chechen or Ingushian names. This would see the emergence of both the *nationality* and *commonly shared history building blocks* aggravated by chosen traumas for the Terek Cossacks.

With the Cossacks removed from the Sundhza Line, the veritable buffer zone between the Ingushians and the Ossetians ceased to exist. This resulted in territorial disputes between the two groups and the subsequent emergence of the *nationality building block* in their own conflict. Additionally, the loss of stability caused a widespread increase in banditry throughout the area.

1943–1944: The Ingushian (and Chechen) Tragedy

Following accusations of "collaborating with the Nazis" during the early stages of WWII, 91,260 Ingushians (and 387,229 Chechens)—almost the entire population of the region—were deported to the Kazakhstani Steppes. The journey was arduous; many died on the road to their new home. This resulted in an *unresolved and acute chosen trauma* for the Ingushians and Chechens alike.[75]

- March 7, 1944: The Supreme Soviet Presidium of the USSR officially abolishes the Chechen-Ingushian ASSR.

Following the dissolution, the Prigorodnyi District was almost entirely granted to North Ossetia, barring its southernmost part (which went to Georgia). Afterward, toponymic repression began once again: Ingushian place names were replaced by Ossetian names (which were the original names of the Cossack stanitsas).[76]

- February 1956: The *Twentieth Congress of the CPSU* openly condemned Stalin's "distortions of Lenin's nationality policy."
- January 9, 1957: The Chechen-Ingushian ASSR was restored and Chechens/Ingushians were allowed to return to their homelands. All territories were returned to their respective natives save for one group: the Chechen-Akins, who had previously populated several districts of Dagestan and most of the now North Ossetian Prigorodnyi District. The reason for this exception was that, in the intermittent time, the area had been populated by approximately 55,000 Ossetians, 26,000 of whom were forcibly transferred from Georgia, 15,000 from other districts of North Ossetia, and 14,000 from Russia proper.[77] North Ossetian authorities then imposed a moratorium on distributing "residence permits" to allow settlement in the Prigorodnyi District. Over a long period of time, however, Ingushians began resettling there by paying bribes to the local bureaucrats.
- 1957–1985: "Accidents" and even full-on riots (including the previously mentioned 1981 Ossetian riot that targeted the resettling Ingushians) took place during this period with ever-increasing frequency. This resulted in mutual violence and even murder between the two groups.

(2) Current Cycle: 1988–Present
1988–October 31, 1992: Stirring-Up Stage

- 1988: The seemingly continuous chain of mutual provocations/violent incidents, together with the spread of ethnocentric nationalism (see examples in chapter 6 regarding behavioral patterns), culminated in the formation of the powerful ethnocentric sociopolitical movement *Niiskho* ("*Justice*") in Ingushetia, headed by the clergy and the *Council of Elders*. Keenly caught in the shift in the political climate in favor of the peoples who had been subjected to mass repressions and deportations, the Ingushian ethnocentric nationalists of *Niiskho*—in unison with the Russian liberal intelligentsia—demanded territorial administrative rehabilitation (i.e., the Ingushian right to *communal* control over their "primordial" ethnic homelands).
- 1988: *Triggering event*—Niiskho organized the *First Congress of the Ingushian People*, which demanded that the Soviet authorities "partition [off] the Chechen-Ingushian Republic and restore the Ingushian Republic to its 1924–1934 boundaries which would include ... [the] Prigorodnyi District."[78] Thus, the *nationality building block* of the Ossetian-Ingushian ethnic conflict would reemerge in force.
- November 1989: *The Soviet Council of Nationalities* repealed the 1982 decree responsible for "restricting the issuance of residents' permits in the [Prigorodnyi] District."[79]
- 1989–1990: Niiskho conducted twelve mass meetings where they accused the North Ossetian authorities of continuously restricting the Ingushians' ethnic rights, including their Islamic faith, by "prohibiting" visitations to the abandoned and otherwise neglected Muslim cemeteries in the Prigorodnyi District and through open persecution of Kunta-Khadji zikrist meetings (see chapter 1 for more about Kunta-Khadji). Thus, the *religious building block* of the conflict emerged.

- 1989–1990: The "*War of Historians*"—Historians in both republics produced a litany of literature using the same archeological, ethnographic, and anthropological sources, but interpreted in different ways. Ultimately, this proved to be a source of ethnic satisfaction (and indignation) of their respective populations, as it depicted the long-running issues over the territorial "originality" and "primordiality" of their ancestors that was then, with the aid of different powers, stripped away from them by their neighbors. For example, some theories regarding the founding of Vladikavkaz—the capital of North Ossetia—state that it came about some "3,000 years ago." This is especially absurd and has no basis in actual history, but this theory, and the others like it, soon became exalted in the minds of their target demographic.[80] Not only did the *biological building block* find a new source of "legitimacy" within these ideas, but it also contributed heavily to the *commonly shared history building block* of the conflict at large.

- March 13–15, 1990: Mass meetings in Nazran—the capital of Ingushetia—resulted in an echoing call to arms and an insistence toward the return of the Prigorodnyi District. Additionally, those present at those gatherings accused Ossetian authorities of restricting the linguistic rights of the Ingushians in all areas of the educational sphere (i.e., schools) within the Prigorodnyi District. From this, an Ingushian version of the *linguistic building block* emerged. Both groups then continued to adhere to the aforementioned anthropological and linguistic arguments that the aboriginal populations of this area—the Sarmato-Alans—were their ancestors and only their ancestors.

- 1990–1991: The collective behavioral patterns of both groups became characterized by the concepts of group mentality, self-assertive and integrative tendencies, mass behavior, conformity, and mutually displayed ethnic prejudices. Furthermore, and by the end of the *stirring-up stage*, these sides assumed the more vividly ethnocentric features of authoritarianism and brotherhood within/warlikeness without behavioral patterns (for example, see the above-cited pull among students of either side).

- March 24, 1990: The previously mentioned *Rebirth movement*, composed of the remnants of the Terek Cossacks and encouraged by Ossetian leader Akhsarbek Galazov, added more momentum to the issue and subsequently infuriated the Ingushians. This fury was driven by the idea that, with the help of the Ossetians, the Terek Cossacks might be able to reclaim their rights over the lands of the Prigorodnyi District, which had been confiscated from them during the 1918–1921 Genocide at the hands of the Bolsheviks.

- April 17, 1991: During the anniversary of the tragedies of 1921, Aleksandr Podkolzin, Cossack leader of the Sundzha District of Ingushetia, was assassinated by an Ingushian terrorist cell. Following his death, attacks on Russian and Ossetian commoners alike increased dramatically within the Prigorodnyi District.[81]

- April 26, 1991: Russian exacerbating factor. Russian legislation (namely the Supreme Soviet) passed a law *On the Rehabilitation of the Repressed People*. Article 6 of this new law, which would directly contradict the Constitution of the Russian Federation, granted such peoples the right to "restore the national-territorial boundaries, existing before their unconstitutional and forcible change."[82] In addition, Boris Yeltsin, during a visit to North Ossetia, assured the peoples of the republic that Moscow would assist it in maintaining its territorial integrity. The very next day, during a similar visit to Nazran, he contradicted himself by promising to create a separate republic for the Ingushians within the accords of their wishes and the spirit of this law. Alongside the Prigorodnyi District, the

Ingushians demanded the right bank of Vladikavkaz, which temporarily housed their administrative headquarters in the 1920s–1930s (as they lacked an appropriate building in Nazran proper). One may see the promotion of these lofty promises as an irresponsible move. But during this whole debacle, I understood that Yeltsin wanted to territorially separate Ingushetia from Chechnya, which, under the leadership of Dudayev, was about to declare its own independence. Therefore, he promised the Ingushians everything that they wanted in order to keep their republic a part of Russia. This ploy ultimately succeeded, but it also contributed to further regressive development of the Ossetian-Ingushian ethnic conflict.

- September–October 1991: Following Yeltsin's departure, a spontaneous and rapid militarization of the region took place. Galazov ordered the creation of an informal force of armed North Ossetians (which was an unconstitutional decision). At the same time, Dudayev began to build his own Chechen military, and by October 1991, the Ingushians had also formed their very own *National Guard of Ingushetia*, composed of 15,000 well-armed men and even an equestrian regiment.[83]
- September 15, 1991: The *Congress of the People's Deputies of Ingushetia* adopted a declaration regarding the creation of an official *Ingushian Republic*, which incorporated both the Prigorodnyi District and the right bank of the city of Vladikavkaz (which would serve as their new capital).
- October 1992: Violent clashes between official and informal armed groups from both republics became more and more frequent.

October 31–November 5, 1992: Hot Stage

- October 31, 1992: *Triggering event*—at 7:30 a.m., armed groups from Nazran and other local Ingushian settlements attacked a police station in an Ossetian border village, Chermen. After the police were dealt with, the pogroms of the Ossetian residents began. Full-scale armed clashes between both sides saw armed groups of Terek Cossacks siding with the Ossetians.
- November 2–5, 1992: Russian troops began arriving in the area to try and stop the fighting. But during the chaos, armed groups of Ossetians would purge most of the Ingushian population from the Prigorodnyi District and Vladikavkaz, burning down homes and chasing down civilians.

Casualties from the *hot stage*: Aside from the dead and wounded, a staggering 50,000 Ingushians were forced to flee from their homes in Vladikavkaz and the Prigorodnyi District (though some Ingushian authors put it closer to 60,000). Additionally, more than 3,500 homes were burned to the ground.[84]

November 5, 1992–Present: Smoldering/Frozen Stage

More than 40,000 Ingushians would gradually return to North Ossetia–Alania and to the Prigorodnyi District. Occasional incidents along the border still occur, albeit rarely. After 2009, the conflict fully entered its Frozen Stage with the Russian pacification of Chechnya and a progressive crackdown on underground armed groups and the adherents of *Emirate Kavkaz* and *ISIS/ISL*

- **Mild, middle-ground, and extreme forms of ethnic cleansing during the conflict:**

Mild and middle-ground forms of ethnic cleansing during the conflict: Regarding the *biological building block*—I (1, 4, 5); regarding the *use/abuse of language*—II (1, 2); regarding *religious expression*—III (1, 4); regarding the *commonly shared history building block*—IV (2, 3);

Extreme forms of ethnic cleansing during the conflict: Regarding the *biological building block*—I (2); regarding the *use/abuse of language*—II (2, 3); regarding *religious expression*—III (3); regarding the *commonly shared history building block*—IV (1, 2, 4, 5, 6); regarding the *nationality building block*— V (1, 2, 3, 5, 6, 7); *state organizations practiced*—VI (1, 2, 3, 4, 7, 9); and *economic measures*—VII (1, 4).[85]

- **Type of Conflict:** Irredentist
- **Principal building blocks of the North Ossetian–Ingushian violent ethnic conflict in terms of importance:**
    - **Primary Building Blocks**
        1.1.11. Nationality
        1.1.12. Commonly shared history aggravated by unresolved acute chosen traumas
    - **Subsidiary Building Blocks**
        1.1.13. Religious expression
        1.1.14. Linguistic

(VI) Russian-Chechen Violent Ethnic Conflict: 1991–2008

(1) Historical Prerequisite of the Modern Conflict: 1859–June 1991

The Chechens (along with some of the ethnic groups native to Dagestan) showed a great deal of stiff/ intermittent resistance to the Russian Imperial conquest between the late eighteenth century and late nineteenth century. In reviewing a collection of Russian and Chechen primary sources, as well as both domestic and foreign literature, I noted that the Chechens (sometimes partnered with the Ingushians)

FIGURE 8.15   Flag and Coat of Arms of Russia

FIGURE 8.16   Flag and Coat of Arms of Chechnya

initiated at least twelve uprisings or riots against Russian dominion from the end of the Caucasian War in 1859 well into the 1980s: (1) 1859–1865 saw a mass uprising as a result of the loss of the lowlands in Northern Chechnya; (2) 1877–1878 saw a series of uprisings and raids on Russian settlements propagated by land disputes; (3) 1905 brought about not only a mass uprising but periodic raids and robberies of Cossack-Russian settlements, private estates, and cities (notably Grozny, Vladikavkaz, and Kizlyar); (4) 1913 brought with it uprisings and raids on Russian settlements; (5) the violence of 1918–1921 resulted in the massacre of Cossacks living in the stanitsas on the *Sunzha Line*; (6) 1922–1924 saw the spread of "banditry" (Russian term)—encompassing raids on Russian colonial properties and the assassinations of Russian officials; (7) similarly, 1925 was rampant with predatory/retaliatory raids on Russian settlements and the assassination of important Russian officials; (8) 1928 had several uprisings; (9) prior to the start of WWII, massive uprisings against Soviet collectivization ranged from 1930 to 1936, resulting in the persecution of the Chechen intelligentsia and wealthy farmers by the Soviets (otherwise known as the "dispossession of the kulaks")—which was roughly 15 percent of the population; (10) anti-Soviet uprisings from 1940–1941 resulted in waves of exterminatory campaigns by the Soviet secret police—the *NKVD*; (11) 1944 saw the formation of an underlying chosen trauma, with the deportation of the entire Chechen population to Kazakhstan; (12) and finally, the 1970s–1980s mainly consisted of attacks against the Russians, with a particular focus on officials within the Chechen-Ingushian ASSR.[86]

- 1960–1980s: Nikita Khrushchev's policies closed all native-language schools within the autonomous republics and districts within the Russian Federation, including all of the Chechen schools in Chechnya.[87]
- 1970s–1980s: Another collection of documentary material indicates that, during the enforcement of Soviet state atheism, Chechen religious traditions (as well as those of other peoples) suffered under the strain. For instance, the *Naqshbandi*, a major mystical and spiritual order of Sufism based on a clans' *teips'* organization, had faced severe restrictions and persecution within the USSR since 1927. It is important to keep in mind that, from the eighteenth century onward, open resistance by the mountaineers (the Chechens in particular) had been carried out under the ideological banner of *gazavat* (the war against the infidels). It is therefore worth noting how during the recent cycle of ethnic conflict with Russia, Mufti Akhmad-Khaji Kadyrov (backed by Dzhokhar Dudayev, head of the breakaway Republic of Ichkeria), revived this ideology and called upon all Chechens to engage in a holy war against Russia: albeit this time in the form of a total jihad.

Thus, these and other previously cited examples mark the origin of the highly complicated relationship between Russia and Chechnya that has persisted for more than 300 years. For those three centuries, the ethnic building blocks have been periodically radicalized and, especially during the last cycle of ethnic violence, would emerge again through discrepancies over its principal building blocks: namely the *nationality, commonly shared history* (aggravated by unresolved acute *chosen traumas*), and *religious building blocks*, with the *linguistic building block* playing a subsidiary mobilizing role.[88]

June 1991–December 1994: Stirring-Up Stage

- June 1991: *Triggering event*—ethnocentric nationalists Zelimkhan Yandarbiev, Movlady Udugov, and Said-Khan Abumuslimov organized the so-called "second stage" of the *Congress of the*

Chechen People. Soon after, Dudayev would join the organization in a leadership role. Together, they founded the *Vainakh Democrats*, a highly ethnocentric political party. They then assumed the political direction that they deemed necessary to attain the "true liberation of the Chechen people" and that "it was necessary to stay away from the Russian Federation and the USSR." They likewise called upon their compatriots to mobilize all available resources to initiate an *armed rebellion* in order to "throw off the Russian colonial yoke once and for all."[89]

- 1991–1992: The ambivalent, inconsistent, and provocatively exacerbating policies of the Russian government exacerbated tensions throughout the region (see timelines and examples cited in chapters 5 and 6).
- October 27, 1991: Dudayev was elected president of the Chechen Republic.
- October 1991: Yeltsin's announcement of the *Introduction of Martial Law in Chechnya*i nfuriated the Chechen masses, leading to their consolidation around Dudayev and his ethnocentric nationalists. This in turn triggered the enacting of middle-ground forms of ethnic cleansing containing trace elements of the more extreme forms against the local Russian-speaking population. According to Chechen journalist Arbi Arbiev, more than 300,000 Russian residents lived in Chechnya (and Ingushetia) prior to 1991; but afterward, only half of the population remained in the area (see cited examples in chapter 6).[90]

Beginning in 1991, the behavioral patterns of ethnocentric nationalism were primarily centered on mass behavior, conformity, authoritarianism, and brotherhood within/warlikeness without, with rapid subsequent regression into uncritical obedience to charismatic leadership and unrestricted aggressiveness. Additionally, widespread lawlessness and mafia-style banditry began overlapping many of the socio-cultural spheres of the Republic (see examples in chapter 5).

- 1992: A total of 60,000 Russians (including many highly qualified specialists and trained professionals) fled this persecution, resulting in the deterioration of educational quality and industrial output within the fledgling republic. This outmigration of the highly skilled workforce marked the beginning of the demodernization process in Chechnya.[91]
- 1993: At this time, more than 150 armed bands were operating within the republic completely independent from any local or national authority.
- June 4, 1993: Dudayev initiated his coup. Chechen forces killed many members of the prodemocracy opposition and stormed their stronghold—the municipal council building—effectively establishing a dictatorship.
- October 1993: Yeltsin's forces subjugated nearly all parliamentary opposition in Moscow.
- December 1993: The Moscow-based "Party of War" pushed Yeltsin into making a fatal decision, resulting in his call for a direct assault against Chechnya.

December 24/25, 1994–August 30, 1996: First Hot Stage

- December 24–25, 1994: A direct Russian invasion of the Chechen Republic of Ichkeria took place throughout the 24th and well into the night of the 25th.
- December 1994–1996: Any and all military action at this time was usually accompanied by the immense suffering of the local civilian population, be they Russian or Chechen. Russian bombing

runs targeted the city of Grozny, resulting in an almost indiscriminate loss of life and the destruction of the urban infrastructure. Afterward, intense close-quarters fighting raged through the streets of the city. Several extreme forms of ethnic cleansing were levied against the remaining Russian-speaking population. Artillery barrages and missile strikes plagued otherwise inconspicuous settlements around the city. Additionally, this conflict was marked by the several unsuccessful Russian attempts to take Grozny, which is notable, given the massive damage the city had sustained. This tenacity was one of the catalysts that transformed this conflict from an ethnic resistance against Russia into part of a regional jihad, thereby strengthening the *internationalization of the conflict* through the terrorist dimension of the global jihadist movement (for more context on the driving forces and opposing sides of this conflict, see examples in chapters 5 and 6, respectively).

- May 1995: Shamil Basayev, the man responsible for effectively organizing the defense of Grozny, lost eleven members of his immediate family, including his wife and two children, in a Russian bombing raid.

Apparently in retaliation for their deaths, Basayev and a group of around 130 fighters under his command drove north into the Russian heartland in order to stage a major act of reprisal. After being stopped by traffic police in Budyonnovsk, Stavropol Krai, Russia, they seized control of a local hospital and held some 1,000 people as hostages. After two unsuccessful attempts by Russian forces to enter the building and rescue the hostages, Basayev negotiated their release with then Russian Prime Minister Victor Chernomyrdin on live TV, with the condition that he and his men would be allowed to safely return to Chechnya. This daring act, combined with the tale of his suffering, effectively made Basayev a hero in the eyes of many Chechens.

- August 1996: Basayev played a key role in the recapture of Grozny, which resulted in the tentatively named *Khasav-yurt Accord*, which officially ended the *first hot stage* of the conflict.[92]
- August 22, 1996: The creation and signing of the *Khasav-yurt Accord* followed a formal cease-fire agreement (which was itself signed that same day by General Aleksandr Lebed' and General Aslan Maskhadov in Novye Atagi). This document covered aspects regarding the demilitarization of Grozny, the creation of a joint headquarters to mitigate looting in the aftermath of the violence, and the withdrawal of all Russian forces from Chechnya by December 31, 1996. Thus, the *first hot stage* technically ends in a Chechen victory, and sees the Chechen Republic of Ichkeria become de facto independent.

August 22, 1996–August 1999: First Smoldering Stage

- January 1997: Aslan Maskhadov was elected president of the Chechen Republic of Ichkeria.

Overall, *lawlessness* became the most obvious characteristic displayed by Chechnya and other adjacent areas in the North Caucasus. The spread of Islamism/Wahhabism, the creation of *mujahedeen* training camps (as explained earlier in chapter 6), and the founding of underground jamaats (communities of Islamists) who trained in them came to influence the entire North Caucasus, turning Chechnya into a maternal ark of jihadism. Additionally, and despite the presence of the *Khasav-yurt Accord*, thousands of Russians and foreign nationals remained within the country as hostages to these groups. According to Magomet Tolboyev, then head of the Dagestan Security Council:

> Islamic fundamentalists strengthened themselves in the area; they received ... skills and experiences of carrying out military operations. ... People are sick and tired of them: [the] raids of brigands, kidnapping, stealing of cattle, murder and assassination ... I warned [the] Interior and Foreign Ministries of Russia many times [not to] let people come to the North Caucasus regions [of] Kabarda, Dagestan, and Ossetia. I know how [kidnapped] people live there ... they sit like slaves in dungeons ... If you want to be kidnapped, go to Chechnya, Dagestan, Kabardino-Balkaria, and Ossetia. Maybe you will be ransomed afterwards, maybe you will not. If not, [then] you will be killed ... [The officials in Moscow] do not understand what the Caucasus looks like.[93]

- 1996–1999: Prior to the dawn of the new millennium, the recently revitalized illusion of Russia being a great power, instigated by their recent defeat, humiliation (which is, in fact, one of their chosen traumas), and nationalistic (specifically anti-Chechen) hysteria, threatened Russian affairs well beyond the Caucasus.[94]
- Mid-November 1996: Yeltsin and Maskhadov sign an agreement that dictates the economic relations between Russia and Ichkeria, as well as the payment of compensation to those Chechens who had been affected by the 1994–1996 *hot stage*. However, the previously discussed schemes of the Chechen mafia ultimately took advantage of this agreement, all but wrecking any further constructive rapprochements. Similarly, the local *OSCE mission* would make great efforts to promote a more solidified peace agreement, only to be undermined by radicals pursuing their own agendas.
- Summer 1999: Basayev aligns himself with radical Islamists headed by Osama bin-Laden's aforementioned envoy, Emir al-Khattab, who sought to establish an *independent Islamic state* in the North Caucasus (*Emirate Kavkaz/Caucasian Emirate*).

August 1999–March 2008: Second Hot Stage

- Early August 1999: Working with Field Commander al-Khattab, Basayev launched the "ill-fated incursion into neighboring Dagestan that impelled the Russian leadership to embark on a new war."[95]
- 2000–2008: All five building blocks *were* activated under societal tension. The prolonged use of more extreme forms of ethnic cleansing—which rested on the brink of genocide—saw a heavy loss of Chechen life and the near-total disappearance of the Russian population (for examples, see chapter 6). The radicalization of the religious building block fully transitioned this once separatist/secessionist intrastate ethnic struggle into a regional aspect of the global jihadist movement perpetrated by radical Islamists. This transition also shortened and spread the terrorist dimension of the latter's struggle in the region. By this point the so-called "balance of terror" between both sides was built on "filtration camps," illegal prisons, the deployment of "death squads" by the Russians, and terrorist attacks of Islamists on civilian populations and infrastructure—in this

case, the *Riyad-us as-Saliheen Battalion* under the command of Shamil Basayev was the veritable vanguard of terror.

List of Major Terrorist Attacks against Russia during the Second Hot Stage and Afterward, 1996–2013.

- November 1996:In Pyatigorsk, Stavropol Krai, the bombing of an apartment building housing Russian border guards; sixty-eight people were killed.
- March 19, 1998:In Vladikavkaz, North Ossetia, a bomb went off in a busy market place; eighty-two people died, 160 were wounded.
- August 1999: In Vladikavkaz, North Ossetia, three separate explosions went off in an apartment complex located in the "Sputnik" suburb; twenty-seven civilians were killed, eighty-one wounded.
- May 9, 2002: In Kaspiysk, Dagestan, an explosion during the Victory Day military parade killed thirty-two—including twelve children—and injured 130 others.
- October 23, 2002: In Moscow, the infamous Moscow theatre hostage crisis. Terrorists took 850 hostages within a theatre; thirty-three terrorists and 200 hostages died as a result of the rescue operation.
- 2003: In Mineral Waters, Stavropol Krai, the bombing of electric trains killed over 100 civilians.
- January 24, 2004: In Moscow, a powerful bomb was set off by a suicide attacker inside Domodedovo International Airport; thirty-seven lay dead and 173 more were wounded.
- August 24, 2004: In Moscow, twin female suicide attacks occurred on flights from Moscow Domodedovo International Airport; all ninety passengers on the flights were killed.
- September 1–3, 2004: In Beslan, North Ossetia, the infamous Beslan High School 1 siege. Of the 1,254 hostages taken during this incident, 341 died (according to the figures released so far), including 181 children, first graders, and infants. Another 700 people were injured.
- October 13, 2005: Islamist militants launched attacks in the city of Nalchik, Kabardino-Balkaria Republic. More than 100 people were killed.
- November 27, 2009: The high-speed rail link from Moscow to St. Petersburg was hit by a suicide bombing, killing twenty-eight and injuring 130.
- December 29–30, 2013: In Volgograd city, two suicide bombings a day apart targeted the public transport system. A total of thirty-four people were killed weeks before the start of the 2014 Winter Olympics being held about 400 miles away in the Russian Black Sea resort of Sochi.

Editorial remark: Aside from other observations, this list is a bright demonstration of my thesis in chapter 2 of the theoretical generalization that each of such violent ethnic conflicts has a dangerous potential of transformation from the local ethnic conflict to a national and even international problem.

The *"Chechenization of the Conflict"*—the last transformative phase is mainly characterized by a set of two contradictive developments. The first is known as *"Chechenization"* and refers to the policy of the Russian Federation, specifically under the leadership of Putin, to organize elections in Chechnya in which pro-Russian leaders are inevitably elected. After their positions are secured, these leaders, as well as their Chechen supporters, assume the responsibility of battling the Islamists. The second development can be described as the *"Palestinization"* of the conflict, which sees efforts put into turning the North Caucasus into a homeland or Caliphate exclusively for Muslim habitation.[96] Despite each opposing the rhetoric of the other, both developments are closely linked to the same drastic changes—particularly of the demographic variety—within the social structures, ethnic composition, and confessional characteristics of Chechen society as a result of fighting two devastating wars and harboring the growing influence of radical Islam. Ultimately, Putin prevailed, thanks to the majority of the Chechen people and clergy—the latter of which was headed by Akhmad-Khaji Kadyrov (who had at one point proclaimed a jihad against Russia)—who were afraid that their traditional Chechen Sufi Islam would be erased by the puritanical radical Islamists. Now allies, the Russians and the Chechen majority both fight against the followers of radical foreign trends, especially those who adhere to the "pure" Arabic version of Islam.

Casualties of the conflict in totality: According to the 1989 Union census, there was an estimated 1,270,429 people living in the Chechen-Ingushian Autonomous Soviet Socialist Republic (ASSR). This number encompassed (from greatest to least) 734,501 Chechens, 293,771 Russians, 163,762 Ingushians, 14,842 Armenians, 14,824 Tatars, 12,537 Nogias, and 4,085 Jews.[97] Before the *first hot stage* from 1995 to 1996, approximately 397,000 people resided in Grozny, with around 210,000 of them being Russian and/or Russian-speaking.[98] According to several different sources, more than 200,000 of those Russian/Russian-speaking people left the republic from 1989 to 2002 as a result of military action, several different forms of ethnic cleansing, attacks by Islamist militants, total economic collapse, and a wide array of miscellaneous criminal violence. By 2002, only 40,645 Russians remained in the whole of Chechnya, while 5,559 stayed in Ingushetia. At the same time, more than 125,000 Chechens, who either feared the growing influence of radical Islam or suffered cruelties under the pretense of Russian "counterterrorist" operations, had also left their republic.

In 2004, Tauz Dzhabrailov, then chairman of the State Council of Chechnya, told journalists that since the beginning of the *first hot stage* of the Russian-Chechen War in 1994, the "number of victims of the conflict has exceeded 200,000 people." The Russian military alone suffered 25,000 casualties—both killed and wounded. According to different experts, out of those who remained in the republic, approximately 5–10 percent of the Chechen and Ingushian population currently continue to sympathize with and support the radical Islamists. Countless children were orphaned, and at least 20,000 people now struggle with lasting psychological disorders as a result of the conflict. In the mid-2000s, "every month as many as 50 Chechen civilians died for various reasons and every year in Chechnya two to three thousand people are killed, kidnapped, or disappear without a trace."[99]

- March 2008: President Putin declares that the conflict in Chechnya effectively over.[100] The previously mentioned reforms and asymmetric consociational institutionalized federalism (see chapter 6) helped to establish a relatively peaceful restitution for the violent ethnic conflict in Chechnya.

Mild and middle-ground forms of ethnic cleansing during the conflict: Regarding *language*—II (2); regarding the *commonly shared history building block* (aggravated by acute chosen traumas)—IV (1, 2, 5); *state organizations practiced*—V (1, 3); and *economic measures*—VI (1, 4).

Extreme forms of *ethnic cleansing during the conflict:* Regarding the *biological building block*—I (1); regarding *language* (practiced by the Russian state during the 1906s–1980s)—II (2, 3); regarding *religious expression*—III (2, 4, 6); regarding the *commonly shared history building block*—IV (2, 3); regarding the *nationality building block*—V (1); *state organizations* (intensively) *practiced*—VI (1, 2, 4, 5, 6, 7, 10); and *economic measures*—VII (5).

- **Current Status of the Conflict:** *Resolved.* Russia spent approximately $52 billion in order to reconstruct the destroyed sections of Chechnya.
- **Type of Conflict:** *Separatist/secessionist* and *intrastate*.
- **Principal Building Blocks of the Russian-Chechen violent ethnic conflict ranked in terms of overall importance:**
  - **Primary Building Blocks:**
    - 1.1.15. Nationality
    - 1.1.16. Commonly shared history aggravated by acute chosen traumas
    - 1.1.17. Religious expression
  - **Subsidiary Building Blocks:**
    - 1.1.18. Linguistic

Notes

1   David Marshall Lang, *The Armenians*, Report no. 32 (London: The Minority Rights Group, 1987), 6.

2   Lang, *The Armenians*, 6; the nationalist fervor of the Armenians at that period of time was further instigated by the fact that, during these same massacres, Azerbaijanis began their rapprochement with Turkey. See Thomas de Waal, *Black Garden: Armenia and Azerbaijan Through Peace and War* (New York: New York University Press, 2003), 127.

3   Ed. Ziya Buniatov, *Istoria Azerbaijana*, Vol. I (Baku, Azerbaijan: Academy of Sciences of Azerbaijan SSR, 1958), 334–36.

4   Lang, *The Armenians*, 6.

5   Nikolai N. Shavrov, *Novaya ugroza russkomu delu v Zakavkaz'e: Predstoyashchaya rasprodazha Mugani inorodtsam* (St. Petersburg: Sytin, 1911), 59–60; see also *Kavkazskii Kalendar'* (*The Caucasian Calendar*), part V (Tiflis, n.p. 1896), 48–61. Regarding the resettlement policy of the Russian Empire and the resulting waves of migration in and around the South Caucasus, see Anatoly Isaenko, *Polygon of Satan*: *Ethnic Traumas and Conflicts in the Caucasus*, 3rd ed.(Dubuque, IA: Kendall Hunt Publishing House, 2014), 287–89.

6   Farid Shafiyev, *Resettling the Borderlands: State Relocations and Ethnic Conflict in the South Caucasus* (Montreal: McGill-Queen's University Press, 2018), 332; in 1911, Shavrov put the number of Armenians in Transcaucasia at approximately 1,300,000. Of that population, more 1,000,000 were settled there by the Russian government.

7   Lang, *The Armenians*, 6.

8   Lang, *The Armenians*, 7. During the trial, the defense advocates included Alexander Kerensky—the would-be head of the Russian Provisional Government in 1917—and Pavel Milyukov—a would-be minister in this government.

9   Willem van Schendel and Eric Jan Zürcher, *Identity Politics in Central Asia and the Muslim World* (London: I.B. Tauris, 2001); Michael G. Smith, "Anatomy of a Rumor: Murder, Scandal, the Musavat Party and Narratives of the Russian Revolution in Baku, 1917–1920," *Journal of Contemporary History* 36, no. 2 (April 2001): 216–18.

10   Sergei A. Zenkovsky, *Pan-Turkism and Islam in Russia*, 1st ed. (Cambridge, MA: Harvard University Press, 1960), 37.

11   Cited in "Sotsopros: Otvetstvennost' za genotsid armyan nesut," *Transcaucasian Chief-Editorial of Information Agency Regnum*, April 26, 2005, 1–2, emphasis added.

12   Lang, *The Armenians*, 4–5; Isaenko, *Polygon of Satan*, 42, 287–89.

13   Isaenko, *Polygon of Satan*, 290.

14   Dmitri Trenin, "Russia's Security Interests and Policies in the Caucasus Region," in *Contested Borders in the Caucasus*, ed. Bruno Coppieters (Brussels: VUBPRESS-VUB University Press, 1996), 93.

15   Lang, *The Armenians*, 8; I collected all of these facts from primary sources and cited them in Isaenko, *Polygon of Satan*, 76–77, 292–95.

16   Arthur Tsutsiev, *Atlas etnopoliticheskoi istorii Kavkaza (1774–2004)* (Moscow: Europa, 2006), 56.

17   Alexi Zverev, "Ethnic Conflicts in the Caucasus: 1988–1994," in *Contested Borders in the Caucasus*, ed. Bruno Coppieters (Brussels: VUBPRESS-VUB University Press, 1996), 14. Radical nationalists from both the Musavat and Dashnak-Tsutiun parties entered international exile with the establishment of Soviet power in both countries. For the Armenian diasporas in particular, this was the third wave of outmigration that they had to face. Especially strong Armenian diasporas had been previously formed in Russia, the United States, France, Argentina, Lebanon, Syria, Iran, Canada, Ukraine, Turkey, Greece, and Australia. The total population worldwide is estimated at eleven million. Of these, only around three million live in Armenia, with 130,000 in Nagorno-Karabakh and 120,000 in Javakheti (in adjacent Georgia).

18   Zori Balayan, *Ochag* (Yerevan, Armenia: Sovetakhan Grokh, 1984), 21; Additional information can be gathered from another of his books, Zori Balayan, *Between Hell and Heaven: The Struggle for Karabakh* (Yerevan, Armenia: Amaras, 1977).

19   Cited in Tsutsiev, *Atlas*, 110–11.

20   Balayan, *Ochag*, 3.

21   A. Lalaiyan, "Kontrrevolyutsionnyi 'Dashnaktsutiun' i imperialisticheskaya voina 1914–1918gg.," *Revolutsionnyi Vostok*, no. 2–3 (Moscow: Gosizdat, 1936), 76.

22   De Waal, *Black Garden*, 143.

23   For an example, see Shahen Mkrtchyan, *Istoriko-arkhitekturnye pamyatniki Nagornogo Karabakha* (Yerevan, Armenia: Aiastan, 1988).

24   Ziya Buniatov was a soldier in the Red Army during WWII. In his service, he crossed the entirety of Europe during, and ended the war participating in the taking of Berlin. For his military deeds, he was honored with the highest award in the USSR—the highly distinguished title "Hero of the Soviet Union." This recognition helped him to build a successful postwar career in Soviet Azerbaijan. Thus, and because of his great authority alone, his ethnocentric anti-Armenian activity became especially contagious. In February 1997, both his career and life came to an end as he was mysterious assassinated in the doorway of his home. See de Waal, *Black Garden*, 143, 150–51.

25   De Waal, *Black Garden*, 141.

26   Cited in Yuryi Pompeev, "Krovavyi omut Karabakha," *Zhurnal Samizdat* (2010), http://zhurnal.lib.ru/a/armen/pompeev.shtml, 82.

27   De Waal, *Black Garden*, 141.

28   De Waal, *Black Garden*, 141.

29   De Waal, *Black Garden*, 141.

30   Ziya Buniatov, *Azerbaijan v VII-X vv.* (Baku, Azerbaijan: Elm, 1963); de Waal, *Black Garden*, 152. For details on the mutually exclusive agreements of both the Azerbaijanis and Armenians during the War of Pamphlets, see Isaenko, *Polygon of Satan*, 300–305.

31   De Waal, *Black Garden*, 143, 150–51.

32   See Mahmud Ismail, "Fal'sificatory," *Bakinskii rabochii*, January 5, 1991, 3.

33   G. Glushkov, "Defitsit glasnosti il idefitsit ob'ektivnosti?" *Bakinskii rabochii*, August 9, 1989, 4.

34   De Waal, *Black Garden*, 39; 36.

35   Isaenko, *Polygon of Satan*, 325.

36   For examples of the different forms of ethnic cleansing, see Isaenko, *Polygon of Satan*, chapter 7.

37   The death toll of this incident fluctuates between 213 and 477 persons depending on the source. See de Waal, *Black Garden*, 212–13, note 25; Yevgenii Krishtalev, "Spravedlivost' dlya Khojaly," *Nezavisimaya gazeta*, February 26, 2010, http://www.ng.ru/printed/237387.

38   I constructed the chronology of the *hot stage* based on a collection of different sources from both the Azerbaijani and Armenian perspective. See Isaenko, *Polygon of Satan*, 333–43.

39   Isaenko, *Polygon of Satan*, 343.

40   See "Europe, Narorny Karabakh: Risking of War,"*The Report of International Crisis Group*, no. 187 (November 14, 2007); no. 55 (October 7, 2009); no. 60 (February 8, 2011), http://www.kavkaz-uzel. ru/articles/183747, 3.

41   *The Report of International Crisis Group*, no. 60, 7. On the most updated Western vision of the security in the South Caucasus and in particular in the zone of Armenian-Azerbaijani conflict, see Turgut Kerem Tuncel, "Security and Stability Concerns in the South Caucasus," in *Proceedings of the Symposium Organized by AVIM on 12 June 2015 under the Sponsorship of NATO's Public Diplomacy Division*, Conference Book No. 17, ed. Hazel Cagan and Turgut Kerem Tancel (Ankara, Turkey: AVIM Center of Eurasian Studies, 2015).

42   "Na granitse s Nakhijevanom VS Armenii unichtozhili azerbaijanskuyu tekhniku," *Infoteka 24*, June 1, 2020, zen.yandex.ru/media/infoteka24/na-granice-s-nahidjevanom-vs-armenii-unichtojili-azerba-idjanskuiu-tehniku-video-5ed4ceb066114c67b34fdb41.

43   Mikhail A. Zhyrokhov, *Semena raspada*: *Voiny i konflikty na territorii byvshego SSSR* (St. Petersburg: BHV-Petersburg, 2012), 77–78.

44   Paul Hare, "Who Are the Moldavians?" in *Reconstructing the Market: The Political Economy of Microeconomic Transformation*, ed. Paul Hare, Mohammed Ishaq, and Judy Batt (Washington, DC: Taylor & Francis, 1999), 369–70.

45   Zhyrokhov, *Semena raspada*, 78.

46   Zhyrokhov, *Semena raspada*, 86–87.

47   Zhyrokhov, *Semena raspada*, 96–97; compare to Erica Daily, Jeri Laber, and Lois Whitman, *Human Rights in Moldova: TheTurbulent Dniester* (New York: Human Rights Watch, 1993), 4.

48   Daily, Laber, and Whitman, *Human Rights in Moldova*, 4.

49   Zhirokhov, *Semena raspada*, 97–98.

50   Mark Bliev, *Yuzhnaya Osetia v kolliziyakh rossiisko-gruzinskikh otnoshenii* (Vladikavkaz, Russia: Proekt Progress, 2006), 311-19; *Yuzhnaya Ossetia: Kkrov' i pepel* (Vladikavkaz, Russia: Assotsiatsia tvorcheskoi i nauchnoi intelligentsii, Ir, 1991), 47.

51   See Tsutsiev, *Atlas*, 117.

52   See also all the interviews in Isaenko, *Polygon of Satan*, 145–49.

53   Isaenko, *Polygon of Satan*, chapters 4, 5; these chapters contain full examples of these forms in Georgia, Ossetia, and Abkhazia as transmitted through the corresponding building blocks of ethnicities/conflicts that were radicalized during the *stirring-up stage*, as well as those that manifested through the official legislative actions of state organizations and the formation of economic policies.

54   Isaenko, *Polygon of Satan*, 162.

55   Isaenko, *Polygon of Satan*, 165; see also Alexei Zverev, "Ethnic Conflicts in the Caucasus, 1988–1994," in *Contested Borders in the Caucasus*, ed. Bruno Coppieters (Brussels: VUBPRESS-VUB University Press, 1996), chapter I, 41.

56   Edward Ozhiganov, "The Republic of Georgia: Conflict in Abkhazia and South Ossetia," in *Managing Conflict in the Former Soviet Union: Russian and American Perspectives*, ed. Alexei Arbatov et al.(Cambridge, MA: MIT Press, 1997), 356.

57   Ozhiganov, "The Republic of Georgia"; see also Ghia Nodia, "Political Turmoil in Georgia and the Ethnic Policies of Zviad Gamsakhurdia," in *Contested Borders in the Caucasus*, ed. Bruno Coppieters (Brussels: VUBPRESS-VUB University Press, 1996), 88, note 12.

58   Tsutsiev, *Atlas*, 89; Zverev, "Ethnic Conflicts in the Caucasus," 45.

59   Human Rights Watch: *Bloodshed in the Caucasus: Violations of Humanitarian Law and Human Life in the Georgia-South Ossetia Conflict* (New York: Human Rights Watch, 1992); "Statement of the Russia Government," *ITAR-TASS*, June 29, 1992; Ozhiganov, "The Republic of Georgia," 363.

60   Ozhiganov, "The Republic of Georgia," 342–43; *Rossiiskaya Gazeta* (March 10, 1993); Lara Olson, "Women and NGO: Views from Some Conflict Areas in the Caucasus," *New Bridges to Peace: Enhancing National and International Security by Expanding Policy Dialogues Among Women* (Washington, DC: Women NGO, 2001), 3.

61   Mark Bliev, *Ossetia, Kavkaz: Istoria i sovremennost'* (Vladikavkaz, Russia: North Ossetian University Press, 1999), 326–27.

62   Tsutsiev, *Atlas*, 92.

63   Charles King, *The Ghost of Freedom: A History of the Caucasus* (Oxford: Oxford University Press, 2008), 230.

64   Gruzia Segodnya, "Svoimi glazami," [Broadcast] *Echo Moscow*, October 19, 2009, http://www.echo.rusk.ru/programs/svoi-glaza/027454-echo.phtml.

65   See *EU Independent Fact-Finding Mission Report* (September 2009), http://www.ceiig.ch/pdf/IIFFMCG_Volume _1.pdf.

66   Isaenko, *Polygon of Satan*, chapter 4. All of these facts, as well as other miscellaneous facts within this timeline, are calculated and cited from the most reliable primary sources available.

67   Tsutsiev, Atlas, 60.

68   Ozhiganov, "The Republic of Georgia," 350; Vitalii Sharia, ed., *Abkhazskaya tragedia* (Sochi, Russia: Department of Mass Media of the Krasnodar Territory, 1993), 12; compare to King, *The Ghost of Freedom*, 215.

69   M. Lordkipanidze, *Abkhazy i Abkhazia* (*The Abkhazians and Abkhazia*) (Tbilisi: s.n., 1990), ch. 1; see also G. Zhorzholiani et al., *Istoricheskie i politico-pravovye aspecty gruzino-osetinskogo konflikta* (*Historical and Political-Legal Aspect of the Georgian-Ossetian Conflict*) (Tbilisi: Samshoblo, 1995); see also Zurab Anchabadze, *Istoria Abkhazii* (*The History of Abkhazia*) (Sukhumi: Alashara, 1976),

98–99. The most readily visible pro-Georgian position can be found in Avtandil Menteshashvili and Georgii Pandzhikidze, *Pravda ob Abkhazii (The Truth About Abkhazia)* (Tbilisi: s.n., 1990); Avtandil Menteshashvili and Georgii Pandzhikidze, *Krovavyi separatism: Chto proizoshlo v Abkhazii (Bloody Separatism: What Happened in Abkhazia)* (Tbilisi: s.n., 1993), 5.

70 Menteshashvili and Pandzhikidze, *Krovavyi separatism*, 5.

71 Zverev, "Ethnic Conflicts in the Caucasus," 57; Ozhiganov, "The Republic of Georgia," 342.

72 Concerning the detailed analysis of the positions hosted by either side of the conflict prior to the Five Days, War of August 2008, see Isaenko, *Polygon of Satan*, 215–17.

73 *Izvestia TsKKPSS*, vol. 6 (Moscow, Russia: Izd-vo TsKKPSS "Pravda," 1989), 177–78. The first time this decree was translated into English was by me in *Polygon of Satan, Third Edition*, 236.

74 Anatoly Isaenko, "Golgotha Terskogo kazachestva," *Terskii Kazak*, no. 6 (April 1990), 2-3.

75 For more detail on the suffering of the civilian population during the forcible deportation process, see Edward Radzinsky, *Stalin*, trans. H.T. Willets (New York: Bantam, 1996), 503; Frederick C. Cuny, "Killing Chechnya," *New York Review of Books*, April 6, 1995, 15–17.

76 Pavel Polian, *Against Their Will: The History and Geography of Forced Migrations in the USSR* (Budapest: Central European University Press, 2004), 4.

77 Isaenko, *Polygon of Satan*, 242.

78 Alan Ch. Kasaev, "Ossetia-Ingushetia," November 2, 1998, http://www.rand.org/publications/CF/CF129/CF-129.chapter1.html.

79 Olga Osipova, "North Ossetia and Ingushetia: The First Clash," in *Managing Conflict in the Former Soviet Union*, ed. Alexei Arbatov et al. (Cambridge, MA: MIT Press, 1997), 44.

80 I have collected and presented numerous examples from both sides of this provocative "historical dispute" in Isaenko, *Polygon of Satan*, 231–44.

81 Isaenko, *Polygon of Satan*, 251.

82 Zakon RSFSR, "O reabiletatsii repressirovannykh narodov," *Biulleten' Kongressa Narodnykh Deputatov i Verhovnogo Soveta RSFSR*, no. 18 (1991), Article 6.

83 Georgii Pogrebnov, "Voina," *Shpion*, no. 1 (Moscow: Misticos, 1993), 5.

84 Osipova, "North Ossetia and Ingushetia," 55; see also *Ingushi: deportatsia, vozvrashenie, reabilitatsia 1944–2004* (Nazran, Ingushetia: Humanitarian Fund of Ingushetia, 2004).

85 For more examples, see Isaenko, *Polygon of Satan*, 227–56.

86 Isaenko, *Polygon of Satan*, Table 3-1, "Ethnic Uprisings and Riots, 1859–1908s: From the End of the Caucasian War to the End of the Soviet Period," 108–110.

87 Isaenko, *Polygon of Satan*, 63, 81.

88 See Moshe Gammer, *The Wolf and the Bear: Three Centuries of Chechen Defiance of Russian Rule* (Pittsburgh: University of Pittsburgh Press, 2006).

89 *Ternistyi put' k svobode: Pravitel'stvennye documenty Chechenskoi Respubliki* (Vilnius, Lithuania: Taurus, 1993), 376–77.

90 Arbi Arbiev, "On the Run," *Moskovsky Komsomolets*, April 1998, 2.

91 Emil Pain and A. Popov, "Rossiiskaya politika v Chechne, kriminal'nyi rezhim," *Izvestia*, February 8, 1995, 2–3.

92 *Khasav-yurt Joint Declaration and Principles for Mutual Relations* (August 31, 1996), RU_960831_Khasavyourt_Joint_Declaration_and_Principles_for_Mutual_Relations.pdf.

93 Magomet Tolboyev, "Do Not Come to Us in the Caucasus," *Novoye Russkoye Slovo*, July 6, 1998. For the best full account of the Chechen perspective during the two *hot stage*, see Ilyas Akhmadov and Mirriam Lanskoy, *The Chechen Struggle: Independence Won and Lost* (New York: Palgrave Macmillan, 2010).

94 Isaenko, *Polygon of Satan*, 269.

95 Liz Fuller, "Chechnya: Shamil Basayev's Life of War and Terror," *Radio Free Europe/Radio Liberty*, July 10, 2006, rferl.org/a/1069740.html.

96 "Palestina Na Kavkaze," *Radio Free Europe/Radio Liberty*, March 9, 2009.

97 *Vsesoyuznaya perepis' naselenya 1989 goda* (Moscow, Russia: Glavnoye upravleniye statistiki i demografii, Soyuza SSR, 1989).

98 *Vsesoyuznaya perepis' naselenya 1989 goda*.

99 Isaenko, *Polygon of Satan*, 389. ; Emil Souleimanov, "Is Beslan the Result of Russian Policies in the Caucasus?' *Prague Watchdog—Crisis in Chechnya*, October 20, 2004,www.watchdog.cz.

100 Isaenko, *Polygon of Satan*, 365.

Figure Credits

CHAPTER NINE

Timeline of Russo-Ukrainian Violent Ethnic Conflict, 1989–Present

FIGURE 9.1 Flag and Coat of Arms - Russia

FIGURE 9.2 Flag of Ukraine

FIGURE 9.3 Coat of Arms Ukraine

For the historical prerequisites of this particular conflict, please see the examples and scenarios presented in chapters 1, 3, 4, 5, and 6, as well as the cited literature.

These examples indicate that, during both the Imperial and (especially) the Soviet Periods, glimpses into all five building blocks of ethnic conflict show that they manifested themselves in varying degrees of intensity. However, *language* would invariably become the most important building block of ethnicity and conflict, as it was gradually responsible for the ethnicization of any and all sociopolitical interaction between these culturally approximate ethnic nations in the post-Soviet period. Additionally, and in spite of the fact that the majority of both peoples are primarily Orthodox Christians, the *religious building block* reemerged with full strength in 2018, when the Ukrainian side argued that the Moscow Patriarchate had altered their control over the Kyivan Metropolitan in 1686 and the late eighteenth century, resulting in "further changes" that ultimately "reduced the number of church properties under the Kyivan Metropolitan and local leadership made way for Moscow appointed bishops."[1]

The defined "sides" of this modern ethnic conflict are as follows:

- First Level of Conflict: Ukrainian ethnocentric nationalists and the Ukrainian state itself faced off against the Russian majority in Crimea and the minority pro-Russian "separatists" in the Donbas/Donbass region. Since all of these combatants are technically Ukrainian citizens, this level of the violent ethnic conflict was definitively *intrastate*.

- • Second Level: The Ukrainian nation-state versus Russia, who supported the rebels in Donbas. Following Russia's annexation of Crimea in 2014, this ethnic conflict simultaneously assumed *interstate* characteristics.

In more specific terms, the Ukrainian side has the support of volunteers from various countries (especially those with already hostile relations with Russia), including Mustafa Dzhemilev and Rifat Chubarov's Mejlis of Crimean Tatar People and the various powerful Ukrainian diasporas within Western countries, all flanked by indirect involvement and material support from those same Western nations, as well as international organizations. In a sense, this is the third level of the Russo-Ukrainian violent ethnic conflict, which, under certain stimuli of regressive development, began evolving from the first/second level: this not only holds politico-diplomatic, informational, and economic implications (like the relatively recent economic sanctions imposed on Russia by the West) but also the potential to result in direct military confrontation of the nation-states in question, resulting in subsequent and uncontrolled escalation in the involvement of military amalgamations from both the East and West. As previously stated, the pro-Russian rebels in Donbas have the support of volunteers from Russia and other countries, as well as a hybrid (humanitarian/military munitions) line of support from Russia. Additionally, and as seen in many of the pervious entries, Russia unilaterally distributes documentation of Russian citizenship to those dwelling in this and any other region. By now, approximately 600,000 residents of Donbas have become Russian citizens.

October 1989–February 23, 2014: Stirring-Up Stage

It is necessary to reiterate the fact that during the thawing of the USSR through Gorbachev's perestroika initiative, which lasted from 1988 to 1991, each of the constituent union republics "had rushed to enhance the legal status of its 'own' language."[2]

For the sake of impartiality, which is the only proper way to present this ethnic conflict, I choose to abstain from making any critical assessments of the policies held by either side of this conflict. In this particular timeline, I will simply reproduce the mutually exclusive/radical (ethnocentric) positions of either side corresponding to the principal building blocks of the conflict, with the Russian view described on the left side of the page and the Ukrainian view on the right. I will cite those policies that reflect the benign characteristics of civic nationalism and the actions of compromising outside/international organizations, as well as any additional remarks, down the middle of the page.

October 1989–1996: Emergence of Linguistic Building Block of the Conflict

Russian/Pro-Russian Position	Ukrainian Position
The formation of a unified opposition consisting of people from various backgrounds, including many ethnic Ukrainians from southeastern Ukraine, who	*The Law on Language* appointed Ukrainian as *the sole official state language*. In 1996, it was ratified as a part of the independent Ukrainian constitution. President Kuchma would then

favored Russian policies. Specifically, they argued that it was an "infringement on their rights to be expected to use Ukrainian at work or to have their children schooled only in Ukrainian."[3]

publish a book titled *Ukraine Is Not Russia*, in which he argued that "Ukraine is a state that has to rebuild itself according to some parameters … and [the] most important is the state language." He continued, poignantly concluding that "Ukrainization is the restitution of justice."

With this first step, the most important underlying building block of the Russo-Ukrainian conflict reemerged. As previously mentioned, *language* is the first building block of ethnicity that was fully *radicalized*, resulting in a division between Ukrainian citizens living in the western and southeastern regions of the country. According to the 2001 census, the last all-encompassing record to be taken as of now, only 17 percent of the total population identified themselves as ethnically Russian. However, 83 percent of that particular ethnic group lived in the eastern and southeastern regions of Ukraine, making their influence there noticeably higher.[4]

- 1990s

Russian Position	Ukrainian Position
This mindset dates back to the Imperial practice of denying the existence of Ukrainian as a separate language. Instead, it is considered an adjunct dialect of the more common Russian, Belarusian, and Ukrainian linguistic commonality, similar to how Russia, Belarus, and Ukraine were considered "the same country" that had been violently divided by the actions of hostile forces from outside their region following the collapse of the Soviet Union.[5] (See also the interviews in the Introduction chapter.)	Ukrainian is a completely different and independently developed language, just like the Ukrainian people and nation-state. "Bilingualism" had become a mask used to hide the injection of Russification into their country. "For years 'bilingualism' [was] increasingly directed toward insuring proficiency in standard Russian at the expense of other languages such as Ukrainian."[6]
A variant of this idea states that bilingualism is a naturally existing phenomenon in Ukraine; as in, Ukrainian is a natural mixture of Eastern Slavic dialects—with the prominent inclusion of Russian—similar in nature to the Surzhyk sociolect.	Since the 1990s, many publications have appeared within Ukraine arguing for the naturalness and legitimacy of the newly independent folk, their nation, and their language.[7]
In this same vein, the diversity of dialects is a natural occurrence, and the richness of the language that should be protected, seeing as it is directly linked to the cultural linguistic rights of the people in question.	Many saw Surzhyk as a "disease or a product of Ukrainian self-hate and self-denigration."[8]
	There was a heavy prerogative arguing that the Ukrainian language must be purified/purged from Russisms (as well as Polonisms, etc.) and standardized around the nucleus of Halychyna Mova. Linguists should do so due to their responsibility in forming and legitimizing the Ukrainian ethnicity's ability to define its own social and political future as an integral state.

In general, the "privileged" position of the Russian language was criticized and rejected as "a colonizer's language."[9]

Russian Position	Ukrainian Position
Ethnic Russians living in both Crimea and the southeast of Ukraine both lobbied to have Russian designated as an "official" language. Around this point, President Leonid Kuchma suggested that he might introduce such legislation into the political landscape.[10]	Throughout the rest of Ukraine—and especially in the west—the demand to make Russian an official language was met with strong opposition. The leaders of the *Ukrainian Writer's Union*, the *People's Movement of Ukraine (Rukh)*, the *Ukrainian Republican Party*, the *Democratic Party of Ukraine*, the *All-Ukrainian Prosvita (Enlightenment) Society*, and the Hetman of the Ukrainian Cossacks all signed a petition demanding that this initiative be recalled.[11] They would ultimately prevail, and the constitution of 1996 would declare Ukrainian as the sole official state language.
	Surzhyk was condemned as a degradation of both the Ukrainian language and the culture at large. Overall, these parties demanded that their language *must be correct and pure*, which was coupled with this simultaneous rejection of other languages and ethnic identities as impositions of colonizing rule from other states.[12]

- 2000s

Russian Position	Ukrainian Position
Meanwhile in the east of the country, [ethnocentric] nationalist sentiment was low, though the introduction of Ukrainian in Crimea was met with stiff resistance.	Ukrainian linguists increased their efforts to reject theories of exclusive East Slavic unity.[13] Instead, they started insisting that Ukrainian should achieve a greater degree of "authenticity," "purity," and "correctness."
	"Ukrainian language and [ethnocentric] nationalist inclinations were prevalent in western regions."[14]
	(1) "Urbanized-Peasant Surzhyk," (2) "Village-Dialect Surzhyk," (3) "Sovietized-Ukrainian Surzhyk," (4) "Post-Independent Surzhyk," and (5) "Urban-Bilingual Surzhyk" were subjected to purification efforts in relation to the construction of standardized Ukrainization.[15]

- May 2000–2001

Russian Position	Ukrainian Position
Five out of the thirteen largest newspapers printed in Ukraine continued to be printed in Russian, as they were founded on and given financial support from Russia.	Major protests break out in western Ukraine after the death of Ukrainian songwriter Ihor Bilozir, "who died after being beaten by ethnic Russians who did not like that he was singing Ukrainian songs with his friend in a café" in Lviv.[16]

- April 2004

Five months after its initial introduction, the resolution (see right-hand column) would fail under the immense pressure brought about by Ukrainian broadcasters and politicians in Moscow.[17]	The *National Council for Television and Broadcasting* adopted a resolution stating that national and international companies were required to broadcast their programming in Ukrainian in at least half of the twenty-five regions of the country.[18]

- 2012

Laws passed by Ukrainian President Victor Yanukovych allowed for minorities to teach their languages in regions where *they represented more than 10 percent of the population* (see chapter 6).	Shortly thereafter, ethnocentric opposition to these *regional language* laws were organized in thirteen of the twenty-five national regions, which began fighting to overthrow it.

February 2014–Present: Hot Stage

- February 2014: The *Revolutsiia Hidnisti*, integral (ethnocentric) nationalists, came to power in Ukraine. As a result, President Yanukovych fled to Russia (see chapter 6).
- September 25, 2017:

Russian Position	Ukrainian Position
Russian, Hungarian, Romanian, and (as of now) Bulgarian authorities protested the introduction of this law (see right-hand column), as it seriously undermined the linguistic rights of their respective minority groups living in Ukraine (see chapter 6).	The Verkhovna Rada (Ukrainian Parliament) adopted the *Law About Education*. President Petro Poroshenko would later sign this law, officially integrating it into Ukrainian society.

- May 5, 2019:

Russia's criticism of this legislative action (see right-hand column) is swift, seeing it as a brutal return for the policy of "total Ukrainization." In 1989–1990, there were 4,633 schools in Ukraine that utilized the Russian language. By 2007, only seven of such Russian schools remained in Kiev. By 2017, the total number had dropped to 3,000. In Odessa, where 75 percent of the population speaks Russian, there were only forty-six Russian schools left in the region by 1998 (a drop of nearly 32 percent). By 2003, the Donbas region's sphere of higher learning had been converted to Ukrainian.	President Poroshenko signed the Law About Provisions of Functioning of Ukrainian as the State Language. Its introduction completely overthrew the 2012 Law About the Foundation of State Policy and introduced a mono-ethnic linguistic culture into all levels and spheres of sociopolitical life. The end of this process was the total absorption of ethnicity into the life of the republic itself.

- December 6, 2019: *The internationalization of the conflict within the parameters of the Linguistic building block.* Specifically, the *Venice Commission of the European Council* (of *The European Commission for Democracy Through Law*) called upon Ukrainian officials to *reverse the requirements of the language law* (see chapter 6).

- January 16, 2020

The use of Russian in the medical sphere was completely forbidden (grievances of Russians).	The Verkhovna Rada adopted *The Law about Full General [and] Middle Education*.

- March 13, 2020

Restrictions were imposed on the use of Russian in the TV and radio broadcast spheres of life, as well as in common public occurrences and places (under the threat of monetary fines since January 16, 2021).	President Zelensky signed a newer variant of Poroshenko's law into the mainstream.

In fact, this newer rendition of this law introduced a modern variant of the original Imperial/Soviet categorization of peoples of different ethnic backgrounds into the Ukrainian linguistic-educational sphere, which resulted in Russians being shunted to the lowest possible category (see chapter 6). Aside from that, this legislation also objectively served to strengthen the position of separatist forces, such as those in Donbas, who sought to enact an irredentist plan to "reunite" with Russia, since this legislature symbolized the *end of their federalist state-building project*. The end of this project had signaled the "triumph" of the unitarist ethnocentric plan and ended any and all hope for the creation of consociational power-sharing structures between the titular ethnic group and other minorities, particularly the Russians.

Nationality Building Block of Russo-Ukrainian Violent Ethnic Conflict

October 1989–February 23, 2014: Stirring-Up Stage

- 1989–1991: Ironically enough, the idea of *federalism* with ethno-political underpinnings, being deployed by the separatists, originated with the ethnocentric Ukrainian opposition prior to the dissolution of the USSR.
- March 1990: Viacheslav Chornovil, leader of the *Rukh* and chairman of the Lviv regional council, was the first proponent of this idea and introduced the concept during a meeting of the larger Rukh organization—which served to commemorate the anniversary of the proclamation of the short-lived independent *Carpatho-Ukrainian Republic* (1938–39). "Prior to independence it was a means to emphasize the 'Ukrainian' character of Galicia, but once an independent Ukraine had been established, the idea had been discarded as being subversive of state capacity" by the Ukrainian integral (ethnocentric) nationalists.[19] However, and somewhat ironically, it lived on in the rhetoric of the other ethnic minorities.
- 1990–1991

Russian Position	Ukrainian Position
Ethno-political mobilizations began on a regional scale, with Donbas, Zakarpattya (Hungarians—see chapter 6), and Crimea (see chapter 6) being the most prominent. There was also a small-scale movement in [Odessa] trying to revive the idea of the old province of *Novorossiya*, including the Transnistria, Odessa, Nickolaev, and Kherson regions, as well as Crimea.	

- 1991–1994

The First Referendum: initiated the rise of the Russian nationalist-separatist movement in Crimea.

- 1992

Russian Position	Ukrainian Position
On May 6, a faction of Russian nationalists initiated a Crimean declaration of independence. The resulting regional constitution defined the newly founded *Republic of Crimea* as a *gosudarstvo* or "*state*."	The Ukrainian parliament immediately rejected this constitution and by extension any other legislation stemming from its existence. A compromising constitution was enacted on September 25, stating that the so-called "Republic of Crimea" would exist as a *state within Ukraine.*

- 1994

This tension reached its *apogee* in January, as Yuriy Meshkov was elected to the office of president of the new Crimean Republic. Afterward, a regional referendum finalized Crimean autonomy, established a basis for dual Russian-Ukrainian citizenship of its citizens, and widened Meshkov's presidential powers.[20] Shortly thereafter, a "Russian wave" swept across the peninsula.

A local referendum within the Donbas region approved four separate proposals that (1) established Russian as the state language; (2) established Russian as the official language for administrative protocol within the region; (3) set in motion the *federalization* of Ukraine; and (4) established Ukraine's full membership in the *CIS.*[21]

- March 15, 1995

As a result, many of the Russian movements in the contesting areas were fragmented. Additionally, President Yeltsin refused to meet with Meshkov in any capacity "and showed little enthusiasm for a major conflict in Ukraine."[22]	President Leonid Kuchma cracked down on any and all aspects of "Crimean Separatism." The Verkhovna Rada annulled the "separatist" version of the Crimean constitution from 1992, effectively abolishing the Crimean presidency.

- 1996

Russian Position	Ukrainian Position
	Gradually, the following five-step negotiations between Crimean "officials" and their Ukrainian contemporaries resulted in the establishment of a constitutional autonomy in Crimea. Aside from the obvious changes, this *strengthened the notion of a civic Ukrainian state/nation-building project.*

For the time being, in both Donbas and Crimea, the constitutional process "locked most of the key actors" and complex of ethno-political issues "into a bargaining model" and eventually led "to an institutional compromise." This dialogue was *the key to any and all conflict prevention* strategies/tactics, which would later result in the above-discussed political reforms in Russia as a part of asymmetric consociational institutionalism.

Ethnic tensions further eased over Crimea in 1995, when the two sides agreed in principal to divide [the *Black Sea Fleet*] with both navies stationed in Sevastopol. While a reasonable attempt to balance the scales, it ultimately made each side more wary of the other in the grand scheme.

- 1997: The "Big Treaty" on friendship and cooperation between Russia and Ukraine, as well as other important aspects of economic and cultural partnership (including the finalization of the previously mentioned division of the Black Sea Fleet, with 82 percent of the ships staying with Russia and 18 being transferred to Ukraine), was finalized. It was then all capped off with Russia's reconfirmation of the territorial integrity of the Ukrainian state, with an implicit reference to the status of Crimea. Additionally, "the 20-year renewable lease [on the Sevastopol Naval base] was supposed to expire in 2017."[23]

But prior to this bilateral agreement, on December 5, 1994, the international agreement known as the *Budapest Memorandum on Security Assurances*, which refers to three identical political agreements, was signed at the OSCE conference in Budapest, Hungary. The signatories: the Russian Federation, the United Kingdom, and the United States, affirmed security assurances relating to the accession of Belarus, Kazakhstan, and Ukraine to the *Treaty on the Non-Proliferation of Nuclear Weapons*. This memorandum included security assurances against threats of force against the territorial integrity or political independence of these newly independent states. Between 1994 and 1996, these three countries voluntarily gave up their nuclear arsenals; up until that point, Ukraine had possessed the *third-largest nuclear stockpile of any country in the world*.[24] However, the most relevant piece of information to this conflict came in *Article 1* of the Budapest Memorandum, which reads: "Respect Belarus, Kazakh, and Ukrainian independence and sovereignty in the existing borders."[25]

November 2013–March 16, 2014; March 2014–Present: Hot Stage

- November 21, 2013: *Triggering event*—the crisis began with protests in Kiev against President Yanukovych's decision to reject a deal that allowed for greater economic integration with the EU (for details see chapter 6, *Crimean Case*, and Yekelchyk, *The Conflict in Ukraine*, 104–46).

Russian Side	Ukrainian Side
Unlike the 2004 Orange Revolution, the 2014 Maidan protests were not solely concerned with the use/abuse of power but also about the physical survival of adherents of the Yanukovych regime and many ethnic Russians, as well as their ethnic rights.	After a violent crackdown at the hands of Yanukovych's state security forces, more people were drawn to participate in the protests (now levied against corruption),which escalated the conflict. The *Titushky*, a mercenary force that took the guise of *gopniks* (a local subculture roughly equivalent to football/soccer hooligans), was shipped in from the eastern regions to support the police.
February 18-20, 2014: Violence broke out among the protesters. The Russian side often cites the *BBC*'s report that this started	

when "snipers affiliated with [ethnocentric] nationalistic MP Andrey [Andriy] Parubiy during Maidan shot at policemen and provoked them to respond."[26] From this point on, the scale of violence used by the Ukrainian authorities, who themselves came to power through violence, was unprecedented in its application.

Between assaulting protestors and acting as anti-Maidan activists, their presence only added fuel to the fire.

A May 2013 Gallup poll showed that only 23 percent of respondents in Crimea wanted to become part of Russia; in December 2014, after the armed struggle had already begun, an Oxford polling team found that only 10 percent of respondents wanted to be independent or join Russia, 25 percent wished for autonomy within Ukraine, and more than 50 percent wanted to remain a Ukrainian province. Another poll taken in Crimea showed that 41 percent of the population thought that Russia and Ukraine should reunify into a single state.[27]

- February 20, 2014: According to Yekelchyk, "67 protesters and 13 police officers were reportedly killed, and hundreds wounded. Sixteen more protesters died later in hospital."[28]
- February 21, 2014: Foreign ministers from France, Germany, and Poland arrived in Kyiv in order to mediate negotiations between Yanukovych and the opposition, who sought to resolve accumulated contradictions prior to the approaching December elections. What happened next took two different paths, depending on who you ask.

Russian Version	Ukrainian Version
Armed units belonging to the impromptu "Maidan Self-Defense" force broke the agreement and took over government buildings by force.	The police presence surrounding government buildings simply left their posts. The army either sided with the protestors or simply remained neutral.
Soon after, the president's life was threatened, as the leaders of a "coup" prepared a plan to kill him. In a later press conference, Yanukovych denounced the entirety of this event as a "neo-Nazi coup."	Political elites began defecting to the opposition. Subsequently, the "Parliament voted to restore the 2004 constitutional reform, suspended the minister of the interior, and [returned] all troops to the barracks." *Right Sector* leader Dmytro Yarosh and the "captains" of Maidan Self-Defense, with support from the rowdy crowd, demanded Yanukovych's immediate resignation and the arrest of the interior minister.[29]

- February 22, 2014: In response to the chaos, Yanukovych fled the city; he would eventually end up taking refuge in Russia. Meanwhile, in Kyiv, the office for Yanukovych's *Party of Regions* was burned down "with several of its staff members burned alive, and [the] '*Berkut*' [police] unit and Anti-Maidan movement participants from the south-west of Ukraine as well as members of their families were prosecuted."[30] In addition, there were several attacks on buses carrying Anti-Maidan participants out of Crimea.
- February 23, 2014: In one of the more important developments, the new authorities in Kyiv displayed their own ethnocentric nationalism by pushing an "abolishment of the [2012] law on regional languages" through parliament. Though "acting President Turchinov announced on March 4 that

he would not sign the bill," it was simply too late to stop escalation of ethnic tensions.[31] In chapter 6, I stated that this action was an inadmissible signal for the Russian-speaking population of Crimea and the southeastern regions that the new government would only support ethnic (or, rather, ethnocentric) policy. Thus, this would become a *second triggering event*, polarizing ideologies along ethnic lines and ensuring the consolidation of the pro-Russian forces. It essentially opened Pandora's box, releasing an avalanche of events that would cascade into a fully fledged *hot stage* with all its associated behavioral patterns and mild/middle-ground/extreme forms of ethnic cleansing (see "Crimean Case" and Putin's revitalization of the "*Malorossiya/Novorossiya*" plan in chapter 6).

- March–April 2014: Pro-Russian rallies swept across Donbas and the southeast (in places like Kharkiv, Odesa, Mykolaiv, Kherson, etc.).
- April 7, 2014: Pro-Russian activists occupied government buildings, proclaiming the formation of the *Donetsk People's Republic (DPR)*.
- April 28–29, 2014: The proclamation of the *Luhansk People's Republic (LPR)*.
- May 2, 2014: Pro-government forces, headed by Andriy Parubiy and other Kyivan officials, clashed with Anti-Maidan activists in Odesa. By the time it was over, an estimated forty-eight people who sought refuge in the Trade Unions Building had been burned to death. Though this tragedy has yet to be properly investigated, it nevertheless added momentum to an already burgeoning cycle of violence, which encompassed "a series of murders and mysterious suicides of opposition politicians and journalists (widely known writer Oles' Buzina, former MP Mikhail Chechetov, Oleg Kalashnikov, Aleksandr Peklushenko, and Stanislav Melnik)," and provided more evidence that "the new Ukrainian leaders were ready to eliminate the opposition physically."[32] Repressions and prosecutions resulted in further radicalization of the Russian minority, steadily galvanizing *intraregional* and *sub-regional coordination* between the protest organizations: in Luhansk, the "*Moladaya Gvardija,*" "*Luganskaja Gvardija,*" and the militarized "*South-East Army,*" who proclaimed the formation of the LPR, emerged into the world.
- April 15, 2014: Interim Ukrainian President Oleksandr Turchinov orders the creation of the *Anti-Terrorist Operation (ATO)* in the Donetsk, Luhans'k, and Izium Districts of the Kharkiv region. Its creation aided Ukrainian authorities in reestablishing control over Mariupol, Kirovsk, and Yampil, but many Donbas residents considered it little more than a punitive operation bent on suspending any referendum on joining Russia. Several key figures within the protests—such as Donetsk Governor Pavel Gubarev, his deputy Pobert Donya, and Luhans'k Governor Aleksandr Kharitonov—were summarily imprisoned. However, this shake-up had the unintended consequence of forcing these unrecognized republics to establish proper governing institutions, deal with issues of economic development, and restructure self-organized militia units. However, after the arrest of the moderate protest leaders, their positions were then filled by the more radical politicians, such as how Aleksandr Zakharchenko replaced Gubarev as leader of the Donetsk region and subsequently prompted the idea of an independence referendum.
- May 25, 2014: *Third triggering event*—newly elected Ukrainian President Petro Poroshenko launched "a full-scale military operation, which eventually alienated unrecognized republics" and unleashed a vicious cycle of elite-led violence. From time to time, this violence would regress into more chaotic mass-led unrestricted violence over territory and strategic points (such as

Saur-Mohyla or the Donetsk airport) within the region. From this, a full-fledged *"War in Donbas"* would begin.

- May 2014–Present:

The sides of this conflict are represented as such:

Pro-Russian Insurgency (and Allies)	Ukrainian Side
DPR, LPR, and Russia (The Parliament Assembly of the Council of Europe officially recognizes areas of Donbas as effectively controlled by Russia. However, Russia denies any direct involvement).	

Pro-Russian Forces:

- *Donbas People's Militia*
- *The Vostok Brigade*
- *The Russian Orthodox Army*
- *The Sparta Battalion*
- *Luhansk People's Militia*
- *The Great Don Army*
- *The Prizrak Brigade*
- *The First Cossack Regiment of the above-cited KSOVD*

All of the above-cited formations share the same ideas and goals as the *KSOVD*, which was discussed in chapter 6.

Allies:
- *Russian Armed Forces* (although Russia denies their presence)
- *Registered Cossacks of the Russian Federation* (similarly, Russia claims that only some individuals participate on their own terms)
- *Chechen volunteers*
- *Serb mercenaries*
- *Individual volunteers* from many other countries.

Ukrainian forces:

- *Armed Forces of Ukraine*
- *The Aidar Battalion*
- *Territorial Defense Battalions*
- *Special 383 Operations Force*
- *The National Security Service*
- *Alpha Group*
- *The Ministry of Internal Affairs:*
  - National Guard
  - Azov Battalion
  - Dnipro Battalion
  - Dzhokhar Dudayev Battalion
  - Right Sector
  - The Special Police
  - Noman Çelebicihan Battalion of Crimean Tatars
  - The State Border Guard

- April 12, 2014–June 2, 2020: Between the Siege of Slaviansk in the Donets'k Oblast and several skirmishes between the Pro-Russian and Ukrainian forces, peppered with machine-gun fire and 82mm mortar volleys at Pavlopil, 17 main battles occurred between the sides. Subsequently Poroshenko renamed ATO the Operation of United Forces, revoked the previously mentioned Big Treaty of Friendship with Russia, and officially declared it as Aggressor in a special resolution of Verkhovna Rada. Given the staff of the above-listed forces and participants involved in this conflict, one may clearly see that, during this *hot stage*, the overall flow of the fighting has transformed from an *intrastate* (first level) conflict to an *interstate* (second level) violent ethnic conflict. It has also undergone obvious *internationalization*, given the meddling interference of international organizations to either bolster one side or work out a more amicable cease-fire and elaborate on certain transgressions to find a peaceful resolution.

- June 4–5, 2014: The 40th *G8 Summit*, which was to be held in the Black Sea city of Sochi, Russia, was essentially boycotted by the other seven member states, who decided to meet in Brussels, Belgium. Following this and the official annexation of Crimea, Russia was effectively expelled from the *G8* organization.
- June 6, 2014: The creation of the *Normandy Format*. This new contact group was composed of representatives of four different countries: Germany, Russia, Ukraine, and France, who met during the D-Day celebration in Normandy with the aim to resolve the "War in Donbas."[33] Overall, there were six separate meetings that occurred in this format, with the last taking place on December 9, 2019, in Paris, France, and attended by President Volodymyr Zelensky, who, in his inaugural address that May, had made conducting peace talks with the pro-Russian forces a top priority for his administration.
- September 4/5, 2014–February 2015: At the *2014 Wales Summit of NATO*, Ukrainian President Poroshenko announced a cease-fire, which had been agreed upon with one of the larger pro-Russian separatist leaders and under the terms of Russian President Putin. Ultimately, the leaders of NATO welcomed this development, albeit with a great deal of caution. This cease-fire was soon broken, however, as would be many of the subsequent cease-fires since that point, by both sides, as reported by the *Monitor Mission of the OSCE* working in the warzone.
- September 5–19, 2014: The specific *Protocol* on the results and consultations brought about by the *Trilateral Contact Group*, better known as the *Minsk Protocol*, was officially signed by representatives of Ukraine, the Russian Federation, the DPR, LPR, and the OSCE in the titular Belarusian capital Minsk (Minsk I). However, this agreement failed to end the fighting in Donbas (as mentioned above). It was soon replaced by a new package of measures—Minsk II—which was finalized on February 12, 2015. While this agreement also failed to quell the fighting, it and the general tone set by the *Minsk Agreements* remain the most solidified basis for any future resolution to this conflict.

There are currently thirteen points of *Minsk Agreements* that act as the foundation for a peaceful resolution of the *hot stage* in Donbas, which both sides have fully supported and which have been authorized by their signatures. These points can be easily summarized as follows:

1. An immediate and full cease-fire.
2. The removal of heavy weapons by both sides to an equidistant perimeter, with the aim of creating a security zone with a minimum distance of 50–140 kilometers (roughly 31–87 miles) in order to account for the ranges/calibers of heavy artillery, rocket launchers, and missiles—including the Tornado-S, Uragan, Smerch, and Tochka-U tactical missile systems—with the whole process being assessed by the OSCE.
3. The establishment of an effective monitoring and verification system for the cease-fire.
4. The immediate (i.e., on the first day of pull-outs) establishment of a moderation dialogue centered on the workings of local elections in accordance with Ukrainian legislation and the Ukrainian law "On Temporary Order of Local Self-Governance in Particular Districts of Donets'k and Luhans'k Oblasts," as well as the future of said districts based on the aforementioned law.
5. Provide pardons and/or amnesty to all participants of events that took place in particular areas of the Donets'k and Luhans'k Oblasts of Ukraine. There is to be no prosecution, nor punishment.

6. Oversee the release and exchange of all prisoners and hostages (both legal and illegal) based on the principle of "all for all" by the fifth day of pull-out.
7. Safe access to humanitarian aid for all affected persons.
8. The full restoration of any social and economic connections, including any kind of regular payments or stipends.
9. Restore control of the state border to the Ukrainian government in the whole conflict zone, which must begin on the first day *after* local elections and must conclude following the full enactment of political regulation (local elections in particular districts of the Donets'k and Luhans'k Oblasts are to be held based on Ukrainian law and constitutional reform) by the end of 2015, on the conditional fulfillment of point 11, in consultation and in agreement with representatives of these particular districts of these oblasts within the framework of the Trilateral Contact Group.
10. The removal of all foreign armed formations, military equipment, and mercenaries from the territory of Ukraine under strict OSCE supervision. Additionally, they will oversee the disarmament of all local illegal groups of fighters.
11. Enact constitutional reform within Ukraine—with the key element being decentralization—and the establishment of a special status for particular districts within the Donets'k and Luhans'k Oblasts.
12. All questions related to local elections will be discussed and agreed upon with representatives of the particular districts.
13. An intensification of the work of the Trilateral Contact Group.

In addition, the mentioned Ukrainian law "On Temporary Order of Local Self Governance in Particular Districts of Donets'k and Luhans'k Oblasts" must be adopted. Among the measures related directly to the *nationality* rights (such as the "creation of people's militia units"), this law should guarantee the "*Right of language self-determination*" relating to the most important building block of ethnicity, which is and continues to be the most provocative and mobilizing characteristic of the Russo-Ukrainian violent ethnic conflict.[34]

In this way, the combined efforts behind both Minsk I (September 2014) and Minsk II (February 2015) would serve as a veritable roadmap to establishing a lasting peace in Ukraine. But while these agreements have helped to drastically *deescalate* the fighting, they have done little to stop the *hot stage* of the conflict.

There are several circumstances as to why this occurred, but they may only be fully and accurately understood and assessed when one takes into account the complexity of the building blocks—and their associated issues—in relation to the typical progression of a violent ethnic conflict at this stage:

(1) The Ukrainian forces suffered serious setbacks as a result of the *Battle of Ilovaisk* from August to September 2014, the so-called "*Second Battle*" of Donets'k Airport in January 2015, and especially following the *Battle of Debaltsevo* between mid-January and early February 2015.[35] The prospect of having to face further offensives from pro-Russian "separatists," who had been backed by both Russian specialists and supplies, was not (and still is not) an encouraging prospect for the Ukrainian side: the resulting tentativeness allowed the rebels to capture particularly worthwhile districts in both oblasts. At that time, they could even go so far as to threaten the city of Mariupol—an important port on the Azov Sea that serves as the country's main export hub. (2) Because of this, the Ukrainian side was more or less forced to sign the Minsk II agreement in order to mitigate the relatively unfavorable circumstances,

even when—due to the presence of Russia—there were many obligations (and more importantly, *specific sequences of fulfillment*) that were dramatically gainful for the pro-Russian rebels. (3) Those deals were so quickly hammered out that the Ukrainians, after regaining control of the situation, began to argue that the deals "were vaguely worded" and insisted that the sequence to usher in peace should be altered; the Ukrainian side must regain control over the border with Russia (in other words, to reoccupy the particular uncontrolled districts within Donets'k and Luhans'k), all illegal formations must be disarmed, all "foreign" (i.e., Russian) troops must be driven out, and then the subsequent elections must be conducted under Ukrainian law.

(4) Of course, both Russia and the pro-Russian rebels would then insist on the previously established sequence of steps, which had been verified, signed, and published by both sides. In this way, the Ukrainians could only establish control over the border—as per point 9 of the agreement—*after* the elections had taken place in these districts, as well as the enactment of points 1–8. (5) Additionally, if "*language self-determination*" is similarly guaranteed—much like the remaining "*nationality*" rights–based criteria of points 9–13—then the *federalization project of state building in Ukraine*, which had been hated by ethnocentric nationalists, would again realign with the present political agendum. That is why Poroshenko, who had signed off on the original sequence of this political "road map," subsequently did everything in his power (with the full backing of far-right ethnocentric organizations [and as mentioned above, backed by Washington, DC, for his linguistic law package]) to topple the fulfillment of these agreements. It is for this reason that he initiated the previously discussed package of language laws, which were later signed into law by Zelensky (see chapter 6). Zelensky, who was working on the logic of his political predecessor and the ethnocentric nationalists, applied this law to the educational sphere, further delaying the fulfillment of the *Minsk Agreements* in both a de facto and de jure fashion. (6) In 2016, while looking for a way to break the political deadlock, Frank-Walter Steinmeier—the German foreign minister (now president)—proposed what one may call a "simplified" version of the *Minsk Agreements*. In fact, it may have even been possible "to get Ukraine and Russia to agree on the sequence of events outlined in Minsk" by doing so.

This new formula "calls for: (1) elections to be held in the separatist-held territories under Ukrainian legislation and the supervision of the OSCE. (2) If the OSCE judges the balloting to be free and fair, (3) then a special self-governing status for the territories will be initiated and (4) Ukraine will be returned control of its easternmost borders."[36]

On October 1, 2019, this newly crafted formula was signed by representatives from Ukraine, Russia, and the DPR and LPR, as well as the OSCE, in Minsk. Immediately after this, far-right ethnocentric activists organized mass public rallies in protest, referring to Ukraine's agreement to Steinmeier's Formula as "*zrada*" ("defeat" in Ukrainian) and nothing more than Zelensky's "capitulation" to the demands of Moscow.

A recent poll taken by the Kiev-based *Rating Group* indicates that a little under two-thirds of respondents were unable to rate the effectiveness of the formula, while 23 percent opposed the idea and 18 percent supported it.[37] In 2017, Western survey results showed that 80 percent of people living in Ukraine and 73 percent of people living in Donets'k and Luhans'k supported the notion that pro-Russian controlled areas should remain a part of Ukraine. Around 60 percent also believed that the state of Ukraine was not doing enough regain the lost territories as a result of the *Minsk Agreements*.[38] A fairly recent poll (published June 4, 2020) taken by the *Kievan International Institute of Sociology (KMIS)* shows that, by the end of April 2020, 50.5 percent of Ukrainians believed that Ukraine would inevitably defeat Russia, with 10.5 percent supporting the opposite claim, and 37 percent consider that Ukraine will emerge victorious because "Russia is a weak backward state and Ukraine enjoys the support of the [Western] civilized world."[39]

Under the pressure of proactive ethnic organizations, Zelensky and his team once again adopted an unreasonably belligerent position. Dmytro Kuleba, Zelensky's minister of foreign affairs, promised that when Kyiv regains control over the whole of Donbas—including the DPR and LPR—the latters would be liquidated.[40] Zelensky himself has even said that Ukraine agreed to hold local elections in the Donbas region on the condition that they were done so under Ukrainian law and "*only after Russian forces are withdrawn and Ukraine regains control of the state border.*"[41] Thus, he has obviously overthrown the preplanned sequence of events for both sides as detailed in the *Minsk Agreements* and the *Steinmeier's Formula*, with Kuleba reiterating how Ukraine "will not go to the direct dialogue with occupation admin-istrations, neither [will we] agree with the [federalization invented by the Kremlin]."[42] And once again, deadlock and stalemate would prevail.

In the meantime, the "War in Donbas" continues. Between January and June 2020, the OSCE moni-toring mission noted and resolved several dozens of skirmishes, shoot-outs, artillery barrages, and minor battles held in the so-called "gray zone" that rests along the contact line: as a result, infrastructure is being destroyed and nearly 80 percent of the casualties are the civilian residents of Donbas alone.[43] During an interview, former Justice Minister Olena Lukash stated, "All the rights and freedoms are restricted: residents of the region [of Donbas] are being treated like sub humans ... and power does not do any-thing to stop military actions." While referencing information provided by the *United Nations Children's Emergency Fund (UNICEF)*, Lukash pointed out that "since the beginning of the year [2020] in Donbas [ten children were hurt, and nine schools were destroyed]." According to OSCE and UN reports, both Ukrainian troops and the *Security Service (SBU)* continue to participate in "torture, robberies, violence, uncontrolled kidnappings of people, and killings," all under Zelensky's oversight.[44]

Since February–early March 2021, the situation in the zone of the conflict in Donbas has drastically deteriorated. The OSCE Mission has fixed a sharp increase in quantity of skirmishes and shellings along the entire line of separation. In an outright transgression of point 2 of the *Minsk Agreements*, the Ukrainian side is rapidly deploying a massive military force very well-trained by the NATO military instructors' per-sonnel, with heavy artillery, tanks, and rocket launchers. The Ukrainian Army is deploying military rear hospitals and other logistic facilities, mine fields. At the front are operating diversant, reconnaissance, and sniper groups and other special divisions. Drones had been prepared too. The law about mobilizing reservists had been signed by President Zelensky. At that time everything pointed to the fact that the Ukrainian side was inspired by the successful blitzkrieg of the Azerbaijani army in September–November, 2021 in the Caucasus, and Ukraine's authorities are seemingly tempted to repeat the same blitzkrieg in Donbas. Commander of the Ukrainian Army Ruslan Khomchak recently said that his forces had been trained to carry out operations in the "urban environment." It is not difficult to guess that he means the Donets'k and Luhans'k urban conglomerations. Backed by strong political support of the United States, and urged by the "party of war" in his own circle amid deepening all-sided crisis, President Zelensky, who has already mopped up the abovementioned oppositional media resources and rival oligarchs, ultimately may give a fatal order to his armed forces. Special information groups had been dispatched to Donbas to cover possible developments from the pro-Ukrainian point in order to denounce "Russian provocations" that supposedly may follow.

However, knowing Zelensky, one may also suggest that this demonstrative activity is a mere tactical maneuver, testing Moscow's reaction, making it nervous, and then in due time throwing in on the table of negotiations a new reduction of *Minsk Agreements* in a plan gainful for the Ukrainian side concerning the previously discussed sequence of the fulfillment of its points, or to incorporate the United States as a full-time member of the new format of negotiations. If it is so, in any case, this is a very dangerous blackmail. Knowing also Putin, one may suggest with a great degree of confidence that Moscow will never agree to any amendments of the *Minsk Agreements* that have been adopted and verified by the signatures of all contractual sides. Anyway, if such a situation in the Security Zone persists, even without a direct order of Zelensky, he early on delegated authority to the military commanders and soldiers in the field to open fire on their own decisions, and they can pull the trigger for a full-fledged military confrontation with the militias of the self-proclaimed Donbas republics, whose forces on March 3 had also received from their de facto authorities the right to open fire in response to the Ukrainian shellings of their own positions and residential areas. And they are doing so in ever-increasing incidents. Thus, like in the previously discussed cases of the Caucasian ethnic conflicts, this overheated atmosphere may explode on its own at any moment, and neither authority in Kyiv, Moscow, or in the Western capitals could be able to get the genie back in the bottle.

As a matter of fact, Putin has already declared that Russia "will not abandon Donbass under any circumstances," and the speaker of his Foreign Ministry, Maria Zakharova, has recently called on the "Ukrainian side and them who support it" (meaning Western allies) "to chill out their heads" amid this dangerous escalation. All this suspiciously resembles the situation in the beginning of August 2008 in the area of Georgia–South Ossetia on the eve of the *Second hot stage* of their violent ethnic conflict, but with an even more perilous possible resultant confrontation between West and East. It looks like "Saakashvili's syndrome" is highly likely reemerging in Ukraine. In a worst-case scenario, possible clashes may not be limited to the boundaries of Donbas alone.

Early on, Pavlo Klimkin, a former minister of foreign affairs of the Poroshenko administration, had added a mite of "fact" all his own. On his Twitter account, he declared that the Crimean Peninsula cannot be returned unless it is fully retaken by force, as "nobody in Russia would give it up voluntarily."[45] Ukrainian authorities rather provocatively invite NATO air forces to use Crimean airspace otherwise closed by de facto Russian control. On the other side of this debacle, Nikolai Azarov, former prime minister of the Yanukovych regime, declared on his own Twitter account that the modern Ukraine, which came to be in 1922 as a USSR union republic, did not have any measure of lasting authority over Kharkiv, Kherson, Odessa, Donetsk, Luhansk, Crimea, or Lviv. Instead it simply "received all these territories while it was in the USSR for free."[46]

All the while, the DPR and LPR follow their own uncompromising line of confrontation too. The People's Council of the DPR adopted a law dictating that the Russian Ruble is the only acceptable currency, while the use of the Ukrainian *hryvna* was prohibited. Russian was quickly established as the official state language, with another law "About Prohibition of Rehabilitation and Heroization of Fascist Collaborators of the Time of the Great Patriotic War of 1941–1945" following soon after. According to this verbosely named law, members of the OUN-UPA and other "nationalistic formations" (which were already prohibited in Russia) are banned, with any and all glorification of them or their leaders in DPR and LPR mass media outlets being punishable by law. Soon after its introduction, it entered common circulation under the moniker of the "Anti-Banderites' law."[47]

This in and of itself is a plain indication of the reemergence of yet another provocative building block of the current Russo-Ukrainian ethnic conflict.

Commonly Shared History Building Block

For more information on the specific efforts of Ukrainian historians in constructing and exacerbating their nation's chosen historical traumas, please refer to chapter 6. One of the results of these efforts, known as the *Day of Memory of the Victims of Political Repressions*, was established in 2007 on the order of Ukraine's third president, Viktor Yushchenko. Held annually on the third Sunday of May, the acting president is to take and place flowers at the *National Historical Memorial Complex* in the Bykovnyanskii Forest, known as *Bykovnyans'kie mohyly*, which serves as the resting place of the victims of the NKVD prison executions in 1938. During one of his own visits to the memorial, President Poroshenko once stated: "The tragedy of communist terror must be a teaching lesson for the future; it must be a reliable safeguard from the attempts to reanimate the 'Russian World' on our Ukrainian land."[48] Since 2007, all historical events—be they from the Middle Ages, World War II, or the Postwar Period—have been given completely and mutually exclusive interpretations in official state discourse, the history classes taught in schools and universities, distributed textbooks, and all forms of mass media in Ukraine and Russia. As such, Ukrainian interpretations of key historical events during their long-standing relationship with Russia—during the Imperial, Soviet, and post-Soviet periods—are wrought with vivid anti-Russian (if not explicitly Russophobic) stamps and stigmas, as the above-cited example demonstrates. Simultaneously, Ukrainian historians tend to glorify the history of the Ukrainian people as ancient founders of human civilization and distance their historical narrative from the history of Russian people as far as possible, bringing the history of Ukrainians as close as possible to the history of Western peoples. For instance, the authors of a recently published textbook on eighth-grade geography state that the ancestors of numerous peoples originated from Halychyna: "The geographical names of western and southern countries and peoples, such as Galatia, Galileans, France (Gaul), Galicia in Spain or Portu-Gallia (Portugal), point to the fact that the ancestors of the contemporary French, Spanish, Portuguese, Jews, and Turks [may have come] to the places of their dwelling from the Ukrainian Halychyna." Additionally, authors will provide a table of words that sound the same between the Ukrainian, Belarusian, Polish, Slovak, and Czech languages but are drastically different in Russian.[49]

But this endeavor is not mutually exclusive. Even Putin is guilty of utilizing this same tactic, engineering the "ancientization" of Russian history in a way similar to how Tsarina Catherine the Great honored the Baptism of the Rus' when she named two newly founded cities in Crimea:

> With this name we are also renewing those most famous designations that Russian history conserves from the depth of antiquity, that our people is of one stock and is a direct off-shoot of the ancient Slavs, and that Kherson was the source of Christianity for Russia, where after Prince Vladimir took baptism, the light of the divine faith and true religion shone and became established in Russia.[50]

Following the Crimean Anschluss, Putin, following in the logic of the above-cited speech, referred to the monuments of Sevastopol, which commemorate the heroes of Russia and the Soviet Union, as well as the historical site of the Baptism of the Rus' thusly: "Each one of these places are dear to our hearts, symbolizing Russian military glory and outstanding valor." He cursed the mere idea of abandoning the site of one of the most important symbols of Russian history, welcoming those living in the city back into their "native harbor"—Mother Russia.[51] In this regard, I fully agree with my student McBarrett Good, who noticed that "what Putin's speech resembles is a prime example of using history to prove one's point, remembering the past in a way that enables the future."[52]

Under the leadership of Volodymyr Viatrovych (who was succeeded by Anton Dobrovych on December 4, 2019), the previously mentioned *Ukrainian Institute of National Remembrance* (founded in 2006) actively participates in the "Decommunization of Ukraine." In May 2015, then President Poroshenko signed four laws that all concerned decommunization in Ukraine, with Vyatrovych involved in drafting two of them. According to these acts, everyone who refused to recognize the new heroes and/or hindered the decommunization efforts would be arrested and sentenced for criminal charges. Article 6 of one law, *On the Legal Status and Honoring of Fighters for Ukraine's Independence in the Twentieth Century*, effectively criminalizes the denial of the role of recognized individuals/groups in the struggle, including, for example, the *Ukrainian Insurgent Army (UPA)*. As such, this act makes it unlawful to express a critical view of Stepan Bandera, Roman Shukhevych, and others like them. On the other hand, the *Institute of National Remembrance* defined 254 historic persons of Russian-Soviet descent whose memory is to be dashed out from Ukraine's history. Monuments memorializing them erected during the Soviet period should be (and actively are) demolished (stunningly similar processes are unleashing before our eyes in America and Europe today), while places and streets bearing their names are to be renamed after Ukrainian heroes like Bandera. In the face of these changes, author Halya Coynash dares to compare such methods, which are a veritable war on history, with those practiced by the totalitarian Communist regime of the Soviet Union that the Ukrainians so despise.[53]

Oleksiy Honcharenko—an MP from Poroshenko's *European Solidarity Party*—reasons that Ukraine has no right "to be neutral in Putin's war with history." In fact, he precisely expressed the intended goal of the Ukrainian "counteroffensive": "We have to place Ukrainian aspects [of history] in the broader international context, in order to emphasize the central role of [our] country in European history, beginning with the time of the Kyivan Rus' and ending with the Ukrainian experience in the epicenter of totalitarianism of the twentieth century. The crisis because of the corona virus may be a breaking point which will manifest the dawn of the new era. After Centuries in the shadows, Ukraine will have a chance to take over the initiative and give a repulse to the suppressing Russo-centric interpretations ... In order to provide the future of the country, Ukraine [should first] win the battle for the past."[54]

Common Biological Origin Building Block

By 2007, the Ukrainian intellectuals had already fully developed their so-called "early medieval conception of the origin of Ukrainian people" from the Antes, Dulebs, and Sklavini tribes (fifth through eighth centuries), who then later transformed into the "proto-Ukrainian tribes of [the ancient] chronicles: the Volyniani, Drevlyani, Polyani, White Croats, Ulichi, Tivertsi of North-Western Ukraine. The latter were the genetic foundation of the Southern Rus'." Later on, between the tenth and thirteenth centuries, the proto-Ukrainian imperial Kyivan Rus' (in the most primordial meaning of the designation) colonized some of the Baltic and Finnish tribes living in the forest steppes of Eastern Europe. After these groups were sufficiently "Russified," they would go on to become the ancestors of the "young Balto-Rus' (Belarusians and [Pskov-Novgorod] people) and the Finno-Batlto-Rus' (Russian) people" respectively. This conceptual shared origin between the Ukrainians and Russians was intrinsically designed to show that they are *biologically/genetically* completely different peoples, with the first of them being the older and politically *superior* among them—a classic ethnocentric pattern (see the definition of *ethnocentric nationalism* in chapter 6). Alongside this "biological" evidence, these groups also differ in style, clothing, food, music, and anthropology, among other things. Overall, this theory states that "Belarusians, [Pskov-Novgorod] people, and Russians—are the product of synthesis of proto-Ukrainians of [the] Southern Rus' and colonized the Baltic and Finnish tribes of the forest zone of Eastern Europe."[55] As stated above, this theory was then augmented by anothers—which was fully endorsed by the Ukrainian Ministry of Education for teaching—that discusses the direct origin of Ukrainians from the Tripoli (Tripilje) culture of the fourth to third millennium BC.[56]

In its most radical (ethnocentric) form, this concept serves only to categorize the Ukrainian population into groups of "pure" and "not pure"—i.e., "genetic trash"—people. On November 21, 2016, during the "Freedom of Speech" broadcast on the ICTV channel, Yevhen Nishuk, the then Ukrainian minister of culture, stated that: "In the East of Ukraine there is no genetics, because the cities were populated at the behest of Soviet power" by Russians. Throughout this travail, Nishuk repeatedly espoused the ideas presented in the above-cited eighth-grade textbook, which was recommended by then Minister of Education Lilia Grinevich for educational application. In this textbook, one may read that "Slavic-speaking Russians have Ugro-Finnish origin, and [though Belarusians and Poles are closest to Ukrainians,] they also have different genetic origins: Poles—Slavic and Belarusians—Baltic." In this way, Ukrainians are the Slavianized Germans and are, therefore, the oldest nation in the world.[57]

Meanwhile, the contemporary Russian concepts still reflect on the Imperial/Soviet paradigm regarding the common biological origin of Russians, Ukrainians, and Belarusians, with them all stemming from the same abovementioned Eastern Slavic/Rus' tribes. However, they severely criticize the Ukrainian concepts, labeling them as renewed Nazi theories that have no basis in actual science—specifically genetic studies.[58]

Religious Building Block

- 2019: Poroshenko carried out his second presidential campaign, sporting the motto: *Mova, Armya, Vira ("Language, Army, and Faith")*. This particular slogan symbolized his achievements during his first term and expressed his hope to reestablish the superior status of the Ukrainian language (especially over the Russian language—see the linguistic laws discussed above), ultimately strengthened by the Ukrainian Army, which "stopped and defeated Russian aggression," and the hopes of long-desired independence of the Ukrainian Orthodox Church from the Moscow Patriarchate.

In January 2019, following Poroshenko's 2016 request, Bartholomew I—the ecumenical patriarch of Constantinople—signed the *tomos of autocephaly*, which officially recognized and established the *Orthodox Church of Ukraine* and granted it *self-governorship*.[59]

Kyiv obviously took this as a victory, since it had continuously claimed that "Moscow-backed churches in Ukraine are a Kremlin tool to spread propaganda and support fighters in the east." Needless to say, several churches with confirmed ties to the Moscow Patriarchate strongly denied these claims. Prior to this, even President Putin warned that "a heavy dispute, if not bloodshed" would take place if there were any attempts to reassign ownership of church property. In short, the Russian Orthodox Church, which has controlled the Ukrainian parishes since 1686, could lose nearly a fifth out of its 150 million Orthodox followers.[60]

In response, the Moscow Patriarchate interrupted communion relations with the Constantinople Patriarchate; this action, in and of itself, signaled the beginning of a rift in Orthodox Christianity.

- January 30, 2019: President Poroshenko signed a new law, according to which state authorities would recognize the right of religious communities to alter the subordination of their religious center, whether that be to stay away from the Moscow Patriarchate or to join the newly established jurisdiction of the Orthodox Church of Ukraine. However, those who wished to stay under the Russian Orthodoxy quickly found themselves under pressure from both ethnocentric nationalist organizations and the authorities themselves. As such, the *Security Service of Ukraine (SBU)* reportedly carried out several raids across the country specifically targeting churches following the Moscow Patriarchate, intimidating/interrogating priests and accusing them of being agents for the Russian government, with supposedly even metropolitan Pavel being subjected to this treatment.[61]

Thus, a strictly religious matter soon turned into an entirely new building block of violent ethnic conflict, thereby enhancing the process of ethnicization within the political sphere and coalescing with the other building blocks to add more fuel to an already blazing *hot stage*. Unsurprisingly, this makes even the mere notion of the *peaceful return* of lands taken in the east and Crimea very problematic.

Mild and middle-ground forms of ethnic cleansing: Regarding the *common biological origin building block*—I (1, 2, 3, 4); regarding the *use/abuse of language*—II (1, 2, 3,); regarding *religious expression*—III (1, 2, 3); regarding the *commonly shared history building block*—IV (1, 2, 4, 5, 6); *state organizations practiced*—V (1, 2, 3); and *economic measures*—VI (1, 4).

Extreme forms of ethnic cleansing: Regarding the *common biological origin building block*—I (1, 2); regarding the *use/abuse of language*—II (1, 2, 3, 4); regarding *religious expression*—III (4, 5, 7); regarding the *commonly shared history building block*—IV (1, 2, 3); regarding the *nationality building block*—V (elements of 1, 2, 4, 5, 6); *state organizations practiced*—VI (1, 2, 3, 4, 5, 6, with elements of 7, 9, 10); and *economic measures*—VII (4).

Casualties: An estimated 13,000–13,200 were killed, with 29,000–31,000 wounded. As it now currently stands, the Ukrainian side has 4,431 killed, 70 declared missing, and 9,500–10,500 wounded (predominantly military personnel); the Pro-Russian/Russian side has 5,665 killed and 12,500–13,500 wounded (predominantly civilian residents of the Donbas region—around 3,350—with an additional 312 dying between 2016 and 2020).Internally displaced Ukrainians: 1,414,708 people, with around 925,500 of them fleeing abroad.[62]

Peace talks and fulfillment of the Minsk Agreements. Mostly a stalemate encircled by political deadlock, except for the exchange of several detained persons and a limited retraction of heavy weaponry by both sides (most recently violated again) (see points 2 and 6 of Minsk II).

- **Current Status of the Conflict:** *Hot stage*; a violent ethnic conflict with all five building blocks, with second-level *intrastate* and *interstate* conflict that holds the potential to transition into the third level: direct confrontation between East and West—Russia and NATO.

- **Principal building blocks of the Russo-Ukrainian violent ethnic conflict ranked by overall importance:**
  - **Primary Building Blocks**
    - 1.1.1. Language
    - 1.1.2. Nationality
    - 1.1.3. Commonly shared history aggravated by acute, unresolved chosen traumas
  - **Subsidiary Building Blocks**
    - 1.1.4. Religious expression
    - 1.1.5. Common biological origin

Conclusion to Chapters 8–9

The content of chapters 8 through 9 effectively demonstrates that all of these violent ethnic conflicts have passed through the same recurrent stages of the cycle: as in, all of them have followed cyclical patterns. Additionally, their gradual evolutions are also subjected to the same repeatable regularities. This was no better illustrated than during the process in which their *stirring-up stage* gradually radicalized certain building blocks of ethnicity at the hands of the ethno-political elites of the super-ordinate/dominating/titular ethnic nations, who activated their ethnocentric/mono-centric state-building projects and affected both the principal and secondary constituents of subordinate ethnic groups/ethnic nations. This then ignited reciprocal ethnocentric mobilization in the form of defensive secessionist/irredentist plans and actions. The sociopolitical and economic life of both sides of these conflicts became increasingly absorbed and consumed by ethnic paradigms. Co-ethnics living in outside nations began interfering on behalf of their "brothers and sisters," providing different types of aid that all added momentum to the regressive development of the conflict as a whole and further encouraged the secessionist/irredentist drives of the corresponding minorities—sometimes to the extent of turning an *intrastate* conflict into an *interstate* conflict (as seen in the individual timelines). In response, the titular ethnic nations mobilized all potential options to constrain these drives, in many cases utilizing mild *and* middle-ground forms of ethnic cleansing, which only evoked additional military resistance. This gradual escalation would invariably result in the application of more extreme forms of ethnic cleansing, which reflect the particular grievances behind each particular instance and initiated the more uncompromising *hot stage* of these conflicts. The stages were then set in motion by the triggering events. These timelines show the ranking importance of particular building blocks in each conflict, in which they reflect the frequency of complaints and public discussions of either side of the conflict, as well as the general chronology of their stages. It is crucial for international organizations/kin states to recognize that, despite their initial feelings, they should not give unilateral support to "their" side and instead find ways to stall further regressive development of these conflicts before it is too late.

As listed in the timelines, the current status of these conflicts reveals that only six have passed through all the associated stages. Some were resolved through the victory of one side and the establishment of a consociational institutionalized regime (Russian-Chechen conflict). Others still remain planted in the Smoldering or Frozen Stages, effectively placing them at an impasse rather than a peaceful resolution (Russo-Moldavian, Georgian–South Ossetian, Georgian-Abkhazian, North Ossetian–Ingushian, and Armenian-Azerbaijani conflicts). Meanwhile, the Russo-Ukrainian conflict is still well within its *hot stage*, which is accompanied by extreme forms of ethnic cleansing in regard to all five building blocks that constitute ethnicity. And while the Minsk Agreements currently serve as the "road map" for its eventual resolution, the current situation—propagated by both internal and external forces—effectively prevents its realization. As such, outside forces have and continue to play a critical role in all of these violent ethnic conflicts, with a particular importance being seen in the Russo-Ukrainian clash. This factor directly relates to the final aspect of my theoretical model: the expression of a "security dilemma," which, for the purpose of understanding ethnic conflict, was elegantly described by Barry Posen, Raymond Taras, and Rajat Ganguly.

Notes

1   Omeljan Pritsak, "Kiev and all of Rus': The Fate of a Sacred Idea," *Harvard Ukraine Studies* 10, no. 3/4 (December 1986): 275–91.

2   Dominique Arel, *Language and the Politics of Ethnicity: The Case of Ukraine*, Ph.D. Dissertation (University of Illinois at Urbana-Champaign. Ann Arbor, MI: University Microfilms International, 1993), III, 4–8, 57–58; Laada Bilaniuk, *Contested Tongues*: *Language Politics and Cultural Correction in Ukraine* (Ithaca, NY: Cornell University Press, 2005), 14.

3   Bilaniuk, *Contested Tongues*, 15; Leonid Kuchma, *Ukraïna-Ne Rossya* (Moscow: Vremya, 2003).

4   Dominique Arel, "Double Talk: Why Ukrainians Fight over Language," *Foreign Affairs*, March 19, 2014, http://www.foriegnaffairs.com/articles/141042/dominique-arel/double-talk.

5   Fred Kaplan, "Moscow Homecoming Greeted by 5,000, Solzhenitsyn Ends Trip with Renewed Attack," *Boston Globe*, July 22, 1994, 2; Alexandr Isaevich Solzhenitsyn, *Kak nam obustroit' Rossiiu? Posilnye soobrazheniïa* (Paris: YMCA Press, 1990); Alexandr Isaevich Solzhenitsyn, *Rebuilding Russia: Reflections and Tentative Proposals*. Translated and annotated by Alexis Klimoff (New York: Farrar, Straus and Giroux, 1991).

6   Cited in Bilaniuk, *Contested Tongues*, 9.

7   Ya Hoian, *Introduction to M. Hrushevskyi, Pro Ridnu Movu i Ukrainsku Shkolu* (Kiev: Veselka, 1991); V. Ivanyshyn and Ya. Radevych-Vynnytskyi, *Mova i Natsiia* (Drohobych: Lvivska Oblasna Orhanizatsiia Tovaristva Liubyteliv Knyhy, 1990); Svatoslav Karavans'kyi, *Secrety Ukraïnskoi Movy* (Kiev: Kobza, 1994); See also Svatoslav Karavans'kyi, "Do pytannia pro nepereladnist," *Ukraïnska Mova ta Literatura* 2, no. 162 (2000): 8; Olexandra Serbenska, ed., *Preface to Anty-Surzhyk* (Lviv, Ukraine: Vydavnytstvo Svit, 1994); Bilaniuk, *Contested Tongues*, 8–9.

8   Bilaniuk, *Contested Tongues*, 9.

9   Bilaniuk, *Contested Tongues*, 19.

10 "Editorial Article," *Krymskaia Pravda*, July 23, 1994, 1; *Literaturna Ukraïna*, July 21, 1994, 1.

11 "Editopial Article," *Krymskaia Pravda*, July 23, 1994, 1.

12 Bilaniuk, *Contested Tongues*, 20.

13 For examples, see Vitalii Radchuk, "Implementatsiia chy vprovodzhennia?" *Shliakh Peremohy* 32 (2015): 10; Vitalii Radchuk, "Surzhyk jak nedopereklad," *Ukraïnska Mova ta Literatura* 11, no. 171 (2002):11–12; Vitalii Radchuk, "Mova v Ukraïni: stan, funktsii, perspektyvy," *Dyvoslava* 2, no, 540 (2002):2–5.

14 Bilaniuk, *Contested Tongues*, 40.

15 Bilaniuk, *Contested Tongues*, 125–31.

16 Bilaniuk, *Contested Tongues*, 179.

17 Helen Fowkes, "Ukraine Drives to Keep Russians off Busses," *BBC News Online*, June 18, 2004, http;// news.bbc.co.uk/go/pr/fr/./2/hi/europe/3783353.stm, cited in Bilaniuk, *Contested Tongues*, 178–79.

18 Jan Maksymiuk, "The End of Russian-Language Broadcasting in Ukraine?" *RFE/RL Analytical Reports* 4, no. 8 (April 22, 2004).

19 Gwendolyn Sasse, "The 'New' Ukraine," in *Ethnicity and Territory in the Former Soviet Union: Regions in Conflict*, ed. James Hughes and Gwendolyn Sasse (London: Frank Cass, 2002), 80.

20 Sasse, "The 'New' Ukraine," 88–89.

21 Sasse, "The 'New' Ukraine," 85.

22 SerhyYekelchyk, *The Conflict in Ukraine: What Everyone Needs to Know* (Oxford: Oxford University Press, 2015), 125.

23 Regarding the exact details of the deal, as well as the subsequent Russian-Ukrainian relations from a pro-Ukrainian perspective, see Yekelchyk, *Conflict in Ukraine*, 126ff.

24 Volodymyr Vasylenko, "On Assurances without Guarantees in a 'Shelved Document,'" *Den'*, December 15, 2009, day.kyiv,ua/en/article/close/assurances-without-guarantees-shelved-document.

25 United Nations, CD/1285, December 11, 1994, undocs.org, emphasis added.

26 "Snipers at Maidan: The Untold Ukraine Story," video (London: BBC Newsnight, 2015), http://www.youtube.com/watch?v=mJhJ6hksOJg.

27 Both polls are cited in Yekelchyk, *Conflict in Ukraine*, 128, 141.

28 Yekelchyk, *Conflict in Ukraine*, 109.

29 Yekelchyk, *Conflict in Ukraine*, 111.

30 Richard Sakwa, *Frontline Ukraine: Crisis in the Borderlands* (London: I.B. Tauris, 2015), 87.

31 Yekelchyk, *Conflict in Ukraine*, 142.

32 See Ivan D. Loshkariov and Andrey A.Sushentsov, "Radicalization of Russians in Ukraine: From 'Accidental' Diaspora to Rebel Movement," *Southeast European and Black Sea Studies* 16, no.1 (2016): 73.

33 "Russia's Putin Says Supports Future Normandy Format Talks on Ukraine," *Thomson Reuters Foundation*, September 5, 2016, news.trust.org/item/20160905143052-wd0nm.

34 "Minsk Agreement on Ukraine Crisis: Text in Full," *The Daily Telegraph*, February 12, 2015, telegraph.co.uk/news/worldnews/Europe/ukraine/11408266/minsk-agreement-on-Ukraine-crisis-text-in-full.html.

35 Peter Leonard, "Civilians Flee East Ukraine Town as Fighting Intensifies," *Associated Press*, January 31, 2015.

36 Christopher Miller, "Explainer: What Is the Steinmeier Formula—and Did Zelensky Just Capitulate to Moscow?" *Radio Free Europe/Radio Liberty*, October 2, 2019, rferl.org/a/what-is-the-steinmeier-formula-and-did-zelensky-just-capitulate-to-moscow-/30195593.html.

37 Miller, "What Is The Steinmeier Formula."

38 "Ukraine Poll: Majority Wants Donbas to Remain in Ukraine," *International Republican Institute*, June 7, 2017, iri.org/resource/ukriane-poll-majority-want-donbas-remain-ukraine.

39 "Pochemu ukraintsy schitaiyut, chto pobezhdaiyut Rossiiu?" *Vzglyad*, June 8, 2020, yandex.ru/turbo/s/vz.ru/world/2020/6/8/1043680.html?promo=navbar8cutm_referrer=https%3A%2F%2Fzen.yandex.com.

40 "Editorial Article," *Gazeta.ru*, May 27, 2020, gazeta.ru/politics/2020/05/27_a_13098421.shtml?utm_source=smi2&utm_medium=exchange&es=smi2.

41 Miller, "What Is the Steinmeier Formula," see note 36.

42 "Kiev vyzyvaet Moskvu na sebja," *Kommersant* 99 (May 6, 2020): 3, kommersant.ru/doc/4366959?utm_source=smi2_agr.

43 For a relatively accurate overview of the conflict at large, see "Timeline of the War in Donbass (2020)," *Wikipedia*, retrieved on [April 5, 2020,] en.wikipedia.org/wiki/Timeline_of_the_War_in_Donbass_(2020).

44 "Eks-minister: Ukraina zayavila o nevozmozhnosti vozvrasheniia Donbassa," *Izvestia*, June 8, 2020, iz.ru/1020969/2020-06-08/eks-minister-ukrainy-zayavila-o-nevozmozhnost-vozvrasheniia-donbassa.

45 "Na Ukraine nazvali yedinstvennyi sposob vernut' Krym," *Lenta.ru*, June 20, 2020, leuta.ru/news/2020/06/10/klimkin/?utm_source=smi2&utm_medium=exchange7es=smi2.

46 Natalia Sergievskaya and Polina Poletaeva, "Eks-premier Ukrainy Azarov napomnil o eiye territoriyakh do vstupleniia v SSSR," *RT*, May 31, 2020, Russian.rt.com/ussr/article/751060-ukraina-territorii-nikolai-azarov?utm_source=smi2.

47 "V DNR zapretili 'geroizatsiyu banderovtsev," *Rosbalt*, May 26, 2020, rosbalt.ru/world/2020/05/26/1845527.html?utm_source=smi2.

48 "V Kyive vzyvayut k zhertvam terrora: Rossiiu obviniayut v politike stalinskogo rezhima," *Kommersant*, May 17, 2020, kommersant.ru/doc/4347727?utm_source=smi2_agr.

49 Petro O. Maslyak and Svetlana L. Kapyrulyna, *Pidruchnyk. Geografia 8 klas* (Kam'yanec-Podils'kii, Ukraine: Aksioma, 2016), cited in "The Ancestors of Ukraine Could Once Have Left Ukraine—Geography Textbook," *Regnum IA*, May 16, 2020, regnum.ru/news/society/2951814.html. This conceptual approach characterizes the majority of most recently published textbooks on history for the seventh form in Ukrainian schools. See N. M. Sorochin'ska, O. O. Gissem, *Vsesvitnya istoriia. Pidruchnyk dlya 7 klassu zakladiv zagal'noi serednjoi osvity* (Ternopil', Ukraine: Navchalna kniha—Bohdan, 2020), 176 s. Similar ideas propagate six other textbooks of other authors published in Kyiv, Khr'kiv, and other cities.

50 Cited in Andrei Zorin, "Eden in Taurus: The 'Crimean Myth' in Russian Culture of the 1870s–'90s," in *By Fables Alone* (Brighton, MA: Academic Studies Press, 2014), 102.

51 Vladimir Putin, "Address by the President of the Russian Federation," *President of Russia website*, March 18, 2014, http://eng.kremlin.ru/news/6889.

52 McBarrett S. Good, *How to Alienate a Culture: Soviet and Imperial Russia's Role in the Current Russo-Ukrainian Conflict*. Senior Honors Thesis (Appalachian State University, 2019), 29.

53 Halya Coynash, "'Decommunization' in Ukraine Carried Out Using Communist Methods," Kharkiv Human Rights Protection Group, September 6, 2016, khpg.org/en/index.php?id=1462928536; One may find a slew of additional details on this "war" between "histories" in Anna Wylegała and Małgorzata Głowacka-Grajper, eds., *Burden of the Past: History, Memory, and Identity in Contemporary Ukraine* (Bloomington: Indiana University Press, 2020). Ironically enough, we see similar "wars" taking place regarding historical monuments in America today: while the particular ideological guises are different, the methods are the same.

54 Oleksiy Goncharenko, "Ukraine Cannot Be Neutral in Putin's War with History," *Atlantic Council*, April 26, 2020, inosmi.ru/politics/20200426/247327937.html.

55 These statements were collected and cited in Good, *How to Alienate a Culture*, 29–30.

56 Roman Lyah and Nadiya Temirova, *Istoria Ukraïni. Pidruchnyk dlya 7-go klasu* (Kyiv: "Geneza," 2005), 6.

57 Maslyak and Kapyrulyna, *Piqruchnyk. Geografia, 8 klas*, 246.

58 See the university textbook by Aleksandr G. Kuzmin, *Istoria Rossii s drevneishih vremen do 1618 goda. Kniga pervaiya* (Moscow: Gumanitarnyi izdatel'skii tsentr VLADOS, 2004), glava II. After comparing the DNK haplo groups of Russians, Ukrainians, and Belarusians, Professor Anatoly Kolesov, the Russian specialist in DNK genealogy, came to the conclusion that all three historically "constituted one people." See Kolesov's interview given to Julia Alekhina, "Raskryta taina proiskhozhdeniya russkogo naroda," *Komsomolskaya Pravda*, December 16, 2019, kp.ru/daily/27068/4138133/?utm_referrer=https%3A%2F%2Fzen.yandex.com.

59 "Patriarchal and Synod Tomos for the Bestowal of the Ecclesiastical Status of Autocephaly to the Orthodox Church in Ukraine," *Ecumenical Patriarchate*, patriarchate.org/-/patriarchikos-kai-syno-dikos-tomos-choregeseos-autokephalou-ekklesiastikou-kathestotos-eis-ten-en-oukraniai-ortho-doxon-ekklesian.

60 Harriet Sherwood, "Ukraine: New Orthodox Church Gains Independence from Moscow," *The Guardian*, January 5, 2019.

61 "Ukraine Raids Orthodox Churches with Russian Ties," *France 24*, March 3, 2018, france24.com/en/20181203-ukraine-raids-orthodox-churches-russian-ties-putin-poroshenko-azov-crimea.

62 "Office of the United Nations High Commissioner for Human Rights Report on the Human Rights Situation in Ukraine 16 November 2019 to 15 February 2020," Office of the United Nations High Commissioner for Human Rights, March 12, 2020, 29thReportUkraine_EN.pdf. More updated data are cited in "Casualties of the Russo-Ukrainian War, https://en.wikipedia.org/wiki/Casualties_of_the_Russo-Ukrainian_War.

Figure Credits

■ CHAPTER TEN

Outside Exacerbating Factors

Conflict Propaganda, the Eurasian Debate in Russia, and Its

Impact on Current Russian Policy toward Ukraine and the West

"At [the] bottom of [the] Kremlin's neurotic view of world affairs is [the] traditional and *instinctive Russian sense of insecurity* [italics added] … This thesis provides justification for that increase of the military and police power of the Russian state … Basically, this is only the steady advance of uneasy Russian nationalism, a centuries-old movement in which conception of offence and defense are inextricably confused."

—George Kennan

The Provocative Role of Mass Media

I have already dealt with the enticing and deliberate misrepresentation of the highly complex violent ethnic conflicts that took place in the Caucasus and former Yugoslavia as seen in mass media, which brings to mind a "prophecy" from the last Caucasian Chechen "Robin Hood"—the *abreck* (an outlaw folk hero seeking revenge against both the tsarist and Soviet administrations) Khasukha Magomadov. In the 1930s, Magomadov claimed that Communism would collapse by the end of the twentieth century, with *Shaitan* (*Satan*) sending his last "reserve"—a new, blistery people—who "*will mix lie and truth*. They will let loose their charms in listeners in order to set them [into] killing one another through [the] deliberate distortion of facts and false accusations."[1]

With this in mind, I wish to voice my agreement with historian Anatol Lieven, who composed the most carefully argued account of the Chechen War, when he said:

Misrepresentation has been equally general, and has been engaged in by all parties to the conflict and by the Western [and, I may add, the Russian] media and commentators. Misrepresentations by the participants [and by the Russians] has of course been deliberate, and for propagandist purposes. In the West, the reason has been rather a tendency to see the conflict through wider prisms which may or may not be appropriate to the local participants of the conflict themselves.[2]

The representation of the previously discussed events of the Russo-Ukrainian conflict, as well as those of the other ethnic conflicts, vividly confirms this observation as fact. Oliver Boyd-Barret aptly outlined several principles of Western propaganda that are more than applicable to the particular topics of ethnic conflicts. Among them are:

(1) *An Attack of an Army against Its Own People*—As shown in the previous chapter's timelines, when some violent ethnic conflicts reached the intrastate phase, this phenomenon became a realistic occurrence, which I qualified as an extreme form of ethnic cleansing. Boyd-Barret refers to such and similar cases as occurring when "a regime is favored by the West" and it "deploys its army against its own people [rebels], as happened when the authorities in Kiev [Kyiv] attacked and ravaged the separatist movements in Donbass [Donbas], then that is perfectly excusable and is also a pretext for western aid to the regime against regime opponents."[3]

(2) *Context*—If Western governments target a specific country—like post-Maidan Ukraine, for instance—in order to co-opt them into NATO, then the majority of Western media would choose not to criticize (or even mention) any "long-standing weaknesses" or the "non-democratic instincts of their oligarch classes ... Nor need they consider as relevant to Western motivations the loot for Western corporations that are consequent on the IMF and other Western loans."[4]

(3) *Democracy*—A strong executive (almost authoritarian) branch that exists within an asymmetric consociational democratic institution—which prevents the regressive dynamics of ethnic conflicts from returning and creates social conditions for *benign, civic*, and *liberal*-type nationalism—usually does not garner support in Western media. However, an oligarchic regime that supports a system of wild frontier crony capitalism—which reproduces the conditions best suited for *ethnocentric integral*–type nationalism (in its practical realization toward ethnic minorities and the transgression of their basic human rights)—as seen in Ukraine, tends to "deserve" any and all appraisals/support, as they hold a staunchly pro-Western orientation and "exhibit the trappings of modern democracy such as regular elections, diversity of choice, etc."[5]

(4) *Elections*—Elections in those countries approved by Western interests are always treated as legitimate, even if they are held in "the most unpromising of circumstances." The opposite is true in places like Russia and/or Crimea, where nearly every election is severely criticized or painted as a sham.

(5) *Evidence*—As in the case of the complicated characteristics of the Ukrainian ethnic conflict, any and all evidence of blatant *intrastate* interference at the hands of Western nations is mostly ignored and/or hidden on the fringes, while any evidence of Russian "aggression" or direct military involvement, be it unsubstantiated or otherwise, always makes the front pages. "The absence of evidence is never an insurmountable problem for Western propaganda: it can be construed as the devilish cunning of the enemy's capacity for subterfuge."[6]

(6) *"Fascism"* (Boyd-Barret's terminology; I myself refer to it as *ethnocentric nationalism*)—ethnocentric forces, usually backed by corrupt oligarchs (such as Mr. Ihor Kolomoyskyi), are attested as being "patriots," with the entirety of the separatist movement—which can be composed of multiple and sometimes distinctly diverse parts—being presented as "terrorists" under the auspices of the Russian command structure.

(7) *Humanitarian Support*—Regardless of circumstances, any aid sent by Russia to the Donbas region is routinely represented as a form of "military action in humanitarian disguise."[7]

(8) *Invasion*—The genuine desires of the majority of Crimea's population to enter Russian protection, fueled by the threats levied against their linguistic rights by the Kyivan authorities, were mostly ignored in Western media. Instead, this concern was substituted for an intensive and still pending condemnation of

the outright and unprovoked aggression of a gambler—President Putin—who took advantage of a temporary weakness in the otherwise legitimate Ukrainian government in order to invade and capture Crimea.

(9) *Protests*—If any protestors arise in opposition of a regime allied with Western powers, both them and their concerns are usually "disavowed" by Western media at large (as displayed by Western attitudes toward protesters in Odessa in May 2015).[8]

(10) *Secession*—During its own secessionist struggle, "Kosovo's assertion of independence from Serbia" was all but welcomed. But "because the leadership of Crimea and [the] Donbass regions did not enjoy Western favor, their respective bids for secession was condemned," even if—with the application of an unbiased approach/evaluation of either case—one may find a great deal of evidence corresponding to the above-cited "moral criteria justifying secession" in the latter case. [9]

(11) *Suffering*—The overall suffering of the Donbas/Donbass population, as well as the murder of activists opposing Kyiv's regime, has not been mentioned in the West "because such people have brought their suffering upon themselves through [an] unwise choice of leaders or alliance." On the other hand, any killings or assassinations targeting those in opposition to Putin's/Moscow's regime, like Boris Nemtsov, or the recent poisoning of Alexei Navalny, are subject to nothing less than righteous condemnation and speculation carried on the forefront of Western media outlets.[10]

Additionally, one may demonstrate the diametrically opposite and contrary coverage of several key events by the media of each side, their kin diasporas, and their political allies.

Some Examples of the Assessments of the Current Ukrainian Crisis's Major Events

Russian Media	Ukrainian/Western Media
Overall, this situation is shown as a war between Ukrainian authorities and its citizens/a civil war with Western intervention on the side of the Ukrainian government.	Generally, the conflict is considered a war between Russia and Ukraine, spurred on by the former's aggression and its illegitimate occupation of both Crimea and particular sections of the Donbas region.
The US government has helped to carry out a coup—overthrowing a legitimately elected (and Russia-friendly) Ukrainian administration.	Russia's leaders "fear a stable, prosperous, and Western-leading democracy on their doorstep." Because of this, "Russia's leaders will keep destabilizing Ukraine to prevent such a democracy until stopped by Western force or sanctions."[14]
A more radical assessment produced by Sergei Kurginyan depicts the conflict as a "War of the West together with Nazi Ukraine against Russia."[11]	
The image of an external enemy—Russia—was created in order to fortify a Western alliance (NATO in particular) under the leadership of the United States.	"The Kremlin leader's ambitions stretch beyond Ukraine and ... he [Putin] strives to reassert a Russian sphere of influence in Eastern Europe ... [The West] should be contemplating a range of responses—including extending sanctions on Moscow and providing defensive military assistance to Kiev—in anticipation of Mr. Putin's next act of aggression."[15]
Sergei Shoigu, the Russian minister of defense, openly stated: "The utmost danger for Russia's military security comes from the Western strategic direction."[12] In this sense, Russia has legitimate security interests in stopping a hostile military alliance [NATO] from reaching its doorstep.	
Causal Factor of the Conflict: The 2013 financial crisis in Ukraine saw the Kyivan authorities turn to Moscow for help, which then spiraled out of control.	"NATO—an institution in crisis—did not threaten Russia, and the Kremlin, with its many spies in Brussels, knew it ..."[16]

The US State Department and American Embassy in Kiev [Kyiv] had already been planning both a coup d'état and the composition of a new pro-West government, ultimately using the protests against Yanukovych's loan from Russia as the impetus to escalate the situation.

The active snipers who fired on the Maidan protests were agents and provocateurs sent in by those truly responsible for instigating the protests.[13]

Crimea (see also chapter 6)

As previously mentioned, the Russian version of events argues that the triggering event took place on February 23, 2014, when the Verkhovna Rada revoked the Russian language's status as a regional language.

Putin stated that the need arose to supply some armaments and troops to Crimea.

Russian media argued that if constitutional behavior had completely broken down in Kiev [Kyiv] as a result of this "illegal coup," then there was no reason to preserve it in Crimea. It is for this reason that the referendum preceding the peninsula's "incorporation" as a part of Russia was a legitimate foundation. In fact, if you were to compare it to Kosovo's secession from Serbia (which many Western powers recognized and supported), you could easily argue that the Crimean case was more legitimate than that, as Kosovo had no popular referendum to justify their actions in the first place.

The Ukrainian narrative, which was shared by Western media, states that the turning point—triggering event—came on February 27, 2014, when Russian "invaders" seized public buildings in the city of Simferopol—capital of the Republic of Crimea—in an act of "blatant aggression."

This act would therefore constitute a Russian invasion of Ukraine.

Ukrainian/Western media submit the opposite argument. They argue that the referendum was conducted in a hurry, in the absence of an independent international observation, and in the presence of armed Russian troops, which resulted in a "lack of transparency in counting procedures."[17]

Donbas/Donbass

In this case, the Russian side admits to the presence of Russian volunteers within the ranks of the DPR/LPR militias.

The Russian media quoted the weekly German publication *Der Spiegel* (March 2015)—sporting references to sources from the German Chancellor's Office and Federal Intelligence Service—arguing that the United States exaggerated Russia's supposed role in Donbas. Furthermore, they proposed that US representatives worked to erect "hindrances" during their "search for a diplomatic solution to the Ukrainian conflict ... to pave the way for weapon deliveries" to the Ukrainian forces.[18]

Both Ukrainian and Western media outlets heavily covered the supposed presence of regular Russian troops and munitions permeating the region.

The media intensively cited NATO's supreme allied commander in Europe—US General Philip Breedlove—as saying that Russia-backed separatists had prepared "over a thousand combat vehicles [and] sophisticated air defense battalions of artillery" in Donbas; "it is getting worse every day."[19]

Based on the findings of specialists who analyzed the propaganda that arose from these conflict, it is easy to agree that "there is no social or cultural border between the eastern provinces of Ukraine and western Russia"; despite any argument to the contrary, the language is effectively the same (excluding regional differences in accent or dialect); many intermarriages between the two groups usually result in a situation where "many Russian men and women with close kinship ties to Ukrainians on the other side thought it is a 'natural duty' to go and defend their relatives" against what in their perception was an attempt by Kiev [Kyiv] and western Ukrainians (whom they called "Banderites") to "subordinate or expel them. … On the other hand, there is no doubt that some regular Russian soldiers have been fighting alongside Russian-speaking Ukrainians, including leaders of whole combat units."[20]

Odessa (see also chapter 6)	
Following the Odessa Trade Union building incident on May 2, 2014, in which forty-eight people were killed as a result of the fire, Russian media outlets pinned the blame on the "fascist pro-Kiev paramilitaries from outside of the city who had formed units of the National Guard" under the direct leadership of the interim government's head of security, Andriy Parubiy. They also quote the nationalist songs and slogans belted out by the perpetrators: most notably, "Burn, Colorado, burn" (with "Colorado Beetle" being a sobriquet for the protesters—which is itself a reference to their flag). A supplementary report also states that between seven and twenty people were killed by this very same group of "thugs" a week later on May 9, as they literally put the torch to a police station.	Ukrainian media stated that the incident was an accident, which saw protesters burned themselves due to carelessness. Western media (and especially mainstream US media) "referred to the killers as 'volunteers; or 'self-defense forces.'"[21]

Concerning the more "crude" forms of ethnic cleansing being displayed—otherwise denoted as "war crimes" (see the corresponding chart regarding the Russo-Ukrainian ethnic conflict in chapter 9)—Western media often echoes the tone and information provided by Ukrainian media sources. Boyd-Barret provides a number of examples to this point, including: "When a [Ukrainian] missile hit the regional administration building [in Donbas/Donbass] in early June [2014], U.S. mainstream media dutifully reported [the] Kiev government's version of events as fact, namely that the anti-Kiev forces had blown up their own head-quarters, just as several weeks earlier Kiev had claimed that the anti-Kiev forces in Odessa [Odesa] had set themselves on fire."[22]

Samples of Hate Speech in the Media

In May 2020, the Russian *Information Agency Regnum* informed the Russian people that former Ukrainian MP Iryna Farion (whose escapades at a primary school were mentioned in chapter 6) had openly declared that those who participated in the Odessa killing on May 2 "must visit Ukrainian schools and tell the pupils how to correctly burn separatists."[23] This statement, which was readily broadcasted by several Russian media outlets (TV Channel 1, etc.), propagated negative feelings and emotions (including but not limited to seething rage) among Russian listeners and readers as a constructed reaction to this ethnocentric escapade.

May 29, 2020, saw Ostap Drozdov, Lviv's television front man, posted an episode of his YouTube-based talk show in which he declared: "I am a staunch supporter of the total, deaf, categorical blockade of Crimea and Donbas ... If it was my will Crimea would be sitting without water and electricity, without anything. I would close everything for them ... Let them croak. Let them wash themselves in the mud, guzzle water from the continent ..." In addition, he claimed that any and all financial returns going into the rebellious territories, be they business ventures or the distribution of government pension, should be cut off as soon as possible.[24]

At one point, the commercial website of the online Ukrainian store *Nu Sho* featured an image of a T-shirt printed with the phrase "Ty sho jid?" which translates to "Are you jid?" (with *jid* being a derogatory term for a Jew and using colloquial speech to define a "greedy person"), which is a highly spread ethnocentric stereotype surrounding Jewish people. Blatant anti-Semitism as the underlying sentiment behind this phrase is far more striking. According to a poll taken by the *Anti-Defamation League*, an astounding 72 percent of participating Ukrainians agreed that "the Jews have too much power and influence in business" in Ukraine. Based on these results, it should come as no surprise that Ukraine hosts the second-highest anti-Semitic mood among all European countries.[25]

In another instance, former Ukrainian MP Oleksiy Zhuravko was outraged that canned foods labeled as "separatists in oil" and "pieces of Russian bosom babies" were being sold on the shelves of Ukrainian grocery stores. Though prior to this, a similar fervor had already broken out in Odesa/Odessa after a local restaurant debuted a new dish on its menu under the name "Fried Colorados"—an obvious allusion to the victims of the previously mentioned May 2 tragedy.[26]

With just a simple glance, one can find many more examples of this mindset, be they broadcasted through media outlets, presented openly in public places, and even noted in the day-to-day speech of pedestrians—all of which serve as a plain indication of how broadly and deeply an ethnocentric ideology (alongside its corresponding behavioral pattern) is embraced by the masses. In fact, this malignant ideology becomes so prolific (read: infectious) that it transcends any political or socio-cultural mandate and becomes a kind of mass phenomenon.

The Minsk Agreements

Russian Media View	Ukrainian/Western Media View
Russia is not the side of the conflict; it is a guarantor of peace agreements just like France and Germany.	"The Minsk-II agreement will only succeed if Mr. Putin has decided to tone down his confrontation with Ukraine and the West. But there is no sign that he is willing to do so."[28]
Following the conclusion of the *Normandy Four* conference of ministers, Russia accused the Ukrainian minister of foreign affairs, Dmytro Kuleba, of refusing to carry out any of the agreed negotiations with representatives from the DPR and LPR.	
Zelensky again reiterates his desire to regain control of the Ukrainian-Russian border before discussing the implementation of any additional measures. Both statesmen held firm to positions that "vividly contradict [the] Minsk agreements" (see the Russo-Ukrainian chart in chapter 9).[27]	

If one were to summarize these and many other similar samples of *ethnic conflict propaganda*, one may conclude that the destructive messages of both sides are successful because they follow many of the same universal methods and trends utilized in other, similar conflicts. Among them are: (1) the chosen framing of the issue; (2) the use of specific emphasis and omissions to tailor the narrative; (3) the "privileging of certain sources" and ignoring other perspectives; (4) the suppression and/or distortion of information regarding possible alternatives, thereby rendering them in a twistingly incorrect manner; (5) using the kind of language—both verbally and physically—that assists in propagating these methods and their effects; (6) accusing the other side of falsifying sources and information—wherein each side claims that only its own accounts are objectively true/genuine; and (7) the occasional adherence to the invention and propagation of gossip-esque rumors and falsified information.

Curiously enough, the inventors and consumers of these kinds of propagandistic clichés have gradually become hostages of this notorious and piercing propaganda, which, in fact, does not allow them to move beyond a very limited range of discourse. This is because the nature of the propaganda itself undermines any attempts at critical thinking, further polarizes the peoples involved in the conflict, and endorses/stimulates the typical behavioral patterns of ethnocentric nationalism on a massive scale. Thus, the situation effectively becomes one of the *most provocative exacerbating factors within the realm of violent ethnic conflicts.*

Needless to say, both Ukrainian and Western media coverage of this conflict and its associated proceedings lean heavily on a miasma of Russophobia. The mindset behind these portrayals follows a discourse previously formulated by the prominent *RAND Corporation* analyst Paul Henze regarding the Caucasian ethnic conflicts:

> Russia must be at least *minimally supportive* of investigative and mediation efforts undertaken in the North Caucasus; the same applies to the Transcaucasian governments [and, if I may add, to the Ukrainian government] in issues that affect them, or issues between them and Russia.[29]

But all of this is only the tip of the iceberg, as it rests on and reflects the most fundamental rivalry/conflict between the East and West and is, in fact, the *most powerful exacerbating factor* of post-Soviet violent ethnic conflicts, with a particular intensity in the highly complicated and dangerous Russo-Ukrainian strife. It is for that reason that the next part of this final chapter is crucial to understanding this phenomenon at large, as it is absolutely necessary to provide rational (not propagandistic) explanations of the choices and motives driving the actors in this new edition of *The Great Game* (or if I may say, a suspiciously resembling new edition of Cold War), with a particular focus on "Putin's Russia."

Figure 10.1 is significant because it demonstrates hate speech. Early on in this book, I gave an example of the derogatory monikers that both Russians and Ukrainians

FIGURE 10.1   Photograph of a magnet depicting a Cossack wearing traditional clothes and eating traditional foods. The text reads "Thank you, oh God, that I am not a Moscal' [Russian]".

abusively used against each other as manifestation of the so-called habitual nationalism (bytovoi nat-sionalism), also referenced in chapter 6. One of this broadly derogatory monikers that the ethnocentric Ukrainian nationalists use against their Russian neighbors is "Moskal'," as seen in the photograph. The character on the magnet is depicted wearing traditional clothes and eating food and alcohol in front of the Ukrainian flag. This caricature demonstrates what the "*svidomyi*," or righteous patriot should look like, as well as that the Russians have no right to claim first priority on the right to be recognized as the first inventors of this particular native food. The magnet implies it belongs only to genuine Ukrainians. In addition, figure 10.1 demonstrates a part of the first aspect of the theoretical model pertaining to the cultural boundary markers of ethnicity: namely special ethnic food as an Index Feature, discussed in chapter 1. It further demonstrates a persuasion of the author of this image that the real Ukrainian patriot should emulate in life genuine Cossack behavior as it has been established by their Cossack ances-tors. And one of such behaviors is to demonstrate that God almighty has created them as the chosen people—great freemen and warriors superior over the Russians, whom they consider to have stemmed from the miserable slaves of Mongols and Moscow lords.

The Introduction of New Policy

In the previous chapters, I aimed to demonstrate that Ukraine (as well as all the newly established polities along the southwestern perimeter of the "new" Russia) has a complex balance of ethnic intermingling and underpinnings that constitute a genuine "borderland between two increasingly antagonistic blocks." In his own research, Richard Sakwa also cited Anatol Lieven, who in the 1990s "asked whether it was wise to try to force Ukraine to choose between integration into Western institutions, notably NATO, and its traditional orientations to the east."[30] I very much agree with Sakwa in this regard, as one can clearly see that the Western imposition of such a choice has led the gradual transformation of the intrastate relationship, which was originally a "fraternal rivalry," into the deadly stage that threatens "to tear the country apart and endangers world peace."[31]

As such, this part of the chapter homes in on one of the reasons for this new rivalry between West and East over the "remnants" left in the wake of the Soviet collapse—with Ukraine being a territory of particular importance. While personalities play a major role, especially those of Presidents Putin and President Biden, as well as the leaders of NATO and the EU, the ideological perceptions also figure prominently, and they will be highlighted here.

The death of President George H. W. Bush reminded me of his and President Mikhail S. Gorbachev's cooperation in many areas—such as the reunification of Germany and the refinement of nuclear treaties—but also of promises that were not kept. As Putin is quick to remind his country and the world, the most important of these unfulfilled agreements was how the West (i.e., NATO, the EU, and the United States) promised to *limit the propagation of its own influence beyond fairly specific areas of distinctly Russian influence*. In this case, the principal areas of contention are *Ukraine* (including *Crimea*), *Moldova* and *South Ossetia and Abkhazia* (*i.e., Georgia*), and now *Belarus*—the areas that later produced the most violent ethnic conflicts. These potentially overlapping areas must also be seen in the context of new independence as a consequence of the collapse of the Soviet Union in *the Baltic and the Central Asian states*. Of course, this also corresponds to the loss of Russia's control of other major satellite states, such as *Poland, East Germany,* and *Georgia*.

Putin has a trio of very specific reasons for wanting to reestablish the territory that was lost during his lifetime. The first, as odd as it may sound, is that his first name is Vladimir. Putin shares this name with the medieval Vladimir the Great of Kiev, and as such sees himself as a successor to him and the other Russian tsars who also are called "the Great." The second reason is based on his understanding that Russia undergoes cyclical periods of expansion and retraction. The contractions come about as a result of internal weaknesses and subsequent foreign invasions. To briefly mention the most dramatic contractions to take place through history, there was the collapse after the end of Ivan the Terrible's reign, which was followed by European invasions; the weakening of the Imperial regime prior to Napoleon's invasion; the weakening of the monarchy at the outset of the twentieth century and the collapse of the empire, along with losses of territory; and Stalin's undermining of core Soviet institutions, which was followed by the *Wehrmacht's* invasion in 1941. While growing up, Putin had heard stories of the Russian struggle against the German invaders from his father, which had left a deep impression on the future president. The third and final reason stems from Putin's perceptions about the Soviet Union's recovery following World War II and its ultimate profound victory, only for its underlying weaknesses to ensure its collapse and loss of territory in 1991. He witnessed the internal upheavals—mostly ethnicized uprisings—the failure of the planned economy, and the widespread corruption that permeated the Soviet system and ultimately led to the collapse of the Soviet state, in which he was a rising star.

Putin was not going to let internal weakness bring about another contraction. In the same way that many tsars had done before him, Putin let his internal reforms (see chapter 6) be the starting point for expansion back into some of the traditional Russian areas of influence and ownership. However, he faced (and still faces) several serious obstacles to his approach: principally they are the so-called West; the ethnic conflicts that were suppressed by the Soviet regime, which have since exploded; and the new nations that arose at Russia's borders, especially Ukraine. At the same time, Putin has gained access to and can utilize a revived ideological underpinning. This ideological underpinning is the concept of "Eurasianism," which stands in opposition to the centrifugal ethnocentric nationalism flaring up along the rim of the former Soviet Empire.

As such, this chapter will deal mainly with issues concerning the new states surrounding Russia and hear the voices of the Eurasianist theoreticians, ultimately analyzing how practitioners interpret them in order to regain lost Russian might.

Eurasianism

Eurasianism is not a new concept, but with the collapse of the Soviet Union in 1991, the subsequent ethnic revolutions in some of the post-Soviet states, and the emergence of Putin as the leader of Russia, there has been a resurgence in its relevancy.[32] Because of this, the concept is once again being broadly discussed on both academic and political levels in order to determine its legitimacy.[33] As V. L. Kaganskii noted, "Eurasianism is more and more often being invoked as a powerful scholastic foundation of modern Russian politics, even in liberal editions" and concepts.[34] Interestingly enough, political scientists are also increasingly speaking about Russia's return to the "Big East"—Central Asia—and about its dream to rebuild its influence in Eastern Europe.[35] However, this return is not only hampered by the new nations at Russia's periphery but also by the renewed "Great Game" between West and East, with a particular impetus driven by the expansion of the EU, USA, and NATO into the western regions of the "Big East" as well as the former republics of the Soviet Union.[36]

In addition, a series of ethno-political revolutions began rapidly spreading throughout a number of the post-Soviet/Eurasian (or Neo-Eurasian) states. In spite of the obvious implications, however, this phenomenon has yet to be properly analyzed by the historians, political scientists, and economists of either the localized or global academic community. Regardless of their seeming inability to draw attention, it has already been made apparent that these events have seriously undermined the balance of power that emerged in this part of the world during the 1990s. And while Putin has spent many years attempting to gain some semblance of control over this turbulent cycle, many of the existing ethnic elites were able to propose pronounced anti-Russian discourses (or even a sense of Russophobia) to their ethnic compatriots in order to solidify their independence. As a result, this transitory period was inevitably fraught with serious interethnic collisions. However, without some kind of outside support, their projects could not be realized regardless of the outcome.

Early on in the Caucasus, the Baltic States, and (as of now) Ukraine (and the rising "anti-elite" in Belorussia), such elites enjoyed and continue to enjoy the full support of Western powers. Russia in turn realized that these are the same ethnic elites that were and still are the driving forces behind most ethnic conflicts, with vividly pronounced anti-Russian discourse on the part of the latter. Overall, the political result of Russian perceptions during the early cycle of ethno-political revolutions and of continuing ethnic conflicts (like in Eastern Ukraine now) serve as an example of how exaggerated fears may transform into a paranoid picture of the surrounding world, generating equally paranoid stereotypes, and naturalizing them within the political discourse.

In the case of Russia, the resulting paranoia has also been aggravated by the rivalry over strategic natural resources held between the major world powers. Thus, these ethno-political revolutions, spawned by the rhetoric of ethnocentric nationalism, and the real Western support of these phenomena gave rise to the three stereotypes of social paranoia in the modern Russian political patriotic/nationalistic discourse, which is itself fed by chosen traumas of the past:

1. Vladimir Putin has repeated the first stereotype many times in public. He is of the opinion that "it is not Russia who is guilty in this conflict, but Ukraine with its nationalistic moods, and also indirectly the West that encouraged the present state of affairs."

2. The second stereotype concerns the residents of Western Ukraine. In 2014, during the so-called direct line with the Russian people, Putin said:

    There—where nationalism and even Nazism are flourishing and on the rise—there are the Western parts of Ukraine. Partially [Western Ukrainians] had lived in Czechoslovakia, partially— in Poland and in Hungary ... There they had been people of the second sort, but gradually they almost forgot about it. But deep in the sub-consciousness, in the collective memory [of victimization] they still keep it. Those are the sources and roots of this nationalism.[37]

3. The third stereotype reflects the recognition of deep and profound *chosen historical traumas of the general Russian population concerning the eastern expansion of the Western powers, thereby justifying and exacerbating them.*

The Russian View of NATO and Western Expansion

Concerning the expansion of the Western powers, Russia believes that it is the "aggrieved party," and that any further eastern expansion of NATO represents an "existential threat" to the Russian national security. And thus Russia demands to give her firm legal guarantees not to include Ukraine, Georgia, Moldova to the North Atlantic military alliance, nor to deploy any tactical and strategic weapons on the territories of these countries in the post-Soviet space. By this metric, Russia claims that the United States has failed to uphold the promise that NATO would not expand into Eastern Europe, a deal made during the 1990 negotiations between Presidents Gorbachev and G. H. W. Bush on the details of German reunification.

As a result, Russia is being forced to forestall NATO's eastward march as a matter of "self-defense." The Russian version of this development states that US State Secretary John Baker supposedly vowed that NATO "would not" move "an inch" to the east. While some Western partners object that Russia was never given such a promise, it was apparently a real agreement between the two parties. Joshua Itzkowits argues that "hundreds of memos, meeting minutes, and transcripts from U.S. archives indicate" that the West actually made and agreed to these terms, thereby providing them a legitimate basis. But debating whether it is a legitimate agreement or a fabrication of the Russian nationalist mythology is not the point, as the "histories" of chosen traumas are not written for accuracy. As previously discussed, such "history" performs an important function: it creates (or even recreates) *an image of a cultural/ethnic enemy.*

Regardless, NATO's 1990 pledge to forgo eastern expansion helped to end the Cold War in a mutual way. But after a relatively short hiatus, the West began treating their former rival like the defeated side. Because of this mentality of "victor" and "loser," the West does not want to fully recognize the reality of such social paranoia fed by past traumas and its lasting impact on international relations.

Regretfully, it has become typical for modern Western political thinking and action to ignore this and other aspects of history when dealing with Russia. This is a heinous oversight, as a majority of Russia's lasting grievances are built on a narrative of historically recurrent betrayals, slights, and humiliations. At one point, Mikhail Gorbachev described it as such: "They probably rubbed their hands rejoicing at having played a trick on the Russians."[38] At the 2007 Munich Security Conference, Vladimir Putin similarly asked: "What happened to the assurances our Western partners made after the dissolution of the Warsaw Pact?" He would repeat this sentiment in 2014, arguing that "they [the West/NATO] have lied to us many times; made decisions behind our back … This has happened to [consolidate] NATO expansion in the East."[39]

Russia has regarded several the West's steps in this direction as particularly treacherous and provocative, so much so that they are responsible for producing the above-cited expressions of frustration and indignation from Russian leaders.

(1) For the first of these "steps," it is worth noting that Russia was included in *NATO's Partnership for Peace* program in 1994. Additionally, the passage of the *NATO-Russia Founding Act on Mutual Relations* in May 1997 formally created the *NATO-Russia Permanent Joint Council*, with NATO promising not to permanently station troops in the newly accepted post-Soviet countries. Finally, 2002 saw the creation of the *NATO-Russia Council (NCR)*, which sought to improve diplomatic ties between the former rivals. Despite all of this, trouble began brewing as early as 1998, when, without any formal consultations, the US Senate ratified NATO expansion plans. At that point, George Kennan warned that the "Russians will react quite adversely … I think it is a tragic mistake."[40]

(2) In another instance, on March 29, 2004, all three Baltic States—Estonia, Latvia, and Lithuania—became members of NATO and, on May 1 that same year, joined the EU. Furthermore, the 2008 NATO summit in Bucharest (April 2–4) promised NATO membership to both Georgia and Ukraine, without any measure of consultation from the NRC. Russia had known about Washington's plans beforehand, as in February 2008, US Ambassador William Burns "was called by the Russian foreign minister Sergey Lavrov, who explained Russia's strong opposition to NATO membership for Ukraine."[41] Afterward, Burns reportedly sent a cable back to Washington with the "unusual" title: "NYET MEANS NYET (in Russian: 'NO'): RUSSIA'S NATO ENLARGEMENT RED LINES."[42] On the other side of the world, Russia began strengthening its military, aid, and diplomatic ties to Abkhazia and South Ossetia, as the entire situation was nearing the *Second hot stage* of the above-cited 2008 conflict in Georgia (see corresponding charts in chapter 6).

(3) The Ukrainian Crisis of 2013–2014, which saw the deployment of NATO forces along the Russian border with the Baltics, Romania, and Bulgaria, reawakened dormant memories of the catastrophic consequences following the German invasion of 1941. The significance was not lost on Putin, who, through his father's war stories, is well aware of the details of the devastation brought about by that ill-fated invasion, in which almost all the peoples of European countries subdued or voluntary allied with the Nazis. In full agreement with Richard Sakwa, one may argue that the "inexorable enlargement of NATO prepared the stage for the Ukrainian confrontation of 2014 that was, as Stephen Cohen repeatedly warned, two steps from another Cuban Missile Crisis and three steps from World War III"; in short, "Atlanticism became the new ideology to constrain Russia." As a result, Ukraine has become the *center point* of the West in its own confrontation with Russia and the *raison d'être* of Russian attempts to deter the newly revived Western onslaught.[43]

Putin and a part of his loyal political elite believe that the West will use Romania (Moldova), Ukraine, Poland, Georgia, and the Baltic States as a battering ram in the would-be war with Russia. That is why they believe the West cultivates and tames ethnocentric nationalists in Ukraine and has now taken to providing them lethal weapons that may result only in the escalation of the crisis. It is also for those very same reasons that the Russian government supports the insurgency in Donbas/Donbass.

Essentially, Putin, who is beholden to these stereotypical phobias, sees Russia's actions in Ukraine as a form of self-defense "driven by the need to deter the West." That is what he meant when he invited Russia's elite to the Kremlin's gilded hall in order to announce Russia's "reunification" with the Crimea on March 18, 2014, saying that *the West had crossed the red line* in Ukraine. According to President Putin, Western actions left Russia with no choice but to send troops into the Crimea. Conversely, Putin clearly recognizes that he cannot win a conventional war with the West, which is why he has "quickly raised the stakes to the verge of a nuclear war, believing that the other side would always blink first."[44]

So, in the mind of the Russian people—from the average citizen to the part of loyal political elites—there exists a continuously strengthening image of an unscrupulous opponent who have pathologically broken their promises to the point where they are now not worthy of trust. Worse yet, they see the international settlement and European order established after the reunification of Germany as lacking credible legitimacy. As a result, this lack of solidarity has been one of Putin's main talking points since 2014, especially when addressing the Ukrainian crisis and the Crimean "reunification" or, by the Ukrainian-Western rhetoric "invasion/annexation/aggression." Essentially, Russia believes that the policy of the West, both in previous and current engagements, has never changed and finds its expression in the cynical motto: "West First/America First."

Since 2014, the renewal of *The Great Game* between West and East, ultimately *triggered* by the Ukrainian crisis, has entered a dangerous phase, with the rising tensions between Russia and NATO indicating the transition of the Russo-Ukrainian inter/intrastate conflict into its *third level*: there is only one step that separates the two dominant nuclear powers from engaging in a possibly catastrophic confrontation. As of 2014, Putin has come to understand that saving the Russian populations of Crimea and southeastern Ukraine from the wrath of the Ukrainian nationalists and their infringements against the Russians' *linguistic rights* was a solid pretext to justify the taking of Crimea under the cover of humanitarian considerations. However, this also serves as a part of a key element in the Russian defensive plan, as Crimea can serve as an "unsinkable natural aircraft carrier." After all, this new generation of soldiers, who descended from the very same Russians who fought on the outskirts of Moscow, Stalingrad, and Leningrad to repel the invading fascists, do not have to think too hard to consider the immense implications of having a Western missile base erected in Crimea or Donbas—thereby allowing such ordnance to reach Moscow or Saint Petersburg in mere minutes. In this regard, the *pressing security dilemma* urged Moscow's securing these territories as a matter of the *utmost importance*.

The game has now entered a truly dangerous phase. In it, the Western world has its own principal ideology—Atlanticism. On the other hand, many of the Russian nationalistic intellectuals in Putin's entourage think that the formation of "Neo-Eurasianism" might effectively juxtapose the challenge laid out by Atlanticism.

Among the Russian thinkers of the so-called "Neo-Eurasianists," some of the views pioneered by Samuel P. Huntington are rather popular. In particular, they like to point to the map wherein Huntington drew the conditional line that separates "Western Christianity circa 1500 and Orthodox Christianity and Islam." On this map, among other things, the Baltic States are slated to have belonged to the West. Furthermore, the line that divides Ukraine shows an interesting paradigm: the Western part belongs to Western Christianity, and the Eastern Ukraine (including the southeast and Crimea) belongs to Orthodox Christianity.[45] Putin (as well as Sergei Lavrov, during his above-cited conversation with Ambassador Burns) may have had this exact rendition of a *civilizational fault line* in mind when he said that Western Ukrainian nationalists and Western powers had previously "crossed the red line in Ukraine."

As previously demonstrated, ethnocentric nationalists are now very active in both central and eastern Ukraine. With the encouragement of the current Ukrainian government, Metropolitan Filaret (Denisenko) pulled a counter move and removed the Ukrainian Orthodox Church from the jurisdiction of the Moscow Patriarchate, claiming himself to be the head of a new church with its patriarchal site in Kiev. The Ecumenical Patriarch Bartholomew I of Constantinople in 2019 supported this plan and provided the Ukrainian Orthodox Church with their long-desired tomos.

Since the beginning of the 2000s, these previously detailed psycho-historical underpinnings have been cultivating a fertile soil for rejuvenating Eurasianist thoughts. As a result, its modernized version in many respects and in many heads has gradually become the foundation of the current political discourse in Russia.

Early Views of Eurasia and Eurasianism

Initially, the term "Eurasia" had a purely geographical context. It was designated the biggest continent, being the combination of both Europe and Asia—thereby constituting 40.4% of the Earth's landmass and being home to 74.5% of its population. It was not until much later that this term would acquire a more cultural-historical connotation. Modern Russian Eurasianists understand the concept through the lens of a "historical Eurasia," which represents the "totality of adjacent territories populated by different peoples more or less connected through a common historical fortune, steady interest, and likeness of cultures."[46] In spite of their diversity, one can trace an idea of civilizational polycentrism that ties the myriad cultures into a single whole as a peculiar politico-philosophical system.

The first project into determining the exact nature of this concept stems from the Russian nationalist, economist, ethnologist, philosopher, historian, and ideologue of both the Pan-Slavism and Slavophile movements, Nikolai Yakovlevich Danilevsky (1822–1885). He developed the theory of historical-cultural types that has come to define this "Eurasianist" mindset in a stand-alone monograph.[47]

In this work, Danilevsky openly criticized Eurocentrism and developed the concept of cyclical development of civilizations. This concept was named "the theory of cultural historical types" following the publication of Oswald Spengler and Arnold Toynbee's books on the subject.[48] To Danilevsky, each cultural and historical type represents a local civilization that develops according to its own laws and is not exposed to the decisive influence of external factors. He argued that Russia, unlike other nations, expressed its cultural-historical type through the four major spheres: in the field of policy, Russia's identity is fully expressed by *absolute monarchy*; in the field of economy, its identity is fully expressed by the preservation of a community-centered type of economy; in the sphere of art, it manifested itself through such geniuses as Aleksandr Pushkin, Nikolai Gogol', and others; and as a peculiar cultural and historical type, Russia represents *ethnographic diversity*, the development of a literary language, and political independence.[49]

Some representatives of the modern Russian nationalistic Neo-Eurasianist way of thinking have fully adopted and creatively reproduced these postulates, at which point they begin applying them to cultural and historical characteristics of the Russian patriotic elite. These creatively amended concepts now find their practical realization through many of Putin's state-building projects that encompass all four spheres, with the addition of being included in policy decisions behind military build-up.

Danilevsky also believed that, during the course of its evolution, each cultural-historical type went through stages of "youth, adulthood, and old age," with the last being the end of that type. According to him, the Slavic type was only then passing through its youth stage. Therefore, he viewed the most appropriate sociopolitical plan for its further development as the forerunner of the other types involved in the eventual unification of the Slavic world—with its future capital at Constantinople (Istanbul)—under the rulership of an Orthodox emperor.[50]

Konstantin Nikolaevich Leontiev (1851–1891), a conservative tsarist philosopher, similarly became a precursor of modern Neo-Eurasianism through the development of another important aspect of the political philosophy. In his most remarkable essay, *The East, Russia, and Slavdom* (1885–1886), he, like Nikolai Danilevsky and Fyodor Dostoevsky before him, severely criticized Western consumer society and the cult of material prosperity. He further advocated the establishment of closer cultural ties between Russia and the East in order to repel "catastrophic, utilitarian, and revolutionary influences," thus arguing in favor of Russia's cultural and territorial expansion to the East.

Several decades before Nietzsche and Spengler would craft their own philosophies, Leontiev openly endorsed the theory of the cyclical nature of civilizations. He believed that all societies undergo several stages: "flowering and increasing complexity," "secondary simplification," decay, and death.[51] This political philosophy also included a strong religious context, as Leontiev believed that the Virgin Mary had granted him salvation during a severe illness. As such, he regarded traditional Russian Byzantinism as an antidote to Western liberalization, prophesying that there would be a bloody revolution in Russia initiated by the anti-Christ, who would promote a Western liberal agenda. To Leontiev, only a harsh reaction from the Russian government could prevent such a catastrophe, as only they had the power to make the necessary changes.[52]

Ironically enough, classical Eurasianism (*Evraziistvo*) only truly emerged among Russian emigrants and intellectuals as an ideological-philosophical movement in response to the Russian Revolution and Civil War (1917–1920). Leading the charge of this new political philosophy were ethnologist and linguist Nikolai Sergeyevich Trubetzkoy, geologist and economist P. N. Savitskii (1895–1968), musicologist P. P. Souvtchinskii (1892–1985), and religious philosopher Georgii Vasil'evich Florovskii (1893–1979). Later on, this movement would be reinforced by historian Georgii (George) V. Vernadsky (1887–1973) and philosopher Lev Platonovich Karsavin. Certain aspects of "Eurasian" ideas were also subsequently impacted by other famous members of Russian emigrant academic groups, including such names as M. M. Karpovich, M. T. Florinskii, N. A. Berdyaev, P. Milyukov, P. Struve, L.P. Iacobson, and G. N. Malevsky-Malevich.[53]

These men saw themselves and their movement as responsible for creating a new Russian ideology that "would do justice to its own particular historical and cultural development."[54] The principal ideas of Eurasianism were fully manifested in the joint publication of *Exodus of the East* (1921). In this more cumulative form, it reflected on the contents of Nikolai Trubetzkoy's *Yevropa i chelovechestvo (Europe and Mankind)* (1920), a 120-page manifesto that warned of the imminent Europeanization of the world (with Atlanticism being a modern embodiment). According to Trubetzkoy, this was the direct result of Romano-Germanic chauvinism and colonialism, which saw Western European countries consider other peoples and cultures as inferior to their own. This, in turn, inspired these countries to try and remake these "lesser nations" in their own image. However, Russia "had to stand up to this pernicious influence and follow its own path" if it wished to survive the onslaught.[55]

Regarding their geographical considerations, the Eurasianists divided the enormous swaths of terrain within the Northern Hemisphere into three distinct parts: "Western" Europe, including Poland, the Baltic States, and the Balkans; "Asia"—the Far East, Southwest Asia, and Southeast Asia; and "Eurasia," a separate geographical world between the other two, consisting of relatively flat land extending from the estuary of the Danube River to the basin of the Lena River in Siberia. One may readily notice that this central hinterland corresponds to the territory of the tsarist Russian Empire, the Soviet Union, and modern Russia (including Ukraine).

So, unlike Europe and Asia, the Eurasianists' vision of "Eurasia" is effectively landlocked. It also has a distinct continental climate, with hot summers and very cold winters. This "Eurasia" is populated by a great variety of Slavic and non-Slavic peoples, or as Trubetzkoy called them, the Turanic peoples: including Finno-Ugrians, Samoyeds, Tatars, and Kalmyks.

For the first time, Eurasianists would formally introduce the notion of a "historical and geographical unity" that connects all the peoples populating this hemisphere, much like their languages had done previously. From this point on, Eurasianists under Trubetzkoy's banner began to differ from their nineteenth-century ideological forerunners in that they believed that the Russians were culturally and spiritually closer to the peoples of Eurasia than to their Slavic brothers: namely, the Czechs and Poles. They argued that the latter belong to that completely different civilization, namely, the "West"—i.e., Catholic and Protestant Europe.

With this revelation, Eurasianists had effectively centered on the socio-cultural/political importance of religion long before Huntington identified it as a principal formative building block of world civilizations.[56]

Georgii (George) Vernadsky, a distinguished and Russian-born American historian, was one of the brightest stars among the Eurasianist group. The idea that Russia was neither Europe nor Asia but a world unto itself, Eurasia, runs through much, if not all of Vernadsky's enormous scholarly output. Oftentimes, his contribution to Eurasianist theory is reduced to the theme of highlighting the significance of Mongols in Russian history, though in all fairness, it was not only Vernadsky to do so. First and foremost, Trubetzkoy, as well as other Eurasianists, had previously addressed this topic in great detail. Regardless of who formulated the concept, they all agreed that it was Genghis Khan who first recognized the geopolitical significance of Eurasia when he conquered it in its entirety. Afterward, the Mongol subjugation lasted for more than 150 years, thanks in no small part to the qualities of the land and the people who inhabited it.

Unlike other specialists (especially during the Soviet period) who associated that period with being a "yoke"—a time of stagnation and decline—Eurasianists considered Mongol rule as the true beginning of the Russian Empire. When the Muscovite state defeated the Mongols, it merely continued the process of building a Eurasian state. In fact, the Muscovites were even better suited for promoting the unity of Eurasia, because they included the ideology of the Orthodox Church. As a result, Orthodoxy became one of the most important pillars of Eurasia's historical cultural identity. Contrary to the strict hierarchical structure of Catholicism and the rational/individualistic teachings of Protestantism, Russian Orthodoxy is based not on exceptionalism and closeness but on *sobornost'* ("brotherhood") and is thus an excellent vehicle to unite all the Eurasian peoples: Slavic, Islamic, and heathen alike.[57]

Charles Halperin assessed that "the development of Vernadsky's historical concepts ... [was] far more complex than has hitherto been appreciated."[58] As a matter of fact, the tenets of Eurasianism are present throughout all 8,800 pages of Vernadsky's works. It is the unifying theme behind all of his studies into Russian, Byzantine, Inner Asian, and Northern Iranian history. These investigations in and of themselves demonstrate his belief that the cultural world of Eurasia is of a special and peculiar value that formed in the depths of Internal Eurasia, even at the periphery of the mainland. Mass migrations of the Indo-European peoples, including the Northern Iranians (Kimmerians, Scythians, Sarmatians, Alans—the ancestors of modern Ossetians), Huns, Turks, Slavs, Mongols, and, ultimately, Russians, all had a profound integral impact on this part of the world throughout its history.

In fact, the Russian state itself plays the role of a veritable compendium of all the historical-cultural values and traditions (including those belonging to different religious heritages) of all these peoples in the modern day.[59] Vernadsky considered the date range of this decisive period of mixing as stemming between the conquest of the Mongols under Genghis Khan and Batu Khan, their creation of the Great Mongolian Empire, and the subsequent expansion of the Muscovite state into the Volga region and other areas.

All classical Eurasianists, who at the height of their movement jointly published *Evraziistvo (Eurasianism)* (1926) and developed an idea of a real people's party that would endorse their ideology ("ideocracy") as opposed to Communism, assessed the Romanovs' reign, especially during the Petrine period (1672–1725),as a highly negative affair. Peter's policy to make Russia a European power and the introduction of European innovations at the hands of subsequent Romanov rulers thoroughly disgusted the mentality of Eurasianists: whereas imperialism, militarism, and capitalism were prioritized by the state, liberalism, parliamentarianism, and capitalism had been the concerns of the intelligentsia and others.

The Rise of Neo-Eurasianism

Another key concept in the modern interpretation of Eurasianism argues that the Soviet state was based on European ideas, and thus it failed to begin a new period.

In this instance, there is a clearly distinguishable "watershed" that separates early or "classical" Eurasianists from their successors, the Neo-Eurasianists, who wrote at the end of the twentieth century, with the primary contention stemming from their contesting attitudes toward the Russian Imperial and Soviet periods. In many respects, the new generation of Eurasianists built their ideas on the legacy of classical Eurasianists, minus the abovementioned stance, and on the *ethnogenesis theory* penned by Lev Nikolayvich Gumilev (1912–1992), the son of famous poets Anna Akhmatova (1889–1966) and Nikolay Gumilev (1886–1921).

Much like their older counterparts, Neo-Eurasianists consider Eurasia to be a separate civilization in the scope of the world. In accordance with Gumilev's ideas, they see that the Russians, as a young and fresh ethnos, are able to provide the kind of leadership necessary to break the dominance of the dying European ethnoses, thereby allowing Russia to change the political-cultural map of the world.

But why do Russians represent a "young nation"? To Neo-Eurasianists it is because the last stages in the formation of a separate Eurasian civilization, which had begun in antiquity, were ended under the leadership of the Russian emperors. This period coincides with the transformation of the Russians into a nuclear state and, in fact, a core nation of the imperial state as a center of this civilization. That is how Professor Mark Maximovich Bliev, one of the leading historians of the Caucasus, who fully shared the ideas of Gumilev and Neo-Eurasianists, phrased it:

> One has to take into account the certain peculiarities of Russia itself as a Eurasian Empire that from the very beginning of its origin has revealed a capacity to pull into its orbit different states and peoples irrespective of their racial features or religious affiliations. For all this, the Eurasian essence of Russia consisted in a unique combination of ostensibly opposite foundations: an archaic ingrainment of traditions and progress of industry and culture.

Bliev further argued that, while simultaneously revealing a certain drive (read: passion) for the grafting of territorial space, Russia has been gradually "filling" itself with ethnic diversity, essentially instilling a balance between the two primary civilizations—West and East. This successful "gathering of peoples" was the result of the global evolution of Russian history and of a capacity of the Russian people to see and use the obvious anthropological, and especially lingual-cultural, proximity of other Eurasian peoples to pull them into the orbit of its civilization.[60] But, as we know, classical Eurasianism effectively came to an end by the middle of the 1930s, as Eurasianist literature was not available in the Soviet Union.

Thus, it can be reasoned that Gumilev's own intellectual formation occurred rather independently. However, he obviously shared overlapping interests with the classical Eurasianists, "particularly with their views on the geopolitical, cultural, and ethnic aspects of" the above-discussed "concept of Eurasia."[61] Nevertheless, he would still refer to himself as "the last Eurasianist."

Gumilev later developed the theory of *passionarnost'* (from the words for "passion" and "instinct"/"drive"), otherwise known as *passionarity.* According to this theory, the expected vitality of any given human society could be determined based on the amount of driving or passionate energy that they received from the cosmos itself—an idea often referred to as the "space factor." When closely examining these theories, one can see the obvious continuity between Gumilev and the classical Eurasianists in some of the principal points that they developed. In particular, Gumilev was in constant correspondence with Savitskii for more than twelve years, up until the latter's death in 1968; after that, he continued exchanging ideas with George Vernadsky.[62]

Based on these interactions, Gumilev continued to develop the notion of *mestorazvitie* as a synthesis of geography and history, which had first been developed by Vernadsky and Savitskii, with the latter using it as an introduction to the new science of *geosofia*.[63] Gumilev appreciated how the notion of *mestorazvitie* ("place of development") "could help to explain the phenomenon of cultural continuity" within Russia as "a special geographic world." In other words, he grasped Savitskii's idea that the most important characteristics "of Russian spiritual and psychological character, the distinctness of state system, [and] aspects of economic life ... had certain parallels with the geographical features of Russia-Eurasia." In fact, Savitskii even argued that every cultural-historical type (a reference to the work of N. Danilevsky) correlated to a particular place of development—which spawned the concept of *mestorazvitie*.[64] This line of conceptual thinking had a tremendous impact on Gumilev's ideas regarding the decisive importance of environment in the process of ethnogenesis.[65]

The other primary ideas of Classical Eurasianists saw a creative adaptation into the framework of Gumilev's concepts, from which they then migrated into the Neo-Eurasian political-philosophical agenda. From this point, they further developed through their application in the Eurasian projects of Putin's Russia. In this way, they would eventually become solicitors of the above-identified "ideocracy" and economic/political autarky at the basis of many modern polices.

Despite Gumilev's work on the subject, it was actually Trubetzkoy who first proposed the creation of a new ideological basis for a unified Eurasian state. To him, this state should not follow in the class-based theory of the Soviet Union, because, in the long run, it encouraged "national antagonism" that would lead to "separatism" (ethnic conflicts of the secessionist/irredentist persuasion). Instead, Eurasian nations should be united through a broader "Pan-Eurasian nationalism," which could potentially succeed because the Eurasian people "had an unconscious affinity with each other and shared a common historical state."[66] In this theoretical Eurasian state, this "ideocracy" should coordinate all aspects of a state's life into a joint effort. Additionally, Trubetzkoy was under the firm belief that "Eurasia was also suited to economic and political autarky."[67] And while the USSR was the closest to being the ideal of an ideocratic Eurasian core-state, its communist ideology, which had brought the disparate parts of this Red Empire together, should be replaced by the true Eurasianist ideology.[68]

For the most part, Gumilev agreed with "the main historico-methodological conclusions of Eurasianists." However, he also noted several "substantial differences—the concept of passionarnost' was absent in their theory of ethno-genesis. Generally, they lacked [knowledge] of natural sciences. Nevertheless, the Eurasian doctrine was conceived as a synthesis of humanitarian and natural science, i.e., as a synthesis of history and geography."[69]

Gumilev generally accepted the Eurasianist thesis regarding the geographical separation of Eurasia and Western Europe. However, he saw his main contribution to the Eurasianist movement as uniting the sciences, including history, geography, and natural history. He also added a new factor: namely the idea of "passionary impulses" that, together with geographical factors, "had determined the development of Eurasia." Alexander Titov argues that the most important consideration of ethnogenesis and the role of

Russians for Neo-Eurasian thinkers in view of Gumilev's passionarnost' theory is the thesis that the key to understanding the emergence of the "Great Russian Super-ethnos" was the so-called "positive kom-plimentarnost'." This is, in fact, "the natural affinity of the two main super-ethnoses of Russia: the Russian and the Steppe peoples." According to Gumilev, this affinity "served as a foundation of the Muscovite state, followed by the territorial expansion of the Russian Empire as well as the success of the USSR in World War II." Unlike the other Eurasianists, Gumilev believed that the underlying factor in history was the ambient concept of "passionarnost,'" rather than their particular culture.[70]

In this way, Gumilev bridged the gap between classical Eurasianists and Neo-Eurasianists of modern Russia, for whom the collapse of the Soviet Union was a tragedy. This mindset later found itself firmly established in Putin's regard for this event as a "geopolitical catastrophe." In short, both groups found a rational explanation, but also solace and hope for the future, in Gumilev's theory of rhythmical cycles: especially in terms of the rise and fall of passionarity behavior within the Russian super-ethnos.

Some Russian intellectual emigrants, openly brandishing a specific kind of anti-Western thinking, also had good reason to reflect on these system-shattering events in "a sharp and polemical way."[71] To this end, one may add that the Eurasianists' rejection of Soviet power due to religious and ideological considerations resembles their similar rejection of the Imperial period from Peter the Great onward. Gumilev provided a tool for reconciliation pertaining to the same logical explanations for the underlying complexities of the phases of Russian history, interrupted as they were by system-shattering events, as if on a swing, with the periodic rushing from West to East.

According to Gumilev, Russian history, as seen through the prism of his theory of ethnogenesis, has passed through three main phases: the growth phase, the acme phase, and the crisis stage.

The Growth Phase

The growth phase includes the exclusive role of the church, the rise of Moscow, and the decisive military victory over the Tatars at the Battle of Kulikovo in 1380, which triggered the beginning of the rapid-growth phase and the end of the slow-growth phase. As a final period of the Great Russian ethnogenesis, the latter phase was associated with the reign of Ivan III (1462–1505) and with two principal events of this period: the annexation of the Novgorod Republic by Moscow and the collapse of the last remains of the Golden Horde. The end of the Novgorod Republic signaled a drastic change in behavioral patterns, that is, from the "behavioral stereotypes typical of the *vechevaia* Rus' [which was preserved in Ukraine] to the new behavioral stereotypes based around the centralized government under the autocracy of the Grand Prince of Moscovy." Another key (pivotal) event—the collapse of Tatar rule after the Battle of Ugra (1480)—was a triggering moment for the existence of Russia as "a super-ethnos." During the growth phase, the "komplimentarnost'" of Great Russians were formed as a mixture of "Slavs, the Fin-no-Ugric tribes and the Tatars."[72] It should be noted, however, that Gumilev greatly underestimated the Lithuanian ethnic component also taking part in the ethnogenesis of the Russian super-ethnos at that period, despite noted evidence.

The Acme Phase

The next phase symbolized the highest level of "passionarnost,'" which Gumilev succinctly defined as "*acme*." In terms of its application to Russian history, Gumilev distinguished three peaks of the acme phase, along with two passionary depressions between the peaks of "passionarnost.'" From a simple scan of the associated historical events, it becomes clear that Gumilev associated the peaks of passionarity with great victories, internal conflicts, and expansion, during the course of which the Russians showed the ability to adopt the traditions of the indigenous peoples whom they conquered but in the long run established good relations with them and, as a result, reinforced themselves. This is what is meant by the abovementioned term *komplimentarnost'*—complementarity. One such event, the Battle of Poltava in 1709—which saw the Russians defeat the Swedish—was similarly estimated by Gumilev be the last episode in the Russo-Ukrainian unification, because it ended a long period of attempts by the Ukrainian hetmans to steer Ukraine away from Russia. That is why for the Ukrainian ethnocentric nationalists, Hetman Mazepa is a hero, and for the Russians, he is a traitor in their textbooks, because he had sided with Swedish troops under Poltava. Thus Gumilev rather idealistically assessed the relationship between the two peoples as built on a sense of belonging to the same super-ethnos. Though seemingly out of place, this kind of approach is typical for both classical and Neo-Eurasianists (and even Putin himself).

But as we have previously seen, the Ukrainians have had historically different thoughts about themselves and the Russians; they perceive two different *nations* joined together as opposed to a mono-ethnic nation-state. Gumilev, once again in a traditionally conservative fashion, assessed this type of shift as a depression within this phase, with Peter I's forcible Westernization, which violently changed the behavioral norms of the Russian people.

The Crisis Stage

According to Gumilev, the last phase is undoubtedly the crisis stage, which encompasses the initial period of the crisis phase, the formation of the communist sub-ethnos, and the final period of the crisis, which he associated with the collapse of the USSR. In the context of our research, it is curious that Gumilev identified the dissent, directly inspired by Western ideas (beginning with the Decembrist uprising of 1825 against the monarchy and ending with the liberal opposition of the 1990s), as the reason for the depression stages in passionarnost' (which equates to a loss of energy).

Alexander Titov very aptly rendered Gumilev's attitude toward the Soviet period to its simplest form, which he identifies as "the communist sub-ethnos that existed for about 100 years, as compared to the 1,200 years of existence of a super-ethnos." After the Revolution, and in the course of the Civil War of 1918–1920, "the Russian passionary (ethnic) field split into two opposing sides—the Reds and Whites." As the nucleus of the Communist sub-ethnos, the "Reds" were formed on the basis of the revolutionary socialists' organizations, whose leadership attracted the most passionary—energetic—persons in the Russian Empire, especially from the border areas of the Russian super-ethnos. The "Whites," on the other hand, failed to formulate an attractive ideal, and their disunity (caused by the distinct lack of passionarnost'—energy) "ensured their defeat."[73] As a matter of fact, V. I. Ermolaev would later point out how "40% of leading Communists came from the Baltic states, Ukraine, and Belarus, 25% came from the southern areas of contact with the Muslim super-ethnos (Volga region, Caucasus, Georgia [including Stalin], Azerbaijan), and 15% came from poly-ethnic capitals of the empire."[74]

Interestingly enough, these key geographic areas and the "ethnic *passionarii*" (or passionately energetic people) that lived in them coincided with those areas in which ethnocentric movements sprang up during and after the collapse of the USSR, headed by charismatic leaders—so-called "national communists," notable ethnocentric nationalists—who exploded the Soviet Union from within. This was covered by Gumilev, who argued that the Communist sub-ethnos passed through the same phases of growth, acme, and crisis as its larger ethnic counterparts, albeit at an accelerated rate. It is very symptomatic in how he associated the "acme phase" with Stalin's period: the triumph of the acme phase came in 1929 with the year of the "Great Turn" to collectivization and industrialization, which saw Stalin's new cohort triumph over Lenin's "old guard." However, the acme phase ended with the death of Stalin in 1953, as both the supporters and opponents of Stalin's policy—at least those with the highest level of passionarity—were already dead.

Khrushchev's denouncement of Stalin and unsuccessful attempts to reform Stalin's system marked the beginning of the crisis phase; in the long run, it led to the economic and political crisis that would haunt the Soviet state. This phase, again according to Gumilev, was nearing its end after the collapse of Communism. However, he foresaw a future in which Russia would enter the "golden autumn" of the so-called "inertial phase," accompanied by the slow and steady fall of the *passionarnost'* and the subsequent establishment of law and order. With all things considered, this idea of a "golden autumn" was a rather optimistic prediction.[75] Though, if the country tried to follow this line of logic after Putin—the last Russian passionary—then Russia would crack and, eventually, collapse along ethnic lines—just like the Soviet Union before it. In fact, nationalistic (i.e., ethnocentric) movements, especially those composed of the most energetic people, have become ingrained in the periphery—the fiery rim of this slowly sinking ship—and especially in Ukraine.

Overall, Neo-Eurasianism attempts to adopt the theory of ethnogenesis but, more importantly, in the sense that Gumilev was a "self-acknowledged Eurasian scholar," transfer the conservative tradition of classical Eurasianists like Danilevsky and Leontiev, including the rejection of Westernization and emphasis on the polycentric view of world history, to the Neo-Eurasianist camp. Through the prism of his fall and the subsequent rise of passionarity, Gumilev more or less rehabilitated the Imperial period among his modern contemporaries. Putin's thesis about a multi-polar world is a replica and compendium of this heritage.

The Duel of Civilizations

Aside from this extensive legacy, the ideas and emotions based on the many different interpretations of past traumas and abuses found their way into the minds of Neo-Eurasian nationalistic philosophers, who wrapped them in scholastic form, sometimes quite brilliantly. The most talented representative of this cohort is the radical right-wing Russian geopolitician Aleksandr Dugin. However, as is the case with most Russian thinkers who founded original theories, he based his rhetoric not only on his Russian predecessors but also on some ideas of his Western forerunners. One of these influences, for example, was Alfred Thayer Mahan and his 1890 naval history "The Influence of Sea Power upon History," which strongly influenced Theodore Roosevelt's own vision of American power. Mahan's ideas also influenced Woodrow Wilson, because, like Mahan himself, Wilson believed that "America should develop an overseas colonial empire to dominate global commerce much like Great Britain had done centuries earlier." In congruence with this, one should also be aware of the ideas presented by Halford Mackinder (1861–1947), a leading British cultural geographer, founding member of the London School of Economics, and the author of *The Geographical Pivot of History* (1904). In this book, published in the twilight of the Imperial period, Mackinder argued in favor of a British-Russian accord that would recognize the growing predominance of *land-based powers*, and not only Mahan's *sea-based empires*.[76]

In the preface of a Russian undergraduate textbook, Dugin requests that the students study geopolitics because of the threats posed by foreign "expansionist policies," such as the US-sponsored New World Order, Greater Europe, Greater China, and Greater Turan.[77] At this point, Russia's geopolitical visions mainly revolved around the idea that Russia is (and always has been) a distinct Eurasian entity. The Westernizing orientation heralded by these concepts, which were developed by liberal pro-West intellectuals and dominated foreign policy under Boris Yeltsin, faded into oblivion when Putin came to power. Aleksandr Dugin (b. 1962), a former activist of the small but prominent far-right movement *Pamyat'* ("*Memory*") in the late 1980s, was constantly establishing contacts with some of the most noticeable figures of the Russian imperial nationalists and European New Rightists. Since Vladimir Putin rose to power in Russia, Dugin's prominence has only increased, with Russia's official Eurasian orientation having been further consolidated as a response to Western (NATO and EU) expansion in Eastern Europe. Dugin's most important book, *Osnovy Geopolitiki: geopolticheskoye budushchee Rossii (Fundamentals of Geopolitics: The Geopolitical Future of Russia)*, was published in 1997 with the help of the Department of Strategy of the Russian General Staff Military Academy. Since then, it has been distributed and used as a standard textbook within the curriculum of this institution, which serves as the principal military academy of the Russian Federation.

Dugin's thesis—laid out as a single geopolitical law—is described as "the ceaseless duel of civilizations" or the "great war of continents." The two sides of the duel comprise (1) the land-based societies—"tellurocracies"/continental powers (embodied fully by Russia)—and sea-based societies—thalassocracies (embodied by "Atlanticists" led by Great Britain and, later on, by the United States). If the current geopolitical processes continued in the same direction that they currently hold, it would result in the inevitable annihilation of tellurocracy and, therefore, the real end of history. The opposite tendency, which is the total consolidation of tellurocracy in Eurasia (under leadership of Russia) would more than likely result in real bipolarity. Additionally, if a tellurocracy managed to establish Eurasian control over sea borders, then the end of history would be met under tellurocratic rule.[78] That is why the control of Crimea and the southeast coast of Ukraine is so important for Russia. Dugin and other Neo-Eurasianists believe that after the collapse of the Soviet Union, it was the thalassocracies who took full advantage of the crisis. They immediately put forward and began vehemently realizing their own projects to build "one-polar World" (variants of this idea are known as mondialization or globalization). According to Neo-Eurasianists, this project intends to force the peoples of other civilizations into adopting the "American way of life." By this, they primarily mean the proliferation of liberal-democratic values and gradual universalization. This in turn entails the compulsory adaptation of cultural, social, political, and economic principles that emerged in only one segment of humankind, namely in Western Europe, and reached their own "acme phase" in the Anglo-Saxon ethnic areas.[79]

As a result, it is the historical mission of Russia to meet this Western challenge. Dugin supposes that "the very 'developmental' place of Eurasia (as a reflection of Savitskii's *mestorazvitye*) makes it a fortress in the strategic continental space." Moreover, it makes Russia a core state—the veritable center of Eurasia. Thus, Dugin believes that Russia, as a result of its geographic location, geopolitical gravity, and historical background, is the only player in world politics able to put forward and affirm an alternative to the existing world order, *especially if they could establish a stable alliance with their closest contemporary: China.*[80]

Stemming from this, Dugin proposed the creation of the *Eurasian Project*.[81] If Russia builds itself a "Eurasian strategic block," (in co-partnership with China) then it should come to see itself as "a global alternative and powerful counterbalance to globalization."[82] Following its introduction, the ideas behind this project revitalized a dormant feeling of Russian paranoia and called for the creation of a strong anti-West discourse in the economic, social, cultural, and *politico-military spheres*, which are just now being realized by Putin.

Naturally, the idea of a "one-polar project" has been rejected by the Neo-Eurasianists, who, under the motto of "fighting for independence and cultural originality, national and state specifics," wish to instead promote a new Eurasian project. At the foundation of this approach lies the creation of an amalgamation (if not total union) of the states on the Eurasian continent under the aegis of a Russia that has "risen from the knees."[83]

Dugin in turn has introduced the possibility of enacting a "conservative revolution" that combines left-wing economics and right-wing cultural traditionalism. He also proposed the idea of building a Eurasian empire "constructed on the fundamental principle of the common enemy." In this case, these "common enemies" are Atlanticism, liberal values, and geopolitical control by the United States.[84]

This breed of "right-wing conservative traditionalism" is also strongly represented by Aleksandr Prokhanov (b. 1938), the editor-in-chief of *Zavtra* (*Tomorrow*), a famous and talented writer, chairman of the *Izborsky Club*, editor of *Izborsky Club Journal*, deputy chairman of the Public Council of the Ministry of Defense of the Russian Federation, a member of the Secretariat of Union of Writers in Russia, and so on. Throughout his career, he has authored more than forty works and has been awarded a number of state awards. By his own account, he is "a strong Stalinist."

Initially, Prokhanov was rather critical of Mr. Putin. (Recently Prokhanov has resumed his critical position regarding Putin's support of loyal oligarchs and pro-West liberals in his bureaucracy at the detriment of desired focus on creating the conditions for the growth of the Russian middle class). However, he would change his tune after the latter won a war against "the proud-dwellers in the Caucasus," after which point Prokhanov began calling him the "Emperor of the Fifth Empire." Prohanov's 2012 book, *The Tread of the Russian Triumph,* is a compendium of the views held by numerous right-wing pro-Putin intellectuals and Neo-Eurasianists. It is also a fictionalized account of Russian history that promotes the author's own doctrine of the "Fifth Empire," stating that the current *Eurasian Economic Union* has already started to evolve into a new geopolitical giant and the rightful successor of the four previous empires: the Kievan Rus/Novgorod Republic, the Muscovy Empire, the Romanovs' Russian Empire, and Stalin's USSR.[85] He continued, saying that "there will be a place for everyone in it: the left and right, Orthodox Christians and Muslim fundamentalists, synagogues and big business … like the Bolsheviks used the potential of the Romanovs's Empire, the Fifth Empire is to be composed of all kinds of disparate elements."[86]

In this way, Prokhanov has definitively proven himself not only as an esoteric thinker (for which he was already known) but also as a Neo-Eurasianist; he continued the work started by Gumilev, who was the first to bridge the sentiments of the classical and Neo-Eurasianists. Moreover, he completed a process initiated by Gumilev, who had begun the rehabilitation of a part of the historical-cultural content of the Imperial and Soviet periods with his theory of passionarnost.' Such ideas are very close to Putin, who himself has recurrently speculated about the necessity of establishing an "integral" approach to the history of Russia that would unite all inhabitants on the foundation of true patriotism rather than divide them as antagonistic groups.

As a shrewd politician, Putin has never presented himself as being in the company of these thinkers. However, and especially in regard to the most important aspects and elements of his goal to build up

Russia in the modern world, one can easily detect the strong influence of Neo-Eurasianists and even classical Eurasianists in his actions as of late. Now, with the adoption of the amendments to the Russian constitution initiated by Putin, one may see how many of the above-cited ideas of Dugin and Prokhanov found their way there.

Putin began implementing these ideas with the resolution of the Russian-Chechen ethnic conflict. He took into account the experience of the Imperial armies who conquered the Caucasus in the nineteenth century and of the Caucasian war with the mountaineers that followed.[87] In fact, the two prior incarnations of the Russian nation-state (the Imperial and the Soviet) rarely allowed the Caucasian mountaineers to practice their ways without some hindrance or molestation. The more aspects of mountaineer ethnicity were threatened by Imperial policies in pursuit of total domination of their social and cultural life, the more radical the ethnic mobilization and actions of the mountaineers became. In the long run, this approach would inevitably lead to a history of bloody clashes along ethnic lines.

The customary laws of the mountaineers, being the *Adats* and *Shariates*, were the primary targets of assimilatory policy from both Imperial and Soviet practices. Gumilev and the Neo-Eurasianists understood that these codes represented a compendium of protective norms and values that emerged naturally, which legitimized specific stereotypes and behavioral patterns aimed at self-preservation. In order to incorporate the mountaineers into the growing "Russian super-ethnos," central authorities needed to guarantee these codes by securing the normal functioning of the ethnicity's *principal building blocks*. As I stated above, defending their traditions, the mountaineers responded with armed rebellions that persevered for more than sixty years. Later, the tsarist administration learned the lessons and lifted the ban and guaranteed the administration of justice and punishments according to their *Adats*. In their turn, the mountaineers agreed to accept new Imperial legal qualifications, such as "high treason" and "obstruction of authorities," into their legal makeup. They even agreed to help defend the otherwise fiery rim of the empire.[88] Thus, the traditions were preserved and complementarity was again secured for a renewed growth of Russian super-ethnos, now reinforced by the incorporation of the mountaineer periphery.

In a repetition of history, Soviet power also attempted to assimilate the Chechens, this time with the aim to outright destroy the *Shariates* and *Adats*. But whenever the center was weakened, the mountaineers once again rebelled; in response, they were brutally suppressed and deported.

The Impact of Chechen Independence

Initially, as I stated above, Boris Yeltsin's government promised to allow the mountaineers to "grab as much sovereignty as they want." But when Chechnya declared full independence from Russia, Yeltsin fell back on the policy of his Imperial and Soviet predecessors.[89] Interestingly, the rebellious Chechens were referred to as *passionarii* by several writers who had previously adopted Gumilev's theory. According to the Neo-Eurasianists, all ethnocentric nationalists and their groups (including, for example, Islamist terrorists) are to be designated as passionarii. The reason for this lies in the fact that they will act aggressively, with a sense of apathy for the price that they and others will have to pay for engaging in a more violent approach.

The blatant and pointless Russian aggression under Yeltsin, combined with the brutal actions of the Russian military, only intensified the desire for ethnocentric separatism and its gradual transformation into part of a regional *jihad* led by foreign Wahhabi and Salafi militants.[90]

When Putin replaced Yeltsin in the Kremlin at the dawn of the twenty-first century, he struck a deal with the opponents of the Wahhabists, a coalition of Sufi groups headed by Ahmad Kadyrov. This led to the victory of this pro-Russian group. With it, the *Second hot stage* of the conflict ended in 2008, and traditional Islam was once again reinstated in the Caucasus and in Russia (see the corresponding chart in chapter 8).

With the assistance of Neo-Eurasian advisers, this experience helped Putin to elaborate on the new nation-state building policy, which later became an important part of the Neo-Eurasian project. The undisputed nucleus of this project is the effort to enshrine more *civic criteria* as the identifying factors of Russian citizenship, with "*Rossiyanin*" becoming part of *civic nationality*. Unlike the qualifications of ethnic nationality in Ukraine, Russian civic nationality applies to all territories of the Russian state. Membership in it is generally open to everyone who is born in or is a permanent resident of the national territory and beyond, irrespective of language, culture/religion, or ancestry. Essentially, this civic nationality can apply to any of the many peoples who once lived in the USSR. As a result, the modern Russian state now shows a favorable attitude toward the practice of "traditional religions" like Russian Orthodoxy, Islam, Buddism, and Judaism; while it bolsters a decidedly negative attitude toward so-called "extremist" religious organizations and their associated ideologies (like ISIS, Jehovah's Witnesses, and others).

The current relationship between organized religion and the state can be ultimately described as such: "Today, freed from the secular chains of Communism, the Russian government and the Russian Orthodox Church embrace each other politically, economically, and culturally in brotherly fashion. In consideration of the turbulent conditions in Russia during the 1990s, Patriarch Kirill, the primate of the Russian Orthodox See, rejoiced at Vladimir Putin's leadership: 'Through a miracle of God with the active participation of the country's leadership, we managed to exit this horrible systemic crisis.'"[91] Thus, the Byzantine and Petrine tradition of "embracement" of the church and state has been once again confirmed. Additionally, Glenn Ellis noted that "many of Putin's opponents believe the glowing endorsements and mutual [backslaps] the Kremlin and the Orthodox Church gave each other these days are contributing to ever more tightly defined and religious conservatism, and a growing personality cult around the president."[92]

A Eurasian Economic Union

The next aspect of the Eurasian project centers on the realization of the *Eurasian Economic Union*. This idea corresponds to the following conceptual building blocks of the politico-philosophical agenda of both classical and Neo-Eurasianist thinkers: the concept of global regionalization, a polycentric world order, and the geopolitical concept of the *core area*. Regarding these particular building blocks, Nataliya Vasilyeva and Maria Lagutina argue that Neo-Eurasianist ideas can be viewed from a geopolitical basis that supports the rationale behind the Eurasian Economic Union, which may constitute a more interpretational structure that consolidates the post-Soviet landscape and neighboring regions into a wholly new, and more cohesive, collective.

The treaty defining and establishing the EEU was signed in Astana, Kazakhstan, on May 29, 2014, between Belarus, Kazakhstan, and Russia; it was joined by Armenia and Kyrgyzstan the following year (2015). Today, the EEU covers an area over twenty million square kilometers and applies to a total population numbering more than 179 million. Alongside the provision of unified economic benefits, it is also augmented with additional free-trade zones.[93]

The next integrational projects are *The Shanghai Corporation Organization, the Union State of Russia and Belarus*, and the *Customs Union*. In the military political sphere, it is ODKB—the collective organization on security. This aspect of a bigger Eurasian project is based on the ideal of Eurasianists and indicates that modern Eurasia, under the leadership of the core state of Putin's Russia, has become one of the centers of integrational processes both regionally and globally. This is highlighted by the fact that the EEU is a key element of the new system of so-called "integration of integrations," which provides the backbone of the blustery Putin's global project of a "Greater Eurasia" that stretches from Lisbon to Shanghai.[94] The *Nord Stream* 1 and 2 and *Turkish Stream* gas lines connecting Russia and the EU are but an economic expression of this politico-philosophical paradigm. Given the recent deterioration of the *hot stage* of the Russo-Ukrainian violent ethnic conflict in Donbas, previously discussed in its corresponding timeline in chapter 9, a broad military confrontation, if it happens between Ukraine and Russia, may effectively bury this costly project by the hard sanctions "from hell" that would likely be imposed by the West on Russia following such a highly possible development.

Conclusion

By introducing his asymmetric consociational institutionalism (which I have previously discussed, in chapter 6), which guarantees the all-sided interests of the various ethnic minorities, Putin has successfully (for the time being) resolved many of the acute ethnic problems, prevented ethnocentric secessionism within Russia, and won the Chechens and other ethnic groups over to his side. Thus, to use Neo-Eurasianist terminology, he resumed a complementary strengthening of the Russian state. (Interestingly enough, the Chechen *Vostok* Battalion served as the vanguard of the Russian forces that defeated the Georgian Army in South Ossetia in 2008, with some of its members currently fighting for the DPR and LPR against the Ukrainian Army in Donbas).

Putin is fully aware that the process of Eurasian reintegration within the post-Soviet space is not possible without the inclusion of Ukraine (if at all possible), as well as his opponents in the West. By further promoting his reforms, mainly by providing favorable conditions *for the free functioning of all the principal building blocks of ethnic minorities* and creating conditions for a more civically consolidated *Russian state-building project* with the intention of creating a Eurasian *Rossiikii super-ethnos*, despite his best efforts, he sends a plain signal to the Russian-speaking ethnic minorities in Ukraine, inviting them to take part in the gradual rebirth of the region.

In contrast, the Ukrainian government, by adopting an *ethnocentric unitarist state-building project*, *rejecting the federalist alternative*, and vigorously implementing a policy of *Ukrainization*, have effectively undermined and jeopardized the *principal building blocks of ethnicity*, as well as the genuine interests/ concerns of the *ethno-political elites of minority groups*. Thus, they have successfully produced the optimal conditions for instilling a permanent all-sided societal crisis and ethnic tension within the country. This in turn allowed Putin to turn Crimea into a fortress—a veritable military bastion—against any further NATO expansion and to continue supporting the pro-Russian separatists in Donbas, with both serving as splinters in the side of the pro-West Ukraine.

With its own efforts, the West has done little to truly resolve the issue. By expelling Russia from the G8 organization in 2014, by imposing difficult economic sanctions on Russia and its projects (such as the Nord Stream 2, with which Russia hopes to bypass an openly hostile Ukraine to successfully transport its energy sources to Europe and thereby undermine the unfriendly Kyivan regime), and by providing Ukraine with weapons and support for their ethnocentric initiatives in all spheres of society, the West has been slowly whittling away any possibility of having a diplomatic dialogue with Russia. This in turn has the effect of pushing Russia to seek an alliance with China (see the above-discussed Neo-Eurasianist ideas) and gradually turn Ukraine into a battlefield between the East and West, with increasingly unpredictable consequences. Ironically, one crisis besets another, as the recent efforts of both sides have been significantly weakened by the outbreak of the COVID-19 pandemic. In addition, the West has been further weakened by the outbreak of riots and protests that peculiarly resemble many of the typical regularities of the previously detailed ethnic conflicts. Thus, the outcome of this geopolitical battle for Ukraine, in which both sides play an exacerbating role in the progression of ethnic violence, has become rather vague and concerningly unclear.

Notes

1   Anatoly Isaenko, *Polygon of Satan: Ethnic Traumas and Conflicts in the Caucasus*, 3rd ed. (Dubuque, IA: Kendall Hunt Publishing House, 2014), Introduction, parable.

2   Anatol Lieven, Preface to Emil Soulimanov, *An Endless War: The Russian-Chechen Conflict in Perspective* (Frankfurt, Germany: Peter Lang GMBH, 2007), 13; see also Anatol Lieven, "Through a Distorted Lens: Chechnya and the Western Media," *Current History* (October 2000), 321–28.

3   See Oliver Boyd-Barret, "Ukraine, Mainstream Media and Conflict Propaganda," *Journalism Studies* 18, no. 8 (2017): 1028.For a completely opposite, pro-Ukrainian view on the issue, see Nataliia Ischchuk, "Russian New Media Propaganda About the Events in the Eastern Ukraine and Crimea," *Fundamental and Applied Researches in Practice of Leading Scientific Schools* 31, no. 1 (2019): 71–76, https//doi.org/10.33531/farplss.2019.1.15. See also Maria Snegovaya, *Russia Report I. Putin's Information Warfare in Ukraine: Soviet Origins of Russia's Hybrid Warfare* (Washington, DC: Institute for the Study of War, 2015).

4   Boyd-Barret, "Ukraine, Mainstream Media, and Conflict Propaganda," 1028.

5   Boyd-Barret, "Ukraine, Mainstream Media, and Conflict Propaganda," 1028.

6   Boyd-Barret, "Ukraine, Mainstream Media, and Conflict Propaganda," 1029.

7   Boyd-Barret, "Ukraine, Mainstream Media, and Conflict Propaganda," 1030.

8   Boyd-Barret, "Ukraine, Mainstream Media, and Conflict Propaganda," 1030.

9   Boyd-Barret, "Ukraine, Mainstream Media, and Conflict Propaganda," 1030.

10 Boyd-Barret, "Ukraine, Mainstream Media, and Conflict Propaganda," 1030.

11 On Russian Television, Channel 1, an advertisement depicting this message periodically appeared in the commercial breaks during pro-Kremlin journalist Vladimir Solovyov's daily political talk show.

12 Ilia Zuev, "Shoigu nazval naibol'shuyu ugrozu dlia voennoj bezopasnosti Rossii," *Vechernyaia Moskva*, May 20, 2020,vm.ru/news/801816-shoigu-nazval-naibolshuyu-ugrozu-dlya-voennoj-bezopasnosti-rossii?from=smi2.

13 Eric Zuesse, "Ukraine's President Poroshenko Says Overthrow of Yanukovych was a Coup," *Global Research*, June 23, 2015. The author also reports that George Friedman—founder of Strategic Forecasting Inc. (Stratfor)—once said: "It really was the most blatant coup in history." See note 14 in Robert H. Wade, "Reinterpreting the Ukrainian Conflict: The Drive for Ethnic Subordination and Existing Enemies," *Challenge* 58, no. 4 (2015): 370.

14   See Martin Wolf, "Help Ukraine Seize This Chance," *Financial Times*, February 11, 2015; also cited in Wade, "Reinterpreting the Ukrainian Conflict," 361. See also Robert H. Wade "The Ukraine Crisis Is Not What It Seems," *Le Monde Diplomatique*, March 31, 2015, http://mondediplo.com/blogs/the-ukraine-crisis-is-not-what-it-seems.

15   "A Tactical Pause in Putin's Assault in Ukraine," *Financial Times*, February 13, 2015, cited in Wade, "Reinterpreting the Ukrainian Conflict," 362.

16   Alexander Motyl's own words cited in Wade, "Reinterpreting the Ukrainian Conflict," 364.

17   Boyd-Barrett accurately summarized the general positions within Western media. See his "Ukraine, Mainstream Media, and Conflict Propaganda," 1022.

18   "Ukriane-Krise: Nato-Obserbefehlshaber verargeret Allierte," *Spiegel Online*, March 7, 2015, cited in Wade, "Reinterpreting the Ukrainian Conflict," 367.

19   "Ukriane-Krise: Nato-Obserbefehlshaber verargeret Allierte," cited in Wade, "Reinterpreting the Ukrainian Conflict," 367.

20   Wade, "Reinterpreting the Ukrainian Conflict," 368; US Lieutenant General Frederick "Ben" Hodges, former commanding officer of the United States Army Europe, estimated that there were approximately 12,000 Russian troops operating inside Ukraine as of March 2015. See Mark Urban, "How Many Russians Are Fighting in Ukraine?" *BBC News*, March 10, 2015; see, note 19 in Wade, "Reinterpreting the Ukrainian Conflict," 370.

21   Robert Parry, "NYT Discovers Ukraine's Neo-Nazis at War," *Consortium News*, August 10, 2014, cited in Boyd-Barrett, "Ukraine, Mainstream Media and Conflict Propaganda," 1024.

22   Boyd-Barrett, "Ukraine, Mainstream Media and Conflict Propaganda," 1025. Recently, Daniel McAdams revealed that "the Kiev government lied about the attack on Luhansk and that those lies were accepted by the U.S. government and the vast majority of the U.S. mainstream media," as quoted in Boyd-Barrett, "Ukraine, Mainstream Media and Conflict Propaganda," 1025. Additionally, while local media has only recently begun showing the results of the recurrent shelling of certain areas in Luhansk and Donetsk—specifically those districts under the control of the DPR/LPR—these attacks have never been openly presented to or condemned by the West. This shows that the Ukrainian side has continued to win the informational war against Russia.

23   "The Ancestors of Many Nations Could Once Have Left Ukraine—Geography Textbook," *IA Regnum*, May 16, 2002, regnum.ru/news/polit/2951814.html. For samples of denouncing similar tricks of the Russian conflict propaganda against the Ukrainian state, its leaders, and military, please see Vladimir Sazonov, M. A. Kristina Muur, and Holger Molder, eds., *Russian Information Campaign Against the Ukrainian State and Defense Forces* (Tartu, Latvia: NATO Strategic Communication Center of Excellence, Estonian National Defense College, 2016).

24   "Ukrainian TV Presenter Wished to "Die" the Residents of Donbass and Crimea,"*IA Regnum*, May 31, 2002, regnum.ru/news/polit/2967525.html.

25   "Ukrainian Store Humiliated Jews," *Lenta*, January 16, 2020, lenta.ru/news/2020/01/16/antis/?utm_source=smi2&utm_medium=exchange&es=smi2.

26   "In Ukraine, Outraged by the Sale of Canned Food with 'Pieces of Russian-Speaking Babies,'" *Lenta*, January 10, 2020,lenta.ru/news/2020/01/10/cannedfood/?utm_source=smi2&utm_medim=exchange&es=smi2.

27 "Zatyanuvshiisya fars, ili Minsko-Donbasskii geopoliticheskii pasyans," *Eurasia Daily*, May 18, 2020, eadaily.com/ru/news/2020/05/18/zatyanuvshiysya-fars-ili-minsko-donbasskiy-geopolitich-eskii-pasyans?utm_source=smi2.

28 "A Tactical Pause in Putin's Assault in Ukraine," *Financial Times*, February 13, 2015, see note 683.

29 Paul Henze, *Conflict in the Caucasus* (Chapel Hill, NC: UNC Library, Rand Library Collection, 1995), 19, emphasis added.

30 Anatol Lieven, *Ukraine and Russia: A Fraternal Rivalry* (Washington, DC: US Institute of Peace Press, 1999), cited in Richard Sakwa, *Frontline Ukraine: Crisis in the Borderlands* (London: I. B. Tauris, 2015), 50.

31 Lieven, *Ukraine and Russia: A Fraternal Rivalry*, cited in Sakwa, *Frontline Ukraine*.

32 The idea of Eurasianism first appeared on the verge of the nineteenth and twentieth centuries. Conceptually it was elaborated by many representatives of Russian historical and political philosophical thought. Among them are: N. Ya. Danilevsky, K. N. Leontyev, N. S. Trubetzkoy, G. V. Vernadsky, P. N. Savitskii, and L. N. Gumilev. See *The Color Revolutions in the Former Soviet Republics: Success and Failures* (London: Routledge, 2010). See also https://en.wikipedia.org/wiki/Colour_revolution.

33 V. L. Kaganskii, "Mnimyi Put' Rossia—Eurasia," *Kul'turnyi landshaft i sovetskoye obitaemoye prostranstvo* ("Imagined Way, Russia—Eurasia", *Cultural Landscape and Soviet Inhabited Space*) (Moscow: S.N., 2001), 414.

34 Kaganskii, "Mnimyi Put' Rossia," 414.

35 See, for example, S.G. Luzyanin, *Vostochnaya politica Vladimira Putina. Vozvrashenie na "Bol'shoi Vostok"(2004–2008)(Eastern Politics of Vladimir Putin, The Return of Russia to the "Big East" (2004–2008)),* (Moscow: S. N., 2007).

36 The term "post-Soviet space" was popularized following the collapse of the Soviet Union in the 1990s; as of late, it has been gradually replaced by the moniker of "Eurasian" or "New-Eurasian" space within the lap of the Russian political establishment and general political thought, as the Eurasian project itself began to grow. See Nataliya A. Vasilyeva and Maria L. Lagutina, *The Russian Project of Eurasian Integration*: *Geopolitical Prospects* (Lanham, MD: Lexington Books, 2016), 2–3.

37 See *Glavkom* (17 Kvitnya, 2014). For the Ukrainian perspective on who is guilty in this ethnic conflict, see Pavlo Hai-Nyzhnyk, L. Chupriy, Y. Fihurnyi, I. Krasnodemska, O. Chyrkov, *Aggression of the Russian Federation Against Ukraine: Ethno-national Dimension and Civilizational Confrontation* (Saarbrucken, Germany: LAP Lambert Academic Publishing, 2018).

38 "Russia's Got a Point: The US Broke a NATO Promise," *Los Angeles Times*, May 30, 2016.

39 Christopher Clark and Kristina Spohr, "Moscow's Account of NATO Expansion Is a Case of False Memory Syndrome," *The Guardian*, May 24, 2015.

40 Thomas Friedman, "Foreign Affairs: Now a Word from X," *New York Times*, May 2, 1998.

41 Wade, "Reinterpreting the Ukrainian Conflict," 366–67.

42 "Ex-NSA and Intelligence Veterans Warn Merkel on U.S. Lies Concerning 'Russian Invasion' of Ukraine," quoted in Wade (who added the single quotation emphasis), "Reinterpreting the Ukrainian Conflict," 367. See note 16 for the online address of the source.

43 Richard Sakwa, *Frontline Ukraine*, 47.

44 Arkady Ostrovsky, "Inside the Bear," *The Economist*, October 22, 2016, 11, 13. Here I wish to argue against some statements of professor Daniel Triesman—who had an interesting article published in

Foreign Affairs, in which he dismissed three otherwise plausible interpretations of Putin's move to the Crimea: (1) "[the] Crimean operation was a response to the threat of NATO's further expansion along Russia's Western border." (2) "Putin is imperialist" and (3) Putin as an improviser. It seems to me that Professor Triesman inclines to support the third version. He writes: "In both Crimea and Syria, Putin has sought to exploit surprise, moving fast to change facts on the ground before the West could stop him by reacting boldly to crisis, he creates new ones for Russia and the World." It seems that the bulk of his argument homes in on Putin's tactics. In view of what I said above regarding existent Russian paranoia as a *legacy of tragic history*, there is not really a basis for rational explanations. I do not think that he lied when he said that the "West crossed the red line" in the Ukraine, as Putin truly believes that the very existence of Russia is threatened. See Daniel Triesman, "Why Putin Took Crimea: The Gambler in the Kremlin," *Foreign Affairs*, May/June 2016, 47–54.

45 Samuel P. Huntington, *The Clash of Civilizations?: The Debate* (New York: Foreign Affairs, 1996), 8.

46 I. I. Osinsky, "K chitatelyam," *Yevraziistvo i mir* 1 (2013): 4.

47 N. Ya. Danilevsky, *Rossiya i Yevropa (Russia and Europe)*, retrieved 2013, ch. V. The author distinguishes four particular categories of historical-cultural activity: (1) religious, (2) political, (3) sociopolitical, and (4) cultural. These four categories in turn gave rise to ten historical-cultural types: Chaldean, Hebrew, Arab, Indian, Persian, Greek, Roman (Ancient Italian), Germanic, Hamitic (Egyptian), and Chinese.

48 See Maria V. Rubtsova, Oleg V. Pavenkov, Vladimir Pavenkov, "Identity of Russian Elite in Theory of N. Danilevsky," *Proceedings of the 2nd International Conference on Identity Studies* (Vienna: September 6–7, 2016) Available at: https://ssrn.com/abstract=2919917.

49 Rubtsova et al., "Identity of Russian Elite."See also L. Abalkin, "N. Ya. Danilevsky about Russia, Europe, and Slavic Unity" *Voprosy Economiki (Questions of Economics)* 11 (2002).

50 Danilevsky, *Rossya i Yevropa*, ch. V.

51 See Nicholas Rzhevsky, *Russian Literature and Ideology: Herzen, Dostoevsky, Leontiev, Tolstoy, Fadeyev* (Champaign:University of Illinois Press, 1983), 101f.

52 Rzhevsky, *Russian Literature and Ideology*, 101f.

53 Pavel N. Savitskii, Nikolai Trubetzkoy, Pierre Souvtchinsky, *Exodus to the East: Forebodings and Events: An Affirmation of the Eurasianists*, ed. Georges Florovsky (Marina del Ray, CA: Schlacks Jr. Pub, 1996), Preface.

54 "Eurasianism—Dictionary Definition of Eurasianism," *Encyclopedia of Philosophy* (2017) http://encyclopedia.com.

55 Ilya Vinkovetsky and Charles Schlacks, Jr., eds., *Exodus to the East: Forebodings and Events: An Affirmation of the Eurasians* (Marina del Ray, CA: Charles Schlacks, 1996), Preface.

56 For details on these Eurasianist ideas, see Nicholas V. Riazanovsky, "The Emergency of Eurasianism," *California Slavic Studies*, no. 4 (1967): 39–74; see also Nicholas V. Riazanovsky, "Prince N. S. Trubetzkoy's 'Europe and Mankind," *Juhrbucher fur Geschihte Osteuropas*, no. 12 (1964): 207–20; Dmitry V. Shlapentokh, "Eurasianism Past and Present," *Communist and Post-Communist Studies* 30,no. 2 (1997): 129–51; Ilya Vinkovetsky, "Classical Eurasianism and Its Legacy," *Canadian-American Slavic Studies* 34, no. 2 (2000): 125–39.

57 Nikolai Trubetzkoy, *The Legacy of Genghis Khan and Other Essays on Russia's Identity*, ed. Anatoly Liberman (Ann Arbor: Michigan Slavic Publications, 1991).

58 Charles J. Halperin, "George Vernadsky, Eurasianism, the Mongols, and Russia," *Slavic Review* 41, no. 3 (September 1982): 477–93. This article contains an excellent bibliography of Vernadsky's publications.

59 Charles Halperin, "George Vernadsky, Eurasianism, the Mongols, and Russia," *Slavic Review* 41, no. 3 (2017): 477–93, https://doi.org/10.2307/2497020 (2017). See also George Vernadsky, "Mongol'skoe igo v russkoi istorii" ("Mongol's Yoke in the Russian History"), *Evraziiskii Vremennik* (*Eurasian Calendar*), no. 5 (1927): 153–64; George Vernadsky, *Opyt istorii Evrazii s poloviny vi veka do nastoiyashego vremeni* (*The Experience of the History of Eurasia from the VI-th Century to Nowadays*) (Berlin: S. N., 1934) 11–3, 108, 131–32.

60 Mark M. Bliev, *The Ossetian Embassy to St. Petersburg, 1749–1752: Joining of Ossetia to Russia*, translated from Russian to English by Anatoly Isaenko (Vladikavkaz: "Avri-Asin", 2011), 6–7.

61 The most profound analysis of Gumilev's ideas to date is presented in Alexander S. Titov, *Lev Gumilev, Ethno-genesis and Eurasianism*, PhD Dissertation (University College London, 2005), 184.

62 Titov, *Lev Gumilev*, 191.

63 P. N. Savitskii, *Rossiia osobyi geograficheskii mir (Russia as a Special Geographic World)* (Prague: S.N., 1927), 58–59.

64 Savitskii, *Rossiia osobyi geograficheskii mir*, 63–67.

65 Lev Gumilev, *Ethnogenez i biosfera zemli (Ethno-genesis and Biosphere of Earth)* (Moscow: Eksmo 2007), 667f.

66 Nikolai S. Trubetzkoy, "Obshcheevraziiskii natsionalism" ("Pan-Eurasian Nationalism"), *Istoria, Kul'tura, Iazyk* (*History, Culture, and Language*) (Moscow: Arktogeia, 1995), 417–26.

67 Trubetzkoy, "Mysli ob avtarkii" ("Thoughts about Autarky"), *Istoria, Kul'tura, Iazyk* (*History, Culture, and Language*), 436–37.

68 Trubetzkoy, *Istoria, Kul'tura, Iazyk*, 438–43; 406–16.

69 Lev N. Gumilev, "Skazhu Vam po sekretu, chto esli Rossia budet spasena, to tol'ko kak evraziiskaia derzhava" ("I'll Tell you a Secret: If Russia Is Saved—Then It Could Be Saved Only as a Eurasian Power") *Ritmy Evrazii: epokhi i tsivilizatsii (Rhythms of Eurasia: Epochs and Civilizations)* (Moscow: S.N., 1993), 26.

70 Titov, *Lev Gumilev*, Conclusion.

71 Mark Bassin, "Eurasianism and Geopolitics in Post-Soviet Russia," *Russia and Europe: Conference Proceedings*, ed. Jakub M. Godzimirski (Center for Russian Studies, Norwegian Institute of International Affairs, March 4, 1989), 38; see also Titov, *Lev Gumilev*, 212–13.

72 Lev N. Gumilev, *Ot Rusi do Rossii (From Rus' to Russia)* (Moscow: Eksmo, 2000), 192; Lev N. Gumilev, "Menia nazyvaiut evraziitsem" ("They Call Me Eurasianist"), *Nash Sovremennik (Our Contemporary)*, no.1 (1991), 139; Titov, *Lev Gumilev*, 156–57.

73 Titov, *Lev Gumilev*, 177–78.

74 V. Iu. Ermolaev, "Rossiia 2000—vek voiny ili stoletie mira?" ("Russia of 2000—the Century of War or the Century of Peace?" *Deti Fel'dmarshala*, (*Children of Field Marshal*), no. 12 (2000): 4.

75 Lev. N. Gumilev, "Zakony vremeni" ("Laws of Time") *Literaturnoe obozrenie (Literature Observer)*, no. 3 (1990): 3–9; Lev. N. Gumilev, *Konets i vnov' nachalo (The End and Again the Beginning)* (Moscow: Eksmo, 2001).

76   York Norman, "Prophets of Global Conflagration: Woodrow Wilson, Halford Mackinder, Karl Haushofer and Alexander Helphand Parvus on Democracy, Alliances, and Empire," unpublished transcript presented to Anatoly Isaenko, 2.

77   A full biography and critical analysis of Dugin's ideas is available in Alan Ingram, "Alexander Dugin: Geopolitics and Neo-Fascism in Post-Soviet Russia," *Political Geography* 20, no. 8 (2001): 1029–51, 1031–32; see also Andreas Umland, "Alexandr Dugin, the Issue of Post-Soviet Fascism, and Russian Political Discourse Today," *Russian Analytical Digest*, no. 14 (6 February 2007): 2–5.

78   Alexandr Dugin, *Osnovy geopoltiki: Geopoliticheskoye budushee Rossii* (Moscow: Rossiiskaya Akademia General'nogo Shtaba VS Rossii, 1997), 5, 259–62, 265.

79   I. I. Osinskii, "K chitateliam" ("To the Readers") *Evraziistvo i mir* (*Eurasianism and World*), 5; Alexandr Dugin, *Evraziiskii put' kak natsional'naya idea* (*Eurasian Way as a National Idea*), (Moscow: "Arktogeya-sentr, 2002), 18.

80   Dugin, *Evraziiskii put' kak natsional'naya idea* , 18.

81   Dugin, *Evraziiskii put' kak natsional'naya idea*, 85.

82   Dugin, *Evraziiskii put' kak natsional'naya idea*, 90, 94.

83   Osinskii, "To the Readers,"6.

84   Dugin, *Osnovy geopolitiki*, 259–62; see also Andreas Umland, "Alexander Dugin's Transformation from a Lunatic Fringe into a Mainstream Political Publicist, 1980–1998: A Case Study in the Rise of Late and Post-Soviet Russian Fascism," *Journal of Eurasian Studies*1, no. 2 (2010): 144–52.

85   Aleksandr Prokhanov, *The Fifth Empire Is Getting Born Right Now*, Newstand.com (2012); Aleksandr Prokhanov, *Piataia Imperia* (*The Fifth Empire*) (Moscow: Ecsmo, 2007), Introduction.

86   Cited in Zakhar Prilepin, *Alexandr Prokhanov: The Demiurge, Nurturing an Infant*, Zakhar Prilepin's website, retrieved January 13, 2014.

87   Isaenko, *Polygon of Satan*, 104.

88   Isaenko, *Polygon of Satan*, 194.

89   Isaenko, *Polygon of Satan*, 268–9.

90   Emil Souleimanov, "Islam as a Uniting and Dividing Force in Chechen Society," *Prague Watchdog-Crisis in Chechnya*, October 20, 2004, www.watchdog.cz.

91   An excerpt of "Russian Foundational Identities: Church and State" from Evan Wallace, *Tiertus Romane: An Examination of Muscovite Political Theology*, MA Thesis (Appalachian State University, 2018); Gleb Bryanski, "Russian Patriarch Calls Putin Era 'Miracle of God,'" *Reuters UK*, February 8, 2012.

92   Glenn Ellis, "Putin and the 'Triumph of Christianity' in Russia," *Aljazeera*, October 19, 2017.

93   Vasilyeva and Lagutina, *The Russian Project of Eurasianist Integration*, Part 3.

94   Vasilyeva and Lagutina, *The Russian Project of Eurasianist Integration*, 192.

CONCLUSION

In conclusion, I want to briefly summarize and emphasize the most important observations that I have made within each *aspect* of the *theoretical model* developed and discussed in the corresponding *chapters*.

(I). The *first aspect and corresponding chapter 1* dealt with the nature of ethnicity itself as applicable to those ethnic groups/ethnic nations on the eve of and following the collapse of the Soviet Union in 1991, which have since found themselves embroiled in violent ethnic conflict. An overview of their historical interactions during the Imperial, Soviet, and post-Soviet periods, as well as a comparative analysis of the definitions of other specialists (including anthropologists, linguists, psycho-historians, political scientists, and sociologists) based on their own studies of ethnic groups/nations in different periods of their history and around the world, allow me to argue that all of them, as products of historical evolution, share the same ethnic indications—those attributes and/or descriptors that have remained virtually the same over long stretches of time. Moreover, a comparative study of their traditional cultures indicates that all ethnic groups have been elaborating on the *protective norms* surrounding their most basic constituents/ethnic building blocks. Such norms represent the most essential components of customary law, such as, for example, the Adats and Shariates in the Caucasus. The most protected indications/attributes are *language, commonly shared history* (especially a collective memory of acute, unresolved *chosen traumas*, which have to be avenged or redeemed), *nationality, religion*, and a sense of belonging expressed in terms of *a common biological origin* or *blood relation*.

In the process of building and subsequently functioning within a society, ethnic groups are distinguished by these so-called *cultural boundary markers* and differentiating *index features* (please see the definitions in chapter 1). As a result, any kind of encroachment and/or infringement upon either generates a monumentally negative reaction. As more and more building blocks/cultural boundary markers are threatened by the policies of another dominant ethnic nation, the resulting ethnic conflict becomes more and more uncompromising/acute. In the long history of interactions between ethnic groups within the former Soviet Union, one may find many examples ultimately proving the utmost value of these building blocks and cultural markers for all ethnic groups. For the sake of example, please see in chapter 1the citation from the sermon of Sheikh Kunta-Khadji Kishiev, founder of the Zikrist branch of Sufi Islam in the Caucasus.[1]

(II). The conditional "pyramid" of the *second aspect in chapter* 2 shows the place of ethnic groups within the structures of the modern world. Eight distinct world civilizations occupy the uppermost section of this pyramid. Below them are the so-called "nation-states." Closer to the bottom of the pyramid are the various ethnic groups, with the fourth and final layer consisting of the constituent tribes, clans, and families that have historically built the superseding ethnic groups. I have searched tirelessly for any previously existing definitions for each of these units, a comparison of which allows me to conclude that all four of them share the same building blocks/constituents, as identified and described in the *first chapter*. However, they have one highly essential difference: each slightly prioritizes one building block over the others, despite them all being massively important to all of these sections at large. In the case of the world civilizations, the most formative building block—a veritable cornerstone of their makeup—is *religion*; for nation states—*nationality*; for ethnic groups—*language*; for the tribes, clans, and families—*a common biological origin* is of the utmost importance. Aside from these highlighted constituents and the remaining building blocks, a *shared history* of common struggle and *chosen traumas* also plays a significant role in the functional cohesiveness of these sections.

As a result, if a conflict occurs between ethnic groups, it may easily draw in the involvement of *kin nation-states*. These bodies, which can range from foreign co-ethnic diasporas to entire countries, usually mobilize any and all available resources and power at their disposal to aid their compatriots in defending their "national cause." Since these nation-states may be separated by different religious building blocks into separate world civilizations, some especially sharp ethnic conflicts may occur as a result of their involvement. This would most likely come about when certain ethnic groups, who have close connections to the most powerful of nation-states (especially core states of civilizational units, like, for example, the United States of America—a core state of the Judeo-Christian Transatlantic Western civilization—or Russia—a core state of the Eastern Orthodox Christian civilization), trigger the deterioration in the relationship between nation-states over their support of different ethnic groups. While this support is generally justified due to cultural proximity, it is *mostly* done for the sake of pragmatic geopolitical considerations and/or imagined security dilemmas from the nations involved. In the worst-case scenario, this could even provoke armed conflict between all involved states. Thus, my argument, which is backed by the examples presented in this and other chapters, is such: along the lines of many other interstate/intertribal/inter-clan conflicts, it is ultimately the *associated ethnic conflict that has the most dangerous potential for outreach* in the highly interdependent modern world.

(III). The *third aspect in the third chapter* provides several past examples as to how ethnic groups responded to the challenges imposed by super-ordinate nations in their attempts to subdue or assimilate them. This includes the Imperial categorization of ethnic groups, Stalin's categorization of the Soviet peoples, and the renewed assimilatory ideological campaign in the post-Stalin period of the USSR, just to name a few.

The exceptionally complicated histories of the various Ukrainian sub-ethnic groups living under the aegis of multiple super-ordinate powers, as well as the outright tragic history of the Cossacks as a whole, serve as primary examples of the widespread applications of these challenges. No matter the intensity of their masters' attempts to destroy their most important ethnic building blocks, all efforts to do so soundly failed in the long run. Even if the sub-ethnic groups suffered as a result of their resistance—being beaten down by heavy losses and assimilatory policies—these trials and tribulations only *hardened their basic ethnic constituents*. Furthermore, these groups readily added these very same losses to an ever-growing list of unresolved chosen traumas, encapsulating them in their collective memory of victimization and postponing them until a time that their former masters would become weak, after which they would seek compensation for the losses they suffered, be it in money, territory, or blood. But until then, they would accumulate the energy of their dreams and latently work toward their ultimate revenge for these past offenses. To that end, many Caucasian mountaineers, especially Muslim Chechens and some Dagestani groups, participated in twelve separate rebellions against Russian domination and assimilatory attempts over the last 300 years. In this case, one of the most provocative building blocks behind their resistance was *nationality*—the right to their clans' native land—which had been aggravated by numerous historical chosen traumas, including military defeats and mass relocations. Both the *religious* and *linguistic* building blocks would become major driving forces during the Imperial and Soviet periods, as they would both suffer from assimilatory attempts under a multitude of ideological disguises. In one instance, the Cossacks openly rebelled against the Soviets and became victims of Genocide as a result (though they have made a miraculous comeback following the collapse of the USSR).

The most provocative (or, to use Vernadsky's terminology, "passionate") and educated ethnic activists created a literary base that generated ideas and plans for "national liberation." Sometimes they utilized a very sophisticated combination of "situational," "constructivist," and/or "instrumentalist" tactics to preserve and promote their ethnic identities and constituents—especially language—in otherwise unfavorable environments.

However, if conditions allow for these changes to take root, then there will be a rapid growth in their implementation. Such was the case for the Ukrainians in Galicia when, under the yoke of their Austrian masters (who planned to use Ukrainians living in the region against their neighbors, most notably the Russians), they mustered an educated vanguard of western Ukrainians and immediately took advantage of a precarious situation, for the first time in history outlining a comprehensive ethnic state-building project with themselves at the center. Since that time, Galicia/Halychyna has become the heart and citadel of the Ukrainian integral (i.e., ethnocentric) nationalist movement. Moreover, after the collapse of the USSR in 1991, these same ethnocentric nationalists have become rather notorious in their attempts to rejuvenate this state-building plan in all spheres of the newly independent Ukrainian state pertaining to the building blocks of ethnicity. Needless to say, other subdivisions of the Ukrainian ethnos, as a result of living in other areas of Ukraine, being subject to the effects of a different history and belonging to other ethnic nations that neighbor the core ethnicities, wanted to preserve *their own* regional or sub-ethnic identities. This creates an auspicious basis for the development of uncompromising violent ethnic conflicts on the *intrastate level*, with the almost guaranteed involvement of ethnic diasporas and neighboring home (revisionist) states siding with their co-ethnics. This results in the overt transformation of these intrastate conflicts into an *interstate* form, which can itself result in further *internationalization* and even clashes between entire civilizations.

I remember how, during his 1993 visit to the Caucasus, my friend and benevolent colleague Professor Peter Petschauer told me that he was amazed at how the locals recounted their chosen traumas, some of which had taken place hundreds of years prior, as if they had just happened the day before. They also told him how they would force the new generation of perpetrators to recognize their past offenses and then pay for them dearly. With the outbreak of the current social drama in America (and Western Europe), in which our own historical injustices are haunting us at full strength, all of my colleagues who were critical of this aspect of my theoretical model have a more relatable and readily available avenue for assessing its credibility.

(IV). In the *fourth aspect and corresponding fourth chapter*, I analyzed the impact of an all-sided societal crisis on the ethnic groups/nations of the Soviet Union, both amid and after its collapse. Through this analysis, I succinctly demonstrated how a combination of ontological, decisional, and conjunctural factors coalesced, ultimately resulting in the collapse of the Soviet supranational state. In the context of this research, it is important to emphasize that an all-sided societal crisis, which was further enhanced by the very same collapse it triggered, almost totally destroyed the sociopolitical, economic, ideological, and even moral constraining mechanisms of ethnic confrontation, which had already suffered degeneration since the remote past. However, the most important observation to take away from this chapter is that the prolonged presence of an all-sided societal crisis puts people in a situation where their ability to cope with stress, both on the individual and group level, is slowly exceeded. As a result, they begin responding to the entirety of the situation with anger, anxiety, and (sometimes) depression. And like any other highly charged emotions, these feelings inevitably spill over into the political arena, as the people needed to track down and punish those responsible for their otherwise wretched situation. They also have a need to find those among them who might be able to reestablish some semblance of control within the various local levels of society. When this kind of climate began to permeate the Soviet Union, many conspiracy theories and unfounded motives began to flourish and were usually accepted without any critical thought. People sought strong figures who could (supposedly) handle the situation that they had all inexplicably found themselves in. Thus, they began to rally behind nationalistic leaders and their ethnocentric organizations, which soon came to replace the older structures of their Soviet past and ascend to power in their respective polities.

At the same time, while researching the situations taking place in the new "national" republics within the framework of this aspect and chapter, I found that the thresholds leading to the potential combustibility of these conflicts were seriously lowered through both a regressive political climate and the deterioration of the social system at large. Oftentimes, people were outspoken about the need to establish strong borders between themselves and their ethnic enemies, repeating their leadership's blustery and near-paranoid ideas, while such leaders themselves were acting out of their own primitive aggressive tendencies.

(V). Hence, *the fifth aspect* in *chapter 5* examines the role of the ethno-political elites and charismatic leaders in the post-Soviet states as the driving forces behind continued regressive development of ethnic conflicts. These newly established ethno-political elites gradually grew into an odd combination of formally unassociated groups: the "national communist" nomenklatura, composed of the party, Komsomol, Soviet directors, and other officials, including those from the KGB, Army, and law enforcement agencies, which became newly "elected" nationalistic leaders perched on the various rungs of the equally new sociopolitical ladder; former Soviet "shady" businessmen and legal entrepreneurs; the ethnic mafias; and anti-Soviet (or anti-Russian) national democratic activists, who later became the heads of different "People's" front-sand ethnocentric organizations. Out of this broadly composed group sprang up the powerful oligarchs, flanked by bodyguards and private armies. Using their influence, these people privatized entire sections of political power, staffed by their own handpicked cronies and many of the most important mainstream media outlets. And this doesn't even begin to cover their lucrative economic branches, for which they engaged in intermittent wars to bolster their own power, thereby spreading the same chaos and institutionalized corruption that has prolonged the all-sided crises well into the modern day (with Ukraine being a primary example).

For this part of the chapter, I collected and cited examples of the shared characteristics of such people as presented by leading experts—such as Volodymyr Polokhalo, Serhy Yekelchuk, Richard Sakwa, Taras

Kuzio, and others—who argue that through their implementation, these oligarchs were able to create a structure of wild frontier/oligarchic "crony" capitalism.

On the other hand, charismatic leaders who rose to power out of the aforementioned groups, with the help of ethnocentric activists/organizations on the payroll of different oligarchic groups, gradually formulated their own variety of ethno-political paradigms. (For a list of these ethnocentric organizations and their respective characteristics/paradigms relevant to current ethnic conflicts, see chapter 5.) In most cases, these charismatic individuals simply revitalized and modernized the older ethno-political projects of their predecessors, which themselves had been attempted amid the collapse of the Russian Empire and the subsequent Civil War of 1918–1921. Alternatively, as is the case in Ukraine, modern ethnocentric nationalists retrieved and rejuvenated the state-building policies and ideologies of that same period, as well as the ideologies of the Ukrainian integral (ethnocentric) nationalism propagated during the 1930s. With this in mind, it should by no means be a surprise that these modern violent ethnic conflicts emerged in a manner eerily similar to those of the previous cycle.

The post-Soviet ethno-political elites of the newly established national republics elaborated and enacted state policies and economic measures that generated unbearable conditions in areas populated primarily by ethnic minorities, sometimes to the point of initiating and even leading full-on ethnic pogroms. They endorsed mild and middle-ground forms of ethnic cleansing that I surmised as pertaining to all five building blocks of ethnicity. This kind of ethnic cleansing policy was, in a sense, an attempt to establish borders between one's own ethnic nation and their neighbors/enemies, who had been almost totally demonized by large-scale projective processes. As these mild/middle-ground forms of ethnic cleansing evolved, I saw how symbolic objects—monuments, churches, museums, etc.—dedicated to oppositional activists and cultural representatives of ethnic minorities were attacked with ever-increasing frequency. Supposedly, the intended goal was to debase the "enemy" and rid one's own territory of the symbols belonging to the "evil other." In this portion of the chapter, I provided several such examples from areas around the Caucasus during the initial stages of many separate ethnic conflicts. As a result of these aforementioned policies, the sociopolitical landscapes within these republics had undergone total *ethnic absorption*, setting off a violent exchange of ethnic populations accompanied by an ever-increasing exodus of the Russian-speaking populations.

All of this was performed and sanctified by the then rising trend of ethnocentric nationalism, which I define as *a driving ideology of violent ethnic conflicts*.

(VI). Following this same development in my theoretical model, aspect six in a corresponding *chapter six* deals with the nature of *ethnocentric* (or, as other researchers define it, *ethnic, integral,* or *malignant*) *type of nationalism* and its juxtaposition to the idea of *civic nationalism* (also called *liberal, benign*, etc.). These two forms greatly differ regarding the societal conditions that encourage their individual development, with one often opposing the other. During the course of my work, I investigated the general trends of those societal conditions in the post-Soviet polities that spawned the most violent ethnic conflicts. An impartial and objective analysis of these conflicts reveals that all of them suffered from a seemingly continuous all-sided societal crisis punctuated by noticeably weak economics and unstable political systems. The resulting society was effectively fragmented and polarized, possessing an almost embryonic middle class, authoritarian traditions, weak civil institutions, and ingrained conventions of ethnocentric (integral) nationalism. Furthermore, the contesting groups of oligarchs, as well as the ethno-political amalgamations that they supported through their policies in all social spheres (especially in those related to the five building blocks), generated the kind of environmental conditions fit to promote the continued propagation of ethnocentric nationalism.

Ukraine provides a great deal of practical evidence confirming the accuracy of these theoretical generalizations. A general examination of their society highlights the existence of three major ideological streams that permeate the country, the first of which is (1) the ethnocentric nationalists, who are the most well-organized and represented group in the mainstream media sources, under the control of a group of oligarchs who "tamed" and financed these radical organizations in order for them to meet their own narrow politico-economic interests. (2) The second stream, which rose to prominence following the 2014 Maidan protest, unites ethnic Russians and Russian-speaking Ukrainians (alongside independently driven representatives of other ethnic communities, such as Hungarians, Romanians, Bulgarians, etc.) who outright reject most of the goals and values of the Euromaidan movement. Much like the first stream, I found and researched another similar spattering of oligarchs who invest into and subsequently exploit the ethno-political interests of these people. (3) The third group is a rather amorphous collection that represents those who support *civic nationalism* (other specialists refer to them as "statists"). Unlike the prior two, they reject radicalism of any kind, focusing instead on the dream of all-inclusive statehood, while seeing any "national interests" as nothing more than the preservation of the Soviet legacy in terms of territory, economics, East–West geo-economic ties, Ukraine's neutral status, and the diversity of the population with a strong localist/regionalist component. With this, we see a typical example of a fragmented society under the total domination of oligarchic groups that reproduce an environment of wild frontier/"crony" capitalism, characterized by a weakened and deindustrialized economy oriented around the export of resources (including the possible trade of Ukraine's famously fertile soil),the "presence" of a feeble middle class (making up 1 percent of the population, with 25 percent living beneath the officially established income minimum), and the lack of an integral civic political ideology. There is a silver lining, however, as one would notice that there is a segment of Ukrainian society that ideologically resents everything that, to them, resembles radical (ethnocentric) "Galician nationalism," while another still resents everything belonging to the Russian Imperial/Soviet (i.e., "Leftist") legacy.

This sentiment can be perfectly summed up with an account from one of my western Ukrainian interviewees, who when speaking of their compatriots living in secessionist Donbas, said the following: "We'll never find a common language with them: my hero is Bandera, and theirs—Zhukov [the Soviet "Marshal of Victory" who conquered Berlin in 1945]. It is better for them to leave for their favorite Russia, otherwise we'll show them the way [back to where they came from a] couple of centuries ago: the 'chemodan-vokzal-Rossia' [meaning "Luggage-Railway Station-to Russia"]" (interview, 6, 2019, Isaenko, File II, List 21).

In order to demonstrate the depths of traditional integral nationalism in the state of Ukraine, I included a brief historical survey concerning the principal ideas of a state-building project via its main ideologues—Mykola Mikhnovs'ky, Mykhailo Hrushevsky, Dmytro Dontsov, Yaroslav Stetsko, and others—as well as nationalist organizations—like the OUN-UPA—who briefly attempted to enact their own plans between the late 1930s and early 1940s. Since the 2000s, these ideas have undergone a veritable renaissance in the writings and political practices of the next generation of leaders, including Andrii Bilec'kii, Dmytro Korchynsky, and many others.

More importantly, and especially after the 2014 Maidan protests, many of these ideas found their legal embodiment within the previously discussed linguistic and linguo-educational legislature of Petro

Poroshenko and Volodymyr Zelensky, which introduced a wholly new system aimed at categorization of peoples along ethnic lines, particularly in the educational sphere. Additionally, the efforts of such nationalists have resulted in the formation of a "New History" bent on distancing the Ukrainian people from its Imperial Russian/Soviet past. On a more informal level, ethnocentric nationalists have spread ideas about the existence of genetically "pure" and "impure" peoples living in the western and southeastern sections of Ukraine. All of this heavily factors to its regressive development into a violent ethnic conflict, which is, as of now, passing through its bloody *hot stage*.

Overall, and under a rubric of this particular chapter, I have collected many pieces of evidence proving how, in all seven of the post-Soviet violent ethnic conflicts, an unbiased observer may find several recurrent behavioral patterns of ethnocentric nationalism performed by either side. Among them are the following: the presence of a group mentality, manifested by a sense of belonging; self-assertive and integrative tendencies within a collective behavior; general mass behavior; conformity; mutually displayed ethnic prejudices; brotherhood within/warlikeness without; uncritical obedience to a charismatic leader; authoritarianism; unrestricted aggressiveness; and even a regression into a paranoid-schizoid behavior during ethnic pogroms and massacres. All of these behavioral norms were originally classified by Dusan Kecmanovic and Marta Cullberg Weston, who worked out their individual manifestations through an examination of the violence that broke out across former Yugoslavia. (For my own contribution, I supplied examples/evidence of the most prevalent of these behavioral patterns from the previously mentioned seven conflicts in the post-Soviet space.)

(VII), (VIII), (IX). *Chapter 7, 8, and 9* was developed to demonstrate yet another *aspect* of a theoretical model dealing in particular with the recurrent regularities of these violent ethnic conflicts: the fact that all of them follow a distinct *cyclical pattern*. For this purpose, I compiled individual timelines for each conflict in order to more easily break down their causes and proceedings over the span of history. For instance, the chronology of each conflict vividly demonstrates that, during past cycles (stemming from the collapse of the Russian Empire in 1917 and the Civil War that followed it from 1918 to 1920) and modern cycles (beginning shortly before and continuing well after the collapse of the Soviet Union in 1991) alike, they have gone through the *same stages of development*. I dubbed these stages the "*stirring-up*," "*hot*," and "*smoldering*" stages, which, when certain conditions were met, would eventually enter a "frozen period" or otherwise find some sort of short/long-term resolution. Briefly, the conclusions of these conflicts can be summarized as the following:

(1) The events collected and detailed in these individual timelines in *chapters eight and nine* show that the Armenian-Azerbaijani ethnic conflict, after passing through most of the abovementioned phases, currently rests in the smoldering stage. (2) The Russo-Moldovan conflict over Transnistria/Pridnestrovie has effectively entered its frozen period. (3) The Georgian–South Ossetian and (4) Georgian-Abkhazian conflicts are both well within their smoldering stages. (5) The North Ossetian–Ingushian conflict over the Prigorodnyi District of North Ossetia–Alania is currently in its frozen phase. After 2008, (6) the Russian-Chechen conflict found a resolution within the framework of a bargaining deal in line with the previously discussed system of asymmetric consociational institutionalization, which had been established within Russia for the express purpose of preventing these conflicts in the first place by harmonizing the ties between a federal center and the ethno-political elites of the national republics. And, as is well known, (7) the Russo-Ukrainian conflict is currently passing through its *hot stage*.

During the *stirring-up stages* of both past and present cycles, either side predominantly participated in *mild and middle-ground* forms of ethnic cleansing corresponding to the previously cited behavioral norms of ethnocentric nationalism. During the *hot stages*, however, both sides, regardless of any moral or tactical justification on the contrary, committed atrocities against one another, primarily under the sway of the "unrestricted aggressiveness" and "paranoid-schizoid" behavioral patterns. And almost every time this occurred, it pertained to the most important building blocks of the associated ethnicity, which, in and of themselves, served as the *principal building blocks of violent ethnic conflicts*.

The individual timelines also demonstrate that while all ethnic conflicts may present several or even all of the principal building blocks of ethnicity and their corresponding constituents as contributing to the conflict in some way, their combination in the scope of each particular conflict is noticeably different and affects how they develop on a case-by-case basis. The intensity and diversity behind the implementation of ethnic cleansing, which relates back to the qualities of the most prominently contested ethnic building blocks, is reflected through their listing under the "primary" and "secondary" categories, representing their general importance and mobilizing power. For example, the timeline of the Russo-Ukrainian violent ethnic conflict recognizes that the primary building blocks behind its outbreak are (1) *language*, (2) *nationality* (especially after the Crimean annexation and the rebellion in Donbas), and (3) a *commonly shared history* aggravated by acute chosen traumas. Additionally, the (4) *religious* and (5) *biological origins* building blocks, though still present within the framework of the conflict, only serve as subsidiary mobilizing factors that accent the violence rather than driving it.

Chapter 7, 8, and 9 also introduce a *typology of conflicts* that details their individual evolution during different stages. These range from an *intrastate* conflict (first level) to an *interstate* conflict (second level), which itself has the potential to spill over into a clash between different groups of nation-states representing entire civilizations (third level). During these stages, primarily those dominated by the characteristics of *separatism/secessionism*, certain conditions will cause them to become more *irredentist* in nature, which is also detailed within the individual passports. While they can be triggered by internal developments, such transitions mainly occur as a result of external factors that impact the entirety of the conflict, which I refer to as *outside exacerbating factors*. There are two of them explored in *aspects eight* and *nine* of the theoretical model: *Conflict propaganda* and *exacerbating role of outside powers*, acting out of their geopolitical national interests, different value systems and out of security dilemma as they understand it in a very different way.

(X). *Chapter 10 then first* deals with *aspect eight* about the destructive role of mainstream media on both sides of the conflict, with a particular focus on the media of outside nation-states either directly or indirectly involved through the pursuit of their own, sometimes completely independent, geopolitical interests. Regarding the generalizations within this chapter, it is of the utmost importance to utilize the unbiased and impartial analyses of this so-called "conflict propaganda" provided by the most highly regarded specialists in this field, such as Oliver Boyd-Barret, Robert Wade, Anatol Lieven, and many others. Their accounts demonstrate that the methods utilized by the mainstream media of all sides of the conflict (be they directly or indirectly involved) are all stunningly similar, including the creation of one-sided and uncritical reports (both verbal and visual); the emphasis/omission of facts in regards to their position onto the stereotypical and politically engaged propagandistic clichés; the suppression/distortion of information regarding possible alternatives; and the spreading of rumors, propagation of false information, and any other minor tricks that force the public to look at reported events through, in the words of Anatol Lieven, "a distorted lens."

Such a sophisticated system of conflict propaganda helps either side in maintaining the image of their opponent as ethnic enemies—who are constantly engaged in malicious plots against them—in order to dehumanize them to such an extent that all extreme forms of ethnic cleansing seem necessary and justifiable. By utilizing these methods, the mainstream media of outside players effectively demonize their geopolitical rivals in order to gain advantages through public endorsement, allowing for the imposition of various sanctions and the allotment of military assistance against the so-called "revisionist states."

Finally, *chapter 10* also deals with the nine's aspect of the theoretical model exploring those more powerful *outside exacerbating factors* that support and feed this conflict propaganda. In particular, the Russo-Ukrainian ethnic conflict illustrates that, since the dawn of the new millennium, it has become complicated by the conflictual relationship between Russia and Western organizations (EU, NATO, and the United States). According to the prevailing "wisdom" in the West, the conflict in Ukraine is blamed almost entirely on Russian aggression. Putin in a gambling manner annexed Crimea out of malignant desire to resuscitate the Russian Empire, and he supposedly wants to eventually go after the entirety of Ukraine, as well as other countries in Eastern Europe. In its own turn, Russia believes that the taproot of the trouble is NATO enlargement, the EU's eastward expansion, and the West's backing of the prodemocracy and ethnocentric movement in Ukraine—beginning with the Orange Revolution in 2004, and especially its role in "illegal coup" of 2014. Richard Sakwa's monograph specifically demonstrated that the Atlantic alliance, with Washington, DC, at its head, tries to impede any attempt at forming a "substantive Ukrainian-Russian alliance, which would have created a powerful market of some 200 million people and harnessed the dynamism of the two [culturally proximate] countries to purposes" that obviously contradict the collective interests of Western political elites.[2] This has itself become a *center point* in the long-standing policy of the West: aiming to prevent the potential resurrection of an "expanded" Russian state by the actual expanding of the West's influence along the trails of their historic predecessors. It is for this reason that the Atlanticists put a great deal of interest into former parts/eastern satellites of the USSR in order to create a chain of hostile anti-Russian regimes along its western perimeter. As the biggest and potentially strongest of these "converts," Ukraine has naturally become the most crucial piece on this multinational chessboard. If the West were to secure the support of Ukraine, replace Aleksandr Lukashenko's regime in Belarus with a more Western-friendly equivalent, and help Transnistria and Moldova integrate into Romania, then they will have successfully accomplished their goal of erecting a barrier against perceived Russian expansion. So, to paraphrase Sakwa's above-cited expression of concern, is it not the overall goal of this Western construction project to turn the entirety of Ukraine into a "pawn" to deploy against a "revisionist" Russia?

Consequently, Putin's Russia seeks to prevent this outcome by any means possible. Since the mid-1990s, Moscow adamantly opposed NATO enlargement, and Putin made it many times clear that Russia "would not stand by while their strategically important neighbor turned into a Western bastion." That is why until to 2014, he paid all efforts endeavoring to turn Ukraine into a player that, if not outright friendly, is not hostile/neutral. At the very least, Russian authorities aim to ensure the rise of a new country that is cooperative (especially economically) with Russia and not a member of NATO, the latter of which being a worst-case scenario responsible for triggering an unprecedented reaction by the larger country. If to cast away all other important nuances—particularly the economic and political implications, which are thoroughly investigated in Sakwa's monograph—in the context of the current violent Russo-Ukrainian conflict, this newly reinvigorated rivalry between the West and Russia might be very dangerous to the very existence of Ukraine as an independent state and to world peace at large.

Overall, Washington has essentially revitalized "its nineteenth-century geopolitical representations but tempered by twenty-first-century liberal universalism," with a strong anti-Russian (rather traditional) discourse.[3]

The Western paradigm fits well within the unitarist state-building plan of the Ukrainian ethnocentric nationalists (which is itself strongly backed by the intellectuals of the western Ukrainian diasporas); at the same time, Russia's paradigm under Putin exploits the genuine interests of a considerable part of Ukraine's Russian minority/Russian-speaking population (located primarily in the southeastern parts of the country) in order to further their own goals. But as we have previously seen, the ideal setup of the unitarist project requires Ukrainian citizens to distance all spheres of their society and ethnic identity as far from Russia as they possibly can. It presupposes the unilateral adoption of the "pure" Ukrainian *Mova* (language), which is free from any and all kinds of dialectical "pollution" (such as different types of *Surzhyks*), the acceptance of the "correct" interpretation of Ukrainian history, a "reunion" with the newly formed Ukrainian Orthodox Church, the return of lost territories in Crimea and Donbas, and the recognition of Halychyna as home to the region's anthropologically genuine biological substance. Ukrainian authorities fully rely on the all-sided Western help and direct involvement (including military close cooperation and immediate membership in NATO) to realize all aspects of this state-building project.

On the other hand, Putin's Russia proposes an asymmetric consociational institutional model (which is, in fact, a variant of the near-defeated federalist project that currently is dying in Ukraine) that would guarantee the free functionality of regional languages and dialects, promote a slightly amended and modernized Soviet history, overcome the schism in the Orthodox Church (in favor of the Moscow Patriarchate), and cement the irrelevance of the biological origins and autonomous status of the Donbas territories (with the insistence that the Crimean question is "closed"). In addition, it propagates that Ukraine continue to uphold its neutral (non-joining) status in the military sphere, as well as the reestablishment of economic bridges with Russia that do not interrupt any further economic cooperation with the EU. In other words, the Russian vision for Ukraine sees them taking advantage of their geostrategic position as a natural bridge between themselves and the West, rather than a "pawn" or "battering ram" under Western control. As mentioned before, even the oligarchs, as influential and well-informed as they are, have found themselves divided between these two differing paradigms.

This particular case of Russo-Ukrainian ethnic conflict fraught with a potential transformation from local to global collision clearly indicates that the current situation has reached such a moment that a question of *strategic stability* in the addendum of both West and East (the United States and Russia as the biggest nuclear powers) urgently comes upfront in their very complicated relations and requires from political leadership of both sides much wisdom and courage to begin to discuss it without a delay. As this publication has gone into production, the first round of negotiations between Russia-USA, NATO, and OSCE on January 10–13, 2022, ended with an obvious failure. West unanimously rejected the aforementioned Russian ultimatum demands regarding non-acceptance of Ukraine and other post-Soviet countries in NATO, non-deployment of the strategic and tactical weapons on their territories, and withdrawal of such a military infrastructure threatening Russia from the territories of another Eastern European states-members of NATO. Moreover, Russia threatens that if these conditions would not be accepted by the opposite side she will undertake non-specified "political and military-technical measures." In fact, by delivering these knowingly unacceptable demands Russia achieved quite an opposite result: Western countries have dramatically increased their military aid to Ukraine, and the situation around this country and regarding strategic stability at large is drastically deteriorating. Military building and training on both sides of the Russian-Ukrainian border and in the eastern flank of NATO continues with ever-increasing speed. Wave of hysteria and information warfare when mainstream media of Russia and Western countries are hurling at each other mirror-reflecting accusations of planning provocations along the contact line in Donbas, strongly backed up by the belligerent statements of high profile politicians, reached very dangerous level. In such an overheated atmosphere the stone that would be cast first threatens to set off the avalanche that may bury any hopes for peaceful resolution not only of this violent ethnic conflict, but the conflict between West and East at large as well.

I want to end this volume by citing the well-spoken words of Alexander Lukin, a highly recognized specialist in international economic and political discourse:

> Countries close to Russia are being torn apart by the West's ideologized expansion which has already led to the territorial division of Moldova and Georgia, and now Ukraine is falling apart in front of our eyes [...] the cultural border was drawn across their territories and they could stay undivided only if their leaders would have taken into account the interests of the people living in both the regions that gravitate towards Europe and those that would like to preserve historical [and cultural] ties with Russia.[4]

Postscript

The folks of my generation who grew up in the Soviet Union, probably remember the speeches of our schoolteachers and what they taught us. One of the best of these lessons was how, irrespective of our own ethnic origins, all of us are brothers and sisters who should be as united and eternal as the Soviet Union itself. And we believed them, treating each other exactly as we were told, with no fear of it ever ending. At that time, if somebody had told me that, within my lifetime, I would see these same "brothers and sisters" go for each other's throats in the manner that I have honestly described in this book, I would have considered them either completely insane or a malignant provocateur. However, the reality of this situation successfully overthrows the most convincing ideological dogmas and even the most benevolent of myths. As sad as it is to say, the story of Cain and Abel has, once again, reared its hideous head.

Notes

1   Cited in Anatoly Isaenko, *Polygon of Satan: Ethnic Traumas and Conflicts in the Caucasus*, 3rd ed. (Dubuque, IA: Kendall Hunt Publishing House, 2014), 106.

2   See Richard Sakwa, *Frontline Ukraine: Crisis in the Borderlands* (London: I. B. Tauris, 2015), 247. For a very objective analysis of a crisis-at-large in Ukraine, and in Donbas in particular, I recommend an article of Ivan Katchanovski and the entire book in which it was published: Ivan Katchanovski, "The Separatist War in Donbas: A Violent Break-Up of Ukraine?" in *Ukraine in Crisis*, 1st ed., ed. Nicolai N. Petro (Kingstone, RI: Routledge, 2017), and another book enlightening about the genuine causes of the crisis and about the perspectives of its development, including a thorough critique of notorious

propaganda surrounding this conflict: Agnieszka Pikulicka-Wilczewska and Richard Sakwa, eds., *Ukraine and Russia: People, Politics, Propaganda and Perspectives* (Bristol, UK: E-International Relations Publishing, 2015, New version, 2016); see also Tatyana Malyarenko, "A Gradually Escalating Conflict: Ukraine from the Euromaidan to the War with Russia," Chapter 28, in *The Routledge Handbook of Ethnic Conflict, 2nd Edition*, Karl Cardell and Stefan Wolf, eds. (Washington, D. C.: Routledge, 2016): 349–68. An account from the Ukrainian perspective can be found in Serhii Hakman, *Contemporary Russian-Ukrainian Confrontation: A Look Through the Prism of International Law and Geopolitical Interests* (Chernivtsi, Ukraine: Academia, 2019); Vlad Mykhnenko, "Causes and Consequences of the War in Eastern Ukraine: An Economic Georgaphy Perspective," *Europe-Asia Studies*, 72/3 (2020): 528–60; Nadia Bureiko, Mariia Koval, Hennadiy Maksak, Hanna Shelest, eds., *Ukrainian Prism: Foreign Policy. Analytical* Study (Kyiv, Ukraine: Foreign Policy Council "Ukrainian Prism," Frederich Ebert Foundation, 2019); Hanna Shelest, "Minsk Agreements Implementation: Art of Impossible," *UA: Ukrainian Analytica,* Issue 1(3) (2016): 7–22; Csilla Fedinec, Istvan Csernicsko, "Language Policy and National Feeling in Context of Ukraine's Euromaidan, 2014–2016," *Central European Papers,* no.1 (2017): 82–100; Andrew Makarychev & Alexandra Yatsyk, "Biopower and Geopolitics as Russia's Neighboring Strategies: Reconnecting People or Re-aggregating Lands?," *Nationalities Papers,* vol. 45, no. 1(2017): 25–40. For the Russian perspective on the origin and development of the contemporary crisis, see Stanislav Byshok, *Expert Report: Extremism in Ukrainian Politics, Society, Media, Defense and Law Enforcement*, Issue I (Moscow: Commonwealth of Independent States—Election Monitoring Organization CIS-EMO, 2015).

3 Sakwa, *Frontline Ukraine*, 247.

4 Alexander Lukin, "Chauvinism or Chaos?" *Russia in Global Affairs*, June 7, 2014, http://eng.globalaffairs.ru/number/chauvanism-or-chaos-16709.

APPENDIX

Political Culture of Democracy and a Road Map for the Countries of Post-Soviet Space to Heal the Violent Ethnic Conflicts

American political analysts Carol Barner-Barry and Cynthia Hody outlined "eight assumptions" that have to be developed in the post-Soviet states to create conditions that they regard as a "political culture of democracy"[1] (my notes are enclosed in brackets):

1. Internal political [ethnic] disputes should be solved peacefully. [I suggest that those in conflict should sign obligatory documents of mutual refusal from using force in ethnic disputes.]
2. Government should be limited, and those who govern should be subject to the same rules as those they govern.
3. Those who are active in politics should be able and willing to compromise.
4. The political-economic system should maintain a relatively high level of economic development.
5. There should be widespread [i.e., public] control over politically important resources.
6. Adult citizens should have the right and the duty to take part in their own government.
7. Different racial, religious, or ethnic groups should live together in peace and a spirit of mutual trust.
8. Minorities should be able to vie for control over the government without fear of reprisal.

Another prominent expert, Arend Lijphart, considered the importance of creating in multiethnic states a policy based on "a consociational democracy model." This model rests on the following key features:[2]

1. Cooperation among political elites leading to the formation of coalition governments and executive power-sharing.
2. Formal and informal separation of powers and checks and balances between the various branches and levels of government.
3. Balanced bicameralism through special minority representation in the upper chamber of parliament.
4. The existence of mutual political parties representing different ethnic groups.
5. Proportional representation in parliament.
6. Territorial and non-territorial federalism and decentralization of power.
7. Allowance for ethnic groups to veto legislation affecting their vital interests.
8. A high degree of autonomy for each ethnic community to run its own affairs.

308 | Brothers at Each Other's Throats: Regularity of the Violent Ethnic Conflicts in the Post-Soviet Space

9. A written constitution that explicitly lays down certain fundamental rights that cannot be violated by the government.

Notes

1   Carol Barner-Barry and Cynthia Hody, *The Politics of Change: The Transformation of the Former Soviet Union* (New York: St. Martin Press, 1995), 212–13.

2   Arend Lijphart, *Democracy in Plural Societies: A Comparative Exploration* (New Haven, CT: Yale University Press, 1977); Arend Lijphart, *Democracies: Patterns of Majoritarian and Consensus Government in Twenty-One Countries* (New Haven, CT: Yale University Press, 1984), 23–30. Also cited in Raymond Taras and Rajat Ganguly, *Understanding of Ethnic Conflict: The International Dimension*, 3rd ed. (New York: Pearson, 2008), 17–18.

INDEX

Printed in the USA
CPSIA information can be obtained
at www.ICGtesting.com
LVHW020927090823
754690LV00011B/28